Tony Blair's strong start to his third term, with his pivotal role in capturing
the 2012 Olympic Games for Britain, his statesmanlike handling of the
aftermath of the terrorist attacks on London, his promise of a fresh start to
the European Union and his leadership of the G-8 summit at Gleneagles,
has brought his relatively lacklustre second term into sharp relief. The
foundations of his premiership having been laid in the first term, the
second should have been the time when New Labour fulfilled its manifesto promises. The government enjoyed the tremendous benefits of a
strong economy, a rock-solid majority in the Commons and a quiescent
labour movement. So what changed between 2001 and 2005 and what was
achieved? How far was Blair himself responsible, and what was Gordon
Brown's influence? Were the benefits enjoyed in any way wasted? What
was the impact of the Iraq war? And what of Blair's policy towards Europe?
In their fourth book on the political impact of British prime ministers,
the editors have gathered together leading academics and journalists to
provide an authoritative assessment of Blair's second term, including a
review of the 'Blair effect' from the first New Labour term in 1997 to the
present.

ANTHONY SELDON is the co-founder of the Institute of Contemporary
British History, and is Headmaster of Brighton College and Master Elect
of Wellington College. He is the author or editor of over 25 books of
contemporary history.

DENNIS KAVANAGH is Professor of Politics at the University of Liverpool, and a senior scholar of British politics. He is the author of extensive
publications including the British Election Survey series.

THE BLAIR EFFECT 2001–5

Edited by

ANTHONY SELDON AND DENNIS KAVANAGH

CAMBRIDGE
UNIVERSITY PRESS

CAMBRIDGE UNIVERSITY PRESS
Cambridge, New York, Melbourne, Madrid, Cape Town, Singapore, São Paulo

Cambridge University Press
The Edinburgh Building, Cambridge CB2 2RU, UK

Published in the United States of America by Cambridge University Press, New York

www.cambridge.org
Information on this title: www.cambridge.org/9780521678605

First published 2005

Printed in the United Kingdom at the University Press, Cambridge

A catalogue record for this book is available from the British Library

ISBN-13   978-0-521-86142-7 hardback
ISBN-10   0-521-86142-x hardback

ISBN-13   978-0-521-67860-5 paperback
ISBN-10   0-521-67860-9 paperback

CONTENTS

v

NOTES ON CONTRIBUTORS

Lewis Baston is Research Officer of the Electoral Reform Society and author of *Reggie: The Life of Reginald Maudling* (2004). He and Simon Henig have collaborated on three political reference books, including most recently *Politico's Guide to the General Election 2005* (2005).

Louis Blom-Cooper QC has been an active public lawyer in every sense of the public domain.

Vernon Bogdanor is Professor of Government, University of Oxford and Professor of Law at Gresham College. His books include *The People and the Party System: The Referendum and Electoral Reform in British Politics* (1981), *Multi-Party Politics and the Constitution* (1983) and *Devolution in the United Kingdom* (1999). He is currently working on an interpretation of the British Constitution.

Philip Cowley is Reader in Parliamentary Government at the University of Nottingham, and author of *Revolts and Rebellions: Parliamentary Voting Under Blair* (2002). He runs www.revolts.co.uk and his next book, *The Rebels: How Blair Mislaid His Majority*, is due out shortly.

Andrew Gamble is Professor of Politics at the University of Sheffield and author of *Between Europe and America: The Future of British Politics*, which was awarded the Political Studies Association W.J.M. Mackenzie prize for the best book in political science published in 2003.

Stephen Glaister CBE FICE is Professor of Transport and Infrastructure at Imperial College London. He is a member of the Board of Transport for London and has been economic adviser to the Rail Regulator and to various government bodies.

Howard Glennerster is Professor Emeritus in Social Policy at the London School of Economics. He is author of *British Social Policy since 1945* and numerous books and papers on the economics of social policy in general and health care in particular. He has lectured widely abroad and has spent several sessions as a visiting scholar at the Brookings Institution in Washington.

Simon Henig is a Senior Lecturer in Politics at the University of Sunderland. He is co-author with Lewis Baston of *Politico's Guide to the 2005 General Election* (2005), *Politico's Guide to the General Election* (2000) and *The Political Map of Britain* (2002), and is also co-author of *Women and Political Power* (2001).

Christopher Hill is Sir Patrick Sheehy Professor of International Relations, and Director of the Centre of International Studies, University of Cambridge. He has published widely in the areas of foreign policy analysis and general international relations, his most recent books being *The Changing Politics of Foreign Policy* (2003), and *The European Union in International Relations* (edited with Michael Smith, forthcoming 2005). He was Chair of the British International Studies Association, 1998–2000.

Dennis Kavanagh is Professor of Politics at Liverpool University. He has written 30 books, including the Nuffield series of British general election studies. The latest in the series is *The British General Election of 2005* (with David Butler). He and Anthony Seldon have also co-authored *The Powers Behind the Prime Minister* and co-edited *The Major Effect* and *The Thatcher Effect*.

Raymond Kuhn is Professor of Politics at Queen Mary, University of London. He has published widely on the politics of the British and French media, including the monograph *The Media in France*. His most recent book is *Political Journalism*, co-edited with Erik Neveu.

Iain McLean is Professor of Politics and Director of the Public Policy Unit, University of Oxford. He has worked on devolution and the politics of the nations and regions of the UK for over 30 years. Recent publications include *The Fiscal Crisis of the United Kingdom* (2005) and *State of the Union* (with Alistair McMillan, forthcoming 2005). He has written reports for three government departments and for the Commons Treasury Select Committee on regional public expenditure patterns.

Pippa Norris is the McGuire Lecturer in Comparative Politics at the John F. Kennedy School, Harvard University. She has published almost three dozen books, most recently *Electoral Engineering* (2004), *Radical Right* (2005) and *Britain Votes 2005* (2005).

Peter Riddell is chief political commentator of *The Times* and was the Political Studies Association's Political Columnist of the Year in 2004. He has written several books on British politics. His *Hug Them Close – Blair, Clinton, Bush and the 'Special Relationship'* won the Channel 4 award for Political Book of the Year 2004. His book *The Unfulfilled Prime Minister – Tony Blair's Quest for a Legacy* appears in autumn 2005.

Anthony Seldon is the co-founder of the Institute of Contemporary British History, and is the author or editor of over twenty-five books of contemporary history.

Lord Skidelsky is Professor of Political Economy at Warwick University. His three-volume biography of the economist John Maynard Keynes (1983, 1992, 2000) received numerous prizes, including the Lionel Gelber Prize for International Relations and the Council on Foreign Relations Prize for International Relations. He is the author of *The World After Communism* (1995), and is currently writing a book on globalisation and international relations. He was made a life peer in 1991, and is a member of the House of Lords Select Committee on Economic Affairs. He was elected a Fellow of the British Academy in 1994.

David Smith has been economics editor of the *Sunday Times* since 1989, where he writes a weekly column. He is also an assistant editor and policy adviser. He is the author of several books, including *North and South* (1994), *Eurofutures* (1997), *UK Current Economic Policy* (1999), *Will Europe Work?* (1999) and, most recently, *Free Lunch: Easily Digestible Economics* (2003).

Alan Smithers is Professor of Education and Director of the Centre for Education and Employment Research at the University of Buckingham. He has previously held chairs at Manchester, Brunel and Liverpool universities. He has researched, written and commented extensively on education. Throughout the first two Blair governments he has been adviser to the House of Commons Education Committee.

Peter Snowdon is a freelance writer whose books include *The Conservative Party: An Illustrated History* (2004).

Kitty Stewart is a Research Fellow at the Centre for Analysis of Social Exclusion (CASE) at the London School of Economics and Political Science. Her research interests include child poverty and disadvantage, international comparisons of policy and outcomes relating to poverty and exclusion and employment trajectories for the low skilled. She is the co-editor, with John Hills, of *A More Equal society? New Labour, Poverty, Inequality and Exclusion* (2005).

Mark Stuart is a researcher in the School of Politics at the University of Nottingham. He has just published *John Smith: A Life* (2005), the authorised biography of the Labour leader, and he has also written *Douglas Hurd: The Public Servant* (1998).

Robert Taylor is an adviser to the European Trade Union Confederation. Former labour editor of the *Financial Times* and the *Observer*, he is the author of six books on trade unions and labour markets. He is now writing a history of the Parliamentary Labour Party since 1906.

Tony Travers is Director, Greater London Group, at the London School of Economics. He has acted as an adviser to a number of House of Commons select committees, notably that for Education and Skills. From 1992 to 1997 he was a member of the Audit Commission and has been a Senior Associate of the King's Fund. He has also undertaken many projects for local authorities and published extensively on the subject.

PREFACE

This is the fourth volume in the series which analyses the impact of contemporary government. The earlier volumes, *The Thatcher Effect*, *The Major Effect* and *The Blair Effect 1997–2001*, were published in 1989, 1994 and 2001 respectively.

The approach has been the same as in the earlier three volumes. Leading authorities from academe and the media address common themes in their specialist area:

- What was the state of the area at the June 2001 general election?
- What was the state of that area at the May 2005 general election?
- What had changed and why?
- How successful or effective have any changes been?
- To what extent was change driven by the Prime Minister himself, or from Number 10 in general, by ministers, departments, think tanks or any other factors?
- What was the net 'Blair effect' in that area between 1997 and 2005?

Within this framework, authors were encouraged to develop their own particular approaches. Inevitably some stuck closely to the guidelines, others were freer in their interpretation of their brief. The aim has been to cover only the areas where the second Blair government made a significant fresh impact. Some chapter areas were dropped from the volume on the first Blair government, such as on the civil service, the constitution, defence and Northern Ireland, because little fresh happened to merit writing a separate chapter. The aim in this volume also was to write a shorter, more targeted book than *The Blair Effect 1997–2001*, which was over 650 pages. In the concluding chapter I examine which areas saw the most significant changes and assess how effective the changes have been. I also examine Tony Blair's personal impact, and look at why more was not achieved, and examine whether opportunities were indeed wasted during these four years. Blair's spectacular start to the third term – with his pivotal role in winning the 2012 Olympic Games for Britain, his masterly handling of the national mood after the 7/7 bombings in London, and his promise of fresh hope for Africa and over global warming and a 'new' European Union – highlight the pace of progress in 2001–5.

The series overall seeks to be studiously non-party political. Where an individual author has a particular viewpoint, the aim is to balance this with a contribution from an author of the opposite persuasion.

Because this book was completed after the election, it forms a comprehensive view of what happened and was achieved between the two general elections. The hope is that the book will still have value in 2025, and even 2055. By those dates, all the main evidence will be available and the full consequences of the decisions taken in those years will have been played out. But my guess is that many of the conclusions in this book will still stand, and, even where they do not, it will still be interesting to know what an eclectic group of commentators thought on the cusp of the events being described.

I am delighted to have Dennis Kavanagh back on board as co-editor for this volume. It was his proposal to produce a shorter volume and his ideas and scholarship have been, as ever, *sans pareil*.

Finally, I would like to thank my colleagues at Brighton College yet again for their support for my work, including Lord Skidelsky, my chairman, Simon Smith and Louise Kenway, the deputies, Debra Lewis and also Dorcas Sherwood, my personal assistants, Julia Harris for all her work on typing, Elizabeth Jones for support in the early stages and David Farley for help with research. Cambridge University Press has proved to be an outstanding publisher, calm, decisive and genuinely interested in the book for its own sake. All these qualities are comparative rarities in modern British publishing.

ANTHONY SELDON

PART I

Politics and government

The Blair premiership

DENNIS KAVANAGH

Tony Blair's continuous eight-year tenure as prime minister equals the lifespan of a two-term US president. By the end of 2005, it will exceed that of every British premier in the last century except for Margaret Thatcher. Lack of time in office is hardly a problem. It is therefore not too soon to make a provisional assessment of Blair's impact. Because he has set a date for his departure there is more of the past than the future about him. And the best may be in the past.

The three phases in Blair's leadership are his three years as leader of the opposition and his two four-year terms as Prime Minister. He led his party to a huge election victory in 1997. But concentration on dominating the media agenda and winning that election meant that, with a few exceptions, little thought was given to a programme for government. In private, he has looked back on the first term as largely a wasted opportunity for public service reform and the second term has been dominated by Iraq and its fallout. In 2001 he claimed that he was more experienced in knowing how Whitehall works, tougher and had a clearer idea of what he would do if he achieved 'the historic second term'.

A second term, however, has rarely enhanced a government's reputation and Blair's has been no exception. On a personal level Blair was troubled by health scares and self-doubt after the damage done to his public standing following the war in Iraq. He was on the brink of resigning in 2004 and in the end announced that he would not serve beyond a third term. Although 2001–5 was dominated by the 'war on terror' and then in Iraq, a number of important decisions were taken – on university tuition fees, foundation hospitals, city academies, an independent supreme court and the NHS internal market. His government could point to continued economic stability and massive investment in the public services. It entered the 2005 general election with a handsome lead on all the key issues apart from immigration and appears to have won the argument about the balance between taxation and public spending. The government also began to develop a more – though not completely – coherent approach to modernising the post-1945 welfare settlement based on devolution, decentralisation, diversity and choice.

The third term provides the opportunity to take the reforms further. But the context will be one in which Blair's political capital (a mixture of his reputation and influence) in Westminster has declined sharply and a general election in which his party lost seats and votes.[1]

Blair has often invited comparison with the two agenda-setting prime ministers of the past century, Attlee and Thatcher.[2] He has enjoyed some of the conditions that helped their dominance, including

• a long period of office (he has served longer than Attlee),
• a large parliamentary majority,
• a weak opposition, and
• a favourable climate of opinion.

It can also be argued that Blair inherited a more favourable economic legacy than Attlee or Thatcher, although he and Gordon Brown will dispute the claim.

Yet his record pales in comparison with the accomplishments of Attlee (coping with the transition from war to peace, independence for India, joining Nato, the creation of the National Health Service, and great extensions of public ownership and the welfare state) and Thatcher (trade union reforms, privatisation and curbing inflation). These were, in the jargon, big-picture governments leaving a substantial legacy behind.

If Blair to date has not been an agenda-setting prime minister, despite the above advantages, a main cause may be beyond his control. The great war leaders, Lloyd George and Churchill, faced a dramatic and widely perceived challenge – national survival. The Attlee government was backed by popular expectations that the state could and should play a more positive role in managing the economy and providing welfare than it had previously done in peace-time. In the 1980s Thatcher had to tackle serious problems of trade union power, inflation and declining economic competitiveness that for some commentators raised questions of Britain's governability. But in 1997 Labour's election was the result largely of the voters' wish for a change of government, after 18 years of the Conservatives, and more investment in public services. Blair has not had the

[1] See Richard Rose, *The Prime Minister in a Shrinking World* (Cambridge: Polity, 2001).
[2] See Peter Hennessy, *The Prime Minister: The Office and Its Holders* (London: Allen Lane, 2000). The studies by Rose and Hennessy stand out for their comparative and historical perspective and are less than enthusiastic about Blair's premiership.

opportunity of facing and triumphing over a defining national crisis as the other leaders did.

Indeed, Blair has cast his own verdict on his record so far, because he has felt he needs to serve a third term to create a worthwhile legacy. He comes across as a dissatisfied leader – dissatisfied with his party, its pre-1994 structure and ethos, Parliament, the system of Cabinet government, the civil service and large parts of the public sector. He has presented himself as new, modern and radical – words that reverberate through his speeches and interviews – although the passage of time decreases the credibility of the rhetoric. At times it is possible to see the self-perceived pathfinder, like Mrs Thatcher, as prime minister of the wrong country.

This chapter examines Blair's impact on key aspects of a prime minister's job. He has self-consciously tried to be a different kind of prime minister. He has had distinctive views about himself in relation to his party, Parliament, Cabinet, Number 10 staff and the public. His Labour predecessors have been negative role models because, except for Attlee, they seemed to have failed.

Party

Any assessment needs to accept the electoral crisis facing the Labour Party when Blair took over. Its fourth successive general election defeat in 1992 confirmed that its core vote was among declining sections of the population – manufacturing working class, council estates and trades unions. It had little following in growing Middle England and the aspirational working class. The New Labour 'project' was about changing the party from top to bottom and involved capturing traditional Conservative sections of the electorate, espousing social and economic policies long associated with the political right (including privatisation and flexible labour markets), and creating a formidable election-winning machine.

A consequence of this success has been to weaken the sense of the party as tribe or family. Although he has been attacked for this it can be argued that at a time of declining partisanship and class cohesiveness, his approach has advantages in reaching out to uncommitted voters. Indeed, the current ideas of triangulation (adopting a position independent of one identified with either Labour or Conservative) and spatial leadership positively favour the leader who wears his party ties lightly.[3]

---

[3] M. Foley, *The Rise of the British Presidency* (Manchester: Manchester University Press, 2001).

His promotion of New Labour has depended on distinguishing it from what he regarded as Old Labour, consisting not only of the left but also of the spend and tax social democrats like Lord Hattersley, and defining himself against the party. Constructing a negative and selective recent history of the party' policies, personalities, institutions and values that had made it outdated and unelectable, he consolidated and extended changes in the party's structure, policies and ethos begun under Kinnock.

Blair and his entourage were impressed by the Thatcher brand of forceful leadership, a view reinforced by the failure of Major's more consensual approach. Strong personal leadership would be required not only to change the party and its direction but also to win elections. Traditionally, Labour had rejected a cult of leadership, a feature reinforced by its pluralist structure and democratic ethos; until 1922 the leader was called 'chairman' of the Parliamentary Labour Party (PLP). But sections of the media and many voters took a dim view of Labour leaders from Gaitskell onwards who faced constant and wearying party opposition. Labour modernisers believed that in the modern era a party's message is carried by and through the party leader. Hence Labour had to become what is called an 'electoral-professional party' and market the leader rather than the party. This appeal worked as long as Blair had plenty of political capital and was seen as indispensable if the party was to gain and retain office. By 2005 Blair was no longer an electoral asset.

Indicators of the decline of the traditional Labour Party are several: a reduction in members and activity, trade union protests that they are marginalised, the rise of polling and focus groups as sounding boards of policy rather than the annual conference and party grass-roots, the minimal role of the policy-making machinery on university top-up fees, foundation hospitals, ID cards and Iraq, and the attenuation of many of the traditional checks and balances in the party. Party membership is now fewer than 200,000, some 50,000 fewer than when he became leader in 1994.

Perhaps decay is a highly probable outcome of a party being in government for a lengthy spell – the state of the Conservative Party by 1992, let alone 1997, as well as Labour by 1970 and 1979 are examples. The paradox is that Blair and Thatcher, although they reinvented their parties, also presided over their decline.

But does this decline matter much? Might Blair see the future as one of 'partyless democracy', one where populist leaders seek inclusive or target audiences and communicate with them directly via web sites, Question Time, media interviews, and such television shows as *Richard and Judy*?[4] Perhaps there is less need for mass parties in the age of communication via focus groups, direct mail and call-centres, finance from a mix of wealthy donors and state funding, and policies from think tanks. Parties as electoral organisations can operate as partnership franchises, contracting out key tasks to private and voluntary agencies.

A paradox is that the Labour Party is more dominant than ever in Britain but in some respects is also perhaps weaker than at any time since 1945.

Parliament

Support among party MPs has long been a crucial determinant of a leader's authority. After all, until recently the party's MPs chose and had the right to sack the leader, and prime ministers spent time in the Commons, feeling the need to be physically present and sense the mood of the House. Macmillan, Wilson and Thatcher all confessed to fears before facing Question Time. Late at night in March 1917, a fraught time in the First World War, Winston Churchill was about to leave the House of Commons. Looking around the empty dark chamber he said to a fellow Liberal MP: 'This little place is what makes the difference between us and Germany . . . This little room is the shrine of the world's liberties.'[5] It is difficult to imagine Tony Blair echoing that sentiment.

Since 1979 only John Major after 1992 has had to worry about the passage of his legislation through the Commons, a largely extra-parliamentary electorate now chooses the party leader and governments have other preferred means of communicating with the public. Parliament has been bypassed as prime ministers increasingly 'go public' via the television studio, the *Today* radio programme and town hall meetings, and are drawn to international summits by the growth of intergovernmental institutions.[6]

No leader, however, compares with Blair in searching for opportunities to project himself outside Parliament. He is an extreme example of a

---

[4] Peter Mair, 'Partyless democracy', *New Left Review 2*, March/April 2000.

[5] I am indebted to Peter Hennessy for the quotation in his 'An end to the poverty of aspiration? Parliament since 1979', unpublished paper, November 2004, p. 23.

[6] See Rose, *The Prime Minister*, ch. 7, and Peter Riddell, *Parliament Under Blair* (London: Politico's, 1998).

trend that dates back at least thirty years. George Jones and his colleagues
at the London School of Economics have shown that attendance, votes
and interventions by the prime minister in the House of Commons are
all in decline. Prime ministerial statements, usually about war and international conferences, have also declined. On all the indicators Blair is an
all-time low scorer. The figures may register the changing roles of prime
minister and Parliament and in Blair's case have been emphasised by his
huge majorities in Parliament – although it is worth noting that Mrs
Thatcher had a large majority in 1983.

Parliament can still remind a prime minister of its capacity to bite back.
John Major had a torrid time in the 1992 Parliament and since 2001 Blair
has faced substantial rebellions over Iraq, top-up fees and foundation
hospitals. That Iain Duncan Smith was the preferred candidate of fewer
than half of Conservative MPs undermined his position as a leader from
the start. The factors that allowed Blair to take Parliament largely for
granted – his personal authority, popularity and large majority – have all
weakened. The 2001 Parliament turned out to be the most rebellious in
modern times, and he may have a more troublesome time in the third
term.

Cabinet

Choosing and managing Cabinet remains an important part of the prime
minister's remit. Mrs Thatcher found that her Cabinet colleagues' withdrawal of support in 1990 was fatal. But as a forum for discussion,
decision-taking and bonding it has been in decline for many years,
a casualty of time pressures, overload and leaks. Under Blair meetings are shorter and have fewer papers before them. Increasingly prime
ministers prefer to retreat to Number 10, where they have assembled
their own staffs. The Cabinet system appears to be in decline in other
Westminster systems such as Australia, New Zealand and Canada: in
each there have been moves to a full-blown Department for the Prime
Minister.

The Blair style had been demonstrated in opposition. He had little
time for his shadow cabinet, while the New Labour project, something
of a coup over the party, was largely the work of himself, his entourage
and Brown. No opposition leader's office has ever been as well staffed
as was Blair's; it was nearly as large as the number of civil servants and
political appointees working for John Major in Number 10 at the same

time. Blair had a virtual prime minister's office in waiting, and aides like Campbell, Hunter, Miliband, Morgan, Powell, Allan, Coffman and Hyman, all moved from Blair's office in opposition to Number 10 in government. In government, the key meeting of the week for Blair remains the 9am office meeting with his staff on Monday mornings, sometimes called a 'Tony meeting'. This meeting is designed to give direction for the rest of the week, as staff review progress and take action on points he has thought of over the weekend. Till very recently he held bi-monthly meetings on his agenda with the ministers for education, health, crime and transport, in addition to traditional regular meetings with the foreign secretary and chancellor of the exchequer.

What pluralism there is comes from Gordon Brown's success in carving out his own sphere of responsibility over economic policy and social policy, widely defined. Blair has had no senior economic adviser. His premiership has been overshadowed by the relationship with Brown, stoked up by the war of the books by journalists. These books have been heavily reliant on sources from within the rival camps and reflect on a premiership that has been the most spinned for and spinned against of any. At the last count a dozen journalists had written studies of Blair and or Brown. Once each side has put its own story into the public domain it usually dismisses the book as 'tittle tattle'.

On one level it is soap opera. But Blair has certainly felt constrained by the leeway he granted, implicitly or explicitly, to his neighbour in Number 11 over entry to the eurozone, economic policy and welfare reform. During the first term Brown's aides let it be known that he was the chief executive, in charge of domestic policy while Blair, concentrating on foreign policy and Northern Ireland, was something akin to that of a head of state – a novel thesis of the dual premiership. By the second term, however, Blair increasingly felt Brown was limiting his ability to leave behind a New Labour legacy. Brown, on the other hand, could point to his record of economic stability, New Deal, attack on poverty and his reputation as the social justice chancellor.

This rivalry is an old story in recent British politics. R. A. Butler and Harold Macmillan were the architects of the post-war new Conservatism. They differed little on domestic policy but competed for the leadership. Such agreement on policy seems to nourish personal rivalry. Together Blair and Brown have been perhaps the most formidable partnership in modern British politics, marginalising the Conservative Party for over a decade. But in government it has been an enormous source of tension.

Brown's bold demands for a date for an allegedly 'agreed' handover to take place during the 2001 Parliament, largely on the grounds that it was his turn, have no parallel in recent British history: they put in the shade Eden's expectations that Churchill would hand over power well before 1955. Relations deteriorated to the stage where Blair called off his regular Tuesday afternoon sessions with Brown.[7]

There has been a downside to the Blair style of operations. The decline in number and duration of Cabinet meetings, although this has been reversed somewhat in 2004 and 2005, did little to increase the sense of collective ownership among Cabinet ministers. It has been a Tony and/or Gordon show, resembling court politics, a battle of who is in and who is out of favour with Number 10, and who is a Brownite or a Blairite.[8] The fiefdoms were drawing the life from the Cabinet. Until 2005 ministers and senior civil servants were at times exposed to two narratives not just about the succession but also about the direction of government, notably on the euro and public service reform.

The decline of Cabinet has encouraged more informality in decision-making and allowed the rise of an element of cronyism or, depending on taste, a greater reliance on friends and allies, all exemplified in the Hutton and Butler reports. Lloyd George in 1916 and Churchill, already an old man in 1951, relied heavily on friends and confidants. But they pale in comparison to Blair. Mrs Thatcher in 1979 took two relatively junior appointments with her, a political secretary and a chief of staff (in reality an office manager), as well as John Hoskyns, to head a small policy unit. The tenure of all three was short-lived. Her most renowned and long-serving aides, Charles Powell and Bernard Ingham, were appointed through established civil service procedures. Major took with him only Gus O'Donnell (as press secretary) from the Treasury and Judith Chaplin (as political secretary).

Some are convinced that under Blair there has been a decline in the quality of decision-making in the 'den'. He has gone further in making policy in bilaterals, ad hoc groups and informal discussions, what Anthony Seldon calls 'denocracy'. Mandarins, to quote the former Cabinet Secretary, Lord Butler of Brockwell, complain of 'a lack of reasoned deliberation' and 'too much central control'. Butler has argued that the informality, absence of papers and consultation with other ministers and

---

[7] For an appreciation see Anthony Seldon, *Blair* (London: Free Press, 2004).

[8] Francis Beckett and David Hencke, *The Blairs and Their Court* (London: Aurum Press, 2004).

aides without the presence of civil servants has had its costs. He claimed in the House of Lords:

> The positive features of that system, designed to draw in the expertise available in all parts of the government in a systematic way and subject policy decisions to constructive criticism, and challenge from those political colleagues with a wider perspective than those grappling with the issues day to day, are still worth pursuing.

Butler's long experience at the centre gave him a special authority to claim that the Blair methods represent a serious departure from that ideal, although some cynics might claim that this is Whitehall code for not being sufficiently consulted. But Lord Owen cited the intelligence failure when complaining of the 'the matey, corner-cutting, somewhat shambolic, structure of No. 10's defence and security decision-making which were revealed in the Hutton hearings'.[9] Cabinet colleagues have complained in private that Blair's liking for bilaterals allows people to believe different things about his intentions. This was notably the case with his late decision to hold a referendum on the EU constitution – it was not discussed in Cabinet and took pro-EU ministers by surprise.[10]

Perhaps this will change, as Blair at the outset of his third term has declared his intention to make more use of the Cabinet system and to involve himself more in the Cabinet committees. He has also decided that Cabinet committees will review progress on key targets rather than conduct regular stocktaking exercises in Number 10 with his advisers and the minister.

The centre

Blair began with the assumption that there was a hole at the centre of British government. Many of his predecessors felt the same, but nobody, not even Lloyd George, has matched Blair's energy in creating a personal machine. Yet despite his recurring attempts to increase the number of staff, units and resources at his disposal, he still seems to feel he lacks sufficient levers. Presumably, the levers are over colleagues and departments.[11]

---

[9] Lord Owen, 'The ever-growing dominance of Number 10 in British diplomacy', lecture at London School of Economics, 8 October 2003.

[10] On the evolution of this decision, see Seldon, *Blair*, pp. 648–51.

[11] On problems of dependency and implementation, see Mark Bevir and Rod Rhodes, 'Presidents, barons, court politics and Blair', unpublished paper, April 2005.

Mrs Thatcher left behind a memory of a style of premiership, one that stretched the elasticity of the office and was heavily reliant on personal qualities: her energy, conviction and self-belief. The style died with her demise. Blair, in contrast, may leave behind a set of institutions. In the past, however, there has usually been a reaction against institution builders in Number 10. The role of the Cabinet Secretary was reduced when Lloyd George fell in 1922, and his so-called Garden Suburb was disbanded. In 1964 Harold Wilson talked confidently of making Number 10 into a powerhouse not a monastery. He only managed, in the face of a recalcitrant civil service, to appoint an extra private secretary, a deputy press secretary and Marcia Williams as his political secretary. In 1974 he created a policy unit which Mrs Thatcher was on the point of abolishing in 1979. She did manage to disband the Central Policy Review Staff (CPRS), created by Edward Heath in 1970.

Yet the demands on prime ministers have increased over time and Blair's response is understandable. Number 10 today is certainly much better staffed than it has ever been and has lost much of the famous family atmosphere. Although it is still not large in comparison with the centres available to political leaders in other major Western states, Blair in his first term had created a prime minister's department in all but name.

Blair's chief of staff expressed his leader's determination to have a Napoleonic rather than a Cabinet system. He wanted decisions to flow from a central point rather than from a series of ministerial barons or collective processes. The core of the executive would be in Number 10, which would have a considerable increase in staff, particularly of special advisers, two of whom would have the power to instruct civil servants. From John Major's eight special advisers in Number 10, Blair in 2005 had 28. He increasingly relied on three figures in Number 10 with whom he had regular personal contact: Alastair Campbell, his principal private secretary, Jeremy Heywood and Jonathan Powell. The first left by the end of 2003 and Baroness Morgan of Huyton emerged during the second term as a key confidante.

The creation of a more powerful Number 10 has occurred as a series of ad hoc steps. Over the first term he expanded the staffs of most units and created new ones (e.g. the Strategic Communications Unit and the Research and Intelligence Unit). Having by 2001 doubled the size of the Policy Unit and the private office, Blair combined the two into a new Policy Directorate, consisting of some 30 civil servants and political appointees working side by side, dealing with short- and medium-term policy questions. In 2001 he also established a Strategy Unit to work on more long-term policies and has over 60 staff working at any one time, an Office of Public Service Reform, and a Delivery Unit, based in Number 10 until its move to the Treasury in 2003. The latter oversees the key objectives and monitors the departments' progress on targets and delivery.

The traditional role of the Cabinet Secretary has been redefined. After 9/11 and the growing importance of terrorism, security and intelligence coordination were removed from the Cabinet Secretary, along with honours and various minor tasks. Sir Andrew Turnbull was to concentrate on the core political priority of delivery, centring on 30 key targets. Whitehall managed to fend off attempts by some of his advisers to appoint an outsider as Cabinet Secretary and make the appointee a permanent secretary to the prime minister.

A result is that a larger number of people appear to speak with the authority of the prime minister than ever before. From the start Policy Unit staff took it upon themselves radically to rewrite White Paper drafts from senior Cabinet ministers. An offended Deputy Prime Minister complained about the 'teeny boppers' in Number 10 who mangled his Transport Paper.

Blair has also shown a liking for creating project teams that cut across departments, another indicator of his dislike of departmentalism. In the first four, let alone eight, years of his premiership he presided over more change around Number 10 than had been achieved over the previous fifty years. The purpose of these changes was to establish better linkages between Number 10 and the departments as well as to make the latter more responsive to the former. Blair wanted to drive the agenda. That agenda increasingly is about delivery of public service reform and improved public services. No predecessor has engaged so much with this agenda and tried to break with the traditional 'one size fits all' approach to the public services. Since 2001 he has added the principles of diversity of providers and choice for consumers to the other mechanisms of national standards, flexibility and devolution to the front line. He impatiently warned a gathering of permanent secretaries in summer 2003 that the civil service of the twenty-first century would be judged not so much on the quality of its policy advice (a trend starting with Thatcher) as on its success in delivering quality public services.

Here is another Blair paradox. The constitutional changes under his leadership mean that he has conceded unprecedented powers from Whitehall and Westminster, but his style of party management and governing has been top-down and managerial. Treasury and Number 10-inspired targets are with departments rather than ministers and persist even with a change of minister. The fusion of much of Number 10 and the

Cabinet Office has produced a complex structure and raises the question of how the Prime Minister can actually be in control of it.

The curse of abroad

New Labour leaders claimed to appreciate the interconnections between domestic and foreign policy; after all, they invoked the theme of globalisation when explaining the need for the shift in traditional Labour economic and social policies to make Britain more internationally competitive. But Blair has surprised himself with the amount of his time taken up with Northern Ireland, Europe and wars. Apart from a few seminars with retired diplomats when in opposition, he had shown little interest in international affairs.

Blair revels in being on the international stage. His tendencies to grandstand and moralise have been given ample scope by the proliferation of summits and institutions of international governance. The wars in Kosovo and Iraq were vehicles for him to express his absolutist sense of right and wrong and, like Woodrow Wilson, a passion for remaking the world. His address in Chicago in April 1999 spelled out five conditions for high-minded interventions in the affairs of other sovereign states, a reworking of the case for a just war. His initiative to save Africa has accompanied efforts to find a way through the Middle East quagmire and provide a new direction for the European Union. After the 2001 general election he created a new Overseas and Defence Secretariat in Number 10, drawing functions from the Cabinet Office, a new European Secretariat, again drawn from the Cabinet Office, and appointed two senior civil servants to head them. But there is no denying that Attlee and Churchill were much bigger figures on the international stage when Britain was, however nominally, one of 'the big three' and the centre of a great empire.

Blair has been the most pro-European British prime minister since Heath and, perhaps more than his predecessors, sought to lead the EU by joining or breaking the Franco-German axis. But he has limited his impact in the EU by his acquiescence in Gordon Brown's seizure of the euro decision (accepting that it is an economic decision makes it primarily a Treasury matter), his unwillingness to make – or allow pro-euro ministers to make – the case for entry in the face of a hostile press (although he described it as 'a matter of destiny for us'), and siding with the United States rather than 'old' Europe over Iraq. The Atlanticist thrust of his foreign policy has imposed strains on the party and the PLP. In Westminster the Prime Minister may be a big fish but outside the United Kingdom he is just one of 25 leaders who all have their own electorates to consider. At the Council of Ministers Blair's influence is not exercised by the Labour whips or reliant on the support of the *Sun*, but depends on the cooperation of other states.

Abroad is sometimes a leader's escape from home with its complex problems, political opposition, party critics calling for his resignation, and carping press. But abroad, even when playing the role of the international statesman, can also be politically dangerous. When James Callaghan was in sun-drenched Guadaloupe in January 1979, the winter of discontent was unfolding at home and power was slipping from his grasp. And in Paris in November 1990, Mrs Thatcher, feted by fellow political leaders celebrating the end of the Cold War, learned that her ungrateful MPs wanted her to go.

Blair has been no exception. If Calais was engraved on the heart of Mary Tudor, Iraq may be Blair's epitaph. It has been a case, to quote Robin Cook, of Blair wanting to 'fix the world rather than running Britain'.

Strategy

Blair often talks of strategy and appointing ministers to carry out 'the strategy'. He created a Strategic Communications Unit and, for long-term policy, a Strategy Unit. But few politicians think strategically, least of all when they are so concerned with the media and elections. Even Mrs Thatcher, when asked by an aide what her strategy was on an issue referred to her policy, and, when asked what that was, referred to a speech she had made. 'A speech is not a policy', replied the brave aide. To date, Blair's record hardly compares with the scale of Attlee's major reform programme or Thatcher's relatively clear and consistent sense of direction.

If Thatcherism was in part statecraft to roll back the policy legacy of 1945 and create a vote-winning coalition, New Labour was an acknowledgement of Conservative hegemony in policy and elections in the late twentieth century. In the 1997 general election it succeeded brilliantly in overturning that electoral deficit. It has had mixed success in redefining the parameters of what a social democratic party can achieve in a world of global competition. Blair can point to some successes – Bank of England independence, the minimum wage, constitutional changes and partial reform of public services.

Before 1997 policy preparations had been made only for the Treasury and education: Gordon Brown and David Blunkett were the only two shadow ministers to be promised their positions in advance of the election. It does not help that the average ministerial tenure is two years (for some posts it is less), that recruitment of ministers is confined to what John Hoskyns called a small gene pool of the largest party in the Commons and that appointments also take account of such criteria as political balance, gender and geography.

Blair has taken some positive steps. Departments, at the behest of Lord Birt, have produced five-year plans – although we can speculate how many would survive a change of prime minister in their present form. He has sought to broaden the range of talent at his disposal in making government appointments by giving peerages to the likes of Gus MacDonald, Charles Falconer, David Simon, David Sainsbury and Andrew Adonis. He held bi-monthly progress meetings with his key ministers, with the Treasury, Delivery Unit and senior officials in attendance, which continued to take place during the Iraq war. Most unusually, at the beginning of the 2001 Parliament, he informed the senior ministers at the Home Office, health, education and transport that they could look forward to serving in their posts for the duration of the Parliament. A brave hope, but none stayed the course.

Blair the crisis-manager and headline seeker has hampered strategy. It is inevitable that high-pressure events like wars, Northern Ireland, foot and mouth disease and the petrol protests dominate Number 10. But the Prime Minister called on his aides for 'eye-catching initiatives' and said that he 'should be associated with as much of this as possible'. Many of the interventions have been in Home Office matters. The interest in media-driven initiatives and the assumption that media coverage is the same as action illustrates the dictum of Dick Morris, the American campaign consultant, that every day is election day and a battle for the headlines. The permanent campaign and all too often the style of leadership and policy-making that Labour perfected in opposition has been imported into government.

The misleading presidential analogy

The decline of the above institutions has led to claims that we are moving to a Blair presidency. The Labour MP Graham Allen has introduced a motion calling for the adoption of a proper set of checks and balances to cope with an emerging presidential system.[12] Such a trend precedes 1997;

---

[12] Graham Allen, *The Last Prime Minister* (London: Politico's, 2003).

Blair happens to be a high point in the trend to more leader-oriented parties and government. In support of the thesis, one may point to Blair's personal manifesto and pledges at election time, the increase in the size and influence of his personal staffing in Number 10, the mechanisms established to monitor the progress of departments in meeting targets set by Number 10, the neglect of Parliament and Cabinet, the focus on presentation in all its manifestations, and the increase in 'summitry' as political heads of state confer and negotiate on behalf of their governments.

This analysis is all accurate, but the analogy claims both too much and too little: too much, because, unlike the US president, the prime minister has no guaranteed tenure, as the party's MPs and Cabinet colleagues can withdraw their support; too little, because a prime minister with a majority in Parliament is virtually assured of getting his legislation and budget through. And the blocking role of the Treasury under Brown is difficult to square with presidential ideas of central command.

The public

Blair has shown a remarkable capacity to communicate with the electorate, to demonstrate empathy at key moments and present himself as a 'regular sort of guy'.

He regularly invokes the idea of the people – the people's agenda, the people's princess. But if it is populist it is, as Rose claims, 'managed populism', in which the communication is largely one-way. He uses the Third Way to dismiss the old left and the right and place himself in a virtuous middle, a form of conflict-free politics. But the terms like 'new', 'modern' and 'radical' say little of the direction; they could equally be applied to Thatcherism. The inclusiveness is reflected in the 1999 conference speech: 'Arrayed against us: the forces of conservatism, the cynics, the elites, the establishment . . . On our side, the forces of modernity and justice. Those who believe in a Britain for all the people.' Geoff Mulgan, a former adviser, has argued that the success of New Labour's big tent strategy 'actually weakened it as a transformative project'.[13]

Blair personally, and his government, began with enormous goodwill. Much of his appeal rested on the expectation that he and his ministers would be whiter than white and would restore trust in politicians and the political system, both of which had been damaged during the Major years. Over time, however, he and his ministers have suffered a massive

[13] Geoff Mulgan, 'My time in the engine-room', *Prospect*, May 2005.

haemorrhaging of trust, in spite of building an elaborate communications machinery. Iraq and his exaggerated claims about weapons of mass destruction and his handling of the intelligence exacerbated existing doubts about his trustworthiness. With the departure of Alastair Campbell, Blair tried to create a less media-driven Number 10. The new Director of Communications, David Hill, did not have Campbell's authority to issue instructions to civil servants and Blair held 'on the record' press conferences and took questions from the Commons Liaison Committee.

For the 2005 general election campaign his aides, concerned about voters' disillusion with him, eventually prevailed on him to appear regularly in public with Gordon Brown to minimise the damage to the party. The image was a far cry from the triumphant figure of 1997 and 2001. Indeed the 2005 British Election Study found that the level of voter support for a policy actually fell from its initial level when it was revealed that Tony Blair backed it.

Conclusion

Over the two terms Blair may point to the following achievements:

1. Three successive general election victories – the first time this has happened in the party's history – and two of them by a landslide. Labour now appears as the natural party of government, the Conservative Party has been driven to the margins of debate and some 60% of the electorate vote for parties of the centre left.
2. Substantial, if incomplete, constitutional reform, the most far-reaching for a century.
3. Economic stability and prosperity, so that Labour has seized the mantle of economic competence from the Conservatives.
4. The minimum wage, talked of since Keir Hardie's day, and redistribution to the poorest households largely through the working tax credits and child tax credits.
5. Welfare reform, to encourage work not dependency.
6. Greatly increased investment in public services.
7. The Good Friday agreement in Northern Ireland has been kept and is on course.
8. A stronger centre in Whitehall, based on a better resourced Number 10 and Cabinet Office, has been created.
9. Some improvements in some public services, although there has been no 'transformation' or emergence of 'world class public services'.

The credit for the achievements is not all due to Blair. Some belongs to Gordon Brown, some to previous Conservative governments, and some to forces outside the government's control. Blair, for example, inherited much of the constitutional reform agenda from previous Labour leaders, did not show much interest in it, and when he has become involved – as over the composition of the House of Lords or abolishing the role of the Lord Chancellor – has made a mess of it. Other issues, such as pensions, local government finance, electoral reform and entry to the eurozone, have been put to one side.

Blair has tried to fashion a new-style premiership, mixing populism with a tighter grip over Whitehall and the wider public sector. A risk of his downgrading of party, Parliament and Cabinet is that when blame is allocated it settles on him.

But when set against the opportunities – the large parliamentary majorities, the supportive Labour Party (until recently, at least), initial press goodwill, benign international economy, and the feeble and divided opposition party – one might have looked for more. The bar would be even higher if set against the inflated rhetoric (Britain as a model state for the twenty-first century, the new Britain, and Britain as a pioneer of a Third Way, 'a new style of politics for the centre left in the twenty-first century').

To date the great peace-time prime ministers have been change-oriented or pathfinders; they have sought to make radical changes to British society, economy and/or institutions. Apart from Blair, would-be pathfinders since 1945 have been Attlee, Macmillan, Heath and Thatcher. Of the list only Attlee and Thatcher were achievers. So far there has not been a third.

2

Parliament

PHILIP COWLEY AND MARK STUART

Parliament is one of the most misunderstood aspects of the Blair premiership – and especially of the second term. Critics of the government bemoan the Prime Minister's own lack of interest in the institution – as demonstrated by his poor voting record – and the government's approach to reform of both the Commons and the Lords. They bemoan the decline of Parliament and its increasing subservience to the executive.

Yet the true picture is more complicated – and more balanced – than this melancholy caricature. This chapter examines both the growing independence of Labour's backbenchers and the process of Commons modernisation during the second Blair term. It also examines the two key developments in the Lords during the same period: the cack-handed (and ultimately futile) attempts to enact stage two of Lords reform, alongside the growing activism and assertiveness of the partly reformed Lords.

The combined result of these four developments was that throughout 2001–5 the government faced a partly reformed but much more assertive House of Commons and a partly reformed but much more assertive House of Lords. It is probably fair to say that it is not what the government had intended when it first took office – or what it desired – but it is also a more positive picture than the government's many critics appreciate.

I want to hold your hand

One of the earliest signs that things in Parliament were going to be rather different in Blair's second term came in July 2001, when viewers of BBC's *Frost on Sunday* were treated to the sight of Donald Anderson MP and Gwyneth Dunwoody MP holding hands on live television. The cause of this early-morning tryst – which surely ranks as one of the more disturbing sights of the 2001 Parliament – was the decision taken by the government (in the form of the whips' office) to remove Mr Anderson from the Foreign Affairs Select Committee, which he had chaired since 1997, and to do likewise to Mrs Dunwoody from the transport committee. The government claimed that both had had a fair crack of the whip, and that the committees needed some fresh blood. Critics saw it as an attempt by the government to nobble two independent-minded select committee chairs, thus weakening Parliament's ability to scrutinise the executive. Their early morning appearance on the Frost sofa was a sign of mutual defiance – and was enough to put any watching whip right off their cornflakes.

The following day the House of Commons sided with the hand-holding rebels. The new composition of the Transport Committee was voted down by 308 to 221, that of the Foreign Affairs Committee by 301 to 232. Some 125 Labour MPs voted against the government's wishes in the first vote; 118 did so in the second.[1] Anderson and Dunwoody were promptly reinstated on their committees, which they then went on to chair for the rest of the Parliament. In themselves, the votes were of only moderate importance. It is hardly as if the Foreign Affairs Select Committee has much power (and not even that much influence), ditto for the transport committee.[2] But the dispute was emblematic of several of the key developments in the Commons during Blair's second term.

The first was the continuing lack of interest of many in the government in Parliament, except as an institution that could be controlled to make life easier for the government. The second, however, was the increasing willingness of Labour backbenchers to defy their front bench – and to make life harder for the government. Donald Anderson greeted the select committee result with the claim that it was 'a peasant's revolt and a great day for Parliament'. The select committee votes were just the first public manifestation of that growing independence. The third and perhaps the least obvious factor was the role played by Robin Cook, the new Leader of the House of Commons. Having been moved from the Foreign and Commonwealth Office after the election, Cook had declared privately that he was determined to 'leave footprints in the sand'. Almost his first public act in his new role was to intervene in the Anderson and Dunwoody affair, promising Labour MPs that they would be given a free vote on the issue, and making it clear that the Commons had the potential to reverse the decision should it so wish. The view in the government whips' office was that, had they been able to whip the vote as they wanted to, they would have got their way – but Cook's intervention had stopped them dead in

---

[1] Both figures include tellers.

[2] Although it was to be Mr Anderson's Committee which interviewed the MoD scientist, Dr David Kelly, and concluded, erroneously as it turned out, that he was not the source for Andrew Gilligan's claims about the 'sexing up' of the government's Iraq dossier.

their tracks. This was the first public sign of how Cook would fulfil his role, and until he resigned in 2003 over the Iraq war, he was to prove an activist Leader of the House, intervening in the process of Lords reform as well as attempting to give some drive and direction to the 'modernisation' of the House of Commons begun, somewhat hesitatingly and sporadically, in the first Blair term.

Backbenchers get stuck in

During the first Blair term it became usual to refer to Labour backbenchers in disparaging terms. They acquired a reputation for mindless loyalty and a distinct lack of backbone, routinely compared to sheep, poodles, clones, robots or – most bizarrely of all – daleks. Then, during Labour's second term, a remarkable transformation appeared to come over the Parliamentary Labour Party (PLP). Almost overnight it appeared to develop some attitude. Between 1997 and 2001 Labour MPs had attracted a reputation for asking patsy questions to the Prime Minister during Prime Minister's Questions (PMQs), in what occasionally became a cringe-making competition in sycophancy. It wasn't that Labour MPs were the first to do this – the practice had been rife under previous Conservative governments, many of whose MPs could toady with the best of them – but Labour MPs had certainly taken the practice to new lows. However, in the very first session of PMQs of the new Parliament Labour backbencher after backbencher stood up to challenge the Prime Minister, making clear their opposition to proposed changes to incapacity benefit. It was a remarkably assertive series of questions, which appeared to leave the Prime Minister taken aback by their ferocity. One journalist jokingly described it as 'Day One of the Intifada'.[3]

This was followed by the Anderson/Dunwoody votes, which were then followed in turn by a remarkable series of backbench revolts against the whip. The 2001 Parliament was noteworthy both for the frequency and size of the backbench rebellions that took place. Labour MPs defied their whips on a total of 259 occasions, more than in any other post-war Parliament (save that of 1974–9). But the Wilson/Callaghan government of 1974–9 lasted for five parliamentary sessions, whereas the second Blair government consisted of just four. Measured as a percentage of the divisions (votes) to occur in Parliament, the period from 2001 to 2005 tops the post-war list. It saw Labour backbenchers rebel in 20.8% of divisions,

---

[3] The first private meeting of the Parliamentary Labour Party was similarly argumentative.

more than in any other Parliament since 1945. Some of the revolts were especially large. The 65 Labour MPs who voted against the government in the largest rebellion, over foundation hospitals, in 2003 broke the record for the largest health policy rebellion by Labour MPs against their own government, ten more than the 55 who rebelled against the Wilson government over charges for NHS false teeth and spectacles in July 1969. The 72 Labour MPs who voted against the Second Reading of the Higher Education Bill in 2004, the bill which would have introduced so-called top-up fees, were precisely double the 36 who rebelled over voluntary schools in 1931 (until then the largest education rebellion by Labour MPs) and exactly matched the post-war record for a rebellion by government MPs at a bill's second reading. And the rebellions over Iraq – the largest of which saw 139 Labour MPs vote against their whip in March 2003 – were larger than any foreign policy or defence rebellion ever before against a Labour government.

Indeed, the Iraq revolts were the largest rebellions by MPs of any governing party – Labour, Conservative or Liberal – on any type of policy since modern British party politics began.[4] To find a larger rebellion than Iraq, you had to go back to the Corn Laws in the middle of the nineteenth century. Then Robert Peel had seen two-thirds of Conservative MPs vote against their own administration and just a third backing him in the division lobbies. But since then – since the beginnings of modern British politics in other words – there had been nothing to match the Iraq revolts.

Moreover, foundation hospitals, top-up-fees and Iraq were just the best known revolts. In the four years after 2001 there were also decent-sized rebellions over anti-terrorism legislation (repeatedly), community health councils, smacking, asylum and immigration (again, repeatedly), faith schools, living wills, trial by jury, gambling, the firefighters, the Housing Bill, organ donation, the Enterprise Bill, the European constitution, ID cards and the banning of incitement to religious hatred.

Peter Oborne, writing in the *Spectator* (as the government was struggling to pass its Higher Education Bill) argued, 'Tony Blair has achieved the impossible. Three years after winning a landslide majority of 160, he

---

[4] They shattered all existing records: the 93 Liberals who had voted against Gladstone's proposals for Home Rule in June 1886, the 95 Conservatives who had defied the Major government over aspects of its firearms legislation, after the Dunblane massacre in 1996 (when 16 young children and their teacher were shot dead by a man using legally licensed weapons and ammunition) or the 110 Labour MPs who had rebelled in July 1976, during the passage of the (now long-forgotten) Rent (Agriculture) Bill.

is forced to conduct his business as if he were leader of a minority government.' It was, Oborne concluded, 'a failure of party management on a heroic scale'.[5] The talk of sheep was no more; but how had a group of politicians routinely dismissed as second-rate and cowardly become so rebellious?

It was certainly not because of any change in personnel. Only a handful of seats had changed hands in the standstill election of 2001, with 85% of the Commons exactly the same after the election as it had been before. The people who caused so much trouble in the four years *after* 2001 were therefore much the same ones who had been dismissed as sheep for four years *before*.

Part of the answer was that the sheep and robots of the first term were a myth. Certainly rebellions were relatively infrequent between 1997 and 2001 (although there were still more, for example, than those against the Attlee government), but those that took place were large, and involved a total of 133 Labour MPs, far more than the so-called 'usual suspects'.[6] Another part of the answer was that while Labour MPs became more rebellious in the second term, party discipline did not collapse. The majority of rebellions consisted of fewer than 10 MPs; those that made the whips sweat – such as those over Iraq, top-up fees or foundation hospitals – remained infrequent occurrences. And although more than 200 MPs rebelled at some point during the Parliament, most did so only sporadically. Even the rebels were overwhelmingly loyal. The most rebellious Labour MP, Jeremy Corbyn, voted against his party whip on 128 occasions out of the 1,246 votes to take place during the Parliament: that is, he rebelled against his whip in just 12% of votes. Cohesion therefore remained the norm after 2001, with dissent the exception – and when cohesion weakened, the result was usually splinters rather than splits. The 2001 election therefore did not mark the point at which the PLP changed from being poodles to rottweillers – both because Labour MPs were not poodles before, and because they did not become rottweillers afterwards. But something did change. There were four main reasons why Labour MPs became more willing to defy their whips in the 2001 Parliament, when compared with 1997.

The first was what Tony Benn calls 'the ishoos'. Even the most independent-minded Labour MP does not vote against the party just

---

[5] Peter Oborne, 'Blair downgraded the Labour whips – and now he is paying the price', *The Spectator*, 17 January 2004.

[6] See Philip Cowley, *Revolts and Rebellions: Parliamentary Voting Under Blair* (London: Politico's, 2002).

for the hell of it. It takes the right issues to trigger revolts. Iraq was just such a trigger. So too were many of the pieces of legislation through which the government tried to enact the 'reform' of the public services. Yet a moment's reflection shows that the issues alone do not fully explain the growth in backbench dissent in the period. Compare, for example, the reaction of the PLP to the government's higher education reforms in the 1997 Parliament with those in the 2001 Parliament, when it introduced variable post-graduation fees. The former produced a rebellion of 34 MPs, despite removing grants and introducing up-front fees which were likely to be a far greater disincentive to working-class students than deferred fees. The latter saw 72 Labour MPs vote against their whips – cutting the government's majority to just five – despite the variable fees being deferred and grants being reintroduced for students from low-income families.

A second reason why backbench dissent increased was that the back benches increasingly contained more MPs with personal reasons for being disgruntled with the leadership, including all those who had been sacked from ministerial office or passed over for promotion: what one senior whip called 'the dismissed and the disappointed'. By the end of the 2001 Parliament, almost a quarter of the PLP had been in, but had left, government. The influence of these ex-ministers was as much qualitative as quantitative; they lent the later rebellions gravitas that those in the first term had lacked. Many of the ex-whips now knocking around on the back benches also lent the rebellions some of the organisational flair lacking in the first term. In addition, there was also a sizeable group of MPs from the 1997 cohort who realised that they were now unlikely to make it into government, and who began to rebel as a consequence. This latter group included the much-maligned Helen Clark, who (as Helen Brinton) had become synonymous with excessive loyalty during the 1997 Parliament – loyalty was once jokingly said to be measured in 'Brintons' – but who voted against her whip on ten occasions between 2001 and 2005.

Third, the self-discipline that was exercised by many Labour MPs for much of the first Parliament continued to decline. When first elected to government many Labour MPs, even those on the left, took a conscious decision – motivated in part by the spectre of squabbling Conservatives in the 1992 Parliament – not to rebel unless forced to. Faced with a choice of being seen as clones or being seen as disunited, many chose the clones. As time went on, especially as the Conservatives continued to fail to make any obvious (half-decent) recovery, so the pressure to be self-disciplined receded. Blair's speech to the Parliamentary Labour Party in 2003, in which he appealed to the party not to let disunity allow the Conservatives back in, was an (unsuccessful) attempt to reinstall some of that self-discipline.

Fourth, what made things even worse for the government is that once an MP has rebelled, he or she is much more likely to rebel for a second time (and then a third, and a fourth . . .). Once the taboo of defying the whip has been broken, further acts of defiance become more frequent. And so with each new rebellion, the number of likely rebels for any subsequent rebellion increases. The dangers of recidivism are very real and it was for precisely this reason that the whips' office began the 2001 Parliament with the explicit aim of keeping the number of new rebels down to a minimum. This was not because they were especially worried about the effect of rebellions in Blair's second term, but rather to avoid storing up trouble for the third term. The events of the second term meant that they failed in their aim. By the end of the Parliament, 218 Labour MPs had voted against their whip at least once.

Despite all the revolts, however, the government did still manage to reach the end of its second term undefeated in the Commons on a whipped vote. Prior to 1997, every government since Wilson's elected in 1966 had been defeated at least once in the Commons. By 2001, Blair had survived eight years without suffering a defeat. In part, this was because of the sheer size of the majority enjoyed by the government. For all that large majorities can engender revolts (with MPs knowing that they can defy the whip without it having any consequences for the government) they also provide useful cushions against those occasions when MPs are more seriously disgruntled. Moreover, some Labour MPs were prepared to bark but not to bite, rebelling only on those occasions when they knew they would not defeat the government. Over foundation hospitals (2003) and top-up fees (2004) and the Prevention of Terrorism Bill (2005) there were enough Labour rebels to have defeated the government, had they all voted the same way at the same time. They did not, and so the legislation survived. Also the government frequently gave way on legislation in order to ensure its passage through the Commons. That was true, for example, in all three of the above cases. It was also true on other occasions, with ministers agreeing to water down or amend legislation in order to pacify backbench critics. The lack of defeats should not be assumed to imply a lack of backbench influence.

But perhaps the clearest example of backbench influence came over the proposed ban on fox-hunting (more accurately hunting with hounds). It had long been clear that many at the top levels of government – especially the Prime Minister and both his first two home secretaries – did not want to see a total ban on hunting reach the statute book. But ever since they had voted in such overwhelming numbers for Michael Foster's private members' bill in November 1997, Labour MPs refused to allow their government to wriggle away from the issue. When he was Home Secretary Jack Straw attended a packed meeting of Labour's backbench committee on Home Affairs, at which nearly all of the 100 or so MPs in attendance made it clear that they wanted to see a ban. As he left the meeting Straw was heard to say that he could see no point in 'lying in front of a tank'. Every time the government tried to offer a compromise, or a delay, or some other concession to the hunting lobby – and they did try, repeatedly – their backbenchers refused to concede the issue. In the end (after yet another desperate attempt at a compromise solution), the government relented, and agreed to use the Parliament Act to force the measure past a reluctant House of Lords.

The ban on fox-hunting is on the Statute Book precisely because Labour MPs refused to let it go. As one anti-hunting Labour MP remarked after the final vote: 'I'm quite proud of the PLP for getting us here – shows what one can achieve by polite persistence.' Whatever one's views about the policy, and whether one thinks hunting should continue or not, that aspect of the process is striking. The eventually successful struggle by Labour backbenchers to secure a ban on hunting deserves to go down as one of the clearest examples of backbench influence in the post-war period.

Modernisation

The story of Commons modernisation in the first term of the Blair government was a mixed one.[7] The process was variously criticised for detracting from the ability of the Commons to hold the government to account, for being too piecemeal and for lacking coherence. Some of the Modernisation Committee's proposals – such as removing the requirement for MPs to wear a top hat when making a point of order during a division – had been useful and sensible. Some of the ideas – such as the Westminster Hall debating chamber – did some little good (or little harm, depending on your point of view). But few of the proposals had the potential to enhance the scrutinising role of the Commons. Of the 15 substantive reports published by the House of Commons Modernisation Committee between 1997 and 2001, only two contained proposals to help enhance the power of the Commons in relation to the executive. The others were designed

---

[7] See Philip Norton, 'Parliament' in A. Seldon (ed.), *The Blair Effect* (London: Little, Brown, 2001), pp. 43–64.

for cosmetic or tidying-up purposes, or for the convenience of members. As one observer argued, although many of the changes introduced by the committee were desirable in themselves, 'The basic questions of scrutiny and accountability – of power – have not been addressed.'[8]

One problem had been that neither of the two Leaders of the House during the 1997 Parliament, Ann Taylor and Margaret Beckett, had been especially interested in the process of parliamentary reform, except insofar as it could expedite the government's programme. Robin Cook, by contrast, was a much more reform-minded Leader of the House. In addition to being determined to enjoy a political Indian summer in the post, Cook was anyway temperamentally a more Parliament-focused individual. His own predilections for reform were given extra impetus (somewhat bizarrely in our view) by the low turnout in the 2001 election, which had generated an elite-level perception that the public was dissatisfied with the institutions of representative democracy (as if strengthening select committees, say, would somehow make the voters of Liverpool Riverside happily troop out to vote with a song in their heart). Shortly after the election, the Hansard Society's 'Commission on Parliamentary Scrutiny', chaired by the former Conservative Leader of the House, Tony Newton, published its final report, *The Challenge for Parliament – Making Government Accountable*. It was well received by commentators and practitioners, and added to a growing body of influential literature urging reform of Parliament. June 2001 also saw the formation of a cross-party group of MPs called 'Parliament First', whose first act was a motion stating that 'the role of Parliament has weakened, is weakening and ought to be strengthened'. The momentum for reform was clearly present.

Cook's approach was to push forward a package of reforms, rather than the somewhat piecemeal approach taken before – in order to prevent opponents of reform picking off individual reforms. And so, in December 2001, he published the so-called Cook memorandum, in which he made clear his intentions for a wide-reaching set of reforms.[9] Many of the proposals were similar (in some cases, identical) to the proposals made in the various reformist publications – such as the report from the Hansard Society – with the key proposals addressing select committees, parliamentary hours and the passage of bills.

However, once the Commons began voting on the measures it became clear that while reforms could be *presented* as a package, there was no

---

[8] Peter Riddell, *Parliament Under Blair* (London: Politico's, 2000), p. 248.
[9] HC 440 (2001–2002), *Modernisation of the House of Commons: A Reform Programme for Consultation*, memorandum submitted by the Leader of the House of Commons.

guarantee that the Commons would *accept* them as a package. The first batch of proposed reforms was debated in May 2002, when MPs agreed to improve the resources available to select committees. This included introducing payment for select committee chairs in order to make backbench careers an attractive alternative to entering government.[10] But in response to the Anderson/Dunwoody controversy at the beginning of the Parliament, the Modernisation Committee had also proposed establishing an independent selection panel to choose the members of select committees.[11] The proposal was designed to shift the power to decide which MPs are to sit on select committees away from the Committee of Selection (which was, in reality, controlled by the party whips) to an all-party committee.

Despite Cook's very vocal support, the proposal was defeated by 209 votes to 195. While 133 Labour MPs voted in favour, 103 voted against. There were complaints that the government whips – keen to hold on to their power – had pressurised some Labour MPs into voting against Cook's proposals.[12] The behaviour of the whips certainly did make some MPs vote against the proposals and because the vote was so close the whips' behaviour ultimately explains why the decision went nay rather than aye. But this handful of MPs (and it was only a handful) did not explain why the vote was so close in the first place. There was also much genuine opposition from some backbench Labour MPs. For example, Dennis Skinner – hardly a whip's nark – argued that 'The new-fangled select committee system would have handed over power to the political enemy – the Tories – who were going to sit on a joint committee to select Labour members of Parliament.'

A further batch of changes – a veritable collection of parliamentary reformers Greatest Hits – came up for decision in October 2002.[13] They included:

---

[10] After referring the matter to the Senior Salaries Review Body, it was eventually agreed that most select committee chairs would be paid an extra £12,500 per annum.

[11] HC 224 (2001–2002), *Select Committees*, First Report from the Select Committee on Modernisation of the House of Commons.

[12] See, for example, Alexandra Kelso 'Where were the massed ranks of parliamentary reformers? – "attitudinal" and "contextual" approaches to parliamentary reform', *Journal of Legislative Studies* 9 (2003): 57–76. It was striking, for example, that 11 whips voted no, while the Chief Whip Hilary Armstrong was joined by only three whips in the aye lobby.

[13] HC 1168 (2001–2002), *Modernisation of the House of Commons: A Reform Programme*, Second Report from the Select Committee on Modernisation of the House of Commons. The House also debated (and accepted) reforms proposed by the Procedure Committee on parliamentary questions, which had the effect of making questions more interesting and topical.

- Ending the sessional cut-off, allowing bills to carry over from one session to another, thus stopping the legislative log-jam which routinely occurs at the end of each parliamentary year.
- Further changes to the parliamentary timetable: for the first time there would be a House of Commons calendar (to be announced a year in advance) that would allow MPs an extra week to work in their constituencies; and the Commons would return earlier from its summer recess.
- Changes to the parliamentary day: from Tuesdays to Thursdays the Commons would sit earlier, usually starting at 11.30 am (and finishing by 7 pm rather than 10.30 pm), while constituency business would be given precedence on Fridays.
- More bills to be published in draft form, thus allowing for earlier and routine legislative scrutiny, and a more regular use of time limits on backbench speeches.
- An earlier start to Prime Minister's Questions – at noon on a Wednesday, instead of 3 pm – in order to generate better media coverage.
- More of an effort to connect with the public by improving public access to Westminster, including on Saturdays.

Supporters argued (as they had with all previous votes on modernisa-tion) that the proposals would make Parliament both more efficient and effective – and that these changes would improve the public's perception of the institution. Robin Cook argued the 'the best case for modernisa-tion is that this House will lose its authority if it is seen by the nation to be out of date'. Opponents argued (again, as they had with all previous votes on modernisation) that the proposals simply made it easier for the government to get its business through, and undermined the House of Commons. As Eric Forth, the shadow leader of the House said, 'Every-thing the government is proposing makes life easier for MPs and easier for the government. That surely isn't what Parliament should be about.'

Some of the biggest splits came over the issue of parliamentary hours (and, as a result, this was the issue that attracted most attention in the media). Although a majority of Labour MPs backed the Modernisation Committee's proposals, a sizeable minority (over a third in two cases) opposed the reforms. They argued that there was little benefit in finishing early for MPs who represented constituencies too far away from Westmin-ster to be able to return home at night. Chris Mullin conjured up images of hundreds of MPs 'roaming the streets of the West End with too much time on their hands and too much money in their pockets'.

Despite a fairly heated debate, the modernisers won the votes, albeit narrowly in some cases. The votes were a triumph for Cook and for the modernisers in general. Collectively the reforms of May and October 2002 constituted a more comprehensive set of reforms than would have seemed possible a year before – and more than had been achieved in the preceding four years. They generated a letter to *The Times* from Michael Ryle, a former Parliamentary Clerk and one of the founders of the academic Study of Parliament Group, who argued that the reforms brought 'almost to completion the most systematic package of parliamentary reforms for 100 years'. His letter ended, 'As a campaigner for parliamentary reform for more than 40 years, I can now retire happy.'[14]

Several years on, it is, however, possible to be slightly more sceptical. The impact of several of the reforms has turned out to be peripheral at best. Little in the way of meaningful legislative business has been conducted in the new two-week period in September (although in mitigation reformers blamed the whips for trying to undermine the new timetables by only scheduling unimportant business during the period).[15] The new carry-over facility has been restricted to a very small number of bills, with most sessions ending with the now-familiar legislative ping-pong between the Lords and the Commons over key government bills (see below). The innovation of pre-legislative scrutiny – a favourite of parliamentary reformers for years – has proved less than entirely satisfactory. Several bills that had gone through the process, such as the Gambling Bill or the Mental Capacity Bill, exploded into exactly the sort of partisan controversy that pre-legislative scrutiny was supposed to avoid. Peter Hain, one of Cook's successors as Leader of the House, was to remark that the reformers' zeal for pre-legislative scrutiny had somewhat naively reckoned without the intervention of party politics.

Although many of the reforms made Parliament more efficient and several made it more open and accessible (and doubtless all made it more 'modern'), it was possible to argue – just as it had been in the first Blair term – that few of the reforms did much to strengthen the capacity of the legislature to hold the executive to account. Even if one did not buy the anti-reformers' line that Parliament was weakened as a result of several of the changes, it was hard to make much of a case that the institution had

---

[14] *The Times*, 5 November 2002.
[15] In 2004 the House did use the time to debate all the stages of the reintroduced Hunting Bill, but one of the first moves after the 2005 election was to suspend the September sitting, with no guarantee that it would return.

become stronger. At best, the effect of the reforms was probably neutral. The loss of the vote over select committee nominations was particularly unfortunate in this respect. It was the one reform that would unquestioningly have weakened the control of the whips and created (however marginally) a more independent select committee system – and it was the one Cook reform proposal to be defeated.[16]

It was also unfortunate that the process of modernisation ceased to be a cross-party initiative in any meaningful way. Many of the reforms in the 2001 Parliament were driven through the Commons using the bulk vote of the PLP (albeit on free votes), supported by very few opposition party MPs. Perhaps the most important of any of the reforms in terms of its impact on the legislative process was the automatic timetabling ('programming') of legislation. The process had begun in the 1997 Parliament but was made permanent in 2004 (the House previously voting annually to renew the procedure). The vote to make programming of government bills permanent saw not a single Lib Dem or Conservative MP vote in favour. This did little to weaken the suspicion that many of the reforms were not aimed at improving the scrutiny of government.

Moreover, while Cook showed the impact that a reformist Leader of the House could have, it also meant that his absence – following his resignation over the Iraq war in 2003 – led to the process of modernisation slowing down, and, in some cases, even going into reverse. His immediate replacement as Leader of the House was John Reid, although he was barely in post before being moved on again to be Secretary of State for Health. Reid was in turn replaced by Peter Hain, who combined the role with being Secretary of State for Wales. Under Hain, the process of modernisation continued, but with none of the intellectual verve brought to the subject by Cook, and without any great enthusiasm.

Hain's period as Leader of the House did see some of the earlier reforms bedded down by being made permanent as well as seeing yet further reforms to public access. Symbolically, the terms 'stranger' or 'strangers' when referring to visitors to the House of Commons were replaced by 'the public' or 'member of the public'.[17] This period also saw the partial

---

[16] Independently of the defeat, the PLP did democratise the process by which it produced nominations for select committee membership, thus achieving greater transparency in the process.

[17] One of the golden rules of parliamentary reform is that there is an inverse relationship between the importance of any reform and the amount of coverage it receives in the media. This entirely symbolic reform attracted widespread discussion on phone-in programmes and in the newspapers; the permanence of programming – done at the same time – went without a mention.

reversal of one reform, following MPs' complaints about the new hours, especially those involving a late ending on Mondays, followed up by an early start for committees on Tuesday mornings. As a result, the hours were partially reformed again in January 2005, with the hours of business on Tuesday reverting to those that had existed prior to October 2002: 2.30 pm to 10 pm.

Other Commons reforms

The Parliament also saw two other reforms in the Commons, neither part of the process of modernisation per se, but both equally important. The first was the Prime Minister's decision to appear before the Liaison Committee – the committee consisting of the chairs of the other select committees – twice a year. The first meeting took place in July 2002. The Prime Minister's appearances last for two and a half hours at a time, during which he is quizzed by the MPs in depth. Each session covers a different theme or set of themes, with the Prime Minister knowing in advance the themes to be covered but not the exact questions. These sessions have not attracted the attention that they deserve, partly because the Prime Minister proved rather good at answering or deflecting the MPs' questions, so that the committee rarely landed blows (although the questioning over Iraq was far from gentle). But the innovation remains considerable. It represented a significant advance in the scrutiny of the prime minister; it was the first time for 65 years that a prime minister had been before a select committee – and it will now be very difficult for any future prime minister to refuse to attend such meetings.

The other significant reform occurred in late 2004, when, anticipating the coming into force of the Freedom of Information Act in January 2005, the House of Commons authorities published details of the expenditure claims made by each MP. These revealed that MPs claimed a total of just over £78 million in allowances and expenses between April 2003 and March 2004, an average of £118,000 per MP.

Entirely predictably, the media worked themselves up into a lather of contrived moral indignation, with newspapers depicting MPs as a 'bunch of thieving, fiddling, wasteful, good for nothing, feather bedded spongers', languishing in the Palace of 'Wasteminster'. Most headlines talked of MPs getting an extra £118,000 on top of their salary of just over £54,000. But anyone giving the figures even a cursory glance could see that most of the expenditure was not 'expenses' in the way that the phrase was normally understood. Most of the money went on staff costs (around £72,000 on average), on allowances for second homes if the MP lived outside London (up to £20,000 on average), and office space (again, about £20,000), plus stationery and travel expenses. As Stephen Pound, Labour MP for Ealing North, said: 'This is not about filling our boots. This is not about trousering a lot of money. This is about the money it takes to do the job.'

The majority of the 'expenses' were being spent on the ever increasing constituency work of MPs. Although the growth of the constituency role of MPs dates back to the 1960s, there is little doubt that the large influx of (largely Labour) MPs elected in both 1997 and 2001 has been especially constituency-focused. Seen from this perspective, therefore, it becomes a moot point whether an MP who runs up large expenses may be deemed to be working hardest for their constituents. When Claire Curtis-Thomas was identified as 'the most expensive MP', she said that she didn't 'know whether to be worried or honoured'. However, the consequence of this growth in constituency work is also just as interesting as its cause. The state is now providing around £100,000 per year for MPs to interact with their constituents. Few challengers can afford to cough up £100,000 'working' a constituency (let alone each year) and there is now the potential of a real incumbency advantage developing.

Lords reform, or how not to do it

The first Blair term had seen the government enact what it called Stage One of Lords reform. The House of Lords Act 1999 had removed all but 92 hereditary peers from the Lords. Further reform was to be left to a second stage, preceded by a royal commission (the Wakeham Commission) which duly reported early in 2000. The intention in 2001 was to deliver Stage Two of Lords reform during the government's second term. But – just as elsewhere – the reality did not live up to the intention.

In November 2001 the Lord Chancellor unveiled the government's White Paper, *Completing the Reform*, following Labour's manifesto commitment to implement the report of the royal commission chaired by Lord Wakeham 'in the most effective way possible'. The 92 remaining hereditary peers left over from Stage One would lose their place in the Lords, and the link between the peerage and members of the Lords would be broken, so that future members would not become peers of the realm, but Members of the Lords (ML). A cross-party Appointments Commission would control the appointment of 120 non-party peers but, in defiance of the Wakeham proposals, which proposed that the Appointments Commission should be in charge of all appointments, the political parties would remain responsible for selecting most peers. Quotas would ensure increased representation for women and ethnic minorities, while the number of Church of England bishops would be reduced from 26 to 16. In this transitional period, the Appointments Commission would be handed the almost impossible task of overseeing the political balance of the second chamber. The power of the Lords to veto statutory instruments would be removed, but otherwise its basic scrutiny functions would remain unaltered, and the House of Commons would retain its status as the predominant chamber.

But it was Lord Irvine's plans to allow only 20% of peers to be elected that caused the greatest opposition.[18] Some 140 Labour backbenchers signed Fiona Mactaggart's Early Day Motion calling for a second chamber that was 'wholly or substantially elected', and on 9 January 2002, Labour MPs jeered the Lord Chancellor during a meeting of the PLP. By February, 119 Conservatives had also put their names to Mactaggart's EDM, following the shadow cabinet's decision to support a second chamber or senate of which 80% was to be elected. A majority of the House of Commons therefore had come out in favour of a substantially elected second chamber.

Robin Cook, who had been (not so) privately opposed to Derry Irvine's scheme, admitted early on that he wanted to find a 'centre of gravity' on the Labour backbenches concerning the proportion of the directly elected element. During January 2002, 14 Labour MPs conducted a survey of their 268 backbench colleagues. When Graham Allen, a former whip, collated the survey's findings, the average preferred percentage for the directly elected element in the Second Chamber came out at 58%. This informal survey of Labour MPs was strengthened further by a more official survey carried out by the Public Administration Committee, after which the committee called for 60% of peers to be directly elected.

Cook was forced to ask for patience among the most vociferous of the opponents of the White Paper. But finally, on 13 May 2002, the government announced its surrender. In one of the biggest U-turns since Labour came to power, Cook announced that Irvine's scheme had been ditched and the establishment of a 24-member Joint Committee drawn equally from both houses, and chaired by Jack Cunningham, to draw up a range of options for reform, particularly the thorny question of composition. These options

---

[18] The Wakeham Commission had failed to agree on the proportion of directly elected peers, proposing three options with 65, 87 or 195 elected members – 12%, 16% or 35% of the total – with the remainder appointed.

would then be subject to a free vote in both houses, with the government then introducing legislation in the light of these free votes.

This 24-member body, with 12 members from each House, had several meetings – meetings which were described by one of its senior members as 'the biggest waste of time I have ever been involved in' – which resulted in both houses being offered a wide range of different options, ranging from a wholly appointed house through to one that was wholly elected.

On 4 February 2003, the Lords rejected all the elected options, coming out in favour of a wholly appointed chamber by a margin of three to one. The outcome in the Commons on the same day, however, was less clear-cut. The Commons managed to reject all of the available options for reform. Three – including the 20% elected option that had originally been government policy in *Completing the Reform* – were rejected on a voice vote, with not a single supporter.[19] The option that came nearest to succeeding – an 80% elected chamber – failed by just three votes.

The reasons for this illogical outcome – the Commons rejected an all-appointed house by 323 to 245, yet ended up with almost exactly that – are many and varied.[20] One of the few decisions the Joint Committee did take was to reject the idea of a secret ballot (as the House of Commons has now agreed to use when electing the Speaker), as well as the idea of using an alternative vote system. The latter would have forced MPs to rank their preferences, ensuring that one of the options would have been chosen at the end of the voting. The former might have been problematic in terms of accountability but would have prevented pressure being applied to Labour MPs – especially once the Prime Minister had made his own position clear. On 29 January 2003, during PMQs, Blair came out in favour of an all-appointed house, arguing that the Lords should be a revising chamber, not one that would rival the authority of the House of Commons. Although the votes on Lords reform were technically free, many of the Labour whips – who themselves voted overwhelmingly for an all-appointed house – privately urged MPs to 'support Tony'. It is difficult to estimate how many Labour MPs were persuaded by such calls but it is certainly enough to have made the difference between the success and failure of the 80% elected option.

---

[19] There was an extra division in the Commons after the Speaker accepted an amendment in the name of George Howarth calling for the abolition of the Second Chamber. Their Lordships had not desired a vote on their abolition.

[20] Well discussed in Iain McLean, Arthur Spirling and Meg Russell, 'None of the Above: The UK House of Commons Votes on Reforming the House of Lords, February 2003', *Political Quarterly* 74 (2003): 298–310.

Additionally, the way in which MPs were voting caused problems; there was a group of 10 MPs (nearly all Labour) who favoured abolition of the upper House and who – once that option had been defeated – then voted against all the other options. There was also the difficulty of coordinating MPs' actions. As McLean et al. point out, of those who voted, a majority supported one of the elected options. 'If they could have coordinated their preferences on any one of them, it would have been carried.'[21] But despite the best efforts of Robin Cook and a team of MPs who were trying to organise MPs behind-the-scenes, they were unable to get enough pro-election MPs through the same division lobby at the same time. Moreover there was a group of MPs who voted for the 80% elected option, but against 60%, even when they knew that 60% was the last elected option remaining, and even when the only alternative was no election at all, something they had already opposed. This group – largely Conservatives – may have genuinely preferred zero election to 60%, but they might also have been motivated by a desire to be able subsequently to criticise the government for having failed to deliver on its election promise. Then, lastly, there were those MPs who voted the wrong way by accident. At least four MPs are thought to have voted against 80% elected by mistake (believing they were voting against 80% appointed). These four alone were enough to have caused the 80% elected option to fail.

After the voting, a dejected Robin Cook conceded that it might be a good time to 'go home and sleep' on the events of the day. Few people came out of the episode in a good light. The Commons did not appear able to make what to most outsiders seemed like a simple decision. The Prime Minister had had his position rejected by the House, by the majority of his own MPs, and by four of his Cabinet colleagues and 21 other ministers. The Leader of the House had also seen his own position rejected, and – less noticed – the Conservative leader, Iain Duncan Smith, had seen the majority of the Conservative MPs who voted oppose his party's position.[22] The only winners – albeit largely by default – were those who wanted an all-appointed House. They had lost the vote in the Commons by a substantial margin but the outcome was effectively exactly what they wanted.

The government's initial reaction was to announce that it intended to introduce a House of Lords Bill *inter alia* to remove the remaining 92 hereditary peers, but in March 2004, faced with the parliamentary reality

[21] Ibid., p. 304.
[22] See Philip Cowley and Mark Stuart, 'Still Causing Trouble? The Parliamentary Party', *Political Quarterly* 75 (2004): 356–61.

of trying to enact such a bill, it announced that it would not be introduced until the next Parliament. At roughly the same time, its proposals for the reform of the Lord Chancellorship (and the creation of a Supreme Court), all of which were less glamorous aspects of Lords reform, ran into serious trouble in the Lords but were passed just before the 2005 election.[23]

Their lordships get stuck in

The government's reform of the House of Lords used to be a central part of complaints about Parliament's marginalisation. By removing most of the hereditary peers, the government was said to be emasculating the one remaining check on its dominance of Parliament.[24] For example, of the first 53 defeats the government suffered in the Lords after 1997, all but six occurred as a result of the votes of the hereditary peers. And so, the argument went, remove the hereditary peers and you remove any effective opposition.

In fact, as was clear within a year or two of the House of Lords Act 1999 coming into effect, the exact opposite occurred. The pre-reform House of Lords – conscious that its legitimacy was limited by the presence of so many hereditary peers – frequently practiced a self-denying ordinance, pulling back from many confrontations with the government. But with the hereditaries largely gone, those peers that remain see themselves as more legitimate and have become more assertive than before. If the government hoped it had created a poodle of an upper chamber, then it was very much mistaken. The full consequences of reform became increasingly clear during the second Blair term.

The 2001–5 Parliament saw the government defeated on 245 separate occasions.[25] This was more than double the number of defeats in the first Blair term (108). The (mean) average number of Lords defeats per session during the extended period of Conservative government between 1979 and 1997 was just over 13. The (mean) average for the 2001 Parliament was just over 61. In other words, the Lords were defeating the Labour government of 2001–5 more than four times as often as they defeated the

---

[23] There were other, less glamorous but important, changes to the internal proceedings of the Lords, including a compulsory register of interests. See Philip Cowley and Mark Stuart, 'Parliament: More Revolts, More Reform', *Parliamentary Affairs* 56 (2003): 188–204.

[24] Read almost any Conservative contribution to the parliamentary debates over the House of Lords Bill removing the hereditary peers.

[25] The 2002–3 session alone saw 88 defeats, more than there had been in any one session since 1975–6.

Thatcher and Major governments, and more than twice as often as they had defeated the first Blair government.

These defeats ranged across almost every major piece of government legislation. In the first session, the Lords caused the government serious problems during the Animal Health Bill and the Nationality, Immigration and Asylum Bill (both were passed only after last-minute concessions), with its continued power to stand up to the government best illustrated during the passage of the Anti-Terrorism, Crime and Security Bill. The Lords inflicted no fewer than 13 defeats on the government before the bill became law. The then Home Secretary, David Blunkett, was forced to make a humiliatingly large number of concessions.

As the Parliament progressed, so the Lords became more intransigent and less willing to give way at the end of the session, with the result that the sight of a bill pinging back and forth between Commons and Lords became commonplace. As the 2002–3 session came to an end, for example, the government ran the risk of losing its plans for both foundation hospitals and judicial reform. Peter Hain was forced to make arrangements for the Commons to sit right up until the Queen's Speech, if necessary, before the Lords eventually gave way on foundation hospitals but only allowed the government's plans for jury trials to pass after demanding extra compromises. The 2003–4 session saw a similar dispute over the Pensions Bill, and the final session of the Parliament saw the mother of all ping-pongs, over the Prevention of Terrorism Bill. On 10 March 2005, the Lords dug their heels in over three aspects of the government's proposed legislation. Peers wanted a so-called sunset clause allowing the bill to expire, demanded a higher standard of proof on control orders and insisted that a group of Privy Counsellors review the legislation. The result was the longest day of parliamentary business since Labour came to power in 1997, with the Bill passing between Lords and Commons for twenty-eight and a half hours.

Eventually, as exhaustion set in the government conceded that although no formal sunset clause would be introduced, Parliament would have the opportunity to review or repeal the current legislation when a fresh bill on tackling terrorism was introduced early in the next Parliament. As one opponent of the Bill commented wryly, there was now 'a sunset clause that smells and sounds as sweet by any other name'.

Of the two Houses of Parliament, therefore, it was the Lords that was more of a block on the government during Blair's second term. Government ministers preparing legislation for its passage through Parliament knew that they faced a more serious test in the Lords than in the Commons. Ministers routinely resisted giving too many compromises while a bill was passing through the Commons in order to be able to offer placatory gestures to their lordships. The extra problems which the government faces in the Lords is sometimes ascribed to the greater sagacity of peers, their great wisdom and their increased independence of thought. In fact, as Lord (Philip) Norton has shown, the parliamentary parties in the Lords are no less cohesive than those in the Commons.[26] The difference – and it is a crucial one – is that in the Lords no one party holds a majority. Despite Labour increasing its membership in the Lords throughout the Blair years the government remains permanently in a minority position. The process of Lords reform since 1999 has created a permanently hung second chamber, and one which is willing to stand up to, and regularly defeat, the government of the day. Predictions that Stage One of Lords reform would produce a poodle legislature, packed with acquiescent legislators, therefore now look very silly indeed.

Conclusion

In an interview with the *Spectator* in late 2004, Lord Butler, the former Cabinet Secretary, complained about the weakness of Parliament. 'We should', he said, 'be breaking away from the party whip. The executive is much too free to bring in a huge number of extremely bad bills, a huge amount of regulation and to do whatever it likes – and whatever it likes is what will get the best headlines tomorrow.'[27] Lord Butler's complaints were characteristic of a routine critique of Parliament during the Blair government.

It is at least plausible, however, to argue that the events in Parliament during Blair's second term contradict much of Butler's argument. It is, of course, true that the government's overall record on modernisation of the Commons (especially before and after the period when Robin Cook was Leader of the House) was not especially impressive. Its record with respect

[26] Philip Norton, 'Cohesion without Discipline: Party Voting in the House of Lords', *Journal of Legislative Studies*, 9 (2003): 57–72.

[27] 'How not to run a country', *Spectator*, 11 December 2004. He also criticised the use of the Parliament Act to enact the Hunting Bill. But there is a curious paradox between those who perpetually complained about the weakness of Parliament and the over-bearing dominance of the executive but who complained when the lower House – after a repeated series of votes, and quite clearly against the wishes of the executive – insisted on getting its way. For all the talk about executive dominance, and the weakness of Parliament, fox-hunting was a victory for the latter over the former.

to Lords reform in the second term was even worse. Labour's record in the Lords between 2001 and 2005 consisted of a hapless White Paper followed by a U-turn followed by a farce followed by another U-turn. It was not their finest hour. Labour had still not properly implemented its manifesto pledges of 1997 and 2001 to make the House of Lords more 'democratic and representative'.[28] And it is also true that Parliament does not have the influence that many people – including the authors – think it should have, and that governments today are able to introduce 'a huge number of extremely bad bills'; possibly whenever they think it will get them positive headlines. During the second Blair term, Parliament's influence on legislation and on the activities of government remained sporadic and marginal.

Yet this is hardly new. To blame the Blair government for much of this is about as sensible as blaming it for the loss of the American colonies. Moreover, much of the evidence suggests that things are getting better, not worse. The Blair government – particularly the period from 2001 to 2005 – resulted in a partial rebirth of Parliament. Almost none of this was intentional on the part of Blair or his immediate circle. The House of Lords Act 1999, for example, was not intended to result in the far more assertive body that it created – but it did. Similarly, it was not the wish of the government that its backbenchers, routinely dismissed as weak and feeble during the preceding Parliament, should became increasingly rebellious during the second Blair term – but they did, with the result that MPs are now increasingly 'breaking away from the party whip', with clear consequences for the government's legislative programme.

Such difficulties were rarely enough to block the government's plans, but they did mean that getting its way became more difficult for the government and more politically costly than in the first Blair term. The combination of opposition from Commons and Lords could produce a watering down of legislation in order to achieve its passage far more frequently than would have normally been expected of a government enjoying a Commons majority of over 160.

Even the much maligned record of Commons modernisation had its plus points. If some of the reforms have done little to strengthen the

---

[28] *Because Britain Deserves Better*, 1997, p. 32. By 2001 the phrasing had changed to 'representative and democratic', *Ambitions for Britain*, 2001, p. 35. At best, the government can – at a stretch – argue that things have got slightly 'more' democratic and representative since 1997 (although plenty of people would challenge even that claim); but such achievements as there were all came in the first term.

Commons, they have at least made it more efficient and more accessible, and – in the case of the changes to parliamentary questions – more topical. And, although not part of the modernisation process itself, the Prime Minister's twice-yearly appearance before the Liaison Committee is an unprecedented extension of parliamentary scrutiny.

The Blair effect in Parliament was almost certainly not what Blair had intended – but it was far more positive than many realised.

3

Elections and public opinion

PIPPA NORRIS

Other chapters in this book consider the record of the second Blair government on key policy issues, including the delivery of public services, the issue of constitutional reform and the foreign policy record on Iraq and Europe. There are reasons to be sceptical about whether Tony Blair fully achieved his goals in many of these areas but on one there is no doubt whatever: if nothing else, in terms of the outcome of elections, Tony Blair will go down in the history books as the most successful Labour prime minister we have ever known. One of the most striking features of elections and public opinion in the UK since 1997 has been the predominance of the Labour Party, in contrast to the weakness of the Conservative and Liberal Democrat opposition at Westminster, despite everything which has occurred during Blair's tenure. This electoral success is puzzling given that many polls report continued public dissatisfaction with Britain's involvement in the Iraq war, popular mistrust of Blair's leadership and perceptions of the government's 'failure' to improve delivery of basic social services. Labour has also suffered from backbench rebellions, visible leadership rivalries and policy divisions at the apex of government, which are often believed to damage party popularity. Tony Blair has continued to win elections despite the loss of some of his closest advisers who were thought to be the architects of his victories, including Alastair Campbell and Peter Mandelson. The puzzle of Blair's electoral success is deepened by historical comparisons, notably the extent of Conservative hegemony established under Mrs Thatcher during the 1980s, and by contrast the limited duration of previous Labour leaders in Number 10. In Britain, the Conservative Party has seemed emasculated by Tony Blair, although this is not a broader crisis of the right; elsewhere conservative movements and ideas remain vigorous and thriving, notably the power of the US Republican Party controlling both ends of Pennsylvania Avenue.

In the light of this puzzle, this chapter aims to consider the extent of Tony Blair's electoral success since 1997 in historical perspective. We first compare the results of recent elections, and the monthly series of published opinion polls, against historical precedents. Building on this foundation, we then analyse the relative importance of four main factors associated with voting for Labour during the 2005 general election, focusing upon the personal appeal of Tony Blair compared with the government's performance in office, the ideological location of the Labour Party at the centre of the political spectrum and the social basis of the Labour vote. We also consider the role of partisan bias in the electoral system in contributing toward Labour's electoral success. Last, the conclusion reflects upon the broader implications of Blair's electoral success and considers whether this pattern will continue as an enduring legacy, representing a partisan realignment which will outlast his leadership.

Tony Blair's electoral success in historic perspective

One of the most remarkable achievements of Tony Blair is the fact that no previous Labour leader has ever won re-election with a sufficient parliamentary majority to last a full second term – let alone managed to be re-elected for a third successive time. Clement Atlee's landslide victory in 1945 was followed by a majority which shrank to just five in 1950, with subsequent defeat the next year. Harold Wilson consolidated his 1964 victory by winning a majority of more than 100 in 1966, before Ted Heath trumped him four years later. The 1997 general election first swept Tony Blair triumphantly into Downing Street with a massive landslide of seats, producing a majority of 178, the largest for any post-war government. The 2001 contest confirmed new Labour's ascendancy at Westminster, leaving their majority, at 167, almost untouched. From 2001 to 2005 the monthly opinion polls, and votes cast in the series of local elections, by-elections and European elections, indicated that Blair's honeymoon with the British public was becoming stale. For these reasons, many expected that the May 2005 general election could well produce a close result. Indeed, the regular swing of the pendulum in post-war British politics usually brings a rotation of the parties in power. The election on 5 May 2005 broke records, however, by producing the third straight Labour victory in a row. The closest post-war parallel was Mrs Thatcher's hat-trick in 1979, 1983 and 1987. The 2005 general election returned 356 Labour members, generating a solid 66-seat parliamentary majority for the Labour government, although based on a far lower share of the vote.

Figure 3.1 illustrates the extent of Labour's success since 1997 at Westminster – and the extent of Conservative failure. The shrinkage in the number of Labour MPs in 2005, combined with a greater propensity to backbench rebellions, makes the government potentially more vulnerable

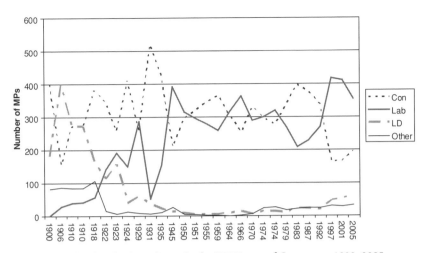

Figure 3.1. The distribution of seats in the UK House of Commons, 1900–2005
Sources: Colin Rallings and Michael Thrasher (eds.) *British Electoral Facts 1832–1999*
(Aldershot: Ashgate, 2000), and *The British Parliamentary Constituency Database,*
1992–2005.

to problems in steering through its ambitious programme of 45 new bills
outlined in the Queen's Speech after the election. The chapter by Cowley
in this volume documents the rise of parliamentary rebellions on key
issues such as student top-up fees. Nevertheless Blair still enjoys a more
comfortable parliamentary majority than Mrs Thatcher had in 1979, as
well as a greater margin than experienced both by John Major in 1992
and by Harold Wilson in 1964 and 1974.

Figure 3.1 also demonstrates how disastrously Conservative numbers
were reduced by the 1997 general election, plunging from 336 to 165
MPs under the leadership of John Major. The party flat-lined in the
next election, making a net gain of just one additional member under
William Hague. Table 3.1 indicates how the Conservatives performed
more strongly in 2005 by making 32 net seat gains under Michael Howard.
The party experienced an infusion of blood with the entry of 53 new
Conservative MPs, including three dozen challengers who defeated
Labour and Liberal Democrat members, while the remainder inherited
Conservative seats from retiring incumbents. This influx is important,
as a source of fresh energy and a broader pool of younger talent which
should help the opposition mount a more effective leadership team in
future contests. The Conservative benches rose to 197 MPs, representing
about a third of the House of Commons.

Table 3.1. *UK general election results 2001–5*

	Share of the UK vote (%)			Number of UK MPs			
	2001	2005	Change	2001 General election[1]	2001 notional results[2]	2005 General election	Net change
Labour	40.7	35.2	−5.5	412	402	355	−47
Conservative	31.7	32.3	0.6	166	165	197	32
Liberal Democrat	18.3	22	3.7	52	51	62	11
Scottish National	1.8	1.5	−0.3	5	4	6	2
Plaid Cymru	0.7	0.6	−0.1	4	4	3	−1
UK Independence Party	1.5	2.3	0.8	0		0	0
Green	0.6	1	0.4	0		0	0
British National Party	0.2	0.7	0.5	0		0	0
Other	4.5	4.4	−0.1	19	19	22	3
Speaker				1	1	1	0
Turnout	59.4	60.9	1.5				
Lab to Con swing			3.3	659		646	−13
Labour majority				165	158	66	−92

[1] The actual results in June 2001. [2] The 'notional' results of the June 2001 election when calculated under the new Scottish boundaries.

Sources: The British Parliamentary Constituency Database, 1992–2005; David Denver, Colin Rallings and Michael Thrasher (eds.), *Media Guide to the New Scottish Westminster Parliamentary Constituencies* (BBC/ITN/PA/Sky, University of Plymouth, 2004).

But any celebration at Conservative Central Office was quickly mitigated by the realisation that, despite the seat gains, the party had made only painfully modest progress in boosting their share of popular support: winning 30.7% of the UK vote in 1997, 31.7% in 2001, and 32.3% in 2005. Indeed their performance in vote share was highly uneven across the nation, falling further in some of their weakest regions, such as Scotland and the north of England, as well as in Labour seats, while recovering best in their own seats and in the leafy suburbs and shires of the southeast and Greater London. They received support from just one fifth of the total electorate. The party essentially speaks for rural England; it has only one MP in the whole of Scotland, just three in Wales, and none in Birmingham, Newcastle, Sheffield, Leeds, Liverpool and Manchester. The following day, Michael Howard announced that he would stand down as leader, after the new leadership selection rules had been agreed within the party, the fourth Conservative leader whom Blair had outlasted.

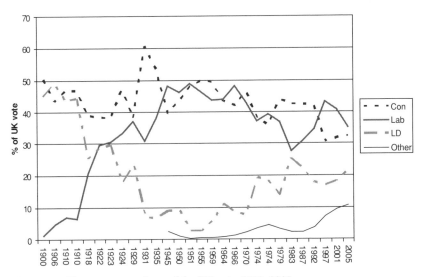

Figure 3.2. The percentage share of the UK vote, 1900–2005
Sources: Colin Rallings and Michael Thrasher (eds.), *British Electoral Facts 1832–1999* (Aldershot: Ashgate, 2000), and *The British Parliamentry Constituency Database, 1992–2005.*

The fall in the Labour Party share of the UK vote by 5.5% in the May 2005 general election did make the party far more vulnerable in subsequent contests; a further 2.3% Lab–Con uniform national total swing in the next general election would deprive the government of its overall parliamentary majority (see Table 3.2). But the electoral challenge facing the main opposition party remains formidable. It would still take a 4.8% uniform national total swing in the next general election to make the Conservatives the largest party in a hung parliament. And it would take a substantial 7.6% swing to propel them back into power with an overall parliamentary majority. The closest historical parallel would be Mrs Thatcher's triumph over Jim Callaghan in 1979, following the Winter of Discontent, which generated an 5.3% swing. The Conservative Party share of the vote would need to be at least a dozen points ahead of Labour in the next general election to be assured of single-party government.

Among the main parties the Liberal Democrats made the greatest progress in boosting their share of the vote in the May 2005 general election. The party won almost six million ballots, representing 22% of the UK vote, up 3.7% from 2001. Their share of the vote strengthened in every region, especially in Scotland and the north, where they made inroads

Table 3.2. *Projections of seat change by uniform vote swing in the next general election*

	% UK Vote			Number of Seats					
Swing	Con	Lab	Lib Dem	Con	Lab	Lib Dem	Other	Govt	Parl.Maj.
−1.0	31.3	**36.2**	22.0	186	**368**	63	29	Lab	90
0.0	32.3	**35.2**	22.0	197	**356**	62	31	Lab	66
1.0	33.3	**34.2**	22.0	216	**341**	59	30	Lab	36
2.0	**34.3**	33.2	22.0	231	**326**	58	31	Lab	6
2.3	**34.6**	32.9	22.0	235	**323**	57	31	–	–
3.0	**35.3**	32.2	22.0	249	**309**	57	31	–	–
4.0	**36.3**	31.2	22.0	263	**294**	58	31	–	–
4.8	**37.1**	30.4	22.0	**281**	278	57	30	–	–
5.0	**37.3**	30.2	22.0	**284**	275	57	30	–	–
6.0	**38.3**	29.2	22.0	**302**	258	56	30	–	–
7.0	**39.3**	28.2	22.0	**313**	248	55	30	–	–
7.6	**39.9**	27.6	22.0	**326**	235	55	30	Con	6
8.0	**40.3**	27.2	22.0	**332**	229	55	30	Con	18
9.0	**41.3**	26.2	22.0	**350**	214	53	29	Con	54

Note: The estimates assume a Con–Lab uniform national swing across the UK with no change in the share of the vote for the other parties.
Source: The British Parliamentary Constituency Database, 1992–2005.

into traditional areas of Labour support. After the election, the Liberal Democrats were left in a promising position to make further advances in subsequent contests, placed second in more than one hundred Labour seats, twice as many as before. But under Charles Kennedy, on 5 May the party still failed to make a decisive breakthrough at Westminster, gaining only 11 more MPs (compared with the 'notional' 2001 results) to swell their parliamentary ranks to 62. This represents their largest parliamentary representation for eighty years, but nevertheless they had hoped for far more seat gains.

Trends in public opinion

Nor was the 2005 general election a fluke; instead, it reflects a broader pattern of Labour predominance according to many indicators. The standard

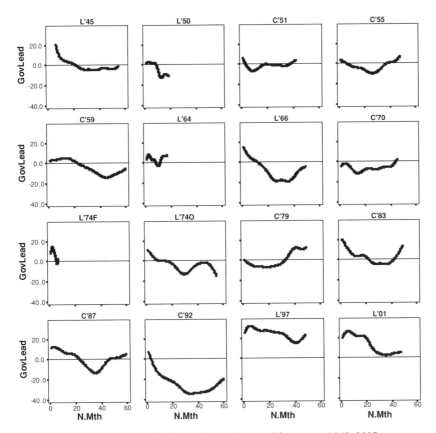

Figure 3.3. The government lead over the main opposition party, 1945–2005
Source: Estimated based on voting intentions expressed in Gallup polls 1945–99 and MORI polls 2000–5.

measures of party popularity in the monthly opinion polls usually report that after a post-election honeymoon period, governments experience a mid-term slump in support. This well-known electoral cycle has been found in Britain and elsewhere.[1] Figure 3.3 illustrates the government's lead in voting intentions over the main opposition party in the series of monthly opinion polls published in Britain since the war by Gallup and MORI.[2] The time series has been standardised for each administration

[1] Andrew Gelman and Gary King, 'Why are American presidential election polls so variable when votes are so predictable?' *British Journal of Political Science* 23 (1993): 409–51.

[2] It should be noted that Gallup discontinued their series in 1999. The MORI monthly polls may produce some discontinuity in the post-war series but nevertheless when both

against the month in office. The horizontal line across each graph indicates whether the government ends in positive or negative territory against its main rival. The dip in support is found throughout the series although the precise timing is unpredictable; sometimes it occurs earlier, sometimes later. Most administrations usually stage a recovery as polling day nears, and they then go on to win the subsequent general election, for example the Conservatives under Harold Macmillan in 1959, or again under Mrs. Thatcher in 1986–7. Others, however, continue to haemorrhage support, or at least fail to mount a sufficient bounce back, for example Harold Wilson's second administration in 1966–70, or John Major's government after the Exchange Rate Mechanism (ERM) debacle in September 1992.

Does support for Tony Blair's government fit the general pattern? A comparison of the graphs illustrates how far the government's lead from 1997 to 2001 defied trends; Blair's lead over the opposition was more substantial than that of any other post-war administration, remaining in positive territory throughout. There was indeed a slow slide then a dip during this period (with the nadir in September 2000, around the time of the fuel crisis), but Labour support recovered sharply as the 2001 general election approached. The second Blair administration experienced a stronger and more sustained fall in the Labour lead, starting around the 20th month. Nevertheless once again Blair defied political gravity by remaining ahead of the Conservatives throughout this period.[3] No other prime minister in post-war history has retained his or her lead over the opposition party through one administration, let alone two. Obviously the government's lead was reduced during Blair's second term, and moreover this pattern could be attributed to Conservative weakness as much as Labour's popularity. But the government's lead still remains unprecedented in the half-century since polling records began.

By-elections, local and regional elections, and European elections

What of other types of contest? Was Labour equally successful? Here the evidence remains more mixed. There were only half a dozen by-elections in 2001–5, in part because the government has been careful to avoid these

companies were publishing monthly polls of voting intentions, there was a strong correlation between both series. Where two or more polls of voting intentions were published by each company in a month, the figures used reflect the average for each month.
[3] There was one month (September 2004) where the average of the MORI polls recorded a –1% Labour lead, but this was within the margin of sampling error and not part of a general trend in 2001–5.

Table 3.3. *By-elections 2001–5*

		Seat	Change in % share of the vote			
Constituency	Date	Change	Con	Lab	LD	Turn
Ipswich	22/11/2001	*Lab hold*	−2.1	−8.0	7.2	−16.9
Ogmore	14/2/2002	*Lab hold*	−3.7	−10.1	−4.0	−40.6
Brent East	18/9/2003	*LD Gain*	−2.0	−29.4	28.5	−13.7
Birmingham Hodge Hill	15/7/2004	*Lab hold*	−2.7	−28.4	26.1	−10.0
Leicester South	15/7/2004	*LD Gain*	−3.4	−25.2	17.7	−16.4
Hartlepool	30/9/2004	*Lab hold*	−11.2	−18.5	19.2	−10.4
Mean 1979–83	17		−11.4	−10.9	18.3	−14.5
Mean 1983–7	16		−13.9	0.4	12.3	−10.0
Mean 1987–92	23		−11.0	−0.8	−0.6	−17.5
Mean 1992–7	17		−19.9	7.4	5.0	−23.8
Mean 1997–2001	13		−0.6	−11.1	4.6	−27.8
Mean 2001–5	**6**		**−4.2**	**−19.9**	**15.8**	**−18.0**

Source: *UK Election Statistics: 1918–2004*, House of Commons Research Paper 04/61 July 2004.

contests by encouraging older or ill Labour MPs to retire in general elections. The six by-elections which were held after 2001 were all in Labour seats with majorities of 20% or more in the previous general election (see Table 3.3). Labour retained four of these seats, although its share of the vote fell (especially in Birmingham Hodge Hill), while the Liberal Democrats gained Brent East (with a Lab–LD swing of 29%) and Leicester South (with a 21.5% Lab–LD swing). The historical benchmarks show that the government's share of the by-election vote fell by 11.1% in 1997–2001, about the same as Mrs Thatcher experienced during her first term. The Labour vote fell by almost twice as much (19.9%) after 2001, similar to the scale of the losses experienced by the Major government and by the second Wilson administration. This could have been a cause of concern to Tony Blair but, in contrast to previous periods, however, the

Conservatives made no vote gains in any of the by-elections held since 2001, and it was the Liberal Democrats who emerged with the most cause for satisfaction.

Another test of government support was the election to the European Parliament, held under a regional list proportional representation system on 10 June 2004. Labour suffered a fall in their share of the votes and seats (down 5.4% and six MEPs, respectively, compared with 1999). But, once more, Labour deserters did not flock to the Conservative Party, which actually experienced an even worse slump in its share of both votes (−9%) and seats (−8). Instead, the main victor to emerge was the UK Independence Party, which had adopted the strongest Euro-sceptic stance. UKIP rose into third place in their share of the vote, almost doubling its vote share (to 16.1%), and sending a dozen MEPs to the Brussels parliament they seek to abolish. The 1999 contests had been greeted in Britain with overwhelming apathy; voter turnout was 24%, the lowest in Europe. In 2004, turnout increased to 38.2%, which may be attributable, at least in part, to the fact that these were held simultaneously with the local contests, as well as to the extension of postal voting and to voters' perceptions that they had a wider choice of parties and policies.[4] Blair therefore lost support in the European contests but, as in by-elections, this did not benefit his main opposition rival. So long as any slump in government support flows to different parties in different contests, this poses far less of a threat to the government.

The local elections also present mixed fortunes for each of the main parties. The picture is particularly complicated to interpret because of the way in which different types of councils in England, Scotland and Wales are elected in alternative years. The easiest way to evaluate standardised trends in party performance in these contests is to compare the Rallings and Thrasher estimated national share of the vote since 1997, based on the change in the share of the vote in a sample of wards, as shown in Figure 3.4. The trends suggest that Labour suffered a 14-point fall in its share of the vote from 1997 to 2000, reflecting the more modest erosion in vote intentions that we have already observed as gauged in the monthly opinion polls during this period. The 1999 local elections were a particularly bad result for Blair, as Labour lost over 1,000 councillors to the Conservatives. This was followed by a very positive result for the Conservatives in 2000 under William Hague, when they gained almost

[4] John Curtice, *The 2004 European Parliamentary Elections in the United Kingdom* (London: The Electoral Commission, 2004), also available at www.electoralcommission.org.uk.

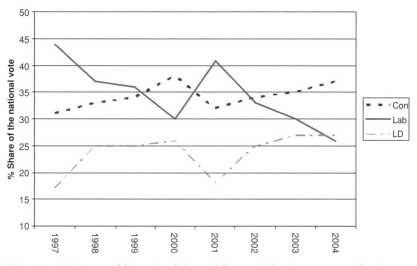

Figure 3.4. Estimates of the national share of the vote in local government elections,
1997–2004
Source: *UK Elections Statistics: 1918–2004*, House of Commons Research Paper 04/61,
July 2004.

600 local seats. The following year, however, Labour recovered its share
of the local vote in the simultaneous local and general elections. The government slid back into second place in the vote in 2002, with modest seat
losses, before falling further into third place in 2004. In historical context,
the Labour Party share of the national vote in the 2004 local council elections, at 26%, was the lowest it had ever achieved since estimations were
first calculated based on the 1979 local government reorganisation.[5] The
Conservatives benefited from this slump, with 37% of the vote in 2004,
although this was slightly less than William Hague achieved in 2000 before
going down to defeat in the general election. The 2004 local elections saw
the Labour Party losing 461 seats and eight councils, including Newcastle,
Swansea and Leeds. The Conservatives gained 259 seats, while the Liberal
Democrats gained 137. The loss of Labour votes in local contests, and
their third-place rank, therefore generates stronger challenges to the thesis
of Blair's electoral success. This erosion of support is politically important for control of town halls up and down the land; both of the main
opposition parties have benefited by gains in local councils and in seats.

[5] Although the Conservative share of the national vote was estimated to be lower (25%) in
1995.

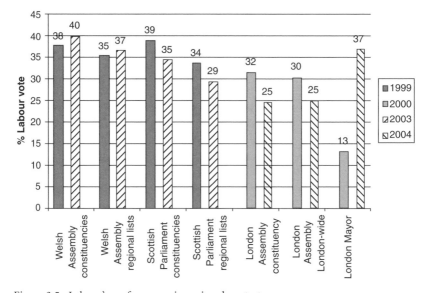

Figure 3.5. Labour's performance in regional contests
Source: *UK Elections Statistics: 1918–2004*, House of Commons Research Paper 04/61,
July 2004.

Local councillors form a grass-roots base which can be a long-term springboard to national power, as this widens the pool of experienced activists
who can be selected as parliamentary candidates. As both the 2000 and
2004 results demonstrated, however, the performance of the main parties
in local elections proved a poor predictor of their support at subsequent
Westminster contests.

There are also complicated patterns when interpreting support for Blair
indicated by the election results since 1997 to the devolved bodies. This
includes contests for the Scottish Parliament and the National Assembly
for Wales held in 1999 and 2003 under the 'additional member' system of
election, the London Assembly election in 2000 and 2004, and the London
Mayoral supplementary vote elections in 2000 and 2004. Although the
national media often want to regard these as second-order referenda on
government performance, in fact the particular outcome may be strongly
influenced by local circumstances, including the use of different electoral
systems, regional patterns of party competition and salient issue concerns
in each area, such as evaluations of the performance of Holyrood Parliament north of the border, and the public's reaction to the congestion
charge introduced for London by Ken Livingstone. Figure 3.5 provides a

simple summary of the Labour results in these contests. Their support goes up slightly in Wales, but down in Scotland and the London Assembly, while the result of the mayoral election in London was heavily influenced by Ken Livingstone's switch from independent in 2000 back to Labour in 2004.

The reasons for Blair's success

So why has Tony Blair managed to achieve such remarkable electoral success, a feat which eluded his predecessors? And, can it be established that it was Blair's leadership and personal appeal which were essential for electoral success in May 2005, rather than other plausible reasons, including the policy performance of the government, the ideological location of the Labour Party or the social basis of the Labour vote?

Social and partisan cues

Ever since Butler and Stokes, traditional structural accounts have long emphasised the importance of the social background of electors as strong predictors of voting behaviour in Britain.[6] In particular, during earlier decades social class and long-term partisan attachments were thought to exert a critical influence in determining Labour and Conservative Party support. Since the early 1970s, however, numerous studies in Britain and elsewhere have emphasised a process of social and partisan dealignment, where voters have become more detached from traditional loyalties.[7] This process is likely to have been accelerated by Blair's emphasis that Labour needed to develop a broad cross-class coalition in middle England, with policies which proved attractive to university-educated public-sector professionals, such as social workers, teachers, local government officials and doctors, as well as to the shrinking Labour base of skilled and unskilled blue-collar workers in manufacturing industry. There have also been important developments in the other social characteristics of British voters, with the rise of the gender-generation gap, where younger

---

[6] David Butler and Donald Stokes. *Political Change in Britain* (New York: St. Martin's Press, 1974).

[7] See, for example, Ivor Crewe and Katarina Thomson, 'Party loyalties: dealignment or realignment?', in Geoffrey Evans and Pippa Norris (eds.), *Critical Elections* (London: Sage Publications, 1999). See also Geoffrey Evans, Anthony Heath and Clive Payne, 'Class: Labour as a catch-all party?', in Evans and Norris, *Critical Elections*.

women have increasingly shifted towards the Labour Party.[8] Accordingly, we need to see how far social background and Labour Party identification continue to predict Labour support.

Straddling the centre ground

Classic Downsian explanation of voting behaviour emphasises the location of the parties across the political spectrum and their closeness to the median voter.[9] For Downs, rational voters select the party closest to their policy preferences and rational parties compete by positioning themselves to greatest advantage, given the normal distribution of public opinion on the major issues. According to this perspective, one plausible reason for Labour's success is the way in which Blair dragged the party towards the centre of party competition.[10] This process started earlier; from 1983 onwards, under the leadership of Neil Kinnock and then John Smith, the Labour Party gradually located itself clearly in the middle of the political spectrum, abandoning its tribal socialist loyalties and advocacy of the unpopular policies of redistributive taxes, trade union power and subsidies for nationalised industries. The transformation of the Labour Party clearly preceded Tony Blair, but he probably took this strategy further and faster than would have occurred under his predecessors. Blair's strategy adopted the Lyndon Johnson adage: hold your friends close, and your enemies even closer. Like a chameleon, he ruthlessly stole any popular new ideas from other parties and claimed them for himself. He embraced constitutional reform from the Liberal Democrats, pro-business policies from the Conservatives and devolution from the nationalists. The one bold, risky, and historic initiative based on deep convictions which he did make in foreign policy – to support US President George Bush in the Iraq war and to commit British troops in this conflict, proved so unpopular with the public and his party that it deeply damaged his personal popularity and trust in his leadership. In response to Blair's centrist strategy, the Liberal Democrats leapfrogged over Labour by gradually shifting leftwards under Charles Kennedy's leadership, advocating the abolition of student top-up fees and their replacement by higher public spending

---

[8] Pippa Norris. 'Gender: a gender-generation gap?', in Evans and Norris, *Critical Elections*.
[9] The classic argument is presented in Anthony Downs, *An Economic Theory of Democracy* (New York: Harper and Row, 1957). See also James M. Enelow and Melvin Hinich (eds.), *The Spatial Theory of Voting* (New York: Cambridge University Press, 1984).
[10] Pippa Norris and Joni Lovenduski. 'Why parties fail to learn: electoral defeat, selective perception and British party politics', *Party Politics* 10(1) (2004):85–104.

on universities, substituting local property taxes for a local income tax, adopting the most pro-European stance and becoming the fiercest critic of Britain's intervention in the Iraq war. Meanwhile the Conservative Party became punch-drunk from Blair's electoral triumphs since 1997, emasculated by its disastrous fall from the Thatcher glory days and confused by the faltering nature of its steps back to power. Uncertain how to regain public popularity, William Hague, Iain Duncan Smith and then Michael Howard have vacillated uncertainly and schizophrenically between emphasising compassionate and moderate conservatism committed to public spending, and alternatively pursuing a line of clear blue water between themselves and Blair by adopting more hard-line right-wing policies, including Thatcherite tax-cutting and anti-immigration rhetoric.

The performance of the Labour government

Yet positional accounts have come under strong challenge, in particular from theories emphasising the importance of the public's evaluation of government performance. Such accounts are most common in the literature presenting economic theories of voting behaviour, but they do not necessarily rest upon economic criteria alone.[11] Other chapters in this volume evaluate the broader record of the second Labour administration. The government promised improvements in a wide range of policy areas, including the delivery of better public services in health, education and transport, the attempts to modernise the constitution, and changes in transatlantic and European relations determining Britain's role in the post-9/11 world. Some commentators, notably Toynbee and Walker, highlight the success of government initiatives in schools, hospitals and the pocket-book economy.[12] Devolution was enacted. The Good Friday peace settlement was agreed. The minimum wage was implemented. Extra teachers and nurses were provided. New hospitals and clinics were built. Crime fell. Overseas aid rose. Perhaps most importantly, under Gordon Brown Labour developed a reputation for competent macroeconomic management, combining fiscal prudence with solid economic growth. Britain's prosperity during the Labour years has been a remarkable

---

[11] See, for example, Michael Lewis-Beck, *Economics and Elections: The major Western democracies* (Ann Arbor: University of Michigan Press, 1988).

[12] Polly Toynbee and David Walker, *Better or Worse? Has Labour Delivered?* (London: Bloomsbury, 2005).

success story, especially compared with the performance of major rivals such as France, German and Italy, as well as the European Union as a whole.

Was this the basis of Labour's electoral success on 5 May? In particular, the investigators of the 2001 British Election Study (BES) presented a strong case that what mattered for voting behaviour in that contest was less the ideological location of the main parties than the public's satisfaction with the performance of the Labour government on important issues.[13] Similarly, during the 2005 campaign, when people were asked which party was best on a range of policy areas, polls reported that Labour had a strong lead over the Conservatives on most issues, particularly those of greatest concern to the public: health, education and the economy. By contrast, the Conservatives were only ahead of Labour on two issues: asylum-seekers and immigration, and crime.[14] According to this perspective, people voted for the Labour Party primarily because they were regarded as the more competent team to deliver the services about which people were most concerned in Britain.

Blair's appeal

The key question is whether the third Labour term can also be attributed to the personal appeal of Tony Blair, over and above the ideological position of the party and Labour's performance in office. Considerable debate surrounds the question of leadership effects on voting behaviour; some theorists have argued that British elections have become increasingly 'presidential', with a growing focus during the campaign on the personality, experience and qualities of the party leaders.[15] Popular commentators and journalists often attribute considerable importance to how the public judged the leaders, including how far any erosion of trust in Tony Blair might damage Labour's prospects. Yet at the same time the literature has often reported that party leaders exert only a minimal effect on voting choices in Britain, once party preferences are taken into account.[16]

---

[13] Harold D. Clarke, David Sanders, Marianne C. Stewart and Paul Whiteley, *Political Choice in Britain* (Oxford: Oxford University Press, 2004).

[14] Christopher Wlezien and Pippa Norris. 'Whether campaigns matter and why', in Pippa Norris and Christopher Wlezien (eds.) *Britain Votes 2005* (Oxford: Oxford University Press, 2005).

[15] Michael Foley. *The Rise of the British Presidency* (Manchester, Manchester University Press, 1993).

[16] Anthony King (ed.), *Leaders' Personalities and the Outcomes of Democratic Elections* (Oxford: Oxford University Press, 2002).

To compare the relative importance of each of these factors, we can draw upon data derived from the 2005 BES Rolling Campaign Panel Survey. The dependent variable for the analysis is whether someone reported voting Labour or not, based on the third wave of the survey conducted immediately after polling day. The independent variables are measured using the first wave of the survey, conducted just before the official campaign was launched in early April.[17]

There are numerous indirect ways in which Blair's leadership could matter, notably by positioning the Labour Party on the centre ground of Westminster politics, as well as by spearheading the reforms improving the delivery of public services. In terms of *direct* effects, however, leadership effects on voting behaviour are usually understood in terms of affective feelings towards the personal qualities of each of the party leaders, such as public perceptions of their honesty, veracity and likeability. In particular, the Conservatives focused a good deal of attention during the campaign on Blair's personal character, with Michael Howard going so far as to call Blair a liar in his parliamentary statements over the existence of weapons of mass destruction in Iraq. Loss of trust in the Prime Minister was emphasised by the press as a critical Achilles heel for Labour. In turn, Labour responded in kind, with personal attacks directed against Michael Howard and Oliver Letwin. Character also featured in the Liberal Democrat campaign, with considerable emphasis on Charles Kennedy's likeability. Accordingly feelings towards Tony Blair were tapped for analysis by affective measures of three specific leadership qualities which are commonly regarded as important to voters, each measured using 11-point scales: how far Blair was regarded as competent, responsive, and trustworthy, as well as by a more general 'feeling thermometer' summary assessment gauging how far people liked Tony Blair.

To compare these measures against the importance of the ideological location of the main parties, we can analyse their perceived position on the classic issue of taxation and public services. This issue summarises much of the debate between left and right in British politics and the trade-off between taxes and services played an important role in the 2005 campaign, notably by the forced resignation of Howard Flight as deputy chairman of the Conservative Party in the debate over their tax-cutting or spending priorities. The position of parties on this issue was measured in the survey using an 11-point scale, where people could pick a point ranging from '*government should cut taxes a lot and spend much less on*

---

[17] Full details of the survey, methodology and questionnaire can be found at www.essex.uk/bes.

health and social services' (0) on the right to *'government should raise taxes a lot and spend much more on health and social services'* (10) on the left. Respondents were asked to indicate their own position on the scale, and then to identify the position of each of the main parties. From this, we can calculate the perceived distance of each voter from each party on taxes and public services. In Downsian theory, rational voters support the party closest to their own preference.

Last, performance theories argue that what matters to voters is 'delivery, delivery, delivery' on issues of concern to the electorate, such as health and education. In this regard, parties seen as competent at managing the economy and public services should gain most votes. Economic voting accounts suggest that given Britain's economic growth, combined with low inflation and unemployment, it was essentially Gordon Brown who won the election for Labour, not Tony Blair. Retrospective economic evaluations, without any reference to the party in government, included judgements whether economic conditions had got worse or better during the previous 12 months, both in the respondent's own household and in Britain as a whole. Prospective economic evaluations were measured by how far people thought that the financial situation in their own household and in the country would get better or worse during the next 12 months. After testing these items using factor analysis, the retrospective and prospective measures were added together into a single scale of economic performance. Moreover, performance theories also emphasise that in May 2005 other issues besides the economy were commonly cited by the public on their list of concerns about the most important problem facing the country, including the priority given to health care and education. To assess this, the general performance of the government was gauged by a scale constructed from questions which asked people to evaluate how well the present government had handled a series of issues, using five-point responses from 'very well' to 'very badly'. The survey included evaluations of the government's handling of the issues of crime in Britain, the education system, the number of asylum-seekers coming to Britain, the NHS, the risk of terrorism in Britain, the condition of Britain's railways, the economy in general, the situation Iraq, the level of taxation and pensions.

The models in Table 3.4 use binomial logit where the dependent variable is voting for Labour versus not voting for Labour, using the weighted BES data from the pooled campaign panel survey. Model 1 includes age, education, gender and occupational status, as well as partisan identification with the Labour Party, since these factors are all commonly

Table 3.4. *Predictors of voting Labour, May 2005 general election*

	Model 1			Model 2			Model 3			Model 4		
	B	Sig.	s.e.	B	Sig.	s.e	B	Sig.	s.e.	B	Sig.	s.e.
Social background and party identification												
Age	.01		.01	-.01		.01	-.01		.01	-.01		
Gender	-.13		.09	-.21	*	.10	-.16		.11	-.27	*	
Education	.01		.01	.02		.01	.03	*	.01	.03	*	
Occupational status	-.03		.02	-.02		.03	-.02		.03	-.04		
Labour party identification	2.05	***	.13	1.29	***	.15	1.15	***	.15	1.00	***	
Leadership												
Blair's leadership affect scale				.14	***	.01	.14	***	.01	.08	***	
Ideological proximity to parties on taxes v. sending												
Labour							.03		.03	.04		
Conservative							-.09	***	.02	-.04	*	
Liberal Democrat							-.11	***	.03	-.12	***	
Performance												
Labour government performance										.11	***	
Economic evaluations										.07	***	
Model Summary												
Nagelkerke R^2	.10			.47			.50			.53		
Percentage correctly classified	75.1			81.3			81.7			83.3		

Note: The table present the results of binary logistic regression analysis where the dependent variable is whether the respondent voted for Labour or not. Model 1 enters social background and party identification, understood as long-term stable cues in voting behaviour. Model 2 adds the scale measuring affective feelings towards Tony Blair. Model 3 adds the ideological proximity of voters to parties on the taxation v. spending scale. Model 4 adds the indicators of government performance, and the economic evaluation scale. See text for details of the construction of these scales. P ≤ .05, ** P ≤ .01, P ≤ .001.

Source: British Election Study 2005, *Rolling Campaign Panel Survey*, weighted N. 2843

regarded as closely associated with Labour support. Of these, only Labour
Party identification proved to be consistently and significantly related to
voting Labour in 2005. The results suggest that after applying these controls, the personal assessment of the qualities of Tony Blair were significantly related to voting for Labour, including evaluations of his competence, trustworthiness, responsiveness and likeability. Knowing just two
factors – whether someone identified with the Labour Party and whether
they were positive towards Tony Blair – could predict 47% of the variance
in the Labour vote. Models 3 and 4 enter the remaining factors, including ideological proximity and the performance measures. Closeness to
the Conservative or Liberal Democrat positions on taxes and spending
reduced the probability of voting Labour, as expected, although proximity
to Labour on these issues proved insignificant. Last, positive evaluations
of the Labour government's performance on a range of policy issues, as
well as rosy economic evaluations, also increased the probability of voting Labour. Nevertheless although Models 3 and 4 slightly strengthen the
summary statistics, the improvement of fit proved very modest. While
none of the potential explanations common in the literature can be dismissed on the basis of this analysis, what the results demonstrate is that
attitudes towards Tony Blair's leadership exert a significant effect on voting Labour, even when controlling for a wide range of alternative factors
which are commonly thought to explain Labour's popularity.

The electoral system

So far we have considered the factors contributing towards Labour's share
of the vote. What matters for the outcome, however, is not simply popular
support but also the distribution of seats at Westminster. This raises the
question: how far did Blair's victory in May 2005 depend upon the workings of the electoral system and what factors contributed towards electoral
bias in this contest? Majoritarian electoral systems, including the single
member plurality system of first-past-the-post used for Westminster contests, are intended to generate a 'manufactured majority' for the party in
first place. This type of electoral system aims to turn even a close result in
the popular vote, such as Harold Wilson's wafer-thin victory in 1964, into
a solid working parliamentary majority for the party in government. It is
intended to facilitate a decisive outcome where the party with the largest
share of the vote forms a single-party Cabinet, producing 'strong' government, clear accountability and transparent decision-making. Such a
system allows the winning party to implement their manifesto policies and

to take difficult decisions during their term in office, when assured of the support of their backbenchers, without the need for post-election negotiations and compromise with coalition partners. Proponents of majoritarian systems argue that the bias is also intended to reduce the representation of minor parties, especially those such as the British National Party and the Greens, with voting support widely dispersed across constituencies. The effective vote threshold facing fringe parties and independent candidates reduces parliamentary fragmentation and penalises extremist factions, such as the radical right. But the disproportionality in the UK electoral system does not necessarily operate equitably for the main parties: since the 1950s it has been characterised by systematic bias towards the Labour Party. This disproportionality is a product of the regional distribution of the party strength, malapportionment (differences in the size of electorate within parliamentary constituencies), patterns of differential turnout, and any anti-Conservative tactical voting, where votes are exchanged among Liberal Democrat and Labour supporters.[18]

The Scottish Boundary Commission's revision of the constituencies north of the border sought to address some of the causes of malapportionment. In the past, in recognition of their distinctive interests and concerns, Scotland and Wales were over-represented at Westminster in terms of the size of their population, primarily benefiting Labour as the strongest party in these regions. Following the introduction of the Scottish Parliament and Welsh Assembly, the government decided to reduce the number of MPs at Westminster drawn from these regions. The Scottish Boundary Commission was required to use the electoral quota in England (69,934 electors) to determine the number of Scottish constituencies in the House of Commons. The new boundaries, which came into effect just before the UK general election, reduced the number of Scottish seats from 72 to 59. The average size of the constituency electorates in the region rose from 55,337 in 2001 under the old boundaries to 67,720. Based on calculating the 'notional' results of the 2001 election, the net impact of the introduction of the new boundaries was estimated to cut the number of Scottish Labour MPs automatically by ten, while simultaneously reducing the number of Scottish MPs at Westminster for the Liberal Democrats, SNP and Conservatives by one each.[19]

---

[18] See Ron Johnston, Charles Pattie, Danny Dorling and David Rossiter, *From Votes to Seats* (Manchester: Manchester University Press, 2001).

[19] David Denver, Colin Rallings and Michael Thrasher (eds.), *Media Guide to the New Scottish Westminster Parliamentary Constituencies* (BBC/ITN/PA/Sky, University of Plymouth, 2004).

Despite these boundary revisions, Figure 3.5 shows that in fact, rather than diminishing, the disproportional votes-to-seats ratio for Labour increased again slightly in 2005. The votes–seats ratio for the government was commonly fairly modest during the 1950s and 1960s, at the height of two-party politics. A majoritarian electoral system can be fairly proportional in its outcome where there are only two main parties, for example in the US House of Representatives. The government's votes-to-seats ratio rose greatly in 1983, when voting support for the Liberal–Social Democratic Alliance surged and Labour reached its modern nadir. But the ratio sharply increased to 1.46 with Blair's victory in 1997, then rose again slightly in 2001 and in 2005, when it reached 1.56. This represents the greatest disproportionality in the government's votes-to-seats ratio in Britain during the post-war era.

The projections of seat change by a uniform total vote swing also illustrate the bias in the electoral system. If the Conservative and Labour parties gain about the same share of the vote in the next general election – 33.5% – then Labour remains in power with an overall parliamentary majority. In contrast, as Figure 3.3 shows, for there to be a new Conservative government with an overall parliamentary majority, the Conservative share of the vote needs to rise to about 40%, with the Labour vote share squeezed down to its 1983 nadir at around 28%. The constituency boundary revisions due to go into effect in Wales and England before the next general election will alter these calculations, to compensate for population changes since the 1992 revisions. It is estimated that these changes will probably reduce the number of Labour seats by about ten, while reducing the Conservative seats by about six. But this will not compensate for all the sources of electoral bias existing in the British system.

Conclusions and discussion

This chapter has demonstrated the unprecedented electoral success which Labour has enjoyed under the leadership of Tony Blair. As a consequence, no previous Labour leader has ever enjoyed such untrammeled control at Westminster and such an opportunity to put his stamp on the history books. Critics charge that despite his electoral success, Tony Blair has seemed disinclined to spend his vast political capital, at least during his first two administrations, on launching grand landmark initiatives and on gaining more than modest micro-policy achievements.[20] Clement Attlee will always be credited with the creation of the modern welfare state and the National Health Service. The Thatcherite revolution will forever be indelibly associated with privatisation, trade union reform, and a radical free-market shake-out of the British economy. With a comparable landslide, after eight years in power, it still remains unclear what lasting and distinctive legacy will be associated with Blair. Having announced that he would stand down before the next general election, as if in fear of this assessment by history and with one eye on the clock, Tony Blair launched into a frenzy of activity immediately after the May 2005 election, announcing an ambitious programme of 45 bills in the Queen's Speech. These domestic initiatives were in addition to a whirlwind series of visits on the world stage, including presiding over the G-8 with an agenda focused on climate change and the plight of Africa, and taking over the presidency of the European Union during the crisis of the proposed constitution.

Irrespective of his policy record, one achievement which will be indelibly linked to Blair's name in the history books will be the way in which, under his leadership, Labour was elected for three successive terms. The Conservatives were not just trounced in 1997, but also soundly defeated in 2001 and 2005, despite some modest seat gains in the last general election. This was no small feat, given the way in which Labour's prospects had been written off during the early 1980s, at their nadir, as an outmoded party saddled with a shrinking social base and membership, old-fashioned socialist dogma and unattractive policies.

Was there a trade-off between policy and electoral success? This is difficult to analyse systematically; if so much energy in the Blair government had not been devoted to maintaining public popularity, as monitored by the paraphernalia of focus groups, opinion polls and spin doctors, might there have been a flowering of bolder, more decisive and more imaginative ideas and policies? We cannot know. What has been insufficiently understood, however, is how far Blair's unprecedented electoral success, and the lack of radical policy achievements during his first and second administrations are, in fact, perhaps intimately related. What links these is the centrist strategy which New Labour adopted, which both catapulted Blair into power in 1997 and simultaneously tied his hands in terms of

---

[20] Trevor Smith. "'Something old, something new, something borrowed, something blue": Themes of Tony Blair and his Government', *Parliamentary Affairs* 56 (2003): 580–96.

visionary policy change. So cautious moderation, located in the centre of Westminster politics, has proved both a blessing and a curse for Blair. It has been the bedrock of his popular success and yet the limit of what he can do with his popularity. Blair's middle-of-the-road strategy, located closest to the average voter, combined with Brown's economic management skills and Blair's personal appeal, all contributed towards enduring electoral success. The one risky venture which clearly strayed far away from British public opinion – the Iraq adventure – illustrates the dangers of adopting policies which are clearly deeply unpopular at home. In this interpretation, it is not so much that policy was sacrificed by Blair to the altar of electoral success, but rather that the type of electoral success which Blair enjoyed brought a limited mandate for introducing radical policy change.

Will the electoral success of the Labour Party prove an enduring legacy which will outlast Blair's leadership? This is a complex issue to assess, but there is little evidence of partisan realignment, understood as a process requiring long-term changes in the proportion of the electorate who identify with Labour; instead, party loyalties continue to weaken over successive elections in Britain, as elsewhere.[21] In successive BES surveys, the proportion of the British electorate who identify very strongly with any party and the proportion who identify very strong with the Labour Party have both eroded slightly since 1997, not strengthened. A more persuasive case can be made that Labour has been forging a broader social coalition, at least in some regards, including proving increasingly popular among women and among younger voters. Nevertheless, in the modern de-aligned electorate, Labour's electoral success remains contingent rather than fixed through life-long loyalties. The party leader who succeeds Tony Blair inherits favorable odds, but far from any certainty, that Labour could well win a fourth term, albeit with a reduced majority. In particular, Labour remains vulnerable to two potential dangers in the next general election. One is the political fallout from a serious economic downturn, where the government's reputation for competent economic management is tested and found wanting by the public. Such a crisis could be triggered by a wide range of unexpected events, for example, a sudden bursting of the housing market bubble, a US-led major recession due to government overspending and a weakening dollar, or a Middle East crisis in the house of Saud limiting the flow of oil to the West. If Gordon Brown

---

[21] Russell Dalton and Martin P. Wattenberg (eds.), *Parties without Partisans: Political Change in Advanced Industrialized Democracies* (Oxford: Oxford University Press, 2000).

steps into Blair's shoes, as expected, any eventual economic downturn, if serious, might make Labour more vulnerable to being blamed for any economic problems, not less. The other danger facing Labour comes from the location of the opposition parties, particularly if the Conservatives successfully shift back aggressively towards the centre-right, perhaps under new leadership, or if the Liberal Democrats return to their original position in the middle of the political spectrum. For all these reasons, while Blair's electoral success was indeed remarkable, given the historical precedents, it still remains an open question whether it will form the basis of a lasting realignment in British party politics.

4

Local and central government

TONY TRAVERS

A continuing revolution?

Significant local authority and regional reform had taken place during Labour's first four years. The Blair government had attempted to reduce the central control that the Conservatives had put in place, though they chose to do so using a careful, carrot-and-stick approach. A number of consultative documents had been published, leading to significant structural and public service reform. The 'modernisation' of public service provision was a key element in New Labour's approach. Because local government was responsible for broadly a quarter of all public expenditure, councils inevitably found themselves involved in efforts to change the method or quality of service delivery.

The second Blair government continued to evolve policies that created new service-delivery units for education, health, regeneration, housing and policing. It also sought to create consistency between different providers and to reduce the extent to which Whitehall departments handed down policies that were disconnected from those in other parts of public administration. Local government became 'governance', embracing a number of different organisation and requiring councils to lead coalitions of local service providers. By 2005, the emphasis had shifted towards 'neighbourhood' and 'community' governance.

The perennially difficult issue of local government finance reared its head in 2003–4. An unexpected jump in council tax levels in that year, coupled with a minority of schools suffering an apparent funding shortfall, led to pressure for a major reform to local funding. A Balance of Funding review was set up, which, in turn, spawned a second inquiry into the subject.

The programme of devolution that had started between 1997 and 2001 continued in 2004 with a referendum on whether or not to set up an elected regional government for the north-east of England. The voters rejected the idea, though the possibility of 'city region' government was then proposed. There was no obvious end point to the programme of continuing reform to neighbourhood, local and regional government. It simply continued.

The development of 'new localism'

The second Blair government undertook a number of reforms which, taken together, came to be described as 'new localism'. As different ministers pursued departmental policies, a number of them evolved policies that could be seen as being 'local', though they moved beyond traditional concepts of elected local democracy. Thus the evolution of autonomous schools, hospitals, urban renewal partnerships, social housing providers and crime reduction partnerships made it possible for ministers to argue that a new kind of 'governance' was being developed.

As so often before, the New Local Government Network (a think-tank) proved adept at applying a degree of intellectual coherence to a number of separately evolved policies that had bubbled up from the Blair government. In 2000 NLGN published a document entitled *Towards New Localism: A Discussion Paper*, and in so doing kick-started the wider use of the term 'new localism'.[1] The purposes of the new policy were outlined:

> Councils would develop a Partnership Contract proposal with their local communities setting out how they intend to address the social, environmental and economic needs of their localities, supported by stakeholders to deliver major improvements over a five-year period. As part of this local government would show how they would deliver on central government targets, as in Local PSAs [Public Service Agreements]. Central government would then enter into a Partnership Contract with the council to support the delivery of local objectives and national targets.

This new form of localism would require the council to work with other local institutions to address a wide range of public policy questions, though they would have to do so in such a way as to hit government targets. Whitehall would agree to behave in a way that was consistent with this objective. Local authorities would be the leader of this process, but not the sole provider. Moreover, there was an acceptance of the legitimacy of a significant degree of central intervention.

---

[1] New Local Government Network, *Towards a New Localism: A Discussion Paper*, by Lord Filkin, Professor Gerry Stoker, Cllr Greg Wilkinson and John Williams (London: NLGN, 2000).

Such pragmatism was reasonable. The Blair government, in its second term, showed no intention of reducing the use of targets, performance indicators, audit and inspection that had rapidly evolved during its first period in office. Local government, in common with health authorities, the police, regeneration partnerships and housing providers, was expected to hit dozens of targets that were set for it. Councils and other providers found themselves required to achieve a number of – often inconsistent – objectives set by different parts of Whitehall.[2] One of the purposes of the new localism was to square this particular circle.

Between 2001 and 2005 different departments of state moved to strengthen or create new local institutions as the delivery vehicle for public services. By far the most important of these new 'micro' institutions were NHS Foundation Trusts, first announced in early 2002.[3] In these new institutions, managers of the best performing hospitals and primary care trusts would no longer be subject to strict financial and management control from Whitehall and would, for example, be given the power to set their own pay rates. They would also be able to establish joint venture companies, get automatic access to capital resources, and be subject to less monitoring and inspection. The policy proved very controversial.

But Foundation Trusts were by no means the only new 'micro' institution to be set up or whose powers were to be enhanced during the second Blair government. Schools were to be given greater freedom to determined their own affairs. Indeed, new kinds of partly privately funded schools ('academies') were created alongside many new 'specialist' institutions. From 2006–7, schools' funding would come not as the result of local authority funding decisions but through a nationally determined ring-fenced funding arrangement.[4]

In housing, social provision had for many years been gradually transferred away from local government control. Registered social landlords (RSLs – not-for-profit companies and trusts) had taken the role that up to the 1980s had been the responsibility of local government. By the early 2000s, RSLs designed, built, maintained and managed virtually all new social housing provision and a significant proportion of older stock.

---

[2] Public Administration Committee, *On Target? Government by Measurement*, Fifth Report, Vol. 1: HC62-I, Session 2002–3 (London: The Stationery Office, 2003).

[3] A. Ferriman, 'Milburn announces setting up of "foundation" hospitals', *British Medical Journal* 324 (19 January 2002): 132.

[4] Department for Education & Skills, *Consultation on New School Funding Arrangements from 2006-07* (London: DfES, 2005).

Much council housing had been block-transferred to RSL control. Where this had not happened, the Blair government had required the creation of Arms-Length Management Organisations (ALMOs) or had insisted that authorities redeveloped their housing stock by means of a private finance initiative (PFI) deal.[5]

Social housing was, therefore, in the hands of a bewildering array of RSLs, ALMOs and, in some cases, local authorities. Private developers were also involved because of planning deals that required them to finance a proportion of 'affordable' housing as a condition of receiving planning permission. Regeneration partnerships, which were generally funded either by Whitehall or by regional development agencies, usually had developers, housing providers, local authorities and several other key local players in membership.

Regeneration bodies, along with the police, health authorities, transport providers and a number of regional agencies, were by no means the only other players involved in 'new localism'. 'Faith communities', non-government organisations, business leaders, utilities providers and innumerable government agencies were often drawn in. Taken together, these bodies came increasingly to be known as 'governance'. Each 'stakeholder' had a role to play in the achievement of goals for an area.

Academics, particularly those in the United States studying 'growth coalitions',[6] have long understood the way in which interest groups evolve for particular political and economic purposes within large urban areas. What is interesting about the Blair government, particularly after 2001, is that its strategic core (notably the Prime Minister's Strategy Unit) began to advance policies designed to rebuild social capital in British local areas.[7] The Strategy Unit, led by Geoff Mulgan (who had previously been director of the think tank Demos), was influential in shaping policy in ways designed to encourage capacity building in communities and neighbourhoods.

After a short period at the start of Blair's second government during which different micro-units of provision had evolved, efforts were initiated to encourage councils and other local institutions to work together.[8]

---

[5] ODPM, *The Decent Homes Target Implementation Plan* (London: ODPM, 2003).

[6] See, for example, Harvey Molotch, 'The city as a growth machine', *The American Journal of Sociology* 82(2) (1976): 309–30.

[7] For example, Performance and Innovation Unit, *Social Capital: A Discussion Paper* (London: Cabinet Office, 2002).

[8] ODPM, *Supporting Strategic Service Delivery Partnerships in Local Government: A Research and Development Programme* (London: ODPM, 2001).

Ministers realised that there were difficulties in having innumerable single-service providers operating alongside local government.

A number of policy developments occurred, including Best Value plans, Local Public Service Agreements (LPSAs), Local Area Agreements (LAAs) and, predictably, a raft of further consultation papers. LPSAs were agreements between the Treasury and individual councils about the achievement of particular public service objectives.[9] Additional resources were provided both to fund new initiatives and as a reward if improvements were delivered. LAAs, which evolved in 2004 and 2005, involved replacing a number of different funding streams with a single one that would generally be paid to an area's Local Strategic Partnership (LSP).[10] Such partnerships, which were a further manifestation of New Localism, brought together the council, health authority, police, business, voluntary sector and others into another new local institution.

Writing in 2003, Geoff Mulgan provided a neat summary of the state of New Localism and, indeed, of local government itself. In a collection of essays, published by the New Local Government Network and entitled *Joining Up Local Democracy Governance Systems for New Localism*, Mulgan wrote:

> After several decades of centralisation the pendulum is now decisively swinging in the opposite direction. Politicians and civil servants have recognised the limits of central command, particularly over services which are inherently local . . . The emphasis now is on devolution, fewer targets and more local accountability. But the debate about what 'New Localism' actually means is far from settled. One reason is the uneven capacity and legitimacy of local government . . . A second is the fact that public demands for guaranteed minimum standards are if anything becoming more intense. A third is the inherent difficulty of reconciling equity and diversity.[11]

The final point in Mulgan's summary of the complexities of localism in modern Britain had been considered at length in a pamphlet written by David Walker a year earlier.[12] Walker had stated the case for centralism. In particular, he had championed the need for the state to guarantee

---

[9] See, for example, Local Government Association, *Improving Local Services: Local Public Service Agreements* (London: LGA, 2001).

[10] Office of the Deputy Prime Minister, *Local Area Agreements: A Prospectus* (London: ODPM, 2004).

[11] Geoff Mulgan, 'Foreword' in Dan Corry, Warren Hatter, Ian Parker, Anna Randle and Gerry Stoker (eds.), *Joining Up Local Democracy Governance Systems for New Localism* (London: NLGN, 2003).

[12] D. Walker, *In Praise of Centralism: A Critique of New Localism* (London: Catalyst, 2002).

redistribution and to provide services that were equal to all. Correctly, Walker had articulated an underlying inconsistency between social democracy and local autonomy.

The NLGN's 2003 pamphlet accepted that New Localism risked becoming 'all things to all people'. In particular, ministers and political parties would over-use the term until it had no meaning left. The pamphlet also took issue with the – at the time – rapidly developing idea that new forms of not-for-profit community trusts or companies offered the way forward for local governance. Home Office Minister Hazel Blears had written a Fabian Society pamphlet in which she had argued that 'if "new localism" is to be anything more than the latest political buzz-phrase, it must mean passing real power to local communities'.[13] According to the NLGN authors, the Blears 'mutualist' approach seemed 'dependent on a highly romanticised understanding of likely human behaviour'.

The Local Government Association and its leadership were suspicious of the proponents of New Localism,[14] fearing that they supported measures that would damage traditional local government by encouraging new single-service micro-units of government and/or by accepting the supremacy of the centre in requiring councils to hit targets. The 2003 NLGN paper wrote defensively that: 'New Localism was never conceived by NLGN as some fiendish plot against local government. It is not . . . just a fancy code-word for devolving down service delivery areas to local managers, creating new democratic single-issue boards . . . and so cutting local government out of the picture in a wanton creation of silo accountability.'

By 2005, New Localism had started to evolve into something rather different from the ideas outlined by the NLGN and others in the period from 2000 to 2003. Local Strategic Partnerships and a number of other joint approaches to public service provision had undoubtedly become more common than in 1997 or 2001. But New Localism had not demonstrably improved either the quality of public services or the strength of local democracy in the way its proponents had hoped. For example, the interest shown in elections for membership of foundation hospital boards proved minimal. Partnerships often proved complex to administer and, in the case of some regeneration projects, could actually inhibit effective

---

[13] H. Blears, *Communities in Control: Public Services and Local Socialism* (London: Fabian Society, 2003).
[14] See, for example, J. Beecham, 'Heading back to the silo', *Public Finance*, 21–7 March (London: CIPFA, 2003).

delivery.[15] The very term 'joined-up' government had become a cliché. The time had arrived for New Localism to move on.

From New Localism to community governance

In the summer of 2004, the government published a document entitled *The Future of Local Government*.[16] These proposals were by no means the first Labour had produced, but they can usefully be seen as a summary of the position ministers had arrived at in their continuing search for a new version of local government. The document stated:

> Sustainable communities require an environment of good governance, public participation, partnership working and civic pride. Effective local government is at the heart of each of these. Local government also has a vital part to play in working with local people to create the conditions that underpin a sustainable community: a flourishing local economy; good quality public services; a diverse, vibrant and creative local culture; community cohesion; and a sense of place and pride.

It is difficult to imagine a paragraph that would better summarise the buzz-word-dominated way in which New Labour continued to evolve policy for government beyond the centre. This section of the 2004 document includes the words 'partnership', 'sustainable', 'participation', 'diverse', 'creative', 'quality', 'vibrant', 'community', 'cohesion' and 'governance'. Only 'joined-up' was missing – though it appeared immediately below.

But there was clear evidence in *The Future of Local Government* that real changes were afoot. The government accepted there had been too many central controls, targets and random initiatives. There should be more citizen engagement, better local leadership and improved service delivery. The government believed that greater citizen engagement was an essential element in improving the quality of provision while simultaneously 're-engaging citizens in civic life and building social capital'. 'Alongside local elections, as well as voter turnouts, there need to be more and better opportunities to participate and exert influence on local issues and decisions. Devolution should not stop at the town hall.'

In a document entitled *Sustainable Communities: People, Places and Prosperity*, published early in 2005, the government expanded on its new,

---

[15] Audit Commission, *People, Places and Prosperity: Delivering Government Programmes at the Local Level* (London: Audit Commission, 2004).
[16] Office of the Deputy Prime Minister, *The Future of Local Government: Developing a 10-Year Vision* (London: ODPM, 2004).

community-based, policy.[17] The government's 'programme of action' for communities would provide 'opportunities for all communities to have more control over their own neighbourhoods'. There would be a 'Neighbourhoods Charter' which would allow communities to own local assets (for example, playgrounds or community centres), to trigger action by public authorities, to have devolved budgets and to use bye-laws. Schools, health services and the police would be required to be 'more responsive'. Local councillors would provide democratically legitimate leadership for any new neighbourhood arrangements.

Yet another document,[18] published at the same time as the *Sustainable Communities* paper cited above, explained that the government wanted to use new forms of community and neighbourhood governance to change the very nature of British democracy. 'Western democracies are all facing a decline in interest in conventional forms of politics. Voter turnout at elections in England has generally declined. The gap between local and national turnout remains high … Fewer people are willing to participate in political parties and traditional democratic processes. All this has serious implications for the legitimacy of existing political institutions and the priorities they set for public services.'

The overwhelming message of the government's research and analysis was that British democracy is not working effectively. A large volume of research evidence[19] was published to back up the proposed 'community' direction of new local governance. It is worth quoting a passage from this research volume to demonstrate the final drawing-together of an array of approaches and ideas that had percolated through Whitehall, think tanks and universities during the period between 2000 and 2005.

The Office of the Deputy Prime Minister (ODPM) researchers quoted a collection of essays on 'The Adaptive State'[20] published by Demos. The introduction to these essays offered, the ODPM officials believed, a description of the context within which New Localism had developed and how it had attempted to 'offer their citizens security and reliability' while also providing 'choice', 'diversity', 'flexibility' and 'responsiveness'.

---

[17] Office of the Deputy Prime Minister, *Sustainable Communities: People, Places and Prosperity* (London: ODPM, 2005).

[18] Office of the Deputy Prime Minister and the Home Office, *Citizen Engagement and Public Services: Why Neighbourhoods Matter* (London: ODPM, 2005).

[19] Office of the Deputy Prime Minister, *Citizen Engagement, Neighbourhoods and Public Services: Evidence from Local Government* (London: ODPM, 2005).

[20] T. Bentley and J. Wilsdon (eds.), *The Adaptive State: Strategies for Personalising the Public Realm* (London: Demos, 2003).

Also identified was the difficulty in demonstrating 'how their promises
convert into coherent action and tangible outcomes'. It was suggested that
casting this as a battle between centralism and localism missed an important dimension of the argument, and that reform 'depends not only on the
level and scale at which decisions are taken or performance is measured;
it will require greater "*adaptive capacity*" in organisations at every level
of the system . . . We need systems capable of continuously reconfiguring
themselves to create new sources of public value.'

ODPM had quoted Demos in attempting to illuminate every nuance
and possible objective of New Localism. Later in the research document,
and in its companion consultative paper, a new policy was outlined that
would bring together the objectives of New Localism with those of the
new desire for greater levels of neighbourhood involvement. It was now
proposed that there would be new neighbourhood arrangements in all
areas, of different kinds and for different communities. In the best traditions of the modern British state, there was to be a 'national framework'
for neighbourhood arrangements which would set out what people could
expect, in their most immediate home vicinity, from central and local
government and other service providers.

The precise form of the proposed new neighbourhood institutions was
not prescribed. Parishes were one model that might be used more widely.
The government would remove the existing barrier to urban parishes
that existed in London. Under new legislation, parish councils would
have powers to levy fixed penalty notices for environmental crimes such
as litter, graffiti and fly-posting.

Wards or parishes might be the basis of neighbourhood arrangements,
though other units were not ruled out. It would be possible for these new
bodies to write contracts with local authorities and other service providers
(presumably including the NHS, the police or social landlords). Local
councils would be allowed to pass new bye-laws to allow neighbourhoods
to control particular activities within their areas. The costs of the new
neighbourhood governance would be limited, but not zero. Arrangements
were 'principally about using existing resources more effectively, not about
increasing expenditure overall'.

Thus, by the end of the second Blair government, New Localism had
evolved into a new, neighbourhood-oriented, variant of itself. This new
type of institutional mechanism would have to operate in a way that
allowed choice and which was responsive. It had to take account of the
needs of a wide variety of groups, including faith communities, pensioners, patients, the young, those concerned with transport and, of course,

local residents within a geographical area. But in operating successfully, these new bodies also had to adhere to public service requirements for equity, fairness and accountability.

Crucially, this new kind of micro governance did not really exist in the comprehensive way Whitehall now intended it to. The new government that took office in May 2005 would have to reconcile the large number of different and difficult objectives now set for new neighbourhood governance. One thing was for sure, local government (in its traditional form) would have to be the local agent to create the new arrangements. No other existing institution had the local legitimacy or capacity to bring about such change.

Targets, inspectors and regulators

The rapid development of mechanisms and institutions designed to improve local government performance that had occurred between 1997 and 2001 continued in the first two years of the second Blair government. Indeed, many of the targets that had been set during that earlier period should have been achieved between 2001 and 2005. As it became clear that a number of targets would not be hit and also that some of them created perverse incentives, pressure grew to have fewer, more locally determined, ones.[21]

But local government also faced an array of auditors and inspectors, many of which had been created in the years since 1997. The most important of these, Ofsted (schools), the Social Services Inspectorate (personal social services) and HM Inspector of Constabulary (police), had each been reformed or strengthened since 1997. New institutions such as the Police Standards Unit were created under Labour. The Audit Commission, which had existed since the early 1980s, was responsible both for probity and value for money. During the second Blair government, the Commission was given the additional duty of creating Comprehensive Performance Assessments (CPAs) for each council in England and Wales.[22]

CPAs were a conscious attempt to bring together a number of the regulator's tools. Inspectors' reports, performance indicators and financial information were combined into a single assessment. Authorities were

---

[21] Public Administration Committee, *On Target? Government by Measurement* (Fifth Report, Vol. 1: HC62-I, Session 2002–3, London: The Stationery Office, 2003).

[22] Audit Commission, *CPA – The Way Forward* (London: Audit Commission, 2003).

graded 'excellent', 'good', 'fair', 'weak' or 'poor'. Although there was some initial complaint from local government – and a number of challenges from individual councils – the CPA process was well handled by the Audit Commission and bedded in with relative ease.

Other regulators continued to oversee local government and to publish reports about its activities. League tables were produced. But, by 2004, the costs of compliance had become an issue. The government's Better Regulation Task Force, which was attempting to produce an assessment of the impacts of red tape, accepted that there were now so many regulators that it was impossible to list them all.[23] As a result of this and other analyses of the growth of regulation, the Chancellor announced in 2005 that the 13 main public-sector regulators would be rationalised into four.[24] In the aftermath of this announcement, most of the regulators with local government responsibilities made efforts to reduce their impacts on councils. Local authorities then found themselves under pressure to undertake more self-assessment in place of external inspection and audit.

The 'Balance of Funding' issue

As far back as its original, 1997, manifesto the Blair government had committed itself to making the local authority finance system 'fairer'.[25] A major review of local authority funding was undertaken during 1999 and 2000, leading to a consultative paper in late 2000.[26] This document ruled nothing out and nothing in, though it was clear that council tax would be retained. More radically, the possibility of significantly increasing councils' freedom to borrow was proposed.

Thus the second Blair term of office inherited the unfinished business of the first. Local government continued to complain about the 'balance of funding' between central and local government. Three-quarters of council revenue income derived from Whitehall grants, with only a quarter coming from council tax. This balance meant that, at the margin, if a council added 1% to its spending, there would be a 4% increase in local taxation (and, of course, vice versa if spending were reduced). Within government this phenomenon was referred to as 'the gearing effect'.

---

[23] Better Regulation Task Force, *Local Delivery of Central Policy* (London: Cabinet Office, 2002).

[24] P. Gosling, 'Dawn of the super regulator', *Public Finance*, 8 April 2005.

[25] Labour Party, *New Labour because Britain deserves better* (London: Labour Party, 1997).

[26] Department of the Environment, Transport and the Regions, *Modernising Local Government Finance: A Green Paper* (London: TSO, 2000).

Worries about the gearing effect were compounded by the annual need to determine grants for each authority in England. (In the years since devolution, the Scottish and Welsh governments had handled their own council funding systems.) Revenue Support Grant (RSG), the annually set source of central funding to local government, was endlessly contentious. Because authorities were so dependent on grant, the process of determining expenditure need (the basis of a significant proportion of grant) was complex and highly political. Indeed, it was these need assessments – then known as Standard Spending Assessments (SSAs) – that Labour had promised to reform in their 1997 manifesto.

By the end of 2002, the government could no longer put off the reform of SSAs. The RSG for 2003–4 would be based on new 'Formula Spending Shares', a somewhat reformed version of the old SSAs. Then, in January 2003, a review was set up, under the chairmanship of Nick Raynsford, to consider the balance of central and local resources for councils.

The Balance of Funding (BoF) review was overseen by a steering group consisting of ministers, civil servants, Local Government Association members and officers, an international expert, academics, a trade unionist and a corporate affairs executive from a large private company. The membership was not dissimilar in type to that of the Layfield Committee, which had reviewed local government finance for an earlier Labour government between 1974 and 1976.

Just as the BoF review was getting under way in the early months of 2003, the impact of the grant reforms introduced in the RSG settlement began to bite. Because grant was redistributed – albeit modestly – the heavily geared impact of these reforms led to an average rise in council tax of 13% over England as a whole. More awkwardly for the government, many schools found they were receiving far less additional cash than ministers had suggested they would from a settlement that was, overall, intended to raise education expenditure to a rate well above inflation.

The ensuing complaints from head teachers, governors and parents led Education Secretary Charles Clarke to accuse councils of withholding money from schools. The LGA retaliated angrily. Relations between the centre and local government briefly returned to the deep freeze of the Thatcher years.

Later in 2003 the Audit Commission published a report[27] that came close to blaming the government alone for the problems outlined above. A

[27] Audit Commission, *Council Tax Increases 2003/04: Why Were They So High?* (London: TSO, 2003).

second report from the Commission suggested that, in fact, councils had allocated more money to schools than the government had originally projected.[28] There had never really been a significant funding 'crisis', though some schools had fared less well than they expected because of the redistribution of government grant between authorities and because a number of specific-purpose grants had been abolished.

As a result of the difficulties (real or imagined) that had faced schools funding in 2003, the Department for Education and Skills announced that, from 2004–5, there would be a 'minimum funding guarantee' for each school. Starting in 2006–7, schools' funding would be ring-fenced and, in effect, removed from the general resources provided to local government. The long era of local authority involvement with education which had begun with the Education Act, 1870, was, arguably, drawing to a close.

The 13% jump in council tax in 2003 led the government to decide to threaten to reuse their briefly dormant capping powers. Having scrapped the universal capping of local tax they had inherited from the Major government, Labour now found themselves under intense pressure – particularly from pensioners – to limit or abolish council tax. Like John Major and Margaret Thatcher before him, Tony Blair had discovered the terrible dangers hidden within the apparently simple issue of local taxation.

Because of the problems afflicting council tax and schools' funding during the spring of 2003, the Balance of Funding review came under sudden and unexpected pressure to produce a solution to the local government funding problem. Like Layfield in the 1970s, Raynsford found himself operating within a pressurised political environment.

Research was commissioned to examine how international experience, public awareness, efficiency and electoral turnout might throw light on local government funding issues. Work was undertaken on a local income tax and on reforms to council tax. The Local Government Association produced an all-party agreed proposal for reform, the so-called 'combination option'. The LGA's document involved a shift in the balance of funding by creating a new set of local taxes, including a reformed property tax, a re-localised business rate, a local element of income tax and, possibly, the introduction of a number of smaller revenues.[29]

[28] Audit Commission, *Education Funding: The Impact and Effectiveness of Measures to Stabilise School Funding* (London: TSO, 2004).

[29] Local Government Association, *The Balance of Funding – A Combination Option* (London: LGA, 2004).

Other proposals were made by think tanks and individuals. The New Local Government Network was essentially cautious about reform, citing difficulties that might arise from greater fiscal devolution. Such difficulties included a reduction in Treasury macroeconomic control, high administration costs, reduced equity and inefficient territorial competition.[30] Policy Exchange was more radical, proposing a move towards local income tax, re-localised business rates and the retention of council tax.[31] The New Policy Institute published research about the possibility of making council tax more progressive.[32]

The Raynsford review published its final report in July 2004, addressing the central issue of whether the existing balance of funding between councils' central and local resource-raising was, in fact, a problem. In paragraph 1.33, it concluded that 'there are strong arguments in favour of a shift in the balance of funding, but the case for any shift depends on the feasibility and desirability of any measures which might be used to achieve it'. Gearing 'can cloud the accountability and transparency of local spending decisions and can contribute to unsustainable council tax increases'.[33]

The acceptance that there were arguments in favour of a change in the balance of funding was heavily tempered by the idea that 'the feasibility and desirability of any measures which might be used to achieve it' should be a constraint on reform. Indeed, it would have been easy to read the latter words as an effective bar on any radical change.

Raynsford went on to consider a number of possible reforms to the council tax, and accepted a 'clear case for reviewing' the number of tax bands and the ratios between them – at the time of the next revaluation. Regional banding 'should be considered'. Council tax benefit take-up should be 'improved'. Much 'further detailed work' was needed.

Business rates could be re-localised, with safeguards for business. Alternatively, national non-domestic rates (NNDR) might remain a nationally determined revenue, but with the inflation-related cap lifted. A third

---

[30] New Local Government Network, *Balance of Funding – April 2004: The New Local Government Network's Response* (London: NLGN, 2004).

[31] Policy Exchange, *I'm a Local Councillor Get Me Out of Here!* (Tony Travers and Lorena Esposito) (London: Policy Exchange, 2004).

[32] New Policy Institute, Paper submitted to Balance of Funding Review, published as *Paper 16: Options for Reform of Council Tax* (London: ODPM, 2004).

[33] Office of the Deputy Prime Minister, *Balance of Funding Review – Report* (London: ODPM, 2004).

possibility would have been to allow a limited retention of business rates, building on the example of initiatives such as Business Improvement Districts. These options would 'have different potential impacts on the balance of funding'. None of these options was either recommended or rejected by the review.

A local income tax was examined, including issues such as administration costs, implications for business and the treatment of particular categories of income. The possibility of less-than-full equalisation was, controversially, raised. But the overall conclusion, as with other parts of the review, was that 'considerable further work would be required' to address technical, administrative and distributional impacts.

Smaller taxes and charges, e.g. a local tourist bed tax, a localised vehicle excise duty or green taxes, could not, the review stated, have achieved a significant shift in the balance of funding. 'The case for and against each of these options should be judged on its own merits.' The review itself did not, however, offer views on such merits.

The Balance of Funding review considered the pros and cons of most of the major proposals put forward in the 1990s and early 2000s as possible ways of reforming the way in which taxation is raised locally by local government. It explicitly avoided coming down in favour of or against any particular proposal.

An assessment of the Raynsford review's cautious conclusions would have to be aware of the words – published in the report and stated by ministers – that the study was 'conducted for the Government, not by the Government'. This deliberate distancing of Whitehall from even the heavily qualified conclusions of the review made it clear that the Blair government remained seriously worried about the distributive (and thus electoral) results of any reform to the system of local authority revenue-raising.

The House of Commons ODPM Select Committee, in a report published in parallel with Raynsford, concluded that 'any fundamental review of local government finance will touch on constitutional matters. Apart from Parliament, local government is the only institution in England with democratic legitimacy. The "balance of funding" between local taxation and centrally determined sources will affect local authorities' capacity to act autonomously and, therefore, the extent to which they can be a check or balance on the power of central Government.'[34] The willingness of

---

[34] ODPM Committee, *Local Government Revenue*, Ninth Report of Session 2003–4 Volume 1: Report, HC 402-I (London: TSO, 2004).

the Blair government to tinker with the British constitution was not, of course, confined to local government.

On the day Raynsford reported, the government announced that Sir Michael Lyons, head of the Institute of Local Government Studies at Birmingham University, would head a follow-up inquiry to complete the work partly undertaken by Raynsford. Lyons's report was due to be published in December 2005 and was expected to produce detailed exemplifications of some of the possible changes touched on by Raynsford. The government's decision to implement a revaluation of the council tax base in England in 2007 (a revaluation took place in April 2005 in Wales) created an additional dimension to Lyons's work.

Optimistic commentators read the Raynsford review and concluded that nothing had been ruled out. An official committee, including ministers from ODPM and the Treasury, had not said 'no' to council tax changes, local income tax or to the re-localisation of the business rate. Reform was still a possibility. Pessimists were less encouraged, believing Raynsford had simply played local government finance into the long grass. Only Lyons's report (in December 2005) and the government's response to it – expected during the spring or summer of 2006 – will determine who was correct.

If the future of revenue funding remained in the 'pending' tray throughout Labour's first eight years in office, capital finance was reformed in a way that was, at least in intent, expected to decentralise political control. A system of 'prudential rules' was introduced to replace the belt-and-braces controls that had previously been used to limit councils' freedom to spend on major capital projects. The new arrangements made it possible for authorities to incur new capital spending so long as they adhered to a number of common-sense rules concerning their capacity to make repayments and the total of their outstanding debts. Unfortunately, the freedoms offered were not widely taken up because councils were concerned about the long-term impacts of new borrowing on their revenue expenditure. That is, they feared that extra debt charges would lead to future capping.

Leadership in the cities

Deputy Prime Minister John Prescott had, since taking office in 1997, seen the renaissance of urban England as a key public policy objective. Rapid de-industrialisation and a taste for rural living had led to catastrophic decline for many of Britain's older cities. Prescott had commissioned the architect Richard Rogers to chair an Urban Task Force, whose 1999 report[35] became the starting point for several years of renewed interest in city development and government.

By the end of Blair's second term in office, there is no doubt that the central areas of Birmingham, Leeds, Manchester, Liverpool and Glasgow had been transformed. Newcastle and Gateshead had, for marketing purposes, become the twin-city of Newcastle/Gateshead. Even Manchester and Liverpool had made serious efforts to bury decades of competitive enmity and work in a more cooperative way. Iconic cultural structures continued to be built as a way of signalling the modernisation of older cities. The New Art Gallery opened in Walsall, the Sage (a centre for music and the performing arts) was built in Gateshead, while Birmingham saw an extraordinary new Selfridges store enter its urban fabric. In London, Mayor Ken Livingstone championed taller buildings and denser development.

London's city-wide government had been restored in 2000. During the years 2001–5, Livingstone established himself as a more moderate politician than the one who, as leader of the Greater London Council, had twenty years previously so appalled Mrs Thatcher. Politics had advanced. In the period since the early 1980s, some of Livingstone's ideas, for example on minorities, had moved from the political extremes to the mainstream. But in other ways, for example on the role of private enterprise and wealth, it was the Mayor who had changed.[36]

Moreover, Livingstone showed considerable bravery in introducing congestion charging to the capital. In February 2003 the world's largest urban road charging scheme was introduced in central London. In the months prior to the charge's inception, there was aggressive opposition from the media and elsewhere. Having withstood this challenge, charging started on time and with an effective operating system. Bus provision was improved with financial support from central government. On the other hand, Livingstone continued to oppose the so-called public private partnership (PPP) that the Treasury had promoted to rebuild the London Underground. Finally, in early 2003, the PPP contracts were signed and the rebuilding went ahead on the government's terms.[37]

In advance of the second London mayoral election in 2004, Ken Livingstone was readmitted to the Labour Party. He faced Steve Norris as Conservative candidate for a second time with Simon Hughes as Liberal

---

[35] Urban Task Force, *Towards an Urban Renaissance* (London: E&FN Spon, 1999).
[36] T. Travers, *The Politics of London: Governing an Ungovernable City* (Basingstoke: Palgrave Macmillan, 2004).
[37] C. Wolmar, *Down the Tube: The Battle for London's Underground* (London: Aurum Press, 2002).

Democrat challenger. Although Norris slightly narrowed Livingstone's lead, the latter was returned to City Hall for a further four years. The fact that Ken Livingstone had successfully created and run the executive part of the new Greater London Authority led ministers to consider the possibility of extending the London model to other cities in England. Mayors in other major authorities such as Doncaster, Newham, Lewisham, North Tyneside, Middlesborough and Hartlepool had also been judged a success in government and beyond.[38]

A further consultative document, published in early 2005, stated the government's enthusiasm for extending the mayoral experiment beyond the minority of authorities that had already adopted it. 'The Government will be consulting on proposals to develop, in partnership with local authorities, a new approach to develop more mayors with more powers to transform our major cities'.[39]

Professor Gerry Stoker, whose views were often a good guide to developing Whitehall thinking, wrote later in 2005 that 'a full-scale reorganisation is necessary, built around the "super-sizing" of cities, towns and counties, in tandem with genuine community-level neighbourhood governance'.[40] Elsewhere, Stoker encouraged the idea of directly elected mayors to run these new, wider, city areas. The possibility of rolling out directly elected leaders to new super-sized cities is clearly a serious option for the third Blair term.

Nations and regions

By 2001 Labour had created new, devolved, governments in Scotland, Wales and London. In Northern Ireland, devolution had produced self-government, though the assembly was suspended in 2002. In the rest of England, regional development agencies (RDAs) had been created, as had putative regional assemblies. These assemblies, originally called 'chambers', were joint committees of the counties and districts within each of the eight English regions outside London. Originally created to provide an element of democratic oversight of the RDAs, the chambers were to assume a far wider role during the years from 2001 to 2005. Indeed, during the second Blair government, it was to the regions of England that devolutionist attention was turned.

---

[38] A. Randle, *Mayors Mid-term: Lessons from the First Eighteen Months of Directly Elected Mayors* (London: NLGN, 2004).

[39] Office of the Deputy Prime Minister, *Vibrant Local Leadership* (London: ODPM, 2005).

[40] G. Stoker, 'England expects . . .', *Public Servant*, 27 April 2005.

Scotland and London had each voted – in referendums – by a convincing majority to create their respective governments. The referendum in Wales was won by the narrowest of margins. The four forms of devolved government (Scotland, Wales, London and Northern Ireland) operating within the United Kingdom in 2001 were, predictably, significantly different from each other. In May 2002 the Office of the Deputy Prime Minister published a consultative document on the creation of regional governments within England.[41] The next stage of devolution was under way.

The government outlined a model of regional government for England that was substantially different from those already adopted for other parts of the UK. English regions were to be given a weaker form of assembly than that operating in London. However, unlike the London system, those for other parts of England would not have a 'mayor', but would instead (like Scotland and Wales) select a leader from among assembly members. Thus the rest of the English regions were to use a form of government based on the traditional British parliamentary or local government model. Only the capital's regional arrangements would feature a directly elected executive.

The powers to be devolved to the new English regions would include the economic regeneration responsibilities already given to regional development agencies, plus strategic planning, the allocation of social housing resources to local authorities and a requirement to publish a number of strategies. These strategies would, separately, allow the region influence over skills and employment, transport, waste, health improvement, culture and biodiversity.

Paragraph 4.17 of the government's consultative document made it clear how modest the English regions' powers would be:

> elected assemblies will have a significant **influencing** role. The proposals
> are designed to give assemblies influence on issues that have a regional
> dimension, but where it is important that this is balanced with national
> and local needs. Its influencing role will include:
>
> - **scrutiny** of the impact of higher education on economic development;
> - **advising** the Government on the allocation of local transport funding;
> - **requesting** call-in of strategic planning applications;
> - being **consulted** by other bodies, such the [sic] Learning & Skills Council
>   (both local and national), and securing a commitment from them to assist
>   the elected assembly in the effective delivery of its strategies;

[41] Department for Transport, Local Government and the Regions, *Your Region, Your Choice – Revitalising the English Regions* (London: HMSO, 2002).

- making **appointments** to other bodies, such as the boards of local learning and skills councils;
- **coordinating activity** in the region by bringing relevant actors together – for example, to further links between business and education to increase employment opportunities and improve economic performance.

The use of the words in bold type (which is there in the original document) was doubtless intended to give the impression that the new regional assemblies would have a number of important roles. In reality, the words themselves gave a significant clue to the modest powers being offered by central government. Even the appointment of members of RDAs would require the region to consult the government on each appointment to each board.

The capacity of the regions to raise their own resources was also heavily circumscribed. Assemblies were to be given the same power to set a council tax precept that had been given to the Greater London Authority (though not, oddly, to the Welsh Assembly). However, the government proposed 'initially to limit assembly precepts through arrangements comparable to the existing local authority capping regime' (paragraph 5.9). The new English assemblies were to be capped before they had even been created.

The new authorities would be elected using the additional member system, a form of proportional representation that had been used in Scotland and Wales and for the London Assembly. Where a region voted to introduce regional government, any areas with two-tier local government (i.e. non-metropolitan counties and districts) would be required to move to a single tier of unitary councils. The government did not believe that the electorate would be prepared to accept three levels of government below Westminster.

Supporters of devolution gave the government's proposals a modest cheer. Many saw the proposed assemblies (which would only be created following a region-by-region referendum vote in favour) as a starting point for a process of further reform. But the Local Government Association (LGA) complained 'that government plans could see future regional assemblies "sucking" power from town halls, rather than taking it from Whitehall'.[42] The LGA also warned the assemblies foreshadowed a patchwork constitution across England.

A Regional Assemblies (Preparations) Act received Royal Assent in May 2003, allowing the government to move ahead with referendums and other preparatory work, such as the need to review local government

---

[42] Peter Hetherington, 'Soundings on devolution in England', *Guardian*, 3 December 2002.

boundaries within regions where regional assemblies were to be created. Also during 2003 the government undertook a 'soundings' exercise – including opinion polling – to see which regions were likely to show the greatest interest in holding a referendum. As a result, local and regional government minister Nick Raynsford announced in July 2004 that people in three northern regions would be allowed to vote later that year on whether or not to set up regional governments in their areas.

Later in July 2004 the government published a Draft Regional Assemblies Bill. On the same day ministers made it clear that they were to postpone the referendums planned for the North West, and Yorkshire and Humberside regions: only the North East of England would vote in November that year.

In the approach to the referendum, it became clear that opinion was running against the proposed regional authority. While the 'yes' campaign received the support of a wide range of regional Establishment and media figures, the 'no' campaign publicised their message using an inflatable white elephant which, they believed, symbolised the bureaucratic and feeble nature of the proposed new government. Even visits from a glittering array of Labour and Liberal Democrat politicians, including the populist Mayor of England's only other regional government, Ken Livingstone, could not win the vote.

On 4 November 2004, in an all-postal ballot, the voters of the North East rejected an elected regional assembly by 78% to 22%. The turnout was 48%. Electors in every district in the whole region voted 'no'. It is hard to exaggerate the scale of the rejection.

The reasons for the 'no' vote were suggested by the Housing, Planning, Local Government and the Regions Committee of the House of Commons in a report published a month after it occurred. 'The Committee thought that the scope of the powers and responsibilities which the Government was prepared to give to Assemblies was disappointing and would limit their effectiveness . . . The ODPM and to a lesser extent the DTI were the only Government departments prepared to devolve powers to the assemblies. There were major concerns that the powers and responsibilities proposed for assemblies would be taken away from local government rather than passed down from central Government.'[43]

Most damningly, the Committee concluded that 'Voters in the North East were not convinced about the 'cost-benefit' calculation in regard

---

[43] ODPM Committee, *The Draft Regional Assemblies Bill,* First Report of Session 2004–05 Volume 1, HC 62-I (London: TSO, 2004).

to elected assemblies. They were unable to see in the modest powers of assemblies sufficient prospects of concrete improvements in their daily lives to vote for their introduction.'

The electorate in Scotland had, in their 1998 referendum, been offered a parliament with legislative powers over virtually all matters of domestic policy. In London the Greater London Authority (GLA) had been given substantial responsibilities for transport, a matter of deep city-wide concern. The North East evidently judged that the assembly offered them very little devolved power.

In recent years there have been few such clear-cut expressions – at the ballot box – of voter distaste for the misjudgement of national politicians. Given how many members of the Blair government (including the Prime Minister himself) sat for constituencies in the North East or in Scotland, this failure of understanding is doubly perplexing. Deputy Prime Minister John Prescott conceded on 8 November 2004 that devolution to the English regions was to be abandoned for the foreseeable future. There would be no referendum in either the North West or Yorkshire and Humberside. The voters of the North East had, in the event, spoken for the whole of England.

In Scotland, responsibility for local government had transferred in 1999 to the new Edinburgh Parliament. The Scottish Parliament decided in 2002 to change the electoral arrangements for Scotland's local government from first-past-the-post to proportional representation.[44] This was a reform that could, in the longer term, have profound implications throughout Britain, particularly in the light of pressures for reform in England and Wales.[45]

In Scotland and Wales, day-to-day local government policy was handled by the national governments in Edinburgh and Cardiff. From 2001 to 2005, councils in England were subject to a barrage of new policies. Reforms, described earlier, including Best Value, Comprehensive Performance Assessments, New Localism, the Balance of Funding review, the centralisation of schools' funding, the reintroduction of capping and, eventually, moves towards neighbourhood governance. Gentler and less activist policies were pursued in Scotland and Wales. In this sense, devolution had made a significant difference.

---

[44] Scottish Executive, *Proportional Representation (Local Government Elections) Scotland Bill* (Edinburgh: TSO, 2002).

[45] See, for example, *The Missing Modernisation: The Case for PR in Local Government Elections* (London: Make Votes Count and the Electoral Reform Society, 2004).

Gershon and the efficiency agenda

The second Blair government presided over a rapid expansion of public expenditure from 2000–1 to 2005–6. Some local government provision, notably education and personal social services, enjoyed a significant share of the additional resources, while others, in particular the local environment and roads, grew at a significantly slower rate. Because of concerns that this boost in public spending might lead to inefficiency, the Chancellor appointed Sir Peter Gershon to undertaken an investigation of how better value might be achieved. The Conservative Party appointed their own efficiency expert, David James, to produce an even more radical set of proposals.

The Gershon Review, published in July 2004,[46] proposed that all parts of the public sector, including local government, should make efficiency savings equivalent in most cases to 2.5% per annum. All the local institutions that delivered services, including schools, were also expected to achieve this level of efficiency. Savings were supposed to occur as a result of greater use of private contracting, improved procurement and increased use of information technology. Early evidence suggested that local government had been able to demonstrate that efficiencies had been made.[47]

In one particular sector, the fire and emergency services, the Blair government made radical efforts to achieve 'modernisation'. Efforts to renegotiate the terms and conditions of firefighters led to a number of strikes during 2003 and 2004 which, in turn, required the army to provide emergency cover. Eventually, the government was able to impose the productivity reforms it sought in the face of continuing opposition from the Fire Brigades Union.

Whitehall and the core of central government

For all the reforms made to local authority structure, functions and finance, the core of central government remained largely untouched by 'modernisation' or by heavy oversight from auditors and inspectors. Whitehall departments, overall, continued with broadly the functions they had had in 2001. However, there was some reorganisation of functions, for example when the Office of the Deputy Prime Minister was created in 2001.

---

[46] P. Gershon, *Releasing Resources for the Frontline: Independent Review of Public Sector Efficiency* (London: HM Treasury, 2004).
[47] Local Government Chronicle, '£1.05BN' in *LGC*, 26 May 2005, London: Emap, 2005.

Departments had been subjected to some elements of the 'targets' regime that had been imposed on local authorities and other local institutions between 1997 and 2001. Public Service Agreements were made between the Treasury and each department of state, requiring outputs to be delivered in exchange for increased public expenditure. In some cases, these outputs were easy to measure, while in others they were more generalised (and thus less simple to quantify). Treasury influence over service departments increased in the period from 2001 to 2005. The use of instruments such as PSAs was backed up by teams within the Treasury who created their own expertise on particular policies or services.

At the core of government, within the Cabinet Office, a number of different units and posts co-existed. Organisations such as the Office of Public Service Reform sought to drive improved performance throughout the public services. The Strategy Unit continued to act as an official 'think tank' within the centre of government, providing the Prime Minister with advice and policy ideas.

There was no fundamental or continuing effort to modernise central government in the way that local authorities were subjected to New Localism, moves to neighbourhood governance or efforts to reform its funding. However, the Gershon Review required efficiency savings from all Whitehall departments, while another Treasury-appointed review by Sir Michael Lyons (published well before his local government finance report) proposed moving 20,000 civil servants away from London and the south-east.[48] As a result of Gershon and Lyons, some civil service reductions and relocations commenced during 2004–5. An inquiry by the Public Administration Committee of the House of Commons considered the operation and independence of the civil service, concluding[49] that there was a need for a new Civil Service Act to enshrine this independence. The inquiry had been instigated following suggestions that governments (notably Labour since 1997) were putting officials under greater pressure than in the past to behave 'politically'.

Conclusion

Tony Blair's second government maintained the restless and reforming approach to local and regional government that had started between 1997

---

[48] Lyons Review, *Well Placed to Deliver? Shaping the Pattern of Government Service, Independent Review of Public Sector Relocation* (London: TSO, 2004).

[49] Public Administration Committee, *A Draft Civil Service Bill: Completing the Reform*, First Report, Vol. I, HC 128-I, Session 2003–04 (London: The Stationery Office, 2004).

and 2001. One clear development was a new interest in governance at the neighbourhood level. The process of policy development, as in the first term, was dominated by a small number of individuals, think tanks and units within Whitehall. A tiny number of academics, local government officers and companies were also involved. New ideas emerged in reaction to what government departments were doing at the local level. In some cases new policies led reform, in others they appeared to follow.

Despite devolution to Scotland and Wales, local and regional government within England remained subject to detailed central control. Efforts to find a new 'balance of funding' that might make local authorities more financially autonomous, failed. A further inquiry into local authority finance may yet lead to reform, though radical change appears as unlikely as ever.

Blair himself had published a pamphlet on local government back in 1998.[50] The concerns articulated in this document, including low electoral turnout, weak local leadership and poor council performance, remained government concerns throughout its first eight years in power. But the relentless initiatives that emerged from Whitehall changed their emphasis as the years rolled past. Labour needed to congratulate itself on improving public service performance, yet the improvements were not sufficient to convince the centre that local government could be trusted to any significant extent. Efforts to decentralise power were limited and minimal.

Leading commentators pondered the state of local government during Tony Blair's second term. Gerry Stoker of Manchester University, who was as close as any outsider to the government's policy-making core, concluded, 'New Labour has offered an unusual mix of rationalist confidence and fatalistic distrust of others in approaching the reform of the state. It believes that it can make the world a better place but it is not sure how and who to trust, and in particular it is uncertain about the role of community governance.'[51] Labour should be 'braver and bolder'.

Simon Jenkins argued for a bold, 'Big Bang', solution to the endless centralisation of the British constitution and government.[52] Jenkins supported a short, sharp move to localism – a rare point of view among Britain's leading political commentators. His proposals included elected

---

[50] Tony Blair, *Leading the Way: A New Vision for Local Government* (London: Institute for Public Policy Research, 1998).

[51] G. Stoker, *Transforming Local Governance From Thatcherism to New Labour* (Basingstoke: Palgrave Macmillan, 2004).

[52] S. Jenkins, *Big Bang Localism – A Rescue Plan for British Democracy* (London: Policy Exchange, 2004).

mayors for all municipalities; a variety of local taxes; local government control of the NHS; central grants to be 'general' and not tied to particular services and no more local quangos. Whitehall regional structures would be abolished in favour of county government, though Scotland and Wales would be given greater powers. There would be a bonfire of targets and league tables.

The Big Bang approach was necessary, Jenkins argued, because more gradualist ones would be likely to fail. The evidence of the period from 1997 to 2005 was suggestive of a time when initiative was followed by initiative, but with no clear democratic end point in view. 'Modernisation' and 'New Localism' were continuing themes. But, just as with other constitutional reforms such as the House of Lords, the Supreme Court, devolution and human rights legislation, efforts to reform local government lacked any stated end point. With the exception of Scotland and Wales, caution and a lack of certainty about objectives together ensured that centralisation in Britain remained as powerful as ever.

There had been no civil service reform by 2005. The core of central government had grown increasingly complex throughout the years from 2001 to 2005, building on the approach during the first Blair government. Legislation and initiatives to reform public services, criminal justice and – following the attacks on the United States in September 2001 – to increase protection against terrorism were introduced. Civil servants, however, were arguably less important in the generation of policy than in the past.[53] Their role moved further towards the implementation of government policies that had increasingly been generated (as the earlier sections on local government suggest) by think tanks, individuals and within the politicised core of government itself.

Taken together, the approach to local, regional and central government can be seen to be episodic and lacking in a final destination. The continuing evolution of the British constitutional arrangements had moved uncertainly during the second Blair government. Determination and certainty in foreign policy was not matched on the home front.

[53] C. Foster, *British Government in Crisis* (Abingdon: Hart Publishing, 2005).

5

Media management

RAYMOND KUHN

The major focus of media management during Blair's second term was on the war in Iraq. During the prolonged run-up to the outbreak of hostilities in spring 2003 the government used the news media to put across its case, albeit with mixed success in terms of influencing public opinion regarding the legitimacy of military action in the absence of a second United Nations resolution. During the pre-war phase, the war itself and the weeks immediately following the downfall of the Saddam Hussein regime, Downing Street pursued a bitter campaign against the BBC regarding the Corporation's alleged anti-government bias on the issue of Iraq. The breakdown in the relationship between Number 10 and the Corporation finally came to a head over allegations made in late May on the Radio Four *Today* programme by its defence and diplomatic correspondent, Andrew Gilligan, that the government had knowingly misinformed the public in presenting the case for war. This broadcast, which indirectly led a few weeks later to the suicide of the government scientist and former weapons inspector, Dr David Kelly, was at the heart of the inquiry led by Lord Hutton into the circumstances surrounding Kelly's death. The Hutton Report,[1] published at the start of 2004, exculpated the government from responsibility and instead directed its fire at the BBC. Its publication was swiftly followed by the resignation of the chairman of the BBC Board of Governors, Gavyn Davies, the Director General, Greg Dyke, and Gilligan himself.

In a separate though related process, the government introduced a series of reforms to its news media management operations, such as the introduction of monthly televised prime ministerial press conferences. The single most dramatic event in this context was the resignation in the summer of 2003 of the government's Director of Communications

---

[1] Lord Hutton, *Report of the Inquiry into the Circumstances Surrounding the Death of Dr David Kelly C.M.G. by Lord Hutton*, HC 247 (London: The Stationery Office, 2004). http://www.the-hutton-inquiry.org.uk/content/report/index.htm

and Strategy, Alastair Campbell. Since becoming Blair's press secretary in 1994, Campbell had come to symbolise New Labour's approach to media management and was often presented by his critics as the embodiment of the art of spin. His departure was followed by the introduction of structural changes in the organisation of government communications in line with the recommendations of the Phillis report published at the start of 2004.[2] Yet despite these structural and personnel changes towards the middle of Blair's second term, the New Labour government seemed saddled with a reputation for media manipulation which persisted up to the 2005 general election.

News management in Blair's first term, 1997–2001

While the process of modernising the Labour Party's approach to political communication in the contemporary era began during Neil Kinnock's leadership in the 1980s,[3] it was only after Blair was elected party leader in 1994 that proactive news management became such a central, even obsessive, concern. By the time of its first general election success in 1997 New Labour had established a hugely positive reputation for its media operations, with sharp contrasts drawn by political journalists between its highly focused activities and the uncoordinated and ineffectual approach of the Conservatives under John Major. During Blair's first term the government's approach to news management was characterised by three key features: centralisation, professionalisation and politicisation.[4]

First, Campbell went even further than Bernard Ingham, Mrs Thatcher's press secretary between 1979 and 1990, in concentrating control over news management in Number 10. As an alternative governmental source for the media, Charlie Wheelan, Gordon Brown's press officer at the Treasury, was viewed with suspicion and even hostility by Campbell. Wheelan was regarded by Campbell as working for Brown to a different agenda from that of Number 10 and therefore being distinctly 'off message' in Blairite terms. Not suprisingly, Campbell derived immense satisfaction when Wheelan was forced to resign at the start of 1999 over his role in leaking information about Peter Mandelson's loan from Geoffrey

---

[2] Bob Phillis, *An Independent Review of Government Communications* (London: The Stationery Office, 2004), http://www.gcreview.gov.uk.

[3] Eric Shaw, *The Labour Party Since 1979* (London: Routledge, 1994).

[4] Bob Franklin, 'The hand of history: New Labour, news management and governance' in S. Ludlam and M. J. Smith (eds.), *New Labour in Government* (Basingstoke: Macmillan, 2001), pp. 130–44.

Robinson.[5] In addition, government ministers who departed from the official line in their dealings with the media found themselves reprimanded by Campbell for not adhering to his centrally imposed rules.

Second, a highly professional approach to news management was evident in the various innovations introduced by Campbell at Number 10. These included the establishment of a Strategic Communications Unit to coordinate government news announcements across departments so that a clear, focused policy message was distributed to the media on any particular day. Former journalists were employed to ensure that a media rather than bureaucratic mindset informed the process. In terms of trailing policy announcements, the rebuttal of critical statements, the 'pre-buttal' of opposition criticisms not yet disseminated in the public sphere, the proactive planting of stories via favoured journalists and speedy reaction to possible negative stories, the New Labour government's media management operations pushed back the frontiers, going further than any of its predecessors in Britain and even acquiring a glowing reputation internationally. Campbell's attention to detail became legendary, as did his facility for the appropriate soundbite, such as the 'people's princess' used by Blair on the occasion of Princess Diana's death in 1997.

Finally, politicisation of news management was evidenced by three important developments. First, although clearly operating in a partisan capacity on behalf of New Labour in general and Blair in particular, Campbell was allowed to give orders to civil servants. Second, Campbell's belief that the non-partisan civil servants acting as ministerial press officers in the Government Information Service would be insufficiently proactive in pushing the government's case with the news media led to many of them being weeded out and replaced in the early months of Blair's first term. Third, the New Labour government appointed a host of special advisers with media-related responsibilities to ministerial departments. The huge expansion in their numbers during Blair's first term in comparison with the Major premiership was further testimony to New Labour's desire to be proactive in setting the news agenda. New Labour supporters argued that inasmuch as these three developments represented a politicisation of government communication, this was a necessary accompaniment to the professionalisation of news management. For New Labour critics, however, politicisation broke with long-standing traditions of civil service

---

[5] Raymond Kuhn, 'The first Blair government and political journalism', in R. Kuhn and E. Neveu (eds.), *Political Journalism: New Challenges, New Practices* (London: Routledge, 2002) pp. 47–68.

neutrality and overstepped the dividing line between party political and official information.[6]

The New Labour government enjoyed a prolonged honeymoon period with much of the news media, which extended well into Blair's first term. This is not to say that all was plain sailing during the first couple of years in office: the Ecclestone affair, the first resignation from the Cabinet of Peter Mandelson and the persistent in-fighting at the heart of the executive between Blair and Brown and their respective spin doctors – all provided good 'knocking copy' for political journalists. Nonetheless, potentially explosive stories, such as Robin Cook's affair with his secretary or the resignation of Ron Davies following his nocturnal wandering on Clapham Common, were skilfully dealt with by New Labour's media handlers to minimise any adverse publicity for the government.

From around the beginning of 2000 New Labour's capacity to shape the news agenda and influence the framing of coverage started to run into difficulties as a series of highly problematic issues came on to the political and policy agendas. The Millennium Dome fiasco, the successful campaign for the mayorship of London by the rebel Ken Livingstone standing as an independent against the official Labour candidate, the protest against the rise in fuel taxation by lorry drivers and the foot-and-mouth disease crisis in the countryside were all issues which New Labour found difficult to manage in news terms. In 2000 Campbell passed on the onerous responsibility of the twice-daily lobby briefings to two career civil servants, Godric Smith and Tom Kelly, and assumed a more strategic role as Director of Communications and Strategy at Number 10. This move was designed to take Campbell away from routine front-line contact with journalists and to remove him from an environment where his increasing frustration with the coverage afforded New Labour frequently spilled out in abrasive comments to journalists. Campbell argued that the real spinners in the interrelationship between government and news media were the journalists and that as a result the government's message was being distorted in various media outlets.[7]

If the change of Campbell's status was intended to depersonalise and heal New Labour's increasingly fractious relationship with sections of the news media, then it failed. In part this was because Campbell could

[6] Bob Franklin, 'A Damascene conversion? New Labour and media relations', in S. Ludlam and M. J. Smith (eds.), *Governing as New Labour: Policy and Politics under Blair* (Basingstoke: Palgrave Macmillan, 2004), pp. 94–8.
[7] Bill Hagerty, 'Cap'n spin *does* lose his rag', *British Journalism Review* 11/2 (2000): 7–20.

not resist continuing to try to shape the news to Blair's advantage and in part because some sections of the media were now implacably hostile to the Prime Minister. In the run-up to the 2001 general election, New Labour's obsession with news management had arguably become counterproductive as journalists filed stories critically unpacking the spin for their audiences. For some commentators 'spin' was becoming for the Blair premiership what 'sleaze' had been for Major's government – a critical label used as shorthand to sum up the perceived deficiencies of an administration.

Campbell, the BBC and the Iraq war

The events of 11 September 2001, marked by the searing television pictures of aircraft deliberately flying into the twin towers of the World Trade Center in New York, irrevocably altered the development of Blair's second term. His support for the Bush administration in the subsequent 'war on terror' led to British military involvement in two foreign conflicts: first in Afghanistan in late 2001 to remove the Taliban regime which had given succour to Osama Bin Laden and his Al-Qaeda terrorist network and then, more controversially, in Iraq in 2003 to find and destroy Saddam Hussein's weapons of mass destruction. Although a cessation of hostilities was announced by President Bush in a highly mediatised event on board a US aircraft carrier on 1 May 2003, the impact of British involvement in the Iraq war was to continue right up to the 2005 general election.

In any evaluation of the New Labour government's handling of the media over the Iraq war it must be remembered that all governments in democratic societies are particularly sensitive to news coverage during periods when their country is engaged in armed conflict and the lives of military personnel are at risk. In such a situation the role of the media in the accompanying propaganda war is inevitably subject to critical scrutiny from across civil society and the political spectrum. In a liberal democracy the news media have a responsibility to inform their audiences about the stakes involved in war and to hold the government to account for its decisions: these are part of the public sphere functions of information provision and 'watchdog' which the media routinely perform in their 'fourth estate' role.

There is a tendency, however, for governments to believe that at times of military conflict the media should fulfil the function of mobilising public opinion in support of the official policy: the tabloid newspapers' 'back our boys' approach. In particular, the myth that television coverage was responsible for undermining the US position during the Vietnam war in the 1960s and 1970s[8] has reinforced the perceived importance for the authorities of the media being kept 'onside' during such politically sensitive periods. This was perfectly illustrated during the Falklands conflict in 1982, when certain programmes on the BBC which sought to be even-handed in their coverage of the official British and Argentinian positions regarding the issue of the islands' sovereignty and the conduct of the ensuing military conflict were severely criticised by Prime Minister Thatcher and her Conservative supporters.[9] Broadcasters' notions of balance and impartiality, which are normally used to underpin news coverage and thus avoid charges of deliberate partisan bias, may be seen as irrelevant or even damaging when applied to coverage of a military conflict in which the nation's armed forces are involved. Broadcasters know, therefore, that in these circumstances they have to be especially sensitive to the construction of the news agenda and the framing of stories.

The war in Iraq brought these concerns to the surface in a particularly acute fashion for the New Labour government and the main public service broadcaster in Britain. While in the run-up to the war public opinion was fairly evenly split, the intensity of feeling in the opposition camp was clearly evidenced by the large anti-war demonstrations held across the country, notably on 15 February 2003 when the 'Stop the War' rally in London represented the biggest demonstration in British history. The mainstream political parties were also divided, with the Conservatives supporting the government, the Liberal Democrats opposed to military intervention and the parliamentary Labour Party split, with a massive backbench rebellion of 139 Labour MPs refusing to support the government in the vote on taking the country to war. There was, in short, no political or popular consensus for the BBC to reflect in its coverage of the issue of Britain's participation in a war in Iraq.

The government had sought to prepare public opinion for conflict through the publication of dossiers designed to support the government's position regarding Iraq's possession of weapons of mass destruction.[10]

---

8 Daniel Hallin, The 'Uncensored War: The Media and Vietnam (Oxford: Oxford University Press, 1986).

9 Robert Harris, Gotcha! The Media, the Government and the Falklands Crisis (London: Faber & Faber, 1983).

10 Mark Phythian notes that 'The process of producing the September dossier needs to be seen in the context of the propaganda requirements involved in preparing nations, particularly democracies, for war.' 'Hutton and Scott: a tale of two inquiries', Parliamentary Affairs 58/1 (2005): 136.

The second dossier, published in February 2003, was quickly shown to have had large sections plagiarised from an academic thesis which was in any case out of date. Changes had also been made to the original document, such as Iraq's 'aiding opposition groups in hostile regimes' becoming 'supporting terrorist organisations in hostile regimes'. Soon discredited, this 'dodgy dossier' was later described by the Foreign Secretary, Jack Straw, as 'a complete horlicks'. Yet no senior official in the government's communications apparatus considered it appropriate to resign in the wake of its publication.

The first and much weightier dossier, published in September 2002, argued that Iraq could use some of its weapons of mass destruction within 45 minutes of an order being given to deploy them, and it was this claim which was given particular prominence in British news media coverage. Jonathan Powell, Head of Policy at Number 10, sent an email to Campbell during the drafting process in which he asked: 'Alastair – what will be the headline in the *Standard* on day of publication? What do we want it to be?'[11] In the event the headline could not have been better for the government: '45 Mins From Attack' was the *Evening Standard* front-page headline on the day of the dossier's publication. The *Sun* was even more apocalyptic the following day: 'Brits 45 Mins From Doom'. Only the *Daily Mirror* and the *Independent*, both of which were to campaign consistently against the war, were hostile in their coverage.[12]

The September dossier became the subject of particularly intense scrutiny after the end of the war was declared as a result of the now infamous two-way exchange between Gilligan and John Humphrys on the *Today* programme just after 6 am on 29 May 2003, during which the government was accused by Gilligan of having 'sexed up' the dossier. Gilligan's assertion further fuelled Campbell's running feud with the BBC. During the war the relationship between the government and the Corporation had been strained to near breaking point over the latter's coverage of the build-up to the conflict in Iraq and of the war itself. Campbell had written to the BBC's Director of News, Richard Sambrook, on several occasions to complain that the BBC's coverage was skewed – '12 separate complaints before that which he sent on Gilligan'.[13] Blair himself wrote to both the Corporation's Director General and the chairman of the Board

---

[11] Hutton, *Report of the Inquiry*, p. 138.
[12] James Humphreys, 'The Iraq dossier and the meaning of spin', *Parliamentary Affairs* 58/1 (2005): 163.
[13] John Lloyd, *What the Media Are Doing to Our Politics* (London: Constable, 2004), p. 80.

of Governors to complain that the BBC had gone too far and that 'he had been shocked by some of the editorializing of our [BBC] interviewers and reporters'.[14]

In terms of his relationship with the BBC Campbell had what in police circles would be called 'form', particularly evident when Britain was engaged in a military conflict. During the Kosovo crisis in 1999, for instance, he had criticised the reporting from the Serb capital Belgrade of the BBC's foreign correspondent, John Simpson. Campbell's views had been given to the political editor of *The Times*, Philip Webster, and they formed part of a front page story in which 'senior government officials accused [Simpson] of. . . swallowing Serb propaganda'.[15] During the war in Afghanistan Campbell had also complained about some of the reporting of the BBC correspondent Rageh Omaar as being too sympathetic to the Taliban regime, after the reporter had spoken of 'an alleged blunder by Allied bombers which, according to the Taliban, had caused civilian casualties'.[16]

Did the government have a case regarding the BBC's coverage of the Iraq issue? It was certainly true that the Corporation did not simply act as an apologist for the conflict; nor did it serve as a mere transmission belt for government views; nor did it act as a cheerleader for the authorities as Rupert Murdoch's Fox News did for the Bush administration in the United States. However, the argument that the BBC was somehow institutionally opposed to the war and that this stance was evident in its news coverage is not supported by the evidence. For example, an academic study conducted at Cardiff University of British television coverage of the war in Iraq examined 1,534 news reports during the war on all weekdays from 20 March to 11 April inclusive from the evening news bulletins on BBC1 (6 pm), ITV News (6.30 pm), Channel 4 News (7 pm) and Sky News (10 pm).[17] On the basis of their detailed research, the authors of this study concluded:

---

[14] Greg Dyke, *Inside Story* (London: HarperCollins, 2004), p. 253. 'The Prime Minister wrote: "I believe, and I am not alone in believing, that you have not got the balance right between support and dissent; between news and comment; between the voices of the Iraqi regime and the voices of Iraqi dissidents; or between the diplomatic support we have, and diplomatic opposition."' Dyke, *Inside Story*, p. 254.

[15] Peter Oborne and Simon Walters, *Alastair Campbell* (London: Aurum, 2004), p. 255.

[16] Oborne and Walters, *Alastair Campbell*, p. 281.

[17] Justin Lewis and Rod Brookes, 'Reporting the war on British television', in D. Miller (ed.), *Tell Me Lies: Propaganda and Media Distortion in the Attack on Iraq* (London: Pluto Press, 2004), pp. 132–43.

our research suggests that the wartime coverage was generally sympathetic to the government's case. This manifested itself in various ways, notably: the focus on the progress of war to the exclusion of other issues and non-military or governmental sources; the tendency to portray the Iraqi people as liberated rather than invaded; the failure to question the claim that Iraq possessed weapons of mass destruction; and the focus on the brutality or decadence of the regime without putting this evidence in context.[18]

The authors' conclusion, therefore, suggests that the BBC was far from anti-war. Indeed, based on this study, 'the government's complaints would have been better directed against Channel 4, which emerges as significantly more unfavourable to coalition policy than the BBC'.[19]

A second academic study, this time comparing a sample of German television news with the BBC's main evening bulletins and the US ABC news, showed that in comparative terms across a range of indicators including information and commentary the BBC was *relatively* impartial and even-handed in its coverage of the war.[20] Where the BBC was out of line was in giving *less* coverage to the anti-war movement in Britain; this can hardly be interpreted as unhelpful to the official position of the UK government. Finally, a third study which among other media coverage examined BBC1 news (6 pm) and ITV News (6.30 pm) between 20 March and 17 April 2003 concluded that there was 'substantial homogeneity between the two main terrestrial channels' bulletins'.[21]

Three further points need to be borne in mind in any evaluation of BBC coverage of Iraq. First, there are the general conceptual and method-ological problems related to notions of objectivity and bias in journalism, especially the political variety, which make the search for consensus in the interpretation and assessment by different parties – including *inter alios* the government, BBC editors and journalists, lobby groups, audiences and academic researchers – of the same news reporting necessarily elu-sive.[22] To put it crudely: one person's flawed coverage is another's factual account. Second, some of the particular targets of government criticism of the BBC – the *Today* programme (Radio Four), *The World at One* (Radio Four) and *Newsnight* (BBC2) with their interview formats and at times highly adversarial style of questioning – were not included in the academic

---

[18] Lewis and Brookes, 'Reporting the war', p. 142.
[19] Howard Tumber and Jerry Palmer, *Media at War: The Iraq Crisis* (London: Sage, 2004), p. 98.
[20] Media Tenor analysis, quoted in Tumber and Palmer, *Media at War*, pp. 96–8.
[21] Tumber and Palmer, *Media at War*, p. 111.
[22] Vincent Campbell, *Information Age Journalism* (London: Arnold, 2004), pp. 153–77.

studies of the Corporation's war coverage mentioned above. Third, these studies focused on television coverage during the period of the war itself, not in the long run-up phase. Despite these caveats, however, it is clear that these studies furnish no evidence that BBC television news had an explicit anti-government agenda in its reporting of the Iraq war. Nor do the studies support the view that BBC television news coverage was even inadvertently skewed in an anti-government direction on a systematic basis.

The Hutton Inquiry

The increasingly conflictual relationship between Campbell and the BBC did not cease with the formal end of hostilities in Iraq. Instead it was to flare up dramatically following the Humphrys/Gilligan *Today* interview and an article a few days later written by Gilligan for the *Mail on Sunday* in which Campbell was accused – this time by name – of having exceeded his presentational remit in the construction of the September dossier. Campbell used his appearance at a meeting of the Foreign Affairs Committee (FAC) on 25 June to launch an attack on BBC journalism and followed this up on 27 June with an impromptu, highly agitated appearance on *Channel Four News*. The FAC subsequently cleared Campbell of substantively altering the dossier, but only on the casting vote of the chair, with the committee simply dividing on partisan lines in the relevant votes.[23] It is an open question as to how the relationship between the government and the BBC would have evolved over the summer of 2003 if events had unfolded differently. The suicide in July of Dr Kelly, who had emerged as the single source for Gilligan's critical assertions, ensured that the September dossier, the government's case for war and the standards of BBC journalism remained firmly in the news for the following six months.

On 18 July 2003 the government requested Lord Hutton to conduct an investigation into the circumstances surrounding the death of Dr Kelly. The inquiry was played out as a piece of political theatre during the late summer and autumn, with apparently all the key dramatis personae including the Prime Minister appearing before Lord Hutton to give evidence. The proceedings of the inquiry were published in full on the Internet, almost in real time. With evidence from email exchanges, personal diary entries and witness statements, the proceedings laid bare the

---

[23] Robert P. Kaye, '"OfGov": A commissioner for government conduct?', *Parliamentary Affairs* 58/1 (2005): 178.

decision-making processes at the heart of the Blair administration, as well as the editorial procedures at the BBC.

With regard to the issue of the preparation of the September dossier, Hutton exonerated Campbell from the 'sexing up' charge where 'sexed up' was defined by Hutton as embellishing 'with items of intelligence known or believed to be false or unreliable to make the case against Saddam Hussein stronger' (what one might call substantive sexing-up) rather than an alternative weaker interpretation of the term to suggest that 'the dossier was drafted in such a way as to make the case against Saddam Hussein as strong as the intelligence contained in it permitted' (presentational sexing up).[24] With regard to the conduct of the BBC, Hutton was damning. Gilligan's allegations on the *Today* programme were deemed to be 'unfounded';[25] the BBC's editorial system was 'defective';[26] BBC management was at fault 'in failing to investigate properly the Government's complaints' regarding the Gilligan broadcast;[27] and the governors were criticised 'for themselves failing to make more detailed investigations into whether this allegation reported by Mr Gilligan was properly supported by his notes and for failing to give proper and adequate consideration to whether the BBC should publicly acknowledge that this very grave allegation should not have been broadcast'.[28]

The Hutton Report was much criticised at the time of its publication for having delivered a 'whitewash' pro-government verdict.[29] One of the sternest critics, not suprisingly, was Dyke, who devotes a significant chunk of his autobiography to a criticism of Hutton: 'it was Lord Hutton, not the BBC, who got it fundamentally wrong'.[30] Among other things, Dyke condemns Hutton's narrow interpretation of his terms of reference; the inquiry's failure to call Kevin Marsh, the editor of the *Today* programme, as a key witness; the report's blanket condemnation of the BBC's editorial procedures; and its selective interpretation of the evidence.[31] For others, however, the main culprit was Gilligan and his flawed report of 29 May.[32] For example, in an excoriating attack on the culture of the media in contemporary Britain, John Lloyd argues that Gilligan's broadcast was 'carelessly done'[33] and that 'it was a grave charge, but it was lightly made'.[34]

---

[24] Hutton, *Report of the Inquiry*, p. 320.   [25] Ibid., p. 212.
[26] Ibid., p. 213.   [27] Ibid., p. 213.   [28] Ibid., p. 214.
[29] Alan Doig, '45 minutes of infamy? Hutton, Blair and the invasion of Iraq', *Parliamentary Affairs* 58/1 (2005): 120.
[30] Dyke, *Inside Story*, p. 287.   [31] Ibid., pp. 287–317.
[32] See, for example, Anthony Glees, 'Evidence-based policy or policy-based evidence? Hutton and the Government's use of Secret Intelligence', *Parliamentary Affairs* 58/1 (2005): 145–52.
[33] Lloyd, *What the Media*, p. 6.   [34] Ibid., p. 7.

Others try to steer a course in between these two opposing views. Kaye argues that

> The specific allegation of the BBC broadcast that the government included, or even fabricated, evidence in the dossier against the wishes of the Joint Intelligence Committee was demonstrably false. The wider belief, that the dossier had included unreliable claims against the advice of some members of the intelligence community, seemed to have been borne out. This, and the removal of caveats, clarifications and qualifications, would, for many, amply justify the sobriquet 'sexed up'.[35]

In similar vein, the director of BBC News contends that 'we [i.e. the BBC] got some things right and we got one big thing wrong'.[36] Certainly the official position of the BBC in the aftermath of Hutton was that mistakes had been made inside the Corporation, notably by Gilligan in the wording of his report: '. . . a core script was properly prepared and cleared in line with normal production practices in place at the time, but was then not followed by Andrew Gilligan'.[37] An internal review headed by Ronald Neil, former director of BBC News and Current Affairs, made a variety of recommendations regarding the handling of external complaints, the appropriateness of live two-ways in breaking stories containing serious or potentially defamatory allegations and the usage of material supplied by anonymous single sources. In the run-up to the debate on the renewal of its Charter, it was clear that the BBC was determined not just to put its house in order but to be clearly seen to be doing so.

---

[35] Kaye, '"OfGov": A commissioner for government conduct?', 185.

[36] Richard Sambrook, 'Tragedy in the fog of war', *British Journalism Review* 15/3 (2004): 12. 'At the time it seemed very complicated. On reflection, it was quite simple. *Today* set out to broadcast a report about genuine and, as we now know, well-founded reservations among parts of the intelligence community about the September 2002 Iraq dossier. That was the script which the programme approved. In a live interview Andrew Gilligan used a form of words which wrongly suggested bad faith on the part of the Government. The BBC, concentrating on what it had intended to broadcast, was slow to recognise the significance of this departure from the script. Alastair Campbell launched a sweeping attack on the BBC before the Foreign Affairs Committee. From that point on there could be no happy ending. The Government was defending its integrity and the BBC was defending its independence. For each side, those two principles are non-negotiable, and it could only end badly. Part of the tragedy is that the BBC didn't set out to accuse the Government of bad faith and I don't believe the highest levels of Government set out to threaten the BBC's independence. It just seemed that way' (Sambrook, 'Tragedy in the fog of war', 12–13).

[37] Neil Review, *The BBC's Journalism After Hutton*, June 2004, p. 26. http://www.bbc.co.uk/info/policies

Clearing out the stables after Campbell

The view that New Labour was obsessed with spin was not assuaged by three stories – the Jo Moore affair, the Queen Mother's funeral and 'Cheriegate' – which hit the headlines between the 2001 election and the outbreak of the Iraq war. All were framed by the news media in terms of the government's propensity for deceit. While all three provided critical headlines, the Jo Moore episode was by far the most damaging for the government, since it alone raised the structural issue of the partisan politicisation of government communication.

The possibility of the inherent tension between the partisan role of special adviser and the avowedly neutral function of civil servant communication officer exploding into overt conflict was always present under the news management arrangements introduced by New Labour after 1997. The surprising aspect when conflict did erupt was that it happened not in one of the major ministries such as Health, Education or the Home Office, but in the relative backwater of Transport. The desire of Jo Moore, special adviser to the headlines-obsessed minister Stephen Byers, to use the events of 11 September 2001 as a 'good day to bury bad news' can be sympathetically regarded as simply an example of the mindset of the communication professional at work. In Moore's defence it could also be pointed out that at the time she sent the email enjoining her colleagues to make use of the events unfolding in New York and Washington as an opportunity to release 'bad news stories' into the public realm, the full extent of what was taking place on the other side of the Atlantic had not yet been appreciated.

Against the background of a government with a reputation for spinning its way out of trouble, however, Ms Moore's comments represented an open goal for New Labour's critics, since her remarks could be presented as consummate evidence of the cynicism at the heart of the government's communications machine. In the event, Ms Moore initially managed to survive the negative publicity, albeit at the cost of a highly mediatised public apology. However, her unfortunate email came back to haunt her when she later became involved in a highly public dispute with the civil servant in charge of communication at the department, Martin Sixmith. In a battle for control of the department's links with the news media, Sixmith revealed that Moore was apparently intent on using the occasion of the funeral of Princess Margaret to publish potentially damaging statistics on rail industry performance in the hope that these would not be given prominent media coverage. Sixmith protested and in the ensuing dispute both Moore and Sixmith left their respective posts, while Byers himself later resigned in a media 'feeding frenzy' which had all the hallmarks of attack journalism.

The row over the Queen Mother's funeral arrangements in the spring of 2002 illustrated the extent of the falling out between Campbell and some media. The much publicised attempt by Campbell to have the Prime Minister play an enhanced role in the funeral backfired disastrously and was presented in some media as an attempt by Blair to hijack the occasion for his own aggrandisement. Not only was the media response to the prime ministerial initiative hostile, but the attempt by Campbell to involve the Press Complaints Commission in an official complaint against the coverage of the incident by the *Evening Standard* and the *Mail on Sunday* was abandoned, leaving Campbell looking foolish.[38]

The third negative media story for New Labour prior to the Iraq war was the coverage generated by the so-called 'Cheriegate' saga. The purchase of two flats in Bristol by the Prime Minister's wife was perfectly legal. However, the transaction brought to public notice the influence on Cherie of her style guru Carole Caplin, who herself was associated with a known fraudster, Peter Foster. This gave the *Mail* newspapers the opportunity to pursue their long-standing anti-Blair agenda. The story was damaging for the Blairs' public image and Cherie exacerbated the situation by committing the cardinal error of being economical with the truth when her version of events was initially challenged. The public apology made by Cherie in front of the television cameras helped provide closure to the story. However, not only was Campbell angry at the way in which the negative coverage had dominated the headlines for days; but the episode also played into a broader media narrative centred on the concept of trust, an issue which, with the Iraq crisis dominating the political agenda, was becoming a central feature of Blair's premiership.

Conscious of the counterproductive nature of its reputation for spin, the government had already introduced changes to the lobby system of briefing in spring 2002, including broadening the number of journalists allowed to participate in briefings. Yet this apparent opening up of the system of news management was criticised by some of the old lobby guard as a false liberalisation, since in the new system it was actually more difficult than before, so they argued, for journalists to follow up on their original questions. In any event, however, these changes were overtaken by the fallout from the Jo Moore/Martin Sixmith affair: a critical

[38] Oborne and Walters, *Alastair Campbell*, pp. 303–12.

parliamentary investigation into the role of special advisers in government followed by an independent review of government communications. The review group was chaired by Bob Phillis, chief executive of the Guardian Media Group and initially consisted of 13 members, representing communications experience within government, across the media and in advertising and public relations. Its terms of reference were

> to conduct a radical review of government communications. This will include the examination of different models for organising and managing the government's communication effort, the effectiveness of the current model based on the Government Information and Communication Service, and the roles played by other civil servants, including those special advisers who have a responsibility for communications.[39]

The final report of the review was published almost contemporaneously with that of Lord Hutton in January 2004. The Phillis report argued that there had been a three-way breakdown in trust between government and politicians, the media and the general public, which had led to popular disillusionment and voter disengagement from the democratic process. In particular, the aggressive approach of Labour and 'their increased use of selective briefing of media outlets, in which government information was seen to be being used to political advantage, led to a reaction from the media that has produced a far more adversarial relationship with government'.[40] On the particular issue of the use of special advisers by New Labour, the report commented that many of them 'concentrate their limited time on the political reporters in the "lobby" and on a handful of specialists . . . this has created an "inner circle" of reporters who have good access, but a disenfranchised majority who do not'.[41]

Among the 12 specific recommendations of the Phillis report was one for a stronger communications structure at the centre, headed by a new Permanent Secretary, and a clearer definition of the roles of the Prime Minister's official spokesperson – a civil service appointment – and that of his politically appointed Communication Director. Phillis thus supported two separate but complementary communications teams at the centre of government: one a strong civil service-led communications unit, based in the Cabinet Office, and the second a well-resourced communications team supporting the Prime Minister, based at Number 10 and including both civil servants and political appointees.[42] Phillis also recommended that

[39] Phillis, *An Independent Review*, p. 1.   [40] Ibid., p. 7.
[41] Ibid., p. 10.   [42] Ibid., p. 13.

the Prime Minister's Director of Communication should not have Order in Council powers that enable special advisers to manage civil servants.[43]

With regard to the system of lobby briefings, Phillis argued that the system was no longer working for either the government or the media, with ministers and officials complaining about media distortion and deliberate misrepresentation while journalists complained about information 'being used as the currency in a system of favouritism, selective release and partisan spinning'.[44] Phillis recommended that the lobby briefings should be televised, with full transcripts made available promptly online and with proceedings webcast. The review also recommended that goverment ministers should play a bigger part in the daily briefings rather than official spokespersons, thus bringing the daily meetings 'closer to the model of the Prime Minister's monthly press briefings'.[45]

Blair had already accepted the break-up of Campbell's role into its constituent parts when Phillis had published its interim report in September 2003, just a few weeks after Campbell's resignation. Because of the special nature of the relationship Campbell had enjoyed with Blair, nobody could in any case have convincingly stepped into the former's shoes once he had left. In that sense the style of New Labour media management after Campbell was always going to be different. In addition, however, the circumstances surrounding Campbell's departure and the widespread feeling that he had become too public and controversial a figure meant that the debate about his succession was not just confined to a question of individuals but also covered appropriate structures, norms and procedures. Campbell's replacement in the new slimmed down post of Director of Communication at Number 10 was David Hill, who had previously been head of communications at Labour Party headquarters. Hill was regarded as a dedicated and intelligent professional, trusted by journalists, and a less keen advocate of pre-emptive spin than his predecessor. However, he was also seen as not nearly so close to Blair.

The bigger question is whether the structural changes proposed by Phillis make sense. While the recommendations in reaction to the perceived excesses of the Campbell era are understandable, some have argued that the distinction between partisan and non-partisan information is fundamentally flawed. Sir Bernard Ingham, for example, contends that it is possible to have only one spokesperson at Number 10, either a civil servant or a party political appointee.[46] Gaber not only agrees with this

---

[43] Ibid., p. 21.   [44] Ibid., p. 25.   [45] Ibid., p. 26.
[46] Tim Luckhurst, 'No 10: more cuddly, less in control?', *Independent*, 27 January 2004, p. 11.

criticism, but also argues that the Phillis recommendations simply strengthen the communication power of Downing Street: 'Phillis has based many of its recommendations on the unsustainable assumption that this Government's communication effort is weak and uncoordinated and that the remedy lies in the path of greater centralisation.'[47]

Conclusion: the end of 'spin'?

In terms of personalities and structures the New Labour government's news management operations were very different at the end of Blair's second term from what they had been at the start of his first. By the time of the 2005 general election Campbell had been gone from Downing Street for more than 18 months (though he was brought back to help with New Labour's general election campaign) and several of the organisational changes recommended by Phillis had been implemented. Yet while Campbell's resignation in the summer of 2003 seemed to mark a turning point in government–media relations, the reality is more complex. By spring 2002 New Labour had already recognised that its relationship with the news media was in need of substantial repair following a prolonged period of deterioration, the origins of which pre-dated the 2001 election. Conversely, even after his departure from Downing Street Campbell's role in government communication and his style of media management featured prominently throughout the Hutton Inquiry and in the aftermath of the publication of Hutton's report. It is, therefore, more appropriate to talk of a *process* of flux and movement in the interdependent relationship between the New Labour goverment and the news media between 1997 and 2005, albeit one punctuated by symbolically and substantively important single events such as the Jo Moore fiasco and the Gilligan affair.

It is also relevant to question the extent to which the post-Campbell changes in personnel and structures may be accompanied by corresponding changes in attitude and behaviour on the part of those who now fill the key posts in government communication, including Blair himself. For some this might be interpreted as asking the question: does the departure of Campbell mean the end of New Labour spin? Yet this is not a helpful formulation. 'Spin' is a term whose lack of conceptual rigour and pejorative overtones make it too all-encompassing and

[47] Ivor Gaber, 'Going from bad to worse: Why Phillis (and the Government) have got it wrong', paper presented at the conference 'Can Vote, Won't Vote: Are the Media to Blame for Political Disengagement?', Goldsmiths College London, 6 November 2003.

value-laden to inform an evaluation of government–media interdependence. In a 24/7 rolling news culture, competitive journalistic environment and frequently hostile media coverage, a government has no alternative but to manage its mediated communication in the public sphere – 'spin' as positive and necessary. At the same time some of the news management techniques employed by New Labour under Campbell pushed up against and sometimes transgressed the boundaries of reasonable behaviour the public expect of politicians and their close advisers – 'spin' as negative and undesirable. Meanwhile, on the media side many journalists welcome spin to help them make sense of official documents and statements; yet they are also prepared to condemn it as manipulation and deception.

Finally, if Phillis is correct in his diagnosis of a breakdown of trust in the process of political communication, then the news media themselves have an important part to play in any reforms. In the wake of Hutton, the BBC through the implementation of the Neil review recommendations seems willing to recognise its stake in a reformulated relationship with government. It will be immeasurably more difficult to persuade many national newspapers – whose behaviour in the 1980s and early 90s was so instrumental in persuading New Labour to professionalise its news management activities – that it is in their commercial interests to change their habits and adopt a more civic-minded journalism or subscribe to a voluntary code of ethics in political coverage.

6

The Labour Party

LEWIS BASTON AND SIMON HENIG

Introduction

In estimating the 'Blair effect' on the Labour Party, particularly during the period from 2001 to 2005, one is confronted with a paradox. On perhaps the most important level, it has been wholly beneficial. The Labour Party has been in power with overwhelming (and even after 2005 certainly comfortable) majorities for over eight years. It has at long last achieved Harold Wilson's ambition of becoming the natural party of government; forming a non-Labour government still seems a distant dream to the opposition parties, even as the third term begins.

Despite this political and electoral ascendancy, the tone of much discussion of the Labour Party, including discussions between members, is anything but triumphalist. As an organisation, Labour seems to be in the process of atrophying – shedding members, short of money, internally divided and with a diminishing presence in the life of local civil society in much of the country. Labour also seems unsure of its purpose. Roy Hattersley is fond of recalling Wilson's cry to the 1962 Labour Party Conference that 'This party is a moral crusade or it is nothing', and shuddering at the modern implications of this statement. Internal critics frequently allege that what Blair is actually doing in government has very little to do with the core aims of the Labour Party.

In what follows, we attempt to chart the 'Blair effect' on the Labour Party, examining different aspects of the question in turn before placing the question more broadly in the context of the British party system. Our conclusion, in fine Blairite fashion, will attempt to reconcile our apparently irreconcilable starting points.

The Labour Party as an organisation

Membership

The initial Blair effect on Labour Party membership was entirely positive. He inherited a membership of around 250,000 in 1994, a figure that had gently declined since 1980 when the figures were accurately collated for the first time. Prior to this date individual constituencies affiliated members in blocks of a thousand, which bore little relation to the actual number of members of the party and produced a wholly artificial minimum national membership of just over 600,000. Interestingly, the previous occasion on which there was a similar surge in individual membership of the party was immediately before and following Labour's first great landslide election win in 1945. It seems clear that however it was counted, membership then went into slow decline from a recorded peak in the early 1950s, falling throughout the next three decades despite a short-lived reversal of this trend in the early 1960s. Although some commentators and Labour Party members still talk of a 'golden age' of high membership and packed party meetings before Blair, we would probably have to go back as far as the Attlee years for this to be an accurate picture.

Over the years between 1994 and 1998, the strong tide in public opinion towards the party served to add a massive number of members, around 200,000. The party's organisation, after years of reform started by Neil Kinnock in 1985, was working efficiently under general secretaries Tom Sawyer and Margaret McDonagh, and after 1994 John Prescott gave his main priority as deputy leader to building up mass membership. The 1994–8 increase was a pronounced reversal of the general tendency for participation in party politics to decline over time, and was a remarkable achievement.

Many of the new members did not become activists in the traditional sense, choosing not to have much of a relationship with their local party organisation but instead treating Labour membership like membership of other affinity groups – paying subscriptions by direct debit and receiving centralised mailings about the party's activities. Revealingly, a study of Labour Party membership in the late 1990s found that there was only one activity in which the new members were more willing to engage than the traditional members – donating money. While there was considerable grass-roots activity in 1997, this could not be sustained in less important elections even as early as the 1999 European elections, when there was a clear shortage of volunteers to deliver election material.

The new mass membership (even at its peak in 1997–8, it represented a much smaller proportion of the public than the memberships of other parties of the European left) did not long survive the experience of government. Membership was on a declining path after 1998 and was clearly heading south of 300,000 by the 2001 election. Labour was losing a lot of fair-weather friends as discontents built up with government policies, and

as in the late 1960s some traditional party activists were becoming disaf-
fected and unwilling to engage in campaign work because of grievances
over particular policies. The war in Iraq in 2003 marked a further decline
in the fortunes of the Labour Party as a membership organisation. The
war was unpopular with Labour members, as was the close identification
of Blair with Bush, and activism took another downward turn. By the
time of the 2005 election the party's membership had fallen to 200,000.
This represented not just a falling-off from the heights reached in 1997–8
but a continuation of decline from the trough reached before 1994. The
Conservatives now have measurably more members, not so much because
of their own increasing numbers but because of Labour's decline.

For Labour as a membership organisation, Blair is very much a Duke of
York, who marched membership to the top of the hill and marched it down
again. But the continuing difficulties of the Conservatives in attracting
members (one of William Hague's objectives was to build a membership
of a million, but the party has not been able to sustain any great rising
trend) point to the wider problem that affects parties as organisations,
namely the continuing downward trend in popular participation in party
politics. It is easier to rally people in opposition to something rather than
in support of the inevitably mixed record of a government – but even that
is still difficult.

Structures

Although it seems that Blair as prime minister has lacked the close interest
in party structures displayed by many of his predecessors, there was an
early determination that a New Labour government would not suffer at
the hands of its own members as previous administrations, notably in
the 1970s, had done. Within a year of Blair's election as leader, a special conference voted to replace Clause IV of the party's constitution, a
change which had defeated Gaitskell at the height of revisionism several
decades earlier. In another departure from tradition, a plebiscitary referendum of party members was held on the draft manifesto prior to the
1997 election, though the most far-reaching change to party organisation
was to be agreed at annual conference shortly after Labour's triumphant
return to power. A new policy-making process, 'Partnership in Power',
was introduced, based around a 'rolling' policy programme, a key role for
the 180-delegate-strong National Policy Forum (NPF), originally set up
in 1993, and the creation of individual policy commissions to draw up
party policy in specific areas over two-year periods.

A direct consequence of these reforms was the effective end to the tradition of annual conference debating and voting on individual policy resolutions. Although conference would still have the final say (the extent to which conference ever really determined party policy is debatable), this was to take the form of rubber-stamping reports from each policy commission. In recent years conference has also been given the opportunity of voting on a small number of 'alternative' policy positions to those in the reports. In addition, conference is permitted to debate a number of 'contemporary resolutions', the subjects to be determined by delegates each year.

Other changes to party structures included amendments to the composition and rules for election to the party's National Executive Committee; a reduction in the dominance of the trade union block vote at party conference (which dated back to the OMOV reforms agreed in 1993); and finally the apparent maintenance of a vice-like grip by the leadership on all party structures, including the selection of candidates. It is noteworthy that more radical changes (such as the once-mooted replacement of traditional party structures and fee-paying members with a looser network of individual 'supporters') have not as yet materialised; as with wider constitutional questions it could be argued that the Blair revolution remains incomplete.

The most obvious effect of the reforms that have taken place has been to reduce dissent significantly or at least to push it behind closed doors where it is easier to manage. Since 1997 the Labour leadership has suffered very few conference defeats in front of the full media spotlight and compared with previous periods of government would appear to be enjoying a very easy ride from its members. However, it is now at NPF and policy commission meetings that key policy discussions take place and agreements are hammered out. The most notable example was the Warwick forum in July 2004 at which trade union delegates claimed significant policy concessions from the leadership, paving the way for their full support for Labour's 2005 general election campaign. Arguably this private gathering of a couple of hundred or so participants was far more significant than any recent annual conference.

Adherents of the new system argue that the new machinery of local, regional and national policy forums has involved more members than were ever directly involved in policy debates in the past. It is also argued that, away from the glare of the media, the new system creates more considered and comprehensive policy positions than the set-piece conference debates and decisions of the past. Further, it has dispensed with the previous ritual of 'compositing' where conference delegates traded bits of their organisation's resolutions late into the night. Critics, however, point to the marked absence in any policy commission discussions and reports of controversial proposals such as student top-up fees, foundation hospitals and Iraq. They claim that the new process is little more than a charade, with important policy decisions more than ever originating in the Number 10 Policy Unit and then dictated to the party. It is also argued that although just as many deals are made between union leaders, rank and file and the leadership as in the past, they now take place in secret.

Whatever the pros and cons of 'Partnership in Power', one clear consequence has been a diminution of interest in party conference, with many constituencies failing even to nominate delegates in recent years. Declining engagement in party structures has also resulted from reforms to the party's ruling national executive committee (NEC). The NEC has lost its role overseeing policy-making to a joint policy committee (which includes ministers, NEC members and NPF representatives). Reforms to the NEC's electoral college introduced after 1997 divided constituency representation from that of members of Parliament, ending the annual 'beauty contest' of MPs from different wings of the party competing for the votes of individual party members. With the absence of big names such as Tony Benn, David Blunkett and Robin Cook from ballot papers, turnout in NEC elections has plummeted. This is starkly demonstrated by a comparison of turnout at the 1997 contest (the last under the old rules), at which four candidates polled in excess of 100,000 votes, to that in 2004, when the winning candidate attracted barely a fifth of that total. Even though constituency members have continued to elect left-wing representatives from the 'grass-roots alliance' to the NEC, the outside world now barely bats an eyelid.

Blair's lack of sympathy for traditional Labour Party structures was perhaps best illustrated by his creation of the new Cabinet-ranking post of party chairman in 2001, even though the post of chairman (albeit annually elected by the NEC) already existed. The introduction of a post similar to that traditionally employed by the Conservatives is perhaps symbolic of the style of party leadership Blair prefers, though realpolitik has dictated that a party traditionalist with strong trade union links, Ian McCartney, has held the new post since 2003. Critics of Blair have long complained of 'control freakery' or the 'Millbank tendency' (even though Labour have now departed their former Millbank offices). Notorious interventions in candidate selections have included the blocking of Ken Livingstone from standing as Labour's candidate for Mayor of London in 2000 and Rhodri

Morgan from becoming First Minister of Wales from the outset, thanks in each instance to union block votes cast without balloting members. Both attempts ultimately failed to prevent their targets from attaining power and Blair ironically backed the readmittance of Livingstone to the Labour Party prior to the 2004 mayoral election. This may perhaps reflect a newer openness in an attempt to re-engage with the party membership, or more plausibly that Blair no longer saw such internal battles as worth fighting.

Trade unions and finance

From the party's creation in 1900 onwards, trade unions traditionally supplied the bulk of finance, reflecting the far larger number of members 'affiliated' by trade unions (more than 6 million in the early 1980s) compared with the total individual membership (less than 300,000 in the same period). This was also reflected in the 90% voting weight unions enjoyed at annual conference, block votes from the largest unions regularly ensuring that the Labour leadership won key votes in the face of internal dissent.

Change began to take effect from the early 1990s. It was under Neil Kinnock's leadership that Labour began to court endorsements and individual donations from business and celebrity individuals. John Smith's short term of office saw the significant OMOV reforms narrowly agreed, which reduced the voting weight of trade unions at conference to 50% in a series of stages and cut them out of parliamentary selections (subsequently to be determined by ballots of local party members) altogether.

Since 1998, trade unions have taken their place on the national policy forum, but were given only 42 places out of a total of 180, an even lower share than their reduced weight at conference. Unions were also reduced to 12 places on the 32-person national executive committee, both changes reflecting the confidence of the leadership in handling the new structures and also perhaps a suspicion that unions would be more troublesome to the Blair leadership than individual party members. This concern has been borne out in recent years by two high-profile conference votes, on restoring the pensions–earnings link in 2000 and reviewing the private finance initiative (PFI) in 2002, at which union votes ensured rare defeats for the leadership despite a majority of constituencies coming out in support.

The reduced reliance on trade unions within party structures has been reflected in donations to the party, which since 2001 have been openly available for inspection via the Electoral Commission. These figures reveal

Table 6.1. *Registered donations to the Labour Party, covering the period from 1 January 2001 to 31 March 2005*

	Cash (£)	Non-cash (£)	Total (£)	Share (%)
Trade unions	40,399,429.89	316,578.88	40,716,008.77	64.5
Individuals	17,932,027.14	62,210.00	17,994,237.14	28.5
Companies	1,655,312.75	1,224,589.00	2,879,901.75	4.6
Partnerships	65,468.00	55,300.00	120,768.00	0.2
Friendly societies etc.	62,180.00	8,900.00	71,080.00	–
Unincorporated associations	829,294.72	73,138.50	902,433.22	1.4
Total	60,943,712.50	1,740,716.38	62,684,428.88	

Source: Electoral Commission register of donations to political parties.

that although unions still provide the bulk of Labour's funding, the proportion has fallen to less than two-thirds, while individuals make up almost a third of the total, much of this made up of a small number of very large donations. For example in the first quarter of 2003, Lord Sainsbury donated a sum of £2.5 million according to the Electoral Commission, which exceeded the amount provided by all affiliated trade unions put together over the same three months. The period following the 2001 election was notable for much sabre-rattling from disgruntled unions threatening to reduce the size of donations to the party or even disaffiliate altogether in response to a perceived lack of influence with the leadership and specific policies such as PFI. Ultimately the 2004 Warwick forum seems to have put an end to such talk for the time being at least, with union donations again almost certain to have provided the majority of Labour's funding for the 2005 general election, as they had done in 2001 (see Table 6.1).

The politics of the Labour Party

Declining membership and grass-roots activity have been symptoms of disillusionment among people who have previously been members of and activists in the Labour Party. However, the picture of a vastly dissatisfied membership needs some serious qualification. Blair and 'New Labour' more generally have had a greater influence than is usually conceded on the politics and ethos of the Labour Party membership. A particularly revealing moment was the vote at the 2004 party conference on a motion about renationalisation of the railways, when the constituency party (CLP) delegates voted to support the government and carried the day against the trade union delegates. This repeated the balance of forces in the 2000 conference vote on indexation of pensions. To veterans of the party, who recalled the occasions in the 1970s and 1980s when the unions rode to the rescue of the party leadership against the left-wing CLPs, this has been an astonishing change. The sense in which 'socialism', however defined, was a central reference point in the party's politics, and the belief of a broad spread of party opinion in a large state-run sector of the economy, are no more.

The lasting change in the politics of the Labour Party, coinciding with falling membership, suggests that the pattern of events has been different from that under the principal comparable case, the Wilson government of 1964–70. During that period, membership and activism fell steeply for similar reasons to the fall since 1999, but the politics of the party membership shifted sharply to the left and set the scene for the left's sweeping successes within the party in the 1970s. There is no comparable surge to the left now; dissatisfied members have tended to use the 'exit' rather than 'voice' option, moving out of the party mostly to single-issue groups like anti-war or anti-globalisation movements, or occasionally to other parties such as Respect or the Lib Dems.

Where there has been a shift to the left, as in the late 1960s, is in elections to leadership positions of the trade unions. The left, in one form or another, has won most significant union elections since 1999 and union votes at party conferences have become increasingly critical of government policy. However, there has been no 'In Place of Strife' style breach with the government. Instead, there has been an effort through the Warwick Agreement of summer 2004 to bind the unions more closely to the party, and in the 2005 campaign Labour was able to rely on strong trade union support.

Within Parliament, the difference has been not so much a gradual trend than a sharp break either side of 2001. The 2001–5 Parliament marked a departure both from 1997–2001 and to some extent all previous parliaments. It was easily the most 'rebellious' in modern history, with the scale of some revolts – especially over the Iraq war in 2003 – being the largest since the Corn Law crisis that broke Peel's government in 1846. In one of the Iraq votes, 139 Labour MPs defied the whip.[1] By the Whitsun recess of 2004, 204 Labour MPs had some degree of 'form' as

---

[1] Philip Cowley and Mark Stuart, 'Rebellions by Labour MPs', in Simon Henig and Lewis Baston (eds.), *Politico's Guide to the General Election 2005* (London: Methuen, 2005) pp. 53–4.

parliamentary rebels against the whip. These numbers suggest a loosening, if not breakdown, of the bonds of party discipline, but that is far from the whole story.

The hard core of rebels, known dismissively by the whips as 'the usual suspects' and drawn mostly from the Campaign Group on the left of the party and a number of disenchanted former ministers, number around 20 at the outside. This is relatively small compared with the Tribune Group in its militant days in the 1970s, when it could marshal larger numbers and inflict defeats on important aspects of government business such as devolution, taxation and, fatefully, incomes policy in the winter of 1978–9. Wilson's and Callaghan's whips' offices would have loved to have such a low proportion of malcontents as Blair has even after 2005.

While rebellions have become more common, the situation is mitigated, apparently paradoxically, by the large number of MPs involved in some way or another. Most MPs combine rebellion on one issue or another with loyalty on most other issues. Backbench dissent is broad but shallow. Blair for the most part has responded to criticism in a rather measured fashion, taking care, for instance, to acknowledge respect for those who disagreed about the Iraq war. Unlike Wilson, whose paranoid style of party management summoned plots and factions into existence, Blair has not created any opposing factions that did not exist before 1997 (such as the group around Gordon Brown, the old left and the trade union MPs).

The risk for the 2005 Parliament is that the habits of rebellion that developed in parliaments with large majorities carry over into a narrower situation (as they did in the Conservative Party after 1992) and that the pool of what John Major called the 'dispossessed' and 'neverpossessed' grows constantly. Blair has taken care on several occasions to restore former ministers to office, and in his 2005 reshuffle appointed some experienced backbenchers. A lesson of history has clearly been learned.

Blair's leadership style and the broad but shallow pattern of rebellion in the 2001 Parliament are closely related. Blair's approach – both as a shadow cabinet member and as leader – has consistently been to assert his will against the party's instincts as much as to represent the party to the public. The record – from the closed shop, to 'tough on crime', to Clause IV, to lone parent benefit cuts, student fees and war on Iraq – is of making the party do things it does not necessarily want to do. In each case, a significant element of the party has more or less grudgingly accepted the necessity of Blair's substantive point, but others have not been able to reconcile it with their values and have chosen to rebel. Provoking rebellion, and reintegrating the rebels, has been an almost essential technique in Blair's style of party management.

New Labour was originally defined in contradistinction to 'Old Labour' (a historical term which never had an identity of its own, covering as it did both the ministers of the 1974–9 government and their backbench internal opposition). The process was designed to emphasise Blair's strength as leader, the break with the problematic aspects of Labour's history and Blair's moderation. It is a modified version of a strategy known in the United States as 'triangulation', by which Clinton defined himself in opposition both to 'old Democrats' and the Republicans. Triangulation is essentially a selfish strategy. While it worked for Clinton, the congressional Democrats are still suffering the consequences. It produces rather shallow electoral support for the leader who uses it, but damages the structure and image of the party. Triangulation is ultimately to saw off the branch on which the party leader and government sit.

The original Blairite approach to party management envisaged a permanent revolution, but it may be time to reconsider. The high level of dissent masks a more startling fact about Blair and the Labour Party – the extent to which it has absorbed his ideology and his assumptions about party and power. The internal ideological wars within the Labour Party that have been fought ever since the party's foundation are over, and Blair has won. The worst period of the party's civil wars was between 20 and 30 years ago; to continue operating on the assumptions of that time is as absurd as it would have been for Edward Heath constantly to exorcise the ghost of Neville Chamberlain.

Dissent and loyalty are both faces of the predominant 'Yes, but' response to Blair and Blairism within the party. There are comparatively few in the party who are prepared to offer an across-the-board 'No', and even fewer who have a coherent and attractive alternative package to support instead. There may be many takers in the party for Blairism without the Iraq war, Blairism without student fees, Blairism without ID cards, even Blairism without Blair . . . but remarkably few who offer a break with all its core features. Blair's market neo-liberalism, interventionist foreign policy, mild social liberalism, work-based social policy and modest redistribution all now seem features of Labour ideology for most MPs and even most party members. There is simply no need any more to win victories by taking on the party. The next leader will offer tweaks to one or more of these aspects, or add another, but even if the change is presented as a break from Blairism the reality will be much less significant.

Table 6.2. *Party votes in general elections, 1945–70*

	Maximum (%)	Mean (%)	Minimum (%)
Labour vote	48.8 (1951)	46.0	43.0 (1970)
Conservative vote	49.7 (1955)	45.3	39.8 (1945)
Liberal vote	11.2 (1964)	7.0	2.5 (1951)
Turnout	84.0 (1950)	77.4	72.0 (1970)

Table 6.3. *Party votes in general elections, 1974–92*

	Maximum (%)	Mean (%)	Minimum (%)
Labour vote	39.2 (1974)	34.3	27.6 (1983)
Conservative vote	43.9 (1979)	40.7	35.8 (1974)
Liberal, etc vote	25.4 (1983)	19.5	13.8 (1979)
Turnout	78.7 (1974)	75.5	72.7 (1983)

Table 6.4. *Party votes in general elections, 1997–2005*

	Maximum (%)	Mean (%)	Minimum (%)
Labour vote	43.2 (1997)	39.7	35.2 (2005)
Conservative vote	32.3 (2005)	31.6	30.7 (1997)
Lib Dem vote	22.0 (2005)	19.0	16.8 (1997)
Turnout	71.5 (1997)	64.1	59.4 (2001)

The Labour Party in the party system

There have been three broad eras in British electoral politics since 1945. In the first, which spanned the elections from 1945 to 1970, there was a two-party system in which Labour and the Conservatives were roughly evenly matched (Table 6.2).

The February 1974 election broke this stable pattern; while Labour had a fairly narrow lead in the October 1974 election the next period was dominated by the Conservatives (Table 6.3).

The events of the 1992–7 Parliament broke the Conservative ascendancy and started a new period for the party system in which Labour has dominated although turnout has fallen sharply (Table 6.4).

So far, the tendency has been for the Labour vote to fall from its initial peak, the Conservatives to stand nearly still and the Liberal Democrat vote to increase. The configuration of the party system and the electoral system has produced a stable foundation for a sustained period of Labour government. While it is not possible to look ahead with any certainty, it is at least as possible that the 2005 election marks a temporary trough in Labour's vote as that it is a point on a declining trend.

Tony Blair overtook Attlee as the longest continuously serving Labour Prime Minister in August 2003, and Wilson as the longest serving Labour Prime Minister in total in February 2005. Labour has never before successfully sought a third term. On only two pre-Blair occasions (1945 and 1966) has Labour won a majority bigger than that of May 2005, and these were in early flushes of enthusiasm for the party rather than after a gruelling period of government.

In what follows, we examine how Labour fits with the other two main elements of the party system.

Labour and the Conservatives

The Conservative Party has endured a period of electoral disaster in the years since Blair became leader of the Labour Party. Assuming that the 2005 Parliament lasts at least two years, 1997–2007 will be the longest exclusion from power in the history of the Conservative Party (1905–15 being the current record). The Conservatives' previous identity as a flexible, relatively non-ideological party of power has been shattered.

Under Blair, the Conservative share of the vote plummeted to a new low in 1997 at only 30.8% and had recovered only to 32.3% in 2005 (see Table 6.4). Never before had the party polled less than 35%; under Blair and post-Blair, getting as high as 35% is a challenging strategic objective.

The Conservatives' failure to recover much popular support has been reflected in the instability of their leadership (in the eight and a half years since the 1997 election, they will have had five party leaders) and the debates about their broad strategy and ideology which are still unresolved. The Conservatives, the traditional 'court' party of the establishment, have been usurped by Blair and have adopted the classic oppositional technique of accumulating disgruntled, anti-modern interest groups in an inverse rainbow coalition. From time to time they ponder the merits of tolerance, inclusion and the pursuit of a 'modern' social agenda, but then back off on realising that social conservatism is the principal remaining appeal the party has for its core voters and members. The party has gained little from populism and law-and-order politics in 2001 and 2005, although in 2005 it did also try harder to present its appeal in terms of managerial competence and contrast its integrity with Blair's alleged lack of it. However, the alternative courses of tolerance, radical tax-cutting, libertarianism, English nationalism and social conservatism all still have their adherents and adversaries within the party.

The party has, without getting much recognition, reformed itself radically as an organisation, replacing the irrational but traditional structures it had in 1997 with a more centralised and efficient structure. In some respects, the party has emulated New Labour in terms of structure and campaigning techniques; its 2005 championing of 'hard-working families' was from the 1992 Clinton campaign via Blair in 1997. The ill-advised changes to the leadership election system in 2001, which created an awkward two-stage election with the membership having a final say, was devised looking over Labour's shoulder. It was supposed to introduce a greater element of intra-party democracy to encourage a new mass membership. However, the members' mandate could not override the lack of confidence the MPs had in Iain Duncan Smith and the situation was untenable. The 2003 leadership crisis was effectively a temporary reversion to the pre-1963 system of magic circles, men in grey suits and a winner 'emerging'; the party went back to the drawing board in 2005. In party management terms the Conservatives could still learn something from the plebiscitary, Napoleonic democracy of Blair's Labour Party.

However, in some respects the Conservative Party has also improved on the Blair formula. Its 2005 election campaign was professional and disciplined and in some of the marginal seats clearly superior to and better supported by volunteers than Labour's defensive work. It has been willing, as Labour was after the Clinton campaign in 1992, to learn from successful foreign practitioners of election campaigning – in their case Lynton Crosby, who had overseen four election victories for the uncharismatic John Howard in Australia. But, even if they wavered before May 2005, they retain a healthy respect for – and perhaps an unhealthy fascination with – Labour's expertise in the campaigning arts.

However, the traffic has not been entirely one-way. Michael Howard wittily observed in the Queen's Speech debate after the 2005 election:

> The day after the election, the Prime Minister set out his priorities, the priorities that are meant to be reflected in the programme before us today: controlled immigration, school discipline, cleaner hospitals and police. Come to think of it, they sound rather familiar to me. In fact, it is almost a complete set. We had no idea that he was thinking what we are thinking.

Howard's jibe captures the essence of Blair's approach to the Conservatives. While Blair is surprisingly tribal about the Conservative Party as an institution, he is willing to borrow and steal ideas and policies from them. This stems both from his pragmatism about public policy ('what matters is what works') and also that very tribalism, which is expressed in his fear of a Conservative revival and his determination not to allow them any political space to regroup and fight back. If that requires co-opting the Conservative phrases and policies that resonated most in the 2005 campaign, so be it.

Blair, more than any previous Labour leader, employs a deliberate strategy of doing things that will most discomfort the Conservatives – for example, promising a referendum on Europe and cutting civil service employment to reduce the Tories' opportunity to promise tax cuts. In the past, Labour leaders have been more preoccupied with the need to balance factions within the Cabinet and the wider Labour movement – the wrecking tactics Blair has employed against the Conservatives show the extent of his room for manoeuvre, at least in terms of political tactics.

The ruthless crushing of the Conservative Party as an electoral force is attributable to a considerable degree to Blair personally. It is often said that any Labour leader could have won the 1997 election, but the difference Blair and New Labour made was to make that victory so overwhelming. That initial pulverising blow, and the continued squeeze on the Conservatives ever since, was made possible by Blair and his anti-Conservative electoral strategy. It was perhaps only with the second landslide of 2001 (which made 2005 practically impossible for the Conservatives to win) that the longer-term importance of the Blair effect became apparent. Blair added new parts to Labour's electoral coalition, and those middle-class and skilled working-class New Labour voters have been more loyal to the party than some earlier adherents. Despite all the personal criticism of Blair that dominated the election campaign of 2005, many swing voters were unworried, retained confidence in Blair and clearly preferred him to Howard in a head-to-head contest.

While the Conservative Party has remained a sickly plant, deprived of light and oxygen under Blair's shadow, Labour's votes have slipped away to abstention and the smaller opposition parties. The student, academic and metropolitan liberal voters who flaked away particularly in 2001 and 2005 were not part of the initial Blair effect – they had been acquired for the most part by Neil Kinnock in 1987 and 1992 – but their loss most certainly is a Blair effect.

Labour and the Liberal Democrats

Perhaps the most noticeable change in the party system between 1997 and 2005 is the swing away from the close relationship that had existed between Labour and the Liberal Democrats. Prior to 1994 there had been a gradual rapprochement at the highest levels of the two parties, after the bitterness of the 1981 SDP breakaway had faded and the Conservatives had won successive election victories despite the apparent existence of a 'progressive' majority. Paddy Ashdown abandoned 'equidistance' between the other parties; John Smith was committed to Scottish devolution and made common cause with the Lib Dems on this issue. The accession of Blair in 1994 seemed at first to promise an ever-closer relationship between the two parties. Blair told Ashdown on election day 1997:

> I do want you to know that I am absolutely determined to mend the schism that occurred in the progressive forces in British politics at the start of this century. It is just a question of finding a workable framework. But we are now in a position of strength and I intend to use that.[2]

Blair, however, wavered even during the 1994–7 discussions with Ashdown on how far he might go towards the ultimate 'progressive' reform of politics – a proportional electoral system and the promise that, after that change, the twenty-first century might be mostly progressive after the 'Conservative century'. Blair was, and is, much influenced by easily grasped historical trends and parallels. But by the end of the first Blair term this prospect had receded and in 2005 was barely on life support, tended only by a civil service departmental committee.[3] The special Cabinet Committee that included Lib Dems played a significant role in the first term, was suspended in the second and formally wound up at the start of the third.

Labour's dominant position in Parliament and electorally, and Blair's increasing comfort with power, and the traditional Whitehall ways of exercising it, weakened the prospects for a cooperative form of government. For Blair, the gains involved in playing the coalition or consensus game with the Lib Dems were not worth the sacrifice of the goodwill of Labour tribalists, particularly John Prescott, of whom he was already asking a lot.

After 2001 increasing political differences with the Lib Dems were a further source of friction. Blair's lack of enthusiasm for constitutional change

---

[2] Paddy Ashdown, *The Ashdown Diaries*, vol. 1 (London: Penguin, 2000), p. 555 '1 May 1997'.
[3] See Anthony Seldon, *Blair* (London: Free Press, 2004), ch. 20, for a discussion of Blair's attitude to electoral and constitutional reform.

after the initial burst of action in 1997–9 reduced the number of things on which he and the Lib Dems could agree. The eclipse of the Conservatives served eventually to open wider areas of electoral combat between Labour and Lib Dem. The rancorous Littleborough and Saddleworth by-election in 1995 was a straw in the wind that cooperation could be strained by competition on the ground. Lib Dem competition in local elections opened up not just in the long-besieged Labour cities of Liverpool and Sheffield, but spread to the inner London boroughs, Birmingham, Newcastle and even smaller cities such as Southampton and Leicester by 2003. Labour's grass-roots, always inclined to dislike the Lib Dems, gained further reasons for this feeling year by year (and also vice versa). In the 2005 general election, for more or less the first time ever, the Lib Dems made significant gains of seats against Labour.

The dominance of foreign affairs in the Parliament of 2001–5 sharpened the division at the highest levels. Lib Dem opposition to war in Iraq, and a good deal of Blair's foreign policy beyond the single issue of Iraq, drove a wedge between Kennedy's and Blair's parties that simply did not exist in the time of Ashdown. The Lib Dems' stance in the 2005 election was decidedly antagonistic to the Blair government on domestic issues such as civil liberties and student finance as well as foreign policy. Charles Kennedy announced that he would not serve in government with Blair (a huge contrast to Ashdown's willingness to do so in 1997), and would have been unwise to have held his breath waiting for the phone call requesting his presence even if Labour's majority had been a lot less. The 'project' was well and truly dead.

The Blair effect on relations with the Lib Dems has been inconsistent – the initial warming and the later deep chill have both been connected with Blair's personal decisions. His initial enthusiasm for a progressive front, and his later increasing conservatism about issues of process and power, have been part of his evolution as a politician.

But there have always been constraining factors. Blair could not be sure that Labour could win outright in 1994–7, and it was a rational calculation to keep his coalition options open; electoral arithmetic has since repeatedly demonstrated that Labour alone is a powerful enough electoral vehicle. Nor could he, in 1997, have anticipated that the Lib Dems would be as dedicated, and more numerous, opponents of his public policy agenda as what remains of the die-hard Labour left.

In his last election, Blair has left the Lib Dems with a dilemma. Their strong showing in 2005 was in its way as dangerous a result as their previous post-1910 peak of 1923, which left them the pivotal party in the

Commons. After that election, they first installed a Labour government and then put it out again, earning enmity on both sides and being crushed in the election of 1924. While the Lib Dems gained a haul of seats from Labour in 2005, these were an unusual collection. All of them had fairly recent non-Labour histories. Bristol West, Falmouth and Camborne, and Leeds North West were Conservative until 1997; Birmingham Yardley, Cambridge, Cardiff Central, and Hornsey and Wood Green until 1992; and Manchester Withington and Dunbartonshire East until 1987. Lib Dem near misses in seats such as Aberdeen South (1997) and Edinburgh South (1987) also conform to the pattern. Inverness and Rochdale were Lib Dem prior to 1997. Even in Labour's last pre-Blair election victory in October 1974, Labour won only Yardley among these seats. Meanwhile, the Lib Dems suffered a net loss to the Conservatives in 2005, a predictable enough consequence of trying to appear to the left of Labour. Many Lib Dem seats remain vulnerable to the Conservatives, while there are few more easy targets from Labour and massive margins to make up in the real Labour heartlands.

The risk of continuing to be a left opposition is that they will shed seats to the Conservatives, while Labour could regain some of its losses once Iraq and Blair are out of the way.

Conclusion

The years from 2001 to 2005 were for the most part a continuation of the trends that were apparent in 1997–2001. While the weakening of the party in local elections and at the grass roots, and the increasing incidence of rebellion, were more apparent in 2005 than 2001, this was a deepening of existing trends rather than a change in direction. The same is true of the changing ethos of the party – what had been a tentative experiment in 1994–7 that electoral failure in 1997 might have reversed had bedded down by 2001 and become permanent by 2005.

In 2001–5 the Labour Party, while becoming the natural party of government, has become much weaker as an organisation. Membership and activism have continued to fall, and the party's defeats in the 2003 and 2004 local elections have gravely weakened its base. The party is in divided and uncertain mood after the Iraq war and after the various contentious and divisive issues that came up during the second Blair term. Although Labour won a more than adequate majority in the 2005 general election it depended more than ever on a centrally controlled media and advertising strategy. The party was also the beneficiary of the electoral system that translated a vote share not much higher than it reached in 1992 into a comfortable victory.

Despite all the uncertainties and the withering of the party in some respects, it is relatively easy to plot the course for a fourth Labour victory. The party first of all needs to choose an attractive leader when Blair steps down. The extent to which ideological divisions within the party have been blurred or abolished will probably make this more likely. It is hard to imagine the party choosing a candidate, as it did in 1980 with Michael Foot, with a view to resolving internal difficulties rather than appealing to the wider electorate. The logical approach for a new leadership candidate, both in winning an internal election and in preparing an appeal for the general election, is to continue many Blairite policies but adopt a less confrontational manner in doing so.

Labour in government also needs to avoid antagonising natural elements of its electoral coalition. It survived losing large chunks of the left of centre electorate in 2005, and it could have been worse had it not been for the unattractiveness of the Conservative alternative. The obvious thing to avoid is having another divisive war. Many of the losses of 2005 could be temporary.

Labour also needs to avoid an economic recession. Stable economic growth and low interest rates have underpinned the party's support base even when the political weather had turned nasty, and enabled the party to hold on to what used to be archetypal swing voters. A third successive Labour victory in suburban seats across the country such as Wirral West, Wansdyke and Broxtowe is a remarkable demonstration of how completely Blair has destroyed the aspirational Toryism that took shape under Thatcher. But the loyalty of these voters could be fickle indeed if a Labour government stops delivering the goods. A sharp rise in interest rates and/or higher taxes could kill off the party's appeal.

It is correspondingly difficult to imagine quite what choices the Conservatives and other parties need to make to dislodge Labour from power; they remain dependent on Labour's mistakes and misfortunes if they are to make progress, and even then they need to be politically astute enough to capitalise on the opportunities.

The Blair effect on the Labour Party has been to carry it to an unprecedented position of strength – dominating government and the public policy agenda – while radically altering it as an institution. The general assent – particular policy points aside – to the Blair agenda within the party, and its continued electoral success, suggest that a viable political entity has emerged from the process of creative destruction. It is called the

Labour Party, but it is very different from what it was in 1994 and bears only the most fleeting resemblance to what it was before 1985. There has been, to coin a phrase, a fundamental and irreversible shift in the politics of the Labour Party, and Blair's personality and decisions have been very important contributory factors in this change. While his successor will naturally have a different style of leadership, the politics and to a large extent the organisational structure bequeathed by Blair will live on.

However, the final word on Blair must be that while he leaves the Labour Party somewhat changed and compromised, it is as nothing compared to the turmoil he has wrought on the other parties.

7

The Conservative Party

ANTHONY SELDON AND PETER SNOWDON

How far was Blair responsible for the Conservatives' plight?

Tony Blair's effect on the Conservative Party, direct or indirect, has been comparable to his effect on the Labour Party. After Blair became Labour leader in July 1994, the Conservatives suffered three successive general election defeats and four changes of leadership. By 2009, the party will have been out of office for 12 years, its longest uninterrupted period in opposition since the Great Reform Act of 1832.

Labour's second term in government from 2001 to 2005 coincided in particular with one of the Conservative Party's most aimless performances. Reeling from a second historic landslide defeat in 2001, the party seemed destined to suffer another four years of disarray under a relatively unknown and inexperienced leader, Iain Duncan Smith. A dramatic, but bloodless coup in October 2003 offered the party the chance to recover, when Michael Howard's elevation to the leadership presented the first real Conservative challenge to Blair since 1994. But the opportunity came and went. Although the 2005 general election produced a closer result than the preceding two elections, the Conservative Party failed to present itself as a credible alternative government – the minimum requirement of the principal party of opposition. To have made so little mark against an increasingly vulnerable Blair was remarkable.

This chapter will examine why the Conservative Party between 2001 and 2005 squandered its opportunity, making only the limpest of recoveries. It will also examine how far Blair himself was responsible for the Conservatives' plight, and to what degree the party was the author of its own lack of success.

Blair, in association with his fellow architects of New Labour, above all Gordon Brown, certainly did the Conservatives great harm. By completing the journey, begun in 1985 by Neil Kinnock, of moving Labour into the centre ground, they emasculated the Conservative Party. It was pushed out to the right in search of voters, while its natural 'friends' in business, the establishment and the media were stolen. Blair ruthlessly jettisoned traditional Labour positions which might alienate the centre ground voter, such as its close relationship with trade unions and its ambivalence on defence, particularly nuclear weapons. In their place, he pursued policies traditionally associated with the right, including a tough line on law and order and immigration, choice and target-setting in welfare, a pro-enterprise economic policy and the most belligerent foreign policy pursued by any party for fifty years. Repeatedly the Conservatives came up with a good idea: repeatedly, if attractive to the middle ground, Blair stole it.

Blair's strategy was explicit. He wanted to destroy the old-style Conservative Party, which he characterised as being backward looking, obsessed with looking after only its own, and insular. He set out to make the twenty-first century the 'progressive' century, in contrast to the 'Conservative' century that had preceded it. In this new century, he wanted there to be no place for the traditional Conservative Party; rather power would alternate between progressive parties, with New Labour predominant. Blair toyed with the idea of an anti-Conservative government coalition of Labour and Liberal Democrats, perhaps to be entrenched by proportional representation. But he shied away from this 'project' after 1997 in the face of the solid opposition from many of his senior lieutenants, notably John Prescott and Gordon Brown.[1] Thereafter, Blair continued to put the squeeze on the Conservatives electorally, losing no opportunity to humiliate the Conservatives, or, as again in early 2005 with Robert Jackson, recruit former Conservative politicians into Labour ranks. But it was a mark of Labour's crushing hegemony that Blair did not in fact need the Liberal Democrats to marginalise the Conservatives.

Blair and his lieutenants were not, however, wholly responsible for the Conservatives' troubles. If one examines the opinion poll ratings since January 1990 (Figure 7.1), one sees the Conservatives averaging only 35% of popular support until John Major succeeded Mrs Thatcher as leader in November 1990. The party then achieved ratings in the low to mid-40s, through their general election victory in April 1992. This 16-month honeymoon period ended abruptly when Britain was ejected from the Exchange Rate Mechanism (ERM) in September 1992 (on 'Black Wednesday'). Conservative popularity sank to the mid-20s even before Blair became Labour leader in July 1994. In other words, the Conservatives

---

[1] Anthony Seldon, *Blair* (London: Free Press, 2004), pp. 265–77.

Party ratings and Labour leadership

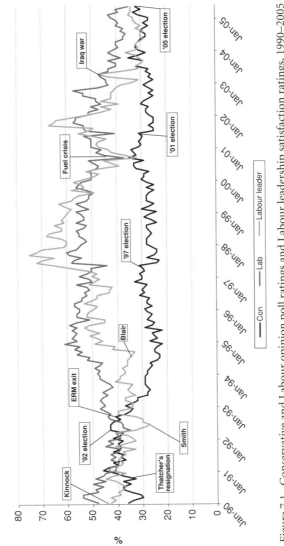

Figure 7.1. Conservative and Labour opinion poll ratings and Labour leadership satisfaction ratings, 1990–2005
Source: MORI long-term trends polls: party opinion poll ratings, January 1990–May 2005; satisfaction ratings for Labour leaders, January 1990–May 2005. http://www.mori.com/polls/trends/voting-all-trends.shtml

had already hit their own 'ground zero' while John Smith was Labour leader (1992–4) and before Blair succeeded him.

Many factors accounted for the loss of Conservative popularity, including boredom with the party after so long in office after 1979, revulsion at some of their policies, notably the poll tax and on Europe, and dissatisfaction with their economic performance. At the same time, Labour's leaders were making their party look more appealing and centrist than its leaders had in the past. Under Kinnock, the party's poll rating in 1991 reached almost the mid-50s, while under Smith, it was in the mid-40s, some 15 percentage points ahead of the Conservatives.

Under Blair, the party's opinion poll ratings soared to the mid-50s until the 1997 general election. But Blair, one must be clear, did not initiate the eclipse of the Conservatives. Neither, incidentally, as right-wing Conservative Eurosceptics have argued, did 'Black Wednesday', though it took the Conservatives to new lows. Nor indeed was John Major mostly to blame: Labour's ascendancy over the Conservatives pre-dated his arrival at Number 10: a year and a half before the 1992 general election, the Conservatives stood far lower in the polls against Labour than they were a year and a half before the 2005 general election. Indeed snatching a fourth successive victory from the jaws of defeat was Major's remarkable achievement in 1992. Blair's achievement was, for eleven years to date, to prolong the agony, by keeping the Conservatives down in the low 30s in the opinion polls.[2]

Placing too much emphasis on Blair himself is wrong for another reason. It reduces the culpability of the Conservatives themselves. Major, for long the scapegoat of the party, had little room for manoeuvre as prime minister, the victim of a party deeply divided over Europe which had lost its traditional self-restraint and deference to the leadership, with a small and dwindling majority after April 1992, an economy suffering from the after-effects of Lawson boom of the late 1980s and lacking any clear sense of mission on which it could agree in the post-Thatcher world.[3] It remains conventional wisdom that Major led the party into the gloom. Few, however, have suggested realistic alternatives he could have pursued, while still trying to achieve his primary objective of holding the party together. Successful leadership is much about timing, and there Major was as damned as Blair was blessed.

---

[2] Despite being the most electorally successful Labour leader, Blair has failed to surpass Major's record-breaking achievement (in terms of votes) in 1992, when 14.1 million voted for the Conservative Party.

[3] See Anthony Seldon, *Major: A Political Life* (London: Orion, 1997).

But after the 1997 general election defeat, the party, with a new leader, William Hague, did have the chance to break free from the constraints.[4] What the party needed to do was to meet the minimum requirement for opposition, of offering a clearly understood raft of sensible policies, presented by credible and increasingly well-known faces, ready to capitalise on Labour's woes once it began to lose its sheen. But, under Hague between 1997 and 2001, the party provided no such platform, and bar a freak episode in late 2000 – a fuel crisis – never made any impression on Labour's great lead (see Figure 7.1).[5]

Hague was determined to make his mark as a forceful opposition leader, and embarked on a period of organisational reform. He introduced a plebiscitary form of democracy to the party membership on major policy announcements, and, in a move much criticised subsequently, the grassroots were given the final say in leadership elections. Too many of Hague's reforms were rushed and poorly devised, and made little difference to the party's standing in the country. More serious were Hague's errors on policy, above all his failure to provide strategic consistency. Midway through his period in office he abandoned his broad policy platform in favour of a right wing/populist appeal focusing on issues such as 'saving the pound', crime and asylum. Inevitably, it detracted from a clear image of what the party stood for under Hague. Although there was some creative thinking in the party's 2001 manifesto, it did not amount to a serious programme for government. Unlike previous periods in opposition, such as 1945–51 and 1964–70, Hague had not undertaken a thorough-going review of policy. The so-called 'core vote' (i.e. right wing/populist) strategy diminished further the party's support in the 2001 election among those sections of the population and areas of the country which had swung heavily towards Labour in 1997. Brilliant oratory by Hague in Parliamentary Questions against Blair was no substitute for real leadership. Hague was too young in every sense for the task of Conservative leader. His was one of the weakest periods in opposition that the Conservative Party had ever experienced.

More surprising still, the Conservatives subsequently failed to apply the lessons in 2001–5, and the leadership behaved with little more strategic understanding than it had from 1997 to 2001. By acting as they did, Duncan Smith and Howard proved that it was not only Blair who was

---

[4] See Daniel Collings and Anthony Seldon, 'The Conservatives since 1997', in Pippa Norris (ed.), *Britain Votes 2001* (Oxford: Oxford University Press, 2001).

[5] See Anthony Seldon and Peter Snowdon, 'The barren years 1997–2005', in Stuart Ball and Anthony Seldon (eds.), *Recovering Power: The Conservatives in Opposition Since 1867* (London: Macmillan, 2005).

responsible for the party's poor showing. Inept leadership, and failure to capitalise on Labour's vulnerabilities, assisted Blair's task in the same way that Michael Foot's guileless leadership of Labour from 1980 to 1983 greatly helped Mrs Thatcher.

Lessons unlearnt, 2001–5[6]

What might a wise Conservative leadership have done from 2001 to 2005? Much as suggested above. Appoint a broadly based and capable front bench and leave them in post so that they could gain widespread recognition and a reputation for competence. Insist on absolute party discipline (as did Blair) across all levels of the party. Spend the first year researching deeply into practical policies that would be true to Conservative principles and which would gain broad support, and then stick with them. Tease out Labour's vulnerabilities, personal and policy, and pursue them relentlessly, while also working to identify the reasons the centre ground had for rejecting the party, and then set out a clear course to win them back. Build friends across business, academia, commentators and the professions. Deepen support across constituencies (particularly in urban areas) and the existing membership. Above all, repeatedly demonstrate that they were a principled party, deserving of respect, capable of regaining a reputation for trust and competence among all sections of the electorate. What the party had to avoid at all costs was being seen to 'flip-flop' on policy, appear opportunistic or to fail to establish itself by 2005 with a range of familiar and trusted faces on their front bench. It should not have been beyond the party to have achieved all, or at least much, of the above.

Duncan Smith shared many of the problems which had faced Hague after 1997: a defeated and demoralised party, seemingly incapable of undertaking real thinking about the reasons for its unpopularity and still deeply riven by ideological uncertainty and personality clashes. It did not take long for the underlying weakness of his position, and still more the inadequacies of his leadership style, however, to reveal that he was not up to this task, and to bring his short tenure to an end.

Duncan Smith's triumph in the final round of the 2001 leadership election, winning by a margin of three to two over Clarke, settled the debate over Europe on the sceptical side, but otherwise it was a hollow victory. Unlike Hague, he failed to win support from a majority of his colleagues

[6] This section leans heavily on Seldon and Snowdon, 'The barren years 1997–2005'.

in the parliamentary party; indeed, in no ballot did he win more than a third of its votes. Securing second place in the final round of the MPs' ballot revealed all too visibly that Duncan Smith had not received the acclaim of the party in Westminster. Popularity with the rank and file in the country was no compensation. Many on the Conservative benches, including former whips and ministers from the Major government, questioned why they should demonstrate loyalty to a man whose Eurosceptic behaviour had threatened the very survival of the party in office in the mid-1990s. Here was also a figure, who, having declined to serve in the Major administration because of his opposition to its European policy, had never held even the most junior ministerial office.[7] As shadow social security secretary and shadow defence secretary under Hague, Duncan Smith had achieved a certain profile, but his personality, and views on anything other than Europe, remained a little known quantity outside the precincts of Westminster.

Duncan Smith began promisingly. One of his first acts as party leader was to announce a thorough review of policy. Aiming to restore the Conservatives as the 'party of ideas', he declared that the process would be conducted with 'urgency and energy'. He instigated a reorganisation of the Conservative Research Department, and commissioned sophisticated polling and market research. A wider range of outside advice was drawn on from businesses to think tanks and professional organisations. All this suggested a more thoughtful and inclusive approach to policy renewal than had occurred under Hague. Duncan Smith sought to focus on the salient issues of the 2001 election, moving beyond the narrower 'core vote' focus of Hague. He demonstrated decisive leadership in calling on the party to close down its discussion of Europe completely and to examine health, education and transport as well as crime.[8] Reforming the public services and helping 'the vulnerable' in society were to become his mission, striking a very different tone from that of his predecessor, or indeed from the kind of right-wing policies those on the centre and left of the party feared he might espouse. Duncan Smith's vision of 'Compassionate Conservatism' (first espoused from a Glasgow housing estate) stemmed in part from his Christianity and sense of social justice, but it still did not convince the political world that he had yet found a coherent agenda the party could

---

[7] Duncan Smith was the first leader of the Conservative Party not to have served as a Cabinet minister before becoming leader: P. Snowdon and D. Collings, 'Déjà vu? Conservative problems in historical perspective', *Political Quarterly* 75 (2004).

[8] G. Clark and S. Kelly, 'Echoes of Butler? The Conservative Research Department and the Making of Conservative Policy', *Political Quarterly* 75 (2004).

pursue. His case was also weakened because key figures in his shadow cabinet were not convinced about his 'compassionate Conservatism'.

Duncan Smith decided to steer clear of organisational reform and instead focused on the need to give the party a better public image. A marketing director and marketing department were thus established within party headquarters.[9] Under the chairmanship of David Davis and then Theresa May, Central Office tried to encourage more women and ethnic minority candidates to apply and be included on the centrally approved candidates list, but hardly any progress was made and the Conservatives very visibly lagged in this area behind Labour. Local associations continued to assert their autonomy, often choosing candidates who conformed to the white, male, middle-class stereotype, though openly gay and ethnic minority candidates were selected in a handful of seats. Membership continued to decline after the 2001 election, but the party's revitalised youth wing, Conservative Future, saw its membership increase to over 10,000 by mid-2003.[10] Party finances showed little sign of improving, with corporate and individual donations remaining at relatively low levels, whereas the number of individual donations made to the Liberal Democrats increased dramatically after the 2001 general election and Labour's cash tills continued to ring. Worryingly for Duncan Smith, some former donors chose to withhold support from the party unless it changed its leader.

In a claim that came to be seen as naïve and hubristic, Duncan Smith had announced that people would be able to form a judgement on his leadership after only three or four months. Only two days before his election as leader, the al-Qaeda attacks on New York and Washington heralded the beginning of the 'war on terror'. The world after 11 September 2001 offered Blair opportunities to ensure that his international statesmanship would come even more to the fore, leaving Duncan Smith's Conservative Party in the shadows. The latter's pledge of unqualified support for military action against Iraq brought him short-term approval from Washington and plaudits from the right-wing press, but no long-term political gain, and shackled the party to wholeheartedly supporting a war and its prosecution about which many clear-thinking Conservatives, such as former Foreign Secretary Lords Howe and Hurd, had significant qualms.

---

[9] See J. Lees-Marshment, 'Mis-marketing the Conservatives: the limitations of style over substance', *Political Quarterly*, 75 (2004).

[10] *Sunday Times*, 29 June and 2 November 2003.

Continuing prosperity during Labour's second term ensured that Conservative efforts to dent the government's economic record made little impact. However, cracks in the New Labour edifice began to appear after 2001. Its divisions and policy difficulties, including university tuition fees and foundation hospitals as well as over Iraq, offered Duncan Smith opportunities for making political capital that had not been available to Hague. Yet, by 2002, Duncan Smith's stock had fallen so low with the press, with the exception of the *Daily Telegraph*, that his voice struggled to be heard.[11] His 'quiet man' image (launched at the 2002 Conservative Party conference) failed to excite the electorate, as opinion polls continued to show Blair and the Liberal Democrats' Charles Kennedy as the more popular leaders. The Liberal Democrats capitalised electorally on the government's discomfiture, winning a series of safe Labour seats at by-elections. By contrast, the Conservatives' poor performances, particularly at Brent East in September 2003, were the final straw for many Conservative MPs who lost whatever confidence they may have once had in their fledgling leader. As with Hague, he suffered from the fatal perception that no one saw him as a convincing prime minister-in-waiting. Despite exhibiting some promising instincts, such as trying to make the party again an inclusive, centrist force in politics, his fundamental weaknesses of personality counted too heavily against him.

Michael Howard began his leadership in November 2003 with advantages enjoyed by neither of his immediate predecessors. He had political experience at a high level (notably as Major's Home Secretary), having first become a minister under Thatcher. No Conservative leader since Edward Heath in 1965 came to the post with so much experience. Unlike Hague and Duncan Smith, he had the benefit of being elected unopposed, and was clearly seen as the man most likely to unite the party after years of quarrelling. The party, having absorbed the disappointing leaderships of Major, Hague and Duncan Smith, now had a vested interest in seeing Howard succeed and, laying aside personality and ideological differences in favour of a common end, defeating Labour. Although clearly a man on the Eurosceptic centre-right of the Party, his personal friendship with the 'big beasts' on the left of the party – Ken Clarke, Michael Heseltine, Malcolm Rifkind and Chris Patten – resulted in them holding their fire.

---

[11] Even the normally loyal Conservative commentator, Bruce Anderson, called on Iain Duncan Smith to resign, arguing that he did not possess the 'judgement, the personality, the intellect, the leadership skills or the self-confidence to lead his party anywhere near victory', *Spectator*, 5 May 2003.

Howard claimed that he had never briefed against anyone and expected no one else to do so, and said that he was determined to restore discipline to the party – and, unlike Duncan Smith, he could do so with some credibility. The media were in agreement that at last the Conservatives had found a heavyweight figure and, crucially, a potential prime minister, as their leader. Moreover, by late 2003, Blair and New Labour had further lost their sheen and some of their popularity with the electorate and the press. The war on Iraq and its aftermath, party divisions (notably over tuition fees) and personal fatigue were dragging Blair downwards. Howard had an extraordinary opportunity. He had sparred with Blair very effectively in the Commons ten years before, and was considered at least Blair's equal as a debater. The political world held its breath in expectation at the first sustained Conservative onslaught on Blair since he became Labour leader in 1994.

Howard began well: on the day he declared his candidacy for the leadership, he delivered a speech (drafted by Francis Maude) at the Saatchi Gallery in which he declared 'when the government gets things right I won't oppose for opposition's sake'. The speech appeared statesmanlike, suggesting that he wanted to reclaim the moral high ground, almost unknown territory to the Conservatives for several years. It also suggested that he understood that the principal opposition party had to look and sound like a government-in-waiting. However, as one colleague commented, 'the problem was that Michael didn't really connect with the words he uttered. He kind of did, but not fully. Before long, day to day pressures intervened.'[12] For all his qualities, the virtue most needed in a leader succeeding in 2003, strategic clarity and consistency, was the one he most conspicuously lacked.

Howard changed the tone heard in his Saatchi Gallery speech in the first three months of 2004. It was partly that the more consensual line he had articulated did not chime with the sympathies of those two assertive voices of Conservatism, the *Daily Telegraph* and *Daily Mail*. But it was also not in Howard's personality to be a consensual figure: he was by nature combative, and by profession a forensic lawyer, and these facts combined to make him want to be on the front foot against Labour. In the first quarter of 2004, he tried to convey his own personality and mission to the electorate. He set out to achieve this in a variety of ways, including his 'I believe' statement, which listed, initially in a double-page spread in *The Times* in January 2004, his personal credo. He developed

---

[12] Private interview, 21 November 2004.

his theme in a series of speeches. At Burnley he attacked the far-right British National Party, which revealed his passionate, as well as profoundly anti-racist, side. In Berlin he delivered a speech outlining his pragmatic Eurosceptic line towards the European Union, and at home he delivered another powerful 'British dream' speech, in which again he expounded on his vision for the country. The early signs were encouraging. In January 2004, one poll showed the Conservatives with 40% support, the highest since Black Wednesday, and ahead of Labour. Howard and his team hoped to build on this momentum when the Hutton Report on the build-up to the Iraq war was published, and expected it to be far more damning of Blair than it was. Instead of opting for a measured response, Howard acted as if he was the prosecuting counsel and was portrayed as opportunistic: it was his first serious miscalculation as leader, and, with hindsight, can be seen to be the turning point of his leadership.

Howard had still to entrench in the public's mind either his branch of Conservative policies or, indeed, the faces of his frontbench team. Instead of offering positive and constructive policies, he opted for pugnacity and negativity. From March to June 2004, under the influence of his new joint party chairmen, Maurice Saatchi and Liam Fox, he moved into a new phase which was a prolonged attack on Labour, accusing it of having 'let down' the electorate. The view was taken that the forthcoming June local government, European and London Assembly elections should be viewed as a referendum on the performance of the government and that the Conservatives would be seen to be failing if they did not lay bare the government's weaknesses as they saw them.

The results were scarcely an unqualified success, as we shall see later in this chapter. Yet another shift in strategy was now unleashed. The summer of 2004 saw positive campaigning on the Conservatives' new policies on public services. Private polling suggested that health and education were seen as two negative issues for the Conservatives, so Howard determined that he should put forward fresh policies to counteract the criticisms that his party's policies were out of touch or unrealistic. By the late summer, polls were indeed suggesting that the party was slightly ahead of Labour on education. The leadership had also commissioned a far-reaching review of public spending under City trouble-shooter David James, to identity public sector 'waste' and propose savings in government expenditure to allow the party to announce its new fiscal policy before the general election.

However, it was again over Iraq where the Conservatives that summer failed to win the argument. In an interview in the *Sunday Times*, Howard had suggested that he would have voted with the Labour rebels in March

2003 (while still supporting the war) if he had known the full facts about weapons of mass destruction at the time. This troubled the parliamentary party so that, when it came to the debate in the Commons on the Butler Report, it was not fully behind the leader, and his performance lacked credibility and stature. Blair's conduct of the Iraq policy remained his greatest vulnerability, but Howard failed to push home his case, or, worse, even to identify a consistent Conservative line.

From the autumn, the final phase of Howard's leadership before the general election began: the so-called 'Timetable for Action'. His office had decided that it would be 'inconceivable that the general election would be on any other date than in May 2005',[13] so this phase was thus all about preparing for the election. Based on focus group research undertaken over the summer, Saatchi in particular argued that the electorate was disillusioned with the failure of Labour to deliver on its promises (one might ask whether the party really needed focus groups to tell them this). The leadership decided that it needed to give not only specific policy pledges but also a clear timetable for delivery if it was to gain any credibility. Howard's speech to the Conservative conference in October, a masterpiece of inoffensiveness, set out the party's stall for the general election, which was more centrist than the party had produced in 2001, with an emphasis on health and education; Howard's personal qualities as a potential prime minister were also highlighted in contrast to what his team saw as an increasingly vulnerable Tony Blair. 'We want the general election to be a presidential contest between the two leaders,' one aide said.[14] The party's private research had led them to form this conclusion, which would seem counterintuitive to many seasoned watchers of the political scene.

By early 2005, as some of his close team acknowledged at the time, Howard had still failed to find an 'over-arching narrative' to explain what his Conservative Party was all about, and why people should vote for it rather than for Labour or the Liberal Democrats. Howard set great store by the party's spending proposals, which would match (and in some areas exceed) the government's own plans for the public services. The James Review had recommended £35 billion of savings, of which £23 billion Howard and Oliver Letwin, the Shadow Chancellor, pledged towards reinvestment in 'front-line' public services, while £8 billion would help to reduce government borrowing. The remaining £4 billion would finance 'targeted tax cuts', aimed at helping savers, first-time house buyers and pensioners. These announcements in the run-up to the election

---

[13] Private interview, 19 November 2004.   [14] Private information.

campaign produced mixed messages about the party's priorities on taxation and spending, leaving many commentators to conclude that Howard and his team were trying to please everyone, while satisfying none.

Howard's task would have been easier had opinion polls suggested, after his early success, that he was continuing to dent Labour's lead. However, poll after poll since March 2004 has shown little change in the Conservatives' low levels of support at little over 30% – no higher than under Hague and Duncan Smith. The *Economist*, which in January 2004 had praised Howard for creating 'a resurgent and reinvigorated' party which was again 'a disciplined fighting force', had by November decided to write him off: 'the once impressive Mr Howard has shrunk in the job'.[15] Ambitious figures began to position themselves for the post-election (and post-Howard) world. There was much journalistic talk in the months leading up to the general election of the 'Notting Hill' set (David Cameron, George Osborne, Ed Vaizey and Michael Gove) as the new hopes for the party.

Howard's age (62) was a drawback, and he did not look or sound sufficiently appealing on television. His image still suffered from the killer comment of his one time junior minister at the Home Office, Ann Widdecombe, that there was 'something of the night' about him. Like Blair, he is a barrister who excels at oratory and debating, but not in thinking strategically about policy. Howard had announced that he was 'going to put in place a clear strategy which is designed to win the election and I won't be blown off course by opinion polls or newspaper headlines'. This statement displayed flawless logic. Yet that is precisely what happened. No more than Hague nor Duncan Smith did he analyse correctly how to make the most of the opportunities before him, nor did he plot a consistent course and stick to it. Yet, of the three, Howard had the easiest task, and his failure thus was the greatest.

2005 campaign

By the beginning of 2005, a clear 'grid' outlining the precise strategy week by week was in place for the final stage of the 'long election campaign'. By then it was evident from private polling and published opinion polls that the government's lead on the key issues of the economy and public services was too large to reverse before the expected start of the official campaign in early April, let alone by polling day. Howard's team was

---

[15] *Economist*, 10 January and 6 November 2004.

now under the firm influence of celebrated Australian campaign director, Lynton Crosby (architect of the victories of Premier John Howard). He worked on the assumption that a positive promotion of Conservative policies in these areas would not make the impact the party needed to challenge Labour.[16] Instead, the party should fight a highly disciplined but negative campaign on specific issues, such as hospital-acquired infections and indiscipline in schools, where Labour's record was perceived to be at its weakest. It was believed that a strategy which sought to depress Labour's vote and boost the Conservative core vote with some additional support could bring about a dramatic collapse in Labour's working majority.

For a time, Crosby's tactics appeared to bring dividends. By highlighting individual cases where patients and pupils had suffered as a result of government policies and targets, such as the case of Margaret Dixon, the 69-year-old whose shoulder operation was repeatedly cancelled, the Conservatives scored points against Labour as the long campaign reached its climax. The party had seized the news agenda, with the right-wing press rallying to its cause, as the Alan Milburn-led Labour strategy of highlighting £35 billion of 'Conservative cuts' to public services faltered. The opinion polls began to show a steady narrowing in Labour's lead. But the 'hit and run' tactics belied the weaknesses in the Conservative strategy. While some aspects of the Conservative offensive appeared to work, others only served to reinforce the impression among many voters that the party was still unfit for office. Howard's attack in March on the abuse of planning laws by gypsies was designed to regain the initiative and reclaim the headlines after Brown's pre-election budget. But the attack invited more criticism than praise, reviving memories of the 'bandwagon populism' pursued by Hague in the pre-election period four years earlier.

What had begun as a tight and disciplined long campaign began to unravel only weeks before the start of the official campaign when Howard Flight, party deputy chairman and one of the architects of the Conservatives' tax and spending proposals, declared at a private meeting that the potential for efficiency savings was greater than those announced in the James Review. It gave the impression that there was a secret agenda drastically to cut public spending.[17] Determined to avoid the party being

---

[16] Private information.

[17] Matthew d'Ancona, 'The battle of the two Howards had to be fought', *Sunday Telegraph*, 27 March 2003.

cast as untrustworthy on the public finances, Howard swiftly demanded Flight's resignation and de-selection as a candidate. His departure was damaging not only to party morale and cohesion on the eve of the official campaign; it also helped to revive a beleaguered Labour's attempts to portray the Conservatives as a threat to the public services, and called back into question what exactly the Conservatives did believe in.

The party was, however, in some ways more fully prepared for the 2005 general election than for those in 1997 or 2001. Activists were better mobilised, benefiting from an injection of younger recruits from the party's revitalised youth wing, and were bolstered by more than 8,000 Conservative councillors (although still fewer than the 12,000 councillors who were able to campaign for Mrs Thatcher's first election victory in 1979). Conservative Central Office was renamed Conservative Campaign Headquarters, and in July 2004 had moved to modern premises in Victoria Street, close to the Palace of Westminster. Crosby's disciplined approach quickly filtered throughout Campaign Headquarters and in the field, while an influx of donations after Howard became leader enabled the party to invest in sophisticated computer software and equipment.[18] The 'voter vault' system, successfully pioneered by Karl Rove and the Republicans in the United States, which was procured by Liam Fox in mid-2004, enhanced targeted campaigning in marginal seats. The party's new machinery concentrated resources on 900,000 swing voters, and was helped by a number of regional call centres, the largest based near Birmingham.[19] Despite efforts to boost the resources for candidates in a number of marginal contests, the party, however, still lagged behind Labour and the Liberal Democrats in channelling resources and manpower into target seats.[20] The task of winning all 159 target seats to form an overall majority required a national swing of 11.5%, a task that was made all the more difficult by an electoral system that heavily favoured the Labour Party.

The party nevertheless went into the official campaign on 5 April in a buoyant mood. In the first few days after Blair announced the election, polls showed the Conservatives trailing Labour by only 1 or 2%, on 35–36% of the vote, a far stronger position compared with the equivalent position in 1997 and 2001. Indeed, the British Election Study analysis

[18] J. Fisher, 'Money matters: the financing of the Conservative Party', *Political Quarterly* 75 (2004).

[19] P. Oborne, 'The mean machine', *Spectator*, 20 November 2004.

[20] *The Times*, 26 May 2005.

revealed that the Conservatives were even ahead of Labour among those most likely to vote at the start of the campaign, particularly in marginal seats.[21] It was a picture which was to bring a false sense of security and confidence in the strategy adopted months beforehand. The Conservative manifesto, published on 11 April, several days before the manifestos of Labour and the Liberal Democrats, was, at only 28 pages long, one of the thinnest ever produced. Its title, *Are You Thinking What We're Thinking? It's Time for Action*, was also the party's main slogan for the first half of the campaign. But as *Sunday Telegraph* journalist Matthew d'Ancona pointed out, the message could be interpreted as one, not of empathy, but of 'grubby conspiracy: whispered words, and noses tapped' about concerns such as 'uncontrolled immigration'.[22] Another figure, Michael Portillo, called the party's programme nothing more than a 'Victor Meldrew manifesto'.[23]

Howard indeed pressed the message of 'controlled immigration' to the fore in the first two weeks of the campaign.[24] The other campaign themes, 'cleaner hospitals, school discipline, more police and accountability' came over less clearly as a consequence. Crosby, whose record in highlighting immigration in Australian elections was well known, later insisted after the election that Howard 'only gave one speech and one press conference on [immigration] in 34 days'.[25] This is utterly disingenuous. The Conservatives' emphasis and tone of the policy of yearly quotas and caps on both asylum seekers and immigrants exceeded the rhetoric used in Hague's unsuccessful campaign four years earlier. Howard's team asserted that immigration was a legitimate part of the leader's self-declared 'battle for Britain', and blamed the media for hyping the issue.[26] But by the end of the second week, there were criticisms from senior Conservatives, including Lord Parkinson and Ken Clarke, that the 'public had enough of immigration' and that the Conservatives were in danger of becoming a 'one-issue party'.[27] As most opinion polls indicated, immigration was high on the

---

[21] See The British Election Study Rolling Campaign Survey, 2005: voter intentions among likely voters, University of Essex at http://www.essex.ac.uk/bes/

[22] D'Ancona, 'The battle of the two Howards'.

[23] Michael Portillo, 'The Conservatives undone by their Victor Meldrew Manifesto', *Sunday Times*, 24 April 2005.

[24] The Conservative website boasted at the start of the campaign than Michael Howard had 'thrust immigration into the forefront of the campaign'.

[25] Alice Thomson, 'We lost but the Conservatives are back in the game', interview with Lynton Crosby in *The Spectator*, 19 May 2005.

[26] Private information.   [27] *The Daily Telegraph*, 24 April 2004.

list of salient issues before the official campaign began, but by 5 May it had receded in importance.[28] It is also clear from polls taken during the campaign that the public's rating of the Conservatives' campaign performance fell dramatically from +2% at the beginning to −18% at the end.[29] Leading pollster Peter Kellner pointed out that the party's lead on immigration actually fell during this period, indicating that the issue was a turn-off to potential supporters, and that there was little electoral gain to be made because 'the constituency that wants to be tough on immigration is much tougher than the Conservatives'.[30]

As the official campaign entered its final stages, it became clear that Howard had dominated the party's presentation. With private polling research continuing to suggest that Howard was perceived to be more in touch than Blair with the detail of people's problems, his advisers were keen to place him at the forefront of the campaign.[31] It was further felt that Howard needed to counter Blair's 'presidential' style of campaigning, but Conservative strategists either failed to notice or ignored the fact that Blair never seemed far apart from Brown for most of the campaign. Letwin, on the other hand, was conspicuously absent in the last two weeks of the campaign, not just because he was fighting to save his own seat in Dorset. Indeed most of the Conservative front bench were barely visible as Howard bestrode the campaign trail in front of a watchful media. Despite Blair's popularity ratings taking a tumble (as Figure 7.1 earlier in this chapter shows), the public's perception of Howard's prominence and performance went into free-fall as the campaign drew to a close.[32] Only 21% by 5 May believed that he would make the best prime minister, 14 points behind Blair.[33]

Realising, belatedly, that the Conservative campaign was weakening the party's support rather than strengthening it, the leadership sought

---

[28] See Christopher Wlezein and Pippa Norris, 'Whether and how the campaign mattered', in Christopher Wlezein and Pippa Norris, *Britain Votes 2005* (Oxford: Oxford University Press, 2005).

[29] See The British Election Study Rolling Campaign Survey, 2005: campaign performance index, University of Essex at http://www.essex.ac.uk/bes/

[30] *Economist*, 14 May 2005.   [31] Private information.

[32] Blair's performance in the campaign fell from −0.8 at the start of the campaign to −1.8 at the end, whereas Howard's dropped from −2.7 to −19.4. See The British Election Study Rolling Campaign Survey, 2005: leader campaign performance index, University of Essex at http://www.essex.ac.uk/bes/.

[33] See The British Election Study Rolling Campaign Survey, 2005: Who would make the best Prime Minister?, University of Essex at http://www.essex.ac.uk/bes/

to lower the temperature of the immigration theme and to broaden the party's message. 'Are you thinking what we're thinking?' was replaced by 'Taking a stand on the issues that matter', a slogan which also gave little indication about what the party stood for. The focus of the campaign, which had so far been predetermined by the Crosby grid, now veered off onto the territory of Iraq and the events which led to Blair's final decision to go to war in early 2003. Crosby admits that Iraq was a problem for the Conservatives in the final week of campaigning. 'People remembered why they had lost trust in Tony Blair', he argued, 'but they couldn't see any real difference between the Conservatives and Labour so we lost out on that.'[34] Howard's earlier claim that he would have gone to war irrespective of the Attorney General's advice sat uneasily with his accusations that Blair 'lied' in the case he made for war. Just as Howard was at sea after the Butler Report on the intelligence on Iraq's weapons of mass destruction, he now weakened his hand in the argument about the legality of the war in Iraq. The issue, which looked as if it would wound Blair deeply, and did to some extent, also harmed the Conservatives, who were already defined by their original support for the war.

Appealing to the electorate in the last days of the 2005 general election campaign to wake up to a 'better, brighter Britain' by voting Conservative on polling day, Howard's almost only positive message of the campaign fell on deaf ears. The voters would not buy what Howard was selling them. The long campaign had begun so promisingly. For the better part of the 'long campaign' and the first week of the official campaign, the party had the edge over Labour, although only on the issues of asylum and law and order did the party enjoy leads over Labour; yet, even here, its advantage decreased by the end of the campaign.[35] On all other issues, including the economy, health and education, voters viewed the governing party (somewhat grudgingly) to be the more competent team on offer. Fighting on their chosen strategy, the Conservatives under Howard were highly unlikely to reach out beyond their core vote by more than 5%. The fact that the party barely increased its vote on its 2001 performance is testament to a campaign that, for all its claimed discipline and vigour, failed utterly to offer the voters a convincing alternative to an unpopular government.

---

[34] Thomson, 'We lost but the Conservatives are back in the game'.
[35] The Conservative lead over Labour on immigration dropped from 11% to 8% by the end of the campaign, while the lead on law and order dropped from 6% to 0%. See ICM Research at http://www.icmresearch.co.uk/reviews/pollreviews.asp.

Electoral impact, 2001–5

But was the Party destined in 2005 to have performed no better? To answer this question requires a longer perspective. New Labour's command of the electoral landscape after 1997 had looked initially unassailable, with healthy leads over the Conservatives in every age and occupational group, except for the over 65s and AB professional classes.[36] The size of Labour's majority, 179, would, most purists thought, almost certainly ensure two full terms in office at the very least. The outlook facing the Conservative Party under Hague, leading a rump of just 165 MPs, was grave: 4.5 million voters had deserted the party between 1992 and 1997. Within four years a further 1.2 million would leave the Conservative fold; fewer voted Conservative in 2001 than Labour in 1983, at its own lowest point under Michael Foot. With a mere 1% increase in the share of the vote, producing a net gain of just one seat, the 2001 general election defeat ranks as one of the worst performances in the party's history and a clear vindication of New Labour's electoral strategy.[37] Labour and the Liberal Democrats continued to advance in former Conservative seats, particularly in the key battlegrounds of the Midlands and the south-east.[38] The Conservatives improved their standing in their safest seats, but fell back in Labour and Liberal Democrat-held marginal seats. While a recovery in Scotland and Wales remained elusive (apart from a solitary gain in south-west Scotland), the party failed even to come second in any of the Manchester or Liverpool constituencies. Labour's bias in the electoral system added to Conservative woes: the party required a massive 10.5% swing to win a bare majority in 2005.[39]

It was always going to be a long and arduous journey for the Conservatives to claw their way back into contention. The electoral dimension of the Blair effect had weakened morale and lowered the bar of expectation among observers and the media about the party's chances of making a strong recovery after the nadir of 2001. Despite a collapse in the Labour

[36] David Butler and Dennis Kavanagh, *The British General Election of 1997* (London: Macmillan, 1997), pp. 244–6.
[37] It was the lowest popular vote for either main party since the 1931 general election, when the Labour Party was split by the formation of the National Government.
[38] Labour held 23 of its 30 most marginal seats and increased its majorities in many of the leafy, suburban seats, such as Enfield Southgate, Wimbledon and Bristol West. Pippa Norris (ed.), *Britain Votes 2001* (Oxford: Oxford University Press, 2001) p. 13.
[39] Progress made in the mid-term elections in the previous four years, particularly in the European and local elections in 1999 and 2000, had failed to be built on to produce anything like the 11.6% swing the party required to regain an overall majority in 2001. Norris, *Britain Votes 2001*, p. 4.

vote in the mid-term elections in Blair's second term, mainly due to the fall-out surrounding the Iraq war, the Conservatives under both Duncan Smith and Howard showed little sign of progress. In the six by-elections during the 2001–5 Parliament, as luck would have it all held in relatively safe Labour seats, the Conservative share of the vote fell on average by 4.2%, compared with the 0.6% fall in Blair's first term.[40] Far from challenging Labour, the party slipped into third place in Birmingham Hodge Hill and Leicester South and fourth, behind the United Kingdom Independence Party (UKIP), in Hartlepool. In the elections to the Scottish Parliament and Welsh Assembly in 2003, the party remained in third place behind the nationalists, while in the London mayoral and assembly elections the following year some strides were made – pointing to the revival in the party's fortunes in Greater London at the general election.[41] The European Parliament elections in June 2004 provided the most disappointing result for the Conservatives. Although the party came first in the poll, it only secured 27% of the vote (9% lower than Hague's performance in 1999) and saw a loss of eight seats. Labour's collapse (to 23% of the vote) and UKIP's success (coming third with 16%) obscured the fact that the Conservatives suffered their worst ever performance in a national election. It was only in that summer's local government elections that the party built on the local recovery begun under Hague. By 2004 the Conservatives had once again become the largest party in local government with over 8,000 councillors and had made important gains in urban areas in the Midlands and the north-west. Bad though these mid-2004 elections were for Labour, they were also the elections that helped fortify a depressed Blair and made him realise he could convincingly win the coming general election as Prime Minister.[42] Howard also failed to match Hague's local election success of 2000, when the party won an estimated 38% of the vote (Figure 7.2)

None of this made the prospects of defeating Labour in 2005 look encouraging. Howard and Crosby nevertheless believed that a disciplined and carefully targeted campaign could deprive Labour of a working majority – and indeed there were indications before the start of the campaign that this objective was within their grasp. Labour's final vote was indeed

---

[40] These are changes in the party's overall share of the vote at by-elections compared with recent general election results. See House of Commons Research Paper 04/61 July 2004.

[41] In Scotland, the Conservative vote rose by 0.6% and in Wales 3.3% compared with the 1999 elections; in London (the GLA elections) the vote fell by 2% compared with 2000, but the Conservatives became the largest party in the GLA.

[42] See Seldon, *Blair*, pp. 628–55.

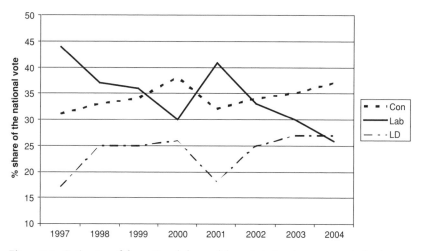

Figure 7.2. Estimates of the national share of the vote in local government elections, 1997–2004

Source: *UK Elections Statistics: 1918–2004*. House of Commons Research Paper 04/61. July 2004.

on the verge of collapse (falling by 5.5% since 2001), but the electoral system cushioned the blow and provided Blair with a comfortable third term majority despite securing a very low 35.2% of the vote. It was the Conservative Party, improving its share of the vote by a mere 0.6% to 32.3%, which had failed to capitalise on Labour's woes and, as in 2001, merely reinforced its core vote rather than won over additional support from the centre ground. The Liberal Democrats rather were the repository for disgruntled Labour voters, gaining 3.8% since 2001. Nevertheless, Howard claimed that the party could 'hold its head up high' on the back of 33 net gains on 5 May. So, in the face of all the odds stacked against it, was the Conservative campaign a success?

The Conservative performance varied considerably across the country, as Table 7.1 shows. Only in the London, South East and East of England regions did the party stage anything like a recovery. Yet even here the Conservative share of the vote only rose between 1 and 2% and the gains in seats were sporadic. Successes in Enfield Southgate, Putney and in a cluster of seats in Hertfordshire were offset by near misses in places like Hove, Harlow and Crawley, where Labour held on by the narrowest of margins. Aside from Wales and Scotland, where there was some progress, the Conservative share of the vote fell in the five northernmost regions of England compared with 2001. In the crucial battlegrounds of the East

Table 7.1. *Conservative performance by region, 2005 General Election*

Region	Seats won	Change since 2001	Votes 000s	% share	% change since 2001	Swing Lab to Con
UK	198	+33	8,773	32.3	+0.6	3.0
England	194	+29	8,103	35.7	+0.5	3.3
Wales	3	+3	298	21.4	+0.4	3.1
Scotland	1	+1	369	15.8	+0.2	2.2
N. Ireland	0	–	3	0.4	+0.1	n/a
North East	1	–	214	19.5	−1.8	2.4
North West	9	–	846	28.7	−0.6	2.5
Yorks & Humber	9	+2	641	29.1	−1.1	2.0
East Midlands	18	+3	747	37.1	−0.2	3.0
West Midlands	16	+3	835	34.8	−0.1	3.1
East of England	40	+6	1,147	43.3	+1.5	4.2
London	21	+8	932	31.9	+1.4	4.9
South East	58	+5	1,754	45.0	+2.1	4.6
South West	22	+2	985	38.6	+0.1	3.7

Notes: Based on notional 2001 results for new Scottish boundaries; 'swing' is calculated as the average of the percentage change from 2001 to 2005 in the Conservative share of the vote and the Labour share of the vote
Source: House of Commons Research Paper 05/33, 17 May 2005; *The British Parliamentary Constituency Database, 1992–2005*; BBC.

and West Midlands, the party only gained six seats – well short of the number needed to displace Labour's majority. The party continues to have no representation in Birmingham, Newcastle, Leeds, Liverpool and Manchester. To form a government at the next election, the Conservatives have to win seats in the urban north, but the task will be made even harder now that the party invariably languishes in third place behind the Liberal Democrats.

More troubling for the Conservatives is the failure to reverse the socio-demographic trends in voting behaviour that first became evident in the mid-1990s. In some cases, the party has fallen back even on its 2001 performance. While New Labour's support consistently fell across all age, class and housing tenure groups, Conservative support improved slightly or even fell compared with 2001. Yet again, it was the Liberal Democrats

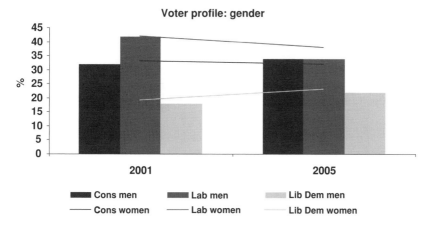

Figure 7.3. Voter profile: gender (change since 2001)
Source: MORI Aggregate Analysis, data cited in *The Parliamentary Monitor*, May 2005, Issue 127.

who gained at Labour's expense, rather than the main opposition party. Polling analysis of voter profiles and preferences in the 2005 general election suggests that women, once the most dependable source of support for the Conservatives, continue to desert the party, while in the 25–34 age group the party has been relegated to third place (see Figures 7.3 and 7.4). Even among the AB professional and managerial classes, the party's support has fallen by 2% since 2001, while the only improvement was among C2 and DE voters, where Labour enjoys large leads (see Figure 7.5). In the crucial C1 category, the party simply trod water as the Liberal Democrats gained at Labour's expense. Despite Labour's downward trend in most social and occupational classes, it continues to lead the Conservatives among mortgage owners – a group that once placed its faith the party of Thatcher and Major, but now remains loyal to Blair and Brown (see Figure 7.6).

Clever targeting of resources and campaigning tools enabled the party to make modest inroads into Blair's majority, but the story of the 2005 general election is much more about New Labour's success in holding on to just enough support to provide victory.[43] The Conservatives' failure in

[43] Christopher Wlezien and Pippa Norris argue that the 2005 campaign did have an impact on the result. Their research of opinion polling before and during the campaign compared with the result (using *The British Parliamentary Constituency Database, 1992–2005*) suggests that the Conservatives could have gained another 38 seats, leaving Labour with a majority of around 18 rather than 66. See Christopher Wlezein and Pippa Norris, 'Whether and how the campaign mattered', in Wlezein and Norris, *Britain Votes 2005*.

Voter profile: age

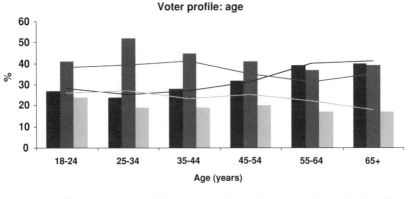

Figure 7.4. Voter profile: age (change since 2001)
Source: MORI Aggregate Analysis, data cited in *The Parliamentary Monitor*, May 2005, Issue 127.

Voter profile: social class

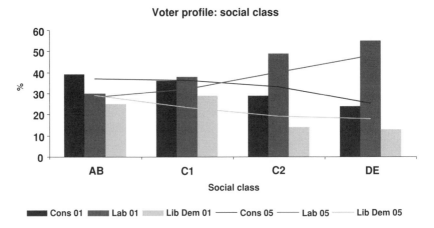

Figure 7.5. Voter profile: social class (change since 2001)
Source: MORI Aggregate Analysis, data cited in *The Parliamentary Monitor*, May 2005, Issue 127.

2005 among women, AB voters and the young in particular points to the failure of the Howard/Crosby strategy either to damage Labour, who have a solid working majority for its third term, or to provide a springboard for the Conservatives for the next general election. The party will have to gain between 120 and 140 seats to form the next government with a

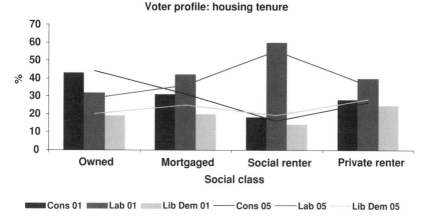

Voter profile: housing tenure

Figure 7.6. Voter profile: housing tenure (change since 2001)
Source: MORI Aggregate Analysis, data cited in *The Parliamentary Monitor*, May 2005, Issue 127.

bare working majority, an awesome (but not impossible) undertaking. To see the 2005 campaign, and Howard's leadership, as anything other than a complete failure is not only disingenuous: it is also dangerous if the Conservatives are at last to learn lessons and move forward.

Conclusion: the Conservatives' effect and the Blair effect

'We are far too slow in learning the lessons from Blair,' admitted a senior Conservative after the 2005 defeat.[44] Only indeed after that defeat is there evidence of some Conservatives trying seriously to analyse the whole New Labour phenomenon. Prior to 2005, the aping of New Labour was confined largely to tactics and campaigning devices (copying the war room, 'instant rebuttal', the 'grid' and discipline over the central message) rather than understanding the whole New Labour philosophy, of moving into the centre ground, 'neutralising the negatives' (the reasons which accounted for the party being deemed unattractive to 'middle England'), iron discipline and a pursuit of power above all other considerations.

This late conversion underlines the truth that, for much of the period since 1994, it has been Blair who has been far more influenced by the Conservatives than they have been by him or by New Labour. Mrs Thatcher was the political figure who had more influence on Tony Blair than any

[44] Private information.

other.[45] From her, or mirroring her, he learned the importance of leading the country from the front, of dominating one's party while standing apart from it, of keeping close to the United States, of the supremacy of the market economy and limiting the role of the state, and of being unafraid to be a strong war leader. From the Conservatives in general, he learned the supreme importance of 'hugging the centre ground'. He realised that no party, either Conservative or Labour, ever won elections and *held on* to power by occupying the flanks, either right or left. Blair's achievement has been to appropriate the Conservative Party's hegemony, and to 'steal' the two strategies that had been the keys for two hundred years of its electoral success: its hunger for power at all costs, and its willingness to adapt its policies and its organisation to adjust to new circumstances. So blatant was he, and so blind were the Conservatives, that it took them many years to realise exactly what he had done.

The Blair effect on the Conservative Party has to date been devastating, but was made much worse by the leaderships of Hague, Duncan Smith and Howard. The party, in effect, stood still for eight years, with very little prospect of improvement in the long term. Duncan Smith failed to provide conviction or authority to the important changes he identified. Howard's failure is more surprising. In the year and a half before the election, he achieved barely any of the goals set out above at the start of the 'Lessons unlearnt, 2001–5' section. Rather than listening to intellectuals and historians, or indeed those in his own party who have a deep understanding of the Conservative Party and of the ingredients of its success over two centuries until appropriated by Blair, he opted to listen to electoral mercenaries like Crosby. He must bear the blame himself for choosing those whose advice he opted to follow. During the campaign itself, his failure to adopt a clear policy platform based on Conservative principles, or to promote a credible frontbench team, were cruelly exposed, as they always would be. If the Conservatives under new leadership cannot learn the lessons for 2009–10, the party's very survival could be at stake. But if they can, they can overhaul Labour's lead. The 'Blair effect' on the Conservatives may yet prove to be temporary, while, under his own successors, it is far from established that the Blair effect on Labour will definitely outlast him.

[45] Seldon, *Blair*, pp. 441–54.

PART II

Economic and social policy

8

The Treasury and economic policy

DAVID SMITH

On 15 June 2004 Gordon Brown passed an important milestone. A politician whose stock after-dinner joke is that there are two types of chancellor, 'those who fail and those who get out in time', became the longest-serving holder of the office in the modern era. In beating David Lloyd George's twentieth-century record (7 years and 43 days) in a job whose modern-day pressures far exceed those of the past, Brown's achievement was considerable. Under his economic management the Blair government had avoided economic crises, something that every previous Labour administration had succumbed to. It had maintained, indeed added to, its reputation for economic competence, by achieving the low-inflation stability that too often had eluded governments of all colours. The Treasury's pre-eminence in Whitehall, often in doubt during the Thatcher and Major years, was unquestioned. So was Brown's own political stature. If it was ever open to question during Blair's first term, nobody in the second term seriously challenged the notion that when it came to the Cabinet it was Blair, Brown and the rest some distance behind.

As Brown surveyed the scene in summer 2004, he had much to be satisfied about. Blair was politically weakened and privately doubting his ability to carry on. The chancellor, untainted by Iraq, was getting much of the political credit for the improvement in public services beginning to come through. His crystal ball might not have predicted how pivotal a role he would have in the May 2005 election campaign, acting as what lobby correspondents dubbed a 'human shield' for Blair. But he had no doubt, then or later, that the economy would be a powerful vote-winner for Labour. The economy is also fundamental to the durability of the Blair–Brown relationship. Commentators have often sought to draw comparisons between it and, for example, Margaret Thatcher and Nigel Lawson. Thatcher and Lawson's relationship only fractured, however, when the economy got into trouble. John Major sacked Norman Lamont in May 1993 because he lacked belief in his ability to manage and sell to the public an economic recovery neither man had much confidence in. Economic stability, in contrast, has been the glue that has held Blair and Brown together through political thick and thin. Given the economic record, Brown not only cast away the Labour party's economic demons but, uniquely among modern chancellors, made himself unsackable.

According to the National Institute of Economic and Social Research, in a spring 2005 assessment,

> Labour's economic record has been very satisfactory. Nothing has gone badly wrong with the economy over the period since 1997. Inflation has been low and stable and output growth has also been stable, at a rate consistent with most views about the trend rate of growth. By contrast with earlier periods, the public finances have been reasonably well controlled and our current position is better than that in both France and in the United States in that respect. Employment conditions have improved markedly, continuing earlier trends, so that by 2004 employment rates of prime-age workers were higher than in both France and the United States.[1]

Economic stability in Blair's first term was a source of mild wonderment, even to those responsible for it. During the second term it came to seem natural. The question, though, was whether Labour had achieved enough given that platform of stability.

Safe with the Bank of England

In February 1997, three months before Blair's first landslide, Gordon Brown and Ed Balls, then his adviser, later chief economic adviser in the Brown Treasury, travelled to the United States. The trip, which included a Labour fundraising party in New York organised by Tina Brown and Harold Evans, was partly for fact-finding purposes, partly to raise the international profile of the chancellor-to-be. It was on the Washington leg of the trip, however, that the two discovered real policy gold. After a day of meetings with Alan Greenspan, chairman of the Federal Reserve Board, and Robert Rubin, the then US Treasury Secretary, the way forward became clear. As they were driven back to Washington's Dulles airport on 20 February, Brown and Balls turned to each other and smiled. The talk at the Fed had been all about monetary policy – interest rates and the control of inflation. At the US Treasury, in contrast, the discussion had been about

---

[1] National Institute of Economic and Social Research, *National Institute Economic Review* (London: Sage Publications, April 2005), p. 9.

long-run economic issues such as productivity. The differences between the US and British systems were striking.

Brown knew well the history of previous Labour chancellors, bogged down from the start by sterling crises and a failure to win the confidence of the financial markets. Chancellors of all governments had spent too much time considering and being constantly badgered about interest rate changes. On arriving back in London he announced new initiatives. Not only would Labour target inflation at 2.5%, but it would establish a monetary committee of Bank of England insiders and outside appointees. He tied with it an announcement that a Labour-run Treasury would also have a US-style council of economic advisers. Even then, he still had to win Blair over to the idea of immediate Bank of England independence. That decision was taken on 28 April, three days before the 1 May general election, according to Geoffrey Robinson, a close ally of Brown and Paymaster-General in the Treasury for part of Labour's first term. It was not announced, however, until 6 May, five days after Blair was safely in Downing Street, and it came as a surprise. Labour's pre-election policy position had been that independence could occur, but only after the bank had 'proved itself' through the quality of its advice to the chancellor, under the system of 'quasi' independence – public advice on interest rates and the bank given a specific responsibility for monitoring and forecasting inflation – established by Lamont. Lamont, in fact, had wanted to go the whole hog and make the bank independent in the autumn of 1992, but was blocked by Major. Kenneth Clarke, his successor, was not an enthusiast for central bank independence, leaving it as an 'open goal' for Labour to score. Even so, Labour's pre-election spin had suggested that it was far from happy with the bank and its then governor, Eddie (later Sir Edward) George.

Bank operational independence – the requirement that its monetary policy committee (MPC) of nine insiders and outsiders achieve an inflation target set by the government – provided the basis of Labour's economic stability. The details of the policy arrangements also provided reassurance to concerned Labour backbenchers, such as Diane Abbott, then a member of the Commons Treasury committee, who wondered publicly whether the 'inflation nutters' would take over. The 2.5% target would operate symmetrically, with as big a penalty (a public letter of apology from the bank governor to the chancellor) for undershooting it by more than a percentage point as for overshooting it by a similar amount. It is important, however, to distinguish between the bank's roles in the first and second terms. 'Bank independence was the ideal commitment device

for Labour,' said Willem Buiter, the economist, one of the founder members of the MPC. 'Independence got the markets off Gordon Brown's back
and, equally importantly, it got the Parliamentary Labour Party and the
unions off his back. He could say to them, "I feel your pain, but I don't set
interest rates". That gave him time to focus on serious fiscal consolidation
instead of monetary policy panic.'[2]

The bank's task in the 1997–2001 Parliament was to achieve credibility for the new arrangements. Even when Labour was first elected, the
period of low inflation in the UK was long-lasting by comparison with
past periods. It was only a matter of time, doubters argued, before the
economy resorted to its inflation-prone type. That it did not owed much
to the MPC's almost immediate grasp of the task in hand. Interest rates
were initially raised quite sharply but then cut in the autumn of 1998 in
response to a multi-faceted international financial crisis, which focused
on Russia's bond default and the failure of the Long Term Capital Management (LTCM) hedge fund. As well as maintaining low inflation and
establishing credibility, the bank also contrived to have interest rates falling
in the run-up to the 2001 election. The electoral cycle of falling interest
rates as polling day approached had been preserved in an era of central
bank independence, if only by coincidence.

From fighting inflation to preserving growth

Establishing the anti-inflation credibility of a newly independent central
bank was a tough enough task. The second-term task, however, was if anything more demanding. The long global economic upswing of the 1990s
came to an abrupt halt around the time George W. Bush succeeded Bill
Clinton by winning the November 2000 US presidential election, although
the extent of the slowdown was not apparent until several months into
2001. The 11 September 2001 Al-Qaeda attacks on the United States,
which hit business, consumer and financial market confidence, and had a
direct and negative effect on many sectors of the economy, reinforced the
downturn. OECD growth dropped to just 1.1%, that for the wider world
economy to 2%. The United States experienced two quarters of declining gross domestic product (GDP), at least on initially available figures,
meeting the standard definition of recession. So did most other major
economies. The 2001 downturn marked the beginning of a prolonged
 period of extremely weak growth for France, Germany, Italy and the
majority of the 'euroland' economies, the single-currency members.

---

[2] Quoted in David Smith, 'Brown to break record', *Sunday Times*, 6 June 2004.

The British economy, however, continued to grow, not least because of the bank's swift actions. Interest rates, which had been falling even before the 9/11 attacks, were reduced to just 4%, their lowest since 1963, in their aftermath. When confidence was further threatened by the uncertainty generated by the invasion of Iraq in 2003, the bank cut rates again to just 3.5%, their lowest since 1955. For comparison, the average level of short-term interest rates under Margaret Thatcher was 12%, and their lowest was 7.5%. The highest rate in the era of bank independence had been 7.5%. It worked. If Britain's economy was traditionally inflation-prone, it was also in the past more subject to recession than other economies. This time, largely thanks to the bank's actions, it had barely skipped a beat, without a single quarter of declining GDP.

Why was this? Charles Bean, the bank's chief economic adviser and an MPC member, suggested that the reputation acquired quickly during the immediate post-independence period soon began to pay off. 'As the counter-inflationary credibility of monetary policy increased, so central banks found themselves better able to offset disturbances without the danger of destabilising inflation expectations,' he said in a speech in 2005.[3] In the past, in other words, policy-makers would have been constrained from cutting rates for fear of setting off a wage-price spiral or an adverse reaction in the financial markets, or both. By anchoring inflation expectations the bank was able to avoid this. In every budget and pre-budget report the Treasury produces, a chart shows how inflation and inflation expectations have been locked together since about 1998, when individuals, businesses and the financial markets came to believe that the MPC would indeed achieve its central aim of meeting the inflation target. The novelty of independence may also have helped. In other countries, where central bank independence was well established and taken for granted, there may have been less of a positive impact on confidence as in the UK, where the avoidance of monetary policy errors was unusual. The European Central Bank, which came into being in January 1999, just over 18 months after the MPC, had a tougher time establishing its credibility.

Not everybody recognises the contribution of Bank of England independence to the success of Blair and New Labour. In one account by two journalists sympathetic to the New Labour cause but not overly familiar with economic theory or policy, MPC members were 'the monetarists to whom democracy had been delegated'. The old left-wing charge, that

---

[3] Charles Bean, *Monetary Policy in an Uncertain World* (London: Bank of England, 22 February 2005).

central bank independence was a policy that operated against the interests of the working classes, and was the brainchild of free-market economists like 'Mrs Thatcher's one-time guru, Friedrich Hayek' has not entirely gone away.[4] To some critics, the bank's success is merely a by-product of low worldwide inflation and a small gain in return for the loss of political control of monetary policy.

A more credible strand of criticism is that the bank has not been monetarist enough. Critics point to the rough trebling of house prices in the UK since the mid-1990s, the rise in the household debt burden from 100 to 140% of annual disposable income – equivalent to £1,100 billion – and strong increases in money and credit over the period of independence, as indications that monetary policy has been too lax. On this view the bank, like Alan Greenspan at the Federal Reserve Board in Washington, has given too big an emphasis to the avoidance of short-term economic pain, risking longer-term problems of inflation and economic instability.

Staying out of the euro

At the end of Blair's first term there was a general expectation, encouraged by Downing Street, that while the first four years had been all about proving that Labour could run the country and the economy competently and without outside interference, that would change during the second term. The Prime Minister had committed the government to a reassessment within two years of the five economic tests for membership of the eurozone, designed by Brown and Balls. A brief assessment of those tests in October 1997 had concluded that Britain was not ready to join the single currency at its inception on 1 January 1999. But the five tests – 'are business cycles and economic structures compatible?', 'if problems arise is there sufficient flexibility to deal with them?', 'would joining create better long-term conditions for firms wanting to invest in Britain?', 'what would be the impact on Britain's financial services industry?', and 'would joining promote higher growth, stability and a lasting increase in jobs?' – were not seen as an insurmountable barrier to entry. Some independent economists said the tests had already been met. More common was the argument that they could be fudged to produce whatever outcome was politically convenient.

---

[4] Polly Toynbee and David Walker, *Better or Worse? Has Labour Delivered?* (London: Bloomsbury, 2005), p. 136.

Journalists and commentators became used to briefings and counter-briefings from Downing Street and the Treasury. As early as 10 June 2001, three days after the election, the *Sunday Times* was reporting, on the basis of Treasury briefings, a slap-down for the Foreign Office. The story, that the focus of the second term would be on public service delivery, and that the new foreign secretary, Jack Straw, should adopt a more critical attitude to the euro than Robin Cook, his predecessor, was an early drawing of the battle lines. It was preceded by a report in the *Independent* that Blair favoured a referendum on single currency membership in the autumn of 2002, and would 'kick-start a national debate on Britain's future in Europe' at the annual conference of the Trades Union Congress in September 2001. A common criticism from Britain in Europe and other pro-euro groupings was that the government in general, and Blair in particular, had failed to challenge the predominantly sceptical mood in Britain. Brown's official position, set out in his Mansion House speech on 20 June 2001 was one of 'pro-euro realism'. Few people who had contact with the Treasury could, however, detect that there was much that was pro-euro about its approach. As it turned out, Blair's own pro-euro speech to the TUC was scheduled for the afternoon of 11 September 2001 and was never delivered. Understandably, he hurried back to London from the Brighton conference when news of the Al-Qaeda attacks on the United States broke. He did, however, return to the theme in his speech to the Labour Party Conference three weeks later. In what many saw as a jarring note in a speech about the post- 9/11 world, he said: 'If they (the five tests) are met, we should join. And if met in this Parliament, we should have the courage of our argument to ask the British people for their consent in this Parliament.' The war on terror, it seemed, had an echo in the battle with the Eurosceptics.

Even Blair, however, could not force a positive verdict. Robert Peston, in his book *Brown's Britain*, has detailed the tensions the euro produced in the Blair–Brown relationship, to a degree that barely seems credible to those outside the relationship. Thus: 'On Wednesday April 2, 2003, Blair asked for Brown's resignation in a fit of frustration at his inability to influence the decision on whether the UK should join the euro and Brown duly offered it to him – though when tempers cooled, they returned to their roles as though nothing had happened, much in the way that dysfunctional partners in a marriage would do.'[5] Westminster was also constantly awash with stories, many of them detailed by Peston, that Blair was prepared to

---

[5] Robert Peston, *Brown's Britain* (London: Short Books, 2005), p. 217.

stand aside in favour of Brown in return for the latter's agreement to join the single currency. In Treasury-inspired versions of such stories, Brown was never prepared to sacrifice the national interest for his own personal ambitions.

The five-tests assessment

What is undoubtedly true is that the Treasury was aware from an early stage that if it was to be a 'no' verdict, the assessment had to be rigorously conducted. The October 1997 exercise had been relatively cursory. The 2003 assessment, by contrast, would be the most thorough of its kind ever conducted. Gus (later Sir Gus) O'Donnell succeeded Sir Andrew Turnbull as Treasury permanent secretary in July 2002, having been its managing director for macroeconomic policy and international finance. His main concern was to ensure that the Treasury could not be accused of a lack of thoroughness in its work, and that – assuming a 'no' verdict – pro-euro supporters would not pick on holes in the analysis. To that end, O'Donnell commissioned 18 supporting studies, several of them from academic economists, to back up the main five tests assessment. They included a historical study of the United States as a single currency area, the likely effect of European monetary union (EMU) on trade, the role of fiscal policy, the equilibrium exchange rate for sterling against the euro and the relationship between the housing market, consumer spending and monetary union. The Treasury's rationale, set out in a speech by Balls in December 2002, was that unlike previous big decisions affecting the exchange rate – the 1925 return to the Gold Standard, the 1949 and 1967 devaluations and, most notably, 1990 membership of the European exchange rate mechanism – this one was being subject to the fullest possible economic analysis. 'The reason why the five tests are so important is because they ensure that a proper and long-term economic assessment of the national economic interest will precede an irreversible decision of great long-term economic and therefore political significance,' Balls said in his Cairncross lecture.

Brown had intended to publish the 18 studies, together with the five tests assessment, in his budget on 9 April 2003. But Blair insisted that the assessment be delayed. Not only was it too big an announcement to be slipped out in the budget but it would also reinforce the impression that the Treasury had full control of the decision. So he insisted that the 18 technical studies be circulated to all members of the Cabinet, and that the announcement be delayed until June. When it came, on 9 June 2003, few could have been surprised by the verdict: 'No, not yet' or, as

Downing Street preferred it, 'Yes, but not yet'. The only glitch from the Treasury's perspective was that it chose a release timetable that meant that the technical studies were released ahead of the overall assessment. Some of those studies, particularly one outlining the potential benefits for trade, appeared to put a more enthusiastic slant on entry than had been intended. Officials were quick to point out that the overall assessment remained cool on euro membership, and suggested that very significant barriers remained. Despite this, the exercise was a success. The Treasury was praised for the thoroughness of its approach. Only one of the five tests, that euro membership would be good for the UK's financial services industry, was met, as it had been in 1997. Overall, the verdict was: 'Despite the risks and costs of delaying the benefits of joining, a clear and unambiguous case for UK membership of EMU has not at the present time been made and a decision to join would not now be in the national economic interest.'[6]

Brown did, however, show willing. He announced a change in the Bank of England's target inflation rate from 2.5% under the old measure – retail prices excluding mortgage interest payments – to 2% on a new measure, the 'harmonised' index of consumer prices, later just the consumer prices index, to bring inflation targeting in Britain in line with that of the European Central Bank. There is some mystery about this change. The Treasury says that it was demanded by Downing Street but Downing Street insists that it was not a change it was either looking or asking for. Brown also announced a number of minor measures to attempt to improve Britain's convergence with the economies of the euro area.

Fundamentally sceptical?

There are two views about Brown's attitude to euro membership. One, favoured by this author, is that the Chancellor's pre-May 1997 enthusiasm for the single currency was genuine enough but that it changed in office as a result of two factors. The first was that the success of the UK's monetary and fiscal framework, and in particular bank independence, surpassed expectations. If Labour's home-grown framework worked so well, why should it look elsewhere? The prospect of euro membership, held out by Brown before he took office, was an insurance policy that turned out not to be necessary. To this should be added the fact, for Brown, of dealing with fellow European Union finance ministers. Not only did the

---

[6] HM Treasury, *UK Membership of the Single Currency: An Assessment of the Five Economic Tests* (London: HM Treasury, 9 June 2003).

post-EMU arrangements establish an apartheid between ministers whose countries belonged to the euro and those outside it, something resented by a politician who always craves being at the centre of things, Brown became dismayed by his colleagues' willingness to flout openly the single currency's fiscal rules – the stability and growth pact – and their unwillingness to engage in the kind of reforms needed to make the EU economy more flexible. The euro, in other words, became a club that Brown had no desire to join. His scepticism, and that of the Treasury, runs deep. Such a view, it should be said, has been quietly encouraged by the Treasury.

The alternative view, as argued by Derek Scott, Blair's former personal economic adviser, is that Brown's opposition to the euro was tactical rather than fundamental. Tactically, it suited the chancellor to have a battleground on which he could challenge Blair, knowing that public opinion and most newspapers were on his side. If it came to the crunch, and one of the many Blair–Brown battles on the issue ended up with the Chancellor being forced out or resigning on a matter of principle, he would be an exile with powerful political support. In a mirror image of Margaret Thatcher's downfall, set in train by Sir Geoffrey Howe's resignation in protest at her anti-European stance, Blair's end could have been precipitated by his determination to force through a pro-European agenda, against the protests of his chancellor. But according to Scott, in his book *Off Whitehall,* there is no evidence that Brown's opposition to the euro runs deep:

> In 2003, some commentators took the view that Gordon Brown had become convinced that it was not in Britain's long-term interests to join EMU. He might even be a closet sceptic! It is true that if that had been the case Gordon Brown would have had to adopt a policy similar to the one he did adopt: procrastination and postponement. But that was not his position at all. There was no evidence that Gordon Brown thought that membership of EMU was undesirable and no reason to doubt that, if he (or any other likely successor) were to become Labour's next prime minister, he would want, like Tony Blair, to take Britain in, though his strategy and tactics might be different.[7]

Where does that leave prospects for the UK's membership of the euro? After the June 2003 'Yes, but not yet' assessment, and the minor policy concessions made in its wake (notably the change in the Bank's inflation

---

[7] Derek Scott, *Off Whitehall, A View from Downing Street by Tony Blair's Adviser* (London: I.B. Tauris, 2004), pp. 228–9.

target and a commitment to an annual review, but not a full assessment, at the time of each budget), Treasury officials and advisers conceded that it would be difficult, perhaps impossible, to say 'no' again. After two negative assessments there would be a strong presumption of a positive outcome for the next one. But when? At the start of Blair's third term, the European question revolved on whether Blair could secure a 'yes' vote in a referendum on the proposed EU constitution, not the euro, a question soon rendered irrelevant by the French and Dutch referendum 'no' votes. The notion that the Prime Minister could sweep Britain into the single currency on a wave of post-Iraq enthusiasm had been shown to be 180 degrees wrong. Even if Brown's attitude was equivocal, establishing the political conditions for euro entry seemed more problematic than ever. The risks, both to the government in general and his own position in particular, were considerable. Brown's own line of attack, that Britain needed to be sitting at the European table to force through the economic reforms needed, had little resonance among voters. The catch-22, it seemed, was that only when the UK economy was in trouble would the public warm to the idea that the grass would be greener in Europe, as happened in the late 1980s over ERM membership. By the same token, though, any such economic problems would rebound badly against Labour. The Treasury, in 2003, had found a long and elegant way of rejecting euro entry. It may also have ensured that the issue remains off the agenda for the indefinite future.

Prudent for a purpose

Until Gordon Brown arrived at the Treasury in May 1997, the annual budget 'red book', the financial statement and budget report, was a dull document. It is hard to imagine any of his predecessors sitting down and taking time to come up with a title for this annual production, or allowing it to run to 200 pages or more. That changed with New Labour. All Whitehall documents became not so much statements of fact and policy as vehicles of government propaganda, lengthy ones at that. A run through the titles of these annual documents is instructive. This, New Labour's first budget in July 1997, was 'Equipping Britain for our Long-Term Future', followed in March 1998 by 'New Ambitions for Britain' and, a year later, 'Building a Stronger Economic Future for Britain'. The significance of those first three budgets was that, while long-term policies were put in place, such as the New Deal for the unemployed, the working families' tax credit and the launch of the productivity and competition agenda, the fiscal arithmetic remained extremely tight. Brown in 1997 had inherited public spending plans described by Clarke, his Conservative predecessor, as 'eyewateringly tight'. He had raised taxes from his first budget, including a £5.2 billion windfall tax on the privatised utilities and the £5 billion annual 'raid' on pensions through the abolition of the dividend tax credit. He had also increased personal taxes by stealth, partly by abolishing well-established reliefs such as the married couples' allowance and mortgage interest relief. The aim was clear. Blair and Brown had learned from the history of previous Labour governments. The standard response on taking office after a period of Tory rule was to relax government spending, thus cheering their supporters among the public-sector unions and their members. The problem with this approach of spending first and asking questions later was that it quickly ran into economic trouble. Harold Wilson in 1964 thought the circle could be squared through raising the economy's growth rate. Ten years later Wilson, this time with Denis Healey as his chancellor, thought a Keynesian injection of government spending would see the economy through the first OPEC (Organisation of Petroleum Exporting Countries) world recession.

So Brown, with Blair's support, did things in exactly the opposite way. First he raised the taxes, and provided the cushion of very healthy public finances, helped by the April 2000 auction of third-generation mobile phone licences, which raised an astonishing £22.5 billion; £380 per head of the UK population. Then, and only then, did Brown relax spending. The transition between the two policies is evident from the title of his fourth budget, in 2000, 'Prudent for a Purpose: Working for a Stronger and Fairer Britain'. The spending increases announced in the 2000 budget, foreshadowed in Tony Blair's January television interview that year with Sir David Frost – in which he pledged to raise health spending in Britain to the EU average – would not take effect until 2001–2, the start of Labour's second term. The inference was clear; the first term had been all about creating the fiscal room for manoeuvre that would allow big increases in public spending, targeted particularly at the NHS and education, during the second. That was the purpose of Brown's early prudence.

Tax and spend

Although the March 2000 budget signalled a much higher rate of growth of public spending looking forward, there remained considerable nervousness in the Treasury about this sudden change of tactics. Would independent economists not conclude that Labour had resorted to type, admittedly after a three-year delay? How could Treasury officials, having defended a strategy of squeezing public-sector budgets as the best way to squeeze out greater efficiency, defend the government's new policy of turning on the spending taps? By the time of the June 2001 election there was scepticism on two fronts: the ability of Labour to transform public services by increasing budgets, and their ability to do this without significant additional tax increases. The March 2001 budget barely addressed such concerns, and went back to a safe title, 'Investing for the long term'.

March 2001 did, however, announce the arrival of Derek Wanless on the scene. Wanless, the former chief executive of the National Westminster Bank, would, the Treasury announced, 'undertake a review of the technological, demographic and medical trends over the next two decades that will affect the Health Service. The review will report to the Chancellor in time to inform the 2002 Spending Review'. The appointment of Wanless was significant. During the first term Brown had often used businessmen to rubber-stamp policy decisions, the rationale being that voters would respond favourably to policy endorsements by senior business people, rather more than they would to politicians. Martin Taylor, former chief executive of Barclays, had advised on and endorsed the working families' tax credit, while other senior businesspeople were hauled in to chair taskforces on other aspects of Treasury policy.

Wanless's task was to quantify 'the financial and other resources required to ensure that the NHS can provide a publicly funded, comprehensive, high quality service available on the basis of clinical need and not ability to pay'. He was not asked to judge whether reliance solely on public funding was necessarily the best option for the increase in health spending he determined was necessary, to his reported frustration. Wanless delivered his interim report in November 2001 and his final report in April 2002. The first set out the scale of underfunding and the extent to which Britain fell behind other advanced industrialised countries on a variety of health outcomes. The second detailed the additional resources needed over a 20-year period under three different scenarios: 'solid progress', 'slow uptake' and 'fully engaged'. All three built in real increases in NHS spending of more than 7% a year for the first five years, even though Wanless warned that such rises were 'at the upper end of what should sensibly be spent'. His concern was over the ability of the NHS to absorb an increase in funding of this magnitude without huge waste. He also warned that 'higher spending inputs do not necessarily imply better health outputs and outcomes'. The subsequent record would appear to have proved these warnings justified.

Despite the caveats, however, Brown had got the answer he was looking for and, indeed, had expected. The April 2002 budget, 'The strength
to make long-term decisions: investing in an enterprising, fairer Britain',
incorporated not only new and more generous figures for NHS spending, it also set out how they would for. The 1% rise in National Insurance contributions much speculated about before the 2001 election was
announced, raising an extra £3.5 billion a year from employees and £450
million from the self-employed. Individuals were also hit with a £700m
tax increase from the freezing of personal tax allowances. The surprise,
though, was that Brown also hit businesses with a 1% National Insurance
hike, the hated 'tax on jobs'. The Confederation of British Industry (CBI),
which had expected the tax increases to be targeted solely at the personal
sector, reacted with 'deep dismay'. Suddenly, those parts of the Wanless
report that stressed the importance to business of a healthy workforce
made sense. But the episode soured relations between government and
business for the remainder of the Parliament. The April 2002 budget,
however, maintained the Blair–Brown pattern. As in 1997, the bad news
of higher taxes was got out of the way at the earliest opportunity in the
Parliament, although on this occasion the National Insurance hikes would
not take effect until April 2003.

No longer so prudent

The National Insurance hike announced in April 2002 marked a significant
change from the character of the first term. This time the tax increase was
explicit and in the open, rather than 'stealthy', even if half of it had been
raised from business. It was also aimed at a specific purpose, the NHS,
even though the government stopped short of hypothecation and, in fact,
the extra revenues went into the general taxation pot. Saying that the hike
was necessary to pay for tax credits or defence spending would have been
less politically astute. The tax hike would also, however, ensure not only
much faster growth in public spending – more than 5% a year in real
terms over the three years from 2003–4 – but that such spending could
be afforded without risking Brown's own fiscal rules. The Golden Rule of
balancing the current budget over the economic cycle and the Sustainable
Investment Rule of keeping government debt below 40% of gross domestic
product would be met, whatever happened, he insisted. Before the end of
the year, however, that boast was looking rather less assured.

The November 2002 pre-budget report marked an important point
in the Brown chancellorship and in Blair's second term. Brown, in

announcing big increases in public borrowing – including a near-doubling of the 2002–3 figure from £11 billion to £20 billion – crossed from being the 'iron' chancellor to one who began to give a fair impression of his spendthrift Labour predecessors. The rise in borrowing gave him the worst headlines of his period at the Treasury, as prudence was seen by the headline-writers to have been dumped in favour of a racier model. It also, for a while, changed the balance of power within the Cabinet. For the first time Brown was vulnerable, Blair loyalists began to speculate about 'life after Gordon' and other ministers, having been subjected to five years of the chancellor's unique brand of power politics, became bolder, sensing that the big beast of their political jungle was wounded. Not only was the rise in borrowing worrying from an economic perspective, it was also bad politics. The risk was that the National Insurance rise, which was not due to take effect until the following spring, would be seen by voters as paying for the government's mistakes and miscalculations, not a better NHS.

Brown did not stay down for long. The March 2003 budget, 'Building a Britain of economic strength and social justice', showed a confidence that had been lacking the previous November. The rise in public borrowing, with more yet to be announced, did however fundamentally change the nature of the second term. By granting independence to the Bank of England, Brown had relieved himself of the question faced by all his predecessors: when are you next going to raise interest rates? Instead, he faced an equally unpalatable alternative: when are you next going to raise taxes? The deterioration in the public finances ensured that, in macroeconomic terms at least, Brown's next three budgets would be non-events, remembered mainly for further increases in public borrowing and the chancellor's dogged insistence that his fiscal rules would be met. So the 2003 budget, 'Building a Britain of economic strength and social justice', 2004, 'Prudence for a purpose: A Britain of stability and strength', and 2005, 'Investing for our future: Fairness and opportunity for Britain's hard-working families', simply rehearsed familiar lines.

What would have changed if the government had had more fiscal breathing space? Possibly very little. The fiscal rules were set up in such a way that they were always intended to be met with a margin to spare. The detailed debate the Treasury found itself locked into over whether the Golden Rule of balancing the current budget over the cycle was met or not was never meant to happen. Martin Weale, director of the National Institute of Economic and Social Research, insisted that the Treasury 'moved the goalposts' by changing the way it specified the Golden Rule mid-cycle. In a sense that did not matter. 'Our own assessment is that the economic cycle has just ended and the latest government borrowing figures suggest that the Golden Rule has been broken', wrote Weale and his colleagues in the spring of 2005. 'No great economic importance can be attached to this and the breach of the rule is indicative of a flaw in the rule rather than an inherent indicator of economic mismanagement.'[8] That is not quite how it was seen by the Treasury, and by being forced into a debate that came down to decimal points Brown had demonstrated that he was sailing too close to the wind when it came to meeting his own rules. Soon after the May 2005 general election another cloud appeared on the horizon with an announcement from the Office for National Statistics that it was reviewing the classification of debt under private finance initiative (PFI) projects. Were that review to result in a significant increase in the stock of public debt (because risk had not been transferred to the private sector), Brown's other rule, of keeping government debt below 40% of GDP, would also be threatened.

The upshot is that if the public finances had been healthier the Treasury would have been able to breathe easier; any spare funds would not have been used mainly for additional public spending, or for tax cuts. Some of it, however, might have been. By the time of the 2005 election, rationalising the fiscal position in which he found himself, Brown insisted that tax cuts were the things only irresponsible Tories offered. Labour was, however, sensitive to the charge, not only that it had not done enough to ease the tax burden for those on low incomes, but that it had dragged large sections of middle England, including teachers and senior nurses, into higher rate tax. The number of higher-rate taxpayers rose from 2.1 million in 1997 to 3.3 million in 2005. That and the prospect of third-term tax hikes was a cloud over the economic record. Blair, it seems, was more concerned than his chancellor about the adverse impact on UK competitiveness and incentives about a rising tax burden. According to Scott: 'Within No. 10 he took the view that direct taxes need to be cut significantly over the medium term for the vast majority of the population who were or who aspired to be middle class.'[9] Brown, however, had a different view: 'Gordon saw tax as something that could be altered and tweaked to meet other objectives that he, or the government, thought desirable and, moreover, he thought that the British electorate had been brainwashed into thinking that a rising burden of tax is a bad thing.'[10]

---

[8] National Institute of Economic and Social Research, *National Institute Economic Review*, p. 6.
[9] Scott, *Off Whitehall*, p. 29.   [10] Ibid.

Some token tax reductions ahead of the 2005 election might have helped to alter that impression, but this was not to be; the fiscal arithmetic did not allow it. Instead, the Treasury briefed that Brown had deliberately eschewed short-termism and the gimmicky tax cuts associated with previous pre-election budgets. Voters were not fooled. Polls taken during the election campaign showed that while Labour remained well ahead of the Conservatives on the key question of economic competence, the overwhelming majority of voters expected taxes to go up during Blair's third term. That was never part of the Prime Minister's plan.

Competition and productivity

In his November 1997 pre-budget report, six months into his chancellorship, Brown set out his priorities. 'The first challenge is to increase our productivity,' he said. 'Britain today is some 20% less productive than our main competitors and has been for years. Second, the challenge of employment; 3½ million working age households – almost 20% – have no one earning a wage. And third, the challenge of stability. For forty years our economy has an unenviable history, under governments of both parties, of boom and bust. Stop-go has meant higher interest rates, less investment, fewer successful companies and lost jobs. It has been the inevitable result of a failure to take the long-term view.'

Few would argue against the claim that the third of those three aims, stability, was achieved. The employment record was also good, with the Labour Force Survey measure reaching 28.6 million by the time of the 2005 election, 2.1 million up on its May 1997 level. Only part of that was due to rising public-sector employment. Independent assessments suggested that the New Deal had made a contribution to the reduction in youth employment, as had the chancellor's tax credits, although in both cases the effect was modest. The national minimum wage, introduced mainly as a political gesture but also to stop employers 'free-riding' on the government's tax credits (in other words leaving the state to pick up the wage bill for low-paid workers) did not have the negative effect on employment predicted by critics. One interesting point is that the 'workless households' measure of unemployment cited by Brown in 1997 showed only a small improvement, mainly because of persistently low employment among single parents. It was on the third of those priorities, raising Britain's productivity performance, that the record has been wanting. According to Paul Krugman, the US economist and columnist, 'productivity isn't everything, but in the long run it's almost everything'.

Brown set out a plausible agenda for raising productivity. It included higher levels of education spending, a renewed emphasis on skills and training, correcting Britain's 'historic' underinvestment, increasing the amount of research and development activity, removing supply bottle-necks, including those arising from an inadequate transport system, and, intriguingly, a new competition regime. Most of the measures were straight out of the productivity primer, their main shortcoming being that no government had deliberately neglected these things before. The new competition regime was quintessentially New Labour and represented a clear break with the party's past. Previous Labour governments, under pressure from the unions, had been sympathetic to the idea of protecting domestic firms from competition, particularly international competition. The competition regime established by Brown and Blair, effectively giving independence to the Office of Fair Trading (OFT) and the Competition Commission, changed that. The philosophy was that British companies could only become competitive internationally if they were competitive at home. 'The competition regime that Gordon Brown established was probably the most liberal (in a free-market sense) anywhere in the indus-trialised world', wrote Derek Scott. 'If it is maintained, it could have a beneficial effect in ten years or so that will outweigh any other single economic decision he made, except making the Bank of England inde-pendent.'[11]

The productivity agenda, however, was slow to work, if it was working at all. By 2005 there was no sign of a break in the previous trend. Produc-tivity growth since 1997 on an output-per-hour basis had averaged 2.2%, in line with its long-run average, and slightly below the 2.5% annual rate achieved in the four years before Brown became chancellor. One expla-nation could be that change takes a long time; it may take a generation to improve education and skills to the point where they have a decisive impact on productivity. Another argument is that, while Brown put a framework in place, notably in the area of competition, it was never fully utilised. There was disappointment, including from within the govern-ment, that the OFT had not made more of its cartel-busting powers. The Competition Commission had significantly less work to do under the new competition regime than when it was tasked to investigate monopolies by ministers. Productivity may have suffered, in addition, from the 'new worker' problem – in a time of expanding employment new entrants tend to be less productive than existing workers and it takes time for them to

[11] Scott, *Off Whitehall*, p. 31.

catch up. To this can be added the problem of low public-sector productivity during a period of rising government spending and employment.

The Economic and Social Research Council, in an autumn 2004 assessment which concluded that the productivity gap in relation to competitor countries was as large as when Labour came to power, came up with a variety of explanations, including 'a relative failure to invest, failure to innovate, poor labour relations, trade distortions attributable to Empire, antagonism towards manufacturing,"short-termism" among business leaders and financial institutions, technological backwardness, lack of entrepreneurship, over-regulation of business, an overly-instrumental attitude to work among employees, and the rigidities of the class structure. The list is not exhaustive.'[12] That would point to the problems Brown was attempting to tackle as being ingrained and long-term, if not necessarily intractable. But what if Labour's supply-side policies, far from taking the country forward, were taking it back?

Squandering a golden legacy?

While economic stability provided the basis for Blair's third election victory, the narrowness of that victory, at least in terms of the popular vote, suggested that, as well as Iraq and other factors, the spell was beginning to wear off. Labour party strategists suggested that this was because voters had begun to take stability for granted, which was why the party's election posters included a bloodcurdling, if highly implausible, warning of a return to the instability and 15% interest rates of the past, were the Conservatives to be elected. There may, however, have been other factors; the sense that the rise in house prices and household debt under Brown was unsustainable, that taxes would inevitably rise further to pay for the expansion of public services, and that the government's economic boasts did not square with the economic reality faced by the majority of people.

There was also a strong sense, curiously much more in 2005 than in 2001, that Blair and Brown were claiming a little too much for their economic management. The longest run of continuous economic growth since 1701 cited by Brown in his March 2005 budget, 51 successive quarters by the time of the May 2005 election, was impressive. But simple arithmetic showed that more than a third of those were achieved under the Conservatives. Labour's claim, to have inherited an economy with

---

[12] Romesh Vaitilingam, 'The UK's productivity gap: What research tells us and what we need to find out' (London: Economic and Social Research Council, September 2004).

worrying problems and put them right, was wearing thin. Ruth Lea, in a Centre for Policy Studies paper, quotes an incident cited by Tom Bower, in his biography of Brown: ' "These are fantastically good figures," the official concluded."The state of the economy is much better than predicted." Eyes swivelled to Brown."What am I supposed to do with this?" he snarled."Write a thank-you letter?" '[13] According to Lea, the economy's performance under Brown was mainly due to two factors he inherited: the supply-side reforms of the 1980, including trade union reform, privatisation of the utilities and the reform of the tax system; and the post-ERM (exchange rate mechanism) transformation of macroeconomic policy under Lamont, including the introduction of inflation targeting, an enhanced role (quasi independence) for the Bank of England and a programme of fiscal consolidation.

On this view, not only was the economy's post-1997 performance mainly a function of Labour's 'golden' economic legacy (the May 1997 election defeat for the Conservatives was unusual in the context of a strong economy) but on many measures performance had deteriorated. Thus the current account of the balance of payments, in broad balance in 1997, was heavily in deficit by 2004, including a record £57 billion trade deficit; economic growth was slightly higher in the 1992–7 period than afterwards; unemployment was already falling sharply, including youth unemployment, and, crucially, the inflation dragon had been slain. 'He [the Chancellor] is keen to inform the electorate that he has transformed the economy since 1997; and he likes to give the impression that the country was floundering in a swamp of economic chaos prior to 1997', she writes. 'Nothing could have been further from the truth. And secondly, the economy is not currently performing as well as it did when it was under the Major government.'[14] Others, while putting it less forcefully than Lea, agree. 'Essentially what happened was that we got a sensible policy established in 1992 and 1993 and it changed a bit when Labour came to power,' said Martin Weale, director of the National Institute of Economic and Social Research.[15] Willem Buiter, a founder member of the MPC, puts it more colourfully. 'The foundations for greater macroeconomic stability were laid when the UK left the ERM and the Bank took up inflation targeting,' he said. 'That was Mervyn's work [Mervyn King, now Bank governor], long before Balls was even a twinkle in Gordon's eye.'[16]

---

[13] Ruth Lea, 'Whatever happened to the golden legacy?' (London: Centre for Policy Studies, March 2005).
[14] Ibid., p. 2.   [15] Quoted in Smith, 'Brown to break record'.   [16] Ibid.

By the end of the second term, and looking into a future in which he would expect to succeed Blair, Brown still had much to prove. Economic stability had been maintained but in other respects there was little to praise. His budgets, most of them containing little of note, had been characterised by tinkering, and the creation of an extraordinarily complex tax system, clogged up with tax credits. 'He's made a terrible mess of the tax system,' said Lamont. 'Instead of tax neutrality or simplicity, it has been a little relief here, a little relief there.'[17] 'The trouble is that we've had this endless tinkering,' said Lea. 'He's been the best chancellor on earth for the accountancy profession.'[18]

Increased tax complexity, a rising tax burden and the re-regulation of the economy were all characteristics of the Brown chancellorship, with Blair unwilling or unable to stop him. The IMD World Competitiveness rankings, from the Swiss-based International Institute of Management Development (www.imd.ch), show the UK dropping from ninth place in 1997 to twenty-second in 2004. Two weeks after the May 2005 general election, Brown was admonished by John Sunderland, president of the CBI. 'Business must be free to fulfil its responsibility to create wealth for the country and help build a fairer world, without being held back by increasing tax and damaging regulation, he said.[19] According to Scott,

> The long-term impact of the Blair–Brown partnership on the British economy remains to be seen, since it takes several years for the full impact of policies, for good or ill, to take effect. In the next few years, Britain's economy should continue to outperform many of our nearest neighbours, but there are limits to the length of time public spending can increase at a faster rate than growth in gross domestic product without causing problems, and by the time I left Downing Street [in December 2003], Britain was approaching, or perhaps even past, that limit. The regulatory burden had been increased, the tax system become more complicated and the tax burden was rising too. Over the medium term this matters and it is easier for governments to mess up an economy than it is to improve it.[20]

Wasted years

If Scott and other critics are right, 2005 could have been the last election Labour would be able to fight with such a clear run on the economy, and

---

[17] Ibid.   [18] Ibid.

[19] John Sunderland, 'Annual Dinner speech', 17 May 2005, London: CBI (available at www.cbi.org.uk).

[20] Scott, *Off Whitehall*, p. 31.

such a clear lead over the Conservatives. Brown was lucky enough to be the beneficiary of a favourable economic inheritance. His successor may not be so fortunate. The question, however, is why he did not do more with the platform of economic stability that, having inherited, he managed to sustain.

One explanation is that Labour's economic ambitions were always limited to the achievement of economic competence. Had Brown and Blair been presented in 1997 with a future in which the economy ran for eight years without a recession, an inflationary episode or a run on sterling, they would have seized it with open arms. If, at the same time, that future held out the possibility of a sustained increase in health and education spending, they would scarcely have believed their luck. Supply-side reforms, on this view, were merely an add-on, not central to Labour's economic strategy in the way they had been for the Tory opposition in the 1970s. Not only that but such was the overriding ambition of being perceived as competent that, in the end, it got in the way of other aims. William Keegan's *The Prudence of Mr Gordon Brown* has as its central thesis the argument that Brown overdid the prudence and caution in the first term. This was not so much to disguise his Old Labour roots as to build up a reservoir of trust, in the financial markets and among voters, to permit the second-term relaxation of public spending:

> First there was a famine; then a feast, with public spending rising fast and newspaper advertisements replete with job opportunities in the public sector. But the early years of prudence had served to make the problems of the public sector either worse than the inheritance or, at the very least, to have delayed improvements in, for example, the Health Service and the rail network. A Labour government elected with an enormous majority was pusillanimous in its approach.[21]

Brown was fortunate in the timing of the spending relaxation, but it was not necessarily good economic management. Public investment fell to a post-war low as a proportion of GDP in 1999–2000, so the subsequent recovery was from a shrunken base. Throughout the public sector there was widespread scepticism when the extra billions finally came through, partly because they followed such an intense squeeze, and partly because Brown had used the language of expansion when still applying

---

[21] William Keegan, *The Prudence of Mr Gordon Brown* (London: Wiley, 2003), p. 333.

that squeeze, most notably in 1998. This undoubtedly contributed to the lacklustre performance of public services even when budgets were being genuinely expanded. The fact that Brown was so anxious to keep the financial markets onside may also have inflicted damage in other ways. Keegan and others argue that excessive prudence and caution contributed to a prolonged overvaluation of sterling which undermined the efforts of industrial exporters. By spring 2005, a million jobs had been lost in manufacturing since May 1997. Nor did Brown's prudent beginnings buy him that much time. The reputational shift he suffered from 'iron' chancellor in the first-term to something close to dangerous spendthrift in the second was swift and savage. He would argue that it could have been a lot worse and, despite the criticisms, the financial markets remained on board, in a way they clearly had not during earlier Labour regimes.

The second explanation for the second-term disappointment is that Brown was continually frustrated by Blair, and vice versa. The Treasury, in other words, would have been much more radical and redistributive if the Chancellor had been given a freer hand. Downing Street would have been much more aggressive in its pursuit of public-sector reforms had it not been for Brown's constraining hand. On the first, evidence produced by the Institute for Fiscal Studies in April 2005 found that there had been a reduction of 700,000 in the number of children in poverty compared with 1996–7, and that there were 800,000 fewer poor pensioners. On the key measures of inequality, however, it found that 'despite a large package of redistributive measures, the net effect after seven years of Labour government is to leave inequality effectively unchanged'.[22] The government, moreover, did not achieve its own target for reducing child poverty and had presided over a small increase in the incidence of poverty among working-age adults without children. Was Brown held back by Blair? There is scant evidence of it. The disputes between the two did not impact on the government's redistribution efforts. There is plenty of evidence that Blair was sceptical about Brown's tax credits, none at all that he restricted them in any way. As Scott puts it: 'Tony Blair gave Gordon Brown unprecedented authority over a range of domestic policy but that was his choice. They were jointly responsible for the economic outcome.'[23] Where problems

---

[22] Mike Brewer, Alissa Goodman, Jonathan Shaw and Andrew Shephard, *Living Standards, Inequality and Poverty* (London: Institute for Fiscal Studies, April 2005).
[23] Scott, *Off Whitehall*, p. 31.

arose, particularly for policies such as tax credits, they often lay in the way they were designed and administered.

There is a stronger argument that progress in reforming the public sector was held back by differences between the Treasury and Downing Street. That was true for foundation hospitals, which Brown effectively neutered. It was also true in education. Brown eventually backed tuition fees, but only after the government faced defeat by its own backbenchers. As the controller of the purse strings, Brown was ideally positioned to insist on far-reaching public-sector reforms. Whether it was for fear of upsetting the unions (despite tough talk) or because he genuinely believed money was the solution, he failed to do it. One of the big frustrations for Blair was the slow pace of public-sector reform during the second term. Part of the blame for that, at the very least, has to lie with Brown.

The third explanation is that Brown's overweening leadership ambitions, and Blair's ability to frustrate them at every turn, were ultimately damaging. The Blair–Brown rift did not result in a run on sterling, as was the case when Thatcher and Lawson fell out. It did set the tone for economic policies that were less than optimal. In Peston's sympathetic (to Brown) account, the Chancellor is either protecting his own empire from a Downing Street assault or engaged in expanding his influence across Whitehall under the terms, as he would see it, of the Granita deal. As described by Scott, Brown's obsessive budget secrecy extended to unprecedented degrees in not even letting the Prime Minister know what was coming. As described by Peston, it was Brown and his allies who more frequently felt under pressure: 'All the time a campaign was being fought against us, claiming that we were anti-reform – equating reform with "marketisation" and privatisation and then saying we are anti-reform and centralisers on that basis. There was a limit to how much we could do while staying in the government.'[24]

This is not the time to rerun all the accounts of the Blair–Brown rift. The simple question is whether it led to good government, or not. The answer must be that it did not. Whatever they were up to behind closed doors, Blair and Brown competed to announce 'eyecatching' initiatives. A prime minister obsessed with headline-grabbing initiatives probably does not do too much damage; a chancellor who clutters his budgets with them probably does. At one stage late in the second term, a sulky Brown tellingly says he will 'just get on with being chancellor of the exchequer', almost as though this was not what he had mainly doing

[24] Peston, *Brown's Britain*, p. 332.

up until then. Nobody could say that the economy went badly wrong during Labour's second-term. The macroeconomic record over the period 1997–2005 was good, although it was no better than in the period from autumn 1992 to May 1997 under John Major. In some respects, such as the economy's unbalanced growth and the sharp widening in Britain's external deficit, it was worse. Many would argue that more could and should have been done. Divisions at the top were at least partly to blame for that.

9

Mr Blair's British Business Model – capital and labour in flexible markets

ROBERT TAYLOR

It is a sign of the complete transformation of British politics that we can claim to be the party of the economy and the Conservatives are the threat to it.

> Tony Blair, speaking to a business audience in London's Canary
> Wharf complex, 14 April 2005

Business has a responsibility to make profits, using the money invested by shareholders and making it grow. Profitable businesses create sustainable employment and the pursuit of profitability stimulates innovation and productivity.

> Labour Party's 2005 general election business manifesto

The challenge of globalisation needs a strong and vibrant trade union movement standing up for its members in a coherent and intelligent way.

> Tony Blair speaking at the TUC annual conference,
> September 2002

The partnership between us is essential and I intend to ensure that it remains positive and firm.

> Tony Blair speaking at the Confederation of British Industry
> annual conference on 17 November 2003

Labour believes in strong trade unions that are representative of the diverse workforce and which play a positive role in securing the success of their workplaces. Labour wants to work in partnership with the trade union movement to help such unions grow.

> The so-called Warwick Agreement, September 2004

The making of the British Business Model

Tony Blair – in his third successive elected term as prime minister – has made it clear that he would like to carry through an irreversible transformation of the British economy so that it can become one of the world's leading centres for successful private enterprise, wealth creation and investment in research and development and technological innovation. He believes that Britain under his leadership is turning into a Business Model of how an advanced post-industrial economy can meet the formidable challenges posed by the competitive forces of globalisation and technological change. Blair's ambitious purpose is to advance a much more radical strategy of liberalisation and deregulation of markets – financial, product as well as labour. It represents a further significant shift in the Labour Party's attitude towards the virtues of a more lightly supervised capitalism which is based primarily on the supposed neo-liberal virtues of the US model of the political economy. As Blair explained at the launch of his party's third general election manifesto specifically designed to meet the perceived needs of the business community on 28 April 2005,

> Labour as a party not only believes that economic dynamism and social justice must go hand in hand, but that creating and maintaining the right environment for enterprise and wealth creation is a policy priority. It is business and not government that creates wealth but I do not accept the dogmatic view of the Conservatives that government can have no role in fostering enterprise and innovation.[1]

On that occasion Blair emphasised that the British state had to perform many important roles – to maintain macroeconomic and financial stability and thus reassure business that it could invest and innovate with less risk of uncertain results; to create a competitive tax regime under which entrepreneurs and companies could flourish through greater personal rewards for commercial success; to equip employees with the appropriate skills and formal education for application in modern workplaces; to invest far more than in the past in science, technology and innovation; and perhaps above all else to propagate widely a national popular culture of private enterprise to be inculcated across society – from among children in primary schools to the world of adult paid work. Blair has insisted that his own personal economic vision was not of a controlling or centralised state that assumed it knew what was best for business. Instead, the state was to act more as a catalyst and an enabler, ensuring the necessary conditions around an agreed minimum framework of legal rules and regulations within which private enterprise could grow and flourish.

---

[1] Labour party press release, 28 April 2005.

At the end of his second term as prime minister, Blair spoke proudly of Britain having been transformed under his leadership since May 1997 into a distinctive national model which was markedly different and significantly more successful than what he regarded as the sclerotic social market economies of western Europe that were for so long the post-war engines and paragons of growth and prosperity. He and his chancellor Gordon Brown liked to point to the supposed failures of the continental European approach in reforming their supposedly rigid labour markets and in particular to the relatively high levels of open unemployment and lower employment rates being suffered in competitor economies such as France and Germany. By contrast they liked to draw attention to the allegedly more effective British Business Model of flexible labour markets and lightly regulated workplaces they were creating. They argued that the British way was far more attuned to meeting the challenges of increasing globalisation and the rapid application of communications and information technology in advanced market economies. Their declared aim, for Britain's period in the European Union presidency from July to December 2005, was to try to set an example and lead the rest of the EU into a willing acceptance and implementation of an economic reform programme that was based broadly on the neo-liberal principles of flexibility and freedom that they believed had been the necessary foundations for their own country's recent economic achievements. Central to the Blair vision of the new political economy was his government's positive and activist approach to the avowed needs and demands of the business community.

Much of Blair's programme of radical economic reform stemmed from the bold ambitions that were first laid out in the so-called 2000 Lisbon agenda that was agreed to by all the heads of European Union member governments at a ministerial summit meeting held in the Portuguese capital. Its principal stated objective was to make the whole of the EU the most competitive and advanced economy in the world by 2010 through the implementation of a commonly agreed strategy that would advance liberalising and flexible policies to stimulate higher investment and deregulation. The so-called Lisbon agenda was actually designed to build on the achievements of the EU presidential era of Jacques Delors in the 1980s which first led to the creation of the single European market for labour and capital, goods and services by 1992. To Blair and Brown the programme would involve a determined effort to roll back or at the very least water down and halt many of the labour and social regulations that had been introduced by Brussels. The original EU aim had been to create a Europe-wide free market economy which would contain as an integral part a substantial social dimension with legal protections and labour rights for workers whatever their employment status. The Prime Minister liked to argue that the EU social action programmes of the 1990s had been in part responsible for the high level of unemployment and poor record of job creation in many continental European countries compared to that of Britain. What the whole of the EU needed, he insisted, was a much more determined effort to achieve the ambitious Lisbon goals through a more full-hearted commitment to deregulation and labour market flexibility that would liberate employers from unnecessary red tape and loosen the burden of legal restrictions so that they could hire and fire workers virtually at will. Many across the European democratic left, especially inside the trade union movement, regarded such an objective as an Anglo-Saxon attempt to Americanise continental Europe and undermine its social market models. The decisive rejection of the EU constitution by the French and Dutch electorates in their 2005 national referendums was blamed in part on the widespread popular opposition to the neo-liberalism which many voters feared was contained inside the constitution's complex provisions. It is this broader perspective, posed by the dual challenges of globalisation and the EU social policy framework, which needs to be recognised if we are to understand Blair's second-term attitude to employment relations and labour markets.

Many British trade union critics of New Labour used to complain that during his second term as prime minister, Blair had simply failed to create a coherent grand narrative for the political economy and establish an overall strategy for employment relations and labour markets with which they could amicably work and cooperate. They liked to contrast what they believed to be his government's barrenness of achievement in those policy areas with the substantial advances made on a social market agenda that they experienced between May 1997 and May 2001. It is true that during his first four years the Prime Minister presided over the introduction of a national statutory minimum wage to abolish poverty pay as well as comprehensive legislation to provide for statutory trade union recognition from employers and to strengthen a number of individual worker rights such as holiday entitlement and parental and maternity leave. In addition, Blair agreed to end the UK's opt-out from the social chapter of the 1991 European Union Maastricht treaty achieved by his Conservative predecessor John Major. As a result, a flow of Brussels-inspired social regulations poured into Britain on such contentious issues as legal limits on the length of the working week, measures to ensure greater work/life balance for all workers, legal protections for agency and part-time workers and stronger health and safety regulations.

The stark contrast drawn by the trade unions between a productive first term of employment relations reform and a second term of limited progress and retreat was not entirely fair. It was simply not true to argue that very little of real substance was provided by the government for workers and trade unions during Blair's second term. The Labour Party published a general election manifesto for 'people at work' in May 2005 that was designed to complement its business document. This contained a detailed account of what had been achieved between May 2001 and May 2005 in the betterment of the workplace. 'Labour has always believed in equality, dignity and opportunity for all. We have worked hard to deliver on those values through more jobs and better rewards and conditions at work', the Prime Minister explained in his personal preface to the document.[2] The so-called Warwick Accords, negotiated between the Labour Party and the trade union leadership in September 2004, also provided a detailed account of what the Blair government had actually carried through during its second term that was of a positive benefit to workers in general whether they were members of a trade union or not.

But despite evidence of such tangible achievements there did appear to be an apparent drift and incoherence in much of the government's policy on labour markets and employment relations. Both Blair and Brown found it increasingly hard to argue and defend their overwhelmingly pro-business position from growing trade union criticism, especially when they both began to challenge the need for any further social regulation from Brussels more forcefully. But they were successful in May 2005 in preventing the ending of the UK's opt-out from the working time directive on the 48-hour working week. Their defence of Britain's long hours work culture may have incensed the trade unions, which pointed to the health and safety consequences for many employees who worked more than 48 hours a week, but it was in line with the pressures coming from companies that feared that they would lose their competitive edge if they were unable to ensure that their workers did not work longer hours than those employed in their competitor firms. Blair was also keen to press for a legally enforceable EU services directive that would have opened up the EU to cheaper and less protected professional labour from low-cost central and eastern European countries and thereby undermine existing standards of worker treatment in the west.

[2] 'People at work. Forward not back', Labour Party, 1 May 2005.

It was also true that Blair was keen to adopt a restrictive attitude towards any further steps to reform employment relations in such a way that it would strengthen the bargaining position of the trade unions. At best, he expressed support for only a consolidation and minor modification of what had been achieved during his first term under the government's 'fairness at work' agenda. A review of the 1999 Employment Relations Act brought only limited modifications to the existing regulations, despite demands from the TUC for sweeping improvements. Blair resisted trade union pressure to extend legally enforceable worker rights to those who were employed in firms with 20 or fewer workers, mainly as a result of successful business lobbying from the Federation of Small Businesses. A government reform of alternative dispute resolution procedures was more balanced in its intentions but substantial cuts in the budgets of surviving tripartite public institutions in the employment field such as the Advisory, Conciliation and Arbitration Service and the Health and Safety at Work Commission did not suggest that Blair was in any mood to address seriously vexatious issues of workplace justice and equity.

Certainly the Prime Minister failed to focus positively on any further steps towards the creation of a genuinely social market economy in Britain in line with the various European models that might receive the acclaim and support of the trade unions. But then his whole approach to capital and labour during his second term grew much more ambitious as it moved in a direction totally different from what many of his trade union allies might have hoped for before 2001. The Prime Minister had never regarded his first-term changes to improve workplace fairness as a kind of belated reward or compensation for Britain's trade unions after more than 18 years of remorseless decline in their power and influence in the political economy. Indeed, most of the important reforms contained in the 'fairness at work' agenda and carried out during Blair's first four years were first promised by his two Labour predecessors Neil Kinnock and John Smith, and they did not reflect his own modernising intentions. Indeed, he always maintained that the industrial relations reforms introduced during his first term as prime minister needed to be seen as an important means to improve the performance and profitability of companies and they were to be regarded as only a limited part of a much wider programme that was designed to enhance competitiveness by creating a modern framework of rights and responsibilities within which British business could thrive. After May 2001 he continued to warn the trade unions that he would not restore for them the kind of special and bilateral relationships they used to enjoy under previous Labour governments in the post-war years. He believed he had provided them with some important, useful but limited opportunities to grow again by removing the more excessive anti-union regulations that he had inherited from the Conservatives. But he refused to contemplate any wholesale repeal of the industrial relations laws introduced by Margaret Thatcher's governments that were designed to cut back trade union power. Those changes were all to remain firmly in place despite trade union opposition. A second term in office for Blair still meant that there would be no legislation passed for a return to the lost world of trade union-imposed closed shops, secondary picketing in strikes or the toleration of solidarity actions by workers. More importantly, it became increasingly apparent between 2001 and 2005 that under Blair's public policy agenda for labour market reform and employment relations the trade unions were to play only a small and rather marginal role, mainly as voluntary learning organisations designed to help improve corporate performance and assist in the eradication of obsolete labour practices through the formation of high performance workplaces.

The unrealistic demands of the Fire Brigade Union in 2003–4, for example, to protect and advance their pay by as much as 45% without changing the system under which their members worked failed to impress the government. The resulting national firefighters' strike was met with firm ministerial resistance. The lesson from what turned into an embarrassing debacle for the union was clear enough – workers in the public services could not expect to enjoy real improvements in their pay and conditions unless at the same time they agreed to cooperate in the modernisation of their organisation of work carried out in measurable ways. Indeed, the Prime Minister took a robust view of public service workers and their trade unions in general during his second term. Between 2001 and 2005, there was what the independent research body Incomes Data Services called 'the largest overhaul of pay and bargaining arrangements in the public sector for a generation'.[3] Under the banner 'Agenda for Change', sweeping modernisation of the organisation of work was introduced into the health service, education and local as well as central government employment. The reforms were carried out, however, not according to any central plan dictated from Number 10 or the Treasury. On the contrary, the reforms were negotiated between reward managers and their trade union counterparts. Their common features involved moves towards single

---

[3] Incomes Data Services, 'Pay in the Public Services 2005', p. 9.

status terms and conditions for manual and non-manual workers, new national pay spines with local flexibility to meet labour market conditions, commitments to gender equality around equal pay, harmonising of working hours and moves to end poverty pay.

Trade unions may have felt themselves to be marginalised, treated as embarrassing elderly relatives at a family reunion (as TUC general secretary John Monks once famously described them), but Blair and his Chancellor were unconcerned by such a perception. Instead they were determined to ensure that Britain was transformed into a new business model that would become the envy of its competitors around the world. This meant ensuring that the needs of business and not those of trade unions or employees should become the main priority of employment relations and labour market policies.

It is true that on some occasions Blair was compelled to retreat in his personal resistance to what he saw as intrusive and anti-business social regulation emanating from the European Commission. After a prolonged period of stubborn opposition in strategic alliance with Europe-wide employer organisations, the Prime Minister found himself isolated among EU heads of government and he was forced to accept the introduction of a modestly worded and legally enforceable EU directive that required private firms employing 50 or more workers to consult and inform their employees on issues of strategic importance to the company. The measure was to be introduced in stages which were spread over three years beginning in April 2005. But as Sir Digby Jones, director general of the CBI, declared, 'These new rules will be irrelevant to most companies because they already have systems that employees are happy with for discussing developments with them.'[4] Such an insouciant attitude from Sir Digby seemed rather surprising after his organisation's prolonged and passionate rearguard opposition to what was always regarded as a modest measure by continental European standards.

However, the CBI found they had little genuine to grumble about in Blair's general approach to the business community, even if the country's leading employer organisation continued to complain loudly and constantly about red tape smothering enterprise and the onerous nature of 'stealth' taxes being imposed on the wealth creation efforts of its member companies. The continuing failure of Blair in his second term to honour his 1997 general election manifesto commitment to introduce

[4] Confederation of British Industry, press release, April 2005.

legislation to deal with corporate manslaughter did not suggest that the Prime Minister intended to give urgent priority to action making private companies liable collectively for damages in corporate disasters such as the Potters Bar and Ladbroke Grove rail crashes. It is true that there was the belated promise of legislation on corporate manslaughter contained in the May 2005 Queen's Speech for the first session of the new Parliament, but few expected that this would cause any real problems for most companies in their risk audit assessments. The call from Blair and his Chancellor for the introduction of a 'lighter' touch in the inspection of businesses to prevent breaches of existing health and safety laws did not suggest that the Prime Minister was intent on making life more difficult for companies in the handling of their labour needs in the way they wanted. Indeed, fatality and accident figures for 2003–4 in Britain's workplaces indicated that the government's own targets to reduce their incidence under an ambitious ten-year plan were not being met. Nor did Blair make any public criticism of the evidence of widespread corporate excess, seen in the quite extraordinary post-2001 upsurge in the general level of executive board remuneration in bonuses and share options. The rewards of business even went to senior managers whose companies were either under-performing or failing to make a profit. It is true that the Department of Trade and Industry decided in May 2005 to establish a full-scale public inquiry into the circumstances surrounding the rescue and then the ultimate collapse of the MG-Rover company in April 2005 with the closure of its Longbridge car plant in Birmingham. But perhaps this was unavoidable. The stark contrast between the brutal treatment of the Longbridge workers who lost their jobs as a result of the liquidation with minimum compensation and derisory pensions, if none at all, for their years of service, and the enormous personal gains accumulated by John Towers and his executive associates in the so-called Phoenix project who had presided over the company's demise was hardly a positive example of the wonders of a British Model of business behaviour. The Prime Minister also continued to reward many rich business people with peerages, titles and public service contracts for their companies. Nor was Blair's enthusiasm for the rich and powerful confined to entrepreneurs who were ethically responsible in their business activities. The extraordinary promotion of the tycoon Lord Drayson, for example, to Defence Procurement Minister in the post-election government reshuffle in 2005 was indicative of the Prime Minister's uncritical admiration for men of wealth, especially those who donate substantial sums of money to the Labour Party.

Britain's business community may have complained continually about government policies, but Blair never lost the opportunity to flatter private entrepreneurs as well as listen carefully and respond sensitively to their demands. Just after his 2005 general election victory the Prime Minister was prepared to criticise the Sarbanes-Oxley Act in the United States, which even President George Bush was forced reluctantly to accept. Blair believed the measure had been too draconian in its attempts to deal with corporate fraud, although the Act had been designed specifically to tighten up financial regulations in order to try and prevent further scandals like those at Enron and WorldCom companies which had done so much to discredit US free market capitalism. Blair even criticised the UK's Financial Services Authority for its alleged zeal in pursuing corporate misconduct and thereby allegedly making it difficult for law-abiding companies to operate freely.

By contrast, trade union leaders during New Labour's second term and beyond felt themselves to be increasingly unloved and out in the cold. Blair liked to lecture them on their failings and patronise them on his occasional visits to the Trades Union Congress. He was particularly irritated by the public service unions whom he believed were stubbornly resisting his plans to privatise central and local government activities because they wanted to defend public-sector inefficiencies and their restrictive labour practices. Blair displayed an increasing lack of concern for professional standards and the whole concept of the public interest. His avowed purpose was to achieve value for taxpayer's money in the public services by means of a regime of individual performance targets, assessments, audits and benchmarking. The belated modernisation of hospitals and schools was to be mainly achieved by forcing public-sector workers into an acceptance of the cultural values of the private market. The operations of an increasing range of public services were to be subcontracted to profit-making business organisations through long-term legally enforceable agreements under private finance initiatives (PFIs). Many of those private companies were to be heavily subsidised or underwritten by the government in their spending programmes. In addition, Blair decided to advance the private-sector culture into areas of the public sector that Margaret Thatcher and John Major had always feared to go because of expected Labour Party opposition. The transfer of the country's air traffic control system from state to private ownership was followed by the expensive break-up of structure of the London Underground and the selling-off of its component parts to a variety of operating companies at enormous cost to the taxpayer but with a bonanza of rewards for auditors, lawyers and construction firms. The latter plan was partly based on the failed model of the privatised national railway network which had been carried out by the Major government. Blair argued that it would have been too expensive to return the entire railway system to state ownership. Instead an estimated annual sum of £16 billion of taxpayers' money was to be poured into the coffers of the private railway operators and contractors in the name of modernisation.

Trade unions may have continued to provide the party with most of its funds for election purposes, but their influence on the government's policies seemed extremely limited, even if they believed they had won the Prime Minister's approval in the 2004 Warwick Accords to prevent the establishment of a two-tier workforce in the public services, whereby those who were employed on private-sector contracts received lower pay and worst employment benefits and conditions than their counterparts who remained in the public sector.

Blair continued to urge his trade union audiences to embrace what he called partnership unionism, a form of social collaboration between employers and trade unions that was centred primarily on the improvement of corporate performance and the creation of high performance workplaces. His government provided some limited funding to encourage such arrangements, but a growing number of trade union leaders and their members after 2002 showed little enthusiasm for their introduction. By 2005 the word 'partnership' was gradually being erased from the lexicon of the trade unions as many of them turned away with relief from such cooperative practices and started to give a higher priority to more aggressive organising membership drives against employers.

What was now becoming most apparent in the New Labour business approach was the virtual absence not only of trade unions and their leaders but also of workers from any recognisable form of social dialogue. Only the quality of workers' education and skills seemed to retain the focus of close ministerial attention. Blair and his Chancellor shared no apparent common interest in furthering a comprehensive workplace reform agenda that would have strengthened employment rights and social justice. Britain continued to uphold some of the most restrictive labour laws in the Western democratic world, some of which were in continued and clear breach of fundamental International Labour Organisation conventions that previous British governments had signed. Blair did not favour giving any substantial extension to the responsibilities and power of the trade unions in a partnership approach between labour and capital at the national level in the management of the British economy. Every other government in western Europe, except for Britain – and irrespective of their economic performance and the political complexion of their government – continued to provide such a crucial role for trade unions through forms of national policy coordination. None of this was to be found in the newly conceived British Business Model.

Nor was there any suggestion that the New Labour approach was likely to move in a more sympathetic pro-trade union direction in the immediate future. On the contrary, during Blair's second term as prime minister his approach to labour markets and employment relation reform became much more visible than it had been between May 1997 and May 2001. He made it clear that he was now intent on the further accommodation of the interests of the business community, even if this was done at the expense of the trade unions. The Confederation of British Industry, the Federation of Small Businesses and the Engineering Employers' Federation seemed to have become more successful lobbyists of the government in Number 10 and at the Department of Trade and Industry than the Trades Union Congress and its new generation of more left-wing trade union leaders who were elected to power after the summer of 2002. Neither Tony Woodley of the Transport and General Workers' Union and Derek Simpson of Amicus, who defeated the Prime Minister's favourite trade unionist Sir Ken Jackson in a surprise result, seemed to secure attention or respect from the Prime Minister. The so-called 'awkward squad' of trade union leaders embarrassed Blair at the 2003 Labour Party Conference when they coordinated their block votes to defeat government policy. But the Prime Minister ignored those adverse decisions and the trade unions were powerless to do anything about it. If Blair has his way – despite the large cut in the size of his overall parliamentary majority at the May 2005 general election – the pace of radical change in business and labour market policy is likely to grow faster and not slow down during his final third term in Number 10. Nor does it seem likely that his probable prime ministerial successor Gordon Brown would make any substantial difference to the government's central strategy of trying to make Britain one of the most competitive and profitable free market economies in the world through the introduction of more rigorously neo-liberal measures that are hostile to employment rights and social justice.

Indeed both men were at one in their clear-sighted determination to modernise Britain's world of paid work in the name of enterprise, profitability, productivity and innovation. Of course, previous Labour governments – from those of Ramsay MacDonald and Clement Attlee to

Harold Wilson and Jim Callaghan – had never been ideologically hostile to the existence of markets and private enterprise, even if they had been eager to plan the country's industrial progress from Whitehall and ready to use the power of the central state to subsidise or nationalise specific private industries in what they perceived to be the national interest. But what Blair had done was to abandon any genuine attempt to establish a new kind of social contract or even a national understanding with the trade unions in the management of the political economy. For their part, the new generation of trade union leaders also appeared to have abandoned the social partnership approach that John Monks, the TUC's general secretary, had pursued with admittedly modest and limited results during the late 1990s until his departure to Brussels in 2003 as a disappointed and frustrated man in order to lead the European Trade Union Confederation. Back in May 1997, at the time of New Labour's first general election victory, most trade union leaders had believed or hoped that a New Labour government would establish a strong and fruitful alliance with them that was based on the values and policies of social citizenship that lay at the heart of the European social market models. It is arguable whether their organisations were really structured or had developed internally in such a way that would have led to their successful commitment to such a project. In the event, they were not given much opportunity to shoulder the burdens of social partnership in the European way. On the contrary, the newly acclaimed British Model was to provide only a limited role for the trade unions, even if the reform of labour markets was to be an important and integral part of the model's basic components.

Britain's labour market – an audit of success and failure

Blair used to argue that one of the greatest and undisputed successes of his government between 1997 and 2005 came in the formation and implementation of an active labour market policy that was based predominantly on the ethical principles of individual responsibility, of rights combined with obligations to work for the unemployed. The steady and inexorable reduction in the level of open and registered unemployment, coupled with an impressive net growth of paid jobs in the British economy were certainly apparent in both the first and second terms of his New Labour administration. The aggregate national labour market statistics appeared to speak for themselves. The percentage of the working age population in paid employment increased from 70.8% in 1997 to 74.7% by the end of 2004, while the number of people in paid work climbed from 25.7 million to 27.4 million over the same period to a record total. The

Prime Minister used to point to such overall aggregate figures as clear evidence of his government's achievement in delivering employment and unemployment rates which were the envy of other European countries and not seen in Britain for more than thirty years. Certainly the general trend in overall job performance during his second term paralleled that of his first four years in government. The substantial reduction in the level of youth unemployment looked particularly impressive. Ever since the mid-1970s successive Labour and Conservative governments had wrestled with the problem of how to respond in a positive way to the lack of paid employment for 16- to 23-year-olds in the labour market. Now it looked as though that particular difficulty had been resolved. Moreover, the Blair years also witnessed a decided reduction in the number of adults suffering long-term unemployment – being without paid work for 12 months.

The New Deal or £3.6 billion welfare-to-work programme, first introduced in April 1998, was highlighted by the Prime Minister as the main explanation for his government's success in reducing unemployment and raising the country's employment rate. Over the first seven years of its existence the New Deal programme was refined and expanded to deal with a range of different and vulnerable social groups who needed assistance in their return to the world of paid work. The 18- to 24-year-old long-term jobless were given the initial priority for governmental action. But others followed – the older long-term unemployed, lone parents, the disabled, the self-employed. The government claimed that the New Deal had assisted around 1.2 million people into paid work between 1998 and 2004, including 535,000 young people and 200,000 unemployed adults. But, as Simon Briscoe has argued, 'very little information is available about the value of the schemes, in other words how people's lives have been changed by them'.[5]

In fact, the overall figure given of those who benefited from involvement in the New Deal was seriously misleading. Up to the end of 2004 it has been estimated that only 130,000 people actually moved directly from participation in the government's programme into unsubsidised employment at the end of the process which provided most participants with four options – training, work on an environmental project, subsidised employment or voluntary work.

Of course, we need to separate New Labour political hyperbole from the labour market facts in any overall assessment of Britain's employment

[5] Simon Briscoe, *Britain in Numbers: The Essential Statistics* (London: Politico's, 2005), p. 134.

achievements as a consequence of the Blair effect. As Simon Briscoe pointed out; 'The employment rate in Britain in 2005 was not exceptional – there were several countries with a higher rate – and neither was the rise in recent years.'[6] All the Nordic nations, for example, enjoyed far better employment performances after 1997, even though they continued to maintain both generous welfare state benefits for those who were without paid work alongside active labour market policies for getting the unemployed back into paid work. Such an achievement was coupled in the Nordic countries with high rates of taxation and public spending in open market economies. The social democratic projects of northern democratic Europe were still capable of combining economic prosperity and social justice with significant success in a globalising world of more free trade and mobile capital. Blair's British Business Model was apparently by no means the only one that was capable of providing an alternative. Moreover, the country's labour market during New Labour's second term was by no means as dynamic or healthy as the Prime Minister liked to assert.

Considerable debate continued on the exact number of people in Britain of adult age who were either actually seeking paid work or had simply disappeared from the formal economy. It was, for example, estimated that 2.7 million people of working age in 2004 were still claiming incapacity benefit or severe disability allowance at a total annual cost of more than £19 billion to the Treasury. The problem of incapacity was especially apparent among prime-age and older male workers.

The rise of this phenomenon had not only occurred during periods of recession such as the early 1980s and early 1990s; it also continued to grow during times of employment growth, including the years that covered Blair's governments. The main reason for this growth appeared to be the dramatic weakening in demand for unskilled labour, a trend that was first recognised as long ago as the mid-1970s.

But an even more serious statistic that modified the labour market record was the proportion of people of adult working age in Britain who remained economically inactive. In 2004 this numbered as many as 7.8 million and made up 21% of the country's entire paid labour force. It is also necessary to examine where most of the new jobs were coming from under the Blair effect. The ever-expanding public services sector turned out to be one of the main sources for the net increase in the amount of paid employment, with a growth of more than half a million between

---

[6] Ibid., p. 124.

1998 and 2005. A net increase also occurred in construction over the same period. By contrast nearly a million net jobs were lost in the private manufacturing sector during the first eight years of Blair's premiership. In 1997, 4.1 million were employed in manufacturing; by 2005 that figure had fallen to 3.2 million, despite sporadic ministerial declarations of support for manufacturing. Nor was it clear that growth in the private sector of the economy was due to any dramatic upsurge in the expansion of well paid, high quality full-time employment in the labour market. Much of the success story in the private sector of the British labour market came from the net growth in part-time and temporary employment opportunities but often in relatively lower-paid sectors of the economy such as retail, hotels and catering.

Moreover, Britain continued to lag behind the Nordic countries in its experience of growing employment opportunities in information and communications technology. The country's much acclaimed labour market flexibility tended to make its greatest impact at the lower end of the private services sector, where trade union membership was virtually non-existent and collective bargaining almost unknown. The newly discovered British Business Model seemed at its best in generating poorly paid work with an inbuilt culture of longer working hours rather than in providing decent jobs with generous pay and civilised benefits and employment security in the more advanced sectors of the modern economy. In 2002 the UK – among western European countries – had the highest proportion of employees working 45 hours a week or more. As many as 56% of Britain's male workers did so, compared with only 17% in Sweden.

The most significant trend in the labour market under Blair was a continuing polarisation in the earnings level of workers, with a relative decline in the position of those who found themselves on the lowest wage rates. The LSE's independent Centre for Economic Performance concluded in 2005: 'Rather than reducing labour market inequality per se, the national minimum wage seems to have had an effect in preventing wage inequality rising further since 1999. This may be a signal that the wage inequality between middle and low earners may be rising again after the pause in the 1990s.'[7]

The resulting inequalities were also found to be the most acute in the country's more economically depressed areas – in its inner cities, the northern region of England, Scotland and Wales despite the undoubted

---

[7] Centre for Economic Performance, 'Election analysis 2005: the National Minimum Wage' (London: LSE Centre for Economic Performance, 2005).

overall rise in material prosperity for most people who remained secure in paid and rewarding work. It was not just the intractability of low pay and poor working conditions – despite the undoubted, if limited, impact of the national minimum wage – that characterised the new world of paid work under Blair. Low social status, lack of respect and limited self-worth were also seen as equally important consequences of what was happening to paid employment.

An employee opinion survey carried out in 2000 for the Economic and Social Research Council's future of work programme suggested that class still retained its salience in the workplace as a cause of social division, especially when it was reinforced by the persistent gender inequalities apparent in pay and other benefits.[8] Women employed in low skilled manual jobs, especially if they were in part-time work, suffered in particular in the new labour market from the growing pressures of rising work intensity as they sought to balance their work and family responsibilities. In July 2004 the Prime Minister announced the formation of a Women and Work Commission, chaired by the former trade union official Margaret Prosser, to examine the tenacity of the gender pay gap and the persistent problems that continued to challenge women who are in paid employment. It is due to report late in 2005. Despite the introduction of the limited but minimalist rights at work since 1997 the British labour market seemed in important respects to have returned to the divisions and complexities, the degradations and uncertainties that had characterised the Victorian labour market of early industrial capitalism.

Some continental European commentators may have been impressed by what they regarded as the undoubted success of the British Business Model in its apparent ability to create more jobs, even if many of them were unskilled and casual.

But the country continued to suffer from longer term labour market difficulties that had been familiar to observers more than thirty years previously. The marked decline in trade union power and union membership density since 1979, the end of Britain's relative strike proneness and the absence of any return to the ravages of wage push inflation that continued under Blair's premiership had done little to improve underlying structural and supply side problems. The most obvious trouble remained with Britain's relatively low levels of labour productivity, however, measured by comparison with other advanced economies. The National Institute for Economic and Social Research concluded in its April 2005 assessment

---

[8] Robert Taylor, 'Britain's world of work: myths and reality', Future of Work Programme (London: Economic and Social Research Council, 2003).

of the economy that 'no obvious improvement' in productivity had taken place since Mr Blair had come to power.[9] It is true that the UK was no longer falling still further behind France and other European countries in the way it had done for the first forty years after the end of the Second World War. But the NIESR also noted that 'we are not obviously closing the gap with France and we may have stopped closing the gap with the United States'.

Even a Treasury discussion paper, published in December 2004, admitted that Britain continued to suffer as it had done in the past from a 'poorer skills mix than many other countries'.[10] It found that the country lagged behind many of its international competitors with a greater proportion of Britain's adult workers suffering from either low or no recognised skills. The primary cause for the intractable nature of the country's poor productivity performance seemed to lie in the depressingly serious lack of a large enough supply of effectively trained workers who could satisfy the needs of a modernising economy. In 2004 it was estimated that as many as a third of people of working age were still without any recognised skills at all or had at best low skills. This was found to be a much higher proportion than in competitor countries such as France and Germany, whose labour market performances were often criticised by the Prime Minister. Moreover, Britain continued to lag far behind most of the Western industrialised world in the number and proportion of its workers who also lacked any intermediate educational qualifications that were required in the more demanding world of paid employment. It is true that continuous official efforts were made under Blair's exhortation to rectify those depressingly familiar problems. His predecessors had also made sporadic efforts to remedy the situation. In the 1960s industrial training boards were established to encourage industries to increase their training provision for their employees, while in the 1970s the training of the young unemployed became a high priority for government. But the introduction under the Blair government of the Learning and Skills Councils and the formation of Regional Development Agencies had made surprisingly little noticeable initial impact by 2005 on an improvement in the quantity and quality of the country's supply of skilled labour. An official report in 2004 warned of the dire consequences of such persistent labour market failure when it asserted: 'Unless the UK has the requisite stock of skills, including entrepreneurship, innovation, managerial effectiveness and

[9] National Institute for Economic and Social Research, *National Institute Economic Review*, no. 192 (London: National Institute for Economic and Social Research, April 2005).

[10] HM Treasury, 'Skills in the global economy', Treasury Discussion paper, December 2004, p. 3.

technical capability then the goal of achieving a high value-added high productivity economy will remain elusive . . . The extent of the skills gap far exceeds recruitment problems.'[11] To some extent Mr Blair sought to close that gap through an officially encouraged strategy of managed migration from less developed countries. But the influx of skilled and highly qualified people from central and eastern Europe or the developing world could hardly be regarded as a sign of the success of the British Business Model. By any comparative international standards the skills level in Britain remained low and far behind that of the country's main competitors.

'The British skills distribution is becoming bipolar, with large numbers obtaining high levels of qualifications and skills equivalent to graduate level but also a long tail of low achievers who continue to exist with no or only low level qualifications to their name', concluded the LSE's Centre for Economic Performance in 2003.[12] The government's modern apprenticeship scheme aimed to help young workers to combine vocational learning with skills experience but although it was on target in 2005, its overall effect seemed unlikely to provide a solution to the poor quality of the country's skills base. Blair announced in early 2005 that plans were under way to try and remedy the problem during his third term. A national training programme for employers was to be launched in 2007 by the government, with subsidies to encourage firms to train their existing employees to higher skill levels. But the problem of poor skills could not be treated as of marginal importance in the overall labour market picture. The long tails of poorly motivated and under-qualified workers as well as inefficient and poorly managed private companies continued to put a serious question mark over Britain's ability to ensure that it could establish and maintain a future competitive advantage in globalising markets. As the government's 2004 skills audit declared, 'Skill strategies go hand in hand with policies and strategies to increase levels of capital investment within companies, develop new products and processes and capture new markets.'[13]

Britain's persistently poor productivity performance was also blamed on the inability of firms to innovate through a systematic increase in their research and development programmes in new products and services.

[11] The Skills Audit 2004.
[12] Richard Dickens, Paul Gregg and Jonathan Wadsworth (eds.), *The Labour Market Under New Labour: The State of Working Britain* (Basingstoke: Palgrave Macmillan, 2003), p. 249.
[13] The Skills Audit 2004.

'In recent years the aggregate amount of spending on research and development in the UK has lagged behind that of our international competitors', complained a 2004 study from the Office for National Statistics. It spoke of a 'comparative lack of entrepreneurial spirit' among the country's employers compared with those of the United States and the poor quality of management, with many lacking basic qualifications.[14] The study pointed out that in 1999 the United States invested 25% more capital per hour worked compared with the UK while France invested 60% more and Germany 32% more. In 2004 the pre-budget statement revealed that British business invested 1.24% of gross domestic product in research and development, but this compared with the more impressive 1.37% in France, 1.73% in Germany and 1.87% in the United States. The government admitted that the country was 'less effective at realising the commercial potential of research and business expenditure, and its aggregate level was currently below the OECD average'.[15]

A further profound strategic weakness in the supposed British Business Model lay in the inequalities and insecurities that continued to be embedded in the country's labour market. Overwhelming opinion survey evidence failed to suggest that employees felt more at ease in their paid work. Blair may have fought successfully to uphold the long working hours culture in his determined resistance to ending the UK's opt-out from the European Union's working time directive, but it was hard to suggest that such a move reflected the benefits of a flexible labour market. The mainly male manual workers who were compelled to work more than 48 hours a week as a condition for their employment revealed the poor utilisation of labour and the lack of efficiency in the organisation of work. In short, the labour market reforms associated with the Blair effect were of mixed success. It is true that Britain after 1997 did achieve a better overall employment performance than its main west European competitors in the number of jobs created. Moreover, for those in work living standards continued to rise. But the insecurities of the world of paid work, coupled with a persistently poor record on training and skills, productivity and innovation, did not suggest that the British Business Model was as effective as Blair liked to claim. Nor was it apparent that the labour market had grown more socially equitable, despite the national minimum wage, more child support schemes and tax credit measures to subsidise the low

---

[14] Craig Lindsay, 'Labour productivity', in *Labour Market Trends* (Office for National Statistics, November 2004).
[15] HM Treasury, 'Pre-budget report' (London: HM Treasury 2004), p. 57.

paid. At best, it could be argued that the Blair effect had been to slow down or halt the existence of widening overall workplace inequalities. However, the British Business Model could not yet be seen as a sensible and credible way of reconciling economic efficiency and social justice in a modern market economy undergoing profound structural change.

The Blair effect and the British Business Model – an assessment

Blair and Brown appeared to preside over an extraordinary transformation in the health of Britain's political economy after a long period of almost continuous decline. But it is highly questionable just how much of the country's better business performance was owed directly to the Blair effect. To a great extent, the Prime Minister was the fortunate beneficiary of the positive economic and labour market reforms that were first introduced under his Conservative predecessors Margaret Thatcher and John Major. The promotion of an enterprise culture based on free markets and a strong state that was at the heart of the New Labour project was first argued thirty years ago by Sir Keith Joseph and others within the intellectual circles of neo-liberal think tanks such as the Institute for Economic Affairs and the Centre for Policy Studies. For the most part, Blair carried on from where previous Conservative governments had left off. It was not to be Year Zero in 1997. Much more continuity than change was apparent in the development of the British labour market than the Prime Minister's admirers were prepared to admit.

It is true that the 'welfare to work' New Deal programme was advanced successfully after 1998 to deal in a systematic way with troubled and excluded social groups such as lone mothers and long-term youth jobless on the margins of the labour market. But the origins of that achievement owed much to the arrival of a more activist state approach to the provision of job placement and benefits for the unemployed that had firt begun in the middle 1980s under Lord David Young when he was employment secretary. The necessary modernisation of the employment service with the introduction of the Job Seekers Allowance and the 'actively seeking work' principle as well as the integration of social benefit provision with the function of the job centres occurred in 1996 as a result of an information technology revolution that speeded up the process of work placement. The Blair/Brown vision of 'employment opportunity for all' may have been more ambitious and comprehensive in its intent and scope, but it was building on what had already been established by Conservative governments.

Moreover, New Labour's labour market reforms came into force during a period of net employment growth in the economy, a trend which had first begun early in 1993 in the aftermath of Britain's precipitous departure from the European exchange rate mechanism in the previous autumn. However, an overall assessment by the Institute for Economic and Social Research concluded in April 2005 that 'employment activity rates still remain slightly below those of the boom of the late 1980s', although it also agreed that activity appears to be sustainable while in the late 1980s it was associated with rapidly accelerating inflation.'[16]

What is undoubtedly true, however, is that Blair's effect on labour market reform and employment relations was to guarantee the long-term success of Margaret Thatcher's remarkable achievement in destroying the so-called post-war social settlement and replacing it with a more vibrant culture of business success.

The Prime Minister not only shared her conviction that the trade unions were an important part of the problem and not the solution for the country's relative decline, but also believed that Britain needed a cultural revolution in its attitudes to work and business. Both he and his Chancellor were impressed by the employment success of the American Model during the 1990s, and they were convinced that the social market regulatory regimes of western Europe were incapable of meeting the rising challenges posed by globalisation and technological change. But it was only during his second term at Number 10 that Blair felt able to make his intentions much more explicit. Many on the left liked to argue that Britain needed to become much more like mainland Europe and less like the United States in its approach to labour market and employment relations issues. They spoke and wrote that in the battle of the models of competing capitalisms the country needed to learn and act in response to what countries like France and Germany had achieved in employment growth and workplace equality since the end of the Second World War. The flow of social regulation from Brussels into Britain after 1997 was based on a recognised concept of citizenship derived from the twin ideological influences of social Catholicism and social democracy. But increasingly during his second term Blair and Brown turned against the implications of such a trend for what they came to regard as a successful competing British Business Model. In the third term, Blair and Brown were both determined to export the practices of neo-liberal economic reform that owed so much to the

[16] National Institute for Economic and Social Research, *National Institute Economic Review*, no. 192.

intellectual influence of Thatcherism to a troubled and divided European mainland.

The Prime Minister liked to emphasise that flexibility was the key to the British Business Model's coherent and comprehensive approach to labour markets and employment relations, held together by the slogan – 'employment opportunity for all'. In the record on employment growth and job placement, Britain did become a source of interest in the early 2000s from other advanced countries who were finding it difficult to reform their stagnant labour markets and sclerotic social institutions. From being the sick man of Europe in the 1970s, the country was now seen by some as a model of how modern economies could survive and grow again in a globalising world. But as Blair recognised, most of Britain's underlying labour market problems – poor productivity, the lack of a big enough skilled labour force, insufficient private investment in research and development and innovation – persisted. Unless they could be resolved quickly the country could not expect to prosper in the future world of paid work. The Prime Minister, however, seemed convinced that the way forward did not lie through policy coordination with trade unions or in forms of social partnership with labour and capital. Neither he nor his Chancellor believed that an inclusive strategy of renewal through collaborative and strong institutions at national, local or enterprise level would ensure that Britain could achieve those elusive goals of economic efficiency and social justice. The real and impressive record of the Nordic countries in employment creation and economic reform – particularly Sweden and Denmark – failed to capture Blair's attention or his imagination. He did not share a social democratic view of what was possible. His increasing hostility to the very concept of a social Europe, however, was a surprisingly dogmatic attitude to take and it was based on personal prejudice and instinct, not on an array of empirical evidence. The British Business Model that he identified with increasingly seemed much stronger on spin and hyperbole than on fact. It looked increasingly more like a delusion, a mirage and not a satisfactory answer to the country's underlying labour market and employment relations problems. Margaret Thatcher resolved the trade union 'question' effectively during the 1980s. Blair was to consolidate that particular achievement. But whether he had done sufficient to transform the world of paid work in Britain into a more efficient and equitable entity was to remain highly debatable.

Transport

STEPHEN GLAISTER

Transport was not one of the successes of Tony Blair's first two governments. After the radical reforms by privatisation and deregulation of most of the transport industry under the Tory regimes, the ideology had seemed straightforward to many supporters: to 'integrate', to replace new road building with rejuvenated public transport and to re-establish the role of the public sector.

But Blair initially underestimated the complexities, and other policy areas took his attention. He delegated transport to people who did not deliver. As a result, until 2000 transport policy as implemented amounted to a continuation of the Conservatives' policies. In so far as there was any positive control, it remained with the Chancellor and the Treasury, who continued to determine crucial tax rates, rigidly constrained funds for transport operating and capital purposes, fixed the rules for local authority borrowing, promoted private provision and private finance, laid down criteria for value for money and fought for what they saw as essential national transport policy.

Blair was drawn into transport when things went badly wrong: the fuel price protests in 2000, the unresolved dispute over the London Underground public private partnership (PPP) during the 2001 general election, the collapse of Railtrack in 2001, the resignation of Stephen Byers in 2002, and when his wife was caught in a traffic jam. By the end of his second term the Prime Minister had created several personal sources of transport advice. But the Department for Transport already had an external advisory body and the Chancellor had started to set up yet another advisory body of his own. Coherence and delivery remains elusive.

The importance of transport to the electorate

It took the whole of the first Blair parliament for Labour to respond to the fact that the transport interests of the electorate had been transformed over the previous three decades. In 1962 households allocated about 9% of their expenditure to transport and 33% to food, alcohol and tobacco. By 2003 food, alcohol and tobacco accounted for only 13% while transport was the biggest single item, accounting for 14% of the average £406 per week spending.[1]

Of this 14%, some 12% was on private transport: car ownership is now common. This has been the result of increasing real incomes, demographic changes and generally falling real costs of motoring, and these trends will continue. Meanwhile public transport has become much less relevant with the exception of some special markets such as the commute into London. Nationally, the car now accounts for 85% of all passenger kilometres (excluding walking). Half the population uses a train less than once a year,[2] bus accounts for 6% and rail accounts for 5% (much less outside the London area). Rail now carries 8% of freight tonne-kilometres.

In spite of the attention the national press gives to public transport, opinion surveys consistently show it to be surprisingly unimportant to voters. A MORI/*Evening Standard* poll ahead of the 2005 general election[3] found that healthcare (67%) and education (61%) were the leading issues in helping respondents decide which party to vote for, while public transport (26% nationally and 40% in London) was tenth. Significantly, reports on this survey did not mention private transport, though its cost and quality affects the daily lives of many more people than public transport.

In material appearing under his own name Blair was aware of the importance of catering for motorists. But in 1997 there was little evidence to suggest that Blair suspected how awkward transport could become.

The 1998 Transport White Paper

In 1997 Blair delegated the day-to-day business of transport, environment, land use planning and local government to his deputy, John Prescott, and created an 'integrated', sprawling and ultimately unmanageable department for him: the Department of the Environment, Transport and the

---

[1] UK Department of Employment, 'Family Expenditure Survey' (London: Department of Employment, 1964), and National Statistics, 'A report on the 2002–2003 Expenditure and Food Survey' (London: TSO, 2004).
[2] Strategic Rail Authority, 'Everyone's railway: the wider case for rail' (London: Strategic Rail Authority, 2003).
[3] Joe Murphy, 'Voters care most about health', *Evening Standard*, 14 April 2005.

Regions (DETR). Prescott proceeded to issue a consultation paper in summer 1997 and a year later, a major Transport White Paper.[4] Prescott's sentiment, illustrated in his Foreword, caused concern in Number 10 in case it could be perceived as being 'anti-car':

> we needed to improve public transport and reduce dependence on the car . . . Better public transport will encourage more people to use it . . . The priority will be maintaining existing roads rather than building new ones and better management of the road network to improve reliability . . . persuading people to use their cars a little less – and public transport a little more.

The 1998 Transport White Paper was a large and glossy document but it was generally considered to have failed to resolve many issues – it was memorably dubbed 'Carry on Consulting'. It announced the establishment of a new advisory body to the DETR, the Commission for Integrated Transport. This is a curious mixture of representation of a wide range of interests by senior figures in the transport field and research and policy formulation. At one stage the idea had been to create an independent body, but, crucially, by the time it made its public appearance in the White Paper the word 'independent' had been dropped from its title. Its constitutional position and its relationship to the regular civil service has never been entirely clear.

The White Paper was hopelessly unrealistic in its aspirations to substitute bus and rail for the car. It presaged a major review of the national roads programme, as a result of which many schemes were withdrawn. The unintended consequence was that road congestion must get steadily worse. It did have the virtue of having a consistent approach on environmental policy, the core of which was the commitment to continue a 6% per annum increase in the duty on road fuels above inflation (a policy inherited, at 5% per annum, from the previous government). This was enough to slow down traffic growth – though not enough to reverse it. However, the fuel duty policy contained the seed of the first transport policy catastrophe for the Blair government. This only became apparent after the July 2000 publication of Prescott's Ten Year Transport Plan.

---

[4] Department of the Environment, Transport and the Regions, 'A new deal for transport: better for everyone', Cm 3950 (London: TSO, 1998).

The 2000 Ten Year Transport Plan

The Ten Year Transport Plan[5] was an important attempt to recognise the long horizons involved and Prescott was able to make the remarkable claim that he had a ten-year agreement with the Treasury on the funding for the plan. Its main features were an increase in resources for local authority transport purposes and a major shift of emphasis towards both public and hoped-for private investment in railways. There was a modest increase in budgets for investment in strategic roads which returned the levels to what they had been in the mid-1990s, before the Conservatives had cut spending. This already marked a policy reversal on roads.

More rigorous analysis was attempted in support of the Ten Year Plan[6] than predecessor documents, with the result that the reality of the need to cater for inevitable traffic growth was recognised explicitly. This may have been due to the influence of Lord (Gus) Macdonald who had responsibility for delivering the plan and who had been appointed by Blair as transport minister.

The plan was a good concept and a good document, with proper supporting analysis. It had flaws, such as an imbalance of investment in favour of railways and against buses and roads, an unrealistic view of the capacity of the railway to carry enormously increased traffic – especially while it was being rebuilt. Its provision for new road capacity was still inadequate. However, these things could have been adjusted if, as had been intended, the plan had been revised every year or so as it rolled forward.

The fuel price crisis

But almost immediately things went seriously wrong. Civil protest broke out in the autumn of 2000: a rise in the world oil price, a lead given by lorry drivers in France and the fuel tax escalator combined to cause the public to rebel. Lorry drivers obstructed access to fuel supply depots. The country suddenly came to a frightening halt. There was talk of food stocks running out within days. Fuel for buses, trains and lorries (essential to food supply) had already become scarce. There could not have been a clearer demonstration that outside London the country now depends

---

[5] Department of the Environment, Transport and the Regions, 'Transport 2010' (London: TSO, July 2000).

[6] Department of the Environment, Transport and the Regions, 'Transport 2010. The Background Analysis' (London: TSO, 2000). Not surprisingly, given the novelty of the exercise, the results were mixed.

on roads, not railways. This was a major national crisis demanding the immediate attention of the Prime Minister.

As Seldon observes, 'Taking control of events at home, such as during the fuel crisis in 2000 and the foot and mouth crisis in 2001, confirmed Blair's belief that he alone, assisted by his close team in Number 10, could solve any problem.'[7] One part of the solution was that the Chancellor was persuaded to abandon the fuel tax escalator. Amazingly, the Chancellor claimed on national radio that this change in policy would have no effect on long-term traffic growth – contrary to all the objective evidence. At a stroke this change destroyed such coherence as transport and environmental policy had.

The fuel price crisis further alerted the Prime Minister to the electoral consequences of neglecting the vast majority of transport users. Blair's Foreword in the 2001 election manifesto makes no mention of environment or transport. But in the main document transport comes before health and education, under 'The Productivity Challenge': 'Labour's priority is to improve and expand railway and road travel. Our ten-year Transport Plan . . . offers real hope to motorists and passengers alike . . . Supertrams will transform transport in our big cities, with 25 new light rail or tram schemes . . . Motorways will be upgraded: a hundred new bypasses will reduce accidents and pollution. But environmentally damaging road schemes have been scrapped . . .'

So there was a new balance, including prospects for further new road capacity. 'Integrated transport', an eternal cliché which was pervasive in the 1998 policy, was demoted in this manifesto to the insipid 'Good transport systems offer choices across transport modes. Transport Direct – a phone and internet system designed to plan journeys and sell tickets – will put transport services at people's fingertips . . .'

The withdrawal of Prescott from transport policy and the death of the Ten Year Plan

Seldon noted that 'Number 10 became concerned about Prescott's agenda, and was especially worried about the perception that it was anti-car, with damaging electoral consequences . . . Blair . . . worried Prescott was becoming an "unguided missile" in his huge department.'[8] The change in tone between the 1998 Transport White Paper – Prescott's document, and the

---

[7] Anthony Seldon, *Blair*, 2nd edn (London: The Free Press, 2005), p. 694.
[8] Ibid., p. 416.

Ten Year Plan signalled a more active interest from Number 10 and the end of Prescott's reign in transport policy. This was recorded by Kevin Maguire,[9] who noted that Prescott was now thought to believe that he had made a mistake taking the reins of the complex DETR rather than acting as a Cabinet Office enforcer and that he was widely expected to give up the department after the election.

Transport officials had recognised that the plan would need to be revised, and set up a continuing programme of work. Apart from faults in the plan itself, 'events' quickly made revision urgent. These included the fall-out from the fuel price crisis, from the Hatfield rail accident (see below), the subsequent collapse of Railtrack and a violent increase in the cost of the railways.

Much work was done by officials, and publication of revisions to the plan was eagerly anticipated. But no revision was ever published. The plan withered after 2001 with the appointment of Stephen Byers as secretary of state for transport, one of several 'favoured (and non-Brownite) ministers... perhaps the most conspicuously unsatisfactory of all [Blair's] favoured ministers: his antipathy to his civil servants and his obsession with style over substance epitomised New Labour at its worst'.[10] This was well illustrated by his attitude to the Ten Year Plan. It is said that when, on arrival, the civil service offered a briefing on the plan he declined, dismissing it as a creation of a previous government.

So a major attempt to create a long-term transport policy and to secure 'buy-in' from the Treasury was undermined by the lack of interest of the new, 'Blairite' Secretary of State.

Indecision: the railways

In autumn 2000 the Hatfield railway accident occurred, with disastrous consequences for the economics and governance of the railways.

Railways policy under Blair has proved to be indecisive, ineffective and very expensive. The costly débâcle of the London Underground (see below) came about because of a vague policy delegated to Prescott and hijacked by the Treasury. The failure on the national railways came about because of a disputed decision by Blair to do nothing. In opposition the party had a clear policy which must surely have been cleared by Blair: 'a Labour government will make good its commitment to a publicly owned

---

[9] *Guardian*, 2 January 2001.   [10] Seldon, *Blair*, pp. 416, 633.

and publicly accountable railway'.[11] At the first Labour Party Conference following the 1997 election there was a majority call for re-nationalisation which the leadership had a real struggle to prevent becoming official policy. Blair decided not to change the ownership or governance of the railway. This was consistent with the 1997 manifesto to keep it 'as we find it, not as we wish it to be'. So nothing much happened, although there was a propensity to draw attention to failings and for John Prescott to promise 'action', including (unrealistically) 'renegotiation' of the train operating contracts. The rapid growth in patronage which had started in 1994 continued.

Perceived failings in the structure of the railways did lead the government to announce an intention to create a new Strategic Rail Authority (SRA) in the 1998 White Paper.[12] Reform of the railways may have been close to Prescott's heart, but it manifestly did not catch the Prime Minister's attention: the legislation proved to have great difficulty in finding parliamentary time. It took two and a half years to reach the statute book in the Transport Act 2000.

Of all the traumas experienced by the UK rail privatisation, the failure of Railtrack in autumn 2001 attracted by far the greatest public attention, although the privatised railway would have run into difficulty in any case because of the severe financial problems experienced by the train operating companies (TOCs), unrealistic aspirations and inadequate funding to meet them.[13]

There were two major rail accidents, one in 1997 at Southall in which seven people were killed and one in 1999 at Ladbroke Grove in which 31 people were killed. The extent to which privatisation may have been a factor remains controversial, but the general public laid the blame at the door of 'Tory privatisation'. In this they were encouraged by John Prescott, who started the criticisms on a visit to the Southall accident site and initiated public inquiries rather than normal ones by the Railway Inspectorate. Members of the government promised that they would discipline Railtrack to force it to become absolutely safe, whatever the cost (even though the relevant powers were vested in the independent Rail Regulator and the independent safety regulators). Railtrack

---

[11] Clare Short for the Opposition in SBC Warburg, 'Railtrack Share Offer, Prospectus', 1996.
[12] Christopher Foster, *British Government in Crisis* (Oxford: Hart Publishing, 2005), gives an important account of the deficiencies in policy and legislation concerning the Railways Act 1993 and privatisation in 1996.
[13] See Stephen Glaister, 'British Rail privatisation – competition destroyed by politics', Occasional Paper 23 (Bath: Centre for Regulated Industies, 2005).

was particularly heavily criticised in the press after the Ladbroke Grove accident.

That was a crucial turning point: with sufficient leadership government could wisely have taken the line that this was now a private industry and it was a matter for the independent safety and economic regulators to sort out. The very public intervention by ministers greatly heightened the general public's perception – contradicted by the evidence – that privatisation had made the railways less safe.[14]

These factors became critical after another accident, at Hatfield in October 2000, which was due to the failure of a decaying rail. Four people were killed. The rail in question had exhibited symptomatic cracks before failure. Because of its Ladbroke Grove experience Railtrack feared the response from the press and from government, and consequently after Hatfield all but closed the system. This destroyed the train service and with it its business and those of the train operators.

At about the same time it emerged that Railtrack had mismanaged the major procurement for the refurbishment and upgrading of the West Coast Main Line – a failure by a private company that has not often been remarked by New Labour, so keen to allege that the private sector is more efficient than the public sector. Railtrack appealed direct to the Treasury for several billion pounds to rescue it. Amazingly, the Treasury at first agreed and started to make new grants – thus protecting Railtrack shareholders and lenders from the consequences of their board's errors.

Then, in October 2001, Stephen Byers invoked provisions of the Railways Act 1993 to put Railtrack into railway administration. Byers appeared determined to take an opportunity to destroy the privatised, shareholder ownership structure. Although there are allegations that this move had been planned for some months, none of Byers, Brown or Blair had thought through how the new arrangements for ownership and control might turn out. An option was to encourage a conventional take over of Railtrack and there were companies that showed an interest in this. The normal competitive market for corporate control would have acted to change the management and rebuild the company. That would have kept the structure intact and avoided the damaging hiatus that occurred.

If the Labour Party had seen putting Railtrack into railway administration as a move to renationalise the railway, it was to be quickly disappointed. The Treasury was unwilling to find the funds necessary to buy

[14] See Andrew A. Evans, 'Rail safety and rail privatisation in Britain', Inaugural Lecture, Imperial College London, 2004.

out surviving private interests. In addition Railtrack had considerable and rapidly increasing debt which had been classified by the Office of National Statistics as private debt on the grounds that the company was under private, not public, control. The Chancellor was absolutely unwilling to countenance any move that would place that debt on the public balance sheet.

Railtrack lingered in administration for about a year, at considerable cost. The government was then granted its wish to replace the existing Railtrack by a company limited by guarantee. This is run by an executive accountable to about 120 'members', many chosen to represent public and private interests including train operators, railway employees and passengers. It was described as 'not for profit', thus appearing to deal with the objection to the earning of profit in a public utility – although 'not for dividend' would have been less misleading. The company would be entirely financed by debt, supposed to be serviced out of profits.

There is considerable confusion about the governance of Network Rail: 'who is it accountable to and for what?' Indeed, in order to satisfy the crucial test that allows the debt to continue to be classified as private, off the public balance sheet, it is necessary that the public sector *not* be in control of the company – and yet government is now guaranteeing the debt.

Arguably, the restructuring of Railtrack into Network Rail changed little beyond obfuscating lines of accountability. As the Parliamentary Transport Select Committee observed, it is hard to avoid the conclusion that the government

> added another fudge by creating Network Rail, a private company without any private sector disciplines, seemingly set up simply to keep the enormous costs of the railway infrastructure away from the government's balance sheet.[15]

The government was evidently dissatisfied with the new structure it had created – not least because the Treasury was surprised by the size of the liability it was faced with after the independent Rail Regulator's Extraordinary Review published in December 2003. Alistair Darling, appointed secretary of state in May 2002 on the resignation of Byers, instigated another policy review. The Secretary of State explicitly and publicly recognised that, so long as anything like the current structure of the railway survives,

---

[15] House of Commons Transport Select Committee, 'The future of the railway', HC145 (London: TSO, 2004), paragraph 13.

his predecessor's attempts to weaken the position of the independent Rail Regulator had been unwise.

In July 2004 the outcome was published as a White Paper, *The Future of Rail*. In fact this vague document proposes remarkably little fundamental reform. The one major change proposed is that the Strategic Rail Authority will be abolished and its functions will be transferred into the Department for Transport. It is deeply ironic that this will reverse the only change that Labour made during the whole of its seven years in power. The Railways Act 2005 divides the functions of the SRA between Network Rail and the Department for Transport. Crucially, the Conservatives had deliberately put the rail industry beyond the direct control of government, on the grounds that experience had shown that government interference has been damaging to the successful running of rail businesses. Now, for the first time in history, high-level policy is the direct responsibility of a Whitehall spending department.

The recent review of railways policy leaves most fundamental questions unanswered. There is ambivalence about the role and meaning of enforceable commercial contract. There is ambivalence about whether Network Rail is or is not private, whose interests it serves and whether it is or is not under government control. Most important of all there is little sign of anybody being willing to address the fundamental issue: how big a railway operation is the nation willing to pay for over the long term? And, if it is not willing to pay the likely cost of the present scale of operation, what is to be cut?

Blair versus Brown, devolution versus centralisation: the PPP for the London Underground

The story of the London Underground public private partnership illustrates several aspects of Blair's two administrations: the consequences of delegating without a coherent overall policy; the consequence of blind reliance on advice from management consultants, lawyers and business people if they are imperfectly briefed on the subtleties of public policy; the consequences of allowing policy to develop which is not supported by the evidence; the dominance of Blair and, particularly, Brown over Prescott; and a philosophical disagreement between Blair and Brown over the wisdom and feasibility of devolution of powers to local authorities.

The PPP for the London Underground deserves attention in its own right because of its size. It is far bigger than any other PFI or PPP deal. At the time it was conceived it was bigger than all those others put together.

Announced in 1998 and completed five years later, the two Blair administrations forced it through in the face of several sceptical assessments by the House of Commons Transport Select Committee, one from the Treasury Select Committee, one from the National Audit Office (plus two post-completion), scepticism at the Standing Committee on the Bill and a steady stream of critical assessments from the serious press and independent commentators.

Back in 1997 there was a wide measure of agreement about the problem to be solved.[16] The London Underground was crowded and unreliable. Between £1,000 million and £2,000 million were needed to make good past failures and adequately to maintain and renew the physical assets. New rail capacity was needed.

It was taken for granted that sorting out the Underground would be delegated to John Prescott. But he quickly found obstacles. First, some papers he left in a *Panorama* television studio revealed that early advice offered by officials had been not very different from the Conservative proposals (which had been unrealistic about the financial terms on which the Underground could have been fully privatised). Once these proposals were made public Prescott had to repudiate them. Second, when he proposed an immediate, straightforward capital grant the Treasury flatly refused. Apart from the limitations due to the policy of sticking to the previous administration's spending plans for two years, the Treasury was determined to secure the same kind of managerial efficiency improvements they perceived as having been achieved under the Conservative administrations by the privatisation of the railways and the other utilities. This left Prescott in an impossible position and, arguably, he never retrieved control of policy on the Underground from the Treasury.

At this point Whitehall as a whole was at a loss to know what to do. The Treasury has steadfastly denied in public that the Chancellor and his ministers ever did anything other than give advice and support to the responsible department. But Geoffrey Robinson, who was the Treasury's paymaster general in 1997, helpfully revealed in a Commons debate the Treasury's lead in what happened next:

> We could skin a cat in so many ways, and when it came to public-private partnerships – which were quite innovative – there were many different options available. Number 10 had its view; the advisers to Number 10 had their view; the then Department of Transport, Local Government and

[16] See Stephen Glaister and Tony Travers, 'Governing the Underground: funding, management and democracy for London's Tube' (Bath: Centre for Regulated Industries, 1997).

the Regions had its view; I had a view; the Treasury had a view; and the Deputy Prime Minister had very strong views. We had to find a way that we could all see would carry this forward . . . I convened a group of four businessmen with experience of both the public and private sectors to make a recommendation to us. Essentially, that recommendation is what we have today.[17]

The *Evening Standard* revealed that Robinson had said later that the businessmen were chosen because they had experience of major privatisations: 'they were, therefore, the very best people to advise the Government on what would work'.[18] They were chaired by Sir Malcolm Bates, who had been the author of two reports to the Treasury about how best to develop the private finance initiative. He was appointed chairman of London Regional Transport (LRT) in April 1998 in place of Peter Ford, who had articulated LRT's view that the PPP proposal was close to the bottom of a list of 15 alternative options. Bates was ultimately to see the PPP through to completion and the winding-up of LRT five years later.

Thus a major policy was developed not by the Prime Minister, not by the Secretary of State for Transport, not by the civil service, not by management consultants but by an ad hoc group of businessmen selected by a Treasury minister and against the considered policy of the board responsible for running the Underground.

Prescott announced the PPP for the Underground to the Commons in March 1998, after refinement by management consultants PricewaterhouseCoopers and the law firm Freshfields. Thirty-year contracts based on three roughly equal groups of lines were to be awarded to the private sector, after a competition, for the repair, maintenance and enhancement of the fixed infrastructure, signalling and trains. Two-thirds of the employees would remain in direct, public-sector employment to drive the trains and staff the stations.

One embellishment authored by Prescott was an assurance that staff transferring to the private sector would have their terms and conditions protected. This was an important departure from previous privatisations and private finance deals and, arguably, it compromised one of the main sources of cost reduction that the Treasury was so keen to replicate for the Underground.

Gordon Brown and the Treasury have systematically held the line that the PPP was the sole responsibility of Prescott and his successors. But few

---

[17] House of Commons debate, 27 June 2002.   [18] *Evening Standard*, 28 June 2003.

in Whitehall or in the press saw it that way. The chairman of the Transport Select Committee, Gwyneth Dunwoody, gave the following account in the Commons:

> As a Committee, we were worried that most of the arrangements for the bids had been Treasury led, to the point where Treasury officials appeared to be taking precedence over the DETR in the negotiating, and providing individuals who were themselves directly dealing with the applicants for the bids, and yet we were not able to persuade Treasury Ministers to appear before us to discuss the implications. We said very clearly that we thought that that decision undermined the work of Select Committees, simply because the House of Commons does have a responsibility not just to ask awkward questions but to obtain answers.[19]

The Treasury refused to be scrutinised, but employees of the consultants did appear before the Select Committee to assist transport officials and ministers in explaining the policy, and, on occasion they were put up to explain and justify it at briefings for the press. For instance:

> The Treasury's argument is two-fold. First . . . it does not trust London Underground's public sector management to deliver. But second, it maintains the PFI offers the advantage of transferring to the private sector the risk of maintaining the track, signalling and tunnels. 'Under PPP,' says Tony Poulter of PricewaterhouseCoopers, who is advising the government on the Underground deal, 'it was down to the private sector to sort it out, and they did . . . Bonds may have worked for the New York subway but the British public sector does not have experience of being able to write contracts that successfully deliver what is wanted. Through a PPP, with its long-term transfer of operating and financial risk, it does.'[20]

This illustrates not only that the government was using private consultants to expound and defend government policy, but also that in 1999 it was accepted on all sides that this was, in fact, a Treasury policy. In 2005 the press and the public remain clear that PFI and PPP policies were Treasury policies. One of many illustrations is Will Hutton's comment: 'Over the past eight years, I have had my differences with Brown . . . The Private Finance Initiative and the London Underground Public Private Partnership, in particular, are too poorly designed to advance the public interest.'[21]

---

[19] House of Commons debate, 27 June 2002. [20] *Financial Times,* 27 November 1999.
[21] *Observer,* 13 March 2005.

The extent to which the Treasury had become seduced by what the consultants promised the PPP would deliver is apparent in the Chancellor's 1998 Comprehensive Spending Review which mentions 'the new Public-Private Partnership for London Underground (which is expected to remove the need for public subsidy from 2000/01)'.[22] Thus it was expected that, magically, the Underground's underinvestment problem would be solved and all need for subsidy for the Underground would be removed! The government has never revealed the analysis underlying this, even in the face of repeated demands from members of the Standing Committee of the Commons dealing with the legislation. On analysis of a six-page sketch issued by PricewaterhouseCoopers it immediately looked too good to be true.[23]

Yet ministers and the Prime Minister took the view that PFI and PPP arrangements enabled delivery of projects which could be delivered in no other way – often seeming to imply that the private-sector investor would somehow 'step in' to replace the basic funding that the taxpayer could not, or would not, provide. Thus Geoffrey Robinson declared, '[PFI] is enabling Government to support a significant number of additional projects beyond what can be provided through the public purse.'[24] And the Prime Minister explicitly put the view that the policy was somehow providing public services that the taxpayer could not afford: 'The reason that we are engaged in this public-private investment partnership is so that the infrastructure work, which is urgently needed in the Tube, can be done.'[25] and 'there is no way Government through the general taxpayer can do it all.'[26] This view, that PFI and PPP somehow entice the private sector to provide resources that the taxpayer will not provide, is plainly nonsense. But it has been put so often by Labour ministers that one can only assume they believe it, perhaps because they do not understand the fundamental economics behind what are, by any standards, technically complex procurements.

As the details of the implementation of the PPP were worked up, a philosophical difference between Blair and Brown began to emerge. The

---

[22] HM Treasury, 'Modern Public Services for Britain, Investing in Reform' (Comprehensive Spending Review), Cm 4011 (London: TSO, 1998), paragraph 8.4.

[23] See Stephen Glaister, Rosemary Scanlon and Tony Travers, 'A Fourth Way for the Underground?' (London: Greater London Group, June 1998); and Stephen Glaister, Rosemary Scanlon and Tony Travers, 'Getting Partnerships Going: public private partnerships in transport' (London: Institute for Public Policy Research, April 2000).

[24] Speech to a PFI conference, 27 April 1998.

[25] House of Commons debate, 6 February 2002.   [26] Labour Party Conference, 2002.

legislation to devolve powers to a directly elected London mayor and London Assembly were being developed in parallel. Blair's 1997 manifesto had indicated that this was to be genuine and substantive devolution. Yet the Treasury was concerned at the prospect that the new London mayor and Authority would become profligate. Initially this was independent of the personality of the mayor. The government's plan was to have the Underground PPP completed before April 2000, at which point the new mayor would assume his or her powers.

In the event the negotiations for the Underground dragged on until the end of 2002, at which point, in accordance with the Greater London Act 2000, they and their liabilities were summarily imposed upon the Greater London Authority. Whether by design or by accident, the effect of the PPP was significantly to fetter the mayor's powers over the Underground. Thus the Blair-inspired move towards devolution of London government conflicted with the Brown-inspired PPP solution for the London Underground. The conflict between this and the fact that the successful candidate for mayor had been elected on a ticket of explicit opposition to the PPP and with an alternative solution, formed the substance of an unsuccessful Judicial Review brought by the mayor in the summer of 2002.

One thing that Blair and Brown did have in common was a difficult relationship with Ken Livingstone, who won the first mayoral election in 2000. Having failed to give assurances considered adequate, Livingstone was denied the official Labour candidature and excluded from the party. He promptly stood as an independent and won easily, making the official Labour candidate look flat-footed. Blair and Livingstone have since repaired their relationship, but Brown and Livingstone have not.

Blair did make a public intervention on the Underground PPP in 1999, in the context of Ken Livingstone's alternative proposals. However, both Blair and Prescott must have been ill-advised on the facts concerning how capital had been successfully raised for some time in US cities:

> Rosemary Scanlon, a visiting research fellow at the London School of Economics and former deputy state comptroller for New York City . . . has written to Mr Blair to express concerns about his comments . . . His statement, in an interview with the *Observer* newspaper, was 'an absolute and utter untruth', she said. In the letter to the prime minister, she explains that New York City did have a fiscal crisis in 1975. But the Metropolitan Transportation Authority, a State of New York agency, was set up as a public benefit

corporation in 1981, and has since then issued more than $14bn (£8.6bn) of bonds. 'The MTA reinvestment programme, and its bond issuance, is without question a major success story in New York.' A Downing Street spokesman later . . . added: 'To saddle the city with an enormous amount of debt is a recipe for disaster.'[27]

Apart from this intervention Blair paid little attention to the matter of the London Underground, even though the policy was hugely unpopular both within the Commons and outside it. Negotiations were ugly and were obviously going to stretch on for much longer than had been expected. Ken Livingstone was a popular figure and he had appointed Bob Kiley from New York, one of the world's best, as Transport Commissioner (chief executive of TfL – Transport for London). They had an alternative, tried and tested, proposal for raising capital through the issuance of bonds secured against future revenues and other sources of income; and for procuring services from the private sector through a larger number of much shorter term contracts, which would be easier to manage and to enforce. Several other alternatives were available. The Labour government had rescued the floundering (supposedly privately funded) project to build a fast rail link between London and the Channel Tunnel by guaranteeing over £2.5 billion of borrowing on the markets – a guarantee that, in effect, was subsequently called; and the bond issue method of raising local authority capital became Treasury policy in 2004.

With the 2001 general election approaching Blair appeared to decide that he had to intervene. On 2 February 2001 John Prescott and Bob Kiley reached an agreement under which Kiley would take a lead in achieving the modifications necessary to give TfL and LUL (London Underground Limited) 'unified management control of the Underground' – thus meeting one of Kiley's and Livingsone's core objections to the government's original proposal. Negotiations proceeded throughout February and most of March. The DETR was helpful and, with substantive input from 'Adrian Montague, head of the government's private finance initiative department'[28] and 'Lord Macdonald, a Scots media mogul bizarrely put in charge of London's surface and underground railways',[29] the government made concessions which looked as though they would make a resolution possible.

But Kiley found that the understanding he had reached with Prescott was not respected in subsequent negotiations with government's

---

[27] *Financial Times*, 23 November 1999.   [28] *Sunday Times*, 25 March 2001.
[29] Simon Jenkins, *Evening Standard*, 28 March 2003.

representatives. Agreement was not reached by the end-February 2001 deadline, but the government made a new proposal with a deadline for agreement at the end of March. Again, negotiations foundered, essentially because in Kiley's view the government was still not prepared to allow the public sector to retain direct control over maintenance activities or to hold private contractors accountable for the identifiable capital improvements.

After this breakdown London Underground resumed its negotiations on the original PPP proposal and TfL began to prepare its case for the Judicial Review, due to be held on 12 June 2001 (but later delayed until 23 July). With a general election due on 7 June 2001 the Prime Minister must have been keen to find a resolution to this unpleasant dispute involving several of his senior ministers. It came on 4 May 2001 with handshakes outside Number 10 and the announcement of a new agreement whereby Kiley would be appointed to the additional position of chair of London Regional Transport with the purpose of enabling him to 'finalise the PPP contracts for the Underground, making whatever changes within the framework of the PPP are necessary to address concerns previously raised by TfL'.[30] In a DETR press notice John Prescott said 'I am delighted that we have found a way towards unified management control within the framework of the PPP'. The Prime Minister also commented, 'I warmly welcome and endorse this agreement. I've met with Bob Kiley, heard his concerns and have confidence in his ability to deliver a PPP which meets those concerns and ours and will be good for London. He will have the full support of the Government in his efforts.' Thus, apparently, both Blair and Prescott had publicly conceded the crucial 'unified management control' point.

This move was certainly successful in removing the acrimony from the issue for the duration of the general election. But by early July Kiley had informed Blair and the new 'Blairite' transport secretary, Stephen Byers, that he had been unable to conclude an agreement with the preferred bidders and recommended that the procurement be abandoned and restarted on a new basis. With the election out of the way Byers immediately rejected this suggestion and directed that the government's original plans proceed. By 15 July Blair was again defending the original PPP plan 'as the only way to get a "massive investment" into the ailing network'.[31] On the 17th the government summarily replaced Kiley as chairman of the LRT Board, reinstating his predecessor, Sir Malcolm Bates. The Prime Minister's official spokesman made it clear that the dismissal of Kiley was a

[30] Transport for London Press release, 4 May 2001.   [31] Evening Standard, 16 July 2001.

government decision, approved by Tony Blair and not a personal initiative of Byers.

Press and parliamentary reaction was hostile, sensing that the Chancellor had never had any real intention of giving way and that Kiley's appointment had been a cynical device. An *Evening Standard* leader said that realities should not prevent 'Londoners from venting their fury on the Prime Minister and Mr Gordon Brown, the silent killer in the background of this debacle.'[32]

Polly Toynbee laid the blame firmly at Brown's door:

> Those who are friends of this government are appalled at this feckless squandering of good will. Most London Labour MPs and ministers privately roll their eyes in despair at what is going on in their name – the chancellor's runaway train no one else can stop . . .
>
> As I write, calls rain in from Brown's people claiming incredibly that the PPP has nothing to do with the chancellor, nothing at all. It was all John Prescott's baby – as if. Last week they told me it was all Stephen Byers's responsibility, forsooth.
>
> The chancellor's fistprint on this one is indelible: his people have done the negotiating, he is the one key player who still refuses to meet Kiley.[33]

Kiley and Livingstone repeatedly attempted to persuade the government that in negotiation the deal was becoming even worse value for public money. There were constructive meetings with Blair but none with the Chancellor. Kiley had requested a meeting with Gordon Brown as far back as April 2001, and felt that in a 10-minute meeting they could quickly come to grips with some of the issues. It never happened.

On 5 February 2002 the Transport Select Committee published a strongly argued report that recommended that the government not proceed with the PPP.[34] The arguments were reiterated in a Commons debate led by the formidable chair of the committee, Gwyneth Dunwoody, on 27 June 2002.

Blair did make a personal attempt to understand the issues in detail, to the extent of attempting to read and understand the many thousands of pages of draft commercial contracts. There was a rumour that at a meeting between Blair and Mayor Livingstone in the spring of 2002, Blair showed surprise and concern about the developing long-term financial liabilities

---

[32] *Evening Standard*, 18 July 2001.   [33] *Guardian*, 20 July 2001.
[34] House of Commons Committee on Transport, Local Government and the Regions, 'London Underground', HC387 (London: The Stationery Office, 2002).

for the government and he asked his aides in Number 10 to listen to both sides of the argument and to report back.

In Parliament Transport Secretary Byers seemed to say that he had an open mind pending final reports from consultants (rather than from officials) about the value for money of the deals. Unsurprisingly, when these arrived they were not definitive, but, in any event, the government eventually closed the deals in spring 2003. Final negotiations were painfully slow and the terms of the contracts changed significantly with the effect of reducing the exposures to risk for the private sector, as noted by the critical report from the Committee of Public Accounts (PAC) in March 2005.[35] The government's absolute commitment to completing the policy greatly weakened its bargaining position against the preferred (and, by then effectively the only) bidders.

The *ex post* appraisals are beginning to appear. On publication of a further Transport Select Committee report in March 2005,[36] Gwyneth Dunwoody made the crucial point: 'I welcome the fact that the government is at last putting real money into the Tube. But I cannot see why it needed a PPP to do it.' The PAC found that the PPP had caused years of avoidable delay and the procurement alone had cost the taxpayer getting on for £900 million, about half in fees to advisors and consultants, and half in higher borrowing costs than an alternative promoted by Livingstone, amongst others. Transport for London has published progress reports[37] showing a mixed experience, including an emerging concern that the contractors may fail to deliver the investment programme as rapidly as they had promised and that the predictions of the consequences of lack of management control are beginning to be realised.

An editorial in the *Guardian* (1 April 2005) on the occasion of the publication of the critical PAC report summed up the sorry episode:

> One of the few dents in Gordon Brown's reputation for sound economics is his dogged pursuit of public private partnerships for the underground in London, despite widespread criticism that it would have been much cheaper if the project had been financed by government-backed bonds. Yesterday's report by the all-party public accounts committee will do nothing to restore his reputation . . . Looking back, the whole episode looks like a triumph of dogma and personal prejudice over common sense.

---

[35] House of Commons Committee of Public Accounts, 'London Underground Public Private Partnerships', HC466 (London: The Stationery Office, March 2005).

[36] House of Commons Transport Committee, 'The Performance of the London Underground', HC94 (London: The Stationery Office, March 2005).

[37] London Underground, 'London Underground and the PPP – The First Year' (2004).

Further indecision over London devolution: Livingstone and congestion charging

Road user charging – or congestion charging as the London realisation was to be branded – was another transport subject where Blair showed inconsistency. Charging road users by time and location as a means of controlling traffic congestion while producing revenues was a long-established idea but it had always been thought to be too politically difficult to implement (except, of course, crudely by increasing fuel duty). But the powers for local authorities to implement it were contained in the Greater London Authority Act 1999 in the case of London and the Transport Act 2000 in the cases of other local authorities. Crucially, the legislation insists that the net revenues be applied locally for transport purposes for at least ten years.

This policy is a sensible component of devolution and it represents one of the only sources of locally generated income at the discretion of an English local authority. No doubt the 'economic efficiency' half of the Treasury brain welcomed this move. But the 'control of public spending' half certainly did not: it represented a move towards hypothecation of a 'tax' income over which the Treasury would have no control. But the battle had to be won if the policy was to have any chance of political acceptability. And it was won through the persistence of the Deputy Prime Minister.

One might have expected that Blair, apparently committed to real devolution, would have supported any local politician who sought to make use of the new powers. But once candidates for London Mayor were announced and Ken Livingstone, standing against the official Labour candidate, committed himself to introduce congestion charging, official policy became not to introduce congestion charging. Blair and his colleagues were careful to emphasise the political and technological risks of using the powers they had themselves created. When, on many occasions, back benchers asked ministers to intervene on their behalf the answer was always that this was the responsibility of the Mayor of London and the government had no powers to intervene.[38] The clear expectation was that the policy would fail spectacularly and it would all be Ken Livingstone's fault. However, it is said that Blair was eventually persuaded to support it by an RAC Foundation's briefing on their 'Motoring towards 2050', exercise hence his endorsement of road pricing in his Foreword.[39] In particular, he showed a keen interest in the RAC Foundation's opinion polling results.[40]

---

[38] For example, see the exchange in the Commons with Richard Ottaway, 9 January 2002.
[39] RAC Foundation, 'Motoring towards 2050' (London: RAC Foundation, May 2002).
[40] Sir Christopher Foster, personal communication.

In the event the London congestion charging scheme went 'live' in February 2003, worked well and stimulated considerable interest round the world. In October 2003 Blair gave a fulsome acknowledgement:

> I was very, very sceptical but I think that it has made a difference, and I think that provided the money is ploughed back into transport, then I think it is an interesting example of how we can manage transport policy for the future. I think it is too early to evaluate all the results of it, but you have got to give credit where it is due.'[41]

This success encouraged Alistair Darling, who had been appointed by Blair as secretary of state for transport, to sort out the transport policy muddle left behind by Prescott and Byers, to take the idea seriously at a national level. To have been seen to be considering this would have been unthinkable a couple of years earlier, yet this kind of traffic management forms the core of the Transport White Paper of July 2004. And Blair himself wrote a Foreword. While hardly a strong endorsement for the eventual possibility of national road user charging it is the most one could expect and it is remarkable considering the sensitivity Blair has shown to the power of the motoring electorate.

Meanwhile Livingstone has been allowed to rejoin the Labour Party and seems to enjoy a good relationship with Blair. The growth in London bus patronage – a clear consequence of Livingstone's policies – has been sufficient to allow the national government to claim that national bus patronage is growing, even though it is not outside London. And it is Livingstone and the GLA that is leading the way in implementing the devolutionist Prudential Borrowing regime that allows local authorities a new freedom to borrow within limits of 'prudence' without reference to Whitehall. In December 2004, with a delightful irony, Ken Livingstone successfully launched the first £200 million on to the financial markets: the government had flatly refused Livingstone's proposition that he be allowed to do precisely this as an alternative to the Underground PPP.

Now it is apparent that Livingstone has become an important political ally of the Prime Minister's, as revealed in a MORI Survey for the GLA.[42]

Blair's personal interventions

If Blair showed a general uninterest in high-level transport policy, he showed himself to be perfectly willing to intervene when he was personally affected. In autumn 2002 Transport for London was engaged in a quantity

---

[41] *London Today*, ITV.   [42] *Guardian*, 17 January 2005.

of work in preparation for the introduction of congestion charging. One Friday afternoon some contractors at Vauxhall knocked off leaving behind unattended but defective temporary traffic lights. The Prime Minister's wife was seriously delayed in the ensuing traffic jam.

Action was immediate. Blair required junior transport minister John Spellar to investigate, to make weekly reports and to make recommendations. After some debate about whether it would be better to remove traffic management powers and give them to a 'traffic tsar' (which would have been a bizarre contradiction to the creation of the devolved GLA) it was sensibly decided that highway authorities such as TfL required stronger powers. A Bill was announced in the November 2003 Queen's Speech and the Traffic Management Act had royal assent by July 2004. Blair could certainly make things happen in the transport policy world when he put his mind to it.

Another, less benign, example emerged during evidence given at the Old Bailey concerning corporate manslaughter and health and safety charges arising from the Hatfield railway accident. *The Times* reported evidence given in court that the Prime Minister had applied 'naked' pressure to Railtrack executives to lift the speed restrictions plaguing the network.[43] He had offered to 'syndicate' or share the risks. This is an extraordinary suggestion. It is that the Prime Minister was seeking to influence the professional judgement both of those accountable to their shareholders for running a private company (hence the court case) and of the independent rail safety regulators. It is also unclear what 'syndicating' the risks might mean in practice: had the Prime Ministers' requests contributed to a subsequent fatal accident it is hard to see that there a mechanism in law whereby the Prime Minister could have somehow taken over culpability from those accountable for running a safe railway. If the government or Parliament were discontented with the way Hatfield had been handled then the appropriate response would have been to legislate with due process.

Blair's growing interest in transport

In transport policy documents prior to 2001, if there was a foreword it would be by the Secretary of State for Transport and Deputy Prime Minister, John Prescott. After 2001 it seems that Blair had realised a need to take a closer personal interest. That Blair wrote a warm Foreword to

---

[43] *The Times*, 12 March 2005.

'Motoring towards 2050', an independent report by the RAC Foundation was remarkable. The 2004 Transport White Paper also has a Foreword by the Prime Minister which is only 25% shorter than the Secretary of State for Transport's own Preface. It shows the extent to which Blair had stepped in to impose his own view. The first substantive paragraph includes: 'Over 100 road schemes have been completed. The M25 is being widened . . . we want to see Crossrail in London, road widening and bypasses to tackle the worst areas of congestion . . .' It would have been unthinkable to start a major transport policy statement in this way during Blair's first term.

So, by the beginning of his second term Blair had realised that transport was a problem and that he had lost faith in the ability of his secretaries of state or the Chancellor to solve them. He decided to become more directly involved and to do that he strengthened the resources available to him directly. Lord Birt had silently attended a Cabinet Office seminar in November 2001 where academics and other experts had been invited to express their views about the long-term issues in transport, without having been told that this was essentially an initial briefing for Birt.

The Number 10 Internet site records a press briefing by the Prime Minister's official spokesman (PMOS):

> Asked to clarify exactly what it was about Lord Birt which had so impressed the Prime Minister that he believed he could solve the country's transport problems, the PMOS said it was important to make a distinction between what the Forward Strategy Unit (FSU) – of which Lord Birt was a member – was and was not doing . . . we had set up a small unit within Government composed of people drawn from different backgrounds who could look at some of the longer term issues facing our public services ten or twenty years down the line.
>
> Asked the difference between the FSU and the Policy Unit, the PMOS said that the FSU's role was to look at issues ten or twenty years hence. . . . The new Policy Directorate's role was to look at the short and medium terms.[44]

The Leader of the Opposition was quick to articulate a general concern, particularly within the civil service, that transport policy development was becoming confused and unaccountable.[45] The Commons Select Committee on Transport complained about the way the normal systems of scrutiny were being evaded by Birt's position.[46] Lord Birt had not accepted an invitation to provide oral evidence to their inquiry into the Ten Year Plan.

---

[44] 8 January 2002.   [45] House of Commons, 23 January 2002.
[46] House of Commons Transport Committee, Press notice, 31 January 2002.

Noting that that a couple of members of Lord Birt's team were being paid for by the Transport Department, they expressed the view that it is important that those engaged in policy should be accountable to Parliament through the select committee system.

Neither papers written for Birt, nor reports written by Birt for the Prime Minister, have been made public. But it became known that one proposal emanating from Downing Street was for a new network of tolled motorways. This idea was scotched by Alistair Darling on taking office as transport secretary.[47]

Recent press appraisals of Birt's role[48] report lack of clarity of how, or if, Birt's access translates into real power. They also report irritation in the civil service that Blair had quietly created what was effectively a prime minister's department in which Birt, unelected and unaccountable through civil service codes, is a key part. They note that the number of consultants hired by the government has recently exploded, just as it did at the BBC in the Birtian days. It is reported that senior civil servants moan about the increase in management consultancy 'Birtspeak' in communication from what is referred to disparagingly as 'the Centre'.

As if in confirmation of the suggestion that the Chancellor feels threatened on transport policy by the 'blue skies thinking' seeping from Number 10, in his March 2005 budget Gordon Brown announced yet another transport policy initiative.[49] Sir Rod Eddington, the chief executive of British Airways, is to advise ministers on the impact of transport decisions on Britain's productivity and stability beyond 2015. When he retires from British Airways in September 2005, Eddington will live in Australia but will travel to London regularly to counsel the Department for Transport and the Treasury.

Conclusion

In his introduction to 'The code of practice on consultation'[50] Tony Blair wrote, 'effective consultation is a key part of the policy-making process'. The episodes related in this chapter illustrate that if there is not effective consultation then the process is unlikely to make successful policy.

They support Seldon's view[51] that 'Tony Blair has never been a man who has liked or felt a need to consult widely'. Each of the episodes exhibits

---

[47] *Daily Telegraph*, 2 June 2002.
[48] David Hencke, *Guardian*, 27 January 2005, and Rachel Sylvester, *Daily Telegraph*, 10 January 2005.
[49] *The Guardian*, 17 March, 2005.   [50] Cabinet Office, 2003.
[51] Seldon, Conclusion to second edition, pp. 695–7.

some or all of the following: a lack of a clear overall policy direction; parallel development of closely related policies in several parts of Whitehall including a mystery of bodies in and around Number 10; a willingness to ignore or deny evidence; a reliance on commercial management consultancy and individual advisers rather than accountable ministers and their civil servants; a failure carefully to develop policy and then legislation over a reasonable period of time; an unwillingness to publish or consult on a substantive written account of draft legislation giving the reasoning in support; a reluctance to be exposed to scrutiny.

Had scrutiny and criticism been heeded then some of the mistakes might have been avoided. The 1998 Transport White Paper proposed more consultation rather than specific legislation (except for the creation of the SRA, which took two and a half years to enact) but the generic policies it proposed did not square with the facts of the situation or the reality of electoral sentiment. There soon had to be U-turns on road building and fuel duties which destroyed such coherence as there was.

The Ten Year Plan was a good concept and it did have high-quality public documentation. However, the necessary revisions in the light of unexpected events never happened and a good idea died for lack of attention when Byers, the Treasury and the Prime Minister all lost interest.

The development of the PPP for the London Underground, the destruction of Railtrack, its replacement by a new form of company and the process adopted for the next review of the railways policy were all matters of national significance, involving considerable commitments of public money over many years. Parliament was excluded. Public money was spent on management consultants, yet much of their work was – and remains – confidential. Proposals were published without prior consultation. Rather like the rail privatisation bill of the early 1990s,[52] the Railways Act 2005 was not well defined in advance and had to be put together 'on the hoof' in Parliament.

There was much turbulence in transport policy over the first two Blair terms of office but rather little progress. The Prime Minister's initial attempt to delegate failed. John Prescott at the DETR generated several genuinely new policy initiatives but they were undermined by Number 10 or blocked by the Treasury because they were unrealistic, unpopular or not consistent with Treasury policies on the use of the private sector, on control of public expenditure, on public borrowing and on the needs of the economy. Blair was drawn into attempting to make transport policy in Downing Street, with rather little help from the Chancellor.

---

[52] See Foster, *British Government in Crisis.*

By the 2005 general election it was unclear where, if anywhere, the real initiative lay. Symptomatic is the growing number of internal and official advisory bodies attempting to develop transport policy outside the official Department for Transport, including internal units in the Treasury and in the Office of the Deputy Prime Minister, Lord Birt and the Prime Minister's Strategy Unit in Number 10, the Commission for Integrated Transport advising the Department for Transport and the new Eddington exercise for the Treasury. Overall, the effect has been substantial additional centralisation of powers over transport policy in the hands of Blair and, separately, Brown, but with little clarity about how they ought to be used.

At the end of Blair's second term the situation on the railways continued to look precarious. Otherwise there were some more hopeful signs. Alistair Darling's 2004 Transport White Paper does take a sensible long view. While it takes great care not to give any hostages to fortune by quoting numbers it does, with the endorsement of the Prime Minister in his Foreword, realistically set out major conflicts that future governments will have to deal with. In particular, it shows the beginnings of the unavoidable debate about how best to address the insatiable wish of the electorate to move around in their own private vehicles. A satisfactory resolution of the conflicts – if there can ever be such a thing – will require a return to an analysis of the facts, clear policy subject to scrutiny, building public consensus to a degree unheard of in this area and considerable leadership.

11

Government and judiciary

LOUIS BLOM-COOPER

Background to Blairism

After 18 years of Conservative rule, an incoming Labour administration (old or new) might reasonably, on past record, have been apprehensive of any clipping of its left wing policies by a traditionally conservative-minded judiciary, a feeling further induced by an outcrop of judicial activism over the previous two decades of incremental growth in judicial review. In the immediate pre-election period of 1996–7 there had, in particular, been concern among penal reformers that consideration of criminal and penal policy would stray even further from the norm of moderately liberal policies towards crime and punishment. The United States had already shown the tragic and counterproductive results of mixing conservative party politics with such policy debates, thereby inflaming public prejudice.

The Blair administration, first-time round, showed no disinclination from following the US experience in the penal field, much in the fashion of standing shoulder-to-shoulder with the United States in the international arena. During the last decade of the twentieth century there was nothing to distinguish policies between the two British main parties; each was vying with the other to assuage the perceived punitiveness of the public. Policy has been over-driven by party political considerations that have led to short-term initiatives, excessive legislation in criminal justice, imbalances, and at times the pursuit of contradictory objectives. The Blair watchword, to be tough on crime and the causes of crime, conceded nothing in reality to a policy which aimed at offenders, and resulted in an almost unrelenting increase in the daily average prison population, to a record high of 76,227 as at 1 July 2005.

Our prisons are symptomatic of a general malaise in penal policy. Nothing in the last eight years has curbed overcrowding. Despite a very large investment in prison building, numbers are at the very edge of operating capacity. Overcrowding affects every aspect of prison life; it demoralises

staff and prisoners alike and defeats any positive programme of training and education. The merger of the prison and probation services
in a National Offender Management Service (NOMS) is unlikely to
affect the continuing reliance on imprisonment. Reconviction rates have
scarcely budged and the dismal stage army of offenders trudges through
probation offices and prisons. The one bright spark has been Jack
Straw's setting up of the Youth Justice Board which is poised, opti-
mistically, to recommend an end to the incarceration of very young
offenders.

The watchword – tough on crime and tough on the causes of crime –
was a skilful piece of political rhetoric focusing on electoral advantage
of not being outgunned by the Tory opposition. It avoided any serious
approach to the underlying causes for criminal activity. Indeed, there
were instant legislative actions to demonstrate a concern for the victims
of crime on the wider public assumption, so often off target, of the nature
and extent of crime and court response in sentencing. In all this the Blair
policy reflected a knee-jerk reaction to instant media hype in the tabloid
press.

By 2003 there developed a tension between the Home Secretary and
the Lord Chief Justice, a healthy withdrawal from the battlefield taking
place only on David Blunkett's disgraced departure in December 2004 and
the arrival of Charles Clarke as the new home secretary, clearly desirous
of putting clear blue water between himself and his predecessor. Significantly, the impression now gained currency that Blair was more than a
solid supporter of the Blunkett approach, having been an ardent framer
of New Labour policy on crime and punishment. Blair had also sided
with Blunkett in the struggle to be rid of the Lord Chancellor over the
constitutional reforms and organisation of departments concerned with
the administration of justice. By the time of the election in May 2005, the
Constitutional Reform Act 2005 had timeously reached the statute book,
and a calm in the relationship between Marsham Street (the new Home
Office building) and the Royal Courts of Justice in the Strand prevailed.
With the prediction of a third term for Blair, the judges braced themselves
for a renewed encounter.

Judicial imperiousness

If ever there was any doubt about the independence of the English judiciary it was dispelled on 16 December 2004 in separate judgments of nine
Lords of Appeal in Ordinary. While the majority (of eight to one) in *A*

and others v. *Secretary of State for the Home Department*[1] contained a couple of intemperate remarks from the Bench (which might appear to have weakened the authority of the final court of appeal's decision, declaring unlawful the power to detain without trial a dozen foreigners 'suspected of terrorist activities') the lead judgment of the senior Law Lord, Lord Bingham of Cornhill – 38 pages of pellucid legal prose in the official Law Reports – however, set the tone of constitutional detachment from the executive branch of government: the judiciary has now declared itself as an independent estate of the realm. The judgments stand as a juridical tour de force, the likes of which have not been witnessed since the seventeenth century when the judges sided with Parliament in resisting the Crown. Even the less ecstatic welcome from a distinguished academic commentator described the decision as marking 'the beginnings of a much-belated judicial awakening to the fact that even in the context of national security the courts have a responsibility to ensure that the rule of law is respected'.[2] This time, the judges perfected the parliamentary process by excising, in effect, a provision in an Act of Parliament insisted upon by government exercising its legislative power through its numerical superiority of party members in the House of Commons against a concerted effort by the House of Lords.

Uniquely, there were seven separate assenting judgments – one Law Lord formally agreed, while Lord Walker of Gestinthorpe delivered a notable dissenting judgment supportive of the government's stance. The collegiality of the final court of appeal pervaded only in its emphatic verdict against an anti-libertarian provision. Judicial individualism, so distinctive a feature of the English system of reaching a verdict by an appellate court, served to enhance judicial independence, as well as denoting the independence of each judge.

While the quashing of the Home Secretary's certification of the detainees, pursuant to sections 21 to 23 of the Anti-Terrorist, Crime and Security Act 2001, required reliance upon the Human Rights Act 1998, the judges deployed their reasoning as much from established principles

---

[1] [2005] 2 WLR 87. At p. 135D. Lord Hoffmann said: 'Whether we should survive Hitler hung in the balance, but there is no doubt that we shall survive Al-Qaeda . . .[there are] nations too fragile or fissiparous to withstand a serious act of violence. But this is not the case in the UK.' Lord Scott of Foscote (at p. 152C) said that 'indefinite imprisonment . . . is the stuff of nightmares associated, accurately or inaccurately, with France before and during the revolution, with the Soviet Union in the Stalinist era and now associated . . . with the UK.'

[2] Adam Tomkins, 'Readings of *A* v. *Secretary of State for the Home Department*', *Public Law* Summer issue 2005, pp. 259, 263–4.

of English public law. The only crumb of comfort for the government was that its derogation from the European Convention on Human Rights, permitting detention without trial exceptionally where there is an 'emergency threatening the life of the nation', was upheld.

Lord Hoffmann's lone assault on the government's right to derogate from the provisions of the Human Rights Convention may yet have a lasting effect. His opinion that a greater threat to British liberty comes not from terrorism (or indeed from individual or isolated acts of terrorism) but from reaction of politicians and a gullible populace, and from panic legislation that follows, is unambiguous. There could hardly have been a more incisive pronouncement, and one which evoked discombobulation in governmental circles.

Lord Bingham, not without misgiving, did not ally himself with Lord Hoffmann, who alone dismissed the notion that the fanatical activities of a handful of terrorists, which might kill large numbers of innocent civilians and destroy tracts of property, threaten the life of the nation, however much they might constitute threats to the country's security. The 'emergency' contemplated in Article 15 of the Convention as a valid reason for opting out of the fundamental freedom of liberty, encompassed armed conflict by an invading army or an internal insurrection. A handful of terrorist suspects, however organised and orchestrated in their activities, hardly bears that description.

The ensuing response to the government's loss of power to detain the crop of a few suspected terrorists underlined the impact of judicial independence. In the frenetic, even frantic debates in February 2005 over the new legislation to control the movements and activities of suspected terrorists – whether British or alien – the opponents in Parliament (effectively in the House of Lords) impliedly endorsed the judicial decision; even the government reluctantly accepted that it had fallen foul of the rule of law, although (as we shall see) there were exaggerated mutterings of impermissible judicial interference. Control orders were instantly imposed, none of which included the imposition of house arrest, which alone was a derogable power. The existence of such a power will doubtless excite a challenge hereafter, along the lines of Lord Hoffmann's sole opinion. A fresh test of judicial independence awaits us.

Discrimination (only aliens were caught by the 2001 anti-terrorist legislation) and proportionality (disproportionate remedy for mere suspicion) were the two concepts relied upon for the Law Lords to find that there was incompatibility with Convention rights. They were concepts that were already part of the growing development of English administrative law, as well as principles emanating from Strasbourg. The European influence came from the civilian systems as much as through the ECHR. By the time the Labour party returned to power after 18 years in the political wilderness, accretion of common law powers in the hands of the judiciary had filtered through to control over ministerial decision-making.

The extent to which courts will nevertheless seek to control even political decisions, under the guise of procedural impropriety or illegality, will go in waves, depending on the contemporary political climate. At times, when government appears all-powerful and uncontrolled by Parliament, the judges will incline to supplement parliamentary control. At other times, when the institutional checks and balances on unbridled political power are in place and fully operative, the judges will be inclined to back off from using their weapon of judicial review.

The democratic process is something more subtle than the postulation of rights and duties, powers and responsibilities. One of the niceties of judicial activism is the public sense that intervention by judges in the governmental process needs to be finely tuned to the particular situation. It too calls for judicial review of a different kind. It is not a question whether Mr Justice Cocklecarrot or Sir Humphrey Appleby should make the final decision. Rather it is a matter of variable choice, according to the mood of the times and the circumstance of the topic under decision. Extra-curricularly, Lord Bingham has concluded that our judges are curiously unpredictable: he regards consistency in a judge as a vice.[3]

In the past judges have deliberately avoided any association with public administration, because to show even the slightest awareness of how the executive operates might appear, if not in fact, to destroy the highly prized virtue of judicial independence. But, under the impact of the development of judicial review, courts and administrators no longer keep their respective distances. They sensibly regard the executive and the judiciary, along with the legislature, as discrete parts of a unified system of government (with a small 'g') functioning in harmony, if not in harness. The fact that courts are independent adjudicators of administrative action against the citizen does not minimise the political reality that they are the arms of established government. Joshua Rozenberg in his book, *Trial of Strength*,[4] was wrong to correct Will Hutton, then the editor of the *Observer*, who talked in *The State We're In* of the judiciary as the 'third branch of government'. Courts do not, now at least, operate on the periphery of society', but are vital cogs in the wheels of a well-oiled vehicle of good and sound government. 'Judges', Lord Scarman wrote – perhaps ending on a note

---

[3] *Guardian*, G2, 31 May 2005, pp. 14–15.   [4] London: Richard Cohen, 1997.

of self-fulfilling prophecy – in *The Laws in Transition*,[5] 'always have been political animals. They have always had to act in the marketplace and in the political arena. They operate, of necessity, in a social, political, economic setting . . . The most important thing is that they act judicially.' And the minister or administrator in turn must act judiciously in his/her approach to the law in action. The Blair administration of 2001 to 2005 positively invited judicial activism, although it did not always respond judiciously to judicial decisions.

Bringing rights home

Observance of judicial restraint has always been a feature of a responsible judiciary, but the mood of restraint is necessarily variable. As if in acknowledgement of this fact, the Labour Party, historically hostile to a Bill of Rights, at least recognised the judges' desire to resolve human rights' issues domestically, rather than await the slap on the wrist from Strasbourg. Increasingly, aggrieved citizens had been winning their claims from the European Court of Human Rights, even if their remedies came protractedly. The Blair administration was ready to 'bring human rights home'. The passing of the Human Rights Act 1998 (which came into force in October 2000) to allow judges to declare that legislation is incompatible with the Convention and providing a fast track procedure for Parliament to alter such legislation, if it so wishes, was an ingenious device to preserve parliamentary sovereignty, and thereby to stop short of establishing a constitutional court with a power to strike down unconstitutional legislation. The move obviates the need for a written constitution or even a Bill of Rights in which sovereignty is wrested from the executive and legislature and resides ultimately in unelected judges.

How has the Human Rights Act 1998 fared in its early life in repositioning the judicature and the executive arms of government? Not all the judges enthusiastically embraced their new-found powers. Lord Hoffman, extrajudicially, has been critical of a decision emanating from Strasbourg. He wrote:

> When we joined [in 1950], indeed, took the lead in the negotiation of the European Convention, it was not because we thought it would affect our own law, but because we thought it right to set an example for others, and to help to ensure that all the member-States respected those basic human rights which were not culturally determined but reflected our common humanity.

[5] Child lecture, 1976, p. 12.

Lord Scott of Foscote (another Law Lord) advanced essentially the same argument – this time, judicially. The Convention was officially regarded in the UK, he proclaimed, as being aimed only at preventing a totalitarian take-over, and not at preventing human rights abuses within a democracy. In *Harrow LBC* v. *Qazi*[6] he wrote:

> The Universal Declaration and the Convention were the product of the horrors of fascism which led to World War II and the Holocaust . . . The intention of these instruments was to enshrine fundamental freedoms. It was not the intention to engage in social engineering in the housing field.

He thus imported a restrictive interpretation of Convention rights, in the instant case in the field of local authority housing.

This theme, that the Convention was never meant to curb the freedom of action of the member states of the Council of Europe, except for their 'freedom' to become totalitarian regimes, lies behind the contemporary utterances of the leader of a Conservative Party in prospectively seeking a review of the 1998 Act and, if necessary, its unthinkable (if only because it would mean leaving the Council of Europe) repeal. Michael Howard, following the case of *Thompson* and *Venables*, the two boys who killed the Bulger child, had argued that anyone who had signed the ECHR in the wake of the Second World War's unspeakable horrors would have reacted with disbelief at the Strasbourg Court's 'insatiable compulsion' to intervene. An examination of the Convention's *travaux préparatoires* reveals that the detractors of the 1998 Act are wrong. The controversy over the original intent of the framers of the Convention was resolved in favour of preventing human rights abuses within the democracies of the Council of Europe. The case law of the Strasbourg Court has long since been founded on a teleological emphasis on effectiveness, and also treats the Convention as a living instrument, the interpretation of which can update the law in response to changing social conditions. The 1998 Act requires the courts in the UK to take account of the jurisprudence from Strasbourg, but is not bound by it. So far there is no evidence of any judicial conflict. But likewise, there is no sign of judicial inclination in the Strand to march ahead of Strasbourg. Strasbourg's concession of a margin of appreciation allowable to courts of the member states has provided elbow-room for some different decision-making in the jurisdictions of the member states.

The Blair administration, which imaginatively brought in the 1998 leg-islation, could feel content with the early products of its brainchild. The first encounter with its ultimate sovereign power did not unduly perturb

---

[6] [2004] 1AC 983.

the government, although there were some predictable retorts that the House of Lords was overstepping the political boundary line. What political criticism there has been has been off target. The human right in the Convention most deployed has been Article 6, which guarantees the citizen a fair trial before an independent and impartial tribunal in public. That guarantee perfectly states what any common lawyer in England would have declared to be the law in our unwritten constitution. Paradoxically, the one element in the English criminal justice system which potentially falls foul of Article 6 is trial by jury, the aspect of our system which evokes the deepest commitment by most legal professionals and, one suspects, the populace. The government's attempts to restrict trial by jury in the Criminal Justice Act 2003 met with stiff opposition, if only partial success. Jury trial is claimed as deriving from Magna Carta. The fact that this is historically inaccurate does not deter most vocal advocates, even though they are faintly aware that the Great Charter could properly be described as, one baron, one vote.

The Human Rights Act 1998 can be hailed as a clear demonstration of government adherence to the rule of law (echoed by section 1 of the Constitutional Reform Act 2005 'as affirming the existing constitutional principle of the rule of law'). The constitutional reforms of 2005 provide further evidence of sincere devotion to creating a judicature institutionally separated from both executive and Parliament, while acknowledging overlapping powers within the three arms of modern democratic government. 12 June 2003 will long be remembered as the unheralded revelation of the trilogy of reforms. Two years later, two of the three – the establishment of a Supreme Court and the setting up of a judicial appointments commission – were on the statute book. The office of Lord Chancellor was kept alive, a slimmed-down version, stripped of its headship of the judiciary and probably consigned to a lower status within Cabinet government. The concordat, which was arrived at by the Lord Chief Justice and the Lord Chancellor and which declared explicitly the independence of the judiciary, to be embedded in government action, is of the highest significance.

Between 1997 and 2001 the reforms of the Blair government provided, first, for devolution: Scotland, Wales and Northern Ireland; although strictly speaking the last had achieved that status from 1920 in the Government of Ireland Act of that year, until direct rule was imposed in March 1972. Second, new proportional electoral systems for the devolved bodies, for the European Parliament, and for the new London strategic authority and mayor of London; and, third, the removal of all but 92 of the hereditary peers from the House of Lords. Fourth, there came the Freedom of Information Act which came into force, however imperfectly, in January 2005. Fifth, radical reform of local government took place; and sixth, greater use of the referendum in the form of intended testing of popular vote on the EU Constitution in 2005 (now in doubt) and prospectively on the currency of the euro. If that fasciculus of constitutional reforms did not evince a desire to modernise the institutional framework, the trilogy of reforms proposed in June 2003 could rightly be regarded as breathtaking, even if some of it was hard to stomach by traditionalists.

The creation of a Supreme Court to replace the Appellate Committee of the House of Lords divided legal opinion, but not for policy reasons. The acknowledgement of the present quality of judicial output from the Law Lords appeared not to warrant the change. Other non-traditionalist opposition opposed the move as 'a costly irrelevance'; in the end the hostility was muted. By the time that the Supreme Court is up and running – probably in 2008 – the present Law Lords will have mostly retired.

The second proposal, to take away the Lord Chancellor's patronage in appointing the judiciary, was mostly welcomed. The establishment of a judicial appointments commission was in general accepted; only the composition of the commission and its modus operandi provided discussion and debate which is continuing. The third proposal, abolition of the office of Lord Chancellor, gave the traditionalists their crumb of comfort. Here the traditionalists in the House of Lords were able to preserve at least the post in name and the Department of State in attenuated form. What has not been grabbed by the Department for Constitutional Affairs will remain in the historic Office of State, mainly an overseeing of the administration of the court service. The Lord Chief Justice of England and Wales becomes the head of the judiciary. (Likewise, the two senior judges in Scotland and Northern Ireland will head their own judiciaries.)

The UK Supreme Court

Had the government on 12 June 2003 not announced its proposal for constitutional reform in such a cack-handed manner, much of the criticism heaped upon the Secretary of State for Constitutional Affairs would probably never have surfaced, or at most would have been muted. For some years now the setting-up of a Supreme Court for the United Kingdom, to replace the Appellate Committee of the House of Lords, thereby dissociating judges from legislators, had been generally accepted both within the legal profession and by informed public opinion. The proposals were thus not the product of scribbled notes on the back of an envelope. They had been well signalled, even if, when they came, they were unhappily announced in the context of ministerial reshuffle.

The critics of the bill in the debate in the House of Lords on 12 February 2004 did not doubt the good intentions of the government, but expressed misgivings – some more serious than others – about the transfer. Only Lord Kingsland, the Conservative Party's Lord Chancellor-in-waiting, imputed bad faith. He said that he found it hard not to reach the conclusion that the real intention was 'to undermine the strength of the judicial arm of the constitution' and also that the move was a 'threat to the rule of law'. Despite a later intervention, to explain that he was not imputing to the government the aim of undermining the independence of the judiciary, Lord Kingsland was roundly rebuked, with justification.

If the proposal to end the House of Lords as the final court of appeal for England and Wales, Scotland and Northern Ireland was unsurprising, half of the present 12 Law Lords echoed the motto of the family of the 15th Viscount Falkland (a Scottish peerage created in 1620): 'If it is not necessary to make a change, it is necessary not to make a change.' The truth, though, is that change was necessary, if only demonstratively to insulate the judiciary from the other two arms of government.

The 22 judicial members of the Judges' Council, which issued an 88-page document responding to the three separate proposals for reform – The Supreme Court, the office of Lord Chancellor and a new way of appointing judges – declined to come off the fence, although its chairman, Lord Woolf (the Lord Chief Justice), favoured the changes.

The Judges' Council did permit itself one observation, that 'the Palace of Westminster constitutes an appropriately justified and prestigious setting for a national final Court of Appeal, although it has the drawbacks as to the accommodation available'. That sounded like an echo of what Walter Bagehot (1826–77), the famous economist and journalist, said in 1876 about the recently revived House of Lords in its judicial capacity. (The abolition in 1873 of the House of Lords as the final court of appeal was never implemented.) Bagehot said that gracing the appeal court with the rubric of 'Parliament' served a useful public function. It erected a dignified facade behind which an ordinary court of law could carry out its mundane task of adjudication under an aura of public deference, thereby conferring special weight upon its lofty pronouncements. The Bagehotian thesis would have carried weight if the facade really did enhance the status of the court. But the fact is that the mumbo-jumbo of the judges' procedures (much reduced in recent years), hidden away in a committee room upstairs in the Palace of Westminster, deceived no one involved professionally, and left outsiders with the impression that the Law Lords were, as labelled, a committee of the House of Lords, reporting in the chamber to the full House its decisions in the form of speeches (then later called opinions, now judgments and individual votes). Something similar seemed to sustain the traditionalist posture of the main current opponent for change, the second senior Law Lord. Lord Nicholls of Birkenhead, in a restrained but pained speech, concluded that ultimately the key question was one of appearance. Lord Nicholls observed, indisputably, that the Law Lords enjoy judicial independence from both legislature and executive government, and are held in the highest esteem. But, by their presence in the House of Lords, they are tainted by an appearance of a lack of independence. And again Lord Nicholls doubted if 'a fair-minded and independent observer, alive to our parliamentary conventions and legal traditions could hardly think so'. If this assessment were sound, the case for change would have been undermined.

The fair-minded and independent observer may not, however, quite so hastily appreciate 'our parliamentary conventions and legal traditions'. And even if he or she has some inkling of these niceties of English constitutional attitudes, there is no escaping one demonstrable fact. The curious location of the UK's final court of appeal in the Upper House of Parliament is itself a wonderment to democratic observers from home and abroad, the more so to Europeans since Britain joined the European Union in 1972. Likewise, there is the curious position of the Lord Chancellor, as the head of the judiciary, who hitherto had not only doubled up his legislative role with that of a judge presiding over appeals (as and when he chose to sit) but also trebled up as a member of the Cabinet, chairing many Cabinet committees. Lord Falconer in 2003 declared that he, as Lord Chancellor, would never sit judicially, thus removing an anomaly. The change to the Supreme Court will repair the image of confused overlap of judicature, legislature and executive. While the highest court in the land is as old as Parliament itself, its contemporary functions, since 1876, have borne no resemblance to its predecessor, save for its name and venue.

The judicial function was in fact abolished in 1873 by the Judicature Act of that year, only to be restored by the Disraeli administration three years later, when the membership became confined to professional lawyers. Since then, by practical and incremental stages, rather than by grand design, there had been a growing dissociation of the twelve Lords of Appeal in Ordinary from the legislature, to the point where the physical overlap between them had, it is true, become largely, but not entirely,

ceremonial and symbolic. Ceremony and symbolism, however, are precisely the twin attributes which impinge upon the independent observer's
assessment, 'The significance of the symbols varies with the knowledge
and experience of the mind receiving them.' So said that great US Supreme
Court judge, Mr Justice Cardozo. To the observer, the appearance (even
though a distinct departure from reality) of the Law Lords is that of dual
functioning within the single forum of domestic legislation, hence the
compelling need to break the formal link. The time had clearly come for
our top judges to move out from under the shadow of the legislature.

Constitutionalists might usefully be reminded of the words of Thomas
Jefferson: 'We might as well require a man to wear the coat that fitted
him as a boy, as civilised society to remain ever under the regime of their
ancestors.' It is all together too dramatic to say, as Lord Nicholls said,
that 'when abandoning what we have long cherished, it behoves us to be
exceedingly careful lest we squander valuable elements of our heritage'.
But there is no question of squandering; indeed there is the evident desire
precisely to preserve all the good we have inherited.

The 12 Law Lords will automatically become the Justices of the Supreme
Court. If the extremely high quality of judicial output from the Law Lords
of the past and present is indubitably to be retained under the new guise,
the change of regime does provide an opportunity, not merely to discard
an outmoded public image but also to update some of the ground rules
of practice and procedure, in the expectation thereby of improving the
institution's reputation as a model final court of appeal in administering
criminal and civil justice. Here there can only be disappointment, since
Lord Falconer had said that there will be no change in the rules governing
leave to appeal to the Supreme Court from the courts of England and
Wales, Scotland and Northern Ireland (see below).

It is conceded that the present facilities for the Law Lords and their
secretariat are sadly wanting. The physical conditions in the Law Lords'
corridor at the Palace of Westminster are cramped and under constant
pressure from other departments of the parliamentary administration
requiring space in Parliament. Library facilities and judicial assistance
will be improved in a separately sited building. No one, except a Scots
Law Lord, Lord Hope of Craighead, doubts the desirability and change
on this score. When speaking in November 2001 about possible alternative accommodation for the Law Lords, the then Lord Chancellor, Lord
Irvine of Lairg, an opponent of replacing the Appellate Committee but
contemplating a change of venue, said that a new Supreme Court building
of high architectural merit in the heart of London may be one of the most

worthy of ambitions entertained by the senior Law Lord, Lord Bingham and other proponents of the change. To achieve that ambition, the government today would need to devote resources to finding a building to reflect the most prestigious court of law in the land and to provide facilities that match the dignity of the institution. There should have been no scrimping and scraping from a tight-fisted Treasury. Every speaker in the Lords debate was insistent on this score. The outcome of this issue was less than the best. A new building, architecturally designed to the highest standards, was rejected out of hand. A wing of Somerset House, a preferred judicial option, appeared not feasible. In the end, Middlesex Guildhall, on the west side of Parliament Square, became the selected building, to be refurbished to meet judicial requirements, at a cost of £32 million, rather less than might have been expended to reflect the optimum deference to a prestigious institution. On this score, the Blair administration has done the judicial arm of government less than the best.

The UK Supreme Court should now have exclusive control of its portfolio. The Court of Appeal decides 'cases', many of them a review or rehearing of the fact-finding decision of the trial court. The House of Lords generally decides issues (albeit framed as 'cases'); it does not exist, generally speaking, to correct errors of lower courts. Given complete control of the 'cases' it hears, the Supreme Court would be able to deal with those cases which significantly raise legal issues of general public importance. This move will confirm a general trend towards the second-tier appeal court being reserved almost exclusively for issues of a constitutional nature, chiefly public law cases rather than private litigation. This may make the Supreme Court, now that the Human Rights Act is playing such an important role in the courts, more like (but specifically not a replica of) the US Supreme Court. It will not replicate the latter court's powers to declare Acts of Congress unconstitutional. The UK Supreme Court is always bound to stop at a declaration of incompatibility of Acts of Parliament with human rights. Parliament remains sovereign.

The preservation of the sovereignty of Parliament, if largely theoretical, was a stroke of ingenuity on the part of Lord Irvine. If his Lord Chancellorship ended in tears on 12 June 2003, he will rightly be remembered as the architect of the Human Rights legislation.

That is not the end of the dilemma about the Supreme Court's case-load. It is not intended that the UK Supreme Court will dispense UK justice. Instead, it will still be the final court of appeal separately for England and Wales, Scotland, and Northern Ireland. Scotland presents an oddity. It does not permit criminal appeals to the House of Lords, although devolution issues have thrown up cases involving criminal justice.[7] (The devolution jurisdiction, at present exercised by the Judicial Committee of the Privy Council, will come under the umbrella of the new Supreme Court.) Why not a criminal jurisdiction for all three, or for none? But Scotland is not giving up its finality in criminal cases. In any event, in considering the membership of the new Supreme Court, there will be a strong need to ensure the presence of a judge with experience of the criminal law and practice, even if it is only for criminal cases from England and Wales, and for Northern Ireland.

Scotland has another oddity in the filtering of cases for determination at the highest level of court, which would sit uneasily with the Supreme Court having complete control over its own case-load, and thus developing its own policies and approach about the categories and importance of cases on which it should rule. Currently, civil appeals for Scotland lie to the House of Lords as of right, save that there is a requirement for two counsel to certify the reasonableness of an appeal. The present arrangement is long-standing; there appears to be no desire among the Scots lawyers to change it. All this indicates a plurality within the UK, asymmetrical arrangements and an acceptance of territorial diversity.

Finally, we shall be rid of the present incongruity of Law Lords, unrobed and without wigs, while counsel appear in gown and wig – a full-bottomed wig for Queen's Counsel – as and when, once a year, the Appellate Committee sits in the chamber of the House of Lords to assert its right to sit in the chamber.

Dress normally, without the parliamentary mumbo-jumbo, and a new Supreme Court's dignity can be maintained, even enhanced, to reflect the renowned status of the Law Lords of the past. The appearance of independence will finally match the reality. And the justices of the Supreme Court will no longer have to wrestle with their consciences whether to participate in the legislative deliberations of the House of Lords, although on retirement from the Bench they may take up the opportunity to revert to being legislators. But the duality of function will have disappeared.

Judges as legislators

Much, but not over-much, was made of the personal contribution of the Law Lords to debates, particularly if they avoided (as they did) any controversial issues of a party political nature. Indeed, Lord Bingham, as

---

[7] Twice, on 11 May 2005, the Privy Council reversed decisions of the High Court of Justiciary: see *Holland* v. *HM Advocate* and *Sinclair* v. *HM Advocate*, *Times Law Report*, 1 June 2005.

the senior Law Lord, used the phrase, 'where there is a strong element of party political controversy', in a formal statement in the House of Lords on 22 June 2000.[8] The memorandum did say:

> The Law Lords hope, and believe, that the contribution they make to the work of the House, in committees and in the chamber is of value. For their part, the Law Lords benefit from the wider perspective derived from the closer contact with the legislative process and also from their awareness of debates in the House on matters of public interest. They believe their judicial work would be the poorer without this.

All this was redolent of what Lord Salisbury said over a hundred years ago: 'Practically, they (the Law Lords) have often to make laws as judges, they will do it better from having to make it as legislators'. Lord Wilberforce, a former senior Law Lord and a member of the House for 38 years until his death in 2004, was a loud proponent of the duality of function of the Law Lords. In a published paper, he wrote:

> It does not seem to be disputed that the Law Lords make a valuable contribution to the legislative work of the House of Lords . . . That it was the privilege and the duty of a Law Lord to contribute in this way was impressed upon me by that great lawyer, Lord Reid, when I joined the House.

It is noteworthy that Lord Bingham was a prime promoter of the removal of the Law Lords from their parliamentary setting. The value of the Law Lords, within the legislature, could not be gainsaid. But the loss of their services was outweighed by the constitutional impropriety. Ironically, at the moment of impending demise, the Appellate Committee of the House of Lords is adjudicating on the validity of the Parliament Act 1949 in respect of the anti-hunting legislation. Nine Law Lords as judges will determine whether as legislators they have acted lawfully. Does that fact automatically disqualify them from hearing the Countryside Alliance's appeal?

Judges acting extra-curricularly

If the Blair administration in its constitutional reforms observed the convention of an independent judiciary, it had not always been sensitive of the convention in practice. Judges (mostly Law Lords or Lords Justices of

---

[8] Since then, until 3 July 2003, only Lord Hope of Craighead (4), Lord Hutton (1) and Lord Scott of Foscote (10) among the Lords of Appeal in Ordinary participated in debates: see appendix to the House of Lords Library Notes on the Appellate Jurisdiction of the House of Lords, LLN 2003/007.

Appeal) have over the years been asked to chair commissions and committees, for the ostensible reason that they alone are perceived publicly as
'impartial' and 'independent', and hence peculiarly capable of reaching,
objectively, responses to public scandals and disasters. What has not been
sufficiently appreciated is that to use members of the judiciary for extra-
curricular inquiries has been to expose them to public criticism for their
political pronouncements without the protective device of a structured
legal system, with its inbuilt safeguards of appellate review and constitutional restraints. The Hutton inquiry into the circumstances surrounding
the death of Dr David Kelly in 2003 exemplified the problem and has led
to a movement among the judges to seek curtailment of their services
beyond the confines of the courtroom. The Inquiries Act 2005 did not
directly address the issue, although there are signs of retrenchment in
the practice of serving High Court judges being pressed into service; a
provision requiring a minister to consult the Lord Chief Justice about any
appointment for the chair of a public inquiry should serve to curb the use
of judicial manpower.

Sir Edward Heath, speaking in the House of Commons debate on 8
July 1982 to approve the appointment of Lord Franks (not a member
of the judiciary) to chair the Falkland Islands War Review, said: 'The
plain fact is that we have never succeeded in finding the perfect form of
inquiry.' Two decades and a spate of public inquiries occupying vast acres
of valuable time and effort and substantial resources from public funds
later, the statement is as accurate today. No one could blame Lord Hutton
for a meticulous study of the factual material; far from it. He provided the
material upon which the public could judge. It was the sweep of the judicial
pen, embracing the canvass of public administration and the world of
electronic and print media, that provided the public concern. It has been
the use of judges to conduct inquiries into matters that go way beyond the
precisely framed dispute so familiar to courts of law that evokes the worry.
The fact that the two top officials in the BBC – both outstanding men in
public affairs – resigned in the face of stinging criticism of the 'systems' in
our public service broadcasting for controlling the broadcasting output
that went awry in a single instance of an admittedly bad piece of journalism
seems altogether a result too far away from the public interest. Should the
government be using the judiciary to examine such complex matters if
the issues encompass policies and practices of the nation's institutions?

The undesirability of pressing judges to conduct these inquiries has
long been a thorny topic among the judiciary – many judges would wish
to refuse the invitation from government, but find that their sense of

public duty does not allow them to indulge in such niceties as individual predilection to stick to their professional calling. The point was most tellingly put by Lord Wilberforce (probably our finest judge of the post-war period) in the debate in February 1997 on the report by Sir Richard Scott (now Lord Scott of Foscote) in the Arms to Iraq inquiry. From his experience in the civil service during the war and later as a judge, Lord Wilberforce recognised that the nature of government (with a small 'g') in the formation and carrying out of policy is a very different animal from a litigated dispute. It was difficult to obtain a clear, consistent, easily describable picture, he said; 'The whole thing is muddy and not transparent.' Turning to the Scott Report, Lord Wilberforce said that 'Sir Richard, as a highly intelligent judge, is quite conscious of the possible gap in the relationship and of the difference in methods of thought between the two worlds' of the law and government. In the legal system there are methods of thought, sets of values and conventions that are different and which above all use a different language from the methods, conventions and language used by those who are responsible for government and other public institutions. The judiciary today is replete with men and women who are both learned and experienced in deciding issues between disputants, frequently on one side a government department or a public authority. They are adept at unravelling tricky issues of fact and law. Lord Hutton has been an exemplar of that fine tradition. But that is not enough. Lord Wilberforce ended his speech in 1997: 'Sir Richard had made great efforts to adjust to the other world outside the law, but the difference remains underlying his approach.' That might have been Lord Wilberforce's verdict on the Hutton Report.

Not only are Lord Hutton's strictures regarding the BBC out of kilter with a large section of the public that avidly listened to and imbibed the evidence which was widely published (although Lord Hutton curiously excluded the broadcasting media from direct reporting through audio and visual recordings). But it was also Lord Hutton's judicial stance which can only damage the public image of an independent judiciary pitchforked into public debate and unprotected by judicial garb.

The lesson on the composition of tribunals of inquiry is clear. If it is thought that the subject matter calls for a judicial approach and that the political sensitivities are not too heavily engaged, then government might look to the best judicial talent for seeking the truth of what happened, how it happened and why. Notably, the Inquiries Act 2005 specifically precludes a public inquiry from identifying and assigning liability, criminal or civil, to any person involved in the event under investigation. The aim is to learn the lessons from the inquiry, and not to lambast individual participants in the event under inquiry.

Blunkett's blunderbusses

If the reforms emanating from the Blair administration designedly and conditionally reflected a modern approach to judicial independence, it was not always matched in the outpourings of ministers, either individually or collectively. Indeed, while ministers will often, quietly or not so quietly, fume at the decisions of the court overturning ministerial decisions and seriously negating or impairing governmental policies, they rarely give voice to other than discreet public utterances. The Blair administration must surely be unique in not always and impeccably preserving the niceties of its relationship to the judiciary. It is a paradox that at a time of unsurpassed intellectual quality of the higher judiciary the normal tension between ministers and judiciary should have been exacerbated.

The Home Office is always the most vulnerable of departments of state to judicial review, if only because almost every decision emanating, most acutely, from that source involves a weighing of the public interest against the rights of the individual citizen. Hence, it was no surprise that David Blunkett's arrival as Home Secretary meant a confrontation with the judges. But his frequent spats with the Lord Chief Justice were indicative of a populist attitude that denied even a commitment to the rule of law.

Blunkett's hostility towards the judges erupted in 2003. He attacked the Law Lords for their decision that under the Human Rights Act 1998 a politician was not empowered to play any part in deciding how long a person serving a sentence of life imprisonment should remain in prison; all sentencing is a judicial, not an executive function. This attack was followed by an even more direct attack on a single High Court judge. Other public utterances from the Home Secretary did nothing to lessen the sense of constitutional impropriety on his part. The excessive length of the Criminal Justice Act 2003, with its specific tariff-fixing provisions for categories of murder convictions, was the riposte. It remains to be seen whether this piece of penal machinery survives judicial scrutiny.

The problem is not new and is not confined to one political party. In September 1959 Lord Parker, the new Lord Chief Justice, attacked the Homicide Act of 1957, an attempt by the Conservative government to head off the growing trend to abolish the death penalty for murder. Rab (R. A.) Butler, the Home Secretary, resented the speech and indeed wrote a memo of protest about it to the Lord Chancellor in which he took particular exception to the charge that he had gone in for an indiscriminate commuting of death sentences (in fact, of the nineteen death sentences he had had to consider by the summer of 1959, he had commuted only eight). That did not stop Lord Parker from returning to the charge, at least on the question of corporal punishment, which he strongly favoured. The ministerial response was predictably decorous. The Home Secretary remained publicly silent, but privately was more than a little irritated. A half-century later, that was not Blunkett's style. Privately he sounded off to his civil servants but also felt uninhibited in public. That was not the only difference. Blunkett fulminated at the courts 'reversing the will of Parliament'. This was a direct attack on judicial pronouncements and not just at the extra-curricular statements of the most senior judge. The contemporary ructions between minister and judiciary occur in the context of increased resort to judicial review and the enhanced powers of the courts under the Human Rights Act. The Blair administration could hardly complain of the activism of the top judiciary; their enactment positively invited the test of its legislative programme for its compatibility with the provisions of the European Convention on Human Rights.

If one wanted to find a home secretary in modern times whose approach to criminal justice and the penal system exemplified what the American political scientist, Professor Seymour Martin Lipset, had in mind when he coined the phrase 'working class authoritarianism', it must surely be David Blunkett. Every response from the Home Secretary during his occupancy of the office has exhibited a personal distaste for liberal values and an intellectually impoverished attitude to the independence of the judiciary, accompanied by harsh language in his exchanges with the Lord Chief Justice, bordering on a rejection of the rule of law. Whether the subject matter was asylum seekers, football hooligans or suicides in prison, David Blunkett was upfront with insensitive utterances, never more so than when he publicly declared his desire to toast in champagne the suicide of the wretched Dr Shipman.

What was made worse in the policy-making of the Home Office has been the utter rejection of any question of independent advice or assistance. When the Law Commission, in its impressive report on partial defences to murder, recommended a review of the law of murder, David Blunkett's first instinct was to reject wholly the Law Commission's wise plea. Only after persuasion by political colleagues and Home Office officials did he begrudgingly announce (incidentally overlooking the convention of informing Parliament first) that there would be an inquiry conducted internally within government. The notion that a review of the law of homicide might properly encompass the public outside government epitomised the arrogance (self-confessed, it must be noted) of the Secretary of State for Home Affairs. With the advent of Charles Clarke as the new home secretary the method of review has been reconsidered. This proved to be a welcome, if minor, concession to legal views.

But the Blunkett outbursts may yet have reflected a similar, less outspoken attitude from ministerial colleagues. If so, the relationship between government and judiciary would be taking on a new dimension. In the course of his judgment in the anti-terrorist case of 16 December 2004 Lord Bingham of Cornhill alluded to the powers of the courts in emergency situations. Constitutional dangers exist no less in too little judicial activism as in too much. There are limits to the legitimacy of executive or legislative decision-making, just as there are to decision-making by the courts. The boundary lines have to be drawn so that judicial review does not trespass on the field of executive government. Delineating the two functions of the cardinal feature of the modern democratic state as 'the cornerstone of the rule of law', Lord Bingham concluded:

> The Attorney General is fully entitled to insist on the proper limits of judicial authority, but he is wrong to stigmatise judicial decision-making as in some way undemocratic.

As the government's chief legal adviser and its advocate before the courts, Lord Goldsmith was speaking for the Blair administration. Did he somehow wish to indicate that, in declaring the relevant statutory provisions detaining indefinitely non-British terrorist suspects without trial as discriminatory and disproportionate, and hence non-compliant with human rights, the judges were overstepping the mark of constitutional propriety? Perhaps he was mindful of what the courts might do to a challenge to the government's decision to invade Iraq.

The Iraq invasion

When the Prime Minister received the Attorney General's opinion on 7 March 2003 about the legality of an invasion of Iraq, he cannot have felt that he was getting the green light. By any reasonable standards the opinion was neutral on the issue, pointing out in lawyerly terms the pros and cons for asserting legality. What cannot be gainsaid, now that the full document has been belatedly released to the public, is that any decision to go to war was fraught with difficulties and faced the distinct possibility of a challenge in the courts, both international and even domestic, with uncertain outcome. (In fact there are proceedings afoot by the families of soldiers killed.)

No doubt, ten days later the Prime Minister and his colleagues in Cabinet got the all-clear personally from the Attorney General, who is not a member of Cabinet but attended a Cabinet meeting. The Prime Minister duly got his legal fig leaf. But rather more extensive coverage of the prime ministerial frame is called for when taking such a monumental decision as to commit British troops to armed conflict abroad. Any substantial doubts about the legality of invading Iraq should have been concluded by the aphorism, if in legal doubt, stay out. That should have been the only sensible position for someone to adopt where there was a total acceptance of the rule of law, including the rule of international law. Characteristic of the Blair administration throughout the eight years has been something less than full commitment to the rule of law. One has only to point to the anti-terrorist legislation of 2001, the detention without trial of the Belmarsh prisoners for three years and the riposte to a resounding defeat in the House of Lords last December, and to the replacement legislation in February 2005, empowering the home secretary to issue control orders on suspected terrorists.

The proper approach to the 7 March 2005 opinion from the Attorney General did not moreover depend ultimately on a political judgment about breaches of UN Resolution 1441. Assuming that such judgment could properly be made by a member state of the United Nations (and was not a matter exclusively for the Security Council) and assuming that there was a clear breach by Saddam Hussein, that could not conclude the issue of legality. The Attorney General rightly pointed out that there was a plausible argument – hardly the language of a firm opinion – for saying that a breach of Resolution 1441 revived the power to use force against Iraq under the earlier (1991) Resolution 678. That hesitant, even provisional argument turned on a pure question of a construction of UN resolutions, which are legal instruments that call for interpretation. It did not require anything other than a legal judgment. The Attorney General's opinion pointed to rival legal views. While the government was obtaining favourable advice from a renowned professor of international law, the overwhelming opinion in other academic institutions and in and around the Temple was that no such revival of Resolution 678 could be invoked simply because of a breach a dozen years later in an entirely different situation of international disorder in the Gulf region.

In a lecture to JUSTICE, the independent legal human rights organisation, on 14 October 2003 Lord Alexander of Weedon QC described the contention of the Attorney General, that the authority to use force in Resolution 678 of 29 November 1990 could be effectively revived 12 years later in entirely different circumstances and for a different purpose and contrary to the wishes of the Security Council, as 'risible'.

There was, as the Attorney General observed, every conceivable reason for greatly preferring a second resolution from the Security Council to put the issue of legality at rest. But the failure to achieve that desired state of affairs could only have led to abandonment of putting British shoulders to the United States' mighty wheel.

What happened between 7 and 17 March is still not fully explained. The Attorney General, in giving the all-clear, may or may not have been 'summarising' what he had concluded on 7 March. Only an independent public inquiry can properly determine that matter. The truth is not helped by the unfortunate constitutional duality of the Attorney General as the government's chief legal adviser and at the same time a member of the government, thus confusing independent legal advice and political activity. That too calls for constitutional clarity, supplementing the Constitutional Reform Act 2005.

Though qualified as a barrister and legally tutored by his discarded Lord Chancellor, the Prime Minister displayed few, if any, lawyerly instincts which dictated that it was illegal to go to war in Iraq. Even during his first term, Blair had evinced a desire to endorse the mightier weight of a law and order policy, a hangover from his days as the Labour Party opposition spokesman on home affairs. His overpowering commitment to political dominance allowed for little or no accommodation for legalistic moderation. If that attitude was present from 1997 to 2001, it manifested itself after 2003.

A balanced Blair

Constitutional reform, accompanied by the replacement of Lord Falconer, a chummier legal heavyweight in place of Lord Irvine, the dour, unbending intellectual giant among lawyers, did not instinctively bear the mark of Blairism. If Blair was the architect of modernisation of the legal system he left the parliamentary process to his new Lord Chancellor, a willing agent capable of charming away hostile peers. The fact that the monumental change in the constitution was overshadowed by a clumsy Cabinet reshuffle speaks volumes for the triumph of political power over legislation. Blair, despite (or perhaps because of) his highly successful wife's career at the Bar, barely identified himself with his professional peers.

The legal profession never felt that it had an ally at Number 10. But then practising lawyers have rarely in our nation's history occupied the office of prime minister.

Wholesome detachment of judicature from legislature and executive branches of government awaits completion. Modernisation generally of our constitutional arrangements has come a long way since 1997, subject only to the need for more evident attention by politicians to its practical consequences. If the rule of law has remained secure, the public perception of threatened detachment was ever-present, never more so than over the Iraq invasion.

When you stand at the edge of an abyss it is vital you do not lose your balance. The requirement in the Constitutional Reform Act 2005 that ministers of the crown must uphold the continued independence of the judiciary (and observe the rule of law) might serve to indicate that the Blair administration in its third term of office will keep its balance. If the Prime Minister's loss of credibility within the electorate was due, in part, to his stance over the Iraq war, it was even more marked in judicial and legal circles. Something more, however, than a balancing act by Blair will be needed to restore his credibility among that professional elite.

12

Education

ALAN SMITHERS

When the Blair government came fresh to power in May 1997 it had primary education as it main aim and a close-knit team ready for both Number 10 and the newly merged Department for Education and Employment. David Blunkett, the secretary of state, had been the only member of the shadow cabinet besides Gordon Brown to have been publicly promised his post prior to the election. Estelle Morris, a member of the education team since 1995, became under-secretary for schools and then school standards minister from 1998 when Stephen Byers was promoted to the Cabinet. Professor Michael Barber, Tony Blair's chief speechwriter on schools in opposition, became Blunkett's main adviser and head of the newly created Standards and Effectiveness Unit (SEU) in the department, charged with changing the culture to accept responsibility for delivery as well as legislation. In Number 10, Tony Blair's chief of staff since 1994, David Miliband, an education expert, became head of the newly formed Policy Unit. Andrew Adonis, don and education journalist, who in an article in the run-up to the 1997 election had urged Blair to become his own education minister, was recruited to be Blair's education adviser. From the outset the new DfEE was a whirl of activity.[1] It restructured and rewrote the mission statement and embarked on an ambitious programme of legislation and monitoring. Within days it was setting targets in literacy and numeracy for primary education. Tony Blair was personally involved, regularly meeting the education team at the DfEE. There were tensions, notably over Chris Woodhead, the chief inspector of schools, whom Blair through Adonis ordered Blunkett to keep in post, but generally they were able to hold together to drive the education agenda through Parliament.

By contrast, following re-election in June 2001, the Department of Education and Skills, as it had become, increasingly found itself having to

---

[1] Alan Smithers, 'Education policy', in Anthony Seldon (ed.), *The Blair Effect* (London: Little, Brown, 2001), pp. 405–26.

react to events and live with the consequences of the education policies of the first term. It also turned its attention from primary to secondary and higher education, where there was less of a consensus as to what should be done. There had been some reallocation of roles. David Blunkett was rewarded by promotion to home secretary and Estelle Morris moved up to take his place. David Miliband, by now an MP, was given the job of minister for school standards early in the Parliament. Michael Barber had already transferred to Number 10 to take charge of a new Delivery Unit intended to apply his approach to target setting and delivery across the public sector. Andrew Adonis replaced Miliband as Tony Blair's policy chief. With so many familiar faces, all looked set fair, but soon education policy began to be blown off course. David Blunkett had a lot to do with it, even though he was no longer there. He had left two ticking bombs. His rash promise to resign if the numeracy and literacy targets declared in 1997 had not been met by 2002 contributed to the downfall of his successor, Estelle Morris. His 2001 manifesto pledge ruling out top-up fees for the lifetime of the Parliament was a great embarrassment to her successor, Charles Clarke, as he struggled to get the very same fees on to the statute book. David Blunkett was also indirectly responsible for a further change, when the speeding of his lover's nanny's visa through the Home Office caused him to resign in December 2004 and Clarke was promoted in his place.

In contrast to David Blunkett's reign of nearly seven years there were thus three Education secretaries of state in the one Parliament, with numerous changes also among the junior ministers. Continuity began to be lost. Each new incumbent took time to master the brief and interpreted it somewhat differently. Estelle Morris took a teacher-friendly tone, believing that her predecessor had been too prescriptive. Charles Clarke reversed some of the major decisions of the first term. He closed the Standards and Effectiveness Unit and dropped the numeracy and literacy targets for 11-year-olds. The impression of a department not entirely at ease with itself was borne out when Charles Clarke's successor, Ruth Kelly, found herself at Tony Blair's behest having to reject the main recommendation of the Tomlinson Working Group on 14–19 Reform after it had been allowed two years and three reports to attract considerable support for its views. It is difficult to imagine that Tony Blair would have allowed things to unravel in this way had he not been preoccupied elsewhere with the aftermath of heinous attack on the twin towers and his internal struggle with Gordon Brown.

According to Robert Peston's biography[2] of Gordon Brown, Brown believed that at the infamous Granita meeting domestic policy had been ceded to him. The note of the meeting as quoted reads: 'Gordon has spelled out the fairness agenda – social justice, employment opportunities and skills – and Tony is in full agreement with this.' Brown wanted the second part changed to 'Tony has guaranteed this will be pursued'. Blair refused, but Brown was able to get a report of his 'guarantee' in *The Times* and behaved as if he were in control of the economic and social agenda. Brown, however, has not seemed much interested in the detail of schools policy, leaving Blair the space to progress his avowed priority. Brown's influence has come through more in his old Labour stance on social class, his keenness to promote skills development, but above all through controlling the purse-strings.

A-levels

Ironically, it was one of the better-seeming decisions of the first Parliament that began to derail education policy in the second. On taking office in 1997 Labour had found itself in the early stages of the implementation of recommendations from Sir Ron Dearing on qualifications for 16–19-year-olds. The report had offered three options: retain and improve existing qualifications, introduce an overarching certificate or replace the array of awards with a diploma. The first two (but not the third) were put out for consultation and improving existing qualifications won the day. This looked to be a sound decision, since by the end of compulsory schooling young people ought to know something about what they are good at, what they like doing and where they want to go. The different directions are likely to be better served by a range of courses and qualifications than by trying to fit everything into just one. But the government had not reckoned with the massive increase in assessment and the difficulty of maintaining standards entailed in the new arrangements. Under them A-levels had been divided into a one-year AS and a second-year A2, so that examinations in the lower sixth became a regular feature of the national exam scene for the first time. The first rumbles of discontent came with the rolling out of the AS in 2001, and these blew up into a storm when the first full A-level results appeared a year later.

In her first week as education and skills secretary Estelle Morris commissioned a report from Professor David Hargreaves, chief executive of the

---

[2] Robert Peston, *Brown's Britain* (London: Short Books, 2005), pp. 66–8.

Qualifications and Curriculum Authority (QCA) on the A- and AS-level reforms. His interim report in July 2001 recommended some timetable changes to reduce clashes, and the final report in December concluded that the reforms had been rushed without taking full account of the capacity of the schools and colleges to implement them.[3] In the meantime, Hargreaves had resigned after only one year in the job. While a successor was sought the chairman, Sir William Stubbs, a distinguished educational administrator, took on both roles. In the first results under the new arrangements the A-level pass rate leaped by 4.5 points amid cries in the press that it would soon reach 100%. But the independent schools had different concerns. They claimed to have evidence that examiners had manipulated the marking so that the pass rate would not be even higher. The alleged gerrymandering meant that some of their students were missing out on rightful university places. What inflamed the press particularly were instances where students were getting straight As in their examinations, but only 'unclassified' in the course work. One examination board admitted to having moved the goal posts, and headteachers of maintained schools joined their independent colleagues in demanding that all A-levels should be re-marked. Estelle Morris ordered the QCA to investigate. When the new chief executive, Ken Boston, recruited from Australia, eventually arrived he found himself, in his first week in office, having to check through examination grades. He said that there was no evidence of a systematic fiddle, but he had looked at only those candidates awarded U alongside two A grades. This was not enough to quieten the clamour and Estelle Morris found herself having to ask Mike Tomlinson, who had recently been replaced as chief inspector of schools, to conduct an independent inquiry into the procedures for determining grades and maintaining standards.

A week later Tomlinson handed over a preliminary report[4] in which he found that the chief executives of the examination boards and the QCA had acted 'with integrity', but that the examination boards 'perceived' themselves to be under pressure from the QCA to cut grades to the same level as in 2001. This was taken by the DfES to suggest that Sir William Stubbs in his dual role was in some sense responsible. Relations

---

[3] David Hargreaves, *Review of Curriculum 2000 – QCA's Report on Phase One* (London: Qualifications and Curriculum Authority, July 2001); David Hargreaves, *Review of Curriculum 2000 – QCA's Report on Phase Two* (London: Qualifications and Curriculum Authority, December 2001).

[4] Mike Tomlinson, *Inquiry Into A Level Standards*, Interim Report (London: Department for Education and Skills, September 2002).

had already soured when he had accused Estelle Morris on national television of improper intervention in the inquiry. The Secretary of State first invited him to resign and when he did not do so immediately he was sacked. He hotly contested that he had done anything wrong and in an appearance before the Commons Education and Skills Committee accused the department of spin-doctoring to make him the scapegoat. Sir William sued for wrongful dismissal and the government eventually backed down, paying him £95,000 for legal costs and lost earnings in an out-of-court settlement. Charles Clarke, now the secretary of state, wrote that Sir William had acted in 'good faith' and 'the circumstances which led to your departure were regrettable for all concerned and caused hurt to all parties'.[5]

Resignation

Estelle Morris was obviously under strain and it showed in a photograph published on the front page of *The Times* of 20 September 2002 in which she had her legs drawn back and tightly wrapped around each other. She had begun to look increasingly accident prone – not only over A-levels, but also on individual learning accounts (ILAs), teacher vetting, school exclusions and primary school targets. Not all were her doing, but she carried the can. ILAs, popularised by Michael Barber[6] when he was Tony Blair's education adviser, were seized upon by Gordon Brown as a platform for his skills revolution. Unfortunately, the scheme had been pressed into service without adequate checks to prevent fraud and it had become a licence for the unscrupulous to print money. Any supposed training provider could come up with the names of applicants, real or imagined, and automatically receive £200 for each. The DfES, responsible for overseeing the scheme run by Capita, a facilities management company, was alerted by the police that ILAs had become the target of fraud. By October 2001 the evidence was overwhelming. Estelle Morris' first inclination was to shut it down, but Gordon Brown, who could see the political risks in the failure of one of the new public private partnerships (PPPs), at first refused to do so,[7] which gave the Secretary of State a very difficult time in the Commons, where she announced a 'temporary stop' of a 'successful

---

[5] Richard Garner, 'Warm words and £95,000 for sacked exams watchdog', *Independent*, 6 February 2003.
[6] Michael Barber, *The Learning Game* (London: Victor Gollancz, 1996), pp. 282–3.
[7] Tom Bower, *Gordon Brown* (London: Harper Collins, 2004), pp. 364–6.

programme'. A month later the scheme was summarily closed to prevent further crime. The fall-out from the failure continued through 2002. In May the Commons Education and Skills Committee[8] described it as 'a débacle' and called for compensation to genuine training companies 'devastated' by the collapse. But the government refused. A damning report on ILAs by the National Audit Office was published in October.[9]

Capita also ran the Criminal Records Bureau (CRB) which was another source of embarrassment for Morris. In the wake of the murder of two young schoolgirls in Soham (as it turned out by Ian Huntley, the school caretaker, with previous form) a decision was taken in mid-August to tighten up checks on school staff. The CRB could not cope and some schools were left without their new staff at the beginning of term, with children having to stay at home. Estelle Morris was forced to apologise for the late policy change and to revert to the old system to ease the backlog. At about the same time she intervened in a dispute over two boys expelled from a school in Epsom, Surrey, for threatening to kill a teacher. She said that she was 'outraged' by the decision of an appeals tribunal to overturn the expulsion and said she 'did not think the boys should return to the school'.[10] But it then emerged that she had no powers to act. The final straw seems to have been primary school targets. The DfES had to admit in March 2002 that the key targets had not been met. When asked previously if she would resign if this were to be the case by the Commons Education and Skills Committee,[11] she said, 'No, and I never said I would.' But then the Conservative opposition unearthed an unequivocal commitment she had made on 2 March 1999. Asked in the Commons if she would commit to Blunkett's pledge she said: 'Of course I will; I have already done so. Indeed, I generously commit the Under-Secretary (Charles Clarke) too. We speak with one voice.'[12]

These bungles coming on top of the fuss surrounding A-levels led Estelle Morris to conclude she was not up to the job and she suddenly resigned

---

[8] House of Commons Education and Skills Committee, *Individual Learning Accounts* (London: The Stationery Office, May 2002).

[9] National Audit Office, *Individual Learning Accounts* (London: The Stationery Office, October 2002).

[10] Krishna Guha, 'Expulsion row keeps Morris trapped in spotlight', *Financial Times*, Weekend 12–13 October 2002.

[11] House of Commons Education and Skills Committee, *Minutes of Evidence for Wednesday 24 October 2001, Rt Hon Estelle Morris MP, Secretary of State for Education and Skills* (London: The Stationery Office, 2001), Question 20, Paul Holmes.

[12] House of Commons, *Hansard Debates for 2 March 1999*, Column 948, http://www.publications.parliament.uk

on 23 October 2002. In her letter of resignation she said, 'I'm good at dealing with the issues, and in communicating to the teaching profession. I am less good at the strategic management of a huge department and I am not good at dealing with the modern media.'[13] This seems a very honest and accurate assessment. She had been a successful number two to David Blunkett as Schools Minister and in her first months as Secretary of State she had received a very favourable press. She got on particularly well with teachers who regarded her as one of their own (she had been a teacher for 18 years before entering Parliament in 1992) and she had made considerable progress in reaching out to the teacher unions.

But when Tomlinson finally reported on the A-level saga after she had departed,[14] it appeared that the problem really boiled down to the standards of the AS and A2 examinations not having been agreed at the outset. One board, Oxford Cambridge and RSA Examinations (OCR), had taken the view that since AS exams were of a lower standard than the old A-levels, the A2 exams should be harder to keep the overall standard the same. Tomlinson's sifting of all the results and combinations of them found that only 1,089 students merited higher grades (fewer than in the previous year), a maximum of 168 missed out on their first choice of university and only four changed university during the year. Serious enough, but one can't help thinking that with more skilful management it would not have come to this.

Top-up fees

Estelle Morris passed on a hot potato to Charles Clarke. After the 2001 election the government was already wondering whether its introduction of upfront university tuition fees in 1997 had been wise. While Gordon Brown was concerned about putting off those from poorer homes, Tony Blair feared that the fees might be eroding support among middle-class voters on whom the means-tested charge mainly fell. Accordingly, the DfEE, the Treasury and Number 10 set up a joint project to review the financing of higher education. It was, therefore, a considerable surprise when, on 8 February 2001, David Blunkett announced to the Commons that 'I can now make the government's position clear. If we win the next general election, there will be no levying of "top-up" fees in the next

---

[13] 'Morris resignation – Dear Tony, Dear Estelle', *The Times*, 4 October 2002, p. 5.
[14] Mike Tomlinson, *Inquiry into A Level Standards*, Final Report (London: Department for Education and Skills, December 2002).

Parliament.'[15] This was emphasised further in the election manifesto: 'we will not introduce "top-up" fees and have legislated to prevent them'.[16] Doubts about upfront fees were confirmed for Tony Blair on the doorstep during the campaign and on re-election he pressed ahead with the review. The Treasury's favoured idea was for a graduate tax and this was supported by Estelle Morris, but Tony Blair wanted to be 'bold'. Prompted by his mentor, the late Roy Jenkins, and his policy chief, Andrew Adonis, the Prime Minister became increasingly attracted by the idea of allowing the universities some freedom to price their own courses with students contributing through deferred loans. This would not only provide an additional income stream for universities, but also switch the payments from the parents (who tended to see upfront fees as their responsibility) to the students once they were benefiting financially from having been at university. Brown, on the other hand, in an outburst at the *Guardian's* offices rejected these 'top-up' fees, as they inaccurately became known, as 'madness'.[17]

Proposals from the review were due to be published in November 2002, but with the change of secretary of state this was delayed until the following January. Charles Clarke had initially been attracted to the idea of a graduate tax, but he soon fell in line with Number 10's preference of deferred fees repaid out of income-contingent loans. The difference is that if a student incurs a liability for fees of £9,000, then this is what he/she repays, but under a graduate tax there would be a charge of a few pence per pound on earnings irrespective of tuition costs. A high-earning graduate footballer or pop star would, therefore, find themselves paying huge amounts of extra tax even though their degree had little to do with their success. The method of repayment was a separate issue from whether universities should be held to the same fee or allowed to charge different amounts, but they became inextricably linked. In an attempt to allay concerns that variable fees would put off the poor, the White Paper set out proposals for an 'access regulator' with whom any institution wishing to charge variable fees would be required to reach an 'access agreement'.[18] It

[15] House of Commons, *Hansard Debates for 8 February 2001*, Column 1061, http://www.publications.parliament.uk.
[16] Labour Party, Labour Party Manifesto 2001, 'Higher education – a world leader', http://www.labour-party.org.uk/manifestos.
[17] Robert Stevens, *University to Uni* (London: Politico's, 2004), p. 131.
[18] Department for Education and Skills, *The Future of Higher Education* (London: DfES, January 2003), White Paper Cm 5735.

also indicated that for students from low-income homes part of the fees would continue to be remitted and grants would be re-introduced.

When the blueprint was published, there was considerable resistance from within the Labour Party. This was exacerbated by both the Conservatives and Liberal Democrats also opposing tuition fees per se. In the case of the Liberal Democrats this was not surprising, since they had consistently argued against them, suggesting that extra money could be found out of a 50% tax rate on incomes over £100,000. The response of the Conservatives, however, seemed out of line with their market principles, and the charge of opportunism stuck. Throughout 2003 Charles Clarke used his considerable political skills to win over his backbenchers, but he was forced to make a number of concessions including raising the grant, dropping debt after 25 years and giving more support to part-time students. Significantly top-up fees, if approved, would not come into force until the next Parliament, thereby honouring the manifesto pledge in the letter if not in spirit.

Nevertheless, when the bill came before Parliament in January 2004 it was by no means certain to succeed. The strength of the opposition seemed to be not only because the bill challenged core Labour beliefs, but also because emotions were running high over Iraq (the vote was on the eve of publication of the Hutton Report). In the event the bill scraped through its second reading by just five votes, incredible for a party with a majority on paper of 161. Gordon Brown was praised for helping to secure the victory, but his position throughout seemed ambivalent. Whether this was because of his strong preference for a graduate tax or because he perceived some political advantage is not clear. Many of his known supporters were among the opponents of the bill and he did not intervene until the last moment when he appealed to Labour MPs to back top-up fees and persuaded a friend and leading rebel, Nick Brown, to switch sides after Tony Blair had failed to do so. Even victory in January was not the end of it. Opponents continued the fight through to the final reading at the end of March, when the majority was still only 28. One of Tony Blair's strongest supporters throughout had been Robert Jackson, patrician and Fellow of All Souls, who had been minister for higher education from 1987 to 1990 in Mrs Thatcher's government, which itself had drawn back from introducing university tuition fees. He felt so strongly that Tony Blair was right that he eventually crossed the floor of the House to become an unlikely member of the Labour Party.

Tony Blair's achievement in getting the principle of variable tuition fees on to the statute book should not be underestimated. It opens the way for future governments to give universities more freedom to set their own fees. But in the short term its financial contribution is limited. At the time of the bill the government estimated that variable fees would bring in about £1 billion per year, but that it would take about 13 years for the loan-pot to break even.[19] While welcome this will do little to offset the £9–10 billion shortfall as a result of chronic under-investment over two decades, but it would be additional to the £5 billion[20] or so being provided to the universities from central funds. A step forward, therefore, but whose main benefits are potential rather than actual.

Teachers

Charles Clarke also found himself having to deal with another major flare-up in the press. At the time of the 2001 election one of Labour's greatest worries was that teacher provision would blow up in its face. Headteachers were complaining bitterly that they did not have enough teachers and some were threatening to close their schools for part of the week. The government became very nervous of the likely effects on voters. A promise to recruit an extra 10,000 teachers was included in the manifesto, and teacher recruitment and retention were put under urgent internal review.

Several research reports suggested that workload was a major reason for teachers leaving, and the government accepted recommendations from PricewaterhouseCoopers for reducing it.[21] These centred on transferring a number of tasks from teachers to assistants, plans announced by Estelle Morris on the day before her resignation. Teachers were also to be guaranteed a minimum of 10% of the school week for planning, preparation and assessment – a boon to primary teachers especially, who previously may have had no non-contact time at all. Unfortunately, as part of its proposals, the government left open the prospect of teaching assistants taking classes. This was completely unacceptable to the largest teachers' union, the National Union of Teachers, and a major row developed. (The

---

[19] House of Commons Education and Skills Committee, *Oral Evidence on Wednesday 14 January 2004, Rt Hon Charles Clarke* (London: The Stationery Office, October 2004), HC 216, Q1, Q7 and supplementary memorandum from Charles Clarke.

[20] Department for Education and Skills, *Departmental Report 2004* (London: The Stationery Office, 2004), Cm 6202, Tables 2.3, p. 28, with current contribution of £430 million from upfront fees subtracted.

[21] PricewaterhouseCoopers, *Teacher Workload Study*, http://www.teachernet.gov.uk/ management/remodelling.

other five teacher unions did sign up to the 'Workload Agreement', but the National Association of Headteachers subsequently withdrew, as they did not think enough money was forthcoming to implement it.)

As these delicate negotiations were going on, the budget settlement for 2003–4 became known to headteachers, and some doubted publicly whether they would be able to afford even their existing staff. Although overall the Chancellor had increased the money available for schools by 6%, with 5% more for specific grants, all but two of the 11 percentage points were eaten up by increases in pension contributions, National Insurance and shorter, more generous salary scales. Within the overall settlement there were some big winners and losers resulting from changes to the allocation methods. Not surprisingly, the press heard mostly from the losers and a spate of headlines warned of numerous teacher redundancies. Charles Clarke found an extra £800,000 from elsewhere in the education budget and allowed schools to raid their own capital funds, which began to turn the tide. The number of recruits to teacher training also improved so teacher shortages did not arise as an issue in the 2005 election. But some primary schools had to cut staff as numbers dropped and it remained a touchy subject, as we shall be seeing when we look at news management.

As well as trying to make teaching more attractive, the Blair governments have sought to establish it more clearly as a profession. In 2000 both a General Teaching Council (GTC) and a staff college for headteachers, the National College for School Leadership (NCSL), were launched. Both have taken time to bed down in what is already a very crowded field with the DfES, the Teacher Training Agency, Ofsted, the School Teachers' Review Body and six teacher unions all with their patches. According to a biography of Blunkett[22] the DfES was reluctant to relinquish any of its powers and the legislation setting up the GTC was so poorly drafted as to leave it little more than a talking shop. That is perhaps unduly harsh, but through its wide range of activities, often duplicating those of other bodies, the Council has left itself open to the charge that it is not focusing sufficiently on its core functions of regulation and registration as would be necessary to attain the credibility of, say, the General Medical Council. The National College for School Leadership has also been criticised for lack of focus. A review commissioned by the DfES in 2004,[23] around

---

[22] Stephen Pollard, *David Blunkett* (London: Hodder and Stoughton, 2005), pp. 234–5.
[23] Department for Education and Skills, *End to End Review of School Leadership Policy*, prepared by Review Team July 2004, http://www.ncsl.org.uk/the_college/college-endtoendreview2004.cfm?CFID+1372329.

which time both the chairman and chief executive left, concluded that the College needed to achieve, 'greater role clarity, outcome focus, goal clarity and efficiency' and to develop 'a more productive relationship' with the DfES. Four years may not be long in the life of an institution, but it seems that both innovations have some way to go before reaching optimal effectiveness.

The Tomlinson Working Group on 14–19 Reform

All through Charles Clarke's tenure there were reports appearing from the Working Group on 14–19 Reform, again chaired by Mike Tomlinson.[24] In February 2002 Estelle Morris had published a Green Paper, *14–19: Extending Opportunities, Raising Standards*,[25] in which she had signalled her intention to introduce a matriculation diploma giving equal weight to academic and vocational studies. But with the troubled introduction of the AS/A2 split of A-levels, and her departure, this was put on hold. However, early in 2003 Charles Clarke commissioned Mike Tomlinson on the strength of his A-level reports to look into 14–19 qualifications as a whole. His remit included making recommendations on 'a unified framework of qualifications', which he interpreted to mean an integrated diploma – an outcome which he pursued assiduously. He published and publicised, in turn, a progress report, interim report and a final report, all giving the impression that the end of GCSEs and A-levels was a done deal.

This was surprising since Tony Blair was known to be keen on A-levels. Virtually his first task as Labour leader in July 1994 had been to launch a discussion paper on the party's education policies, including a recommendation to scrap GCSEs and A-levels in favour of a diploma. His speech totally ignored the recommendations and emphasised that A-levels were safe with Labour, and that is what the next day's headlines carried.[26] Against this background it is hard to see why Tomlinson was given his head in the first place. One can only assume that Tony Blair had not fully appreciated what was going on. Reforming secondary education had become a major objective for the second Blair government and a review of the qualifications may have seemed a logical step. In the wake of

---

[24] Working Group on 14–19 Reform, *14–19 Curriculum and Qualifications Reform*, Progress Report July 2003, Interim Report February 2004, Final Report October 2004, http://www.14-19reform.gov.uk.

[25] Department for Education and Skills, *Extending Opportunities, Raising Standards* (London: DfES, February 2002), Green Paper.

[26] Smithers, 'Education policy', p. 413.

the A-level débacle there was pressure from Labour supporters for reform, and David Miliband, by now the minister of state for school standards, was known to be an enthusiast for a matriculation diploma. Indeed, as a research officer at the Institute for Public Policy Research, a left-leaning think tank, Miliband had been one of the authors in 1990 of the original proposal for a 'British Bac'.[27]

Given that Tomlinson had shown himself to be a safe pair of hands in defusing the row over A-levels, it may have seemed natural to ask him to take on a wider brief, but the remit was slanted towards the conclusion that he eventually reached. It is difficult to see, however, why Tony Blair and his advisers did not spot the dangers and one can only assume that terrorism, Afghanistan and Iraq, and top-up fees were taking his attention. He is known, however, to have become concerned and to have asked David Miliband whether GCSEs and A-levels were safe with Tomlinson. He was assured they were, but Tomlinson had been engaging in double-speak. In confirming that GCSEs and A-levels would remain intact he meant that the content would stay but that the qualifications themselves would go. David Miliband at the launch of the report told the assembled reporters, 'Mike says absolutely clearly that the A-level and the GCSE will be reported independently on the transcript, there for all to see.' Commenting, Tim Collins, the Conservative spokesmen, spoke for many when he said the 'mixed messages' had led to 'confusion and muddle'.[28]

Tomlinson took longer than expected over his inquiry, which itself hints at difficulties. Charles Clarke, who was reputedly sympathetic to the proposals, and David Miliband were there to receive the final report, but before it could be taken forward both had gone. In consequence, it fell to the new secretary of state, Ruth Kelly, to publish the government's official response.[29] In order that she should have sufficient time to weigh the arguments this was put back to February 2005. But instead of a holding document as might have be expected just prior to a general election, Tomlinson's central recommendation of an all-embracing diploma was rejected in favour of keeping A-levels and GCSEs. Tony Blair had been consistent in his beliefs (and alert to the voters) and Ruth Kelly had gone along with him, but at the price of alienating much of the educational

---

[27] David Finegold, Ewart Keep, David Miliband, David Raffe, Ken Spours and Michael Young, *A British 'Baccalauréat'* (London: Institute for Public Policy Research, 1990), Education and Training Paper No 1.

[28] 'Tomlinson: exam labels irrelevant', *BBC News* 19 October 2004, http://news.bbc.co.uk.

[29] Department for Education and Skills, *14–19 Education and Skills* (London: The Stationery Office, February 2005), White Paper Cm 6476.

establishment which had been won over to Tomlinson. However sound the decision may have been – and there were doubts because a further review is planned for 2008 – politically, it seems inept in the extreme to have allowed such a welter of expectation to have built up only to dash it.

Diversity and choice

Tomlinson, to some extent, deflected attention from the main thrust of Tony Blair's plans for reforming secondary education. The central idea – derived again from the Conservatives – is that quality of provision can be levered up by allowing parents to choose across a diversity of schools. With money following the pupils a quasi-market is established. The inherent weakness is, of course, that secondary education is compulsory and, as such, should provide equivalent opportunities for everyone, but markets only really work with differentiated provision and some people missing out. Schools are already very diverse in social background with eligibility for free school meals ranging from less than 1% to over 60%. This might be considered a weakness, but Tony Blair and his advisers, principally Andrew Adonis, have nevertheless homed in on 'diversity'. As a concept, it conveniently allowed the government to accept all existing types of schools including the grammar schools, always a red rag to the left wing of the Labour Party. At various times the government has promoted, in addition, faith schools, beacon schools, leading-edge schools, training and extended schools. But the key element is specialism. Since becoming a specialist school can bring in an extra £600,000 every four years, the schools have flocked to sign up. By September 2004 nearly 2,000 secondary schools had become specialist schools, representing over 60% of those eligible, and Charles Clarke was able to look forward to the day when all would be. In the government's view this would be the end of what Alastair Campbell – using a phrase coined by one of Tony Blair's speech-writers, Peter Hyman – publicly labelled the 'bog-standard comprehensive',[30] and Estelle Morris, the school-friendly secretary of state, described as the schools she 'would not touch with a bargepole'.[31] However, the plan for all schools to have a specialism has inherent weaknesses. Parents cannot have unlimited choice across all subject specialisms, even in London. Supposing even that they knew that their son or daughter by the age of 11 was really attracted to

---

[30] 'Writer's "bog standard" regrets', *BBC News* 7 February 2005, http://news.bbc.co.uk
[31] Will Woodward, 'Bargepole jibe angers teachers', *The Guardian*, 25 June 2002, p. 1.

science, but they could only get him or her into a language school. Would it make a difference? If it did, their child could be taken down the wrong path, but if it did not, what is the justification for calling one a 'science school' and the other a 'language school'? Deciding a child's talents at 11 might in any case be thought premature, especially for a specialist school in, say, business and enterprise, or engineering. Since, however, only some specialist schools are allowed to test the aptitude of their entrants – science and maths, for example, are held to be abilities and excluded – and then only up to 10% of the intake, the schools cannot be specialist in the sense of bringing together a critical mass of talent. The variety of schools and the absence of a simple and coherent set of admission arrangements have meant that getting their child into an appropriate school has become a nightmare for many parents.

How could the government have arrived at such a seemingly illogical set of arrangements? A little history may help.[32] Mrs Thatcher was persuaded that business would wholly fund 200 inner-city schools to combat disadvantage and educate future scientists and technologists. In the event only about a tenth of the funding for 15 of these city technology colleges, as they were called, was forthcoming, including an existing performing arts college. In order to rescue the policy and shore up technology, which had just been made part of the national curriculum, some existing schools were allowed to bid to become technology schools, and the principle was extended towards the end of the Major government to include a few language, performing arts and sports schools.

Urged on by the same adviser as the Conservatives had had, Sir Cyril Taylor, Blair has been persuaded that since becoming specialist improves performance, all schools should become specialist. The Office for Standards in Education (Ofsted) published in 2004 an evaluation of the 521 specialist schools that had been running since at least September 2000.[33] It did indeed find that the specialist schools performed significantly better at GCSEs, with 58.9% of pupils achieving five or more good grades compared with the 50.2% in other schools. It concluded that 'Being a specialist school makes a difference. Working to declared targets, dynamic leadership by key players, a renewed sense of purpose, willingness to be a pathfinder, targeted use of funding and being part of an optimistic network of like-minded schools all contribute to an impetus and climate for

---

[32] Smithers, 'Education policy', p. 415.
[33] Ofsted, *Specialist Schools: A Second Evaluation* (London: Ofsted, February 2004), HMI 2362, p. 3.

improvement.' But, interestingly, fewer than half the schools had met their targets in their specialist subjects and had often achieved better results in the others. This led the Common Education and Skills Committee to question whether 'the effect of certified good management practices and of extra funding alone may account for better results regardless of whether a school has chosen to specialise in a particular subject area'.[34] It may be, therefore, that the government has a generalised school improvement initiative masquerading as a specialist schools programme, but nevertheless designating schools with spurious titles. It is also conceivable that relative advantage is the essential ingredient – which, of course, cannot be scaled up to all schools.

Blair's government has also revived the idea of city technology colleges, now called city academies, as an approach to the seemingly intractable problem of educational underachievement in inner cities. The plan is to establish 200 by 2010. They seem a good idea. Where a school has a persistent record of failure, knock it down and start again, invest in attractive new buildings, find a very good headteacher and free up the new school to tackle the deep-seated problems that brought down its predecessor(s). The weakness is that their distinctiveness centres on the unproven value of having a sponsor who in return for putting in at least £1 million in cash or kind has control of the governance and management of what is designated as an independent school. Sponsors have been hard to come by and in order to attract them the contribution threshold has had to be lowered, but it is a moot point whether they are really necessary. When the finances are looked at in detail, city academies, in their present form, do not stack up. While new buildings may look nice and provide photo-opportunities the costs can be as much as £25 million against the £2 million or £3 million for refurbishing an existing property. Moreover, there is evidence that they are taking fewer children eligible for free school meals and are excluding more children,[35] so they may be merely exporting problems to neighbouring schools.

An aspect of diversity which the Blair governments have not fully embraced is the independent sector. Partnerships between independent and maintained schools have been funded to bridge the divide, but the implicit agenda seems to be to make independent schools less popular. The assisted places for bright students from low-income homes were phased

---

[34] House of Commons Education and Skills Committee, *Secondary Education* (London: The Stationery Office, March 2005), HC 86, p. 10.

[35] Ibid., p. 15.

out from the first, charitable status has been called into question and the impression given that it will be more difficult for independent-school pupils to get into university. Blair has declared in major speeches[36] his aspiration for the state sector to become so good that many parents would not feel the need to opt out (as happened following the Butler 1944 Act, when social mobility also increased). The trend in independent-school pupil numbers can, therefore, be taken as commentary on the education policies and in it there is little encouragement for the government. The Independent Schools Council's 2005 census showed that recruitment had been rising ahead of the demographic trend since 2000 and a slight decrease in the raw numbers latterly was due to fewer pupils from overseas.[37] Blair's attempted 'transformation' of secondary education has not so far caused fewer parents to think of independent education, rather the reverse.

Funding

Gordon Brown's main influence on education has been as its paymaster. He has relished the power that being able to spend taxpayers' money has given him. An early indication of this came after a holiday conversation on Cape Cod in 1998 with the president of Massachusetts Institute of Technology when he rapidly facilitated a research link between that institution and Cambridge University, CMI, funded to the tune of £68 million. But the bedrock of his power has been his 1996 innovation – the Comprehensive Spending Review. Every two years there is an assessment of spending which sets departmental budgets for three years ahead. If negotiations proved difficult there was little point in appealing to Tony Blair as Gordon Brown seemed to harden his stance. The Chancellor has sought to go beyond the allocation of money to ensure delivery through public service agreements (PSAs), the theory being that a spending department would agree to produce certain outputs in return for the money received. This has secured a role for the Chancellor in setting targets for education. For example, the Department for Education and Skills agreed that the proportion of young people achieving at least five A*–C GCSEs would rise by 2% a year over the period 2002–5. This has proved largely meaningless since passing at this level has continued to improve at the rate it

---

[36] Smithers, 'Education policy', p. 424.
[37] Independent Schools Council, Annual Census 2005, May 2005, http://www.isc.co.uk/index.php/430

had been since the inception of GCSEs in 1988, but below the apparently required amount. Nevertheless, there has been no clawing back of the money awarded against achieving the target. Gordon Brown's interest in PSAs seems to have been less about ensuring delivery than in keeping the spending departments on a tight rein and to be able to say that he has held to the 'golden rule' declared in 1995 that 'over the economic cycle, government will only borrow to finance public investment and not to fund public consumption'.

Gordon Brown's concern with public borrowing may also explain his conversion to private finance initiatives (PFIs) in education and health particularly. When first introduced by the Conservative Chancellor, Norman Lamont, in 1992, Brown denounced them as a cynical distortion of public accounts. PFIs, or as the government now prefers to call them, public private partnerships (PPPs), involve the public sector purchasing a service, often the provision of property, from the private sector over a long period and paying an annual charge. The costs are much higher in the long run, but the great advantage to the Chancellor is that as they have so far been classified by the Office of National Statistics (ONS) as a contingent liability which is unlikely to be spent, so they do not show up as public borrowing. If at some stage, as has been discussed from time to time, the ONS reclassifies the PFIs, or part of them, the government will be shown to have borrowed much more than appears in present figures. Whether PFIs have intrinsic benefits is open to question. They do enable schools and hospitals to be built immediately, but the claim is also that they transfer risk to the private sector and yield better value for money. But considerable doubts have been expressed even by Labour's favourite think tank.[38]

Funding for education overall under the Blair governments has followed a peculiar trajectory. In order to establish a reputation for prudence Gordon Brown kept to Conservative spending plans for the years 1997–9, even though, as his predecessor Kenneth Clarke admitted, the Tories themselves would probably not have done so. Anxious then to claim credit for putting some money into the public services Brown authorised a statement that education was to receive an extra £19 billion in the three years 1999–2002, but this largesse was to some extent illusory, since it

---

[38] Peter Robinson, John Hawksworth, Jane Broadbent, Richard Laughlin and Colin Haslam, *The Private Finance Initiative: Saviour, Villain or Irrelevance?* (London: Institute for Public Policy Research). Working Paper of the Commission on Public Private Partnerships 1999–2001.

involved triple counting. In the 2000 Comprehensive Spending Review the Chancellor also introduced pockets of money to be paid directly to schools for them to use as they wished. But at the end of the first Blair government the percentage of GDP devoted to education was still less than it had been under John Major in 1995.

In contrast, in the second term the government has been conspicuously generous to education (and also health), with the amount allocated to education rising by an average of 7.7% per year in real terms from 2000–1 to 2003–4.[39] From £33.41 billion, in 1997–8, at the beginning of Blair's time in office, central and local government expenditure on the education sector in England is estimated to have risen in real terms to £46.03 billion in 2003–4. Schools have been the main beneficiaries, with capital funding up by 117% and current funding by 45%. Revenue funding per school pupil rose in real terms from £2,810 in 1997–8 to £3,620 in 2003–4.[40] Further and adult education also had their allocations increased substantially, by 54%, but higher education received only a little extra, 10%, reflecting the policy of a major relative shift of public resources away from the sector. The munificence has not always been felt in schools because of the way in which the money is distributed and the increases in their own costs, which led some to warn of teacher redundancies in 2003–4. But by 2005 schools and teachers seemed more content with their allocations and salaries. The feeling of relative ease may, however, be only short-lived, since expenditure is planned to rise in 2006–7 by only 3.8% and in 2007–8 by only 3.5%, which may well be experienced as a cut. In order to fund the increases in the second term the Treasury was having to borrow a great deal and Gordon Brown was having to go though the contortions we have described to make it appear to be within his self-imposed limits.

Brown's interventions

Gordon Brown had set out his education priorities in the Granita meeting. He wanted a guarantee that social justice and skills development would be vigorously pursued. Neither, on the face of it, should have been difficult for Tony Blair. If Brown's main interest was skills, Blair's was schools.

---

[39] House of Commons Education and Skills Committee, *Public Expenditure on Education and Skills* (London: The Stationery Office, January 2005), HC 168, pp. 6–10.

[40] Department for Education and Skills, *Departmental Report 2004* (London: The Stationery Office 2004), Cm 6202, Tables 2.5, p. 31; Department for Education and Skills, *Departmental Report 2003* (London: The Stationery Office, 2004), Cm 5902, Table 3.5, p. 32.

Both were agreed that education is the key to a more inclusive society. But there were important differences in emphasis. Whereas Blair's view of social justice seems to centre on inclusion into opportunity, Brown's with social class and school background to the fore has more of an old Labour feel to it. In the government's attempts to advance both excellence and equity, Blair has seemed more for the former and Brown the latter. Blair, for example, has been keen to provide for the top 5% of the ability range through a gifted strand in school support and the National Academy for Gifted and Talented Youth based at Warwick University, though Labour's selection taboo has brought ambiguity and ambivalence to identifying this top band.

In higher education Blair's priority has been increasing participation through his 50% target, while Brown's has been widening access. Excellence versus equity was at the root of many of the difficulties experienced with the Higher Education Bill. The conflicting signals have further left the universities unsure whether they should be going all out to attract the most talented students wherever they can find them or to respond to the 'guidelines' (Charles Clarke squashed an attempt to make them quotas) on the proportions expected to be recruited by social class, postcode, and school attended, but significantly not gender or ethnicity. In seeking to comply, universities have become increasingly willing to make different offers according to social factors which calls into question the fairness of the process. Nevertheless, ever since Laura Spence, who was turned down by Oxford University despite projected A grades in all her A-level subjects,[41] the Chancellor has appeared to want to bully the universities into balancing up by background.

Brown launched into his other priority immediately following the 1997 election victory when he put 10 advisers onto developing an employment opportunities and skills strategy aimed at the disadvantaged.[42] He was particularly associated in the first term with the New Deal, training to enable the unemployed gain work, and the University for Industry (UfI), an open-access higher education institution enabling people to update their skills. Neither were notable successes. The New Deal funded initially out of a windfall tax on the privatised industries has led to a number of the unemployed gaining work, but at considerable cost and it is an open question whether they would have obtained work anyway. The National Audit Office reported in February 2002 that only 3% of the participants found jobs that would not have been created otherwise, at a cost of about £8,000

[41] Smithers, 'Education policy', p. 422.   [42] Bower, *Gordon Brown*, p. 285.

for each job.[43] The Ufl had bold beginnings with the vice-chancellor of Sunderland University, Anne Wright, becoming its chief executive, but she resigned after only three years since when it has become a contact point for local 'learndirect' and online centres. These have not become self-financing as originally intended and trainee levels are below target even though the courses are heavily subsidised. Gordon Brown also strongly supported Individual Learning Accounts whose collapse through fraud greatly added to Estelle Morris' discomfort.

News management

Gordon Brown's concern to put the best face possible on his budget figures is characteristic of the government's presentation of its record in general. On occasions, this has been counterproductive because with blatant over-egging it runs the risk of never being quite believed and real achievements disregarded. Nowhere is this more apparent than in the figures on teacher numbers. Teacher supply was a serious concern at the time of the 2001 election and Labour's manifesto promised an extra 10,000 teachers. Four years later the manifesto claimed that there were 28,000 more teachers than in 1997. But the actual statistics are there for all to see[44] and this figure is plainly an over-generous view of the facts. It has been arrived at by including not only additional qualified teachers but also the unqualified and trainees. On this basis there had been an increase of 21,700 'teachers' since 2001, more than double the declared target. But the details reveal that only 8,700 were qualified regular teachers (none full-time), and 13,000 were either unqualified or trainees. Any credit the government might have enjoyed for funding the extra places has, therefore, tended to get lost in the spin.

Another example of active news management which seems likely to be counterproductive is the government's treatment of international studies. These are mainly carried out by two organisations.[45] The International Association for the Evaluation of Educational Achievement (IEA) has been running studies of maths and science achievement since 1964, and

---

[43] National Audit Office, *The New Deal for Young People* (London: The Stationery Office, February 2002).

[44] Department for Education and Skills, *School Workforce in England January 2005 (Provisional)*, National Statistics First Release SFR 17/2005 (London: DfES, April 2005), Cm 6202, Tables 1.

[45] Alan Smithers, *England's Education: What Can be Learned by Comparing Countries?* (London: The Sutton Trust, May 2004).

England generally has shown up poorly in maths though better in science. In 2000 the Programme for International Student Assessment (PISA) run by the OECD entered the field and England did very well, coming eighth overall out of 33 countries and regions. Unwisely perhaps, the government leaped in to claim credit for this, even though the study was of 15-year-olds who would not have been much affected by its education policies. The PISA study was repeated in 2003 and this time England's performance plummeted. So nervous was the government of these figures that it went along with PISA's reservations about the sample when, in fact, the response rate had been higher than in 2000. It issued a pre-emptive press release regretting the failure to be included, set about killing the results, and left the Office of National Statistics, which had conducted the survey, to take the blame.

But the 2005 manifesto showed that the government had not learned its lesson.[46] It contrasted at the head of the education section, '1997: 42nd in the World Education League' with '2005: Third best in the world for literacy at age ten and fastest improving for maths'. Even allowing for the hyperbole of manifestos (and why should we since ministers could not resist using these sound bites), this plays fast and loose with the facts. The results of three separate studies have been run together. The maths finding is based on comparisons with mainly third-world countries, the literacy result is from a one-off study which cannot offer comparisons over time, and what is called the 'world education league' is a collation aimed at assessing the impact of the education systems on the economic competitiveness of countries. There are also sins of omission: the disappointing results for secondary pupils are totally ignored. For all its concern with delivery and monitoring, the Blair government seems to have treated data more as part of the political narrative than as a basis for grounding policy in evidence.

The government's role

When he came to power in 1997 Blair significantly changed the government's role in education. Prior to 1987 this had been essentially legislating and allocating money, with implementation mainly in the hands of the local education authorities (LEAs). The Thatcher governments attempted to weaken the LEAs and give more power to schools. But under Blair there

---

[46] Labour Party, *Manifesto 2005: Britain Forward Not Back*, Ch. 2 'Education: more children making the grade, forward to personalised learning', http://www.labour.org.uk

was the radical departure of assuming responsibility for delivery as well as the legislative framework. It sought to do this through the targets and monitoring, ignoring warnings from the evident failure of centralisation of this kind in the old Soviet Union.

There were early indications of success. Targets and strategies were put in place for improving performance in primary schools and, at first, it seemed to go up by leaps and bounds (continuing what had been happening under Major, since that government's first publication of the test results in 1994). By 2002, however, progress had stalled, but, incredibly, Estelle Morris's response was to raise the targets still higher, putting them further out of reach. In consequence, any recognition the government deserves for the improvements has tended to get lost in the controversy over targets. Charles Clarke, as secretary of state, perhaps appreciating this or perhaps because he had been tied into Morris's rash 1999 pledge in the Commons, abandoned the primary school targets and they did not appear in the 2005 election manifesto. He also closed down the Standards and Effectiveness Unit, by now under David Hopkins, who had taken over from Michael Barber, who moved in 2001 (originally to Number 10, but in 2003 to the Treasury) to spread the gospel of targets throughout the public service. Barber's official role was head of the Delivery Unit, but he became known to the Cabinet, not entirely kindly, as 'Mr Targets',[47] as a result of his slide shows of graphs and figures every couple of months reviewing ministers' performances.

In the early years of the Blair governments, targets seemed to grow exponentially in spite of continual warnings about their distorting effects. But by 2005 even the apparently impressive improvements in literacy and numeracy have had to face a substantial challenge. No less a body than the Statistics Commission[48] clashed with the DfES over whether the better scores are real or come merely from teaching to the test, as suggested by Professor Peter Tymms of Durham University. Elsewhere, numerous examples have come to light throughout the public services of how targets can distract and divert rather than focus and motivate. Whatever the reason, the government towards the end of its second term began to row back from attempts to control public services centrally through target setting. The number was sharply reduced, and even Tony Blair's cherished 50% of

[47] Andrew Grice, '"Mr Targets" on a mission to reform Whitehall', *Independent*, 6 January 2003.
[48] Statistics Commission, *Measuring Standards in Primary Schools*, Statistics Commission Report No. 23; Letter from Permanent Secretary DfES, 3 March 2005 February; Reply from Statistics Commission, 16 March 2005, http://www.statscom.org.uk.

young people into higher education by 2010 may not survive. Following the 2005 victory the Delivery Unit was downgraded and Michael Barber left government service.

Tony Blair's education legacy

Tony Blair has said again and again, both in opposition and in government, that education is his main priority. He has made numerous speeches in which he has promised radical reform, modernisation and transformation. How well do the achievements measure up? He has continued where Margaret Thatcher and John Major left off, taking forward their major reforms of the national curriculum, key stage tests, a strengthened inspection system and financial delegation. He has refocused primary education to make literacy and numeracy its core; in the secondary phase he has wanted all maintained schools to become specialist and to pursue 'personalised' learning; and in higher education he has increased the number of places, attempted to put university finances on a secure footing, and sought to reduce the social class gap in admissions. He has attempted to underline teaching as a profession and make it more attractive, he has sought to encourage more young people to stay on in education after 16, and he has put in place both the means for the under-fives to get a better start and opportunities for adults to renew their skills. All this he has attempted to drive from the centre through targets, monitoring and the allocation of funding, with extra money being found in the second term.

It is difficult to reach a firm conclusion on the actual impact of these changes because their effects will take a long time to really show through. As a nation, we are still suffering the consequences of the Plowden progressive primary reforms of the 1960s. Blair's 'children' – those who began with the literacy strategy in 1998 – had not yet taken their GCSEs at the time of the 2005 election. Nevertheless, it is possible to make an assessment. Toynbee's and Walker's verdict from the Left is, 'good, but not good enough',[49] pointing to the improving test and examination results, the extra money and the expansion of higher education, but regretting the increasing gap between rich and poor. This may be over-generous, since results and places were going up already and funding has been variable.

On the plus side, it has been a considerable achievement to win acceptance as a normal part of the education scene for Conservative reforms

---

[49] Polly Toynbee and David Walker, *Better or Worse? Has Labour Delivered?* (London: Bloomsbury, 2005) p. 328.

that were seen as revolutionary and opposed by Labour at the time they were mooted. Blair has built on those reforms and put teaching children how to handle words and numbers at the heart of primary education. It is also possible that he will come to be remembered for reducing social differences in readiness for formal education through his investment in the under-fives and for increasing participation post-16 through education maintenance allowances if these policies prove a great success. But it is arguable that his lasting contribution in education will come to be seen as having successfully embedded Thatcherism.

On the other hand, there has to be a question mark against some of his own reforms. Neither his secondary education nor his higher education policies have been a conspicuous triumph. The plan for all secondary schools to become specialist seems too flawed to survive him. If some schools are favoured at the expense of others, it is not surprising that they should appear to do better, but this cannot be a recipe for the whole system. Neither is it clear what 'specialist' means, but on a strict interpretation children would be selected for narrow fields at age 11. Failure to come up with a fair means of allocating the places in popular schools has left secondary education uneven and inequitable. In higher education, Blair has succeeded in getting the principle of deferred variable fees on to the statute book and that is no mean achievement. But it looks likely to be left to a future government to implement them fully. The fees in their present form are so hedged around with conditions – including, in effect, being held till 2010 – that they will not free up the universities in the way intended and must count so far as an opportunity missed.

Elsewhere, some of the bright new innovations, like education action zones and the Standards and Effectiveness Unit, have folded. (Brown's own pet schemes of individual learning accounts and the University for Industry have not fared much better.) Further education, which was establishing a clear identity under its own funding council, has receded into the background once more with the new more diffuse arrangements. The General Teaching Council and the National College for School Leadership have not yet done as much for the standing of the teaching profession as might have been hoped. There has been a retreat from 'government as management' with the Delivery Unit downgraded and the chief gone. The distrust engendered by aggressive news management has meant that the improvements in teacher supply and the extra funding for schools have not always been fully appreciated. The Commons Select Committee has questioned the claimed links between increased expenditure and outcomes.

If Blair's impact on education has disappointed, he himself must shoulder a large part of the blame. His superb campaigning skills won power for the Labour Party after 18 desolate years in opposition. He radiated great optimism and inspired people to believe that he knew how to make a difference. But he was always careful not to say anything that might scare off potential supporters or voters. As detailed plans began to emerge Tony Blair increasingly found himself at odds with his own party and an ambitious Chancellor who sought to embody its core beliefs. Tony Blair's far-sighted plans for higher education were seriously undermined by the difficulty he had in taking his massive parliamentary majority with him. When put to the test, the fig leaves of 'standards not structures', 'diversity', and 'equity and excellence' have proved insufficient to cover the deep divisions. The plans for secondary education seem so unconvincing because they duck the fundamental questions of how to provide equivalent opportunities in compulsory education for all children and, more specifically, what should happen when more parents want their children to go to a particular school than can be accommodated. It begins to look more like selection than choice, but the Labour party finds it almost impossible to discuss selection dispassionately. Failure to confront the inherent tension between excellence and equality of outcome has led to the government, on occasions, seeming to face two ways at once, as when Charles Clarke proposed that all schools including grammar schools should take their share of disruptive pupils. It explains why Tomlinson was given so much encouragement for his diploma only for it to be rejected. It is also at the root of the contradiction between apparently wanting to free up the universities to attract the most talented students they can, while at the same time putting pressure on them to balance up the numbers by social characteristics.

Towards the end of the second term the government made a belated attempt to rediscover a shape for its education policies in a five-year strategy for children and learners.[50] It offered five unifying principles, 'greater personalisation and choice, opening up services, freedom and independence, major commitment to staff, and partnerships'. The high level of generality makes it hard to disagree, but it also leaves one wondering whether behind it all there is a clear functional model of how the educational system as a whole should ideally operate. It has not only been an unwillingness to face up to potentially divisive issues that has led to

---

[50] Department for Education and Skills, *Five Year Strategy for Children and Learners: Putting People at the Heart of Public Service* (London: DfES, 2004), Cm 6272, p. 7.

vagueness. On occasions, Blair has recognised and given voice to a problem – as with the oft-quoted 'tough on crime, tough on the causes of crime' – when neither he nor his ministers seemingly have had much idea of what to do about it. This did not improve with experience of office, rather the reverse. At the very end of the second term Ruth Kelly, the then secretary of state, was allowed to promise 'zero tolerance' of bad behaviour in schools which sounds good, but without the practical measures to make it happen.

Failure to get to grips with the fundamental issues greatly reduces the chances of Tony Blair leaving a lasting distinctive education legacy. In the first term we suggested he might have dissipated his political capital through too many initiatives. In the second, it is true he has not been helped by numerous ministerial changes in education, but he chose his government, including Estelle Morris, whose departure set in train the 'musical chairs'. It is true that foreign affairs, including Afghanistan and Iraq, dominated the second term, but Blair chose the world stage and he seemed more at home there than with his own party. It is true that he has had to contend with a Chancellor who has urgently wanted his job, but one who did find him the necessary money to fund his policies in the second term. If he is not wholly satisfied – and the making up of Andrew Adonis, his policy chief, to education minister in the Lords at the beginning of the third term suggests that he is not – then if he is honest with himself he must see that it is down to him. His has been the opportunity and his are the failings. It may be that history will come to recognise Tony Blair as one of the great architects of English education, but to this contemporary observer it looks as if the substance has not always been there to back the style.

13

The health and welfare legacy

HOWARD GLENNERSTER

When Tony Blair took up residence in Number 10 few could have predicted that he would seek to rest an important part of his legacy on profound *changes* to the National Health Service. In fact, it has become something of a personal crusade.

True, Labour had come to power saying it would 'save the NHS'. But in the context of the accompanying slogans in 1997 this was a conservative claim. It implied that Labour would return to the principles and organisational assumptions on which the NHS had been founded in 1946, assumptions that derived from the apparent success of a centralised state in the Second World War. There was no admission that the service was massively underfunded compared with health systems in similar economies. New Labour accepted the Conservative spending plans for its first two years as a way of convincing voters that there would be no increases in rates of income tax. Many economists were proud of the NHS's low spending, including my mentor at the LSE, Brian Abel-Smith.

Yet Blair *ended* his second period in office:

- with health care spending well on its way to matching the high health spenders in Europe;
- with the government implementing a significant change to the way in which health service providers were rewarded – the aim was to give patients more power; money would follow the patients who would make choices about which hospital or service provider they preferred, again a model more familiar in Europe;
- with adult care services for elderly and disabled people following a similar choice-based approach – individuals were to be given the equivalent of their own tax-funded budget to spend on the mix of services they wished to buy.

What difference these changes may make we discuss later. To begin with, though, the question must be – why the change of direction? What part, if any, did Blair play personally?

Health care spending

The United Kingdom's low health spending record has been of long standing. In the 1930s it was funded from a wide range of sources – fees, private charity, National Insurance contributions from lower earners and local authority property taxes. In this mixed system health spending formed about 4% of the then national income.

When the central state took over most health care provision in 1948 the Treasury could dictate almost the whole of the nation's health budget. As a result it fell, first to about 3.75% of national income, then when the Conservatives came to power in 1951 it fell further, to 3.2% in 1953/4. From the late 1950s on political pressure did raise this share but it remained tightly constrained. By 1998 NHS spending was 5.7% of the GDP, one of the lowest in the developed world. (A further 1% came from individuals' own pockets in over-the-counter drug purchases, charges paid for NHS prescriptions and private health care insurance.) By then spending in the EU averaged 8.4% (weighted by member countries' economic size). Our nearest big neighbours, France and Germany, were spending 9.3% and 10.3% respectively.

This more generous share translated into such countries having substantially more doctors and nurses than the UK, more equipment and more hospital beds – many of them empty, their hospitals waiting and eager for custom. As important, in a growing number of countries institutions were rewarded more generously the more patients they treated.

In the UK the opposite incentives applied. Traditionally there has been little relationship between the number of patients treated and the budget gained. Indeed, the longer the waiting times the higher a consultant's private income is likely to be, at least in some specialties. Big waiting lists have always been a good bargaining chip to wrest more money for a hospital department.

None of this was new, though a small but significant change had been introduced by the Conservative GP fundholding scheme in the early 1990s. These GPs had a direct interest in seeing their patients treated quickly and they had the power to choose where to spend their budgets. They gave contracts and cash to hospitals that did see their patients more quickly. Evidence suggested that this had had some effect in reducing waiting times[1] and made services more responsive to patients.[2] The Labour government's first step in its first term was to close down this scheme. It had been unfair, in the sense that only some patients benefited, but it contained some important innovations.

The Department of Health then reverted to old 'remedies': giving more money to reduce waiting lists, in effect rewarding poor performance, verbal bullying of hospital managers and explicit targets. All this, with a near static budget, meant that the indicator Labour had chosen to be judged by – waiting lists – refused to respond and indeed got rather worse in their first two years. Blair could see NHS failure dogging him as it had Mrs Thatcher in the mid-1980s. Yet he had specifically promised to put it right and the NHS was symbolically linked to Labour in voters' minds.

Blair instigated his own review of the NHS, not as part of the Department of Health, not as a large public exercise, but personal to him and his office. It was conducted by Adair Turner, who is conducting the current review of pension policy.

Blair decided that a change of direction was needed. The biggest difference between the UK and most other health care systems was the sheer lack of resources of the NHS.

The complacent view that the NHS was cheap but efficient had been punctured by research pulled together in the Calman-Hine Report[3] while the Conservatives were still in power. It showed that death rates from cancer were worse in the UK than in many other equally rich countries and the reasons lay in inadequate specialist staffing, lack of appropriate technology and the incapacity to treat patients quickly enough. Evidence of poor outcomes for heart disease was being published too.

The government drew up best practice guidelines for the treatment of these conditions, and others, drawn from the best available research – National Service Frameworks – that had been promised in Labour's first White Paper on health.[4] We discuss the impact of these service frameworks

---

[1] Bernard Dowling, *GPs and purchasing in the NHS* (Aldershot: Aldersgate, 2004); M. Dusheiko, H. Grevelle and R. Jacobs, 'The effect of practice budgets on waiting time: allowing for selection bias', *Health Economics* 13 (2004): 941–58.

[2] B. Croxon, C. Propper and A. Perkins, 'Do doctors respond to financial incentives? UK family doctors and the GP Fundholding scheme', *Journal of Public Economics* 79(2) (2001): 375–98.

[3] Department of Health, *A Policy Framework for Commissioning Cancer Services: A report by the expert group on cancer to the Chief Medical Officer for England and Wales* (London: HMSO, 1995).

[4] Department of Health, *The New NHS: Modern: Dependable* (London: The Stationery Office, 1997).

later, but their early significance was that they gave the Department of Health a strong lever with which to bargain with the Treasury.

It had always been part of accepted Whitehall wisdom that there was no way to decide how much money should be spent on the NHS. The ageing of the population was accepted as a legitimate bit of evidence for some growth, together with rising drug prices and other factors, but the Treasury had never accepted that a case could be made for any particular target for NHS spending.

Now the Department of Health could say 'you have agreed that cancer services should meet these standards – this is the bill'. Not only was there now hard evidence for more health spending but the Prime Minister was onside.

Until people write their memoirs we shall not know the full inside story of how the commitment to match European spending was made, but the memories of the now retired Department of Health's chief economist are indicative.[5] He recalls being phoned on the Sunday before Tony Blair was to give his *Panorama* interview and being asked how much it would cost to raise the UK's level of spending to the European average. He was the only person available who had the figures to hand at home on a Sunday!

The Treasury's Wanless Review[6] followed, analysing what NHS spending should be on various scenarios and how it should be funded. It was very important in convincing the Treasury and Gordon Brown of the need for more resources over the long term. Nevertheless, Blair's initial role was clearly decisive and from a historical point of view critically important. Over the whole of the period since the NHS was created, real (after inflation) spending had risen by an average of 3% a year. In Blair's first term real spending rose by 4.8% a year. In his second term the rise was 7.4% a year. Between 2000 and 2007/8 the NHS will be spending 2.5% more of GDP, reaching 9% of GDP. The European target should be reached, though three more years is a long time in economic forecasting! Whether the sums spent will be worth it we discuss later. But the commitment was a decisive break with the past. For long-time watchers of health spending in the UK, like the author, it was quite extraordinary. It could not have happened though if the UK had not been in a period of continuous economic growth. The Treasury would never have accepted it otherwise. The platform that made it all possible was then Brown's – or Brown and

[5] Clive Smee, 'Speaking truth to power', Nuffield Trust Lecture delivered at the Royal Society of Arts, 1 February 2005.

[6] H. M. Treasury, *Securing Our Future Health: Taking a Long Term View. Final Report* (London: Stationery Office, 2002).

Thatcher's according to taste! Once again, trying to distinguish the role of Blair and Brown is somewhat false.

None of this is to say that the issue of health expenditure and how to fund its voracious appetite will not raise its head again. From 2008/9 the high rate of spending growth will slow. The population will age. But the debates will begin again at a higher plateau.

Typical of Blair's approach at the time, too, was the big national discussion launched to discuss how best to use the additional funds over the next ten years. It pulled in people working in the service and outside groups to discuss priorities and practical changes that could be made to improve the quality of services as experienced by patients. Out of this came a whole range of service targets like a maximum waiting time for in-patient treatment of six months by the end of 2005 (later reduced to three months including day cases by 2008), patients to see a primary care practitioner within 24 hours and a GP in 48, the four-hour maximum wait in accident and emergency and detailed plans for cancer treatment, reducing health inequalities and much more.[7] Remarkably, the medical profession and other provider interests were persuaded to sign up to this very demanding set of goals.

The larger funds enabled the government to negotiate significant new contractual arrangements for both consultants and GPs. These are more demanding and require more accountability. Without the extra cash carrot they would not have been possible.

Choice and competition

The other big change of direction in which Blair took a direct role was the decision to introduce a degree of consumer choice and competition into the service in England, not, it should be noted, in Scotland, Wales or Northern Ireland, as Iain McLean makes clear in his chapter. This represented a basic change in Labour core beliefs.

Heat and little light were generated in a furious debate about the degree of independence local hospitals should have both from the Department of Health and from the Treasury – foundation hospitals. This was a particular Milburn initiative that was not designed to privatise hospitals but to free them from detailed central control if they were being successful. On one level this was a simple and typical Blair strategy to snatch the ground from the Conservatives. They were developing a policy to give independence to local hospitals. 'Let's pre-empt them.' Labour backbenchers did not like

[7] Department of Health, *The NHS Plan* (London: The Stationery Office, 2000).

it. The devolved Parliament in Scotland refused to have anything to do with such ideas. Hospitals, the secretary of state for health, Alan Milburn, hoped, would gain not just some freedom from oversight but, crucially, financial freedom to borrow and spend on new buildings. The ideal in his advisers' minds was a new form of not-for-profit public interest company responsible to the local population.

It was here that Milburn ran straight into predictable Treasury opposition. Local hospitals were not going to be allowed to threaten public-sector borrowing limits. Both Milburn and Blair had to retreat. There would be foundation hospitals, but they would not have unlimited borrowing powers and all hospitals would be expected to reach foundation status.

The real change of strategy went largely undebated, indeed barely noticed at the time. That was to give patients, advised by their GP, the right to choose their hospital or other care provider, including some private hospitals. With that choice would go a payment for the costs of treating that patient at a given NHS tariff.[8] This was more radical than anything Mrs Thatcher had dared try. Why?

It partly sprang from frustration with the way in which the NHS had initially responded to its larger budget – absorbing it but producing little extra in the way of treatment provided. It also reflected a growing public distrust of the medical profession. The case of the Bristol Royal Infirmary, where deaths from operations on children went unquestioned, made it possible to challenge clinical autonomy as never before. More generally, Blair concluded that provider-dominated service monopolies had to go. They needed a dose of competition to make them take consumers seriously. Without such a change these valued universal services would not survive. In a world where consumers had seemingly infinite choice in most aspects of their lives, a system that relied on telling people where to go and who to see at a time of a hospital's choosing was doomed.

Blair came to believe that it was his mission to change the assumptive world in which the NHS worked, to make it more respectful of and responsive to the patient. Some clue to the reasoning that lay behind this ideological conversion can be gleaned from the writings of his health policy advisors in this period – Simon Stevens (2001–4) and Julian Le Grand (2004–5). Writing for an American audience, Stevens[9] talks of

[8] Department of Health, *The NHS Improvement Plan: Putting People at the Heart of Public Services* (London: The Stationery Office, 2004).
[9] Simon Stevens, 'Reform Strategies For The English NHS', *Health Affairs* Vol 23 (3) (2004) 37–44.

an increasing appreciation of the fact that health care improvement requires a source of tension to overcome the inertia inherent in all human systems. The past five years have seen England searching for the optimal policy mix to generate that constructive discomfort.

This had to replace a model that 'reflected the view that health professionals want to, and generally will, "do the right thing" if properly funded and accorded freedom from external interference'.

Le Grand similarly argued that those in public-sector organisations respond to a mix of self-interested and altruistic motivations.[10] The trick was to operate on both.

Neither market type incentives nor national guidance and targets were enough on their own. Nationally set professional service standards were necessary. But there had to be good information on local institutional performance *and* the discipline of informed, GP-aided, consumer choice.

The government accepted that if such a strategy were to work there had to be spare capacity and a possibility for the private sector to come in and challenge NHS suppliers. Otherwise providers would form cartels to ensure that there never was any spare capacity or genuine competition. A common price would be set for a given procedure or service related to its complexity and cost, taking into account local labour market conditions. A series of successful pilots were run which proved that people were indeed prepared to choose hospitals other than their local one if they got quicker treatment and that this speeded treatment times (results that replicated the GP fundholding research).

This England-wide 'payment by results' system was to come into operation in stages. It is in place for elective surgery in 2005 but other elements were put back to 2006. Hospitals and primary care trusts (PCTs) said that their accounting systems could not cope. But the change in psychology was palpable. 'We are being asked to think what patients might want', one manger told me, 'we have never done that before!'

For there to be effective choice there had to be a quick infusion of new capacity, and the competitive contracts to provide independent sector treatment centres and diagnostic facilities did exactly that. (These units have treated far more patients per day than the average NHS provider.)[11]

---

[10] Julian Le Grand, *Motivation, Agency, and Public Policy* (Oxford: Oxford University Press, 2003).

[11] Department of Health, *Treatment Centres: Delivering Faster Quality Care and Choice for NHS Patients* (London: Department of Health, 2005).

Alongside the payments system the power to buy or commission services could be devolved down the GP practices if they wished to do so,
effectively an extended version of the old GP fundholding arrangements.
GPs would have the power to commission services that reflected the preferences of their own patients. These powers came into effect in April 2005.
It topped off a remarkable series of financial/organisational changes.

Despite the results of the pilots the full ramifications are difficult to
predict. A lot will depend on there being some spare capacity, on the way
prices are set and whether there is good information readily available on
quality of care and medical outcomes in different hospitals. Nationally
set average cost pricing causes providers to play all kinds of games with
what kind of patients they choose to attract. But people are prepared to
go beyond their local hospital, and there is now much more information
on quality available than ever before analysed by a private company, Dr
Foster. Even so, much better financial control will be required by PCTs.

It is easiest to see the new approach working well in acute specialties
like surgery, where clearly defined procedures can be carried out, where
patients and GPs can see clear outcomes, have good information and have
realistic choices of provider. For continuing care which needs a range of
local services working in harmony the model may work less well. But here
it is possible to see new agencies entering the market place to put together
packages of care for those with chronic conditions. They could be pur-
chased by GPs or PCTs or even individuals themselves. They may be the
best placed to shape the kind of services they need with advice. The essential point is that Blair himself has sparked what promises to be a potential
revolution in the way the local health care system works. Whatever the
rights and wrongs of Blair's personal style of government, this scale of
innovation in such a tradition-bound service would be unlikely without
some kind of drive from the centre. The fact that it did not happen in the
parts of the UK with their own parliaments or assemblies closely linked
to local provider interests, see Iain McLean's chapter, illustrates the point.
Whether it will last remains to be seen.

Health inequalities

Here was a resolutely Old Labour concern. It had been put on the political
map by the last Labour administration in the late 1970s. That government
had commissioned the Black Report[12] which was almost clandestinely

---

[12] Department of Health and Social Security, *Inequalities in Health: Report of a Working
Group* (London: Department of Health and Social Security, 1980).

published by the Thatcher government in 1980. It became a symbolic piece of work for the left in the long Conservative years when ministers hardly ever let the words 'health inequality' pass their lips.

The gap between the life expectancy of the lowest social class males and the highest had been widening through much of the post-war period. There were disputes about how to interpret these measures over time, since the numbers in each social class category had changed so markedly. *Overall* inequality in life expectancy had continued to fall until the early 1990s.[13] But Black's critics did agree that even this measure of inequality had begun to widen in the 1990s.[14]

Inequalities in *healthy* life expectancy remained very high both between social and ethnic groups and between parts of the country. In east Surrey, Kingston and Richmond, wealthy suburbs of London, the expectation of life at birth is 79. The expectation of a healthy life unaffected by disability or poor health is 67 years. In Barnsley the expectation of life is 76 but only 52 years of healthy life.

An early step had been to revise the formulae which determine how much each local health area should receive. This revision produced more ambitious targets to direct more resources to more deprived areas with higher health demands. Since there was little extra to allocate in the first term progress was slow. It moved faster towards the end of the second term. However, giving more money to the health service in poor areas does not directly have much impact on life expectancy or illness.

One of the first actions of the Blair government in 1997 had been to create a small number of experimental health action zones (HAZs). These were designed to pull together local agencies, far beyond the NHS, to address health inequality – to think about transport dangers, education in healthy living, the environmental causes of ill health. Many were successful in getting local authorities and other agencies interested in the health agenda. But the sums of money given to HAZs were tiny. Very early in its first term the government also commissioned a rerun of the Black research, this time led by Sir Donald Acheson. The result contained conclusions very similar to Black, with even more evidence.[15]

---

[13] Julian Le Grand and Polly Vizard, 'The National Health Service: Crisis, Change, or Continuity?' in Howard Glennerster and John Hills (eds.), *The State of Welfare: The Economics of Social Spending* (Oxford: Oxford University Press, 1998).

[14] Franco Sassi, 'Tackling health inequalities', in K. Stewart and John Hills (eds.), *A More Equal Society?* (Bristol: Policy Press, 2005).

[15] Department of Health, *Independent Inquiry into Inequalities in Health Report* (London: The Stationery Office, 1998).

Like its predecessor it advocated a whole range of social policies that had nothing to do with the Department of Health, a tactic not designed to win friends in high places – more redistribution, more attacks on poverty, up-rating social security benefits more generously, better child care and pre-school education, improved quality of homes, better public transport, encouraging walking and bicycling – none of which was costed. It also contained a range of familiar targets – measures to reduce suicide, to promote sexual health and healthier life styles, abolishing tobacco advertising, taxing tobacco more heavily and restricting smoking in public places. There was little hard practical advice on how to achieve many of these goals.

Nevertheless, the government did follow up with a White Paper.[16] The Labour Party manifesto in 2001 contained a pledge to 'close the health gap', unlike its 1997 equivalent. Targets were set to reduce the gap in infant mortality rates by 10% by 2010 and to reduce the difference in life expectancy between areas.

The problem was that no one really knew how to do these things and no one centrally or locally could really be held to account.

Local managers shrugged their shoulders in interviews I did at the time and said, 'all very good but this lies outside our capacity to deliver'. What they did know was that their jobs were on the line if they missed waiting list targets. Every local manager knew that Blair saw waiting times for hospital treatment as the top priority.

The Treasury[17] did undertake a cross-departmental review assessing what practical strategies might work best and then 'a plan for action.'[18] But the results were disappointing. There were a range of indicators across government that targeted factors related to health. Health inequality targets were included as part of the public service agreements for local government as well as the NHS. Cross-departmental machinery was set up that took responsibility for health inequality away from the Department of Health and gave it formally to the Domestic Affairs sub-committee of the Cabinet Social Exclusion Committee, chaired by the Deputy Prime Minister. This was entirely logical in intellectual terms but such cross-departmental machinery is notoriously ineffective even when there are very clear policy levers. Here, there were not.

---

[16] Department of Health, *Saving Lives: Our Healthier Nation* (London: The Stationery Office, 1999).

[17] HM Treasury, *Tackling Health Inequalities Summary of the 2002 Cross-Cutting Review* (London: HM Treasury and Department of Health, 2002).

[18] Department of Health, *Tackling Health Inequalities: A Programme for Action* (London: Department of Health, 2003).

Once more, comparisons with Scotland and Wales are instructive. Health inequalities there are greater but solutions have been seen largely in terms of resource allocation to health services, and for reasons we have discussed this has not proved very successful.

General measures to improve public awareness about healthy lifestyles affect the best educated classes first and hence tend to *increase* health inequalities. Indeed, overall inequalities in life expectancy *have* been increasing slightly in recent years, probably for this reason. Obesity and high alcohol intake has been increasing, the latter especially among young women. The reduction in smoking has levelled off. The proportion of those households reporting poor health *rose* for the poorest and fell for the richest groups over the period from the mid-1990s to 2001–2.[19]

Striking progress has been made, as we shall see, in overall survival rates for cancer, a specially targeted area of NHS care in the Blair years. Absolute improvements have affected all social class groups. But the relative social class gradient worsened, at least up to 2001: the affluent classes' survival chances improved most.[20] Speed of treatment and early presentation are crucial. This lies in the hands of the patient. The more the delay in treatment is eliminated the more the causes of inequality will lie with the individual's alertness to his or her symptoms. Behind those differences in individual actions lie deep reasons – past cultural attitudes towards discussing health issues, education, class inhibitions about accessing and talking frankly to one's GP, accepting that something *can* be done.

One more hopeful piece of evidence emerged at the end of Labour's second term from research on child poverty. It showed that the increased purchasing power enjoyed by poor families was being disproportionately spent on the children in those families and in a healthy way. Relatively less was being spent on alcohol and tobacco, more on vegetables and fruit.[21]

It is difficult not to feel some sympathy with politicians. Deep structural inequalities that affect people's capacity to control their own lives and where they live do seem to be related to health inequalities,[22] but changing these inequalities will take a very long time, if they ever can be changed.

---

[19] Sassi, 'Tackling health inequalities', p. 85.

[20] M. P. Coleman, B. Rachet, L. M. Woods, E. Mitry, M. Riga, N. Cooper, M. J. Quinn, H. Brenner and J. Esteve, 'Trends and socio economic inequalities in cancer survival up to 2001', *British Journal of Cancer* 90 (2004): 1367–73.

[21] Paul Gregg, Jane Waldfogel and Elizabeth Washbrook, 'That's the way the money goes: expenditure patterns as real incomes rise for the poorest families with children', in Stewart and Hills, *A More Equal Society*, pp. 251–75.

[22] Richard Wilkinson, *Unhealthy Societies* (London: Routledge, 1996); Hilary Graham (ed.), *Understanding Health Inequalities* (Buckingham: Open University, 2000).

Waiting lists and waiting times

What the media, and it has to be said the public, did care about was the time it has always taken for non-life-threatening but painful conditions to be treated under the NHS. This was rightly seen as its Achilles heel. It compared badly with continental experience and was one of the few things the Labour Party promised to deliver on in 1997.

Progress in the first term was minimal, as we discussed earlier. But relentless central pressure and the unprecedented increase in resources did begin to produce results in the second. During the Blair second term the service managed to crack the waiting time problem in a way that had seemed impossible from 1948 on, building on progress begun in the Conservative years on very long waits.

In 1997 Labour had committed itself to reduce the total waiting list by 100,000. This was a silly measure. It could be manipulated. It was perverse. Unless someone goes directly to an accident and emergency (A&E) department any access to hospital in the British system requires a referral from a GP. So, the more people the NHS treats the bigger the list of those waiting for some period. In 1949, 450,000 patients were waiting for treatment. By 1999 over 1,200,000 were. This peak figure has now stopped rising and been reduced for the first time since 1948. However, what really mattered to people was not how many other people were waiting in multiple queues but how *long* they had to wait from the time they saw a GP to being successfully treated. The discussions on the NHS Plan in 2000 did sort out this confusion and introduced more sensible targets:

- maximum wait for in-patient treatment – 6 months by the end of 2005
- maximum wait for in-patient and day case treatment – 3 months by 2008
- maximum wait for outpatient appointment – 13 weeks by the end of 2005
- maximum wait from GP appointment to treatment – 18 weeks by 2008
- maximum wait in A&E – 4 hours by 2004
- access to primary care in 24hrs and a GP in 48 hours.

The possible perverse effects of GP waiting time targets were aired in the election campaign. Consultants have complained bitterly about such targets, claiming that they distort clinical priorities but in the absence of a system like payment by results there is little else government can do to encourage speed of treatment. More resources on their own are not enough.

It is worth recalling that in 1988–9 10% of NHS patients in England had waited more than *two years* for treatment! Altogether a quarter of patients waited for more than 12 months. It is this image of the NHS that foreigners still have. The result of Mrs Thatcher's reforms was to remove waits of longer than two years and largely to eliminate waits of over 12 months. These actually grew again in the period up to 2000. Now they have virtually gone. Moreover, the more ambitious targets above look like being met. The mean waiting time for treatment, in patient and day cases, was nine months in 1988 and was less than three months in 2004. The median (middle) wait is now two and a half months. More impressively still, waits for outpatient appointments have fallen. Over 150,000 waited over 26 weeks in 1999 but almost no one did in 2004. Over 350,000 waited longer than 13 weeks in 1999 and only 77,000 did in 2004. The primary care targets of next day or day after action have been met by 99% of practices, give or take some manipulation. Foreigners' opinions of the NHS, in England at least, are now out of date.

The record in Scotland and Wales, which spend considerably more than England on health care and have resisted the Blair medicine for organisational reform, has not been as good. In Northern Ireland and Wales 22% and 16% respectively of waits are for longer than 12 months, with 10% in Scotland.[23] Virtually no one waits this long in England.

Better health?

Cost-effective treatment

Political discussion of the health service has been dominated for decades by structural and economic issues – to charge or not to charge, how many layers should the governance structure have, are Foundation Hospitals a good idea, how should we finance health care, by taxes or not? The real issues that affect people's lives have to do with the quality of care and what doctors and health providers *do* with the money. Discussion of these issues has been largely off the agenda since Aneurin Bevan struck his bargain with the doctors in 1946–8 – we give you the money and let you get on with it.

---

[23] King's Fund, *Audit of the Labour Government's Health Record* (London: The King's Fund, 2005).

The 1997 government did dare to enter this disputed territory. None of this was particularly linked to Blair and indeed was already in train in some form before Labour took office. But the extra money did make a big difference to what was possible.

One step was to create something called the National Institute for Clinical Excellence, an independent advisory body. (This built on work begun by the previous administration and in April 2005 took over the work of the Health Development Agency.) Its task was to examine the efficacy and the cost-effectiveness of health technology, drugs and treatment practices. Which new drugs were so expensive, with worrying side effects or poor results, that they should not be prescribed on the NHS, for example? Other countries have taken some steps down this road, but the scale and central importance of NICE is unusual and was a bold step. The public seem to have accepted that some kind of explicit national health rationing is inevitable. Interest from abroad is considerable.

The same approach was extended beyond medical care with the Social Care Institute for Excellence and related agencies.

National standards of good practice

Another relatively uncontroversial step was to embark upon good practice guidelines – the national service frameworks we have already touched upon. It is rather extraordinary that in something that claims to be a national service clinicians have been left to ply their own trade almost completely untouched by public accountability. There have been the good practice guidelines of the various Royal Colleges for their own members. But nowhere was there a way of saying 'this is the best proven way for the service as a whole to prevent and treat a given condition'.

The government picked a small number of key areas in which to develop this approach and backed them with money: cancer, coronary heart disease and mental health, to be followed by others. The first two were major killers and the third one of the primary causes of distress for families and the individuals concerned. The following draws on a review by the King's Fund.[24]

Cancer

We have already mentioned the concern about the UK's poor record compared with other European countries and the report commissioned by the previous government.

[24] Ibid.

A National Director of Cancer Care was appointed in 1999 to put together a national strategy and a Cancer Plan was produced in 2000. With it came the promise of dedicated funding. This was used to improve equipment and recruit specialist staff. There was to be a maximum wait for those referred by a GP of two weeks to the first outpatient appointment, a one-month maximum wait from diagnosis to treatment and a one-month maximum wait from urgent referral to treatment. Consultants dislike these targets and say that they distort care, but they and the extra resources in combination have speeded up treatment.

Government figures claimed that by the end of 2004, 99.5% of urgently referred patients had been seen in two weeks. The National Audit Office[25] suggested that the record was less good if non-urgent cases were included, but even here there had been improvements. This has been possible because of an increase of a quarter in the number of consultant specialists involved, a near 80% increase in medical oncology and a doubling in palliative medicine. There has also been big improvement in the technology used, though there are still bottlenecks caused by shortages of radiologists.

Has this all reduced deaths? Yes, seems to be the probable answer. Death rates have been falling since the 1970s for men and the 1980s for women, but they are now falling at a somewhat faster rate. A 20% reduction over 1995–7 rates by 2010 looks achievable.

Survival rates after treatment have also improved. Long-term figures truly attributable to the Labour reforms are impossible to calculate yet. There are signs of progress, though other European countries are probably doing still better.

Coronary heart disease

This is the biggest cause of premature death and varies by class and area – death rates in Manchester are three times those in Richmond Upon Thames. The strategy here was similar in many ways to that for cancer – prevention through anti-smoking campaigns and better diet, rapid access chest pain clinics, reduced waits, more specialist staff, but also getting clot busting drugs to patients within 60 minutes of calling for professional help and greater use of statins, aspirin and beta blockers for those at risk.

Long waits have been sharply reduced, notably as a result of the cardiac choice pilots, and significantly more angioplasty and other operations have been performed, though moderate waits are longer. The end result

---

[25] National Audit Office, *The NHS Cancer Plan: A progress report* (London: NAO, 2005).

is positive. There has been a drop of more than a quarter in death rates since the mid-1990s. Reductions in death rates have been in train for several decades, but the rate of improvement is faster than in the past and reaching the government's target of a 40% reduction by 2010 over 1995 is ahead of schedule. We do seem to be catching up other countries in the number of interventions performed and, more dubiously, in mortalities.

Mental health

The Blair administration did give priority to mental illness, drawing up a national service framework and assigning special additional money to particular aspects of that strategy. Nevertheless, the overall record was disappointing and downright perverse in terms of failed legislation and civil liberties.

Severe mental illness of a kind that causes danger to others or, more usually, the sufferer, is rare. It is true that one in six people suffer from less severe illness. But it is usually the very rare more extreme cases that interest the media and hence politicians. The most noticed elements in the mental health national service framework were a range of reforms designed to reach the most serious cases: 'assertive outreach teams', 24-hour services and carer support, more mental health staff in prisons, more medium-secure and secure beds.

The Sainsbury Centre for Mental Health undertook a study[26] of the extent to which money intended for the mental health services was actually reaching them. They concluded that spending on mental health services was growing *more slowly* than that on other services despite its supposed priority, and was less than that needed to implement the national framework. Wanless[27] had estimated that it would need an increase in mental health spending of nearly 9% a year in real terms to implement the government's policy. That is faster than the overall increases planned for the NHS. Yet the study claimed that the sums mental health services had actually received were growing *half* as fast as the average for the NHS. Child and adolescent services have been least advantaged.

About a fifth of all expenditure on mental health is undertaken by local authorities. They have been heavily cash constrained. But the main

---

[26] Sainsbury Centre for Mental Health, *Money for Mental Health* (London: The Sainsbury Centre for Mental Health, 2003).

[27] HM Treasury, *Securing our Future Health* (London: HM Treasury 2002), as reported in the Sainsbury Report.

reason for the shortfall lay in the fact that NHS funds had been diverted. Local acute trusts' deficits, pay, other local pressures, and the need to meet waiting list targets, had taken the lion's share.

This study's data only went up to 2003–4 and the situation may have changed. But the story is not a new one. In the 1970s services for the elderly, mentally ill and disabled were given priority by Barbara Castle. Yet the more newsworthy acute specialties somehow got more than their allotted share.[28] The PCTs are new bodies and are still prisoners of the pre-emptive strikes and well-honed tactics used by the big acute hospital trusts. It is not until there are equally powerful local voices defending mental health interests that this will change.

Mental health requires joined-up government more than most. Work by the employment agencies and the Social Services Department are crucial in the rehabilitation of people with long-term mental health problems. This was recognised by the Social Exclusion Unit but it is still the case that service departments are much less helpful in responding to this group than to the physically disabled.

In the 2004–5 session of Parliament the disability and mental health lobbies pressed for changes to the Disability Discrimination Bill (now an Act). The joint Lords and Commons scrutiny committee recommended that it should be made straightforward for those with recurrent depressive illnesses to return to work in between episodes. They should be regarded as being long-term ill with rights to benefit. The government rejected this, presumably worried about the reaction of the popular press to 'scroungers'.

Nationally driven media fears have, unfortunately, played a worrying role in the legislative débacle of this period too.

There was wide agreement in 1997 that new mental health legislation was needed, covering compulsory treatment and a range of other issues. In essence, little had changed since 1959 except for some legislative consolidation in 1983. Yet big changes in treatment have occurred since then. An expert committee was appointed in 1998 to consider what changes were needed, chaired by the Professor of Public Law at Queen Mary College, London. It reported a year later.[29]

The result was a long-running battle between the Home Office, the Department of Health and almost every mental health and civil liberties

---

[28] Howard Glennerster with Nancy Korman and Francis Marslen-Wilson, *Planning for Priority Groups* (Oxford: Martin Robertson, 1983).

[29] Mental Health Review Expert Group, *Report* (London: Department of Health, 1999); accessible at www.hyperguide.co.uk/mha/rev-prop.htm.

lobby, along with the professions. Driven by some high-profile cases, notably one in 1996, ministers treated the issue, to a significant extent, as one of public safety.

The expert committee accepted that legislation should enable compulsory treatment where someone was assessed to pose a 'significant risk of harm to others'. But treatment or detention should be permitted only where a health intervention of likely efficacy was available. The government proposed that detention or compulsion should be possible to 'manage behaviour arising from (mental) disorder'. This would allow the detention of those with no specific treatable clinical condition who had not committed a crime.

This proved the fundamental bone of contention, although there were many others. A survey of psychiatrists claimed that the majority would not work the law. It managed to unite groups who rarely agreed on much else. The professions argued that it was impossible to predict who would commit an offence and extreme events were very rare. It was impossible and wrong for them to detain large numbers of people on medical grounds if they could not treat those individuals.

This battle continued in England through the whole of Blair's second term. There were a Green Paper, a White Paper, a first draft bill (2002) and then, for the first time ever, a second draft bill (2004). Little change occurred in the government's proposals. The 2004 draft bill for England and Wales was sent to a joint Parliamentary Scrutiny Committee of both Houses of Parliament with instructions to report by March 2005 – before the election in other words. This whole parliamentary procedure was in itself highly unusual. The report[30] came down strongly on the side of the critics. It made 107 proposals to improve the bill and, indeed, to fundamentally recast it.

The Scottish Parliament had long before achieved a consensus with all the groups that were still in contention in England. The Westminster report recommended taking the Scottish legislation as a model! It called for further delay in introducing the bill to permit the necessary workforce to be recruited, and for different legislation for those who cannot benefit from treatment – dangerous repeat offenders – where changes to the criminal justice system would be more appropriate.

All in all this is an extraordinary story. A group of largely sympathetic professionals and pressure groups were largely turned against the

---

[30] Parliamentary Joint Committee, *Report on the Draft Mental Health Bill* (Houses of Parliament 23 March 2005).

government which took a very rigid line. Fear of hostile reaction from the tabloid press to any more liberal line is the only explanation that seems plausible and, on some issues, this has been a Number 10 obsession. Yet in Scotland an acceptable compromise had been possible.

Community care

During the 15 years following Conservative legislation in 1990 these services have been completely reshaped. Blair's government did not fundamentally alter that process though it did modify it, especially in the second term. By 2005 it was proposing to give more direct choice to families in shaping packages of care for the elderly and those with disabilities.

From 1948 'welfare' services – old people's homes, domestic cleaning, home delivered meals, equipment, carers' support and other help for those with disabilities – had been largely provided by local authorities. Smaller residential homes had gradually replaced the old workhouse accommodation from the 1960s. Other services had grown in coverage but were strictly rationed by local authority staff.

The Conservative strategy in 1990 was to encourage, and indeed force, local authorities, to open up this sector to private providers. The results have been dramatic, particularly in the provision of care in people's own homes. In 1993, 95% of home support contact hours were provided by local authority staff. By 2003 64% were provided by the independent profit-making sector. It was a transformation subsidised initially by the use of social security funding, but local authorities continued to fund these private homes and reduce their own. A new industry of private care providers had grown up – over 3,000 were registered with the national inspection agency in 2004. In 1980, 80% of places in residential homes were provided by local authorities. By 2005 the figure was about a quarter.

The continued scale of this transfer was not slowed by the Blair government, nor indeed by the newly controlled Labour councils elected in the mid-1990s. Here was an example of a genuine shift of attitude on the left that came not from Blair but from realities on the ground. Local councillors came to realise that small home providers and voluntary organisations could provide personal services rather more flexibly and better than local authorities. Those from all parties also realised, more brutally, that small owners were at the mercy of local authorities as predominant purchasers of care. This power could be used to force down prices – useful in keeping down council taxes.

What the Labour government did do was to introduce much tougher quality standards for the inspection regimes that registered residential and nursing homes. This led to the closure of many homes and a worry about long-term viability of others.

Local authorities increased the scale of domestic care in people's own homes, but this has been accompanied by a sharp concentration of that care on the most vulnerable rather than the thinner spread that used to occur. Research had suggested that intense home support was more effective in keeping people out of residential care and improved their and their carers' lives. That trend also continued in the Blair years. But some recognition that this approach has gone too far came in a Social Exclusion Unit report.[31] It advocated more emphasis on crisis prevention.

Social care is, therefore, mostly a story of policy continuity from the administration which preceded it and between the first and second terms. Indeed, in one respect Blair has taken the theme of individual choice further than the Conservatives did and has made that the central theme of the most recent Green Paper.[32]

Younger disabled people have been able to take a direct payment from the Social Services Department instead of services. Then in 2000 the Department of Health extended this 'direct payments system' to older people. The 2005 Green Paper proposed extending the idea to a wider range of public support, wrapping together all forms of state help including social security and health care resources into the equivalent of a cash sum over which the individual and his or her family would have control. These direct payments have been taken up less than many thought they would. Local authority workers seem reluctant to push the possibility. It has been particularly slow to take off in Scotland. As with the idea of a mixed market in social care this approach may take time to take hold, even in England, but individuals' control of their own care budgets will surely become the norm in time.

Real achievement?

Taken together, this account suggests that Blair did achieve a significant shift in the UK government's traditional approach to health care spending,

---

[31] Social Exclusion Unit, *Excluded Older People* (London: Office of the Deputy Prime Minister, 2005).

[32] Department of Health, *Independence, Well-being and Choice: Our vision for the future of social care for adults in England* (London: The Stationery Office, 2005).

to his own party's attachment to a counterproductive, nationalised industry model of the way the NHS and 'welfare services' should be run, and a
return to some of its older concerns with health inequalities. Even though
some of the mechanisms adopted to improve consumers' power over the
service had echoes of Mrs Thatcher, or to be more precise Kenneth Clarke,
they were designed to strengthen the appeal of the NHS to taxpayers, not
to reduce its call on tax resources – a crucial philosophical and practical
difference.

Though foreshadowed in the first term, these changes did not come
together, the spending did not begin to have an impact and the hard practical detail was not put on the broad philosophy until the second term.
Indeed, the complex mechanisms of patient choice will not be tested
until the third term. The full potential results are still in the pipeline and
it is too early to make a full assessment, but the evidence does suggest
a marked improvement in things that matter to patients: speed of treatment, improvement in the way killer and disabling conditions are treated,
modern facilities.

Less impact has been made on health inequalities and mental health.
Here the issues go far wider than the NHS. A recent study by colleagues
at the LSE and Bristol University, for example, showed that the quality of
primary care available to children from poor families is not very different
from that available to others in the population once the character of the
practice population is taken into account.[33] That is remarkable when
compared with, say, the United States, but the quality of primary care
does not have a large effect on differences in child health. There is much
more to do here that lies deep in our social structure.

So, with some caveats, philosophy, policy and outcomes have changed
significantly since 1997, but most markedly in the Blair second term. How
much of this was down to Blair himself? The answer is difficult for outsiders to give now but it seems to be – a lot. It was he who sensed that
things were not going well in the first few years and that Treasury-type
outcome targeting was not enough. More resources and more consumer
power were needed. Advisers' roles can be exaggerated. Politicians choose
advisers who see the world and solutions in ways in which politicians
are in sympathy, though clearly Stephens and Le Grand have played an
important part in shaping the programme. Devolved responsibilities for
health to Scotland, Wales and Northern Ireland, where Blair's medicine

---

[33] Carol Propper, John Rigg and Simon Burgess, *Health supplier quality and the distribution
of child health* CASE paper No. 102 . . . . London: LSE/CASE, 2005.

has not been taken (see Iain McLean's chapter), show that there was nothing inevitable about the direction Blair took; it bucked trends for which
sheer inertia would have been responsible in England. They also suggest
that the Blair medicine is working and inertia is not.

Why, then, are many doctors and health staff so grumpy in England?
Part of the answer is that the service has been under continuous reform
since the mid-1980s. Consultants do not like being forced to follow targets
that have to do with consumer concerns as interpreted by politicians.
The scale and importance attached to these targets has been irksome
and counterproductive in many ways, though in the absence of other
consumer levers, probably inevitable in some form. The Bevan bargain
with the profession – join a state service and we shall leave you alone – has
been broken. English doctors' responses reflect that of any set of producers
who have their monopoly status challenged. But it has its counterpart in
attitudes one finds in other countries where health care systems are also
under challenge. This takes the form of budget constraints, limits to what
can be prescribed or done and higher charges on consumers.

Why did it take some time for these changes to crystallise and take
effect? If they had all been in place and implemented from May 1997 the
NHS would be far more secure than it still is. It is easy to say that in
retrospect. The Labour Party Blair and Brown inherited had to convince
voters it could be economically competent, would not tax away middle
England's prosperity, and would break with aspirations for large-scale
public ownership and control. There was little time to rethink fundamental icons of Labour faith where it already had voters' support. To suggest
otherwise is politically naïve.

Does health and welfare policy form part of a wider and coherent
Blair approach to social policy? In my view the answer to this question is
clearly yes. It took time to evolve but a distinctive approach was, in the
end, forged. It is reflected in the 2005 election manifesto and in the stream
of departmental plans that preceded it.

Twenty-five years ago the dominant Thatcher ideology pointed to the
drastic diminution of the state's role in social policy. Private insurance,
for pensions, health and private schooling were all in the ascendancy. At
the 2005 election Conservatives were committed to increased funding for
these services.

The economic consensus is now that there are serious theoretical and
practical market failures in the funding of health and long-term care,
pensions and education through private insurance markets. The state
has a necessary and, indeed, a likely *growing* role as the population ages.

Labour has added universal all-day pre-school provision to the state's future role. This is a complete sea change in the intellectual starting point for social policy.

However, a wider role does not require the state to act as a monopoly provider. Consumers, used to almost infinite choice in the consumer marketplace, are not going to stand for being told where and in what ways their children are to be educated or their parents looked after, which doctor to see. State monoliths, once considered the heartland of old welfarism, are having to change, at least in England!

Reducing child poverty is centre stage while the very word 'poverty' was forbidden to pass Mrs Thatcher's ministers' lips. This is an approach widely admired abroad. (The Brookings Institution in Washington, for example, devoted a whole volume[34] to considering what the United States could do to reduce child poverty taking the UK example for comparison.)

Greater income equality was not to be achieved solely by tax and benefit redistribution but by action to increase the human capital skills of the least advantaged and the work incentives that face them. This last part of the strategy will take a long time to bear fruit. An important transatlantic intellectual tradition does lie behind this new approach, but earlier and similar themes can be found in continental social policy, at least in Scandinavian countries and the Netherlands. Labour administrations in Australia and New Zealand also provided models for welfare reform.

This combination of market incentives in public services with more consumer power, higher public spending on the key universal services, work incentives for the poor, and more redistribution add up to a distinctive approach, whether or not a Third Way! It took time to be coherently worked through and there are still some inherent tensions in its goals,[35] but it is distinctive compared with the pre-Blair period of leadership, and it is difficult to see it not being sustained after his departure, even if Gordon Brown takes over.

---

[34] Isabell Sawhill (ed.), *One Percent for the Kids* (Washington DC: The Brookings Institution, 2003).
[35] Jane Lewis and Rebecca Surender, *Welfare State Change: Towards a Third Way?* (Oxford: Oxford University Press, 2004).

14

Equality and social justice

KITTY STEWART

The society Labour inherited when it took power in 1997 looked dramatically different from the one it had left behind in 1979. During the Thatcher years economic growth had disproportionately benefited the better off, leading to a widening gulf between rich and poor. The dramatic nature of the change can be seen in historical context in Figure 14.1. Poverty more than doubled between 1979 and 1991, and families with children were most affected: between one in three and one in four children lived in relative poverty in 1997. Inequality measures such as the Gini coefficient show a similar pattern.

Some of these changes can be put down to global forces beyond the reach of government policy. Falling demand for unskilled labour had placed an increasing premium on skills, affecting countries across the industrialised world. The impact on the UK was particularly great because of the high proportion of the population with low qualifications. Demographic factors also played a role, with increasing numbers of children growing up in one-parent households. But policy under Margaret Thatcher was also crucial. Curbs on trade union power and an end to the minimum wages councils had removed a floor on wages, while the move to linking benefits to price levels rather than incomes had left those without work, from pensioners to the unemployed, increasingly far behind. At the same time, changes to tax policy had shifted the burden of taxation from the rich to the poor, for example through reductions in the top rate of income tax accompanied by a greater reliance on indirect taxes. By the early 1990s the UK had moved from being one of the more equal European countries to one of the most unequal, more comparable on poverty and inequality measures to the United States than to Europe. The wider consequences of the social changes were reflected in a number of other indicators: teenage pregnancy and homelessness were among the highest in Europe and there

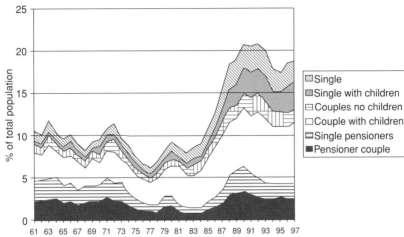

Figure 14.1. Population with below half average income by household type, 1961–97
Note: Share of population living below 50% equivalised mean income, before the deduction of housing costs. Other figures and tables in the chapter use the slightly different poverty line of 60% equivalised median income, but this is not available for the long-run series.
Source: John Hills, *Inequality and the State* (Oxford: Oxford University Press, 2004), Fig. 3.1; updated from Alissa Goodman and Steve Webb, *For Richer, For Poorer: The Changing Distribution of Income in the United Kingdom 1961–1991* (London: Institute for Fiscal Studies, 1994).

were high social class differentials in infant mortality and other health indicators.[1]

In opposition Labour had been careful to avoid making commitments to tackling these problems. Hit hard by successive election defeats and fearful of being tarnished yet again as the party of tax-and-spend, the run-up to the 1997 election saw hardly a whisper of poverty, inequality or social justice. When Tony Blair had taken over the leadership on John Smith's death in 1994, he had made it clear that he intended the party to 'build a new coalition of support, based on a broad national appeal that transcends traditional electoral divisions'.[2] With Blair in charge, the party had worked hard to distance itself from the unions, had abandoned any

---

[1] See e.g. Commission on Social Justice/IPPR, *Social Justice: Strategies for National Renewal* (London: Vintage, 1994); John Micklewright and Kitty Stewart, *The Welfare of Europe's Children: Are EU Member States Converging?* (Bristol: The Policy Press, 2000).
[2] Tony Blair, *Socialism*, Fabian Pamphlet 565 (London: Fabian Society, 1994), p. 7.

commitment to full employment, and had steered clear of being drawn
into pledges on spending. The 1997 election manifesto did emphasise the
importance of addressing educational disadvantage – in 1996 Blair had
famously listed 'education, education, education' as his top three priorities
for government – and also promised to introduce a national minimum
wage and to get 250,000 under-25s off benefit and into work. But to make
it quite clear that this was a 'New' Labour party which could be trusted
with the nation's finances, in January 1997 Gordon Brown guaranteed
that the party would stick to very tight Conservative spending plans for
the first two years of a Labour government, and pledged not to raise either
the basic or top rates of income tax.

Once in office, however, social justice issues rose quickly up the agenda.
Blair's first major speech as prime minister outside the House of Commons was made from a Peckham housing estate, where he promised that
under a Labour government there would be 'no forgotten people and no
no-hope areas'.[3] In August 1997 the creation of the Social Exclusion Unit
was announced, with a starting brief to examine school exclusions, rough
sleeping, poor areas, teenage pregnancy and 16- to 18-year-olds not in
education or training. At the Treasury, one of Gordon Brown's first priorities was a welfare-to-work programme: the windfall tax on privatised
utilities – the only major source of funds available during the first two
years in office – was used to fund the New Deal for Young People and
the New Deal for Lone Parents. Brown was also keen to make sure paid
work made financial sense: on the day after the election he instructed civil
servants to start developing plans for a tax credit scheme for the working
poor, formally announced in the March 1998 budget as the working families tax credit (WFTC). A commission to establish a starting level for the
minimum wage was also established in the first few weeks in office.

Then in March 1999, at a lecture to commemorate William Beveridge,
Blair made a pledge, not just to reduce but to *eradicate* poverty among
children: 'Our historic aim – that ours is the first generation to end child
poverty forever . . . It is a 20-year mission, but I believe it can be done'.[4]
Sources inside the Treasury suggest that not even the civil servants who
wrote the speech were expecting this, that it was a last-minute and unilateral decision taken by Blair. Certainly the assembled academics and

---

[3] Tony Blair, Speech at the Aylesbury Estate, Southwark, 2 June 1997.
[4] Tony Blair, 'Beveridge revisited: a welfare state for the 21st century', in Robert Walker (ed.),
   Ending Child Poverty: Popular Welfare for the 21st Century (Bristol: The Policy Press, 1999),
   p. 7.

journalists were taken by surprise; Polly Toynbee of the *Guardian* has since described the pledge as 'astounding'.[5] The reason the announcement came when it did has been a source of some speculation. Its timing coincided with the end of the commitment to stick with Conservative spending plans: did the government now feel able to declare openly the goals it had all along? Another possibility is that Blair was responding to heavy criticism from the left over the decision to cut lone parent benefits, a policy set in place by the previous government and pushed through as part of the spending plan commitment, though in hindsight it seems unlikely that the criticism was of particular concern to Blair. A third explanation is that the pledge was a response to the growing body of evidence underlining the long-term scarring effects of childhood poverty. In a pamphlet on the Third Way in 1998, Blair had declared the four values 'essential to a just society' to be 'equal worth, opportunity for all, responsibility and community',[6] and since then 'opportunity' had become a government buzzword. Research results such as those released by the Treasury at about the time of the Beveridge speech made it clear that real opportunities of later success in education and the labour market were vastly reduced for children growing up poor.[7] If the government was serious about providing more equal opportunities, it had to start by tackling child poverty.

The child poverty pledge was followed up with concrete interim targets – the first being to reduce the number of children living in households below 60% of median income (adjusted for household size) by one quarter by 2004/5. Successive budgets introduced tax-credits and then reformed the tax-credit and benefit system to make it steadily more generous for families with children for the remainder of Labour's first term and throughout the second: the second interim goal of halving child poverty by 2010 was repeated in both the 2001 and 2005 election manifestos. At the same time, there has been steadily growing interest and investment in services for young children, in part because childcare is key to parents' ability to work, which in turn is seen as key to tackling poverty, but also because of evidence that disadvantage begins in babyhood, and that improving health, education and parenting in the earliest years can make a real difference to the life chances of children in poor households.

[5] Polly Toynbee, 'Time to talk the talk', *Guardian*, 29 November 2002.
[6] Tony Blair, *The Third Way: New Politics for the New Century*, Fabian Pamphlet 588 (London: The Fabian Society, 1998), p. 3.
[7] CASE (Centre for Analysis of Social Exclusion)/HM Treasury, *Persistent Poverty and Lifetime Inequality: The Evidence* , CASE report 5 and HM Treasury Occasional Paper No. 10 (London: London School of Economics and Political Science and HM Treasury, 1999).

While children have been at the heart of the government's anti-poverty
strategy, 1999 also marked the start of a broader attack on social injustice. In September, the first in an annual series of government audits of
poverty and social exclusion indicators was published, *Opportunity for
All*.[8] It promised an 'integrated and radical policy response' to the combined problems of childhood deprivation, worklessness, health inequalities, fear of crime, poor areas, poor housing, pensioner poverty, ill-health
and isolation, and discrimination on grounds of age, ethnicity, gender or
disability. A raft of policies have followed, of which the most significant
are summarised here.[9]

- Welfare-to-work programmes, the National Minimum Wage and tax-
  benefit changes favouring low-income families with children, both in
  and out of work;
- investment in childcare and in nursery education for three- and four-
  year-olds; in Sure Start programmes for under-fours in deprived areas;
  and in longer and more generous maternity leave;
- substantial increases in education and health funding, including changes
  to funding formulae in favour of poorer areas;
- 'floor targets' for achievement in employment, crime, education, health
  and housing in the most disadvantaged areas, backed up with serious
  funding through the National Strategy for Neighbourhood Renewal and
  through a number of additional targeted programmes such as Sure Start
  and the Excellence in Cities programme for schools – the aim to meet a
  pledge arguably even more ambitious than the pledge on child poverty:
  'within 10–20 years, no-one should be seriously disadvantaged by where
  they live';[10]
- education maintenance allowances, paid to those who remain in education between 16 and 18, aimed at increasing the low educational
  achievement of young people from low-income households;
- working tax credits for childless couples;
- improvements in benefits for disabled children and adults;
- for pensioners, an increase in the means-tested income minimum and
  the extension of means-tested help higher up the income scale through
  the Pension Credit; additional special measures including winter fuel

---

[8] DSS (Department of Social Security) *Opportunity for All: Tackling Poverty and Social
Exclusion* (London: DSS, 1999).
[9] For more detail, see John Hills and Kitty Stewart (eds.), *A More Equal Society? New Labour,
Poverty, Inequality and Exclusion* (Bristol: The Policy Press, 2005).
[10] SEU (Social Exclusion Unit), *New Commitment to Neighbourhood Renewal: National
Strategy Action Plan* (London: Cabinet Office, 2001), p. 8.

allowances, free eye tests, free TV licences and increased income tax allowances;

• some action to reduce inequalities in outcomes between ethnic groups, such as ethnic minority achievement grants to local authorities to improve educational attainment.

In most of these areas policies continued to develop as Labour moved into a second term. In particular, employment, education, child poverty, the situation of disadvantaged young people and neighbourhood regeneration, all priorities during the first term, have remained central to the agenda, while the early years agenda and pensioner poverty have both grown in importance over time. The scope and scale of action is very different from anything that could have been anticipated from the election manifesto of 1997. However, it is clear from the outset that a number of issues have not been touched at all, even after the record second term landslide, confirming that these are not areas of concern for a Blair government. Most obvious is the issue of income inequality: the focus has been clearly and explicitly on the situation and opportunities available to those at the bottom, and on the income gap between the bottom and the middle. The gap between the middle and the top is not on the agenda. Second, even concern with income poverty has been confined to specific groups, in particular children and pensioners. Poverty among working-age households without children has been less of an issue. Those without children have benefited from a number of policies provided they are in work, are prepared to work, or are registered disabled, but the situation of the majority of workless people without children has worsened, benefit levels falling in real terms year on year.

In addition, there is one small group of people whose situation has deteriorated rapidly under the Blair government in all the terms the government has considered important for the inclusion of other groups – income, education, employment and housing. This is the category of asylum seekers. Blair's overall social justice record cannot be evaluated without considering the treatment of some of the most vulnerable people in the country.

This chapter assesses Labour's achievements – and failures – in many of these areas, but lack of space means that the discussion is rather less than comprehensive. In particular, for discussion of Labour's record in addressing disadvantage in poor areas, ethnic inequalities and low political participation, the reader is referred elsewhere.[11]

---

[11] See relevant chapters in Hills and Stewart (eds.), *A More Equal Society?*

Table 14.1. *Changes in child poverty across two Labour terms (after housing costs)*

	1996/7	2000/1	2003/4	% change first term	second term	Overall change
All children	**33**	**30**	**28**	**9**	**7**	**15**
Lone parent, FT work	16	13	9	19	31	44
Lone parent, PT work	39	33	27	15	18	31
Lone parent, no work	82	78	74	5	5	10
Couple, one FT, one no work	28	25	21	11	16	25
Couple, one or both PT	62	55	55	11	0	11
Couple, both no work	78	77	77	1	0	1

Note: Share of children living in households with equivalised income below 60% of the median after the deduction of housing costs. There are advantages and disadvantages to the use of both before and after housing cost data, but because of space constraints only after housing cost data are presented here.
Source: DWP, *Households Below Average Income, 1994/5–2003/4*, Table E3.1.

Poverty

Reducing child poverty has been an important goal for Labour. Perhaps less well known is the fact that pensioner poverty has also been taken extremely seriously. In his 2002 Labour Party Conference speech Gordon Brown made a parallel pledge to Blair's promise to end child poverty – 'our aim is to end pensioner poverty in our country'.[12] While this was not followed up with concrete interim targets as in the case of children, the government has introduced a series of measures raising the incomes of the poorest pensioners. However, concern about poverty has not extended to the working-age population without children, and specifically those without work. This section looks at what has happened to levels of poverty for each of these three groups in turn, and considers how far government policy can be said to be responsible.

---

[12] Cited in Alissa Goodman, Michael Myck and Andrew Shephard, *Sharing in the Nation's Prosperity? Pensioner Poverty in Britain*, Commentary 93 (London: Institute for Fiscal Studies, 2003), p. 2.

Children

Table 14.1 shows the change in the share of children living in poverty between 1996–7 and 2000–1 and then between 2000–1 and 2003–4; that is, roughly over the course of each term of Labour government, insofar as data allow.

First, it is clear that there have been substantial drops in poverty over the period as a whole, especially for lone parents in work full-time or part-time, and for couples where one partner works full-time and the other stays at home. These drops are particularly significant when one considers that this is a relative poverty line, measured as a share of median income, and the median rose rapidly over the period. Measures of material deprivation show more striking improvements in real living standards: for example, the share of lone parents stating that they never had money left over at the end of the week fell from 48% in 1999 to 17% in 2002.[13]

However, it is also clear from the table that overall progress on poverty slowed down slightly between the first and second terms – and this is surprising, despite the slightly shorter time-frame allowed by the data, because relevant policies were only introduced from 1999, and tax credits have been made increasingly generous annually since, with a particularly sharp increase in April 2003. The change – or lack of it – between 2002–3 and 2003–4 will have been particularly disappointing to the government. Until figures for 2003–4 came out, commentators were predicting fairly confidently that the government was on track to meet its first target of reducing child poverty by one quarter between 1998–9 and 2004–5.[14] Now the same commentators suggest that reaching the target is unlikely.[15] Let us consider, first, the contribution of policy to the fall in child poverty witnessed in Table 14.1, and second, the explanation for the likely failure to meet the first child poverty target.

The government's strategy for tackling child poverty has been based heavily on promoting employment, through active labour market pro-grammes such as the New Deal for Lone Parents (and more recently the New Deal for Partners), through investment in childcare and through a

[13] Stephen McKay and Sharon Collard, *Developing Deprivation Questions for the Family Resources Survey*, Personal Finance Research Centre (Bristol: University of Bristol, 2003).
[14] Mike Brewer, *Will the Government Hit its Child Poverty Target in 2004–5?* Briefing Note 47 (London: Institute for Fiscal Studies); Holly Sutherland, *Poverty in Britain: The Impact of Government Policy since 1997. An Update to 2004–5 Using Microsimulation* (Cambridge: Microsimulation Unit, University of Cambridge, 2004).
[15] Mike Brewer, Alissa Goodman, Jonathan Shaw and Andrew Shephard, *Poverty and Inequality in Britain: 2005* (London: Institute for Fiscal Studies, 2005).

Table 14.2. *Worklessness and children*

	Children under 16 in workless households		Workless households with children (%)	
	1000s	%	Lone parent	Dual parent
1993	2,400	20.8	61	10
1996	2,600	21.5	60	9
1998	2,400	20.0	57	7
2000	2,100	17.9	50	6
2002	2,100	18.3	49	6

Source: Paul Gregg and Jonathan Wadsworth, 'Workless households and the recovery', in R. Dickens, P. Gregg and J. Wadsworth (eds.), *The Labour Market Under New Labour* (Basingstoke: Palgrave Macmillan, 2003), Tables 2.1 and 2.4.

series of policies intended to 'make work pay', including the National Minimum Wage, reforms to tax and National Insurance which favoured low earners and – most significantly – the system of means-tested tax credits. In particular, the Child Tax Credit (CTC) introduced in April 2003 integrated the systems of support for children in households in and out of work, in principle removing many of the benefit disincentives and uncertainty surrounding the move into a job. The level of worklessness among households with children – the highest rate in the industrialised world when Labour came to power – has fallen steadily, as indicated in Table 14.2, though it remains high by international standards. A strong underlying economy – itself to at least some degree attributable to Labour's macroeconomic management – has been an important factor, but supply-side policies increasing the incentives for parents to work also appear to have been effective.[16]

At the same time, of course, tax credit and benefit changes (including those mentioned above as well as increases to universal child benefit and to the length and generosity of maternity pay) substantially lifted the incomes of families already in employment, reducing poverty for most

---

[16] Tax credit changes between 2000 and 2003 are estimated to have raised lone parent employment by 3.4 percentage points, and that of fathers in couples by 0.9 percentage points, but to have had a slight disincentive effect for mothers in couples. See Richard Blundell, Mike Brewer and Andrew Shephard, 'The impact of tax and benefit changes between April 2000 and April 2003 on parents' labour supply', IFS Briefing Note No. 52 (London: Institute for Fiscal Studies, 2004).

groups – as indicated in Table 14.1. Families with a single earner have benefited most; tax credits appear to have had some disincentive effect for second earners.

But why have these policies not been sufficient to ensure that the child poverty target is met, despite optimistic predictions? One key factor is that according to the Family Resources Survey, which is the official source used to calculate child poverty, worklessness rose slightly between 2002/3 and 2003/4.[17] This may be a statistical blip (other datasources suggest that worklessness continued to fall slowly). However, concerns about the long-term future for further employment gains remain, raising questions about progress beyond the first target. The lone parent employment rate rose to 53% in 2003, compared with 41% in 1996, but the speed of change is far from sufficient if the government is to reach its goal of 70% of lone parents in work by 2010, even though something close to this rate is achieved in many other industrialised countries. Further increases in lone parent employment may be expected as investment in childcare continues, but there may also be limits to how far things can change in the short and medium term, because such favourable economic conditions may not last indefinitely and because of the characteristics of those who remain out of work. For instance, international comparison suggests that the education gap between single and married mothers is particularly large in the UK, and that UK lone mothers are likely to be younger and to have more children than elsewhere.[18] It may be that catch-up with other countries is only possible in the long run, as the factors driving life chances and low skills are addressed (see below).

If this is the case, however, the question of the income of households which remain workless becomes particularly urgent. This issue has not been ignored by Labour: income support for families with children (particularly younger children) has quietly been made considerably more generous. Income support for a couple with two children under 11 increased by 37% in real terms between 1997 and 2004, compared with an increase of just 4% between 1990 and 1997.[19] But as average income has also been rising, these increases have had limited impact on reducing relative poverty, with workless families still living on rates of support which fall well below

---

[17] Brewer et al., *Poverty and Inequality in Britain: 2005*.

[18] Jonathan Bradshaw, Steven Kennedy, Majella Kilkey, Sandra Hutton, Anne Corden, Tony Eardley, Hilary Holmes and Joanna Neale, *The Employment of Lone Parents: A comparison of policy in 20 countries* (London: Family Policy Studies Centre, 1996).

[19] DWP (Department for Work and Pensions) *The Abstract of Statistics for Benefits, Contributions and Indices of Prices and Earnings: 2004 Edition* (London: DWP, 2005).

the poverty line. Indeed, as Table 14.1 shows, while the poverty rate fell by 10% for children in lone parent workless households over the period, it dropped by just 1% for children living with two adults, both out of work. In both household types, some three in four children remained below the poverty line in 2003/4. If child poverty is really to be significantly reduced much beyond the first target, far more substantial resources will need to be found to raise incomes for workless households, despite all the political difficulties this may entail.

One last factor behind the failure to reach the 2004–5 target is the administration of the tax credit system. It is generally agreed that the very large sums of money invested in tax credits (around an extra £10 billion a year by 2003–4, or approaching 1% of GDP) should have had a more dramatic impact on lifting families up and out of poverty – hence the surprise at the most recent income statistics. Teething problems delayed the processing of claims in the first few months after the CTC was introduced, meaning that many families did not receive their entitlement on time. This will have meant that poverty fell by less than it otherwise would have done between 2002–3 and 2003–4. As a result we should see a larger impact of the tax credits over the next financial year. But even without these problems it does not appear that child poverty would have fallen as far as was expected.[20] The annual inaccuracy built into the tax credit system may provide an explanation, and if this is so it will not be easy to tackle. Each year's tax credit entitlement is initially based on the previous year's income, meaning that even with the system running smoothly many families (those slow to report income changes) will not receive the assistance they need in the year in which they most need it, while others will find themselves repaying credits out of incomes which have increased but remain low. Whether child poverty can really be tackled using means-tested benefits, and with incomes often reassessed at long intervals, remains to be seen. Certainly this is not a model followed so far in any of the countries in which child poverty is currently low.

Pensioners[21]

Over a quarter of pensioners were living in relative poverty when Labour came to power. Labour had in the past been keen to restore the link between pensions and earnings broken by the Thatcher

[20] See Brewer et al., *Poverty and Inequality in Britain: 2005.*
[21] This section draws in part on Maria Evandrou and Jane Falkingham, 'A secure retirement for all? Older people and New Labour', in Hills and Stewart, *A More Equal Society?*

administration – this was a central plank in both the 1987 and 1992 manifestos. But by 1997 the policy had been dropped in favour of a broad statement that 'all pensioners should share fairly in the increasing prosperity of the nation.' In the first two years there were very few policy measures aimed explicitly at pensioners, with the exception of annual winter fuel payments of £100, introduced in November 1997.

However, from April 1999 a series of reforms have aimed to improve living standards for the poorest pensioners. Income support for pensioners was rebranded the minimum income guarantee (MIG) in 1999, with above-inflation increases and a commitment to increase MIG in line with earnings rather than prices which was repeated in the 2001 manifesto. In 2003 the MIG was renamed again (and made more generous) as the guarantee level of the pension credit, and the 2005 manifesto continued the commitment to earnings-uprating, at least until 2007–8. By April 2004 the guarantee level was equivalent to around 25% of average earnings for a single person – roughly what the basic state pension would have been if the link with earnings had not been broken. The difference, of course, is that the pension credit is means-tested. At the same time, there have been small increases in the basic state pension as well as the introduction of some universal benefits in kind such as free eye tests and TV licences.

If the guarantee level of pension credit continues to be linked to earnings it will remain just above the poverty line for a single person, though rather below it for couples: in other words, if everyone eligible claimed, lone pensioner poverty would be abolished, but there would still be poor pensioner couples. In practice, the proportion of pensioners who are poor has fallen steadily, from 27% in 1996–7 to 24% in 2000/1 and 20% in 2003/4 (measured against a relative poverty line of 60% of equivalised median income after housing costs) – a fall of more than one quarter over the period as a whole.[22] It is striking that in 2003–4, for the first time since the early 1980s recession, a pensioner was slightly less likely to live in poverty than a non-pensioner, measured after housing costs.[23] The fall in poverty measured against a fixed 1996–7 poverty line has been even more dramatic – down from 27% to just 9% in 2003–4.

Yet against the contemporary line one in five pensioners remain poor, despite available financial support. It is perhaps a little early to judge the pension credit: only once data are available for 2004/5 will the credit's effect be observed throughout a full financial year. However, there does

---

[22] DWP, *Households Below Average Income 1994/5 – 2003/4.*
[23] Brewer et al., *Poverty and Inequality in Britain: 2005.*

appear to be a serious problem with take-up which is unlikely to have disappeared overnight. The latest statistics (which are for the MIG) show that in 2002–3 between 26% and 37% of entitled pensioners failed to claim, compared with between 5% and 15% of the non-pensioner population eligible for income support.[24] Non-claimants were likely to be older (56% were 75-plus), and three in five were in the bottom quintile of the income distribution: the average amount unclaimed (£29 per week) could be expected to make a big difference to this group.

The government is well aware of the need to improve benefit take-up, with a public service agreement in place to increase the number of households receiving pension credit to 3 million by 2006. How easy will it be to increase take-up? One issue concerns raising awareness, which should be straightforward: research examining the barriers to pensioner take-up of MIG found that 57% of entitled non-recipients were unaware of benefits payable to people on low income.[25] But there is also a second issue about addressing the stigma associated with means-tested benefits, and this may be more difficult. Three-quarters of respondents in the same research said they would be more likely to apply if *most* pensioners were entitled to claim, highlighting the preference for universal benefits.

The shift away from universal benefits towards means-testing has been a repeated theme of the Blair government, an attempt to reconcile the enormous pressure a social justice agenda places on public services and social security with the need to keep a lid on public spending. Often the policy has been to protect a little something for everyone while targeting most on the poorest – 'progressive universalism', in New Labour terminology. Support for both children and pensioners illustrates this trend, with small increases in universal child benefit and the basic state pension accompanied by much more significant investment in the child tax credit and the pension credit. A key difference is that nearly all families with children (some 90%) are eligible for some element of support under the extended taper of the child tax credit, and this may have avoided the issue of stigma, though not the administrative and back-dating difficulties highlighted above. In contrast, only 65% of pensioner households are estimated to be eligible for pension credit. For different reasons, then, there may be question marks over the government's ability to reach its goal of eradicating pensioner poverty using the current toolkit, despite the best intentions.

---

[24] DWP, *Income Related Benefits: Estimates of Take-Up 2002/3* (London: DWP, 2005).
[25] DWP, *Households Below Average Income 1994/5 – 2002/3* (London: DWP, 2004).

Working-age households without children

The situation of working age households without children has been conspicuously absent from government targets and indicators. *Opportunity for All* tracks poverty among working-age households overall, but trends are disguised by developments for households which do contain children.

This is not to say that nothing has been done to improve living standards for low-income households without children. The extensive agenda aimed at helping people into work, and at making work pay, has encompassed non-parents as well as parents. Some of the measures, such as the national minimum wage and reforms to tax and National Insurance contributions at the bottom of the income distribution, have benefited all low earners. There have also been a series of New Deal programmes for specific groups, covering young people, the long-term unemployed aged 25-plus, and disabled people (compulsory for the first two groups, voluntary for the latter); these appear to have had a positive but limited impact.[26] Perhaps more strikingly, in April 2003 the working tax credit was extended to include households without children, making it clear that government sees itself as having a role to play in supplementing low wages in general, not just where a low wage is insufficient to support children.

There have also been reforms to the benefit system which have raised incomes for the most severely disabled, while introducing a greater degree of means-testing. But for those who are not disabled, the agenda has stopped with work. Out-of-work benefits have been uprated at the level of prices (excluding housing costs), meaning a steady deterioration in relation to average earnings. A single person on income support in 1997–8 received weekly benefit equivalent to about 40% of median income – well below the poverty line. By 2003–4 this share had fallen to just 33%. This contrasts sharply to the situation in Sweden, for example, where out-of-work benefits for all family types sit safely above the poverty line.[27]

[26] See Richard Blundell, Monica Costas-Dias, Costas Meghir and John Van Reenen, 'The impact of the New Deal for Young People: a four-year assessment', in Richard Dickens, Paul Gregg and Jonathan Wadsworth (eds.), *The Labour Market Under New Labour* (Basingstoke: Palgrave Macmillan, 2003); Karl Ashworth, Yvette Hartfree, Anne Kazimirski, Kate Legge, Candice Pires, Sandra Reyes de Beaman, Andrew Shaw and Bruce Stafford, *New Deal for Disabled People National Extension: First Wave of the First Cohort of the Survey of Entrants*, DWP Research Report No 180 (London: DWP, 2003).

[27] See Christina Behrendt, *At the Margins of the Welfare State: Social Assistance and the Alleviation of Poverty in Germany, Sweden and the United Kingdom* (Aldershot: Ashgate, 2002).

Table 14.3. *Poverty among households of working age without children 1996–7 to 2003–4*

	Before housing costs		After housing costs	
	1996–7	2003–4	1996–7	2003–4
All working-age adults without children	**12**	**13**	**17**	**17**
Single/couple one or more FT self-employed	13	15	16	19
Single/couple all in FT work	2	3	3	4
Couple, one FT, one PT work	1	3	2	3
Couple, one FT work, one not working	8	10	11	13
Single/couple no FT, one or more PT work	17	18	24	23
Workless, head or spouse unemployed	51	61	67	69
Workless, other inactive	30	34	43	46

Source: DWP, *Households Below Average Income, 1994/5–2003/4.*

The result has been that, despite rising employment, poverty among working-age households without children has failed to fall during Labour's time in office, as shown in Table 14.3. Tax credits and other measures intended to make work pay appear to have had an impact in encouraging employment (which is why we see a stable overall figure despite increased risk in each category) but they have not reduced the incidence of poverty for those who are working – although this risk is still very low for households with at least one full-time worker. It is for those without work that the figures are of most concern: more than two-thirds of households in which the head is unemployed lived below the poverty line in 2003/4, alongside between one-third and one-half of those in other inactive households (including those claiming incapacity and disability-related benefits).

How concerned should we be about high and rising levels of poverty among households with no children? A first point is that many households currently without children will include children in the future. In 2004/5 a young single woman becoming pregnant for the first time while on income support would have received £55.65 a week during her pregnancy (or less – just £44.05 – if she was under 25). On the birth of her baby she would have seen her benefits more than double, with an extra £68.60 for her child, in addition to a one-off Sure Start Maternity Grant of £500. This extra financial assistance would surely have been more than welcome. Yet research tells us that maternal diet prior to and in the early stages of pregnancy is crucial to a baby's birth-weight, in turn strongly linked to cognitive development and future health. In his 1999 conference speech, Blair spoke movingly of two babies lying next to each other in a maternity ward, delivered by the same doctors and midwives, yet with two very different lives ahead of them: 'If we are in politics for one thing, it is to make sure that all children are given the best chance in life'.[28] But the reality is that by the time the babies are born and Labour policies for them kick in, it is already too late to give them an equal chance of health and success.

More generally, there are also concerns about the level of benefits going to workless households who will never have (or have already raised) children. There is a pragmatic concern: it cannot be easy to look for work under financial constraints that make basic requirements such as suitable clothes and transport costs problematic. And there is an ideological concern about the nature of a truly inclusive society. The welfare state under Blair is one which accepts only certain reasons for not engaging in the paid labour market as valid, and does not adequately compensate even those. Many of those with caring responsibilities for dependents other than children; those who are in poor health but not severely disabled; and those who simply find participating in working life difficult on standard terms are living in gradually deepening poverty.

Life chances

As already noted, evidence of the impact of poverty in childhood on an individual's future opportunities appears to have been central to the commitment to eradicate child poverty. At the same time, the Blair government has recognised the importance for life chances of non-income factors, in particular education. Alongside income transfers and work-promotion initiatives it has invested heavily in education, including policies aimed at furthering children's development from the very earliest years. Children's health has arguably received less attention.

If the strategy is successful, the next generation of adults will be more highly skilled and in stronger health than the current generation, better placing them to bring up their own children free from poverty. The aim is to replace the intergenerational transmission of disadvantage with a virtuous circle in which today's investment means less need for intervention in the future. The long-term nature of the goal means that full assessment will not be possible for many years, but this section examines the policies

[28] Tony Blair, Labour Party Conference Speech, 28 September 1999.

that have been introduced and looks at early evidence of the difference they are making.

The early years strategy

There have been three key elements to investment in very young children (aside from policies aimed at increasing the number of childcare places, better classified as part of the anti-poverty work agenda). The expansion of paid maternity leave, first to six months, currently paid at £105 a week, and from April 2007 to nine paid months (with a view to an eventual extension to a year's paid leave) follows research evidence that the best place for a baby is at home with a mother who wishes to be there. The greater generosity of maternity leave will surely have enabled more low-income children to spend more time with their mothers in the first few months (although it appears that the same rate of compensation for two weeks' paid paternity leave has been too low to encourage many fathers to take it up).

The second key policy has been the provision of a free part-time nursery place to all three- and four-year-olds, following evidence of the importance of pre-school education for school-readiness and later academic and social outcomes, particularly for children from disadvantaged backgrounds. By 2002, just 7% of children from social classes IV and V were not receiving any nursery education, compared with 17% in 1997.

Finally, the Sure Start local programmes have brought a variation on five key themes to children under four in the 500 most disadvantaged wards – home visiting, parenting support, good quality play, learning and childcare experiences, primary health care and advice, and support for children and parents with special needs. Perhaps mostly because of the playgroups and support groups it runs, Sure Start has been widely popular with parents: in research conducted by the Centre for Analysis of Social Exclusion with parents in deprived areas it was one of few government initiatives spontaneously mentioned as having made a positive difference.[29] But early evaluation is inconclusive about the impact the programmes are having on measurable outcomes. Just one out of 24 child development and parenting outcomes (albeit a very important one) showed a significant Sure Start effect: mothers/main carers in Sure Start areas were observed to treat their children in a warmer and more accepting manner than in

---

[29] See Anne Power and Helen Willmot, 'Bringing up families in poor neighbourhoods under New Labour', in Hills and Stewart, *A More Equal Society?*

comparison areas. However, when 20 indicators were combined into a single score, Sure Start areas performed twice as well as comparison communities, suggesting that different programmes may be having an impact on different indicators – perhaps as to be expected given that programmes are locally designed and run.[30] More decisive assessment will have to wait for future evaluations. It should be remembered, however, that even at their best Sure Start programmes cover just one third of all poor children under four.

Education

Tackling educational disadvantage was an early priority for the Blair government. Since the low point of 1999, when the commitment to stick to Conservative spending plans came to an end, the share of GDP spent on education has risen steadily, from 4.5% to 5.3% in 2003–4, with planned spending rising to 5.6% by 2007–8. This has shifted the UK up the international spending range: 5.6% is getting close to the share spent in, for example, France in 1999 (5.8%), though it still falls well short of the spending share in Denmark (6.4%) and Sweden (6.5%). At the same time, the formula for allocating resources to local education authorities (LEAs) has been revised, increasing the share to those with most deprived populations, although only by half the level recommended in the Pricewaterhouse Coopers report commissioned by the Department for Education and Skills to guide the reform. (In part the decision not to implement the full recommendation was driven by the fact that the LEAs themselves each have their own internal allocation formulae, meaning that there is no way of ensuring that the extra resources reach the most needy schools.)

There have also been a number of targeted initiatives, including Excellence in Cities (EiC), which provides funding for learning mentors and for provision for gifted and talented pupils in the most deprived third of LEAs, and the Ethnic Minority Achievement Grant (EMAG), supporting a range of programmes benefiting schools with high concentrations of minority ethnic pupils. EiC has been found in early evaluations to have had a modest but positive effect on attainment and attendance.[31]

---

[30] See National Evaluation of Sure Start, *The Impact of Sure Start Local Programmes on Child Development and Family Functioning: A Report on Preliminary Findings* (London: Institute for the Study of Children, Families and Social Issues, Birkbeck College, 2004).

[31] Stephen Machin, Sandra McNally and Costas Meghir, 'Improving pupil performance in English secondary schools: Excellence in Cities', *Journal of the European Economic Association* 2:2 (2004) 396–405.

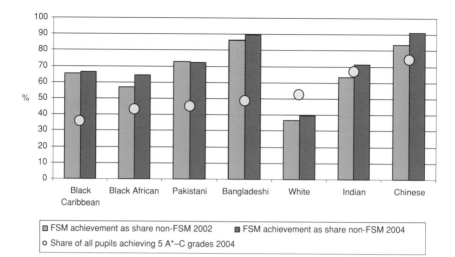

Figure 14.2. Disparities in educational achievement by ethnicity and free school meal status: share of pupils achieving 5 GCSEs at grade A*–C 2004 and 'poverty penalty' for each ethnic group 2002 and 2004 *Source:* Department for Education and Skills (DfES) Statistical First Releases:
http://www.dfes.gov.uk/rsgateway/DB/SFR/s000448/table37-40.xls (for 2002) and http://www.dfes.gov.uk/rsgateway/DB/SFR/s000564/Tables_21_25.xls (for 2004)

Classroom based reform has focused on standards, continuing with Conservative-designed policies such as literacy and numeracy hours, regular formal testing and league table publication; these last now include measures of 'value-added', making them better reflections of a school's performance rather than simply its social and academic intake. In addition, Labour pursued its 1997 election pledge to ensure that no child aged 5–7 was taught in a class with more than 30 pupils. By 2004 the share of such children was down from 28% to 14%.

What has the combined impact of these policies been on inequality in educational attainment? There is some evidence of catch-up to 2001 in the performance in key stage tests of 'rich' and 'poor' schools (those in which respectively less than 5% and over 40% of pupils qualify for free school meals).[32] Unfortunately the government discontinued the publication of these data from 2001, but since 2002 we have been able to look at pupil performance directly. Figure 14.2 shows the share

---

[32] Abigail McKnight, Howard Glennerster and Ruth Lupton, 'Education, education, education . . .: an assessment of Labour's success in tackling educational inequalities', in Hills and Stewart, *A More Equal Society?*

of pupils from different ethnic groups achieving five or more GCSEs at grades A*–C (the circles in the figure), along with the performance of pupils eligible for free school meals relative to that of other pupils (the bars); this has been called the 'poverty penalty'. The figure shows slight improvement in the relative performance of the FSM group for most ethnic groups between 2002 and 2004. But no dramatic transformation is observable and the poverty penalty remains considerable, particularly for the white population: in 2004 white pupils eligible for free school meals were still just 40% as likely to achieve five A*–C grades as their non-eligible classmates.

Interestingly, when we look further down the education system, at pupils who have had more (or indeed all) of their education under a Labour government, we do not see greater signs of change. At earlier key stages smaller disparities are observed across both ethnic group and FSM status, but there is less evidence of improvement between 2002 and 2004. This raises doubts about whether we can expect to see larger step reductions in GCSE disparities as younger cohorts age. At the current pace of change, it is likely to be a very long time before poverty ceases to be a huge obstacle to educational attainment, raising the question of whether more radical changes in funding are not required to start to shift these figures more rapidly.

Health

Health inequalities have been subject to considerable attention during both Labour terms, with a series of assessments and reviews following the report of the independent Acheson inquiry.[33] Four months before the 2001 election the government announced two health inequalities targets: the first to reduce the difference in life expectancy between areas with the lowest life expectancy and the average; and the second to reduce the gap in infant mortality between manual groups and the population as a whole by at least 10% by 2010. Policies, however, have been thinner on the ground – to the extent that a 2004 Treasury review concluded that 'after many years of reviews and government policy documents, with little change on the

---

[33] Department of Health, *Independent Inquiry into Inequalities in Health Report* (London: The Stationery Office, 1998); Department of Health, *Saving Lives: Our Healthier Nation* (London: The Stationery Office 1999); Department of Health, *Tackling Health Inequalities: A Programme for Action* (London: Department of Health, 2003). For further discussion see Franco Sassi, 'Tackling health inequalities', in Hills and Stewart, *A More Equal Society?*

ground, the key challenge now is delivery and implementation, not further discussion'.[34]

The main policy emphasis has been on overall levels of health and increased spending on health care. Health spending has risen as a share of GDP from 5.7% in 1998 to 7.2% in 2004–5 and should reach 9% by 2007–8 – and, as for education, funding formulae have been reformed to channel more resources to disadvantaged areas. In addition, health action zones were set up, aimed at developing local programmes to tackle health inequalities in collaboration with social services, voluntary and business organisations and local communities. However, despite strong evidence of the importance of childhood health as a driver of health in adulthood, there has been no overarching health strategy for children. There have been small initiatives such as the National School Fruit Scheme, which provides every school child aged four to six with a daily free piece of fruit; and late in the second term funding was pledged to improve the quality of school lunches, in the aftermath of celebrity chef Jamie Oliver's high-profile campaign on the issue. But the policy for very early childhood appears to have been reliant mainly on Sure Start, with public service agreements to reduce low birth-weight, emergency hospital admissions, smoking in pregnancy and re-registrations with the child protection register in Sure Start areas. Strikingly, children do not feature among the priorities for primary care trusts for 2002–3, for example, though they were included in 2004–5 – perhaps a realisation of the inadequacy of the strategy to date.

In practice, the share of babies born at low birth-weight remained steady in social classes I–IIINM between 1997 and 2001 but rose slightly among classes IIIM–VI, increasing the social class differential. The class differential in infant mortality has also increased over the period: in this case progress has been made for all groups, but gains have been greater for higher social classes. Similarly, among adults, time trends for coronary heart disease and cancer show absolute improvements for all socio-economic groups, but little change in inequalities between them.[35] For adults it is arguably much too early to judge the impact of any recent changes, given both lags in data and the speed with which policy might be expected to affect health outcomes. But the lack of progress in reducing health inequality for young children is more worrying – both because the challenge of reducing later inequality after an unequal start is far greater

---

[34] Derek Wanless, *Securing Good Health for the Whole Population* (London: HM Treasury, 2004), cited in Sassi, 'Tackling health inequalities'.
[35] See Sassi, 'Tackling health inequalities'.

and because young children's health ought to be quick to respond to effective policy. There are limited indications of improvement in Sure Start areas: smoking in pregnancy fell by 6% in Sure Start areas between 2000–1 and 2002–3, while child protection re-registrations fell by 20% between 2000 and 2004.[36] But this seems a drop in the ocean. We are unlikely to see very significant improvement without a more comprehensive approach to the question of how to tackle inequalities in health from birth, including – as pointed to above – a rethinking of levels of support to low-income women during pregnancy and beforehand.

Income inequality

Reducing the level of overall income inequality has very clearly *not* been a goal for the Blair government. Blair has repeatedly emphasised that his concern is with the bottom half of the income distribution rather than the top half, and with 'equality of opportunity' not 'equality of outcome'. As he put it in a Fabian pamphlet in 2002, 'We favour true equality: equal worth and equal opportunity, not an equality of outcome focused on incomes alone.'[37] Or more colourfully, on *Newsnight* in 2001: 'It's not a burning ambition of mine to make sure that David Beckham earns less money.'[38]

In practice, Figure 14.3 shows that incomes have risen very slightly faster for the poorer groups than for the richer groups under this government. This contrasts sharply to the situation under Margaret Thatcher, shown at the bottom of the figure. While the average annual rate of growth was similar (mean growth of 2.9% under Thatcher compared with 2.5% under Blair), during the Thatcher years growth was skewed heavily towards the richest. Under John Major the lower income groups did best in relative terms, but growth was very low for everyone.

The pattern of growth under Blair has meant, as we have seen, sharp improvements in the real living standards of the poorest, especially for children and pensioners, and slower declines in relative poverty for these groups. But overall income inequality has remained fairly static. Figure 14.4 shows the change in one summary measure of income

[36] Department for Education and Skills, *Autumn Performance Report 2004* (London: DfES, 2004).
[37] Tony Blair, *The Courage of our Convictions: Why Reform of the Public Services is the Route to Social Justice*, Fabian Ideas 603 (London: Fabian Society, 2002), p. 2.
[38] Cited in Tom Sefton and Holly Sutherland, 'Inequality and poverty under New Labour', in Hills and Stewart, *A More Equal Society?*

Blair: 1996/7–2003/4

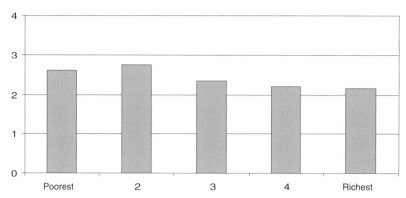

Major: 1990–1996/7

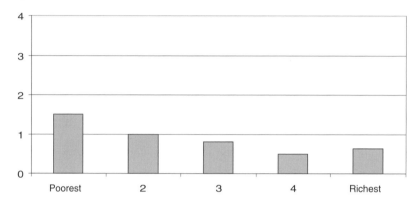

Thatcher: 1979–1990

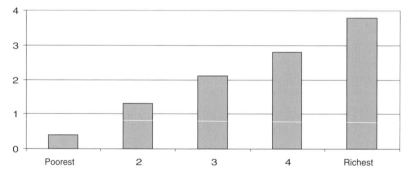

Figure 14.3. Real income growth by quintile group under Tony Blair, John Major and Margaret Thatcher (% per year)

Notes: Averages in each quintile group correspond to the midpoints, i.e. the 10th, 30th, 50th, 70th and 90th percentile points of the income distribution. Incomes have been measured before the deduction of housing costs.

Source: based on Brewer et al., *Poverty and Inequality in Britain: 2005*, Figure 2.4.

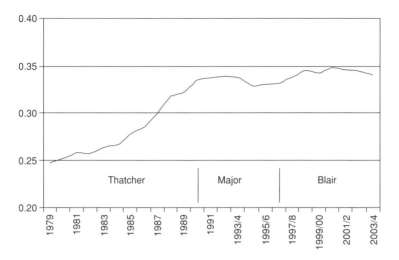

Figure 14.4. The Gini coefficient 1979–2003/4
Note: The Gini coefficient has been calculated using incomes before the deduction of housing costs.
Source: based on Figure 2.7 in Brewer et al., *Poverty and Inequality in Britain: 2005,* using data from Institute for Fiscal Studies website (www.ifs.org.uk).

inequality, the Gini coefficient, which takes a value between 0 (complete equality) and 1 (if one person receives all the income and the others nothing). The Gini rose slightly during Blair's first term to reach a record level, and fell slightly in the second term, but not enough to move back to the 1996–7 starting point. However, both changes are very small in the context of the rise in the coefficient during the 1980s, as the figure shows, and the overall increase between 1996–7 and 2003–4 is insignificant.

Why has inequality not fallen, despite the many measures taken – successfully – to raise the incomes of the poorest? It should be remembered that this has been a time of strong economic growth, and in such periods inequality tends to rise. Certainly tax-benefit changes have had difficulty keeping up with rapid increases in median incomes (which is why relative poverty indicators have been falling so much more slowly than indicators using a fixed income poverty line). Furthermore, income at the very top of the income distribution – in particular among the richest 1% or even 0.5% of individuals – has been increasing far more quickly than average.[39] The income shares of both the top 1% and the top 0.5%, which had been

---

[39] Sefton and Sutherland, 'Inequality and poverty under New Labour'.

falling throughout the century for as far as records go back, have been on the increase since the early 1980s, and have seen a particularly sharp rise since 1998.[40] This has not affected poverty indicators (measured against the median) but has influenced inequality indicators which reflect the full distribution, such as the Gini. The major contributor to income inequality is earnings inequality, and this has continued to widen since 1997, particularly in the top half of the distribution: the ratio between the earnings of those at the 90th percentile and those at the median reached an all-time high of 2.0 in 2003.[41]

Microsimulation by Tom Sefton and Holly Sutherland indicates that the Gini coefficient in 2004/5 is significantly lower than it would have been if the 1997 tax-benefit system had been left in place and just adjusted for inflation: the reduction in the Gini compared to that scenario is about one third of the size of the rise of the previous twenty years.[42] The Gini is also lower than it would have been under a more generous scenario, in which the 1997 system was adjusted for average income growth, though the impact in this case is reduced by about half. In sum, while tax-benefit changes under Labour have been redistributive, they have been working against the tide of pre-tax and benefit growth in equality, and have only been sufficient to prevent further increases in inequality, not to reduce it. Unless there are changes in underlying market factors driving inequality, far more substantial redistribution will be needed to start to bring the Gini coefficient down – and it is unlikely that this will be possible without open debate and commitment to the goal.

Of course this presupposes that income inequality is a problem for social justice. Blair appears genuinely unconvinced of this. There is a wide literature on the impact of income inequality for society, and critics point to a number of potential reasons for concern, from doubts about whether 'equality of opportunity' is really possible when family incomes vary so greatly and can be used to buy private education, to concern that salary packages at the very top are simply so high as to be unjust and unjustifiable, even on meritocratic grounds.[43] There are also pragmatic questions about the use of limited resources: will it be possible to find the

---

[40] Anthony B. Atkinson, *Top Incomes in the United Kingdom over the Twentieth Century*, University of Oxford Discussion Papers in Economic and Social History, No. 43 (Oxford: University of Oxford, 2002).

[41] Sefton and Sutherland, 'Inequality and poverty under New Labour'.   [42] Ibid.

[43] See, for example, Ben Jackson and Paul Segal, *Why Inequality Matters*, Catalyst Working Paper (London: Catalyst, 2004); Edward Miliband, 'Does inequality matter?', in Anthony Giddens and Patrick Diamond (eds.), *The New Egalitarianism* (Cambridge: Polity Press, 2005).

money to eradicate poverty without a greater contribution from those on higher incomes? But the literature is, perhaps inevitably, less empirical and more ideological than the literature on the impact of child poverty, which *has* clearly convinced Blair. Possibly more could have been done by the research community to make the case for reducing income inequality in a way which would have won him over, but it is now most unlikely that we will see the issue any higher up the agenda in a third Blair term.

Social justice with borders: asylum seekers under Blair

Any assessment of Blair's social justice record needs to take into account the treatment of asylum seekers, whose situation has deteriorated rapidly under Labour as the deliberately intended result of policy.[44]

When Labour took office asylum seekers had already faced reductions in their entitlement to support. In 1996, the Conservative administration had removed the right to benefit from asylum applicants who had made their applications from within the UK, rather than immediately on arrival. It had also made things tougher for those who did claim asylum 'at port': these applicants remained eligible for 90% of income support as well as housing benefit and child benefit, but were excluded from waiting lists for local authority housing and restricted from working for the first six months.

In opposition, the Labour Party had called for the restoration of benefit entitlement, but in power it took very different action. The 1999 Immigration and Asylum Act removed benefit entitlement from *all* asylum seekers. Instead, the National Asylum Support Service (NASS) was created, to provide vouchers to cover food and essential items, and to arrange accommodation through compulsory dispersal around the country. Vouchers amounted to a total value of 70% of income support, but in practice were worth less as no change was provided. Furthermore, only certain shops accepted them.

The 2002 Nationality, Asylum and Immigration Act provided for the phased withdrawal even of vouchers, with a view to providing for all the needs of asylum seekers in accommodation centres. In the meantime, while centres were being built, families with children were still eligible for vouchers, but others were excluded unless they had applied for asylum 'as soon as reasonably practicable' on reaching the country. The 2002 Act also

---

[44] This section draws heavily on Tania Burchardt, 'Selective inclusion: asylum seekers and other marginalised groups', in Hills and Stewart, *A More Equal Society?*

extended the ban on working to all applicants and for the full duration of the claim process. The 2004 Asylum and Immigration Act toughened rules further, removing all support from asylum seekers whose claims had been refused.

The cumulative effect of these three acts has been 'the marginalisation of asylum seekers from mainstream services and society – from Income Support to vouchers, from local authority housing to segregated accommodation centres and from the opportunity to support themselves through paid work to exclusion from employment.'[45] Quite simply, limits have been placed on who is covered by the social justice and social inclusion agendas. The government's argument is that such restrictions are necessary to discourage abuse of the system, yet there is no evidence that either the availability and generosity of welfare benefits or the toughness of requirements of the application process are important influences on asylum seekers' choice of destination. Most applicants have little idea of what their entitlement will be and make their decision based on family ties and linguistic and cultural links. The treatment of this already highly vulnerable group places a scar on the other achievements of the Blair government.

Choice, competition and social justice

While many government policies have worked towards combating poverty and inequality, other policies have operated in the opposite direction. The treatment of asylum seekers is clearly an example of this. A second cause for concern, less acute in the immediate term but with potentially widespread and long-lasting effects, is the extension of market-based concepts of choice and competition into the public services. In a 2002 Fabian pamphlet setting out the case for reform, Blair argues that growing individualism means that universal provision is no longer appropriate – greater choice for 'consumers' of health and education is essential.[46] Choice, he continues, has the added benefit of promoting competition: with money following patients and pupils, providers will be forced to compete (and in the health sector this will include competition against private providers), resulting in improvements in standards across the board. Thus everyone benefits, while the use of national floor targets guarantees minimum standards – a sort of Rawlsian maxi-min argument.

---

[45] Burchardt, 'Selective inclusion', p. 224.   [46] Blair, *Courage of our Convictions.*

According to the pamphlet, 'radical reform is the route to social jus-tice'.[47] But commentators on both education and health have voiced con-cerns about the spread of choice and competition in these sectors, and raised doubts about their compatibility with social justice and equity goals.

In the health sector, to take one example, concerns have been raised that the creation of foundation hospitals may affect equity of access and fairness in health care financing in multiple ways.[48] For instance, finance for foundation hospitals will be made on the basis of competition for contracts with primary care trusts, rather than on the basis of local popu-lation need. Successful hospitals will be able to build up a surplus of funds and raise further capital on financial markets, raising the possibility of virtuous circles of performance for the best, and correspondingly lower investment for hospitals already doing less well. Furthermore, founda-tion trusts can generate additional funds from private patients, meaning quality of provision for NHS patients may end up partially dependent on the wealth of the local community.

In education, policies encouraging parental choice and diversity of provision also carry with them the danger of creating a two-tier system. A major problem is that choice mechanisms do not operate in favour of all parents equally, but favour middle-class parents in particular. In part this is because of the importance of understanding how the system works; in part because limitations on school capacity mean that where choice is in operation it is mainly '*the schools that choose parents*, rather than the other way round'.[49] Specialist schools, for example, created by the Conservatives, were permitted in 1998 to admit up to 10% of pupils on 'aptitude'; they were quickly oversubscribed, despite evidence that there was no parental demand for a specialist curriculum.[50] Instead, the hint of selection seems to have been the draw. The vision is for all schools to specialise eventually, and this may improve things – but there is likely also to turn out to be a hierarchy of specialisms, with music and mathematics more highly favoured by the middle class than sports and business studies.

[47] Blair, *Courage of our Convictions*, p. iv.
[48] Allyson M Pollock, David Price, Alison Talbot-Smith and John Mohan, 'NHS and the Health and Social Care Bill: end of Bevan's vision?' *British Medical Journal* 327 (2003): 982–5.
[49] Clyde Chitty, *Education Policy in Britain* (Basingstoke: Palgrave Macmillan, 2004), his emphasis.
[50] Sally Tomlinson, *Education in a Post-Welfare Society* (Buckingham: Open University Press, 2001).

Furthermore, as for foundation hospitals, differences in funding for different types of school threaten to reward success and penalise failure, potentially undermining the changes to mainstream funding favouring more deprived communities pointed to above. Specialist schools and the new city academies receive additional per capita funding and can also attract private sponsorship. Careful monitoring of these policies and their impact on equality of access in both the health and education sectors will be needed over the next few years, but the potential to damage social justice goals is clear.

Blair's legacy: a more equal society?

What will Blair leave behind when he retires from office sometime in the course of his third term as prime minister? Will it be a fairer and more equal society than the one he inherited – and if so, how much can he take the credit?

This government undoubtedly took the levels of poverty and social injustice plaguing Britain in the 1990s far more seriously than many would have expected when Labour came to power on a fairly modest manifesto in 1997. A wide range of problems has been recognised, including child and pensioner poverty, unemployment and worklessness, educational disadvantage, health inequalities and the multiple problems facing people living in deprived neighbourhoods. In many areas targets have been set and policy introduced to try to reach those targets, with a number of clear successes. Reductions in income poverty for children and pensioners are perhaps foremost among these, but there has also been considerable investment in opportunities for children from their very earliest years as well as some progress in improving outcomes in the poorest areas (not discussed in this chapter due to space constraints).

What has been Blair's personal contribution to these changes? Most obviously, his unexpected pledge to eradicate child poverty in a generation has had an enormous impact. Without such a pledge it is unlikely that benefit changes favouring children would have developed as far or as fast, or been given such priority – although a committed Gordon Brown in the Treasury was surely also an essential ingredient (and arguably more important in ensuring delivery). More generally, the 'opportunity for all' agenda, with its emphasis on the importance of tackling disparities in life chances from birth onwards, appears to bear Blair's stamp.

On the other hand, Blair must also be held responsible for the refusal to contemplate taking on – and arguing openly for – wider social justice goals including greater income equality and lower adult poverty rates. Reticence on these matters has been attributed by some to a reluctance to risk upsetting the electorate, but the Blair position on a range of issues from the war in Iraq to university tuition fees and identity cards makes a nonsense of the idea that this is a prime minister unwilling to take on and stick by an unpopular policy. A more likely explanation is that there are limits to the depth of Blair's commitment to social justice, and that his heart and instincts quite simply lie elsewhere. It is telling that Blair has often failed to mention the reduction in child poverty when asked to list Labour's achievements in office. Furthermore, while he described the 2005 Queen's Speech as 'quintessentially New Labour: economic prosperity combined with social justice', the public-sector reform agenda has been given far greater emphasis at the start of the third term than any policies to tackle disadvantage. Where in June 1997 Blair surprised many by speaking up for 'forgotten people' and 'no-hope areas', in May 2005 he probably surprised few in using his first press conference after the election to argue that 'our task is to deepen the change, accelerate reform and address head-on the priorities of the British people in the NHS, schools and welfare reform . . . [Reform] means driving innovation and improvement through more diverse provision and putting people in the driving seat'.[51] Whether poverty will fall further, and how lasting Labour's achievements in furthering goals of equality and social justice will be, depend heavily on the priorities of his successor.

[51] Cited on the BBC News website, 12 May 2005, http://news.bbc.co.uk/go/pr/fr/-/1/hi/uk-politics/4540723.stm.

PART III

Wider relations

15

The national question

IAIN McLEAN

Introduction: four more years of path-dependent devolution

Devolution to Scotland and Wales was already a 'done deal' at the start of
Tony Blair's second term in June 2001.[1] On the face of things, little had
changed in Scotland and Wales at the start of his third in May 2005, while
change in Northern Ireland was for the worse. However, there are subtle
and important changes below the surface. This chapter describes these
changes, and evaluates the Blair effect on them.

Karl Marx wisely said, 'Men make their own history, but they do not
make it just as they please; they do not make it under circumstances chosen
by themselves, but under circumstances directly encountered, given and
transmitted from the past.'[2] The men and women who ran devolution
in the UK between 2001 and 2005 did so under electoral and financial
systems directly encountered, given and transmitted from the past. On
these circumstances depended the path of devolution in the second Blair
term.

In 1994 John Smith, then Labour leader, sonorously proclaimed devolution to be 'the settled will of the Scottish people'. The Scottish referendum of 1997 validated the constitutional settlement proposed by the
Scottish Constitutional Convention that sat between 1989 and 1995. In
a dual vote with a 60% turnout, 74.3% of those who voted approved the
Scottish Parliament, and 63.5% of those who voted agreed that it would
have a power to tax, although to date it has not used that power, nor
does it look likely to in the near future. The Welsh referendum was held
a week after the Scottish one in the hope of generating a bandwagon.
Whether it did so or not, the result could not have been closer. Until the

---

[1] See my discussion of devolution up to 2000 in the previous book in this series: I. McLean,
'The national question', in A. Seldon (ed.), *The Blair Effect: The Blair Government 1997–2001*
(London: Little, Brown, 2001), pp. 429–47.
[2] K. Marx, *The Eighteenth Brumaire of Louis Bonaparte*, in K. Marx and F. Engels, *Selected
Works* (London: Lawrence & Wishart, 1968), p. 96. Originally published in 1852.

very last county reported, it looked all evening as if the Noes were going to win. The National Assembly of Wales was approved by just over 50% of those who voted in the referendum, on a 50% turnout. But devolution is path-dependent. The Scottish Parliament with its massive popular endorsement, and the National Assembly for Wales with its feeble popular endorsement, are equally part of the constitutional landscape. The institutions of politics and civil society adapted to their existence and now have a stake in their continuation. Above all, the Conservative Party has abandoned its historic role as last-ditch defender of the Union[3] in favour of accepting the Scottish and Welsh assemblies and governments. Their systems of proportional representation gave the Conservatives a foothold that they would not have had under the Westminster first-past-the-post system that they continue (inexplicably) to favour.

Ironically, the territory with the strongest popular endorsement for constitutional change is the one where constitutional change has hit a brick wall. In Northern Ireland, the Belfast ('Good Friday') Agreement of 1998 won 71% support; and in the parallel referendum in the Irish Republic, the proposal to abandon the Republic's irredentist claims over Northern Ireland won 95%.[4] Support for constitutional change in Ireland was therefore stronger than in Scotland, and much stronger than in Wales. However, the Northern Ireland Assembly, unlike those in Scotland and Wales, has failed. It has been suspended twice over the failure of the paramilitaries there to disarm. Although a second election to the suspended Assembly was held in 2003, the deadlock has continued, and the new Assembly has never met. The UK general election of 2005 has strengthened the extremes at the expense of the middle. Westminster elections in Northern Ireland always do – partly because of the electoral system, as we shall see in a moment. But opinion in both the nationalist and unionist communities has undoubtedly moved in favour of the hardliners.

Table 15.1 shows how the parties have fared in the Westminster and devolved elections since 1998. Elections to the House of Commons are held under the single-member, first-past-the-post(FPTP), electoral system. Elections to all the legislatures of the devolved administrations (DAs) are by versions of proportional representation (PR). Scotland and

---

[3] I. McLean and A. McMillan, *State of the Union* (Oxford: Oxford University Press, 2005), esp. ch. 9.

[4] Brendan O'Leary, 'The Belfast Agreement and the Labour government' in Seldon, *Blair Effect*, pp. 449–87.

Table 15.1. *Votes and seats in Scotland, Wales and Northern Ireland, 1999–2005*

Scotland

	Scottish Parliament 1999				House of Commons 2001				Scottish Parliament 2003				House of Commons 2005			
	Vote Share	Seats	Seat Share	Seat/Vote	Vote Share	Seats	Seat Share	Seat/Vote	Vote Share	Seats	Seat Share	Seat/Vote	Vote Share	Seats	Seat Share	Seat/Vote
Labour	36.2	56	43.4	1.20	43.9	56	77.8	1.77	32.0	50	38.8	1.21	39.5	41	69.5	1.76
Lib Dem	13.3	17	13.2	0.99	16.4	10	13.9	0.85	13.6	17	13.2	0.97	22.6	11	18.6	0.82
SNP	28.0	35	27.1	0.97	20.1	5	6.9	0.35	22.4	27	20.9	0.94	17.7	6	10.2	0.57
Conservative	15.5	18	14.0	0.90	15.6	1	1.4	0.09	16.1	18	14.0	0.87	15.8	1	1.7	0.11
Other	7.0	3	2.3	0.33	4.0	0	0.0	0.00	16.1	17	13.2	0.82	4.4	0	0.0	0.00
	100.0	129	100.0		100.0	72	100.0		100.0	129	100.0		100.0	59	100.0	

Wales

	National Assembly 1999				House of Commons 2001				National Assembly 2003				House of Commons 2005			
	Vote Share	Seats	Seat Share	Seat/Vote	Vote Share	Seats	Seat Share	Seat/Vote	Vote Share	Seats	Seat Share	Seat/Vote	Vote Share	Seats	Seat Share	Seat/Vote
Labour	36.6	28	46.7	1.28	48.6	34	85.0	1.75	38.3	30	50.0	1.31	42.7	29	72.5	1.70
Lib Dem	13.0	6	10.0	0.77	13.8	2	5.0	0.36	13.4	6	10.0	0.75	18.4	4	10.0	0.54
Plaid Cymru	29.5	17	28.3	0.96	14.3	4	10.0	0.70	20.5	12	20.0	0.98	12.6	3	7.5	0.60
Conservative	16.2	9	15.0	0.93	21.0	0	0.0	0.00	19.6	11	18.3	0.94	21.4	3	7.5	0.35
Other	4.8	0	0.0	0.00	2.3	0	0.0	0.00	8.3	1	1.7	0.20	4.9	1	2.5	0.51
	100.0	60	100.0		100.0	40	100.0		100.0	60	100.0		100.0	40	100.0	

Northern Ireland

	NI Legislative Assembly 1999				House of Commons 2001				NI Legislative Assembly 2003				House of Commons 2005			
	Vote Share	Seats	Seat Share	Seat/Vote	Vote Share	Seats	Seat Share	Seat/Vote	Vote Share	Seats	Seat Share	Seat/Vote	Vote Share	Seats	Seat Share	Seat/Vote
DUP	18.1	10	9.3	0.51	22.5	5	27.8	1.23	25.7	30	27.8	1.08	33.7	9	50.0	1.48
UUP	21.3	28	25.9	1.22	26.8	6	33.3	1.24	22.7	27	25.0	1.10	17.7	1	5.6	0.31
SDLP	22.0	24	22.2	1.01	21.0	3	16.7	0.79	17.0	18	16.7	0.98	17.5	3	16.7	0.95
Sinn Féin	17.7	18	16.7	0.94	21.7	4	22.2	1.02	23.5	24	22.2	0.95	24.3	5	27.8	1.14
Other	20.9	28	25.9	1.24	8.0	0	0.0	0.00	11.1	9	8.3	0.75	6.8	0	0.0	0.00
	100.0	108	100.0		100.0	18	100.0		100.0	108	100.0		100.0	18	100.0	

Notes: Vote share in Scottish and Welsh assemblies: unweighted average of constituency vote and list vote for each party.
Vote share in Northern Ireland assembly: share of first preference vote for each party.
Sources: BBC Election websites 2001, 2005; Electoral Commission; Constitution Unit; Trench, *Has Devolution Made a Difference?*, Figure 4.7.

Wales use the additional member system (AMS); Northern Ireland uses the single transferable vote (STV) system. The three electoral systems in use in the elections covered by Table 15.1 therefore produce very different votes-to-seats mappings. As electors in the DAs have become familiar with the variety of electoral systems in use there, the system also affects the willingness of people to vote for parties of different sorts in different contexts. It is therefore necessary to interpret the figures in Table 15.1 one territory at a time and one electoral system at a time. Vote shares and seat shares each tell an important story, but they are different stories.

In Scotland, Labour has retained its hegemonic position in all four elections since 1999. However, its hegemony in votes is less secure than its hegemony in seats. In the second Scottish Parliament election in 2003, its share of the vote dropped to 32%. It was vulnerable to the left (the Scottish Socialist Party and the Green Party) as well as to the Scottish National Party (SNP). A small Conservative revival was a minor problem for Labour. Indeed, as Table 15.1 shows, Conservative performance in Scotland has been flat. Their improvement from the nadir of the 1997 general election, when they won not a single seat in Scotland, has been entirely due to the votes-to-seats mapping, not to an improvement in their share of the vote. The Liberal Democrats were similarly flat-lining until a remarkable performance in the 2005 general election, which took their vote share from either third or fourth place in the preceding elections to second place, forcing the SNP into third place in Scotland for the first time since 1992. Labour performed better, and the SNP worse, in elections to the House of Commons than in elections to the Scottish Parliament.

In Wales, Labour was also hegemonic, but never to the extent of winning more than half of the popular vote. Unlike in Scotland, the Conservatives made a real recovery between 1999 and 2001, and have retained their slightly higher share of the vote since then. The Liberal Democrats have a similar profile in Wales to that in Scotland, but their gain in 2005 was less dramatic. And Plaid Cymru ('Party of Wales') has done distinctly badly, dropping from nearly 30% of the Welsh vote in the first National Assembly to only 12.6% in the 2005 general election. But as in Scotland, voting behaviour seems to differ in UK and Welsh elections. Labour performed better, and Plaid Cymru worse, in elections to the House of Commons than in elections to the National Assembly for Wales.

In Northern Ireland, each main community contains a relatively moderate and at least one relatively extreme party. With few exceptions, Protestants vote for unionist parties and Catholics vote for nationalist parties. In the unionist community, the relatively moderate party is the Ulster

Unionist Party – UUP in Table 15.1; the main relatively extreme party is the Democratic Unionist Party of the Rev. Ian Paisley – DUP in Table 15.1. Other unionist parties with links to Protestant paramilitaries won seats in the Legislative Assembly elections, but not in general elections. In the nationalist community, the relatively moderate party is the Social Democratic and Labour Party – SDLP in Table 15.1. The relatively extreme party is Sinn Féin, which is widely believed to be intimately connected with the main republican paramilitary organisation, the IRA. Sinn Féin's parliamentary leaders, Gerry Adams and Martin McGuinness, violently deny that they serve on the IRA's governing councils, although Unionists (and some others) believe that McGuinness is a member of the IRA's Army Council. There is relatively little cross-community voting. The non-sectarian Alliance Party has never won seats at Westminster although it did win some at Stormont in 1998 and 2003, as did the Northern Ireland Women's Coalition in 1998. The SDLP's gain of Belfast South in the 2005 general election may indicate the first cross-community voting by Protestants on any scale since the foundation of Northern Ireland.

Throughout the period since 1998, the extremes have been gaining ground at the expense of the centre. The DUP has risen from an 18% share of the vote in 1998 to 33.7% in 2005. Sinn Féin has risen from 17.7 to 24.3 per cent over the same period. The UUP and SDLP have lost votes and seats. Their loss of seats must imperil their future, especially that of the UUP, which was reduced to one Westminster seat in May 2005.

There has been a long-run tendency for the extremes in Northern Ireland to do better in first-past-the-post Westminster elections than in PR local elections. This tendency can neither be confirmed nor contradicted for the period since 1998. True, the centre was annihilated in the 2005 Westminster election, as has happened in Ireland in some past general elections, especially 1885, 1918 and both February and October 1974. However, Table 15.1 shows that the upward gradient for the extreme parties has been continuous since the Good Friday Agreement, so their triumph in 2005 cannot be wholly ascribed to electoral system effects.

Nevertheless, Table 15.1 shows that electoral systems matter profoundly for the future of devolution within the UK. The electoral systems did not change during the second Blair term, but systems introduced at the start continued to work their effects in subtle ways through the politics of representation and finance, to which we go on in subsequent sections of this chapter. Past UK governments introduced proportional representation in (Northern) Ireland and Scotland for quite deliberate reasons, which overrode the winners' natural reluctance to disturb the first-past-the-post system which gave them their victories in UK-wide elections. STV came into both parts of Ireland as long ago as 1918, in order to protect local minorities – that is, Protestants in southern Ireland and Catholics in northern Ireland. In both parts of Ireland, incumbent governments have tried to abolish it in order to bring back the winner's bonus associated with first-past-the-post. In both parts they failed, although in Northern Ireland the incumbent Unionists got rid of it between 1929 and 1973. In Scotland, the architect of devolution, Donald Dewar, was quite explicit. He forced PR through against the will of many of his Labour Party colleagues, who knew that they stood to lose seats. As Labour would probably have easily won an outright majority of its seats on a minority vote had the Westminster system applied in Scotland, Dewar called this 'the best example of charitable giving this century in politics'.[5] However, it guaranteed the legitimacy of the Scottish Parliament and made it harder for the SNP to gain a majority in it. In October 1974, the SNP had come perilously close to winning a majority of Scottish seats on a minority of the vote.[6] PR in the Scottish Parliament makes that unlikely.

Wales, as usual, was an afterthought. There was no comparable reason of Unionist statecraft for imposing PR on the National Assembly, but consistency with Scotland, and perhaps some desire to break up the single-party fortresses of the Valleys, led Labour to introduce the additional member system there too. This accidentally saved Labour's bacon in 2000[7] but in general has constrained Labour more than it has liberated it in Wales.

Votes, seats and electoral systems are endogenous to one another. This makes separating out the unique effects of each on either of the others very difficult. That the SNP and Plaid Cymru do better in devolved than in Westminster elections almost certainly reflects two things: that there are people who sincerely support them in the first but not in the second; and that there is more tactical point in voting for them under PR than under first-past-the-post. For both of these reasons (which we cannot disentangle) they are entrenched in their respective assemblies despite their weakening performance during the second Blair term. The tendency for the centre in Northern Ireland to do better under STV than under FPTP cannot be confirmed for sure during this period. Real reasons of policy almost certainly underlie the weakening of the centre in 2003 and its collapse in 2005, namely the failure of republican paramilitaries to disarm

---

[5] *Parliamentary Debates*, Commons, vol. 312, 6 May 1998, col. 803.
[6] I. McLean, *The Fiscal Crisis of the United Kingdom* (Basingstoke: Palgrave, 2005), p. 67.
[7] McLean, 'National question', pp. 440–3.

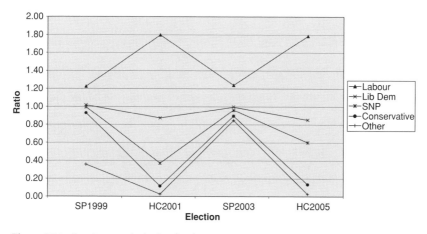

Figure 15.1. Seat/vote ratio in Scotland

and the knock-on disillusionment of unionists with the UUP politicians who had trusted the republicans' good faith.

The simplest summary measures of the electoral system effects on devolution are seat/vote ratios. These are shown in Table 15.1 as the fourth column of figures for each Parliament. The seat/vote ratio for a party is simply its share of seats expressed as a proportion of its share of votes, i.e., the third column in each block of Table 15.1 divided by the first. In pure PR, the seat/vote ratio would always be 1.00. Under FPTP the ratio for the leading party will almost always exceed 1.00, the ratio for the second party is sometimes above and sometimes below 1.00, and the ratio for third and lower parties is almost always below 1.00. The ratio for any party which fails to gain a seat is, of course, zero.

It is easier to visualise these seat/vote ratios graphically. Figures 15.1, 15.2, and 15.3 do this in turn for Scotland, Wales and Northern Ireland. They show how dramatically the path of devolution is set by the electoral systems.

In all three territories, the locally dominant party has a ratio greater than 1 at Westminster elections. For Scotland and Wales, this is always Labour; in Northern Ireland, it was the UUP till 2001, and is now the DUP. Opposition parties whose vote is spatially distributed in a way that is efficient under FPTP may have seat/vote ratios of close to 1.00 – i.e., they may by happenstance be proportionally represented. Examples are the Liberal Democrats in Scotland (not in Wales), the SDLP, and Sinn Féin. The seesaw movements in Figs 15.1 to 15.3 arise from the switching fortunes of other parties, which are penalised under FPTP but do well under

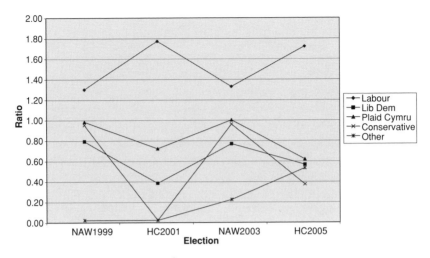

Figure 15.2. Seat/vote ratio in Wales

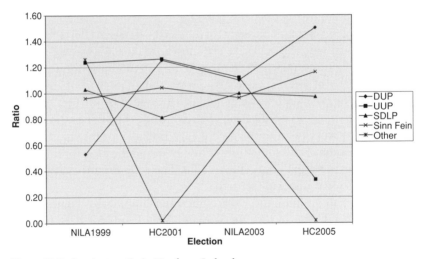

Figure 15.3. Seat/vote ratio in Northern Ireland

PR. This especially describes the Conservatives in Scotland and Wales, and 'Others' (which include the smaller unionist and cross-community parties) in Northern Ireland.

But Figures 15.1–15.3 show that no DA's electoral system is truly proportional. If they were, the ratio for all parties would converge towards 1.00 at both the 1998/9 and the 2003 time points. The DUP had a ratio of only 0.51 in 1998. This is probably an intended effect of STV, which is designed to favour centrists over extremists. If centrists exchanged second preferences for one another's parties, their seat share would be boosted, and that for extreme parties correspondingly depressed. The DUP was a victim of this in 1998, but has not been since then. The Northern Ireland electoral system failed to restrain the more extreme parties in 2003. Disillusionment with the Good Friday Agreement had gone too far by then. This is the biggest, though little remarked, failure of Tony Blair's devolution statecraft during his second term.

In both Scotland and Wales, the incompletely proportional AMS system retained some of the seat advantage that Labour would have had under FPTP. The Labour politicians who wrote the Scotland and Wales Acts 1998 intended this, and they have not yet been disappointed. But the seat advantage was too small to deliver Labour majority administrations. There has been a Labour–Liberal Democrat governing coalition for the whole lifetime of the Scottish Parliament so far. However, Figure 15.1 shows that all parties including 'Others' got a seat/vote ratio close to 1 in the 2003 Scottish Parliament. Two left-wing parties – the Greens and the Scottish Socialists – did well in the regional list vote, and some single-issue candidates did well in the constituency vote. The presence of seven Greens and six Scottish Socialists in particular shapes the policy choices of the governing coalition. In Wales, Labour has governed at times alone as a minority administration, and for a spell in coalition with the Liberal Democrats. In the second National Assembly, since 2003, it has reverted to single-party minority government. Its minority status means that it, too, has to care more about opposition party interests than does its counterpart at Westminster.

Scotland above and below the surface

If you read the papers reasonably attentively, you might think that Scottish politics in the second Blair term was about just one thing, namely the cost of the Scottish Parliament building at Holyrood, at the foot of the Royal Mile in Edinburgh (next to Adam Smith's town house, as it happens). From initial estimates of below £40 million, the cost progressed inexorably to a final bill in excess of £430 million.[8] This was very embarrassing for

---

[8] Lord Fraser of Carmyllie QC, *Holyrood Inquiry: Final Report* (Edinburgh: HMSO, 2004), para. 16.5. Cited from web version at http://www.holyroodinquiry.org/FINAL_report/report.htm.

all the politicians and bureaucrats involved in its construction. It throws an interesting sidelight on the private finance initiative, which has not caught on in Scotland despite its promotion by the deeply Smithian and Scottish chancellor of the exchequer, Gordon Brown.[9] The failures of cost control were many and various, damaging the reputations especially of two eminent deceased people – Donald Dewar, architect of devolution and first first minister of Scotland, and Enric Miralles, the Catalan architect of the building. The Fraser Report specifically exonerates Dewar (but not Miralles). It spreads its blame both before and after the date when the Parliament took responsibility for its own affairs in 1999. Two months after Fraser reported, the permanent secretary to the Scottish executive announced that no civil servants were to be disciplined for their role in the Parliament building fiasco.[10] The building is rather grand, and carries uplifting quotations from Robert Burns on the wall facing the Canongate. When I visited it in January 2005, there were long queues to look round.

The Parliament building fiasco certainly damaged the reputation of the Parliament and government of Scotland. But the damage came early. There is no time-series question specifically on the performance of Parliament or government, nor on the Parliament building. But data from the Scottish Political Attitudes time-series show that the proportion of Scots respondents saying that the devolved institutions have had a beneficial impact on 'giving ordinary people a say in how Scotland is governed' fell from 64% to 44% between the 1999 and 2000 surveys, and has since dropped to 39%. However, a similar 20-point drop occurred in Wales between the 1999 and 2001 surveys.[11] In Wales, there were some issues with the Assembly building, but they were much smaller than in Scotland. The slump in public confidence probably owes more to an onset of realistic expectations than to Holyrood.

Below the surface, devolution was bedding in. Optimists hoped that devolution would bring in a more open and more participatory style of government. To some extent it has – if only because Scotland is a much smaller country than the UK, and the Parliament has modernised some

---

[9] In magnificent mandarinese, Fraser writes, 'I am unable to conclude that the decision to adopt conventional funding, rather than resorting to PFI procurement, was wrong and was the cause of the delay and cost which has plagued this Project' (*Holyrood Inquiry*, p. 241). Never was a double negative more potent.

[10] Scottish Executive news release, 'No disciplinary action after Holyrood Inquiry', 25 November 2004, at http://www.scotland.gov.uk/News/Releases/2004/11/25133828.

[11] John Curtice, 'Restoring confidence and legitimacy? Devolution and public opinion', in A. Trench (ed.), *Has Devolution Made a Difference? The state of the nations 2004* (Exeter: Imprint Academic, 2004), pp. 217–36, Figure 9.3.

Westminster traditions and revived others, such as the acceptance of petitions. Pessimists feared that devolution would not live up to its billing. They are also right, because much of the mass support for devolution probably rested on two things: the correct belief that it would prevent unpopular domestic policies being imposed from London, and the incorrect belief that Scotland used to subsidise England. The consequences of the correct belief have emerged in education and health policy; the consequence of exposing the incorrect belief can only be disillusionment. Even the SNP has ceased making the claim that Scotland subsidises England.

James Mitchell has usefully distinguished between 'redistributive', 'distributive', and 'regulatory' policies in Scotland since devolution.[12] Redistributive politics, which would be core politics in a normal Parliament, are not in Scotland, because the Scottish Parliament spends money that the UK government raises. The SNP flirted briefly with the idea of using the Parliament's tax-raising power but was bitterly attacked, and backed down. This has frozen serious discussion of redistribution and public finance. Distributive politics marked the beginning of differences with the UK government – more by *not* doing things that the Blair New Labour administration was doing in England than by doing things that it was not. However, on free personal care for the elderly – recommended by a UK-wide royal commission but rejected in England on grounds of expense – Scotland acted where Westminster refused to. On student fees, reform of the NHS and use of the private finance initiative to fund public infrastructure, Scotland refused to act when Westminster (or Whitehall) acted. This flows from the history of devolution: from Scottish resentment at being used as an experiment for unpopular policies of a Conservative government, under Margaret Thatcher, that held very few seats in Scotland. That resentment could stick to a New Labour government that, in a sense, held no seats in Scotland. And the Labour–Liberal Democrat governing coalition had to look over its shoulder at the Greens and the Scottish Socialists. The divergence opens up a policy gap among the four nations of the UK, and makes some comparative public policy possible. On education, the comparison mostly shows confusion; on health, it shows interesting contrasts. These are discussed below.

The Scottish Parliament's regulatory politics have been the most distinctive both in what it has done and in what it has failed to do. Mitchell reports that 'most MSPs burst into spontaneous applause when

---

[12] J. Mitchell, 'Scotland: expectations, policy types and devolution', in Trench, *Has Devolution Made a Difference?*, pp. 11–41.

final approval was given to reform of Scotland's antiquated land laws'.[13]
Appropriately: reform of land law is just the sort of thing the Scottish Parliament should be doing. At Westminster, it might have been blocked in
the House of Lords; even if not, it would never have found legislative time.
As it involves reforming Scots law, it is right that Scots law should now
come under the Scottish Parliament, restoring a link that was broken in
1707. Less brave was the Parliament's 2003 ducking of a Green MSP's civil
partnerships bill, which would have extended some of the rights of married people to same-sex couples. This was a matter within the devolved
powers of the Parliament to determine. But in 2000 the Parliament had
been savagely attacked by a cardinal and a busman over its (ultimately
successful) repeal of the misnamed 'Section 28' clause banning the public
endorsement of homosexual lifestyles.[14] This time round, the Parliament
avoided a fight (even though the cardinal had by then died) by passing a
so-called 'Sewel motion'. Sewel motions remit a devolved matter back to
Westminster for legislation. They are a voluntary surrender of devolution.
They have been used much more than commentators expected in 1999.
Sometimes there are good technical reasons why it suits both sides to let
Westminster legislate on a devolved matter. But over civil partnerships, it
was sheer funk.

Wales above and below the surface

The National Assembly's finest moment came in Tony Blair's first term. In
February 2000 its vote of no confidence in Alun Michael, Blair's nominee
as first minister, forced him out in favour of Rhodri Morgan, whom Blair
had been trying to block since devolution in Wales began.[15] The object
of controversy had been additional Whitehall match funding for West
Wales and the Valleys, an artificial confection that was granted 'Objective
One' status by the European Union for the period 2001–6. Objective One
areas are the poorest areas in the Union, with less than 75% of average
EU GDP per head. The actual politics of Objective One are less noble
than the principled defenestration of Alun Michael: namely the distinctly
Old Labour policy of rewarding an area for its poverty and throwing
museums and steam railways at it to get it out of poverty. It will come to

[13] Ibid., p. 30.
[14] Cardinal Thomas Winning, then head of the Catholic Church in Scotland, and Brian
Souter, founder of Stagecoach plc. McLean, 'National question', p. 430. The campaign was
misnamed because it was Section 2A, not 28, of the relevant Scottish Act.
[15] McLean, 'National question', pp. 442–3.

a grinding halt at the next renewal of EU regional programmes, because the accession of ten poor new member states means that nowhere in the UK will qualify for Objective One. It may well have distracted the Labour administration in the National Assembly from growth-promoting economic policy. In December 2002, First Minister Morgan announced that he would put 'clear red water' between Welsh Labour and the Labour government in London. As in Scotland, this would take the form of *not* doing things that the UK government was doing. Morgan singled out foundation hospitals for attack.[16] The Assembly government has also refused to introduce comprehensive performance assessment for local authorities, or league tables of school performance.

Much of the energy of the National Assembly was directed inwards. The Government of Wales Act 1998 gave it the powers and structure of a local authority, and therefore no separate legal recognition of the Assembly government as an entity distinct from the National Assembly. Also, the National Assembly has no primary legislative powers. It has the power to enact secondary legislation (statutory instruments), but these powers are ill-matched to the policy areas that are devolved to it. The constitutional framework therefore rapidly proved unworkable. The Assembly appointed a commission under the Labour politician Lord Richard to review the case for giving the Assembly primary legislative powers. The commission reported in March 2004 (in English, Welsh, Chinese and Urdu). With one dissenting member it called for the National Assembly to be given primary legislative powers on the same lines as Scotland. A tax-varying power, as in Scotland, would be 'desirable but not essential'. The Assembly should be replaced by a legally distinct parliament and executive, as in Scotland. The 60-member Assembly elected by AMS should be replaced by an 80-member Assembly elected by STV.[17]

The mood music at Westminster was discouraging. Secretary of State for Wales Peter Hain said that the criterion of constitutional change should be whether it made the lives of people in Wales better, dropping heavy hints that in his view the Richard proposals would not do so. The commission's

---

[16] Rh. Morgan, 'Clear red water', speech at University of Wales, Swansea, 11 December 2002, quoted by John Osmond, 'Nation building and the Assembly: the emergence of a Welsh civil consciousness', in Trench (ed.), *Has Devolution Made a Difference?*, pp. 43–77, at p. 52.

[17] Lord Richard of Ammanford (chairman), *Commission on the Powers and Electoral Arrangements of the National Assembly for Wales* (Cardiff: National Assembly, 2004), chapter 14. 'Desirable, but not essential' at 14.35. Cited from web version at http://www.richardcommission.gov.uk/content/finalreport/report-e.pdf.

proposal for an 80-member STV National Assembly angered those whose seats it imperilled; its recommendation of greater powers for the Assembly (and hence fewer powers for MPs for Wales) angered 40 MPs, most of them from the governing party. Nevertheless, the May 2005 Queen's Speech announced a Government of Wales Bill, which might (or might not) contain primary legislative powers. A White Paper and possibly a referendum on primary powers are promised.

Northern Ireland: domestic politics under the radar

The Northern Ireland Assembly was suspended in October 2002. The 2003 election was delayed in the hope that the parties could agree on conditions for the lifting of the suspension. No conditions were agreed; the Assembly remained suspended; a delayed election (whose results have already been analysed) was held in November 2003 to an Assembly that has never met and on current conditions is never likely to. The root cause of failure has been the failure of the IRA to prove that it has decommissioned its weapons. This has led Protestant and unionist voters to lose faith in the Good Friday Agreement. A deal on decommissioning seemed tantalisingly close as recently as December 2004, when DUP leader Ian Paisley and Sinn Féin leader Gerry Adams seemed, however improbably, poised to agree terms for resumption of the Assembly. However the talks failed over whether the IRA would be forced to produce photographs of the process of destroying its weapons. Soon afterwards, agreement disappeared over the horizon as IRA members were implicated in rapid succession in a huge bank robbery in Belfast; a money-laundering operation in the Irish Republic; and, most damagingly, in the cover-up after a local Catholic, Robert McCartney, was murdered outside a bar in a republican area of Belfast.

Northern Ireland is therefore governed by direct rule ministers and the Northern Ireland civil service. The most encouraging fact is that life goes on: the incidence of sectarian murders and violence has sharply declined; there have been no terrorist bombs or attacks since the appalling Omagh bomb of 1998, which killed 29 people. Direct rule ministers could do things that elected ministers find difficult, such as close down public services in areas of declining population, or widen the tax base. Northern Ireland escaped the poll tax and still levies domestic rates. The Treasury thinks that Northern Irish householders pay too little towards the cost of local services. In the biennial Spending Review for 2004, they state: 'A major programme of reform to modernise water, rating and public administration will be introduced in Northern Ireland'.[18] For 'modernise', read 'raise more revenue from'. Otherwise, the politics of devolution in Northern Ireland is largely the politics of not changing things that have been changing in England, leading to a natural experiment where education and health have started to diverge.

Divergence in education and health

Since 1918, there have been five distinct school systems in the UK. They did not map exactly on to the four territories. One covered England and Wales. Scotland and Northern Ireland each had two systems. One was non-denominational (which meant 'Protestant'); the other Roman Catholic. The cause of integrated schooling is raised from time to time in Northern Ireland (perhaps curiously, less so in Scotland, although there was a flurry of concern there too about sectarianism in 2003). But the firm opposition of the Roman Catholic hierarchy means that integration is not practical politics. The new responsibility of the National Assembly for school education in Wales has not led to any radical change in the second Blair term. In due course it may become possible to compare the UK's four, or six, school systems using international comparisons of achievement, or on cost per pupil. But the most relevant international comparison has missing data – embarrassingly, too few schools in England supplied data for the latest OECD international comparison of school standards for valid inferences to be made. So the fact that considerably more is spent per pupil in the devolved administrations – especially in Scotland and Northern Ireland – than in England has consequences which are not adequately measured.

It is in higher education that policy has diverged the most. Here policy in the second Blair term has been a mess. Higher education is a devolved function, but scientific research is a 'reserved' function. This cuts across the way that universities are funded. So does that fact that a student whose domicile is in any part of the UK may go to university in any other part of the UK. As indeed may a student from anywhere in the EU (where by EU rules she must pay the same fees as UK students attending the same university). In 2003–4 the UK government decided to enact a Higher Education Bill that made profound changes to university funding

---

[18] HM Treasury, *Spending Review 2004: Stability, Security and Opportunity for All: Investing for Britain's Long-term Future: New Public Spending Plans 2005–2008* (London: HM Treasury, Cm 6237), para. 23.18.

in England. The bill was controversial among Labour MPs. Both main opposition parties saw a handy bandwagon and jumped on to it, opposing the bill's provision for graduates to be liable for a fee of up to £3,000 per annum, reclaimable through their tax bill after graduation and only once their income had crossed a certain threshold. The bill finally scraped through the Commons with a majority of five on Second Reading. If only English MPs had voted on it and MPs from the three territories had refrained from voting, it would have been defeated by six votes.[19]

Ministers and their advisers in the UK government did not stop to consider the knock-on consequences of their bill for Scotland, Wales, and Northern Ireland. Some of these were obvious. There would be a predictable surge of English students to Celtic universities as they sought to avoid the new fees. But the funding for these students would mostly fall on the devolved administrations' budgets. More subtly, the Act and associated spending reviews sharply increase the universities' budget for research. Some of this flows, in England, through the Department for Education and Skills. This money carries a 'Barnett consequential' for the three devolved administrations, so that they get their population share of this flow. But the rest flows through the Department of Trade and Industry, which is the sponsoring ministry for scientific research. The DTI is an all-UK ministry; therefore its own allocation mechanisms (delegated to the research councils) are also UK-wide. The devolved administrations would get their population share of this flow only if their university scientists had exactly the same rate per head of successful grants from the research councils as those in England.

As far as I have been able to find out, a policy with profound implications for the devolved administrations was never discussed before enactment in any of the joint forums set up in 1999 to resolve devolution disputes. This is quite a failure of government – of all four governments involved.

On health policy, an excellent monograph by Scott Greer has tracked the divergence between the four territories of the UK.[20] He characterises the medical politics of the four countries as *professionalism* in Scotland; *markets* in England; *localism* in Wales and *permissive managerialism* in Northern Ireland:

---

[19] Guy Lodge, 'Devolution and the centre: quarterly report', February 2004 (London: Constitution Unit), Fig. 5. Cited from web version at http://www.ucl.ac.uk/constitution-unit/monrep/centre/centre_february_2004.pdf.

[20] Scott L. Greer, *Territorial Politics and Health Policy: UK Health Policy in Comparative Perspective* (Manchester: Manchester University Press, 2004).

The Scottish health policy landscape is . . . densely populated with groups based on very high-status, important medical institutions who are willing and able to participate in policy . . . the channels between officials and professionals that the old Scottish Office opened up in its efforts to govern Scotland remain intact . . . Welsh health policy's guiding themes – new public health, localism, and trust in the public service – stem from a policy community dominated by believers in, and workers in, local public services . . . being an insider with advice and acquiescence still matters in Northern Ireland, while the outlines of policy changes still travel from Britain to Belfast via the civil service.[21]

All three DAs have therefore reverted to a style of NHS politics that antedates the partial marketisation introduced by the Thatcher administration in the late 1980s. England, by contrast, has pressed on. After pulling back in the first years of New Labour, the Blair administration has now taken market concepts such as the purchaser–provider split and contestability among providers further than in the Thatcher era (Glennerster, this volume).

The obvious policy outcome is that the performance of the NHS has visibly improved in England according to tangible measures, whereas in all three other territories it has stagnated or got worse. The latest available news from the Constitution Unit's quarterly 'Monitoring Reports' is:

- *Northern Ireland:* 'an outpatient queue lengthening by more than 17,000 over the calendar year' (April 2005 report, p. 47).
- *Wales:* Assembly Minister for Health removed in January 2005 after criticism of poor NHS performance; highly critical audit report on NHS waiting times in Wales; Secretary of State for Wales Peter Hain interferes in a devolved matter by urging the Assembly government to adopt English methods of cutting waiting times (April 2005 report pp. 6, 23–4).
- *Scotland:* 'Health policy is clearly the area where the Executive is having the greatest difficulty in "delivering". Whichever targets Ministers choose, they not only seem to be missed, but things appear to be getter worse rather than better' (April 2005 report, p. 42).[22]

---

[21] Greer, *Territorial Politics*, pp. 78 (Scotland), 156 (Wales), 193 (NI).

[22] All of these quotations and précis are from the latest available Quarterly Monitoring Reports from the Nations and Regions Programme, Constitution Unit, University College, London. Cited from web versions available from the index page at http://www.ucl.ac.uk/constitution-unit/nations/monitoring.php.

Tony Blair and his advisers may be permitting themselves a sly smile or three.

The Barnett Formula limps on

Devolution in the UK has matured but it is not mature. As I and others have argued for several years, the Barnett Formula, which governs the block grant that finances devolved services in the three DAs, is unsustainable in the long run. It is neither efficient nor equitable; it gives perverse incentives to the DAs; their block grant is a function of a number they cannot control; in turn, their decisions have consequences for UK macroeconomic management which the UK government cannot fully control. For an extensive demonstration of these points readers must look elsewhere.[23] Here are the bare-bones claims which I think are fully justified.

- *The Barnett Formula is neither efficient . . .* because it gives no incentives to the DAs to seek economic (or more narrowly tax) efficiency. All three DAs manage public expenditure. None of them manages public revenue except in a small way (council tax; business rates; domestic rates in Northern Ireland). Any party which suggests using the Scottish Variable Rate of Income Tax is denounced by all the others in Scotland. The National Assembly has asked for a tax-varying power but is unlikely to be given it. Political devolution in Northern Ireland is in cold storage. So in none of the DAs do the decision-makers face a budget constraint. A rational politician would rather spend more than less (because a marginal pound of public spending, financed out of non-local taxation, should always improve her chances of re-election) up to the point where Barnett sets a hard constraint or where the marginal effect of extra taxation *in that territory* outweighs the marginal benefit from the spending. The largest DA (Scotland) contains fewer than 10% of the UK's population. Therefore, extra public expenditure in Scotland would have to cost around ten times the benefit it brings before the Scottish people would rationally rebel against it.
- *. . . nor equitable.* Public spending per head, across the 12 standard regions of the UK, ought to be inversely related to GDP per head. Instead,

---

[23] Especially McLean, *Fiscal Crisis*; I. McLean and A. McMillan, 'The distribution of public expenditure across the UK regions', *Fiscal Studies* 24 (2003), pp. 45–71; D. Bell and A. Christie, 'Finance – The Barnett Formula: nobody's child?' in A. Trench (ed.), *The State of the Nations 2001: The second year of devolution in the United Kingdom* (Exeter: Imprint Academic, 2001), pp. 135–51.

there is no statistical relationship at all between the two. There are three upward outliers from the general trend. They are Scotland, Northern Ireland and London. We have argued elsewhere[24] that their higher relative expenditure per head derives not from greater need but from the more credible threat to the Union of the United Kingdom that they pose, compared with the other nine standard regions.

- *It gives perverse incentives to the DAs.* The incentive to spend what Australians call a '10-cent dollar' (5-cent dollars in Wales; 3-cent dollars in Northern Ireland) has already been mentioned. The DAs have no incentive to broaden their tax bases because they do not see the proceeds; and they have an incentive to switch their block grants from capital spending (which brings benefits after the next election) to current spending (which brings benefits before the next election).
- *Their block grant is a function of a number they cannot control...* because it depends on spending in England on each devolved service. Spending in England is tightly controlled by the Treasury's biennial Spending Reviews, to which the DAs have no input.
- *... But their decisions have consequences for UK macroeconomic management,* notably because of the temptation just mentioned for the DAs to switch money from capital programmes to current spending. This could interfere with the UK government's fiscal rules (currently labelled the Golden Rule and the Sustainable Investment Rule, which are likely to be followed by a UK government of any political complexion).

On the surface, there was little movement over the Barnett Formula in the second Blair term, and the one movement that occurred tended to preserve it, as explained in the next section. But the academic consensus that it was unsustainable was shared, publicly or privately, by civil servants in all three DAs and at the centre. The first green shoots of post-Barnett thought started to appear. Notably, the Fraser of Allander Institute, the leading public policy research institute in Scotland, commissioned a paper on fiscal federalism which turned that from a fine phrase into a careful proposal for the first time. In other work, I have proposed that the Barnett mechanism should be scrapped and replaced by a non-partisan Grants Commission modelled on the Australian system, which would allocate block grant either to the four nations of the UK or to its 12 standard regions.[25]

---

[24] McLean, *Fiscal Crisis*; McLean and McMillan, *State of the Union.*
[25] R. MacDonald and P. Hallwood, 'The economic case for fiscal federalism in Scotland' (Glasgow: Fraser of Allander Institute, 2004); McLean, *Fiscal Crisis*, chs. 8, 9, 11.

The Prescott and Brown agendas in the 2001 Parliament

There was no obvious 'Blair effect' on devolution to Scotland and Wales in the Parliament of 2001–5 because Tony Blair had no interest in reopening in the done deal of 1997–8. However, Deputy Prime Minister John Prescott (representing Hull) and Chancellor Gordon Brown (representing Fife) took a close interest. Their agendas overlapped but were not identical. In the 2001 election campaign, Prescott threatened that there would be 'blood on the carpet' over the apparently unfair distribution of public expenditure around the UK, with the northern English regions getting suspiciously little. He was immediately slapped down by the Prime Minister's press secretary, Alastair Campbell, who denied that Prescott had said the words captured on the journalist's tape-recorder. Nevertheless, Prescott returned to the fray, his then deputy Nick Raynsford telling the bitterly anti-Barnett Newcastle *Journal* in 2004 that the time had come to review the Barnett formula.[26]

The Prescott agenda was zero-sum. Scotland was getting too much; northern England was getting too little; something must be done. The solution might be elected assemblies in each English region, or at least the northern ones. A plan was developed for assemblies with quite limited powers, in those regions that wanted them. If they voted for an elected assembly, the people of any region must simultaneously agree that local authorities in the region would all become single-tier. This provision was said to have been inserted by Tony Blair, anxious that the scheme would not be condemned as 'too many politicians'. But that is exactly what happened in the only region that finally went to a referendum. This was the North East, thought to be the standard-bearer for regionalism, because complaints against Barnett are loudest there. However, the 'No' campaign fought feistily. Its mascot was an inflatable white elephant. The result, on 4 November 2004, crushed the Prescott agenda. In an all-postal ballot with a turnout of 47.7%, the vote against an elected regional assembly was 696,519 (77.9%); the vote in favour was 197,310 (22.1%).[27]

---

[26] Peter Hetherington, 'Scots and Welsh face subsidy axe', *Guardian* 24 April 2001; James Mitchell and Fraser Nelson, 'The Barnett Formula and the 2001 general election', *British Elections and Parties Review* 12 (2002): 171–89; P. Linford, 'It's all to play for', *Journal*, Newcastle upon Tyne, 3 March 2004, p. 1; I. McLean, 'Scotland after Barnett', in G. Hassan, E. Gibb and L. Howland (eds.), *Scotland 2020: Hopeful Stories for a Northern Nation* (London: Demos, 2005), pp. 134–48.

[27] Data from Electoral Commission, at http://www.electoralcommission.org.uk/election-data/index.cfm?epage = q&frmElectionID = 4.

This left only the Brown, non-zero-sum, agenda in play. It owed a lot to Brown's long-standing adviser Ed Balls, chief economic adviser to the Treasury from 1997 to 2004 and Labour MP for Normanton (West Yorkshire) since 2005. Multiple Treasury documents since 2000 – budget books, pre-budget reports, and spending reviews – have drawn attention to unequal economic growth in the regions of England, with London and the South East leading and the rest lagging. The latest Spending Review commits the Treasury and Prescott's department the ODPM to 'make sustainable improvements in the economic performance of all English regions by 2008, and over the long term reduce the persistent gap in growth rates between the regions, demonstrating progress by 2006'. That is a large and tough agenda. To measure improvements in the economic performance of the English regions, governments first need to know what it is. Two reports during the 2001–5 Parliament (the Allsopp and McLean reports) led to improvements in regional statistics being introduced or promised.[28]

Conclusion

Perhaps a chapter on the 'national question' in a book called *The Blair Effect 2* should have been very short: *There was no Blair effect on the national question between 2001 and 2005 because Tony Blair did not intervene on devolution policy except to insist on single-tier local government in the North East were it to vote for an elected assembly, which it did not.* However, I have tried to show that there were longer-term effects, which will continue beyond the 2005 election because the devolution settlement is not yet stable. In Scotland and Wales, neither finance nor representation is stable; in Northern Ireland, nothing is stable.

Finance is unstable because the Barnett Formula is unsustainable. Serious thought as to what might replace it is just beginning. The answer may well not come in the Parliament of 2005–9, but it will have to come soon. In representation, the ancient 'West Lothian question' again reared its head because both university student fees and foundation hospitals were

---

[28] HM Treasury, *2004 Spending Review: Public Service Agreements 2005–2008* Cm 6238 (London: HM Treasury 2004), p. 17; I. McLean et al., *Identifying the Flow of Domestic and European Expenditure into the English Regions* (Oxford: Nuffield College and London: ODPM, 2003), accessible at http://www.local.odpm.gov.uk/research/regeco.htm; C. Allsopp, *Review of Statistics for Economic Policymaking: Final Report* (London: HM Treasury 2004), accessible at http://www.hm-treasury.gov.uk/media/437/68/allsopp_final_ch1to3_384.pdf.

enacted in England only through the votes of MPs from the other territories, where these polices were not to apply. With the reduced Labour majority in the 2005 Parliament, this is likely to recur. The stable solutions are either:

- a more symmetrical federalism, with assemblies for England or the regions of England (unlikely in the near future after the North East referendum), or
- further reduction in Scottish and Welsh seats in the House of Commons. Scotland is represented in proportion to population; Wales is over-represented.

Perhaps the least unfair solution to the West Lothian question is to reduce their representation to about two-thirds of their population share, in line with the arrangements for Northern Ireland when domestic politics was securely devolved, between 1920 and 1972.

Policy divergence is just beginning. In higher education it reveals only confusion all round, while in health real consequences from real decisions are beginning to emerge. A more mature system requires that those who spend are also those who tax, at least at the margin. Then (but probably only then) it will be possible to see whether the coalitional governments likely to be thrown up by PR in Scotland and Wales (and Northern Ireland if and when it returns) truly involve a different style to the majoritarian government of the UK.

Why was there so little Blair effect on devolution? In part, the obvious explanation suffices. Tony Blair is not personally interested in Scotland (although he was educated there), or in regional politics in north-east England (though his constituency is there) or in Wales (although the National Assembly enthroned his *bête noire* Rhodri Morgan there). In Northern Ireland, neither he nor Taoiseach Bertie Ahern of the Republic has been able to stop the collapse of the political centre. But then, neither could Gladstone from 1880 to 1885, nor Lloyd George from 1918 to 1921. It is a failure that Blair shares with eminent predecessors.

Beyond the obvious, this chapter has shown that the dilemmas of devolution are slow-maturing. Everybody in the know realises that the Barnett Formula is unsustainable: but there has been no Barnett Crisis. It is a chronic, not an acute, complaint. There could have been an acute representation crisis over the carrying of English foundation hospitals or university fees on Celtic votes alone. The last time such a crisis occurred was in 1928, when the Celts voted down the Church of England Prayer Book. But none of these three issues sparked the English outrage that would turn the chronic problem of representation in an asymmetric Union into an acute crisis of legitimacy in England. The acute phase may come in the Parliament of 2005. It will surely come, at latest, under the next non-Labour government at Westminster. We live in interesting times but can't quite see what they will be.

16

Europe

PETER RIDDELL

Tony Blair arrived in office in May 1997 on the back of a Labour manifesto pledge to 'give Britain leadership in Europe'. Later, he talked about Europe being 'our destiny'. This commitment always had a double meaning: first, to give Britain more influence over developments in the European Union; and, second, to end the ambivalence in Britain's relationship by persuading the public to embrace a closer involvement with the EU. The Blair government achieved some significant, though partial, successes in the former aim, but failed in the latter. As this chapter will show, the chances of Blair ever achieving his lofty goals were always uncertain and, at key points, would have required him to go against his instincts and to confront the Euro-scepticism of much of the British media and public. The main influences have not just been the policies of Blair and his ministers, or the state of British public opinion, but also changes, and more often the lack of them, within the EU, and elsewhere.

During the course of his premiership, Blair made speeches every six to 12 months about Britain's role in Europe. Carefully drafted by his more pro-European advisers, with help from academics and think tanks, the speeches were presented as evidence that Blair's heart was really in putting Britain in a leading position. But virtually nothing changed as a result of the speeches. There was usually little follow-up, as caution created by electoral worries and the more sceptical rhetoric of the Treasury predominated on a day-to-day basis. Blair posed the dilemma in one of these speeches in Cardiff in November 2002: 'For Britain, there is a simple choice to be made. Are we fully partners in Europe, at the centre of its decision-making, influencing and shaping its direction; or are we at the back of the file, following warily a path beaten by others? For 50 years, that has been our choice. For 50 years we have chosen to follow, first in joining; then in each new departure Europe has made.'[1] His analysis of Britain's

---

[1] Tony Blair, 'The future of Europe: strong, effective, democratic', speech in Cardiff, 29 November 2002.

tendency to catch up on others' terms led inexorably to the conclusion: 'Now we have an historic opportunity to put our relations with the rest of Europe on a more serious footing and choose not to hang back but to participate fully and wholeheartedly.' Yet, despite good intentions, his performance has been nearer his diagnosis than his prognosis.

Early ambiguities

By the time of the June 2001 general election, the ambiguities in the Blair position had already become apparent. When Labour came to power in 1997, there had been a near universal welcome for Blair throughout the EU. He was widely seen as offering a fresh start after the Major years when bitter divisions within the Conservative Party over Europe had resulted in a negative and minimalist approach by Britain. Blair quickly created close links with several of Europe's leaders. Over time, his closest relationships were more with centre-right leaders like Jose Maria Aznar of Spain, Silvio Berlusconi of Italy and, in the early years, with President Jacques Chirac of France, rather than with centre-left leaders like Lionel Jospin of France. Blair's most longstanding ally on the centre left was Goran Persson of Sweden, after the departure of sympathetic, early centre-left leaders like Wim Kok of the Netherlands and Massimo D'Alema of Italy. Although his relations with Gerhard Schroeder of Germany were always cordial, Blair became disillusioned with the Chancellor's inconsistency well before the Iraq war.

During the 1997–2001 Parliament, there were several positive developments. Within a few weeks, Britain had ended its opt-out from the social chapter of the Maastricht treaty and had signed up to what became the Amsterdam treaty. During the British presidency of the EU in the first half of 1998, Blair and particularly Robin Cook, foreign secretary for the whole of the first term, actively pushed enlargement of the EU. Blair played a major role in spring 2000 in sponsoring what became the Lisbon agenda of economic reform to make EU economies more flexible and innovative. Blair followed this up with a series of bilateral initiatives with various countries to push forward reform.

Blair also took the lead in December 1998 at a summit at St-Malo with President Jacques Chirac in launching a joint Anglo-French initiative on European defence. The declaration said: 'The European Union needs to be in a position to play its full role on the international stage. To this end, the Union must have the capacity for autonomous action, backed by credible, military forces, the means to decide to use them, and a readiness to do so, in order to respond to international crises . . . acting in conformity with our respective obligations to Nato.'[2] The reaction in the United States from the then Clinton administration was a mixture of anger at a lack of adequate prior consultation by the British government and suspicion that the primacy of Nato might be undermined by the French suborning the British. The British sought to reassure the Americans that Nato came first: that Europe would only want to run its own operations when the United States did not want to be involved. Meanwhile, the French questioned the sincerity of the British commitment to European defence, especially after the UK participated in US-led raids on Iraq in December 1998, only a few days after the St-Malo agreement.

By the time of the 2001 general election, few of the grand early hopes had been fulfilled. New Labour's vision of Euro-Blairism – the march of the Third Way across the EU – was not shared by all European socialist or social democratic parties. The French socialists, under Lionel Jospin, who took office only a few weeks after Blair, rejected what they saw as 'Anglo-American' talk of flexibility and liberalising markets. Moreover, Blair's attempt to form a common ideological bond with Gerhard Schroeder after the German SPD's victory in September 1998 proved to be short-lived. Their joint paper, 'Europe: The Third Way/Die Neue Mitte',[3] sought to set out a new way forward for social democrats, based on economic reform, a competitive market framework, sound public finance and an active labour market policy to get people back into work via changes to the tax and benefits system. This approach was attacked by the French socialists, as well as by the left of the SPD. Schroeder quickly distanced himself from the paper.

Moreover, the British attempt to break into the core Franco-German alliance by building stronger bilateral relationships, by joint initiatives on defence with Paris and welfare reform with Berlin, did not change the underlying power balance within Europe. Blair talked in a more European, if not always *communautaire* way. But he has always been a committed Atlanticist, and has repeatedly said that he does not see a contradiction between the two roles. So despite the significant advances noted above, Anne Deighton was correct in her view of the first Blair term: 'Despite his personal popularity, Blair has failed to turn public opinion substantially

---

[2] Joint Declaration on European Defence: British–French summit, St-Malo, 3–4 December 1998, www.fco.gov.uk.

[3] Tony Blair and Gerhard Schroeder, 'Europe: The Third Way/Die Neue Mitte', in Andrew Chadwick and Richard Heffernan (eds.), *The New Labour Reader* (Oxford: Polity Press/Blackwell Publishing, 2003), pp. 100–15.

over EMU (economic and monetary union) or enlargement, or to shift the general indifference to the EU that still dominates polling figures.'[4]

Treasury scepticism

Above all, Britain seemed further from, rather than closer to, fulfilling Labour's 1997 election pledge to hold a referendum on taking sterling into the euro. Within only five months of his triumphant entry into Number 10, Blair had surrendered control over the decision to Gordon Brown and the Treasury. Brown, initially the more enthusiastic of the two about euro entry, became more cautious. This was partly because of the influence of the sceptic Ed Balls, his closest political and economic adviser, and partly because of the favourable reception to his decision to make the Bank of England responsible for setting interest rates and controlling inflation. This was seen in the Treasury as a viable monetary alternative to euro entry. So after a period of confusion in October 1997, Brown announced five tests which must be met before the government would recommend entry in a referendum. These five economic tests were and are:

1. Are business cycles and economic structures compatible so that we and others could live comfortably with euro interest rates on a permanent basis?
2. If problems emerged, is there sufficient flexibility to deal with them?
3. Would joining EMU create better conditions for firms making long-term decisions to invest in Britain?
4. What impact would entry into EMU have on the competitive position of the UK's financial services industry, particularly the City's wholesale markets?
5. In summary, will joining EMU promote higher growth, stability and a lasting increase in jobs?[5]

Whatever their meaning for economists, the tests have been a shield for the government to hide behind. At the insistence of Blair, Brown did not rule out the possibility of entry in that Parliament, but that was how the announcement was widely seen. Moreover, Brown made it clear in his statement announcing the five tests that the Blair government did not

---

[4] Anne Deighton, 'European Union Policy', in Anthony Seldon (ed.), *The Blair Effect: The Blair Government 1997–2001* (London: Little, Brown, 2001) p. 325.
[5] *UK Membership of the Single Currency, An assessment of the five economic tests*, HM Treasury, June 2003, Command 5776, p. 1.

see any constitutional objections to entry, as the sceptics did. For New Labour, it was a matter of economics. But by announcing the five tests, Blair had given Brown a permanent veto over British policy on the euro.

The Treasury was generally a sceptic voice in any European discussions, partly reflecting long-established institutional suspicion of Brussels (and, indeed, of all potential rivals) and partly because of a desire to preserve Britain's competitive position against new regulations. There was a long and bruising battle in the early years of the Blair government over plans to harmonise EU taxes on savings. The British fear was that harmonisation would both push up tax rates and threaten financial markets in London. So, using his threat of a veto, Brown forced changes in the proposals away from harmonisation to exchanges of information to prevent tax avoidance. But this was a formative experience for him and the Treasury in taking a critical attitude towards new EU initiatives of all kinds, from new regulations to the draft constitutional treaty. Brown was widely regarded as distant by many of his fellow European finance ministers and by members of the Commission.

After the euro was successfully launched in January 1999, Britain was outside the most important EU development. Brown was excluded from the increasingly important meetings of eurozone finance ministers, which were held before the full meetings of Ecofin, the economic ministers' council. As the 1997–2001 Parliament continued, with no sign of an entry decision, other European governments became more sceptical about Blair's pro-European and pro-euro statements. During the 2001 election, the Labour leadership tried to avoid making Europe an issue in the face of warnings by William Hague, the Conservative leader, that the country only had ten, night, eight etc. days left to save the pound. Europe and international affairs were not decisive issues during the campaign.

Whitehall reshuffle

After the election, Blair unexpectedly removed the born-again pro-European Robin Cook from the Foreign Office and replaced him with the more sceptical Jack Straw. This was partly to reduce conflict with Gordon Brown at the Treasury. However, Blair's main foreign advisers in Number 10 were strongly pro-European, notably Sir Stephen Wall, who combined the roles of head of the European Secretariat of the Cabinet Office and being Blair's personal adviser on Europe, and had an office in Number 10. Roger Liddle, Blair's political adviser on Europe, and a strong pro-European, worked closely with Wall. The only counter-voice was Derek

Scott, Blair's economic adviser, and like Liddle a former member of the SDP, but who became increasingly Euro-sceptic. The promotion of Wall and the creation of a separate, senior European post inside Number 10 have had ambiguous results. European policy has been run by a senior official with direct access to the Prime Minister. This has enabled the Prime Minister's office to take a leading role on European policy, not just in the various joint statements with other EU leaders but also, for instance, in pressing in autumn 2003, after the Iraq war, for a new initiative on European defence planning, despite the doubts of the Atlanticist Ministry of Defence and even parts of the Foreign Office. So Blair has had an ability directly to influence European developments separately from other departments in Whitehall. This has reduced the Foreign Office's influence, though the Treasury has been closely involved over a wide range of European issues.

But splitting the work of the European from the main foreign affairs private secretary also had a downside. The latter has become in effect a national security adviser on the US model, dealing primarily with Washington but also Russia and the Middle East. The foreign affairs private secretaries – initially John Sawers, then Sir David Manning from September 2001 until summer 2003 and then Sir Nigel Sheinwald – and the European advisers – Wall until summer 2004, then Kim Darroch – got on well. But the division of responsibilities meant that European concerns were not always taken into account as much as they previously had been when international crises arose, particularly during the months leading up to the Iraq war. The European viewpoint was neglected in discussions with Washington.

Transatlantic strains

The biggest influence on Britain's relations with Europe in the second term came, however, from across the Atlantic. The arrival in January 2001 of the new Republican administration under President George W. Bush had already created transatlantic tensions over missile defence, over the US intention to withdraw from the 1972 Anti-Ballistic Missile Treaty, over its denunciation of the Kyoto agreement on climate change and over its opposition to the proposed International Criminal Court. The dismissive manner in which these decisions were announced without consultation fed European suspicions. Blair sought to minimise differences and act as the bridge between the United States and Europe, in the manner of most of his predecessors in Number 10. France and Germany disliked talk of a 'bridge', and Chancellor Schroeder was reported as saying that the traffic across Blair's bridge always seemed to be in one direction.

The 9/11 attacks on New York and Washington instantly, temporarily and misleadingly produced transatlantic unity. European leaders rushed to offer both their sympathy and practical support. In France, *Le Monde* proclaimed with a Gallic flourish 'nous sommes tous Americains', while Schroeder expressed 'unlimited solidarity'. But it was Blair who instinctively understood the significance of the attacks for the United States, and particularly for the Bush administration. It was then that he decided that the United States must not be left on its own, and that Britain should remain closely alongside. This reflected fear that the United States might react, or rather overreact, unilaterally. This view dominated his thinking over the following 18 months up to the start of the Iraq war in March 2003. At each stage, he was more concerned with what the Bush administration was thinking and planning than with the opinions of his fellow European leaders.[6]

The strains appeared quickly in the autumn of 2001. Europe discovered that the emotions and solidarity of mid-September did not mark a change in the Bush administration's approach. International support had to be on US terms and, and, apart from British military involvement in the Afghanistan campaign, European help was mainly secondary.

Moreover, in this period, Blair in effect became Bush's ambassador at large, covering more than 40,000 miles in the eight weeks after the September 11 attacks while having 54 meetings with other leaders. Blair's independent actions, initially with Chirac and Schroeder, did not go down well in the rest of the EU. A meeting of the three leaders during the Ghent EU summit in mid-October 2001 was criticised by Romano Prodi, the president of the European Commission, as a 'shame' and as 'solo diplomacy'. These tensions descended into farce when Blair arranged a Sunday evening dinner in Number 10 on 4 November 2001, on the eve of a short visit to Washington. The guest list, originally just the French President and German Chancellor, expanded over the preceding days as other leaders were invited, or invited themselves. The list included the leaders of Italy, Spain, Belgium (which held the EU presidency) and the Netherlands (arriving late during the meal). Blair was trying to be both a messenger between Europe and the United States and a missionary around the world

---

[6] For a fuller discussion of Tony Blair's transatlantic balancing act in this period see Peter Riddell, *Hug Them Close: Blair, Clinton, Bush and the 'Special Relationship'* (London, Politico's/Methuen Publishing, 2003).

on part of President Bush. In neither role did he appear to be acting in the EU's collective interests.

But these difficulties were nothing compared with the open divisions of the following 18 months. The alarm bells began ringing in late January 2002, when during the annual State of the Union address to Congress, President Bush described states such as North Korea, Iran and Iraq as 'an axis of evil, arming to threaten the peace of the world'. In Europe, Herbert Vedrine, the French foreign minister, said that US policy had become 'simplistic', while Chris Patten, the EU's external affairs commissioner, reflected the worries of transatlantic multilateralists in warning that the United States was in danger of going into 'unilateralist overdrive'. As ever, Blair publicly played down the differences, even though there was considerable private anxiety in London. The real issue was increasingly Iraq, where, by spring 2002, Blair privately accepted that the United States would probably take military action and that Britain would almost certainly participate, provided the right diplomatic conditions were met. This meant a new United Nations Security Council resolution and the return of weapons inspectors to Iraq. All the time Blair was saying that no decision on military action had been taken as he attempted to maintain a common US/EU position. But even the façade of unity was undermined during the summer of 2002 as Gerhard Schroeder took a strongly anti-war line in his party's campaign for re-election that September. This infuriated Bush and his advisers, who saw Schroeder's attacks as a personal betrayal. Their relationship was permanently damaged. A common transatlantic position was reached during October and November over what became UN Resolution 1441. But the lengthily negotiated wording only papered over the cracks between the US belief that another vote was not needed before military action and the French and Russian view that 1441 did not provide an automatic trigger for war. The unanimous Security Council vote on 8 November 2002 was the deceptive high point of transatlantic unity, with the British deluding themselves that their successful diplomacy might avoid war.

Revival of the Franco-German alliance

Blair's attempt to reconcile these differences was publicly destroyed in the first three months of 2003. The transatlantic bridge collapsed, exposing the contradictions in his foreign policy. The British government, at least Number 10, failed to recognise the signs of a revival in the Franco-German alliance, which had been distant over the previous four years because of coolness between Chirac and Schroeder. At an EU summit in Brussels in late October 2002, Britain, and particularly Blair, was out-manoeuvred by a surprise joint French and German initiative on the future financing of the Common Agricultural Policy. Chirac and Blair clashed openly on these proposals. Chirac complained that he had never been spoken to in this way before. This may have been absurd but it led to the postponement of the planned Anglo-French summit until the New Year. The renewed closeness of France and Germany frustrated one of the Foreign Office's most longstanding, and invariably disappointed, hopes: to form stronger bilateral relations with both Paris and Berlin to create a three-way, rather than a two-way, leadership in the EU.

The gulf became wider in early 2003 as the US determination to take military action became more apparent, and as French and German opposition became more vocal. Blair was increasingly seen as an advocate for the US side. Two events symbolised the breach. First, on 22 January 2003, Donald Rumsfeld, the US defence secretary, sought to divide Europe when asked about European opposition to military action. 'You're thinking of Europe as Germany and France. I don't. That's old Europe. If you look to the east, Germany has been a problem, and France has been a problem. But you look at the vast numbers of other countries in Europe. They're not with France and Germany on this, they're with the United States.' That was partly correct, but only partly, since the divisions were much more complicated. There were differences between the views of heads of government, like Jose Maria Aznar of Spain who backed President Bush, and his electorate, who were strongly opposed to military action. (The hollowness of the attempt to classify Europe into old and new was exposed in March 2004 when Spain overnight moved from the second group into the first after the election of the socialists under José Luis Rodríguez Zapatero. He had been very critical of the war and immediately withdrew the 1,300-strong Spanish contingent from Iraq.) Rumsfeld's remarks were both provocative and indicated a big change of policy. For most of the post-1945 era, the United States had encouraged a united Europe; now, there seemed to be a deliberate attempt to divide the EU and work with ad hoc coalitions of the willing. That put the Blair government on the spot as a supporter of transatlantic cooperation through the EU.

The second symbolic event came at the end of January 2003, when eight heads of European governments – of Britain, Denmark, Italy, Portugal and Spain among existing EU members, and of the Czech Republic, Hungary and Poland among new entrants – signed a widely publicised article backing the enforcement of Resolution 1441. This was backed up a few days later when the leaders of 10 other central and eastern European countries signed a similar pro-US letter. These letters appeared to confirm Rumsfeld's claim and infuriated French and German leaders.

Blair's isolation

Blair was left looking increasingly isolated over the following weeks, as he faced growing domestic opposition and was spurned by the French, German and some other EU leaders. At the same time, he was unable to secure a majority for the further UN resolution to authorise the use of force. The final, open breach in Europe occurred in mid-March when President Jacques Chirac appeared on French television to say: 'My position is that, regardless of the circumstances, France will vote no because it considers this evening there are no grounds for waging war in order to achieve the goal we have set ourselves – to disarm Iraq.' There has been much dispute about whether Chirac was referring just to the resolution proposed by Britain, or, whether as Blair claimed, to any resolution setting a timed ultimatum requiring Saddam to comply or face the automatic use of force. But Chirac's use of the phrase 'regardless of the circumstances' gave Blair an opening to argue that a further resolution had been unreasonably blocked. There was then a spate of French-bashing, led by Jack Straw and enthusiastically joined by the jingoistic tabloids. This helped to ease the short-term pressures on Blair, but at considerable long-term cost.

The conclusion drawn in much of the rest of Europe was that, when faced with a strategic choice, Blair had opted for the United States rather than for Europe. On this view, for all Blair's pro-European language, he was like his predecessors: an Atlanticist at heart. More crudely, Blair was widely attacked for being Bush's poodle. Blair's instincts were the same as virtually all his predecessors apart from Sir Edward Heath, even though few would necessarily have been as bold as Blair. So, could the diplomatic train wreck of March 2003 have been avoided? Leaving aside all the subsequent arguments about Iraq's weapons of mass destruction. Blair's desire to ensure that the United States, as the sole superpower and Britain's closest military ally, was not left alone was a plausible objective, as well as one with a long pedigree. Blair took a different view of the post 9/11 United States than many other European leaders who, with their long experience of terrorism, did not believe that the attacks on New York and Washington had 'changed everything', as the Bush administration and many Americans did. Moreover, Blair has rejected as destabilising the vision of a multipolar world advocated by President Chirac and other European centralists in which a united Europe acts as a counterweight to the 'hyper-power' across the Atlantic. Blair believes in a strong Europe acting in cooperation, not competition, with the United States. Even if Blair was over-optimistic about the degree of his real influence in the White House, as opposed to access, this was a more credible foreign policy than his critics have acknowledged.

But could Blair have avoided the divisions with much of the rest of Europe? It is possible that a split was unavoidable in view of the belligerent approach of many in the Bush administration and their desire to divide Europe. Moreover, the weakness of Schroeder led to a revival of the Franco-German alliance on Chirac's terms, making it much harder for Blair to bridge transatlantic differences. Yet these months represented a major failure in British foreign policy, both of intelligence and execution. The government, or at least Number 10, had failed to appreciate either the renewed closeness of Chirac and Schroeder or the firmness of the French determination to oppose military action. Despite frequent telephone conversations, Blair and his advisers did not devote nearly enough time to talking to Chirac, Schroeder and other European leaders as they did to relations with the Bush White House. A more even-handed diplomacy might not have prevented differences over the war in view of Blair's overriding priority of not deserting the United States, but more skilful personal diplomacy by him could have mitigated the consequences.

The Iraq war was not only the over-arching event of Blair's second term, and possibly of his whole premiership, but it also undermined his attempt to present a pro-European case. Talk of old and new Europe and the demonisation of France were hardly the best way of combating Euro-scepticism, let alone of winning a referendum on entry to the euro. Opinion polls showed, for example, a slight increase in opposition to joining the euro after the Iraq war compared with before.

Euro assessment

The odds of early entry had anyway been fast receding, both because the British economy was doing pretty well on its own outside the euro and because the performance of the eurozone economies, particularly Germany, remained sluggish. So it was no surprise when the promised assessment about whether the five tests had been met was negative. The assessment was the largest single piece of work ever undertaken by the Treasury, involving 18 separate studies of various aspects of the impact of

EMU, as well as a 246-page White Paper of conclusions.[7] The intention was to show that the exercise was driven by economics, not politics, though pro-euro supporters argued that the analysis could be read in their direction. The Treasury argued that had the United Kingdom joined EMU at its start in 1999, 'the UK economy could potentially have experienced greater economic instability than has actually been the case'. The conclusion was unequivocal:

> Overall the Treasury assessment is that since 1997 the UK has made real progress towards meeting the five economic tests. But, on balance, though the potential benefits of increased investment, trade, a boost to financial services, growth and jobs are clear, we cannot at this point in time conclude that there is sustainable and durable convergence or sufficient flexibility to cope with any potential difficulties within the euro area. So, despite the risks and costs from delaying the benefits of joining, a clear and unambiguous case for UK membership of EMU has not at the present time been made and a decision to join now would not be in the national economic interest.

Gordon Brown discussed the assessment and conclusions individually with each member of the Cabinet. There was also a lengthy discussion by the full Cabinet in its longest session since 1997, before he delivered his statement on 9 June 2003. To appease the dwindling band of Labour supporters of euro entry, Blair talked about launching a roadshow to make the case for entry – still presented as a when rather than an if – as well as a further review the following year to see whether another assessment was justified. But this was quickly exposed a sham. The government did not pursue a consistent programme of advocating entry and no further assessment occurred. By early 2004, Blair accepted the Treasury view that euro entry was off the agenda for the foreseeable future, certainly in his own premiership, not least because of the problems of the European economies. Instead of the strongly pro-entry language of his early years in Downing Street, he talked in 'take it or leave it' terms, emphasising instead that he had always seen euro entry more as an economic question.

The Constitutional Convention

A new issue was, however, fast appearing to replace the euro as a headache for the Blair government. The failure of the acrimonious Nice summit in December 2000 to agree all the changes needed to make the EU fit for

---

[7] *UK Membership of the Single Currency*, pp. 3–6.

enlargement from 15 to 25 led to the establishment of a Constitutional Convention. This consisted of representatives of member governments and national parliaments as well as the European Parliament and the Commission. This was chaired by former French President Valéry Giscard d'Estaing. Jack Straw, and particularly Peter Hain, initially as Europe minister, were the main British representatives. But in many respects the key British participant was Sir John (now Lord) Kerr, the convention's secretary-general and one of the most experienced and wiliest British diplomats of his generation, who had crouched beside British prime ministers at many an EU summit.

The Blair government accepted that the EU had to change to accommodate 25 member states. Britain urged a largely intergovernmental, rather than a federal, approach. This placed most emphasis on the work of the Council of Ministers, but in a streamlined version with presidencies, or chairmanships, of councils lasting longer than six months. Britain backed the case for more qualified majority voting to remove blocking vetoes in some areas such as asylum and immigration, but not over the most sensitive questions such as taxation, social security, defence, foreign policy and treaty changes. In a speech in Warsaw as early as October 2000,[8] Blair had accepted the case for change, though had argued for a number of different treaties, laws and precedents rather than a single constitution. He proposed a second parliamentary chamber, consisting of representatives of national parliaments. But this idea made little headway in the face of the objections of the European Parliament. The British government at times sounded muddled about its view of the convention: after Hain's early ill-judged reference to a 'tidying-up exercise', ministers veered between emphasising Britain's bottom or red-lines and arguing positively for the package as a means of making an EU of 25 work.

There were two stages: first, in the convention, and, second, by member governments in an intergovernmental conference. The convention produced a package that was intended to meet the concerns of big countries, and particularly Britain and France by emphasising cooperation by member states. This included proposals for a permanent president of the European Council, serving for a period of two and half years. There would be a European foreign minister, combining the roles of the high representative and the commissioner for external affairs. There would also be an EU external action service to provide diplomatic support. Most controversial for Britain was the very idea of a constitution, even though it

---

[8] Tony Blair, speech to the Polish Stock Exchange, Warsaw, 6 October 2000.

was strictly a treaty like the Maastricht, Amsterdam and Nice treaties. But the draft highlighted the supremacy of EU law, which had always been true in areas of community competence, and gave the EU a single legal personality. This provoked sceptic fears about a European superstate. The Charter of Fundamental Rights was seen as providing a loophole for the introduction of new EU laws and regulations affecting British business. This was despite British amendments to ensure that new rights were not introduced into British law. Qualified majority voting was also extended in some areas, notably in extending community competence in justice and home affairs, though in none of the British 'red lines', like taxation. This plan was accepted, with various modifications, by EU leaders in June 2004 at a summit chaired by Bertie Ahern, the Irish prime minister, after a stalemate the previous December at the end of the Italian presidency.

Blair was able to claim that the constitution largely met British concerns, but such was the mood of Euro-scepticism at home that he was on the defensive from the start. A constitutional treaty that was criticised in much of the rest of Europe, particularly on the left, as being too pro-British and too pro-market was attacked in Britain by sceptics, particularly in the Conservative Party, for selling out fundamental national interests by supporting a federal United States of Europe. Opinion polls showed a majority of the public against the constitution. Blair, and especially Jack Straw, were worried that demands for a referendum by the Conservative Party and the vocal Euro-sceptic press would dominate any future election campaign and damage Labour's chances. Consequently, in April 2004, ahead of final agreement on the constitution, Blair was persuaded to announce that a referendum would be held to ratify any treaty. He did this without consulting the Cabinet as a whole. He infuriated several strong pro-Europeans, both in the Cabinet, such as Charles Clarke, and outside, such as his longstanding adviser and friend Peter Mandelson. The announcement was seen as a sign of political weakness at low point in his political fortunes when he was depressed by a family problem, by the stories about the torture and degradation of Iraqi prisoners by US (and in a few cases British) troops, and by anxiety about whether he should lead Labour into a third election.

The referendum announcement removed the issue from the election agenda both in the campaign for the European Parliament that June and ahead of the May 2005 general election. Europe consistently came near the bottom of the public's list of the most important issues facing Britain. But that was as much a negative as positive development. Contrary to his frequent post-Iraq statements about being 'best when boldest', Blair

had opted for a minimalist, risk-averse position on Europe, putting off
awkward positions when possible. He rarely any longer made speeches
about Europe.

The record since 1997

The paradox was that the British position in Europe had advanced in many
ways since 1997. Enlargement of the EU to 25, formally completed in May
2004, not only fulfilled a long-standing British foreign policy goal of
incorporating the former communist states of eastern and central Europe
within the EU, but it also promised a Europe more to Britain's liking:
more Atlanticist on security issues, and more free-market on economic
matters. Britain was more comfortable with enlargement than, say, France
with its worries about losing its previously dominant position in the EU.
French newspapers and politicians complained in 2004 about excessive
British influence in Brussels. On foreign and security policy, also, work
towards a more effective joint EU voice and capability continued, despite,
and to some extent because of, the divisions over Iraq. Shortly after the fall
of Baghdad in April 2003, Jack Straw launched a joint initiative with the
French and German foreign ministers to negotiate with the Tehran regime
over Iran's nuclear programme. This was specifically intended to pre-
empt a more aggressive approach by the Bush administration. Although
the hawks in Washington were highly critical of this European initiative,
the State Department offered guarded support, partly because it did not
have a better alternative in the short term. These tripartite talks were,
however, conducted by the three foreign ministers, not as a specifically
EU initiative. However, Javier Solana, the high representative responsible
for the Common Foreign and Security Policy, had an increasing role,
notably in the Balkans, but also in the Middle East and Africa.

These efforts were in parallel with the development of a European
defence policy, building on the St-Malo declaration of December 1998 and
the Helsinki communiqué a year later. Britain backed both the creation
of the European Defence Agency, to improve common procurement, and
an EU battlegroups initiative. Apart from perennial problems of relations
with Nato, the main problem has been capabilities, with the EU as a whole
falling well behind the Helsinki goal of having up to 50,000 to 60,000
troops deployable within 60 days and sustainable for at least a year in
peacekeeping and related tasks. An ill-judged summit of France, Germany,
Belgium and Luxembourg in April 2003, just after the fall of Baghdad,
launched a core European defence plan to permit autonomous European

operations. This infuriated not only the Americans but also the British, Spanish (then centre-right) and Italian governments. Later in 2003, Blair reached a compromise with Chirac and Schroeder for a modest initiative, including a small EU military planning cell. The Bush administration remained worried about EU defence activities separate from Nato. But the EU's short-term ambitions and capabilities have remained modest, though in 2004 it was able to take over Nato's peacekeeping mission in Bosnia.

The Blair government also shifted its position on justice and home affairs. Labour followed the Conservative policy of maintaining national border controls, unlike the countries within the area covered by the Schengen agreement. However, under the influence of Jack Straw, first as home secretary, Britain has participated in police and justice co-operation, and then, from 2002 onwards, in immigration and asylum arrangements. As concern mounted within Britain about rising numbers of asylum seekers, the Blair government argued that a common European approach was needed to control inflows. After the 9/11 attacks, Britain also pushed for stronger action against potential terrorists by supporting a European-wide arrest warrant.

The Blair government has remained active in pushing economic reform, despite Britain's exclusion from the eurozone. Britain has pressed for completion of the single market in energy, telecommunications and financial services (this last a particularly fraught area), as well as for reductions in regulations and more flexible labour, capital and product markets. The main emphasis in the Lisbon process, agreed in March 2000, has been on setting headline goals to be attained by 2010, and then comparing what member states are doing. The key elements have been innovation, liberalisation of markets, creating new enterprises, reducing regulations and state subsidies, employment creation and social inclusion, and sustainable development. The 'Community' method, where the Commission, the European Parliament and the Council of Ministers have agreed laws, worked well in creating a single internal market, but it has been less suitable for deregulating labour markets or reducing the cost for businesses of pensions and other employee benefits.

Progress has been mixed. A scorecard on the Lisbon agenda, drawn up in early 2005 by Alasdair Murray and Aurore Wanlin of the Centre for Economic Reform think tank, argues that: 'The EU's Lisbon process has reached the half-way stage with few obvious signs of improvement in the performance of the European economy. The EU has already admitted that it will miss a number of key targets.'[9] The scorecard puts the Nordic countries and Britain at the top. In most countries, there is now general acceptance among the political elites of the need for reform, but in Germany, France and Italy proposals for changing welfare benefits and pension entitlements have been fiercely resisted by powerful public service and union interests.

The replacement in November 2004 of the ineffective Romani Prodi as president of the European Commission by Jose Manuel Barroso, a former prime minister of Portugal from the centre-right, and his new Commission raised hopes about a new commitment to economic reform. Barroso, strongly backed by Peter Mandelson, the new British commissioner with responsibilities for external trade, made the revival of the Lisbon agenda, growth and employment the top priority for his term. In its review of the Lisbon process, the Barroso Commission has acknowledged that delivery depends on the attitude of member states. But the Commission immediately ran into problems with the European Parliament and with France over the proposed services directive. This would allow a legally established service provider from any member country to operate in any other state. The Commission was forced to revise the directive. There were fears on the left that this would create a free market for services, according to the laws of the least regulated country, leading to a wave of migrants from the east undercutting local workers. Opposition to a so-called 'liberalising' agenda became an important theme of the French referendum on the constitution in May 2005.

For Britain, and the Blair government, the reform debate has had two key implications. First, the overall economic performance of Europe has been disappointing. Growth in the EU averaged about 2% a year between 1999 and 2004, compared with 3% in the United States, which had been the Lisbon target in 2000. Labour productivity has lagged well behind the United States, so the gap in output per head has widened from 3 to 12% since 1995. Unemployment has also risen in many countries, up to an alarming 5 million in Germany by early 2005, Second, the British performance has been consistently better than the rest of Europe throughout this period, in its overall growth rate and in its level of unemployment. At the same time, the strict fiscal rules of the eurozone's stability and growth pact have been relaxed to suit France and Germany. This has allowed the Treasury to argue that fiscal and monetary disciplines and performances

---

[9] Alasdair Murray and Aurore Wanlin, *The Lisbon Scorecard V. Can Europe Compete?* (London, Centre for Economic Reform, 2005), pp. 83–7.

are superior in Britain. The contrast between Britain's strong economic performance and the poor record in the eurozone has been regularly emphasised by the predominantly sceptic British press. This was despite the fact that, even with divergences in recent growth rates, levels of productivity and standards of living, let alone some public services, were still better in much of western Europe than in Britain.

The recent sluggish performance of the eurozone economies has undermined support for the pro-European position. The argument has been 'we are doing quite well on our own, why do we need to get more tied up with Europe'. Business enthusiasm for the EU has been noticeably on the decline, as shown by opposition to the proposed European constitution for fear that it might provide a back-door way of introducing new regulations and increasing costs. The European argument in Britain has usually been put, especially by Gordon Brown, but also, at times, by Tony Blair, in minimalist terms of red lines, of national interests being defended, rather than highlighting the advantages of membership.

Eurosceptism still strong

Hardly surprisingly, given the negative way in which Europe has been discussed both by politicians and a heavily sceptical media, public opinion has remained hostile to the EU in general and to initiatives like the euro and the constitution in particular. Apart from a temporary blip after May 1997, the arrival of the Blair government has made no difference to public opinion towards the EU. According to MORI, the number of people wanting to get out of the EU since 1997 has been around the same levels of 45% to 50% as during the later years of the Major government.[10] While support for joining the euro rose to around 45% in the 1998–9 period, it has fallen back to well below 40% since then – though nearly half the electorate are described as waverers who are persuadable either way. Polls have also shown overwhelming opposition to the European constitution, though the margin narrows sharply when the precise wording of the referendum question is put to interviewees. A Eurobarometer poll[11] undertaken in November 2004 for the European Commission showed that Britain came second to last among the 25 EU members in the number having heard about the constitution (Cyprus was last). Just 6% of the British claimed to know its contents. The UK also had the lowest level of support for

[10] www.mori.com/europe/mori-eu-ref.shtml.
[11] Eurobarometer, European Commission, January 2005.

the constitution. Another Eurobarometer poll in October and November 2004 showed that the number saying that EU membership was a good thing was lowest in the UK of all 25 member states. For the first time in 20 years, more people think that membership of the EU is a bad rather than a good thing. In 1998, at the high point of Blair's pro-Europeanism, the balance was two to one in favour. Trust in the European Commission and Parliament is also lowest in the UK.

Doubts about the direction of Europe are not just, however, a purely British phenomenon. The Schroeder coalition in Germany suffered a series of very bad regional/*länder* election results because of high unemployment and resistance to the government's reform proposals. In France, the opposition on the left to the European constitution was fuelled by dislike of what Europe was becoming in its enlarged form and by the threat by liberalisation to social protection and the European social model. The overwhelming rejection of the European constitution by the French and Dutch electorates on 29 May and 1 June 2005 raised fundamental questions about the direction of Europe, as Blair immediately acknowledged. The votes were as much about the enlargement of Europe and its response to globalisation as about the details of the constitutional treaty.

These referendum results were initially seen as offering a way out for Blair since the constitution was, in effect, dead and he would not have to hold a highly risky referendum some time in 2006 – especially as a 'no' vote might have ended his premiership. But this was a short-sighted view. The European constitution offered the best hope of the type of primarily intergovernmental arrangements that the Blair government preferred. However much Europe might have to pause to pick up the pieces, and whatever short-term arrangements might be put in place, France, Germany, Spain and possibly Italy (after elections scheduled for 2006) might seek to revive alternative plans for integration unacceptable to the Blair government and to British public opinion. Moreover, the results of the referendum would stiffen existing hostility to economic reform in France and other countries, and therefore slow the pace of liberalisation. In his comments after the referendum of 20 May 2005, President Jacques Chirac specifically rejected 'the Anglo-Saxon' economic and social model. These attitudes would again make it harder to argue the benefits of closer involvement in the EU to the anyway sceptical British public.

In summer 2005, Blair's hopes of giving Britain a leading role and reforming Europe looked unachievable. The Brussels heads of government summit on 16 and 17 June exposed deep divisons with France and some other founding members, not just over reform of the Common Agricultural Policy and the British budget rebate but also over the future direction of the EU. Blair argued that the only way forward was the British approach. In a speech to the European Parliament on 23 June,[12] he argued that the choice was not between a 'free market' Europe and a social Europe. 'There is not some division between the Europe necessary to succeed economically and social Europe.' He argued for modernising the social model to enhance Europe's ability to compete and grow. He also said that Britain was prepared to compromise on the budget rebate, provided there was genuine reform of the CAP. At a time when both the German Chancellor and the French President were in serious political trouble, Blair was applauded for offering leadership. But there was no evidence that his words would bring an early agreement on reform.

Blair failed to make the case for Europe to the British people. He repeatedly said in private – first about the euro and then about the constitution – that he could ratchet up opinion in favour of Europe whenever a referendum was called. But that has always been an illusion. It has always been a case of tomorrow, an occasional big speech, but then nothing. Moreover, even his speeches seldom received backing from other Cabinet ministers: most kept quiet about Europe. The achievements of the Blair government on Europe – backing new proposals on economic reform, enlargement, increased cooperation on defence and home affairs – should not be dismissed. They matter and are markedly different from the record of the previous few years. Despite the divisions over Iraq, Britain has been an active player in the EU. The plans of both the Barroso Commission and the general thrust of the European constitution have been in line with British aspirations. But all this has failed to move British public opinion in a pro-European direction. The whole is much less than the sum of the parts.

Moroever, as Roger Liddle, the former European adviser to Tony Blair and, since November 2004, a member of Peter Mandelson's cabinet in Brussels, has argued, the old coalition of pro-European Tories, big business, the Liberals (now Liberal Democrats) and much of Labour has fractured. The old pro-European arguments of the 1960s and 1970s based on Britain's weakness compared with the rest of Europe no longer apply. 'As Britain's relative economic performance has strengthened, the power of the old "declinist" argument for Europe has weakened. In parallel, the attraction of the European model has itself declined.'[13] Liddle has argued that the centre-left has to change the terms of the European political

---

[12] Tony Blair, speech to the European Parliament, 23 June 2005.
[13] Roger Liddle, *The New Case for Europe: The Crisis in British Pro-Europeanism – and How to Overcome It* (London, Fabian Society, 2005), p. 23.

debate away from the 'no alternative' view of the past. Instead, Blair should make a more positive political argument: that only the EU acting together can deal with the new global challenges and manage social and economic change. Despite being instinctively more pro-European than most previous prime ministers apart from Heath, Blair has been hesitant about taking risks over Europe.

Conclusions

Blair cannot be faulted on his intentions. Better relations with Europe were one of his top priorities on becoming prime minister. He ended the frostiness and isolation of the late Major years by his energy and charm. He developed good relations with a number of key European leaders, launching joint reform initiatives. His personal imprint on these changes was considerable. But his efforts were not sustained. He became frustrated with the way that decisions were taken at EU summits, often returning home as soon as possible.

Given this background and these pressures, were his objectives ever attainable? Only in the most favourable circumstances, and only if Blair had decided from the start, like Heath in 1970, that Europe came first in his order of priorities. But it never did for Blair. That was shown, within five months of the 1997 election, when Blair both deferred a decision on entry into the euro and gave Brown and the Treasury a veto over future assessments and decisions on entry. He would have had to defy a sceptic Treasury, an often euro-phobic press and a public which has been the least enthusiastic about the EU of any of the 25 member states. But he also required luck. That disappeared on 11 September 2001. After the 9/11 attacks, and particularly in the run-up to the Iraq war, maintaining European unity came second to relations with Washington. Blair behaved as a very traditional British prime minister, even if he was bolder than all but perhaps Margaret Thatcher would have been in committing British troops. He was unwilling to jeopardise the Atlantic alliance – and all that implied in military and intelligence links – for the sake of maintaining European harmony.

Iraq was the event that undermined even the modest progress that he had achieved previously. But it has not just been Iraq – as noted above, many other European leaders were disillusioned with Blair before the 9/11 attacks. Even without Iraq, Britain would still have not been in the euro, and there would still have been the divisions over the direction of Europe, between the liberalising free-market vision and the more familiar social/protectionist model that surfaced so dramatically in May 2005 in the French referendum on the constitution. Despite his occasional pro-European speeches, Blair was never willing to adapt or devote himself fully to his European goals. These were all the missed opportunities, limiting what he could have done.

So, after eight years, Blair had failed in his initial aim of ending the decades of British distance, reservation and hesitation about Europe. Britain remains the perpetual awkward partner. This was not all his personal fault. Circumstances were against him. But Europe has been a central failure of his premiership. Moreover, since it was one of his top priorities in 1997, Europe is a failure that will feature heavily in the final assessments of his record in 10 Downing Street.

17

Putting the world to rights: Tony Blair's foreign policy mission

CHRISTOPHER HILL

The second Blair administration is almost synonymous with the crisis which began with the terrorist attacks of 11 September 2001 on the United States, developed into the war in Afghanistan and culminated in the long-drawn-out disputes over Iraq, from 2002 through to the present day. How this crisis will end is still not clear, but its various manifestations continue to shape British politics even after Blair's third election victory in May 2005. Indeed, apart from those few months after the second victory in June 2001, when the Labour Party was governing, exceptionally, with the confirmation of a huge parliamentary majority, the whole of this period was consumed by debate and anxiety about what was happening in the world, and what Britain's role in international affairs should be.

One particular paradox about these events from a British viewpoint is that while they precipitated more public interest in foreign policy than any event since the 1982 Falklands war, and possibly since the 1962 Cuban missile crisis, the actual making of British policy took place in an even more restricted circle than usual. Indeed, most observers have concluded that this was a period of highly personalised foreign policy-making, with the prime minister and a small coterie of advisers driving through policies which were not only highly contentious on the wider political scene, but also the subject of grave doubts on the part of large parts of the Establishment, particularly the Foreign and Commonwealth Office (FCO), as the government department with formal responsibility in this area.

This chapter considers how far the picture of Tony Blair's personal responsibility for the controversial foreign policies pursued in Britain's name (precisely why so many carried 'not in my name' placards during the demonstrations over Iraq) is true. It also attempts to assess the changes which have taken place over the last four years, in terms of the fundamental direction of British foreign policy, and the Prime Minister's reputation at home and abroad, while largely excluding intra-European issues, which are dealt with in this volume by Peter Riddell (Chapter 16). It proceeds for the most part chronologically, concentrating on the events flowing from 9/11, but it begins with a discussion of the ideology of foreign policy which Blair has been developing in office, and concludes with a brief survey of the 'normal' foreign policy issues which continued in the background between 2001 and 2005. The whole analysis is subject to the caveat that in the area of foreign and security policy it is particularly difficult to be sure of what went on behind the scenes – even in a period for which we have the unparalleled resources of the Hutton and Butler reports. Judgements cannot be too confident, for the simple reason that some key witnesses have not spoken, and those that have, will at best have been careful with the truth, and at worst addicted to spin.

The Blair view of foreign policy

Like all prime ministers, Tony Blair quickly became drawn into foreign affairs, despite a relative lack of previous knowledge. His quick-witted capacity to extemporise was in fact well suited to the twists and turns of international events, where planning often comes to nothing and ready-made dramas often drop into a leader's lap. The urge to lead, the presentational skills, the accessible sincerity – key Blair attributes – all found ready outlets in international politics, where the audience is by definition less attuned to nuance, and less sceptical through relentless exposure, than it is on the domestic political scene. Blair thus naturally turned outwards quite early in his first term, and by the time of his second electoral victory had determined on a more pliable partner than Robin Cook in the foreign policy executive team of prime minister and foreign secretary. The moving of Cook and his replacement in King Charles Street by the Home Secretary was a straw in the wind, so to speak, of Blair's determination to assert his power of initiative and personally to embody continuity in foreign policy-making.

It did not take long, even in his first term, for Blair to make a mark on foreign policy. He did not bring with him a ready-made portfolio of ideas on the subject, but he was quick to see who might provide them, and by combining the use of intellectuals such as Robert Cooper and Lawrence Freedman with trusted political advisers like Jonathan Powell (whose brother Charles had been Margaret Thatcher's *eminence grise*) he created the space for intelligent speculation about the principles of foreign policy – an activity which has traditionally been in short supply in the self-consciously pragmatic British political culture. Initially the ground had been taken by Robin Cook's version of an ethical foreign policy, with Blair confined to talking constructively about a new relationship with Europe, but before long the Kosovo crisis led him to make the speech in Chicago of 22 April 1999 which set out a 'doctrine of the international community'.[1] This was one of the most theoretical speeches ever made by a British prime minister on the fundamentals of foreign policy. Its core had been provided by Professor Freedman, but Tony Blair was ultimately responsible, and its underlying values were clearly his own. For whatever set of personal and political reasons, Blair was settling on the position that tyrants should not be allowed to stand unchallenged in international affairs, and that if they seemed also to represent a threat to the general peace, they would have to be dethroned. Any sign of imminent or actual genocide should also trigger interventions, whatever the derogations of sovereignty and of international law. What is more, Blair had no doubt that Britain should be a leading agent of the international community's will in these matters, and (as he increasingly came to say) 'a force for good in the world'.

In all this Blair was in tune with the Western Zeitgeist, albeit ahead of other politicians of his generation. Challenges to the stricter interpretations of state sovereignty had been mounting for some time, especially since the cynical doublethink on the matter of the 'Brezhnev doctrine' of 1968, and genocide was in any case generally agreed to be an exception – even if the challenge of acting to stop it remained a daunting one. The Prime Minister, however, like Mrs Thatcher, thrived on challenges. Unlike her, he wanted both to lead and to be liked, or at least, to have the capacity to maintain consensus at home and abroad. Thus he was also coming to the view that he and Britain (it being all too easy to blur the two) had a unique role as a bridge between Europe and the United States and, indeed, as time went on, between the West and the Islamic world. For Blair a quietist foreign policy would simply have meant shirking his responsibilities, and this instinct became particularly evident in his manic shuttle diplomacy during the crises of the second term.[2] An ambitious

---

[1] For the speech, made to the Economic Club of Chicago, Hilton Hotel, 22 April 1999, go to http://www.pbs.org/newshour/bb/international/jan-june99/blair_doctrine4-23.html. An analysis is contained in Christopher Hill, 'Foreign policy', in Anthony Seldon (ed.), *The Blair Effect* (London: Little, Brown, 2001) pp. 340–3.

[2] The *Evening Standard* front page of 9 November 2001 showed a clearly 'shattered' PM, after a week of '40,000 miles, meeting 17 world leaders – and there's a heavy weekend ahead'. John Kampfner reckoned that in the three months from 9/11 Blair had covered more miles than Colin Powell in the interests of building a coalition against terror, meeting the leaders

form of internationalism was developing in Blair's outlook, whereby he wished to reconnect Britain to its European destiny, to help modernise the EU so that it would be fit for the era of globalisation (a Blair mantra), and above all to stay close to the United States, as the ultimate guarantor of British security. The Prime Minister did not shrink from using power, but always preferred to do it in the company of the hegemon. This last stance followed the line laid down by Attlee and Bevin in 1947–8, just as with the 'bridge-building' metaphor Blair was echoing the 'three circles' formulation of Winston Churchill, an idea which has lurked behind much of the thinking of British foreign policy since it was coined in 1949.[3] Yet although Blair liked to make occasional references to the more poignant moments of the British past, he did not show many signs of thinking historically or of reflecting whether he might not be the prisoner of some long-dead political theorist, to adapt Maynard Keynes.

The lull before the storm

The three months from the second great election victory of New Labour on 7 June 2001 will always be overshadowed by what happened on 11 September, just as the political class returned from its summer break. For foreign policy there were no dramatic events that summer, but much important work. Blair was settling down with his new team, of Jack Straw in the FCO, advisers David Manning and Stephen Wall at Number 10, and John Scarlett as chairman of the Joint Intelligence Committee. He was showing signs of cooling on the issue of entry into the euro, and his priority seemed to be ensuring that he would become the most valued counsellor to the newly elected George Bush. Potential disagreements over the Kyoto protocol, over light arms sales and over the alleged US exploitation for commercial purposes of the electronic spying system 'Echelon', to which the British facilities at Menwith Hill were central, were not allowed to run out of control.[4] Blair had said in March 2001 that 'I've been as pro-America a Prime Minister as it is possible to have. There is not a single issue

---

of more than 70 countries. John Kampfner, *Blair's Wars* (London: Free Press, 2003). George Bush was either not so bothered about coalition-building or happy for Blair to do the work for him.

[3] Geoffrey Best, *Churchill: A Study in Greatness* (London: Penguin, 2002), pp. 286–7.

[4] On this period, see Kampfner, *Blair's Wars*, pp. 90–104. On Echelon , see 'Secrecy, spy satellites and a conspiracy of silence: the disturbing truth about Echelon', *Independent*, 30 May 2001.

I can think of in which we haven't stood foursquare with America.'[5] He had no intention of endangering the fundamentals of his relationship with Washington in the early months of a new president's term. Indeed, it is not implausible that Robin Cook was moved from the FCO because he was seen as having become 'Europeanised', and insufficiently pro-American.[6]

Blair himself was already insouciant about opening up a distance between himself and his French or German colleagues over foreign policy questions. In part this was because of the enormous self-confidence that the Prime Minister had in his ability to make a personal difference on some of the great international issues. Almost by definition this implied that he would be in competition with his peers, Jacques Chirac and Gerhard Schroeder. Bush and the Russian leader Vladimir Putin, by contrast, both represented real power in the unsafe world outside the 'postmodern' European Union, and Blair sought to accommodate and to charm them. This whiff of appeasement in his approach to Washington and Moscow ('we deliberately moderated our language on Chechnya' according to one Blair adviser) means that the prime minister of the past whom Tony Blair most resembles is less Anthony Eden, to whom many people have compared him since the war in Iraq, than Neville Chamberlain, who also displayed a sincere but vain belief in his own abilities to persuade the leaders of powerful and potentially dangerous states to come to reasonable agreements. Ironically, both prime ministers had a touching faith in the power of pure diplomacy – but their own, rather than that of the Foreign Ministry professionals.[7]

The world changes

It is well documented how Tony Blair rose to the immediate challenge of the shock of 9/11, collecting his thoughts and words with remarkable speed and sang-froid.[8] The British system generally proves to be a well-oiled

---

[5] Kampfner, *Blair's Wars*, p. 90.

[6] In his diary entry of 9 August 2001 Cook could not understand how Blair could 'have so readily turned off the tap on the euro, when during the election it sounded as if this was one thing on which he had serious conviction'. Robin Cook, *The Point of Departure* (London: Simon & Schuster, 2003) p. 37. On the concept of foreign policy Europeanisation, see Reuben Wong, 'The Europeanisation of foreign policy', in Christopher Hill and Michael Smith (eds.), *International Relations and the European Union* (Oxford: Oxford University Press, 2005), pp. 134–53.

[7] On Chamberlain's character in this respect, see R. A. Butler, *The Art of the Possible: the Memoirs of Lord Butler* (Harmondsworth: Penguin, 1971) pp. 78–9.

[8] Anthony Seldon, *Blair* (London: Free Press, 2005 edition), pp. 483–512.

machine when confronted by the unexpected, as the dispatch of a naval task force to the Falklands in a mere four days proved in 1982, but it still depends on a forceful figure at the top providing leadership. Blair provided this in September 2001, and on a wider stage than just Britain. The Belgian presidency of the European Union faded into the background as Blair became Europe's self-appointed spokesman.

No doubt the British – and indeed the common European – interest was clear enough at this time: preventing a terrorist attack on our own cities, while helping the United States to realise that a considered response was much preferable to a spasm of immediate violence. The latter fear, in any case, soon went off the agenda, and the former could never be discounted. So Blair's influence on the actual course of international events in the first month after the attacks of 11 September was limited. But he certainly succeeded in cementing a privileged relationship with George Bush and (for better or worse) heightening his own profile as a leading figure in the fight against Al-Qaeda – standing 'shoulder to shoulder' with the United States, in his own phrase. He was also probably a significant factor in ensuring a decisive and united European response in support of Washington, although it should not be forgotten that Chirac and Schroeder were just as unequivocal. Where Blair does deserve particular credit is for his perception very early on that the actions of Mohammed Atta et al. might easily set off that 'clash of civilisations' of which Samuel Huntington had been writing since the early 1990s. Blair was quick to distinguish between 'Islam' and Al-Qaeda, and built on his belief in a liberal, multi-cultural Britain to reassure the Muslim residents of Britain that the government was in no doubt of their patriotism and would protect them from any possible backlash (this was in the days before Guantánamo and Belmarsh). Yet this was also a line to which everyone in his Cabinet must have subscribed. Figures like Clare Short, secretary of state for international development and MP for the multi-ethnic constituency of Birmingham Ladywood, would have been in the van, but even the less politically correct David Blunkett was aware of the Muslim vote in his constituency of Sheffield Brightside.

The Prime Minister's other contribution was to insist on the moral dimension of the 'war' against those who were depraved enough to fly a civilian airliner into office buildings. Blair's sense of conviction and moral certainty, guided by underlying religious belief, made any other outcome unlikely. He has subsequently been criticised for this, on the grounds that it encouraged a sloganeering crusade which would lead to the very kind of stereotyping of Muslims which he deplored. But one must not forget that the atmosphere of September 2001 was extraordinary, especially in those countries like Britain which had lost citizens, and to whom New York was a key part of the cultural landscape. In the weeks after 9/11 ordinary rational calculations did not apply. Emotions were running high and there was a widely shared feeling of living through a cataclysmic event. In that context it was not simply a piece of cheap posturing to say that clear choices had to be made. The normal political nuances, of 'the nicely calculated less or more', in Wordsworth's phrase, were pushed to the margins of polite society, as a press officer in the Department of Transport discovered when she suggested that 11 September might be a good day to 'bury bad news'.

The 'war on terror'

The language of the 'war on terror' was one thing, the practice another. As time wore on more and more people, whether professionals in government or members of the public, came to regret the way in which the discourse of the fight back against Al-Qaeda had been cast. Almost no one thought that doing nothing, or reliance on diplomacy, were options, but many came to doubt the good sense of constructing a 'war' against a shadowy transnational group which could never be definitively defeated. Moreover war, especially the unconditional kind which was increasingly what the Bush administration had in mind, is about the relentless use of military force, with other instruments a long way second. Yet terrorism clearly needs interdicting, and most importantly preventing, by a wide spectrum of different means. Wars also tend to have habit of running out of control, with the initial war aims soon replaced by grander yet vaguer objectives. Lastly, the 'them' and 'us' dichotomy which was natural in the traumatic aftershock of 9/11, became a positive handicap as the need emerged to build a wide coalition of support among a diverse range of states, including those who were nominally adversaries of the United States.

It is likely that Tony Blair realised the force of these arguments all too well, but either could not change the mindset of the angry government in Washington, or judged it a waste of time to try. In any case, he set about encouraging a practical level of cooperation against terrorism among the friends of the United States which rendered much of the rhetoric redundant. The most important task was to ensure the efficient exchange of information, through police and intelligence services, and to smooth out some of the well-known obstacles to judicial cooperation between divergent national legal systems, particularly over extradition. This is a shadowy area of high security, difficult to write about with confidence, but it seems likely that Blair was not actively involved in much of this technical detailed work. He could not be; his workload does not permit it and it is not a good use of prime ministerial time to micro-manage. Blair works hard and masters his briefs well, and has the ability to delegate. He left the detailed work of fostering trans-governmental cooperation to his ministers and senior officials, even if without his permission and encouragement major steps like the release of intelligence material to foreign states (even friendly ones) could not have occurred. It was in this atmosphere of unparalleled uncertainty and high perceived threat that Blair probably came to forge the close relationships between the Number 10 team and the intelligence chiefs which was to rebound so badly during the Iraq crisis. The foundations had been laid during the first term during the Kosovo war, but now many of the conditions for the onset of actual 'groupthink' were in place.[9]

The metaphor of the bridge which Blair preferred when imagining British relations with Europe and the United States may actually have had some meaning in the context of the war on terrorism. The encouragement (and the permission) which the Prime Minister gave for high-level intelligence cooperation with European partners may well have helped to dispel some of the distrust which has habitually surfaced on both sides of the Washington– Paris dialogue, and some of the scepticism which US officials have had about the value or reliability of working with their counterparts in Germany, Italy and the smaller EU states. In the event, there was remarkably rapid progress in the first months after 9/11 in giving the United States access to Europol and to the relatively new Eurojust system of expert legal coordination. Up to this point most Europeans had been defensive about US participation. Cooperation also proceeded rapidly on measures against money-laundering and on the anti-terrorist aspects of asylum and immigration policies.[10]

If Tony Blair's role in the behind the scenes aspects of the war on terror was the indirect (but still important) one of facilitator, in relation to its scope he was both more visible and less effective. There was general

---

[9] By 'groupthink' is meant the concurrence-seeking tendency often to be found in cohesive political elites, which can become a pathology when critical or uncomfortable ideas are screened out. See Irving Janis, *Groupthink: Psychological Studies of Foreign Policy Decisions and Fiascoes* (Boston, MA: Houghton Mifflin, 1982).

[10] For the general context of these developments see Christopher Hill, 'Renationalizing or regrouping? EU foreign policy since 11 September 2001', *Journal of Common Market Studies* 42/1 (2004): 143–63.

agreement among Western governments (and probably their publics too) that Al-Qaeda should be pursued wherever they sought refuge, and if they could not be brought to justice, then they should be extirpated. This was the real meaning of the term 'war'. There was less agreement on the means which should be used in this hot pursuit. The expressed wish of the US President that Osama Bin Laden should be taken 'dead or alive', and the green light given to US special forces to engage in assassination, awoke in the *sioxante-huitard* generation which dominates the current European political class uneasy memories of the worst years of the Cold War. They could also all too easily imagine the reactions in an Islamic world already hostile to the United States over its support for Israel. When to this was added the increasing evidence of the detention without trial inside the United States of Muslim residents merely suspected of complicity with terrorists and (quite soon) the public relations disaster of the prison camp at Guantánamo Bay, unease turned to hostility.

This turn of events represented a major difficulty for Blair. As someone who had positioned himself as the rock-solid friend of an ally in mortal danger, he could not easily turn into a moral critic, or pick and choose his moments of solidarity. This dilemma was shared to a lesser extent by José-María Aznar and Silvio Berlusconi in Spain and Italy respectively, but hardly at all by Chirac and Schroeder. This left Blair exposed to criticism at home and within the EU. The same applied in relation to the 'axis of evil' designation of George Bush's State of the Union address of January 2002. It seems likely that Blair and his team, to say nothing of the regional experts in the FCO, would have blanched at this crude lumping together of the disparate problems of Iraq, Iran and North Korea. They would, it is true, have been relieved at the exclusion of Libya from the list; although the United States would later claim that victory in Iraq had frightened Colonel Gaddafi into renouncing nuclear weapons, in reality the Europeans, with Britain and Italy in the lead, had been working (with carrots and sticks over the Lockerbie trial) to bring Libya back into the fold over a number of years. Nonetheless, Blair knew that even an attack on Iraq would cause him grave political difficulties at home and abroad, and almost certainly would have been relieved if Bush had vetoed the idea (it is a simple but often over-looked truth about the whole Iraq affair, that Britain could never even have contemplated moving against Baghdad had the United States been opposed to the adventure, whatever the facts about WMD).

By the same token, the prospect of wars against Iran or North Korea in which Britain might be expected to take a leading part, must have seemed a nightmare even to the most ardent leader of the international community. Britain had been cooperating quietly but effectively for most of New Labour's term of office with its European partners precisely on a policy of constructive engagement towards both Tehran and Pyongyang. This policy could not have been said to have had dramatic results, but neither had it failed. There was still all to play for. Yet at a stroke President Bush had both rendered the strategy almost nugatory and had put his British friend in the most difficult of positions. Events in Iraq were to complicate matters for both leaders in this respect, and it is noteworthy that Blair eventually allowed Jack Straw to take part in the visit of the 'big three' Europeans to Tehran (together with his French and German counterparts) in the hope of heading off a repeat of the Iraq crisis. The European viewpoint on Iran and North Korea may even have won some adherents in Washington, which was an indication of how Iraq had not at all gone according to plan. Blair himself was clearly desperate to avoid being placed in the same position again, and for once sought refuge in a common European line.

Afghanistan: the habit of victory

Once it was clear that Al-Qaeda had been responsible for 9/11, it was inevitable that the United States would attack their bases in Afghanistan and seek to overturn the Taliban regime which was hosting them. Most British opinion accepted that 9/11 was an act of war which would require the defeat of the enemy, to the extent that it could be traced. The Prime Minister was therefore able to commit the country to the campaign which began on 7 October without great controversy, riding out the protests of those who feared it would lead to a humanitarian disaster for the people of Afghanistan. This was helped by the fact that it took only until 13 November for the Taliban regime to collapse and the invading armies to enter Kabul. The two strategic aims of the campaign had thus been achieved: to force Al-Qaeda from their secure bases in a protective sovereign state, and to remove the regime which had been complicit in their acts of aggression. A third aim, high ranking if not strategic, had been to kill or capture Osama Bin Laden, but in this the Americans failed, in part because they would not allow the special forces of their British ally to participate in the critical operation at Tora Bora. This was typical of the way in which Britain, and other European allies, had been used to provide legitimacy to the operation but had not been allowed to influence its course overmuch. In the post-victory phase it really seemed as if, in the common phrase, the Europeans were left with the washing-up after dinner. Washington was barely interested in the reconstruction of Afghanistan, and graciously permitted an expansion of British troop numbers and the creation of a multinational International Security Assistance Force (ISAF), led by Britain for its first few months.

Tony Blair could nonetheless feel relieved and vindicated by the result of this latest Afghan war. Coming after Kosovo and Sierra Leone it confirmed him in his belief in the principle of intervention to overthrow tyrannies which threatened international peace as well as their own peoples, and in the soundness of his judgement on when to apply that principle. As he was not the only one to draw these conclusions, Blair's reputation was riding high at the end of 2001, and he could not resist the chance to be the first foreign leader to visit liberated Afghanistan on 7 January 2002, even (extraordinary as it now seems, given the risks) taking his wife along for the ride.

There was, however, one set of difficulties which was to prove a harbinger of even greater problems in the future. Blair's confident assumption of leadership among the European allies was increasingly leading to divisions within the EU. As yet, this did not involve spats with France and Germany, as Britain sought to operate on the basis of the long-feared (by the majority) *directoire* of the big three member states. It spilled over into public rows because Blair, Chirac and Schroeder caucused together blatantly before the Ghent summit hosted by Belgium on 20 October, and planned to repeat the exercise in London on 4 November. This time Blair's bluff was called, and he was forced to extend last-minute invitations to High Representative Javier Solana and the prime ministers of Italy, Spain and the Netherlands, as well as the Belgian presidency. Even Blair's affability must have been tested by the atmosphere at table.[11] It was a demonstration that it was not so easy to play the game both ways: that is, relying on European solidarity in times of crisis, but ignoring the EU's procedures when they prove inconvenient. Blair should also have learned the lesson that his own instinctive support for US foreign policy was by no means the rule elsewhere in the EU, even in the exceptional set of circumstances obtaining after 9/11. That he did not was in part the result of others making the opposite mistake. Blair was quick to see – sometimes with justice – other European leaders as simply not grasping the bigger picture of international politics. When, for example, the Belgian Foreign Minister Louis Michel naïvely tried to claim the ISAF as

---

[11] Silvio Berlusconi only managed to get his invitation in time for dessert. Filippo Andreatta and Elisabetta Brighi, 'La politica estera del governo Berlusconi: I primi 18 mesi', in *Politica in Italia: I fatti dell'anno e le interpretazioni*, Edizione 2003 (Bologna: il Mulino).

the first EU military force, he was slapped down at once by both Britain and Germany. While committed to the view that all states had to adapt to globalisation, the British Prime Minister did not agree that this meant the end of national foreign policy. He had every intention of asserting Britain's national foreign policy interests and of using them as a platform for his own statesmanship.[12]

Iraq: the defining event

Despite the evident successes – at least in his own terms – of most of his foreign policy judgements up to spring 2002, it was the sequence of events from that point on, all of them tied to the eventual Anglo-American attack on Iraq of March 2003, which has come to shape Tony Blair's reputation in the eyes of the British people, and quite possibly of history. Buoyed up by a sense of mission, Blair proceeded to make one bet after another on the behaviour of other key actors outside his immediate control, which in going wrong rapidly ran down his political capital. It is to these key judgements that we now turn. The events of the build-up to the war, its sequence and aftermath are by now well known, having already been pored over by a wave of journalistic and academic accounts. The aim here is to stand back a little from the detail, so as to evaluate the contribution and responsibility of the Prime Minister for taking his country to war in the most controversial military adventure since Suez.

Counterfactual propositions are inevitable and useful in the writing of history, if also inherently problematic. Looked at from the perspective of mid-2005, it is difficult to imagine, had Blair been personally opposed to the Iraq adventure, that any of his Cabinet colleagues or his senior advisers would have urged such a course of action upon him. Indeed, Blair himself would hardly have pressed for regime change in Iraq in the absence of US enthusiasm.

That said, the Prime Minister's willingness to support the United States' turn towards Iraq after the end of the Afghan war was consistent with both his policy of unconditional support for the United States on matters of declared vital interest, and his history of antagonism towards Saddam

---

[12] It is of interest that although Blair has always talked the language of multilateralism, his practice, like that of the United States, has been to exploit multilateral fora for unilateral purposes. In this he is hardly alone in the EU, but the style is at odds with that advocated by senior colleagues like Robin Cook, Clare Short – and Peter Hain, in his pamphlet *The End of Foreign Policy? British Interests, Global Linkages and Natural Limits* (London: Fabian Society, Green Alliance and the Royal Institute of International Affairs, 2001).

Hussein from the start of the New Labour period in office (perhaps even beforehand). Blair certainly saw Saddam as a danger to world peace in 1998, when he agreed with alacrity to Operation Desert Fox, whose aim was to damage Saddam Hussein's ability to make and to use weapons of mass destruction, and to demonstrate to him the consequences of violating international obligations. This involved heavy air strikes in southern Iraq from 16 to 20 December 1998, following up the intermittent sorties throughout the 1990s which had maintained the no-fly zone imposed after the end of the first Gulf War. As early as February 1998 Blair had said, while visiting the White House,

> We want a diplomatic solution to this crisis [sic]. But the success or failure of the diplomacy rests on Saddam. If he fails to respond, then he knows that the threat of force is there, and it is real.[13]

The word 'crisis' is highlighted because it is important to note how at this early stage Blair saw Saddam as a front-line problem (as did the Clinton administration) and was envisaging the use of force against him, if only to degrade Iraq's military capability. Yet by the time of Desert Fox 10 months later the generalised crisis had become a specific threat: 'Whatever the risks we face today, they are as nothing compared to the risks if we do not halt Saddam Hussein's programme of developing chemical and biological weapons of mass destruction.'[14] In the same speech Blair had addressed the question of possible regime change:

> Is it a specific objective to remove Saddam Hussein? The answer is: it cannot be. No one would be better pleased if his evil regime disappeared as a direct or indirect result of our action, but our military objectives are precisely those that we have set out. Even if there were legal authority to do so, removing Saddam through military action would require the insertion of ground troops on a massive scale – hundreds of thousands, as the British Chief of the Defence Staff, Sir Charles Guthrie, made clear this morning. Even then, there would be no guarantee of success. I cannot make that commitment responsibly.[15]

[13] Speech by the Prime Minister at his arrival ceremony at the White House, 5 February 1998, cited in David Coates and Joel Krieger (with Rhiannnon Vickers), *Blair's War* (Cambridge: Polity Press, 2004) p. 14.

[14] Prime Minister's statement in the House of Commons concerning Iraq, 17 December 1998. Hansard, House of Commons Debates Session 1998–9 (hereafter HCD 1998–9), vol. 322, column 1102.

[15] Prime Minister's statement in the House of Commons concerning Iraq, 17 December 1998, HCD 1998–9, Col. 1101. His view on the risks of an invasion was widely shared by those few even contemplating the issue at the time. According to one Israeli analyst such an action 'would involve considerable number of casualties, have the potential for

This statement is of great interest in the light of subsequent events. Tony Blair evidently changed his mind about a range of things: the balance of risks, the legal authority for regime change, military feasibility and responsible leadership.

There is no doubt that Blair was genuine in his abhorrence of Saddam's regime from a human rights viewpoint. Equally, in the first part of his period in office he saw clearly that this was not a sufficient reason for launching a military invasion of Iraq. With the passage of time, whether through the run of events, US pressure or the evolution of his own views about international relations (Kosovo and the Chicago speech came only five months after the statement to the Commons cited above), he came to blur the humanitarian argument into that which represented Saddam as a threat to the general peace. This yoking together of internal and external concerns is characteristic of interventionists, given the difficulties caused them by Article 2.7 of the UN Charter, prohibiting intervention in the internal affairs of other states. It was true for Eden over Nasser, Kennedy over Castro and Brezhnev over Dubcek.

If one of the main counterfactuals in this story is fairly clear – the Prime Minister would not have envisaged an invasion of Iraq if the United States had not put the issue on the agenda – another is less easy to read. What position would Britain have taken had Blair's plane been shot down on the approach to Bagram airbase in January 2002, with someone else (presumably Gordon Brown) then ensconced in Number 10? Brown might well have been more sceptical of the case, and less keen to curry favour in Washington.[16] He would also probably have dispensed with the services of Alastair Campbell. Still, any British prime minister would have come under great pressure from the United States, and would have been faced with the misinterpretation of intelligence which we now know took place among the professionals (i.e. not just the politicians and spin doctors) on both sides of the Atlantic. Lord Hutton reported that the infamous dossier of 24 September 2002 was issued by the Government 'with the full approval of the JIC [Joint Intelligence Committee]'.[17] It is true that the

Vietnam-like complications, and risk causing Iraq's dismemberment into a number of entities, consequently strengthening Iran. The political price of all that would be heavy.' Shlomo Brom, 'Operation Desert Fox: results and ramifications', *Strategic Assessment* (Jaffee Center for Strategic Studies, Tel Aviv University), vol. 2/1 (June 1999): 2.

[16] Although Brown made 'a long passionate statement of support for Tony's strategy' at Robin Cook's last Cabinet, on 13 March 2003. Robin Cook, *The Point of Departure* (London: Simon & Schuster, 2003), pp. 320–1.

[17] Lord Hutton, *Report of the Inquiry into the Circumstances Surrounding the Death of David Kelly, C.M.G.*, HC247 (London: The Stationery Office, 28 January 2004) (hereafter Hutton Report), para. 467.

Butler Report subsequently felt that the JIC had been unduly influenced by the Blair team – 'We see a strong case for the post of Chairman of the JIC being held by someone with experience of dealing with Ministers in a very senior role, and who is demonstrably beyond influence, and thus probably in his last post'[18] – but it remains the case that the intelligence provided went in one direction only, towards the conclusion that Saddam was amassing WMD. The whole elite was guilty of tracked thinking and 'groupthink' in this respect, and the dissenters, like Brian Jones or David Kelly in the Ministry of Defence, did not get further than thinking the conclusion drawn was too firm, and had been 'sexed up'.[19]

No one seems to have believed – or had the courage to say – that the conclusion was wrong, and/or that even if it were correct, deterrence was the best way of handling an Iraqi threat. Because the Prime Minister was so committed to (a) combating Saddam Hussein, and (b) supporting the United States, there was an evident tendency, if not to feed him what he wanted to hear, at the least to filter out what he did not want to hear. Given then the impossibility (because of its lack of basis in international law) of mounting a case for invasion on the humanitarian grounds which Blair instinctively accepted, the WMD bandwagon gathered pace and became irreversible. Because of its inherent weaknesses this case then foundered on the by now well-known difficulties, rebounding on the credibility of both the case for war and the reputation of Blair.

The tendency towards tracked thinking was thus personal (Blair), psychological (the need of all involved to avoid the dissonance of holding a policy preference – an attack on a sovereign state – which could not be legally justified) and political (pressure from Washington). It was compounded by the failure of the highest levels of the intelligence services to insist on a scrupulous independence from political motivations. But it was also made possible by the failure of British democracy. Both Parliament and the Cabinet – that is, the two institutions with the formal power

---

[18] *Review of Intelligence on Weapons of Mass Destruction*, Report of a Committee of Privy Counsellors, chaired by Lord Butler of Brockwell (hereafter Butler Report) (London: The Stationery Office, 14 July 2004), p. 159.

[19] Concepts like 'tracked thinking' (i.e. the difficulty of getting off a single-track thought once established) or 'groupthink' (see footnote 9) are familiar in Foreign Policy Analysis. See John D. Steinbruner, *The Cybernetic Theory of Decision* (Princeton: Princeton University Press, 1974), and Janis, *Groupthink*. Groupthink finally made it into public discourse in both the British and the American investigations into intelligence failures over Iraq. See the Butler Report, pp. 16, 110 and 145, and Select Committee on Intelligence, *Report on the U.S. Intelligence Community's Pre-war Intelligence Assessments on Iraq*, (Washington DC: U.S. Senate, 7 July 2004).

and responsibility to act in the public interest – failed to hold the Prime Minister to account. Tony Blair can be criticised for poor judgement, for vanity and for weakness in the face of US pressure, but he cannot fairly be damned for doing what he plainly believed was right, in the absence of sufficiently powerful countervailing voices.

It is not as if there was not enough time given for a proper understanding of the issues to be achieved. When a crisis appears out of nowhere, the foreign policy executive – that is, the prime minister, foreign secretary and a few other confidants – have an enormous advantage in setting the agenda and driving through decisions.[20] But when there is a slower build-up to action, and/or the problem becomes more structured and legalised, it is possible for even those without specific responsibilities to become better informed, and to press for alternative approaches.[21] In the Iraq case there was an almost unparalleled agonising over what might and should happen, from spring 2002 until the attack on Iraq of 20 March 2003. The Americans seemed insouciant about depriving themselves of the tactical advantage of surprise, and the British had to follow their timetable. This had the effect of allowing even mass opinion, which is almost always many steps behind a government in matters of foreign policy, to rally its forces (literally, in the case of the huge anti-war demonstrations of 15 February 2003).

The UK Parliament, despite the time available in which to mobilise, and its advantages of expertise (especially in the Lords), information (the librarians are a formidable resource for MPs) and formal opportunities for scrutiny, did not distinguish itself until it was too late, when a formal vote of confidence on the war (itself a rare event) produced a large but not quite sufficient rebellion of Labour back-benchers. The government's majority, at 164, was too large to overturn given the enormous pressures exerted by the whips. But in the year before, MPs had failed to exert enough pressure on the government to give a decisive helping hand to the doubters in Cabinet. The Foreign Affairs Committee (FAC) might have hit the headlines through its interrogation of the unhappy Dr Kelly, but this became a distraction from the central issue of whether Iraq was a serious threat to British security. The committee is itself too subject

---

[20] See Christopher Hill, *Cabinet Decisions in Foreign Policy: the British Experience October 1938–June 1941* (Cambridge: Cambridge University Press, 1991), especially pp. 224–47 on the nature of the foreign policy executive, and pp. 18–47 on the making of the Polish guarantee, 15–31 March 1939.

[21] Ibid. See chapters 3 and 7, on the decisions to go for an alliance with the Soviet Union in 1939, and to outline war aims in 1940–1.

to party discipline to be truly independent, and its chairman, Donald Anderson, tended to be more often an extra wheel for British diplomacy than a focal point for scrutiny, as, for example, Senator Fulbright had been in the United States during the Vietnam war.[22] Neither the FAC nor the whole House exposed the absurdity of the '45 minutes' claim, when any half-informed observer knew that it must refer at best to battlefield munitions, and that the press was colluding its own manipulation by publicising the 'threat' so uncritically. Nor were the serious issues of the wider impact of the war on international relations, and planning for the post-bellum, given the kind of scrutiny which might have embarrassed the government.[23]

The Cabinet was the key site where debate and forensic analysis might have restrained the Prime Minister. But its position, even in these favourable circumstances for participation (that is, a long-drawn out period of gestation, with ample opportunities to seek information and to debate options) had been structurally weakened by five years of confident prime ministerial leadership. As we have seen, Blair had replaced Robin Cook as foreign secretary with a more pliable figure in 2001. He had also weakened the key post of Cabinet Secretary by hiving off intelligence matters to a special 'security and intelligence coordinator', who does not, however, attend Cabinet. Furthermore, two key posts in the Cabinet Secretariat, those of the head of the Defence and Overseas Secretariat and head of the European Affairs Secretariat were combined with those of the Prime Minister's personal advisers on foreign affairs and European affairs respectively.[24] The net effect was that the Cabinet Secretary, who traditionally has serviced the Cabinet as a whole and not just the prime

---

[22] This is despite the fact that Blair had apparently wanted Anderson's removal as chair, after the 2001 election, only to relent under protest. This gave Anderson the reputation of being a troublemaker, which was helpful both to him and to HMG, even if the record does not bear it out. John Kampfner judges the FAC's investigation of 2002, in which Anderson used his casting vote to exonerate Alastair Campbell on the charge of having tried to exert 'improper influence on the drafting of the September dossier', as 'Haphazard, incomplete and at times unprofessional'. Kampfner, *Blair's Wars*, p. 344.

[23] The ease with which the parliamentary committees were manipulated and side-stepped is exposed in withering fashion by Alex Danchev in his 'Story development; or, Walter Mitty the Undefeated', in Alex Danchev and John MacMillan (eds.), *The Iraq War and Democratic Politics* (London: Routledge, 2005), pp. 238–59. See also Peter Hennessy, who notes the difficulties experienced even by the privileged (and restricted) Intelligence and Security Committee (of both Houses), in his 'The lightning flash on the road to Baghdad: issues of evidence', in W. G. Runciman (ed.), *Hutton and Butler: Lifting the Lid on the Workings of Power* (Oxford: Oxford University Press for the British Academy, 2004), pp. 71–2.

[24] Butler Report, p. 147.

minister, was unable to carry out effectively the functions of ensuring that proper papers were written for Cabinet and its committees (the Defence and Overseas Policy sub-committee did not meet during this long crisis[25]), that full minutes were kept, and that informal inner groups did not have an unfair advantage. As W. G. Runciman has argued,

> It must therefore be possible, and may even be likely, that a Cabinet Secretary with the support and authority that Cabinet Secretaries used to enjoy would . . . have been able to see to it that the Cabinet was more fully and impartially briefed than this Cabinet was . . . the decision to go to war was taken without the extent of informed discussion in Cabinet that would have been normal in the past.[26]

Unfortunately the Cabinet in the past has not always had the 'informed discussion' on foreign policy that would have been desirable.[27] But in this case the opportunities which had been created by virtue of prolonged public debate, were negated by the prime ministerial preference for informal, small group decision-making, dignified with the label of a 'War Cabinet', a practice in which Blair, as so often, followed the presidential tone set by Margaret Thatcher. Britain's leading authority on the processes of central government, Peter Hennessy, has highlighted the critical sections of the Butler Report to show how the Prime Minister's use of 'unscripted' oral presentations meant that even the many discussions of Iraq in Cabinet never produced serious debate:

> Excellent quality papers were written by officials, but these were not discussed in Cabinet or in Cabinet Committee. Without papers circulated in advance, it remains possible but is obviously much more difficult for members of the Cabinet outside the small circle directly involved to bring their political judgement and experience to bear on the major decisions for which the Cabinet as a whole must bear responsibility. The absence of papers on the Cabinet agenda . . . plainly reduced their ability to prepare properly for such discussions.[28]

Yet these other ministers must bear their own share of responsibility for allowing themselves to be carried along in the flow so uncritically. They were, after all, for the most part experienced and hard-nosed. It is difficult

---

[25] Ibid.

[26] W. G. Runciman, 'What we know now', in Runciman, *Hutton and Butler*, p. 11.

[27] Hill, *Cabinet Decisions on Foreign Policy;* and James Barber, *The Prime Minister since 1945* (Oxford: Blackwell, 1991), pp. 110–21.

[28] Butler Report, pp. 147–8. Hennessy, 'The lightning flash', pp. 73–4.

to know why a momentum of concern did not build up. In the absence of publicly available minutes (and if they are not detailed we may not know even after the passing of 30 years) we have to rely on the inherently self-serving memoirs of individual ministers, and leaked information. It seems clear that Robin Cook and Clare Short kept up a barrage of concerned enquiry throughout the period, informed by their experience at the FCO and DfID respectively. Cook, through resignation, gave the Cabinet the opportunity to overturn the dominant policy line, but was let down by Short at the critical moment.[29] Jack Straw tried to finesse an increasingly threatening situation by insisting on the need for a second UN resolution, but Brown's support for Blair (or silence) was a crucial factor in hobbling the emergence of any rebellious tendency in Cabinet. Other senior ministers, such as Prescott, Blunkett and Reid, were too close to Blair to have defected – although that very fact gave them the potential to stop the Prime Minister in his tracks with a considered statement of opposition.

The Cabinet must therefore take full collective responsibility for the evident failures of the Iraq policy. Tony Blair was straightforward as to his ends (if not his means), so that to an insider the coming of the 'war by timetable' was clear enough from early autumn 2002.[30] Parliament made a dramatic last stand, having been given, remarkably, the chance to pronounce on the war before it started (did Blair, 'sub-consciously', to use Lord Hutton's term, hope that the Commons might get him off the hook on which he had impaled himself?). But it had been hobbled during the policy-making phase and had made a hash of the few opportunities presented to it. The Cabinet, in contrast, had had plenty of discussions of the coming war, and ministers could have pressed for proper position papers and servicing of their debates. A groundswell of opposition to the policy could have built up, as it did in the country at large, had there been the will to confront the political, moral and personal difficulties. But the existence of a hard core of senior Blair loyalists in the Cabinet reinforced the natural tendency towards groupthink, with its comfort-zone in which

---

[29] It is revealing that in his published diary Cook makes no mention of Short's decision to stay in the Cabinet despite having announced a week previously that she would resign, calling Tony Blair 'reckless' five times in an interview she herself had requested. Cook, *The Point of Departure*, pp. 316–25; Peter Stothard, *30 Days: A Month at the Heart of Blair's War* (London: HarperCollins, 2003), p. 6 (entry for 10 March 2003).

[30] The Conservative politician John Gummer pointed this out in February 2003. Cited by Dan Keohane, 'The United Kingdom', in Alex Danchev and John MacMillan (eds.), *The Iraq War and Democratic Politics* (London: Routledge, 2005), p. 68.

painful conflicts are suppressed. Truth was not spoken often enough to power.

The Iraq war is one of those events, like Suez, which will remain for decades, if not centuries, as a central myth in British politics. As such, it will always be subject to the sway of competing values and ideological positions. This observer's view is that it has produced at least six notable reference points for future foreign policy-making.

The first continues the theme of Cabinet government discussed above. Although Clare Short eventually resigned two months after Cook, no one was in any doubt that it was over the wisdom and legality of the war. That meant that for the first time since Burns and Morley had left the Liberal government in August 1914, two Cabinet ministers had resigned over a matter of foreign policy.[31] This was a sign of the seriousness of the issue, and of the discontents which it had engendered in the governing party, but also a harbinger of continued political difficulties. And so it has proved. Tony Blair was re-elected in May 2005, but with a much reduced majority. It is generally agreed that it was his personal unpopularity which reduced the Labour margin to 66 (and thus at last gave the Conservatives a whiff of victory at the next election). This in turn was the direct result of concerns about the war and the associated loss of trust in the Prime Minister. Blair seemed temporarily chastened and promised to spend more time on 'listening', in particular on domestic issues. Yet he was soon turning outwards again, preoccupied by multilateral diplomacy in the EU and G-8. On Iraq, indeed, Blair has seemed to feel confirmed in his views by both Cabinet dissent and public antagonism. Perhaps stung by earlier criticisms of him as being led by focus groups, Blair has fallen back on a combination of moralism and the self-image of a statesman who will be vindicated by history.

The second issue with long-term resonance is the best known, thanks to Andrew Gilligan, Alastair Campbell and David Kelly – the politicisation of intelligence. It would be naïve to suppose that intelligence has been free in the past of the tendency to give politicians what they want to hear, but in this case something went badly wrong, as the subsequent official inquiries in Britain, the United States and Australia amply testify. The Prime Minister 'fully accepted Lord Butler's conclusions' and announced various measures to rectify the problems relating to the uses of intelligence. This included accepting that his 'informal group', of 'the key players

---

[31] 'Ministerial resignations (1903–1998)', in David Butler and Gareth Butler, *British Political Facts 1900–2000*, 8th edn (Houndmills: Macmillan, 2000), pp. 74–6.

required to work on operational and military planning and developing the diplomatic strategy', should henceforth 'operate formally as an ad hoc Cabinet Committee'. The careful choice of the term 'ad hoc' somewhat diminished the force of this promise, just as that to fill the vacant post of the chairman of the JIC 'fully in accordance with Lord Butler's criteria' was undermined by the appointment in May 2004 of John Scarlett to be the new head of MI6, despite Butler's clear implication that Scarlett had not been 'demonstrably beyond influence'.[32] Moreover the 'interim' replacement as chairman of the JIC, William Ehrman, was still in place a year later, and was not 'in his last post' as Butler had also recommended.

The third notable strand of the Iraq war is that of civil–military relations. Tony Blair has always praised the professionalism of the British armed services, and has indeed relied on them as the major instrument of British foreign policy during his period in office. On the face of it this is not new; British forces were in engaged in action somewhere in the world in most years between 1815 and 1965, and there were few pauses in the period 1965–97, despite Britain's withdrawal from east of Suez.[33] Nonetheless, Blair engaged his forces in five high-profile and dangerous conflicts in six years: Operation Desert Fox in Iraq, intervention in Kosovo in 1999 and then in Sierra Leone in 2000, followed by the wars of regime change in Afghanistan and Iraq, in 2001 and 2003 respectively. Whatever one's views on the merits of these decisions, there is no doubt that they have both shown up the quality of Britain's military systems and stretched them to the limit. It is as well that the conflict in Northern Ireland has not blown up again, or overstretch would have become more than a rhetorical ploy of the Conservative Opposition. Before the outbreak of hostilities in Iraq, the Chairman of the Defence Staff (CDS), Admiral Sir Michael Boyce, asked the Prime Minister for a commitment that the war was legal – and duly received it.[34] This was an unparalleled signal from the armed services of their concern about getting involved in a possible quagmire. They wished it to be clear where responsibility for the decision lay, so that it could not subsequently be said that gung-ho military attitudes were to blame. Even after the successful onset of the campaign, political enthusiasm ran well ahead of that of the soldiers: 'there have already been a few words [in 10 Downing Street] about how, when it is all over, Britain will celebrate

---

[32] HCD, 20 July 2004, Col. 195; Butler Report, p. 159.
[33] J. D. Singer and M. Small, *The Wages of War 1816–1965: A Statistical Handbook* (New York: John Wiley, 1972), for instance pp. 59–70 and 258–87.
[34] Seldon, *Blair*, p. 596.

victory. Sir Michael Boyce does not seem to think there will ever be much to march down the street about.'[35]

The relationship with the United States might be thought to have been one of the successes of the Blair period. After all, he had been willing to sacrifice the support of many other parties, at home and abroad, in order to sustain it. Indeed, the result of the Prime Minister's success, as advised by Bill Clinton, in being as firm friends with his Republican successor, has been that the United Kingdom is still regarded throughout the United States as both a loyal ally and a major player in world politics. No doubt if the UK's vital interests were seriously threatened, the United States would still provide decisive help, as they did (in the end) in 1982 over the Falklands. But whether Blair's policy provides leverage in less dramatic circumstances has to be open to doubt. Even during the Iraq crisis Washington was often only half-committed to the UN path advocated (and increasingly required for domestic reasons) by its friends in London. The neo-conservatives barely bothered to conceal their view that Britain was a desirable but not essential ally in the big battles they were ready to take on.

Given this context, why did Blair go along with the 'war by timetable', in which he was bound to seem increasingly manipulated? The answer lies partly in the diplomatically inept commitment made early in 2002 to stand beside the United States in the event of a war to change the regime in Iraq. Whatever Blair's subsequent struggles to moderate the US position, to go by the UN route, or to 'twin-track' the Iraqi commitment to the promotion of the Middle East peace process, if President Bush had the impression from spring 2002 that Blair would ultimately decide to join him in a war, then the Prime Minister's freedom of manoeuvre was lost. This is still a controversial issue, and will probably remain so, but there is as yet no evidence to suggest that Blair told Bush at any point that he had reservations over the possibility of going to war. Indeed, a secret high-level meeting with the 'informal group' concluded on 23 July 2002 that 'we should work on the assumption that the UK would take part in any military action' – although there were still options within that commitment, stretching from making available special forces plus the bases in Cyprus and Diego Garcia to the land contribution of 40,000 men on which the Prime Minister eventually settled.[36] One of Blair's senior

---

[35] Stothard, *30 Days*, p. 231 (entry for 9 April 2003).

[36] 'Secret Downing Street Memo, from Matthew Rycroft (private secretary to the PM) to David Manning (PM's foreign policy adviser), 23 July 2002. Secret and strictly personal – UK eyes only . . .[n]o further copies should be made'. The memo was leaked (by whom is

colleagues said in January 2003 that 'if Tony had gone off and done a Schroeder . . . we would have had no influence', but it is clear that the choice was less stark than this.[37] Moreover, if the Prime Minister had kept the United States guessing, he would ultimately have had more freedom to decide at least Britain's own position on the basis of unfolding events.

The other reason for Blair having gone along with the US lead was that he and his colleagues (and here the FCO was involved just as much as Number 10) were committed to what might be called transgovernmental bureaucratic politics.[38] In plain language this means parts of the bureaucracy in one country entering into the politics of competition in the bureaucracy of another, usually an ally. Here it involved the British desperately trying to shore up Colin Powell and the State Department, but perhaps also parts of the US intelligence establishment, against the certainties of the neo-conservative view of the world.[39] For their part, Powell and his colleagues were glad to have the articulate support of Blair and his expert officials, and reciprocated as much as possible – in particular in delivering the President's decision to go for what turned out to be Resolution 1441 at the UN in September 2002. Yet the more Blair and his officials got involved in trying to rein in Dick Cheney and Donald Rumsfeld, and to win the war of the President's ear, the more they both alienated these heavyweight figures and got sucked into the fast-moving US policy process, in which Powell knew that if he lost he would still have to go along with the war. The same increasingly became true for Blair. As one shrewd observer has put it, Blair and Powell 'were bonded, exploited and tarnished together . . . every time Blair made a slight gain he reinforced his delusion of influence. Both overvalued their leverage'.[40]

A fifth significant dimension of the Iraq affair for British foreign policy is that of relations with the other member states of the European Union. The EU's foreign policy is in any case a delicate and slowly growing plant,

---

an interesting question) and printed in the *Sunday Times*, 1 May 2005. The meeting was attended by the Prime Minister, Foreign Secretary, Defence Secretary, Attorney General, Sir Richard Wilson (Cabinet Secretary), John Scarlett (chairman, JIC), Francis Richards (director, GCHQ), Sir Michael Boyce (CDS), Richard Dearlove (head, MI6), Jonathan Powell, Sally Morgan and Alistair Campbell (PM's advisers).

[37] *Guardian*, 15 January 2003, cited in Coates and Krieger, *Blair's War*, p. 52.
[38] A phenomenon first observed by Richard Neustadt in his *Alliance Politics* (New York: Columbia University Press, 1970).
[39] See Stefan Halper and Jonathan Clarke, *America Alone: The Neo-Conservatives and the Global Order* (Cambridge: Cambridge University Press, 2004), pp. 214–15, for one example of cross-cutting sympathies.
[40] Sidney Blumenthal, 'The veneer of fraternity', *Guardian*, 12 May 2005.

but here it was brutally ripped from its seedbed. Blair seems quite early to have realised that he would not be able to achieve European solidarity behind his own preferred position, and accepted the consequences, despite his avowed wish to put Britain back at the centre of Europe and to promote the Common Defence Policy he had himself initiated at St-Malo in December 1998.[41] The United States would evidently have preferred Franco-German support, but was unlikely to worry unduly over the failure of the Common Foreign and Security Policy. Tony Blair, however, should by his own stated principles have been much more concerned over the collateral damage from his Iraqi policy than he has shown himself to be in public. Indeed, the furious determination to make France the scapegoat for the failure to get a second UN resolution revealed his main priorities. Perhaps he had confidence in both his own persuasive powers and an historical process of convergence between the European states, to the extent that rifts within the EU seemed manageable. And this judgement may in time prove correct. At the time of writing, with damaging EU splits over the British rebate, and the stalled constitutional treaty, it looks a shade optimistic.

In perspective

Tony Blair still has time to run as prime minister, although this may only be a matter of a year or two. But much more time will elapse before it will be possible to put the Iraq war into perspective, and even then the arguments will not cease. We are still debating the origins of the English civil war, to say nothing of the Cold War. On the other hand, important events in modern British foreign policy, such as Suez and the Falklands, can now be understood with the benefit of a consensus on their major parameters. Much depends on how far the 'facts' can be established, especially in relation to the outcomes. When a result is clear-cut, as with the defeat of Nazism, consequentialism rules, as it is difficult to imagine a more desirable course of events. With Iraq we are still far from that point, if it ever arrives.

In consequence, Tony Blair will continue to be a controversial figure for the foreseeable future, largely because of his foreign policy. If he had been free of difficulties overseas the election of 2005 would probably have been another coronation. The aftermath of the defeat of Saddam

---

[41] For useful context, see John Vogler, 'The European dimension', in Danchev and MacMillan, *The Iraq War and Democratic Politics*, pp. 77–95.

Hussein, however, turned out to be as difficult as its prologue. The lack of American planning for the post-bellum (as revealed in the 'secret Downing Street memo') meant that it proved even more difficult to pacify the country than had been foreseen by the war's opponents.[42] Britain has suffered relatively few losses compared with the United States (let alone the Iraqis, for whom figures are not released), but that has not prevented some searing criticisms of Blair for wasting British lives without good cause.[43] Furthermore there is no immediate prospect of being able to extract his troops with honour – that is, with the confidence that the original objective of a pacified and democratic Iraq has been achieved. Nearer to home, Britain was, until 7 July 2005, mercifully free of the kind of outrage to which the United States, Indonesia, Turkey and Spain have been subjected, but this was no thanks to the Iraq policy, which has led to a closer association with the United States in the eyes of that country's many implacable enemies. One of Tony Blair's qualities is that he has little taste for triumphalism. There is certainly little cause for it over Iraq.

It is also important to remember that British foreign policy over the last four years has had other concerns beyond Iraq, which has both over-shadowed and distracted from them. The Middle East peace process is the most prominent casualty. Tony Blair almost certainly argued hard in private with the Bush administration that progress on the Palestinian question was indispensable if the Islamic world were not to be alienated by regime change in Iraq. But this did not counter the opposite line being taken by the US's other ally, Israel, at least before George W. Bush had secured his second term in November 2004. Blair never felt able to play the card of serious public disagreement with Washington, not least because he was locked into so much private cooperation on Iraq. In retrospect probably nothing would have changed the US line on Palestine while Arafat lived and until it was clear that Iraq had become a running sore, but Blair's approach prevented the European Union from deploying its diplomatic and economic resources more pro-actively in the region, not least by allowing other member states to hide behind the excuse of British unilateralism.

---

[42] 'The Secret Downing Street Memo', 23 July 2002. In it Richard Dearlove, then head of MI6, is quoted as reporting that 'there was little discussion in Washington of the aftermath after military action'.

[43] The most effective came from Reg Keys, whose loss of a son led him to stand against the prime minister in his Sedgefield constituency at the general election. Blair was caught by the television cameras standing impassively behind Keys during the latter's poignant speech.

There was a similar story on other key elements of external relations. It is only recently that the Prime Minister has come to focus on the issues of climate change, African debt relief (spurred on by Gordon Brown) and the reform of international institutions. Even the continuing tragedies of Zimbabwe, Burma and Darfur have been left to the experts, with little political impetus put behind them. This is partly because of sheer preoccupation with the 'war on terror' and with Iraq, and partly because of the inhibitions on falling out with George W. Bush, who has been immovable on the kind of multilateral cooperation which most Europeans (including Blair) advocate. It may be that there will be a happy ending, with Blair staying for a full third term, and reaching that plinth of admired statesmanship which seems so important to him. But international affairs have a habit of throwing up nasty surprises, and the more involved the leader the greater the potential for disaster. Prime Minister Blair has already taken great risks on many fronts by his determination to act on and see through the Iraqi challenge. It would be a terrible irony if the man who managed to help find a way to peace in Northern Ireland proves to have helped generate another intractable conflict, but one with much wider ramifications.

18

The second Blair government: the verdict

ANTHONY SELDON

In the epilogue to the first *Blair Effect*, I described the Blair government of 1997–2001 as a 'foundation' and as 'a surprisingly restrained' government, and observed that 'no Labour government in history had come to power with so many initial advantages, not even the Attlee government in 1945'. Yet in many spheres the first Blair government's achievements, and especially those which bore the Prime Minister's *personal* imprint, were modest. The major successes – over the economy, welfare reform and the constitution – were primarily due to others. The epilogue concluded by saying that Number 10, as the first term was ending, had come to recognise that it would not see the groundbreaking changes and reforms Blair had foreshadowed. Instead, a new narrative emerged: the first term should be seen merely as an introduction or a prelude, in which the 'foundations' for real change were laid. The radicalism would come in the second term.

The chapter was sceptical, however, as to whether Blair would be able to achieve the great things that he promised for his second term. It observed that, where British governments in history had been radical, the progress had come early on in the life of a prime minister rather than in the middle, and still less in the twilight years. William Gladstone, Benjamin Disraeli, Stanley Baldwin, Clement Attlee, Harold Macmillan, Edward Heath and Harold Wilson thus were prime ministers who saw their best work achieved in their early years in Downing Street. Second-term governments have often proved disappointing in British politics, as they were for Macmillan after 1959, Wilson after 1966 or John Major after 1992. Thatcher in the 1980s and F. D. Roosevelt in the United States in the 1930s were rare cases of political leaders whose achievements built after their early years. It was their example that Blair would have to emulate. The epilogue concluded, however, with the words: 'The edifice may prove more difficult to erect than the foundations had been to lay. Blair has succeeded in re-modelling his party: he has yet to reform his country. The future and the ultimate verdict of history on Blair and New Labour are wide open.'[1]

The reputation of the second Blair government earned a reprieve with Labour's election victory in 2005 (albeit with a lower percentage vote than any winning party since the 1832 Reform Act). Had the majority been significantly less than the 66 achieved, or had Blair not begun the third term so promisingly, the second government might have been viewed far less favourably than currently appears.

Yet the second government has already acquired its critics. Some New Labour loyalists at the heart of government, even with a third term in the bag, are beginning to question whether opportunities were wasted and to ask whether the second-term government was insufficiently radical in the pursuit of its diversity and choice agenda in reforming public services. 'It is as if, even after our second landslide, we still didn't appreciate what a strong position we were in', said one aide.[2] In an article in *Prospect*, Geoff Mulgan went into print with his reservations about the government being insufficiently bold and willing to take on vested interests, which included 'the London media, the super rich, big businesses and the City', as well as 'the major public professions [doctors, teachers and the police]'.[3] In private, many other Number 10 figures are more damning: 'The ideas were there but there wasn't the follow-through', lamented another New Labour aide.[4] Unless the third term sees radical breakthroughs, the sense is likely to grow that major opportunities were lost in 2001–5. Blair certainly spoke the language of radical change in speeches written for him by, in particular Andrew Adonis and Simon Stevens, and he was encouraged in this thinking by other New Labour hawks in Number 10 such as Jeremy Heywood and Jonathan Powell. But did the substance match the rhetoric?

Old Labour and others on the left are, unsurprisingly, more critical of New Labour for not doing more to help traditional Labour constituencies between 2001–5, such as the low paid, public-sector workers and the vulnerable. John Gray's verdict in the *Times Higher* was that 'After coming to power making vast promises of national renewal, Blair will leave with very little to show . . . [his] time in office will go down as the fag end of

---

[1] Anthony Seldon, 'The net Blair effect: a foundation government', in Anthony Seldon (ed.), *The Blair Effect. The Blair Government 1997–2001* (London: Little, Brown, 2001), pp. 593–600.
[2] In private information.
[3] Geoff Mulgan, 'Lessons of power', *Prospect*, May 2005.   [4] Private information.

Thatcherism.'[5] John Lanchester meanwhile in the *London Review of Books* wrote, 'The party's record in government evokes a range of responses on the left – from mild gloom to clinical depression, from irritation to rage.'[6] Kenneth O. Morgan, the doyen of Labour historians, was one of many Labour academics to have become profoundly disillusioned with Blair.[7]

Conservatives, meanwhile, though they were unable to develop a convincing overall critique of Blair, argue that he failed to tackle Britain's underlying problems, including structural weaknesses within the economy, and that many of his own policies were, for all their dressing up, merely recycling the ideas put forward initially by Thatcher or Major. They do not see any consistent domestic agenda for Blair, and criticise as a chimera his assertion that New Labour married economic vitality with greater social responsibility.

If one then factors Iraq into the assessment of the second term, which is the defining issue not just of Blair's second term but of his entire premiership, the record of 2001–5 is called even more into question. Iraq highlights one of several problems with assessing Blair's place in history from the perspective of 2005.

What are these problems? First, this was transparently not government by a prime minister in the way that the governments of Disraeli, Thatcher or even Attlee were. This was a duarchy, with two principals, Blair and Gordon Brown. It promised to be the most productive relationship in British politics since that of Neville Chamberlain and Stanley Baldwin in the inter-war years, or H. H. Asquith and David Lloyd George when the former was prime minister between 1908 and 1916. As in that earlier relationship, much the more creative policy force was not the prime minister but his principal lieutenant. Many of this government's most enduring achievements, above all the management of the economy and in welfare reform, were not principally Blair's but Brown's.

Secondly, and very obviously, although the second term has come to an end, the consequences of its policies are very far from worked through. Blair indeed clung on to office, rather than quitting in 2004 as was once possible, so that he could entrench his reforms and see his decisions, over Iraq and elsewhere, vindicated. Blairites were keen to point out that the

---

[5] John Gray, 'Mimic, missionary and a master of media spin', *Times Higher*, 8 April 2005.
[6] Quote by David Aaronovitch, *Observer*, 3 April 2005.
[7] See Kenneth O. Morgan, 'New Labour in historical perspective' in Seldon (ed), *The Blair Effect*, pp. 583–9.

achievements of the Attlee government were heavily criticised at the time, as were Mrs Thatcher's governments. Only in perspective, they argue, can the true historic importance of her administrations be seen. They argue that the same will be true for the Blair governments.

The official documents are also not yet available, though those released by the Butler and Hutton inquiries were revealing about Blair's 'denocracy', his highly personal style of governing from his 'den' in Number 10. Yet it is doubtful whether the documents will tell us much that we do not already know about the main decisions of Blair's premiership, any more than the official history of the Falklands War (2005) tells us much that was not already known about Mrs Thatcher's war.[8] Of course Blair's second term will look different in 2015, and again in 2025, and one will be able to judge his record with greater perspective. But that in no sense invalidates the importance of making judgements now, in 2005. Every new age will have its own preoccupations and its own perspective. Any verdict will always reflect the predominant concerns of the age in which it is proffered. In that sense, all history is contemporary history.

Intelligent judgements about governments and individuals can only be made by looking at the framework in which they operated. One clearly could not have expected very much from the novice first Labour government of 1924, which had many fewer seats in Parliament than the Conservatives, or the government of 1929–31, which lacked an overall majority and then ran into the Depression. A better comparison for Blair's second term is the Conservative government of 1957–9, after Harold Macmillan succeeded Anthony Eden, which had a solid working majority, or Thatcher's second government, from 1983 to 1987. Both these governments achieved much, domestically and abroad.

And what quite exceptional opportunities the Blair second government enjoyed, better even than the first government, and more favourable than any government in the last 100 years.

Questions that initially bedevilled Labour in its first term, concerning its competence to run the economy and indeed the country, had been dispelled by 2001. Every single previous Labour government had run into an economic crisis after two or three years, in 1931, 1947, 1967 and 1976. The successful stewardship of the economy after 1997, and its largely crisis-free running of the country, were thus real achievements. No one again even thought to ask whether the country was safe in the hands

---

[8] Laurence Freedman, *The Official History of the Falklands Campaign*, vols. 1 and 2 (London: Routledge, 2005).

of a Labour government. Indeed, the electorate had more confidence in Labour's competence than in that of the Conservatives – a tremendous boon for Labour as it set out on its second term.

The landslide majority of 166 in 2001 (albeit it with a low turnout of 59% and marginally down on the majority of 179 in 1997) also gave Labour the ideal launching pad for a radical programme. Blair could afford largely to ignore the Parliamentary Labour Party, so numerous were his MPs, as long as they were managed well – though he needed every vote he could muster when the party, angry with him over Iraq, turned against him in late 2003 and 2004. Blair's standing in the party, which remained ambivalent in the second term as in the first, depended critically upon his electoral success. As long as he looked the figure most likely to achieve victories for the party, he was secure. His task was facilitated by the electoral system, which was heavily skewed in Labour's favour and made him far more secure than he would otherwise have been. His internal party reforms had also tightened the leadership's command over the party at all levels, while the trade unions, for all their periodic growling during 2001–5, posed the leadership few concerns.

The continued disarray within the Conservative Party after 2001 was yet another windfall for Labour. In Iain Duncan Smith, the Conservatives chose a leader who offered centrist policies but lacked the personality and the following in Parliament (only a minority of Conservative MPs voted for him) to provide any effective challenge to Blair. Michael Howard, his successor from November 2003, promised to be a much more serious force, indeed the first real threat that Blair had faced from the Tory leadership since he became Labour's leader in July 1994. Howard's star rose but then fell, and by mid-2004, with the opinion polls not moving in his favour and after his failure to inflict more harm on Blair in the mid-year local and European elections, any serious challenge to Labour was effectively over. Blair took heart, and any thoughts of standing down before the 2005 general election were to be shelved.

Howard's inept conduct of the 2005 campaign was the low point of his very disappointing leadership. If the quality of the Tory opposition had been weak under William Hague in 1997–2001, it was feeble between 2001 and 2005. It failed to land any serious punches on Blair, despite his increasing vulnerability over his conduct of the war in Iraq and his battles with his own party over tuition fees and foundation hospitals. The Conservatives' biggest failure came over their inability to devise a credible line of attack on Iraq, the most divisive foreign policy initiative pursued by any British government since Eden over Suez in 1956. A merely competent opposition party would have caused Blair far more difficulties between 2001 and 2005 than those he faced. The quality of opposition leadership was as ineffective as that of Labour's Michael Foot, from 1980 to 1983, when Mrs Thatcher was first prime minister.

A strong and stable economy was another advantage enjoyed by Labour during its second term in office. Historians will always debate the extent to which Brown himself was responsible for the success, and how far other factors, including Thatcher's economic restructuring in the 1980s and Britain's ejection from the ERM in 1992, were the vital springboards that made the economy flourish. But the fact remains that it was the economic success story which bolstered the government's position in the polls, gave those disillusioned with Labour little reason to abandon it and provided money in the coffers for the hikes in public expenditure introduced by the government during the term.

A final advantage that Blair enjoyed in 2001–5 was experience. He came to power in 1997 as one of the least knowledgeable prime ministers in modern times, never having been a junior minister, and having spent only three years as leader of the Labour Party. By 2001, he was fully blooded, had learnt much about the conduct of government and the job of prime minister at home and internationally. He made it plain to his staff that he wanted to learn from the experience of President Clinton's disappointing second term; papers were written in Downing Street on how to avoid the pitfalls of his administration. Blair knew, moreover, that this time around there could be no excuses and that he had to meet the expectations he had aroused.

Blair's team members, too, were seasoned: with the party out of power for 18 years, very few in 1997 had had any insider experience of government. He deliberately appointed his most proven and loyal ministers in 2001 to run the four key public service delivery departments which he wanted to be at the heart of his second term– David Blunkett at the Home Office, Estelle Morris at Education, Alan Milburn at Health and Stephen Byers at Transport. Shortly after the general election, he told them that he would be keeping them in their posts for the full four years, so that they could have all the time they needed to bring about enduring change to the public services. Blair also benefited from having the largest team in Downing Street in the history of British premiership, containing some of the most brilliant minds from academe and its penumbra in think tanks and institutes that have ever been assembled.

Blair ratcheted up expectations of what the second government might achieve. During the 2001 general election campaign he set out bold aims for his second term in a series of speeches. He would not, this time, he confided to his aides, fail to plan ahead properly.[9] What then were his intentions? He was adamant that he wanted Britain to work much more closely with the European Union and to take Britain into the single currency. In domestic policy, he rejected the breezy rhetoric and millennial promises of a 'New Britain' which he made in 1997, in favour of deliberately downbeat pledges on public services, underpinned by clear principles, 'community not individualism' to achieve 'radical reform to the public services' in the new 'post-Thatcherite political system'. Europe and enduring public service reforms then were to be the cornerstones of his second-term agenda.

But as one of his loyalist New Labour lieutenants admitted, as in 1997 Blair was still far too vague and the detailed planning had not been done on either Europe or the public services. Blair was undoubtedly sincere in his aspirations, and on one level he knew that 2001–5 had to be thought through differently. But, 'we went into the 2001 election with no idea of what we were fighting about', said one aide. 'There was no ambition at all about why we wanted a second term.'[10] In further speeches, in July, September and October 2001, Blair developed his key themes. 'What he was trying to say', said one of his speech-writers, 'was that he was taking Britain beyond the individualism of Thatcherism into a country where community values prevailed, and where the middle classes would want to buy into world-class public services, funded by tax and available to all on an equitable basis'.[11] By 2001, this is what the 'Third Way' in practice amounted to.

Blair did not stint on delivering speeches throughout his second term. In March 2002, with more than a little hindsight, he tried to provide his premiership with a historical coherence (or 'overarching narrative') which it had hitherto lacked. Phase 1, he said, lasted from 1994 to 1997 and was about making Labour a modern social democratic party that could be electable. Phase 2, from 1997 to 2001, was about proving that Labour could run the economy and the country competently while laying the foundations for radical change. Phase 3, the second term from 2001, would see that radical change being delivered.[12] He would remould the post-1945 Attlee consensus, which had been based on an all-knowing state and passive citizen, into a 'Blairite' settlement, which was rooted in

---

[9] Anthony Seldon, *Blair* (London: Free Press, 2005), pp. 461–7.
[10] Ibid., p. 468.   [11] Private information.
[12] Anthony Seldon, 'Tony Blair in history', paper to Blair conference 'Whatever Happened to Cool Britannia?', hosted by University of Montreal in conjunction with McGill University, 4 May 2005.

economic prosperity and reformed public services, offering real choices to active consumers. A noble vision, but did it mean anything concrete? Did it recognise that tough choices would have to be made; for example, should resources be allocated by the state according to market signals?

In May 2003, to re-establish his strategic direction after the Iraq war, he delivered a speech to the Fabian Society, written by Blairites Peter Hyman and Patrick Diamond, in which he set out his vision of public-sector reform in the context of the ambition of a reforming Labour government.[13] In January 2004, he addressed the question, at a joint Institute for Public Policy Research (IPPR)/Vice Chancellors' meeting, of whether a Labour government could combine excellence with equity. Drafted largely by Adonis, it was one of the most intellectually cogent speeches delivered by Blair.[14] That March, spurred on by concerns that he was running out of ideas, he delivered a wide-ranging speech to Labour's spring conference, setting out New Labour's agenda: among other topics he discussed the challenges of lifelong learning, skills, childcare, home ownership, science and the knowledge economy. It was a brave prospectus that promised much. But, yet again, he disappointed New Labour zealots by retreating from these fields in the 2005 campaign. 'Like Baldwin in the 1929 election', lamented one, '"safety first" was the order of the day from the Prime Minister. He retreated, rather than win a mandate for radical change.'[15]

What, then, have been the principal second-term achievements? In such controversial waters, it is helpful to begin with what the Blairites themselves highlight as the government's principal successes.

Blairites argue that the second term was every bit as effective as the first. They say that the government, in almost every case, successfully addressed the predominant concerns of the electorate, which were unemployment, education, health and crime. Only a fifth concern, pensions, was tackled inadequately. The government further provided both economic and political stability. They argue that the second government should also be praised for meeting almost all the targets set out in the long 2001 manifesto, and that this achievement is almost without historical precedent (which is true, though previous manifestos didn't offer detailed targets in the same way). Thus, the targets on waiting lists, primary care, teacher recruitment and numbers, police numbers, asylum applications, rail reliability and a host of other areas were met by 2005. It should be added,

---

[13] Tony Blair, *The Courage of our Convictions: Why Reform of the Public Services is the Route to Social Justice*, Fabian Society Pamphlet 603 (London: Fabian Society, 2002).
[14] Private information.   [15] Private information.

however, that the manifesto did not promise three of the most significant developments of the third term: raising tax, and introducing foundation hospitals and tuition fees. When judged against the manifesto, as opposed to Blair's more Olympian musings, there is, nevertheless, much to praise in the government's work.

When judged against international comparisons, albeit against administrations without the same advantages, the government again comes out favourably, according to its own statistics. In November 2003 and January 2005, strategic studies tried to benchmark UK governmental performance against governments abroad. Although in the second division on key indicators, British performance was seen to be improving.

Turning to specific areas, Blairites highlight a range of successes. The decision to increase spending on health (foreshadowed by Blair when he asserted, in January 2000 on the *Frost* programme, that he wanted health spending in Britain to rise to the European average) was described by one Number 10 figure as 'a defining moment in modern social democratic politics'.[16] The 2002 spending review announced an increase of 8.6% per annum in health and 5.2% in education, to be paid for by a significant increase in National Insurance. Blair shared responsibility with Brown for this change, which was a direct challenge to the Thatcherite consensus on 'tax and spend': it showed that the electorate was content to pay higher taxes, if it could see where that extra money was going. In the first term, Blair had fought shy of raising taxes for fear of alienating the electorate. No longer. Tellingly, in the 2005 general election, the Conservatives said that they would match Labour's spending targets (much as Labour in 1997 had said it would match the Conservatives' plans).

How far the increased spending on health, and Labour's organisational reforms, produced a better and a more responsive health service remains in contention. Blairites point to a host of reforms, including the internal market and the new tariff structure, which they believed delivered a much more efficient service and resulted in the meeting of the key health targets. Morale in the profession and questions about whether the new structures were improving delivery, on the other hand, were hotly debated, while much of the increased spending was seen to be going into enhanced pay for medics and bureaucrats rather than directly into improvements in patient treatment.

The second success highlighted is the reduction in child and pensioner poverty, and the recent reductions in income inequality to 1996/7 levels,

---

[16] Private information.

discussed in *Social Justice* (2005),[17] a book produced by the IPPR. The New Deals and Sure Start were among the first term's policy initiatives that came to fruition and led to real improvements in the lives of the least fortunate in Labour's second term. Tax credits, though controversial, have reduced poverty. But the north–south divide remained a problem: the proportion of the working age population on sickness or incapacity benefits in the north still averaged 13%, compared with just 5% in the south. Blair became frustrated by the failure to get more people off incapacity benefit into work, resulting in a high-level political row late in the Parliament and the decision to ask David Blunkett to publish a Green Paper on the subject early in the third term. Means testing was in large part responsible for the reduction in pension poverty. But the long-term solution, Number 10 believed, was not addressed in the second term, hence Blair's decision to set up the Adair Turner Commission on pensions towards the end of the second term. On this, as on many other topics, Number 10 differed from the Treasury.

Health spending and reduction in poverty stand out as New Labour's two proudest achievements of the second term, while education is a third area where Blairites argue that real progress was made. Although there were not the striking improvements to match those in literacy and numeracy in primary schools in the first term, Blairites nevertheless point to improvements in GCSE results and to numbers remaining in education beyond the age of 16 (a contentious claim), to the growth of specialist schools and 'academies' (both innovations of the Conservatives prior to 1997) and to the introduction of tuition fees in higher education, which, while modest in scope, enshrined the important principle of students paying for an element of their university education. If this is coupled with the foundation hospital initiative, Blairites argue that Number 10, aided by a small group of fellow-travellers in Whitehall, had finally succeeded in carving out a distinctive agenda for public-sector reform. Mulgan highlights 10 innovative approaches that Labour employed across the whole field of social policy which resulted in enhanced performance. Many targets set for the government in social policy were indeed met; it is nevertheless fair to say that Britain by 2005 fell some considerable way short of having the promised 'world class' public services.

In early 2005 Ruth Kelly, Clarke's successor as education secretary in 2004, rejected the recommendations of Mike Tomlinson, former Chief

---

[17] Nick Pearce and Will Paxton (eds.), *Social Justice: Building a Fairer Britain* (London: IPPR, 2005).

Inspector of Schools, for a 'diploma' to replace existing A-levels. She did
so on the advice of Number 10, where it was believed that the whole
debate needed closing down with a general election looming, and it was
thus announced that A-levels had to be 'saved'.[18] This decision upset many
across the education profession, and the lack of clarity by the government
was highlighted when Blair himself subsequently questioned the future of
A-levels. The episode is revealing of a complete breakdown in communications between the Education Department, that knew what Tomlinson
was doing, and Blair.

The record in these areas above is discussed by Howard Glennerster
(health), Kitty Stewart (inequality), Robert Taylor (labour market) and
Alan Smithers, less approvingly (education). The stewardship of the economy was another second-term success, which saw the economic stability of the first term consolidated, though questions came to be asked
increasingly about the sustainability of the performance and the levels of
spending and debt. Some successes were also notched up at the Home
Office by Blunkett (and then by Charles Clarke from 2004), where the
former determined to pursue a much tougher line on crime than his first-
term predecessor, Jack Straw, whom he deemed too liberal.[19] Blair joined
Blunkett in devoting considerable time to asylum, as applications had
reached worryingly high levels by 2001, and by 2005 asylum had fallen
back to 1997 levels. Blair, however, failed in his aim to raise the public discourse on the whole fraught issue to a more sophisticated plain, as seen in
the 2005 election, where immigration again proved inflammatory. Much
work was put into reform of criminal justice and sentencing, but all this
effort resulted in only marginal and uneven reductions in crime figures
by 2005 (as Louis Blom-Cooper discusses), while the prison population
remained high and rising during the second term. The Home Office was
sorely tested by 9/11. The verdict on Blunkett must be that he struggled,
while his attempts to take on the police, community safety officers and the
probation and prison services, in a manner which often lacked subtlety
and political skill, generated more heat than light.

Blair's greatest success in 2001–5 came not in any area of policy at
all. Rather, it was his becoming the most successful Labour leader in
history by winning an unprecedented three general election victories
for his party. Favourable circumstances though he enjoyed, it is still a

[18] Private information.
[19] Stephen Pollard, *David Blunkett* (London: Hodder and Stoughton, 2004).

remarkable achievement. The hard question remains, however, whether he made enough of the opportunities the landslides brought him.

So much for Blair's second-term successes. What of the disappointments? Transport was the final public service (alongside health, education and crime prevention) for which Blair held particularly high hopes for the second term. Transport, however, was to have a poor second-term record. Byers' departure in May 2002 after a series of gaffes, many of his own making, left Alistair Darling, his competent successor, with a difficult legacy, compounded badly by having to clear up after the quasi-renationalisation of Railtrack in 2002 and after John Prescott's ill-considered Strategic Rail Authority.

Transport was further handicapped by the legacy of the fuel protests of 2000, which made the government reluctant to increase petrol duty, which would have relieved traffic congestion. It also would have reduced emissions of carbon dioxide, which contributed to another second-term disappointment, one that in 50 years' time might be seen as one of the most glaring failures – namely, not to have done more on climate change – an omission Blair was pleased to address at the G-8 summit in July 2005.

A steady increase in capital expenditure saw some transport improvements, but it is significant that the most eye-catching initiative in the second term came from Blair's one-time *bête noire*, Ken Livingstone, Mayor of London, with his congestion charging. The irony is that this Old Labour rebel pioneered the principal transport innovation which Labour will extend in its third term. Meanwhile, in aviation, the government was too eager to placate the aviation lobby and thus did not opt to expand regional airports.

Europe was another area of second term failure, all the more significant because Blair highlighted it as one of his principal objectives after 2001. It might well have been right for Britain not to join the euro, in which case Blair should not have made it a key part of his platform. As Peter Riddell discusses, Blair found it almost impossible to achieve the enduringly improved relationship with Britain's EU partners that he had promised. He showed courage in allowing migrants from the EU accession countries to come to Britain, and was instrumental in the enlargement process and promoting the accession of Turkey. But Britain's relationship with the EU by mid-2005 was arguably at its lowest point since it joined in 1973, while his ambitious plans for reconfiguring Europe around a more market based and less dirigiste system will take years to bring to fruition, and years at Number 10 are one commodity he does not possess.

Europe exemplifies both Blair's weaknesses at planning ahead, and his 'Polyanna-ish' belief that 'things will turn out well'.

Constitutional reform was another area of weakness in the second term. Blair tellingly did not appoint a constitution adviser to his large Downing Street team. Advocates of his making a major speech on the subject unsurprisingly lost out to those who wanted him to avoid the topic altogether. The major tranche of constitutional reform – the John Smith legacy – had gone through in the first term. Yet much of the agenda was incomplete or inconsistent, while other areas, including the electoral system and sub-central government, were crying out for fresh thinking.

Blair bodged the completion of the House of Lords reform, with five options being put to the House of Commons for its decision: it offered a textbook example of how not to govern. Robin Cook, the Leader of the House of Commons, failed to carry Labour MPs with him on his proposed changes to parliamentary procedure, while Blair's proposals for a reformed Lord Chancellor's Department and Supreme Court were handled so badly when announced in mid-2003 that two years had to be devoted to clearing up the mess.

A similar story of muddled thinking and poor execution applied to local government and regionalism. A proper settlement was badly needed for local government, with clear decisions taken about its exact role and relationship with the centre. Blair, like many prime ministers, had made positive noises about local government in opposition but grew to distrust it in power (his jaundiced view was deepened by the school funding crisis midway through the second term). The government equivocated on local government, and mixed messages were given out from different departments at different times. Blair himself had favoured elected mayors, which foundered, and he subsequently tolerated, without enthusiasm, Prescott's pet project of regional assemblies, to be heralded in the North East region. But when the proposals were rejected in a referendum, the government's strategy, in as far as it had one for the regions, collapsed. There was no Plan B.

Blair's overseas policy record in the second term did not rival the successes of 1997–2001. There were no Kosovo (1999), no dashing stories like Sierra Leone (2000) or even repetitions of breakthroughs such as the Good Friday Agreement (1998). He failed to make real progress in the second term on African relief or peace in the Middle East, both of which he had spoken about with enthusiasm. He deferred to President Bush, as he had earlier to President Clinton, and with equally slender evidence of having made a significant impression on White House thinking. It will remain to be seen whether his policy on Iraq will bring peace and democracy to the Middle East, or even to Iraq itself. For all Blair's work, Al-Qaeda-style terrorism has shown little sign of abating. It may yet prove that he lost his best opportunity to influence Washington when he had real leverage, in the build-up to the Iraq war when British support was badly needed. Thereafter, the US administration had little reason to change its thinking for the benefit of the Labour prime minister in Britain. Northern Ireland remained mercifully light of sectarian killing, but the outlook for the province was given new hope by the IRA ceasefire of July 2005.

Why, then, did Blair not achieve more in his second term? Innate caution is the first explanation. His entire cast of mind was directed towards winning elections. Initially, he was scarred by the experience of four successive defeats in general elections from 1979 to 1992, but, later, the caution was dictated by his wish to avoid jeopardising what he increasingly saw as perhaps his major claim to immortality in history, his ability to win general elections. Blair was always driven more by the desire to win power than to use power. Winning a third general election for Labour was historic. But it came at a price. As the election approached, he pulled back from pursuing his New Labour ideas to their logical conclusion for fear of alienating supporters and, closer to home, upsetting his delicately poised relationship with Gordon Brown.

Blair failed to work out until too late exactly what he wanted to do with power. His own personal credo, developed in the 1970s and 1980s, had been constructed around the ideas of community, personal responsibility and democracy. But it was an embarrassingly thin and inconsistent agenda for a prime minister. The theorist who had influenced him most was not a socialist but a religious visionary, John Macmurray. Works of history that most inspired him were not those of Labour's great leaders of the past but biographies of Liberal leaders such as Henry Campbell-Bannerman. The political leader who influenced him the most was neither Labour nor Liberal but Conservative – Margaret Thatcher.

During the 1994 elections for the Labour Party leadership, when asked what his personal manifesto was, he said that it would become clear once he was elected leader. Indeed, his first act as leader showed great courage in ridding the party of Clause IV of its constitution, an act of great symbolic (if little policy) significance. But then he went tame on policy and said that the electorate would see his radicalism once he was elected as prime minister. His whole energy up until the 1997 general election was devoted to 'neutralising the negatives', i.e. to removing the reasons the electorate might have for not voting Labour, such as the party being weak on defence, or unable to run a modern capitalist economy. But once in power from May 1997, when he had the opportunity at last, he again showed little sense of having any clear idea about what he wanted to do. His story increasingly became 'let's prove to the electorate that we deserve their trust by giving them competent government: the radicalism will come in a second term'.

Yet he fought the 2001 general election on a policy-light manifesto (a joint Blair–Brown decision), with a still incomplete picture of what he wanted to achieve with power. Neither foundation hospitals nor tuition fees, nor the next steps on social mobility and constitutional reform, were promised in the manifesto. Then came 9/11 and he travelled the world for a year, something which eroded his time for serious thinking. Only in 2002–3 did his thoughts crystallise and did he finally decide what he wanted to do with power domestically. It was not to take Britain into the euro, nor to construct a 'progressive centre' coalition in British politics. It was to have a 'choice and diversity' agenda in the public services. It was a halfway house between the 'whole hog' radicals like Adonis and Roger Liddle and more traditional Labourites like David Miliband and Mulgan. Once elucidated, he drove this policy forward. But it was arguably discovered too late to make a significant impression on policy, at least before the 2005 general election. Blair was also never entirely sure what solution he had arrived at. He was not alone. As a Number 10 aide observed, 'there wasn't agreement even on what we meant by our "choice and diversity" agenda. Some of us in Downing Street wanted it to include an extension of co-payment [i.e. charging] and competition across the public services, others saw it as just a dressed up form of the traditional universal welfare state.'[20] The future, as they say, is history.

Not only did Blair not know what he wanted to do with power, he also never fully worked out how to use it. He had never worked in a commercial organisation nor had he run anything until he became leader of the Labour Party in 1994. His preference had always been for working in small groups, whether as a student with his discussion group around student priest Peter Thomson at Oxford, his conclave of fellow barristers in Derry Irvine's chambers, or the close-knit caucus that formed around the room he shared with Gordon Brown after he entered the House of Commons in 1983. It was a tight-knit clique that developed New Labour, including Brown, Mandelson, Alastair Campbell, Philip Gould and Anji Hunter. This same clique, minus Gordon Brown but joined by Jonathan

[20] Private information.

Powell and Sally Morgan, formed his praetorian guard during his three years as opposition leader from 1994–7.

The formula worked for him as opposition Labour leader, but it transferred less happily when shifted wholesale into Number 10. Blair spent most of his first term believing that he could run the country and manipulate the media as he and his team had done from Millbank in opposition. Gradually he developed an approach to government that relied heavily on central diktat, sidelining the views of most of the civil service, the Labour Party, the Cabinet or Parliament. Policy was run from his own office in Downing Street, the so-called 'denocracy'. The Delivery Unit, from 2001, was to provide the storm troopers of his crusade to transform the public services, and targets and monitoring were to be the strategy. A plethora of other units and offices came and went in Number 10 and the Cabinet Office.

Blair's style of governing came under increasing attack during the second term for ignoring of the conventions of British government as well as for its inefficiency. It was Blair's conduct of the Iraq war that brought the 'denocracy' under a piercing spotlight, notably in the Hutton and Butler inquiries. While absolving Blair of the charges of lying, they were sharply critical of his style of governing. Over Iraq, it is possible that if he had listened more widely, not the least to the Foreign Office, he would have acted in a more considered way: more generally, if he had used the institutions at his disposal better, he might have achieved more in his second term. In recognition of his errors and more so the widespread concern at his methods, and with his departure date approaching, Blair promised in 2005 to govern in a more orthodox way, for example using Cabinet committees.

But Blair's style for much of the second term was to bludgeon rather than to consult. Thus a year to 18 months were lost because Number 10 was antagonistic to the Parliamentary Labour Party and to the trade unions, which convinced themselves that Blair's public service programme was merely privatisation by the back door. Political management by Number 10 was indeed often inadequate in the second term. Relying so heavily on their 'true believer' mentality, Number 10 failed to win hearts and minds, not only in the Labour movement but in the civil service also. Mrs Thatcher, even with her 'one of us' approach, managed to win over many supporters among politicians, advisers and officials. Blairites bemoaned the fact that 'there are so few of us'. But their failure to secure a wider base of support across Whitehall and Westminster, or in town halls, is telling of their approach. Number 10 also failed to develop a cadre of highly capable New Labour Cabinet ministers. Faith was lost in Byers and Estelle Morris, while Charles Clarke was viewed with some suspicion. Blunkett burned himself up at a time when Blair most needed him, while only Milburn, Hewitt and Reid were viewed as (mostly) successes. Number 10 was apt to blame the low numbers of 'believers' among the Cabinet ministers for the failure to achieve more. But Blair and his inner circle must bear responsibility, not least for giving out mixed messages about whether they wanted ministers to be radical or to avoid conflict with the Labour Party.

Blair's path was also not eased by the lack of a clear ideology available to give coherence to his policies. While Attlee and Thatcher each came to power on the crest of an ideological wave, Blair had no such fortune. For all the store set by the Third Way, and the recognition by centre-left countries worldwide that there are limits to what government can feasibly achieve, the reality was that it spawned a slight number of policies. Agenda-changing governments need to have an intellectual and an ideological coherence which was not there for Blair. He was personally handicapped because he lacked an original or a deep-thinking mind of his own: he is not an intellectual, he reads light and is a stranger to much high art and culture. Blair's brilliance, genius even, lies in his quite extraordinary persuasive and presentational skills. His stamina, and mental and physical strength, are also outstanding and have been rivalled by few British prime ministers. He was bristling with bright ideas during the second term, some of which, such as for schools or over crime, were of questionable long-term benefit. But he lacked the intellectual equipment to devise a coherent agenda of his own.

In its place was perpetual policy dissonance with his chief ally and aide, Gordon Brown. While Blair and Brown were at one in their drive to create and entrench New Labour, and then to win as many general elections as possible, they differed on much. This personality clash was made more serious by the cleavage between Number 10 and the Treasury. The latter was opposed to, or sceptical of, a number of those policies which were very closest to the heart of the Prime Minister, including foundation hospitals, the proposals for the funding of higher education, the 'academies' programme of new prestigious schools in deprived areas, and greater freedom from local authorities for state schools. It even had reservations about private provision for certain health services like cataract operations. Almost the only area where the Treasury did not obstruct Number 10 was over the controversial public finance initiative, as for the London Underground. It is not surprising that Blair's most striking and bold stances as prime minister came in the international theatre, where Brown could not deflect him. After 1994 their relationship worked best only when they were conjoined by a desire for a common end, which temporarily obscured their underlying difficulties, as in the run-up to the 2005 general election. Blair might have been much clearer as prime minister with his own agenda, if he had not had Brown to frustrate him, but equally his government would not have been nearly as successful. Indeed, without Brown, he would arguably not even have become prime minister in the first place.

Iraq is a final factor which handicapped the government's progress. Blair certainly spent much of his political capital persuading the Parliamentary Labour Party and the country to support the war, and the payback was felt both in Parliament and at the ballot box. His stance also damaged Britain's relations with the EU. But it is not true that his reform agenda was deflected badly because of his attention to the international stage. Number 10 aides claim that he maintained his regular progress meetings with domestic ministers, and indeed that he spent more time thinking strategically in the second term than in the first.

Thoughtful Blairites like Geoff Mulgan maintain that the second term was a significant success when measured against the yardsticks of what the 2001 manifesto promised and international comparisons, and against historical parallels.[21] The government certainly did achieve most of its manifesto commitments, which were specifically designed to be achievable within four years, and by this specific criterion the government was a success. International parallels are fraught and inexact, but the evidence suggests that the government did perform reasonably well against its contemporaries abroad.

But it is against historical parallels, and the aspirations aired repeatedly by the Prime Minister himself, that the cracks show. So was it a wasted term? For all its achievements, the second term was disappointing in relation to the expectations that Blair himself aroused, to the exceptional advantages the government enjoyed, and in comparison to the achievements of successful second-term prime ministers like Thatcher. Blair must shoulder the blame because he appointed the ministers and the aides, and if they were no good he must take responsibility. He also failed sufficiently to learn the lessons either from his own first term, or from second-term leaders abroad such as Clinton. Put simply, he needed to have finalised his agenda, which he had three years in opposition followed by four in power to prepare, and then to execute it. Blair did none

---

[21] Geoff Mulgan, Closing lecture, University of Montreal/McGill Conference, 4–6 May 2005.

of these adequately. Admittedly, some factors were beyond his control, including 9/11 (though he could have avoided falling headlong into the Iraq war), scepticism towards the EU refusing to abate, globalisation taking more decisions away from national governments, and having such an antagonistic Chancellor and an unsympathetic Treasury.

Blair cannot escape blame also for presiding over a period when trust in and respect for politicians declined so much and turn-out in general elections fell so low (59% and 61% in 2001 and 2005 respectively). So much for the promise of democratic renewal. No issue leached trust quite as much as Iraq, compounded by Blair's repeated pleas of 'trust me'. On Iraq, even if history judges the invasion to have been wise, Blair must still be criticised for failing to stand up to the Bush administration and demand concessions before going to war, for taking the country to war on a false prospectus, and for preparing so lamentably for the 'post-war' world.

Blair loyalists insist that the second term was even more successful than the first. They protest too much. They are now developing a new narrative. Rather like Major's court, Blair's circle claims that the second term was bound to be more difficult because the eye-catching changes, such as the minimum wage and constitutional reform, were executed in the first term (just as Mrs Thatcher scooped the big changes herself, leaving little fresh for Major).

The third term, they say, will see Blair's record consolidated. Confidence in Number 10 was high in the summer of 2005. The 2005 manifesto and the 'five-year plans' would ensure that the new government did not lose direction. The third term duly began in gilded manner, aided by the French referendum rejecting the EU constitution – luck, and his ability to exploit it, were key Blair traits. But Blair's 'Indian summer' should not distract from my fundamental verdict on him – that he earns an 'alpha plus' for presentation and persuasion, but a 'beta gamma' for policy and governance.

It may not be another hundred years before Labour again enjoys such unfettered power. Had Blair realised more fully his historic opportunity, much more could have been achieved. From the perspective of mid-2005, the judgement is that Blair – and others – will look back at the second term and ask 'why were our achievements so modest?' His chance fundamentally to refashion the country as he had remodelled the party came, and went, in 2001–5. 'Blairism' turned out to be a 'crazy salad', consisting of the traditional Labourite belief in the efficacy of centralisation and high spending, mixed with a quasi-Harold Wilson policy of technocratic managerialism, planning and targets within the confines of the existing welfare state, and a neo-Thatcherite adherence to extending markets and pricing into the public services. But this was at best evolution: it was not radical, and it was certainly not revolution.

The foundations were laid in 1997–2001. But the edifice was only half built in 2001–5, and in three different styles. Blair came to power in 1997 promising a 'New Britain'. He commenced his third term promising a 'New Europe'. The first has not happened, and the second will not transpire fully in his political lifetime. Had Blair's mastery of persuasion and presentation extended to policy-making and governing, the net 'Blair effect' might have been considerable: as it stands, the Blair effect on 2001–5 will be remembered as much for its opportunities lost as for its achievements.

Commentary
The meaning of the Third Way

ANDREW GAMBLE

In his Fabian pamphlet on the Third Way, published in 1998, Tony Blair wrote that the Third Way was 'the best label for the new politics which the progressive centre-left is forging in Britain and beyond.'[1] This new politics embraced Bill Clinton's New Democrats as well as the newly elected SPD government in Germany. Tony Blair and Gerhard Schroeder published a joint manifesto, *Europe: The Third Way – Die neue Mitte*,[2] which set out their vision of a new social democratic politics for Europe. The phrase from the start drew criticism, derided by its opponents as being vacuous, little more than a device to conceal a move to the right by centre-left parties. Advocates of the Third Way claimed that it represented a third way between statist social democracy and laissez-faire neo-liberalism, but many of its critics charged that it was in fact indistinguishable from neo-liberalism. Far from opening a new era of progressive politics, the Third Way simply consolidated the neo-liberal consensus.[3]

The critics seemed to win the argument. Since that time of glad confident morning the Third Way has fallen on hard times. Within a few years it was unusual to find any mention of the Third Way by political leaders, and even some of the political thinkers who had popularised the term, such as Tony Giddens,[4] conceded that the term itself was not important. The Third Way, he argued, should be seen as a new form of social democracy, concerned with revising and modernising social democratic doctrines to respond to the new challenges of globalisation and the knowledge economy, finding new ways to achieve the traditional social democratic objectives of social justice and solidarity while ensuring economic efficiency and flexibility.[5]

[1] Tony Blair, *The Third Way* (London: Fabian Society, 1998), p. 1.
[2] Tony Blair and Gerhard Schroeder, *Europe: The Third Way – Die neue Mitte* (London: Labour Party and SPD, 1999).
[3] *Marxism Today*, Special Issue, November/December 1998.
[4] Tony Giddens, *The Third Way* (Cambridge: Polity, 1998).
[5] Tony Giddens, *The Third Way and its Critics* (Cambridge: Polity, 2000).

One reason for the decreasing use of the phrase was that it had become indissolubly linked to the personal political projects of Bill Clinton and Tony Blair – and after 2000 Clinton was no longer in the White House. But the Third Way also came out of the intellectual ferment on the left on how to revise doctrines and policies to make social democratic parties both electable and effective in government in changed times.[6] In Britain, key figures in developing 'Third Way thinking' included Tony Giddens, Geoff Mulgan and Charles Leadbeater, as well as the left-of-centre think tanks, particularly the IPPR, the Fabian Society and Demos, and journals such as *Renewal*.

The Third Way therefore does not have a single meaning. It can be viewed as an electoral strategy, as a new politics and as a new programme. These aspects obviously overlap, but they are also distinct and frequently confused. A rather different assessment of the Third Way is reached depending on which is given priority.

The Third Way as an electoral strategy

This aspect of the Third Way was crucial for both Blair and Clinton. Both were seeking to rebuild the electoral appeal and credibility of a left-of-centre political platform following long periods of the ascendancy of the right. Blair was determined to wrest control of several key issues away from the Conservatives, such as economic competence, crime and patriotism. Rebranding Labour as New Labour was an essential part of this. He wanted to demonstrate that there were, in principle, no areas of policy where Labour could not be trusted more than the Conservatives. For Blair the Third Way also meant liberation from the straitjacket of political debate inside the Labour Party, based on taboos and assumptions which kept reminding voters why they disliked the Labour Party so much. The decision to change Clause IV of the party constitution was of little importance for policy but was of huge symbolic significance, since it directly challenged the identification of the party with a socialist vision of how the economy should be organised, and therefore helped to identify the party as a genuinely new party.

As an electoral strategy the Third Way succeeded beyond the dreams of its progenitors. Winning three consecutive election victories with comfortable parliamentary majorities was unprecedented for Labour, as was the disarray of the Conservatives. Neither had happened since Labour's

[6] Alan Finlayson, 'Third Way theory', *Political Quarterly* 70:3 (1999): 271–9.

emergence as a significant parliamentary force after 1918. The Conservatives were forced to change their leader four times between 1997 and 2005, and in the two general elections after 1997 were unable significantly to raise their share of the vote, in sharp contrast to every previous period when they had been in opposition for a whole parliament.

Conservatives often grumbled that Tony Blair was a magician who had cast a spell on the British people, and had stolen Conservative policies and votes. But Blair had only done to the Conservatives what the Conservatives had so often done to Labour in the past. Labour occupied the centre ground of British politics by making sure that on those issues that most mattered to voters it was either ahead of the Conservatives or only a little way behind them. With Blair the Conservatives found that they could no longer rely on Labour not to compete on some major issues. Blair's Big Tent was in principle limitless. The Conservatives in the past had often conceived politics in this way, ideas like 'One Nation' and the 'Middle Way' functioning in a similar manner to the Third Way. They were means of freeing the Conservatives from attachment to particular dogmas and principles, allowing them to respond to what voters actually thought was most important.

The Third Way has performed the same function for Labour, and performed it very successfully. Although Labour saw its vote share decline sharply in the 2005 election, it still managed to lead the Conservatives in the polls as the party most trusted by voters to handle the issues of policy most important to them (immigration and asylum, and crime were the only major exceptions).[7] Above all, Labour was still more trusted on the economy by a wide margin, the issue that up until 1992 had always been the Conservatives' strongest card. This change was due to the legacy of Black Wednesday and Gordon Brown's stewardship of the economy after 1997, but it was also directly the fruit of Third Way politics, which allowed the Labour leadership to disengage from the policy positions and mindsets of the past, and present Labour in a new light to the electorate.

Critics of Blair argue that his success was achieved by abandoning socialism, just as many previous Conservatives criticised their leaders for abandoning conservatism. But successful leaders almost invariably do revise their parties' platforms and appeal to win votes. In competitive electoral politics the alternative is permanent opposition. Opportunities to shape political attitudes, to lead from the front and to create entirely new political alignments in politics are rare. Most politicians

---

[7] YouGov, *Daily Telegraph*, 12 May 2005.

work within the constraints of the existing patterns of values, beliefs and interests of their electorates. In this at least Blair showed himself a master.

The Third Way as a new politics

The Third Way as originally conceived was not just an electoral strategy but a new politics, to counter the disillusion with both the shortcomings of statist social democracy and neo-liberalism. The promise of the Third Way was that government would be more decentralised and therefore closer to the people, and there would be more participation. The heart of this new politics, as Tony Blair and others expressed it, was to be a strong self-governing civil society. The role of the state would be enabling – it would help families, businesses and voluntary associations to be independent and self-governing, rather than trying to impose outcomes from above. The aim of the new politics was to reverse creeping disaffection with politics and politicians, and to renew civic purpose and confidence. The Third Way would point a new direction by rejecting the 'Whitehall knows best' culture of statist social democracy; but equally it would reject neo-liberal suspicion of the state which had undermined the sense of a public interest and public domain.

The outcomes have been a huge disappointment. Far from reversing disaffection with politics, turnout in British elections slumped in 2001 and only marginally recovered in 2005. Cynicism and lack of trust in politicians and the political process have grown markedly. Although Labour has carried through its promise to decentralise some parts of central government, most notably through devolution of powers to a Scottish Parliament and a Welsh Assembly, and has accompanied this with a raft of other proposals for constitutional reform, including elected mayors, English regional assemblies, freedom of information, reform of the House of Lords, and much more, this has done little to stem the tide. The devolved institutions have struggled to gain legitimacy, and the extension of devolution to England in the shape of the North East Assembly was roundly rejected by voters there. Britain has passed through the most far-reaching set of constitutional changes for 300 years, but it has not reversed the tide of disaffection from the government or from the political process. Similarly, although the government has been assiduous in pushing through reforms in the way in which the public sector is managed and monitored, this has not been experienced as the enabling state replacing the command state. Instead there is growing resentment at the heavy hand of government interference – the target and audit culture, performance indicators and all the other devices of the new public management. These have not actually succeeded in getting government off the people's backs or making people identify more with government, or seeing it as a benign force.

There are many reasons for this, but one of the most important is that the Blair government underestimated the practical difficulties facing the new politics. From the start it clashed with the centralist traditions of British government, and a government concerned with improving delivery of core public services soon went cool on experiments with the new politics. Much of the constitutional programme was in any case not really new but addressed concerns that had been around in British government for at least 100 years. The constitutional reforms were the completion of an old agenda rather than the setting out of a new one. The conditions for renewing civic engagement in public life had drastically changed, most obviously through the new role played by the media. New Labour politicians recognised that the media had become the crucial gatekeepers of the relationship between politicians and the public, but they attempted to deal with it by developing a media strategy of their own which they hoped would enable them to control the news agenda and prevent the government becoming the victims of the media in the manner of the Major government. Although this worked for a time, in the long run it proved ruinous for the government's reputation and for any attempt to introduce a new politics. The culture of spin and news management was turned back against the government by the media, which made the government's attempt to manipulate the media an all-consuming news story. The corrosive effect of modern media on the traditional political process and their role in promoting disengagement and distrust has become pervasive,[8] and the Blair government had no ideas for reversing it. Indeed, it played into the media's hands, and in the process destroyed any attempt to forge a new politics.

The Third Way as a policy agenda

The Third Way has often been derided as having no policy substance. The alternative criticism is that it has policy substance but it is simply neo-liberalism under a different label. Both of these are strange charges, since it is apparent both from the statements of the main protagonists

---

[8] John Lloyd, *What the Media are Doing to Our Politics* (London: Constable, 2004).

of the Third Way and from the experience of eight years of Labour government that the Third Way has a rather firm profile. It sets out to combine economic efficiency with social justice, free markets with universal welfare. In this sense the Third Way is the inheritor of previous revisionist projects, including those of Tony Crosland and David Owen. In his Fabian pamphlet Blair set out four broad policy objectives for a Third Way government: a dynamic knowledge-based economy, a strong civil society, a modern government based on partnership and decentralisation and a foreign policy based on international cooperation.[9] In its first eight years the Blair government went a considerable way towards achieving the first goal. It avoided the kind of financial crisis that had always been the lot of previous Labour governments and achieved steady, uninterrupted growth, low inflation and declining unemployment. It invested heavily in the science base and introduced a number of supply-side policies to raise productivity, with mixed results. But it did succeed in proving itself to be pro-business, pro-enterprise and pro-market. For the first time there was a Labour government to which the business community was not hostile.

For the Third Way to be a genuine third way, however, new Labour had to show that it could use economic success to deliver social justice and social cohesion, the foundations of its second goal, a strong civil society. Many left critics have argued that New Labour may have delivered financial stability and business-friendly policies, but at the expense of giving up its ambitions for social justice, resulting in the gradual alienation of its core vote and the disillusion of its activists. This argument looked plausible at the beginning of the Blair government when the Chancellor stuck rigidly to the plans for public spending inherited from the Conservatives. The excuse was the need to put the public finances on a sound footing and to bear down on public debt, but the squeeze was so severe that by the end of the Parliament in 2001 the Blair government was actually managing to spend less on core public services as a percentage of GDP than the much derided government of John Major.[10] However the position after eight years looked very different. Starting from the plans announced in 1999 the government has presided over the fastest ever increase of funds for the NHS and education. By 2008 the resources available to the NHS will have more than doubled since 1997, and as a percentage of GDP will

---

[9] Blair, *The Third Way*, p. 7.
[10] Maurice Mullard, 'New Labour, new public expenditure', *Political Quarterly* 72:3 (2001): 310–21.

have risen from 6 to 9.4%.[11] There is an argument about how effective the increasing spending is proving, but no doubt about its scale. A Conservative government would not have chosen to increase spending at this rate.

A second line of criticism is the Blair government's lack of concern with the redistribution of income and wealth.[12] This is not accidental, however, but characteristic of its Third Way approach. Instead it stresses opportunity, investment in human capital and the establishment of minimum levels of provision. Pursuing this agenda it has instituted a series of measures to combat poverty, reduce disadvantage and discrimination. These include the minimum wage, Sure Start, family and pensioner tax credits, welfare to work, as well as the improvements in the quality of education and health services. The improvements are incremental and gradual, but, if sustained over three parliaments or longer, will push British welfare standards a long way towards European levels of provision. Whether these improvements can be sustained, especially if there is an economic downturn as many predict, is uncertain. But whatever happens in the future, the eight years of the Blair government between 1997 and 2005 are likely to appear at the very least as a time when Labour did for once manage to reconcile economic efficiency and social justice. Given the crises which so regularly attended former Labour governments, wrecking their domestic agendas and their reputation for economic competence, this is a substantial achievement for the Third Way.

Achievement has been less evident elsewhere. The third goal of delivering a modern government, to improve the delivery and quality of public services, has produced mixed results. Many aspects of the target regime have been counterproductive, and efforts to revive morale in the public sector and restore the public service ethos have not met much success. Although many objective measures show that services have improved, most voters do not think they have. The aim of a more decentralised welfare state, based on the continuance of state funding for public services but delivery through a wide range of alternative providers,[13] has made some progress but much less than the advocates of the Third Way hoped. The task of persuading the middle classes to stay with state-funded public services and not vote with their feet has still some way to go.

[11] Pete Alcock, *Social Policy in Britain* (London: Palgrave Macmillan, 2003), p. 68.
[12] John Westergaard, 'Where does the Third Way lead?', *New Political Economy* 4:3 (1999): 429–36.
[13] IPPR, *Building Better Partnerships* (London: IPPR, 2001).

Most disappointing of all has been progress towards the fourth goal – a foreign policy based on international cooperation. This involved a strong commitment to multilateralism and international cooperation to solve those problems which were transnational, such as crime, drugs, terrorism and the environment. It meant Britain seeking to be at the heart of Europe, and making a success of EU membership. But the Blair government has proved unable to stem the tide of Euro-scepticism, while the decision to support the US invasion of Iraq, rather than to seek a resolution through the multilateral institutions of the UN, severely estranged Blair from many EU leaders as well as from European and (eventually) British public opinion. It is hard to see how his decision over Iraq reflected the Third Way approach to the world he outlined so eloquently in 1998. Rather it reflected an older imperative of British political and diplomatic strategy, the need to preserve British influence in Washington at all costs.[14]

Conclusion

The Third Way as a phrase may have fallen into disuse. But it did identify an underlying coherence to the policy regime Labour inaugurated in 1997, a coherence that is more evident as time has gone on. The Blair government at the time received little credit for its achievements. The gap between policy changes and public perceptions was substantial – most people did not believe the changes that were actually happening.[15] This mismatch, which reflected the climate of mistrust that developed around the government, partly because of the way it behaved and partly because of the relentless negativity of the British media, contributed to the widespread disillusion with the Blair government, despite it staking a strong claim to being the most successful government in Labour's history. For all the criticism, the Third Way in broad terms still indicates the policies, the electoral stance and the political style that are most likely to be successful in present circumstances for a party of the left. Yet a weakness remains. The inability of new Labour to construct a convincing narrative around either its constitutional or its welfare reforms meant that too

---

[14] Andrew Gamble, *Between Europe and America: The Future of British Politics* (London: Palgrave Macmillan, 2003).

[15] Polly Toynbee and David Walker, *Better or Worse? Has Labour Delivered?* (London: Bloomsbury, 2005).

often it appeared vacuous and shallow, with no anchoring principles. In this sense Third Way politics may have proved self-defeating, unable to provide the emotional symbols, the tribal enemies and the fundamental beliefs which had in the past defined left and right politics. Merely getting things to work better and to reduce poverty do not get the same attention or elicit the same passions.

Commentary
The reinvention of Blair

ROBERT SKIDELSKY

In 1992, when Tony Blair was shadow home secretary, Kenneth Clarke, the current home secretary, said of him 'he's so shadowy it's ridiculous', and went on to quote Hughes Mearns's celebrated lines, 'As I was going up the stair, I met a man who wasn't there.' Eight years into his premiership, the question of who Blair is, what he believes in, is scarcely closer to being answered. One is tempted to write of him, as Keynes did of Lloyd George, '[He] is rooted in nothing; he is void and without content; he is an instrument and a player at the same time.' In fact, Lloyd George is probably the prime minister Blair most resembles. Keynes praised Lloyd George's 'natural good instincts, his industry, his inexhaustible nervous vitality', his 'vast stores of spirit and of energy'. But these qualities were not grounded in 'permanent principle, tenacity, fierce indignation, honesty, loyal leadership'.

Other similarities suggest themselves. Like Lloyd George, Blair has no sense of history, he does not read books. He runs a sleazy court, and he is an exceptionally gifted political seducer.(Unlike Lloyd George, Blair is not reputed to be a sexual seducer.) Despite his deceptions – which we shall turn to in a moment – people can't help liking him, and therefore disbelieving in his capacity for lying. This charm, together with eloquence and passion, makes him a formidable public advocate and private persuader. Both Lloyd George and Blair were peaceniks who became war leaders. Keynes concludes, 'If Mr. Lloyd George had no good qualities, no charms, no fascinations, he would not be dangerous. If he were not a syren, we need not fear the whirlpools.'

Blair's political achievement is greater than Lloyd George's. Lloyd George destroyed the Liberal Party; Blair saved the Labour Party, not just by making it electable but by making it more electable than the Conservatives, thus reversing a hundred years of political history. The real Blair effect has been to make Labour safe for the middle classes.(How long this 'effect' will continue when, or if, Brown becomes prime minister is far from clear.) Of course, others had a hand in the business, not least

Margaret Thatcher, who destroyed any lingering attachment on the left for large-scale public ownership. Thatcher made Blair's task in ridding his party of the incubus of Clause IV easier than when Hugh Gaitskell tried in 1959. Nevertheless, the bravery, ruthlessness, and skill with which he fought the battle against the traditionalists showed that there was much more to him than a winning smile.

His legislative achievement is unlikely to equal Lloyd George's. (It might be argued that he has had less opportunity, since the only government office he has ever held is that of prime minister.) Lloyd George's National Insurance Act of 1911 started the Welfare State. Despite Blair's personal passion for education, his government is unlikely to leave a mark on its structure as profound as Balfour's Act of 1902 or Butler's Act of 1944. Both Lloyd George and Blair were constitutional reformers, but Lloyd George's instincts were more radical than Blair's, although his political circumstances were more straitened. It may be, of course, that the era of large-scale social and political transformation is over, and that only incremental change is now possible.

Like Lloyd George, Blair exhibits a kind of unfocused radicalism, which soars above more solidly based 'isms'. Both men viewed Britain as a run-down property, 'in need', as the estate agents have it 'of modernisation'. Modernisation meant adopting 'modern' ideas, whatever their source, and applying them to Britain's decrepit institutions. Lloyd George tried to overcome the class war by establishing a centre party made up of 'patriotic' Labourites, radical Liberals and ethical Conservatives; Blair, more fortunate in his political circumstances, has simply converted the Labour Party into an instrument of his modernising agenda. He has taken over the public private partnership themes paraded by Lloyd George in the 1920s. Blair's attempt to moralise capitalism after the ultra-dry Thatcher episode replicates in a remarkable way the late Victorian effort to overcome the economism of the Peel era. Both rested on a 'social' interpretation of Christianity. Blair imbibed his as an Oxford undergraduate through the writings of an obscure Scottish philosopher, John Macmurray and a circle of Christian friends. He called his creed 'ethical socialism', but it sounds much more like ethical capitalism, and Blair has long since given up calling himself a socialist of any kind. In this, as in other ways, the modernising Blair harks back to the much more fluid intellectual atmosphere which existed before class politics and class ideology became solidified.

In domestic policy, the only obstacles to Blair's ecumenicalism have been those imposed by his party (i.e. the Chancellor). The differences, but also the overlap, in the outlooks of the two men are more fascinating to the observer of political fashions than the humdrum story of their personal rivalry. In a nutshell, and oversimplifying matters, Blair rejects any necessary, or inherent division between the private and public sectors, while Brown insists that separateness is built into their logic. In Blair's view, the private sector should be moralised and the public sector subjected to market disciplines. He has taken up the 'quasi-market' approach to the organisation of public health care and school education, and would probably not be averse to a significant element of private payment for these services – as he pushed through for the universities. In these ways a seamless system of political economy might emerge, with the central ground occupied by organisations which are not wholly private or public. The similarity between this vision and that sketched out by Keynes in his essay 'The End of Laissez-Faire' (1925) is striking. Typically, Brown's analysis is more rigorous, even pedantic. Limits to markets are set by technical 'market failures' so chronic that non-market provision, especially in the health care and education sectors is needed. They must be wholly state-funded, with performance centrally targeted and policed.

More important than these differences is the way in which both men were able to wrap up Labour's traditional commitments to full employment and income redistribution in a post-Thatcherite 'Third Way' language, which reassured the faithful without alarming the prosperous. In his Mais lecture of 1995, Blair accepted the main thesis of Nigel Lawson's Mais lecture of 1984, that monetary and fiscal policy should be aimed exclusively at controlling inflation, leaving it to supply-side policy to reduce unemployment – the exact opposite of classical British Keynesianism, which made full employment the goal of government macroeconomic policy, leaving it to 'prices and incomes' policy to control inflation. However, whereas Lawson and the Thatcherites thought of supply-side policy mainly in terms of freeing up labour markets and accepting whatever level of unemployment resulted, New Labour embraced the notion of active supply-side policy, which aimed at rebuilding labour supply damaged by shocks to demand in the 1980s. Furthermore, improving labour market flexibility was interpreted not just as a matter of removing obstacles to market transactions, but in terms of policies aiming to increase the capacity of the workforce to cope with the competitive challenges of globalisation. Price stability combined with active labour market policy was to be New Labour's route back to competitive success and full employment. So far it has worked wonderfully well.

New Labour's proxy for redistribution was 'investment in human capital'. The flaws in capitalism which had produced inequality were redefined as technical 'market failures', which prevented the private sector from investing sufficiently in education, training and health care. This left a substantial role for public investment which, however, would yield a dividend for the whole society in the form of faster economic growth. From this kind of analysis sprang the reinterpretation of social justice as 'inclusion'. Absent from this repackaging of traditional principles was any commitment to equality as a moral imperative and policy goal. The Blair–Brown approach, while decked out in technical economic jargon (e.g. Brown's notorious 'post-classical endogenous growth theory'), harks back to the 'enabling state' ideas of T. H. Green and L. T. Hobhouse, and the National Efficiency movement of the 1900s. The differences between Blair and Brown about how far market disciplines should be extended into the public sector are much less important than this joint redefinition of Labour's governing mission.

In his often stormy relations with his chancellor, Blair has shown himself the more ruthless of the two in the pursuit and retention of power. He has used to the full the advantages of incumbency in outmanoeuvring his rival. Weakened by Iraq, he was forced to concede that this would be his last term in office even before his prospects for continuing as prime minister were undermined by the reduced scale of his third election victory. But such is his resilence and capacity for passionate reinvention, that it would be foolish to take the succession for granted until it actually happens.

Blair's second term will always carry the taint of Iraq. It is clear to any unprejudiced observer that there was no defensible *casus belli* for the joint Anglo-American invasion of Iraq either in terms of national interest or international law. Saddam Hussein had no weapons of mass destruction, and the most that could be justified was a continued policy of surveillance and pressure to make sure that he did not develop or acquire them. Moreover, this would have been a reasonable conclusion from the course of events since the end of the Gulf War in 1991, and of any military intelligence analysis not pumped up by the demand of its political masters to produce evidence to the contrary. It is now also tolerably clear that Blair agreed to back George W. Bush in a war to overthrow Saddam when the two met at Crawford, Texas, in April 2002. The only problem was to manufacture a plausible *casus belli*, since the objective of regime change could not be openly avowed. WMD was to be the justification and their removal the only ostensible object of their war preparations. Blair's one requirement was that UN authorisation for the use of force should be obtained, if possible, hence the charade of the failed Anglo-American

Security Council resolution which immediately preceded the war. There are no 'smoking gun', no Nixon tapes to nail the conspirators. The truth will only come out in bits and pieces, and then possibly never wholly – just as most insiders knew that Eden had colluded with the Israelis at the time of Suez long before compelling evidence for this collusion emerged.

The fierce debate in Britain as to whether Blair lied, or was misled, or deceived himself, owes its importance to the convention that leaders are not expected to lie to their own people (or in our parlance, to Parliament) on matters great or small. Lying breaks the accountability of ruler to ruled, which is the foundation of democracy. At the same time this convention is a myth. Politicians do lie continually. They are usually caught out on the small lies, and get away with the big ones. The reason they lie is that they believe that real transparency would make effective pursuit of the national interest or welfare impossible. Although Goebbels is thought to have been the inventor of the Big Lie, the true inspiration for Nazi propaganda was the war leader Lloyd George, as Hitler makes clear in *Mein Kampf.*

The necessity for lying in politics was most famously defended by Plato in *The Republic.* Plato puts into the mouth of Socrates a compelling rational case for the rule of the best (philosopher-kings) and for the specialised education needed to fit the best to rule. But for Plato, who accepts this argument, there is a dreadful snag. The rational case for minority rule cannot be made acceptable to the masses. So they must be persuaded to accept it by a 'lordly lie' – the so-called the myth of the metals: 'God . . . has put gold into those who are capable of ruling, silver into the auxiliaries, and iron and copper into the peasants and the other producing classes.' Plato concludes, 'It is the business of the rulers of the city, if it is anybody's, to tell lies, deceiving both its enemies and its own citizens for the benefit of the city.' Plato also understands the precarious line between lying and self-deception: it is even advantageous for rulers to come to believe in their own lies, since this makes their propagation more effective.

A similar case for double standards is advanced by the late nineteenth-century philosopher Henry Sidgwick: 'Thus, on utilitarian principles, it may be right to do and privately recommend, under certain circumstances, what it would not be right to advocate openly.' Sidgwick adds, 'it seems expedient that the doctrine that esoteric morality is expedient should itself be kept esoteric' – an argument which Bernard Williams dubs 'Government House Utilitarianism'.

These considerations are not entirely abstract. The Platonic doctrine of the 'noble lie' was made familiar to neo-conservatives like Paul Wolfowitz around Bush by the conservative political scientist Leo Strauss at Chicago

University, via the teaching of Alan Bloom. President Bush himself may be largely exempt from intellectual influences, but it would be a great mistake to think this is true of some of his highly intelligent and well-educated advisers.

On this kind of reasoning the deception is justified if it produces good results. As the argument for going to war to destroy Saddam Hussein's WMD has faded, Blair, while continuing to insist that he believed his own story at the time, has been increasingly driven to justify the war on the grounds that Iraq and the Middle East as a whole will be a better place with Saddam Hussein gone. This, of course, may turn out to be true.

To me the interesting question is not whether or not Blair lied, but why he chained himself to Bush's mast. Blair and New Labour are much more obviously ideological twins of Clinton and the New Democrats than of Bush and the neo-conservatives. And Clinton, though he lied about his sexual life, was not disposed to invent reasons for going to war. There were no doubt persuasive foreign policy reasons for staying close to the Bush administration. But this leaves out Blair's personality, which is, in one important respect, more akin to Bush's than to Clinton's. This is his missionary zeal. It is not attached to any concrete projects or doctrines. It is a generalised, unfocused, urge to make the world better, to right wrongs, combined with a willingness to use force. Blair's eagerness to put troops on the ground in Kosovo in 1998 contrasted strongly with Clinton's reluctance to do so. In its aftermath came a speech in Chicago which outlined what can only be called a doctrine of ethical imperialism wrapped in the language of globalisation. In this, as in other respects, Blair has shown himself to be a throwback to an earlier era, bypassing the century of socialism.

It is not just, then, that Blair made Labour electable by ignoring the central points in its tradition. He has reconnected British politics to its radical, progressive, pre-Labour roots. And it has been his own lack of roots which has given him the audacity to do so. He remains the most interesting, most striking politician in contemporary Europe, and his course is not yet run.

Commentary
Foreign policy

VERNON BOGDANOR

When Labour came to power in 1997, its policies, and especially its economic policies seemed in many respects a continuation of those of the Conservatives. The real divide in politics seemed less between the Conservatives and Labour than between two wings of the Conservative Party. If, for example, John Redwood had defeated John Major in the 1995 Conservative leadership election, the resulting change in policy would have been far greater than it actually was in 1997.

In Blair's first term, the main conflict between the parties seemed to be on constitutional issues. Indeed, in my discussion of these reforms in the first volume of *The Blair Effect*, I suggested that these reforms comprised a veritable constitutional revolution, albeit a quiet revolution, and one little noticed by the general public.

In Labour's second term, the sound financial basis which it had inherited and maintained made possible a concerted attack on problems of public service provision, accompanied by a new politics of redistribution, which, again, was little noticed. Thus, the general election of 2005 was marked by a high degree of consensus on domestic issues on the part of the two major parties. The Tory critique – controlled immigration, cleaner hospitals and so on – was a critique of detail not of principle. In the 1950s there had seemed to be a consensus that much of the Attlee settlement should be retained. Fifty years later, there seemed a consensus that the broad outlines of the Thatcherite settlement should be retained also.

There was even a consensus in foreign policy, with the striking exception of Europe. Yet this new consensus, unlike that on domestic affairs, was Labour-led, or rather Blair-led. For Blair's stance diverged very markedly from what had been the traditional British approach to foreign affairs.

In the past, British foreign policy had generally been based on a cool and pragmatic calculation of the national interest. We had, it was suggested, permanent interests but no permanent allies. We solicited alliances but did not seek them. The main concern of British foreign policy had been to preserve the balance of power in Europe, whether against Louis XIV,

Napoleon, the Kaiser or Hitler. Moreover, British governments, whether Labour, Conservative or Liberal, sought stability, a reduction in international tensions – appeasement in the best sense of that much-abused term.

It is true that, in the early days of the Labour Party, there was much talk of something called 'a socialist foreign policy', but it was never very clear precisely what this meant. In its first election manifesto in 1906, Labour devoted just one half-sentence to foreign policy: 'Wars are fought to make the rich richer'. The sentence concluded 'and schoolchildren are still neglected'. Keir Hardie felt that foreign policy issues were perfectly straightforward. Indeed, a Labour foreign policy was unnecessary, since the working class in all countries would rise up to prevent the ruling classes making war. Thus, the coming to power of socialist governments would enable foreign ministries everywhere to shut up shop. Had not Karl Marx insisted that the working class had no country? That illusion of course died in 1914.

In 1937, Labour's leader, Clement Attlee, in his book, *The Labour Party in Perspective*, had to confess that, 'The Party . . . had no real constructive foreign policy, but shared the views which were traditional in radical circles.'[1] The foreign policy of the first two, minority, Labour governments had not in practice been very different from that of the pre-war Liberal governments of Campbell-Bannerman and Asquith. In the 1930s, Labour came to stand for an odd and contradictory mixture of collective security and disarmament. After the war, however, under the foreign secretaryship of Ernest Bevin from 1945 to 1951, Labour adopted a more tough-minded version of collective security, and the post-war Labour government played a major role in the setting-up of Nato.

There had, however, been an alternative principle of foreign policy on the left, the policy of humanitarian intervention. Its greatest practitioner was Gladstone. The Grand Old Man certainly did not equate liberalism with appeasement or non-intervention. When he denounced the Bulgarian Horrors in 1876, he was not suggesting that Britain should not interest itself in the Balkans. On the contrary, his complaint was that we were intervening on the wrong side, supporting the oppressor, Turkey, rather than the victim, Bulgaria. Indeed, wherever there was injustice, Gladstone sometimes seemed inclined to imply, Britain should make its voice felt even if this led to armed conflict. For 'However deplorable wars may be', Gladstone insisted in one of his Midlothian speeches, 'they are among

---

[1] C. R. Attlee, *The Labour Party in Perspective* (London: Gollancz, 1937), p. 200.

the necessities of our condition; and there are times when justice, when faith, when the failure of mankind, require a man not to shrink from the responsibility of undertaking them.'[2] Moreover, Gladstone's interpretation of Britain's security needs was as wide as those of the Tory imperialists, requiring as it did the safeguarding of the route to India, which lay through the Suez Canal. This in turn required a peaceful and stable Egypt. So it was that, in 1882, Gladstone inaugurated a humanitarian but 'temporary' occupation of Egypt, an occupation which lasted for over 70 years. On the one occasion on which President Nasser met Anthony Eden, he was invited to dinner at the British embassy in Cairo. Nasser said that he was glad to enter the place from which Egypt had been governed. 'Not governed, perhaps', Eden replied, 'advised, rather.'[3] Perhaps the Americans are saying something similar in Iraq.

It is this Gladstonian foreign policy that Tony Blair has revived. In my book, *Devolution in the United Kingdom*, and in my chapter on the constitution in the first edition of *The Blair Effect*, I suggested that Blair's constitutional reforms were Gladstonian in nature, Old Liberal rather than New Labour. The same is true of his foreign policy. Blair is perhaps the most Gladstonian prime minister to have occupied 10 Downing Street since the Grand Old Man himself.

The impact of Labour's new foreign policy was first felt in the Balkans. John Major's government had resisted involvement in the former Yugoslavia. 'More than any country, at some cost to our reputation, we have been the realists in this', Douglas Hurd, foreign secretary from 1989 to 1995, and the main architect of the policy of non-intervention, minuted to John Major.[4] The Conservatives resisted involvement in the former Yugoslavia, that far-away country of which we knew nothing, to adapt Neville Chamberlain's notorious remark about pre-war Czechoslovakia, because what happened in the Balkans did not affect British interests. Their policy was one of appeasement.

Appeasement, however, works best in a community unified by broadly common values and with some sense of mutuality. But it had as little to offer in the twenty-first-century world of Milosevic and Al-Qaeda, the world of ethnic cleansing and the suicide bomber, as it had in the Europe of the 1930s, the Europe of Hitler and Mussolini. In the Balkans and in relations with Iraq, there was not the remotest semblance of a

---

[2] W. E. Gladstone, *Political Speeches*, ed. Andrew Elliot (Edinburgh, 1880), vol. II, p. 30.
[3] Cited in Mohamed Heikal, *Cutting the Lion's Tail: Suez Through Egyptian Eyes*, London: Andre Deutsch 1986, p. 62.
[4] Douglas Hurd, *Memoirs* (London: Little, Brown, 2003), p. 467.

community or settled order between states. So it was that insistence by
Foreign Secretary Douglas Hurd on an arms embargo in the Balkans
in the early 1990s succeeded only in achieving an amoral equivalency
equating victims and aggressors; and Hurd's suggestion that lifting the
arms embargo would create a 'level killing field' drew from Margaret
Thatcher the stinging retort that there already was a 'killing field the like
of which I thought we would never see in Europe again . . . It is in Europe's
sphere of influence. It should be in Europe's sphere of conscience.'[5]

The Blair government took a different view of the conflict in the Balkans
from that of the Conservatives, and in March 1999 committed troops
to Kosovo to counter what it regarded as a Serbian threat of genocide
against the Albanian Muslim population. Intervention was, the Blair government believed, a moral duty. Of course, ministers also insisted that
Afghan terrorism and Iraqi weapons of mass destruction constituted a
genuine danger to Britain. For, after 9/11, the definition of British security widened. The 'war on terror' meant that security involved more than
mere territorial defence. It meant tackling terrorist networks and financing, and perhaps also removing regimes that promoted or allowed terrorist activity. This broader definition of security came to be intertwined
with humanitarian arguments against the horrible regimes in Kabul and
Baghdad. Part at least of the impetus of Blair's foreign policy derives
from its moral fervour, not from any careful calculation of British interests. We went to war in Kosovo, and to some extent in Afghanistan and
Iraq also, partly on humanitarian grounds. It would certainly be difficult to pretend that what happened in Kosovo affected British national
interests.

In April 1999, one month after engaging in Kosovo, the Prime Minister made an important foreign policy speech in Chicago. 'We need', he
declared, 'to enter a new millennium where dictators know that they cannot get away with ethnic cleansing or repress their people with impunity.'
His next sentence defined Labour's foreign policy. 'We are fighting not
for territory, but for values.' In consequence, Blair went on, 'The principle of non-interference must be qualified in important respects.' We
needed 'a new doctrine of international community [to give] explicit
recognition that today more than ever before, we are mutually dependent'.
In consequence, Britain, together with other countries which sought to
uphold international morality, had a right if not a duty to intervene where

---

[5] Brendan Simms, *Unfinest Hour: Britain and the Destruction of Bosnia* (London: Allen
Lane/The Penguin Press), 2001, p. 50.

necessary to prevent genocide, to deal with 'massive flows of refugees' which become 'threats to international peace and security' and to combat rogue states.

In the past, British foreign policy had been founded largely on national interest and it had on the whole ignored the internal nature of different regimes. Where it was in Britain's interest to form an alliance with a regime whose internal politics were unsavoury, as with the Ottoman Empire in 1853, Russia in 1907 or the USSR in 1941, it would unhesitatingly do so. The twentieth century, however, had seemed to show that the internal nature of a regime could not be divorced from its foreign policy, and that how a country treated its own people might well prove a good indicator of how it would behave in international affairs.

In a remarkable reversal of roles, it was not the Conservatives, heirs of Disraeli, but the Liberal Democrats, successors to Gladstone's Liberal Party, who turned out to be the main opponents of a Gladstonian foreign policy, in Iraq, if not in Afghanistan or Kosovo. The Conservatives, by contrast, hitherto the party of realism in foreign policy, supported Blair in Iraq, although, significantly, every ex-Conservative foreign secretary who spoke out on the crisis – Lord Howe, Lord Hurd and Sir Malcolm Rifkind – was opposed to the war. Moreover, Blair's interventionist foreign policy offended the instincts of many if not most Labour MPs, as it did the social democratic parties of western Europe. For these parties, while being committed to collective security, have in practice been more hesitant than the right when it comes to the use of force. Labour was in fact the only social democratic party in western Europe to support the Iraq war. It is by no means clear, therefore, whether the Blair reorientation of British foreign policy will survive into a new premiership.

Blair's foreign policy aligned Britain with the United States rather than with France and Germany, hitherto the leading powers in the European Union. That is at first sight surprising. For President Bush defined himself as a conservative; indeed as a neo-conservative. Classical US conservatism derives from John Quincy Adams who, in 1821, famously declared that the United States 'goes not abroad in search of monsters to destroy'.[6] Conservatives in the United States have generally adhered to a 'realist' foreign policy, exemplified by the approach of Henry Kissinger, national security adviser from 1969 to 1973 and secretary of state from 1973 to 1977, an approach based on a hard-headed calculation of the US national interest. It was, by contrast, Woodrow Wilson, a liberal, who had asked

[6] Quoted in Henry Kissinger, *Diplomacy* (London: Simon & Schuster, 1994), p. 35.

a very non-conservative question: 'How can the world be made safe for democracy?' – a question which came to seem of some considerable relevance after 9/11. Bush's foreign policy has more in common with that of Wilson than with that of Kissinger. He is a Wilsonian, not a conservative, just as Blair is a Gladstonian; and Gladstone, after all, would have had far more in common with Woodrow Wilson than with Kissinger's realism or the principle of *raison d'état*, another form of realism, which animates Gaullist France.

All the same, Blair's foreign policy alignment with the United States seems paradoxical, since from the time he came to power he had sought to improve relations with the European Union and show himself a good European. He had accepted the social chapter as well as proportional representation for elections to the European Parliament; and, in the St-Malo Declaration in 1998, he had stressed the need for a European defence force. On receiving the Charlemagne prize in May 1999, Blair had insisted that we must 'make full use of the potential Europe has to be a global force for good'. His government seemed the first to display a constructive attitude towards Europe since Edward Heath's administration over 30 years previously.

The paradox, however, is more apparent than real. Blair's ethical foreign policy is incompatible with being a good European only if being a good European is defined in Gaullist terms. In the Iraq crisis, President Chirac simply proceeded to label the French position 'European' and rebuked anyone who could not accept it as *non-communautaire*. Gaullism, however, is not necessarily the same as Europeanism. Indeed, it may be regarded as but a high-sounding name for the pursuit of the French national interest, a pursuit which has dominated French foreign policy under governments of both left and right since the inauguration of the 5th Republic in 1958. Had there, in fact, been qualified majority voting on foreign policy in the European Union, the French position would not have secured a majority. In an enlarged Europe, there would actually have been a qualified majority *against* the French position.

Gaullism rests on a limited conception of Europe in which Germany remained subordinate while Britain kept to the sidelines. Enlargement, however, is already causing a diplomatic revolution in Europe. The ex-Communist states, as the Iraq crisis shows, are far more likely to accept the Anglo-American position in foreign policy than the Gaullist. Indeed, when these states announced that they supported Bush and Blair, President Chirac accused them of being *mal élevé* – badly brought up. Moreover, the ex-Communist states are far more likely to accept the British

COMMENTARY   451

conception of a loosely organised Europe than the more federalist concep-
tions of the German foreign minister, Joschka Fischer. Having struggled
hard to win the right of national self-determination, the ex-Communist
states are hardly eager to surrender their sovereignty to a supranational
organisation. The negative outcome of the French referendum on the
constitution in May 2005 shows, moreover, that President Chirac's conception of Europe is not shared even by a majority of voters in France, let
alone the Continent as a whole.

From the time of de Gaulle's veto of Britain's first application to enter
the European Community, as it then was, in 1963, until enlargement,
France was the dominant power in Europe, and Europe was driven by
a Franco-German motor. The agenda was set primarily by France and
Germany and Britain was cast in the role of spoiler on the sidelines, the bad
boy of Europe. Today, by contrast, Tony Blair, without perhaps realising it
or even intending it, finds himself in a unique position to influence both
the United States and Europe, as both continents find themselves groping
towards a new conception of collective security in the post-9/11 world.

The Blair effect in foreign policy, therefore, is both significant and profound. How paradoxical it is that a policy associated with two men, long
since dead and consigned to the past – Gladstone and Woodrow Wilson –
should now seem a pointer to the future, especially for an administration
such as that of Blair which prides itself on being 'new'. In fact, as with
constitutional reform, the distance between New Labour and Old Liberal
does not seem very great.

Yet the doctrine of humanitarian intervention raises as many questions
as it answers. Who is to decide when such intervention is justified? Is the
doctrine not in danger of leading to universal war for the sake of universal
peace? Where is the 'new doctrine of international community' of which
Blair spoke at Chicago? One obvious, if flawed answer, to the question of
who decides the conditions under which intervention is justified, is that
it should be the United Nations. That, indeed, was the answer given by
the Liberal Democrat critics of the war in Iraq, as it had been the answer
given by Labour critics of Suez in 1956.

Woodrow Wilson's conception of the League of Nations had been that
of a Parliament of Man. The United Nations, however, is hardly that and
perhaps can never be such a parliament, since by no means all of the
member states represented there derive their legitimacy from the consent
of those whom they govern. Perhaps it can be realised only on a more limited basis by those countries whose governments *do* owe their legitimacy
to those whom they govern, i.e. the democracies. Perhaps there is a need

for the democracies to get together, to form a caucus, a new organisation to help secure their interests in the dangerous environment which they face in the post 9/11 world.

The Blair doctrine seeks to discover a middle way between Gaullism and unilateralism. The Gaullists had sought to unite Europe on the basis of an anti-US foreign policy, but such a policy, as the Iraq crisis showed, serves only to divide Europe. It could never unite it. Some in the Bush administration, by contrast, seek a unilateral approach to problems of international terrorism and rogue states. That too would cause a rift in the Atlantic Alliance, and it could never form the basis for a stable international order. The 'new doctrine of international community' must, therefore, be genuinely multilateralist. Working out precisely what that new doctrine should be constitutes the most important challenge facing a Blairite foreign policy as it finds itself grappling to adapt the concept of collective security to the conditions of a new age, the age of post 9/11.

BIBLIOGRAPHY

Allen, Graham, *The Last Prime Minister*, London: Politico's, 2003.

Ashdown, Paddy, *The Ashdown Diaries*, vol.1, London: Penguin, 2000.

Ashworth, Karl, Hartfree, Yvette, Kazimirski, Anne, Legge, Kate, Pires, Candice, Reyes de Beaman, Sandra, Shaw, Andrew and Stafford, Bruce, *New Deal for Disabled People. National Extension: First Wave of the First Cohort of the Survey of Entrants*, DWP Research Report no. 180, London: DWP, 2003.

Atkinson, Anthony B., *Top Incomes in the United Kingdom over the Twentieth Century*, University of Oxford Discussion Papers in Economic and Social History, no. 43, Oxford: University of Oxford, 2002.

Ball, Stuart and Seldon, Anthony (eds.), *Recovering Power: The Conservatives in Opposition since 1867*, London: Macmillan, 2005.

Barber, James, *The Prime Minister since 1945*, Oxford: Blackwell, 1991.

Barber, Michael, *The Learning Game*, London: Victor Gollancz, 1996.

Bean, Charles, 'Monetary policy in an uncertain world', Speech to Oxonia, 22 February 2005.

Beckett, Francis and Hencke, David, *The Blairs and Their Court*, London; Aurum Press, 2004.

Behrendt, Christina, *At the Margins of the Welfare State: Social Assistance and the Alleviation of Poverty in Germany, Sweden and the United Kingdom*, Aldershot: Ashgate, 2002.

Bell, D. and Christie, A., 'Finance – the Barnett Formula: nobody's child?' in A. Trench (ed.), *The State of the Nations 2001: The Second Year of Devolution in the United Kingdom*, Exeter: Imprint Academic, 2001, pp. 135–51.

Bevir, Mark and Rhodes, Rod, 'Presidents, barons, court politics and Tony Blair', unpublished paper, April 2005.

Blair, Tony, *Socialism*, Fabian Pamphlet 565, London: Fabian Society, 1994.

   The Third Way: New politics for the New Century, Fabian Pamphlet 588, London: The Fabian Society, 1998.

   'Beveridge revisited: a welfare state for the 21st century', in Robert Walker (ed.), *Ending Child Poverty: Popular Welfare for the 21st Century*, Bristol: The Policy Press, 1999.

   The Courage of our Convictions: Why reform of the public services is the route to social justice, Fabian Society Pamphlet 603, London: Fabian Society, 2002.

Blair, Tony and Schroeder, Gerhard, 'Europe: The Third Way/Die Neue Mitte', in Andrew Chadwick and Richard Heffernan (eds.), *The New Labour Reader*, Oxford: Polity Press/Blackwell Publishing, 2003.

Blundell, Richard, Brewer, Mike and Shephard, Andrew 'The impact of tax and benefit changes between April 2000 and April 2003 on parents' labour supply', IFS Briefing Note no. 52, London: Institute for Fiscal Studies, 2004.

Blundell, Richard, Costas-Dias, Moncia, Meghir, Costas and Van Reenen, John, 'The impact of the New Deal for young people: a four-year assessment', in Richard Dickens, Paul Gregg and Jonathan Wadsworth (eds.), *The Labour Market Under New Labour*, Basingstoke: Palgrave Macmillan, 2003.

Bower, Tom, *Gordon Brown*, London: HarperCollins, 2004.

Bradshaw, Jonathan, Kennedy, Steven, Kilkey, Majella, Hutton, Sandra, Corden, Anne, Eardley, Tony, Holmes, Hilary and Neale, Joanna, *The Employment of Lone Parents: A Comparison of Policy in 20 Countries*, London: Family Policy Studies Centre, 1996.

Brewer, Mike, Goodman, Alissa, Shaw, Jonathan and Shephard, Andrew, *Living Standards, Inequality and Poverty*, London: Institute for Fiscal Studies, April 2005.

Poverty and Inequality in Britain: 2005, London: Institute for Fiscal Studies, 2005.

Will the Government Hit its Child Poverty Target in 2004–5? Briefing Note 47, London: Institute for Fiscal Studies, 2005.

Briscoe, Simon, *Britain in Numbers: The Essential Statistics*, London: Politico's, 2005.

Brivati, Brian and Heffernan, Richard, *The Labour Party: A Centenary History*, Basingstoke: Palgrave Macmillan, 2000.

Burchardt, Tania, 'Selective inclusion: asylum seekers and other marginalised groups', in John Hills and Kitty Stewart (eds.), *A More Equal Society?* Bristol: The Policy Press, 2005.

Burgess, Simon, Propper, Carol and Wilson, Debora, *Choice: Will More Choice Improve Outcomes in Education and Health Care? The Evidence from Economic Research*, Bristol: Centre for Market and Public Organisation, Bristol University, 2005.

Butler, David and Butler, Gareth, *Twentieth Century British Political Facts 1900–2000*, Basingstoke: Macmillan, 2001.

Butler, David and Kavanagh, Dennis, *The British General Election of 1997*, London: Macmillan, 1997.

Butler, David and Stokes, Donald, *Political Change in Britain*, New York: St. Martin's Press, 1974.

Campbell, Vincent, *Information Age Journalism*, London: Arnold, 2004.

CASE (Centre for Analysis of Social Exclusion)/HM Treasury, *Persistent Poverty and Lifetime Inequality: The Evidence*, CASE Report 5 and HM Treasury

Occasional Paper no. 10, London: London School of Economics and Political Science and HM Treasury, 1999.

Centre for Economic Performance, 'Election analysis 2005: the National Minimum Wage', London: LSE Centre for Economic Performance, 2005.

Chitty, Clyde, *Education Policy in Britain*, Basingstoke: Palgrave Macmillan, 2004.

Clark, G. and Kelly, S., 'Echoes of Butler? The Conservative Research Department and the making of Conservative policy', *Political Quarterly*, 75 (2004).

Clarke, Harold D., Sanders, David, Stewart, Marianne C. and Whiteley, Paul, *Political Choice in Britain*, Oxford, Oxford University Press, 2004.

Coates, David and Krieger, Joel (with Rhiannnon Vickers), *Blair's War*, Cambridge: Polity Press, 2004.

Coates, David and Lawler, Peter (eds.), *New Labour in Power*, Manchester: Manchester University Press, 2000.

Coleman, M. P., Rachet, B., Woods, L. M., Mitry, E., Riga, M., Cooper, N., Quinn, M. J., Brenner, H. and Esteve, J., 'Trends and socioeconomic inequalities in cancer survival up to 2001', *British Journal of Cancer* 90 (2004): 1367–73.

Commission on Social Justice/IPPR, *Social Justice: Strategies for National Renewal*, London: Vintage, 1994.

Constitution Unit, University College, London, 'Quarterly monitoring reports from the Nations and Regions Programme', index page at http://www.ucl.ac.uk/constitution-unit/nations/monitoring.php.

Cook, Robin, *The Point of Departure*, London: Simon & Schuster, 2003.

Cowley, Philip, *Revolts and Rebellions: Parliamentary Voting Under Blair*, London: Politico's, 2002.

Cowley, Philip and Stuart, Mark, 'Parliament: more revolts, more reform', *Parliamentary Affairs* 56 (2003): 188–204.

'Still causing trouble? The parliamentary party', *Political Quarterly* 75 (2004): 356–61.

Crewe, Ivor and Thomson, Katarina, 'Party loyalties: dealignment or realignment?', in Geoffrey Evans and Pippa Norris (eds.), *Critical Elections*, London: Sage Publications, 1999.

Croxson, B., Propper, C. and Perkins, A., 'Do doctors respond to financial incentives? UK family doctors and the GP fundholder scheme', *Journal of Public Economics* 79:2 (2001): 375–98.

Curtice, John, *The 2004 European Parliamentary Elections in the United Kingdom*, London: The Electoral Commission, 2004.

d'Ancona, Matthew, 'The battle of the two Howards had to be fought', *Sunday Telegraph*, 27 March 2003.

Dalton, Russell and Wattenberg, Martin P. (eds.), *Parties without Partisans: Political Change in Advanced Industrialized Democracies*, Oxford, Oxford University Press, 2000.

Danchev, Alex and MacMillan, John (eds.), *The Iraq War and Democratic Politics*, London: Routledge, 2005.

Deighton, Anne, 'European Union Policy', in Anthony Seldon (ed.), *The Blair Effect: The Blair Government 1997–2001*, London, Little, Brown, 2001.

Denver, David, Rallings, Colin and Thrasher, Michael (eds.), *Media Guide to the New Scottish Westminster Parliamentary Constituencies*, BBC/ITN/PA/Sky, University of Plymouth, 2004.

Department for Education and Skills (DfES), *Extending Opportunities, Raising Standards*, Green Paper, London: DfES, February 2002.

The Future of Higher Education, White Paper Cm 5735, London: DfES, January 2003.

Autumn Performance Report 2004, London: DfES, 2004.

Departmental Report 2004, Cm 6202, London: DfES, 2004.

Five-Year Strategy for Children and Learners: Putting People at the Heart of Public Service, Cm 6272, London: DfES, 2004.

14–19 Education and Skills, White Paper Cm 6476, London: DfES, February 2005.

School Workforce in England January 2005(Provisional), National Statistics First Release SFR 17/2005, London: DfES, April 2005.

Department of Employment, 'Family Expenditure Survey', London: HMSO, 1964.

Department of the Environment, Transport and the Regions, 'A New Deal for Transport: Better for Everyone', Cm 3950, London: The Stationery Office, 1998.

'Transport 2010', London: The Stationery Office, July 2000.

'Transport 2010. The Background Analysis', London: The Stationery Office, July 2000.

Department of Health, 'A policy framework for commissioning cancer services: a report by the expert advisory group on cancer to the Chief Medical Officer for England and Wales', London: HMSO, 1995.

The New NHS: Modern Dependable, London: The Stationery Office, 1997.

Independent Inquiry into Inequalities in Health Report, London: The Stationery Office, 1998.

Saving Lives: Our Healthier Nation, White Paper, Cm 4386, London: The Stationery Office, 1999.

The NHS Plan, London: The Stationery Office, 2000.

Tackling Health Inequalities: A Programme for Action, London: Department of Health, 2003.

The NHS Improvement Plan: Putting People at the Heart of Public Services, London: The Stationery Office, 2004.

Independence, Well-being and Choice: Our vision for the future of social care for adults in England, London: The Stationery Office, 2005.

Department of Health and Social Security (DHSS), *Inequalities in Health: Report of a Research Working Group*, London: Department of Health and Social Security, 1980.

Department of Social Security (DSS), *Opportunity For All: Tackling Poverty and Social Exclusion*, London: DSS, 1999.

Department for Work and Pensions (DWP), *Households Below Average Income 1994/5–2002/3*, London: DWP, 2004.

Income Related Benefits: Estimates of Take-Up 2002/3, London: DWP, 2005.

The Abstract of Statistics for Benefits, Contributions and Indices of Prices and Earnings: 2004 Edition, London: DWP, 2005.

Dickens, Richard, Gregg, Paul and Wadsworth, Jonathan (eds.), *The Labour Market Under New Labour: The State of Working Britain*, Basingstoke: Palgrave Macmillan, 2003.

Doig, Alan, '45 Minutes of infamy? Hutton, Blair and the invasion of Iraq', *Parliamentary Affairs*, 58:1 (2005): 109–23.

Dowling, Bernard, *GPs and Purchasing in the NHS*, Aldershot: Ashgate, 2000.

Downs, Anthony, *An Economic Theory of Democracy*, New York: Harper and Row, 1957.

Dusheiko, M., Grevelle, H. and Jacobs, R., 'The effect of practice budgets on waiting time: allowing for selection bias', *Health Economics* 13 (2004): 941–58.

Dyke, Greg, *Inside Story*, London: HarperCollins, 2004.

Electoral Commission, *Register of Donations to Political Parties*, London: Electoral Commission, 2001–5.

Enelow, James M. and Hinich, Melvin (eds.), *The Spatial Theory of Voting*, New York: Cambridge University Press, 1984.

Evandrou, Maria and Falkingham, Jane, 'A secure retirement for all? Older people and New Labour', in John Hills and Kitty Stewart (eds.), *A More Equal Society?* Bristol: The Policy Press, 2005.

Evans, Andrew A., 'Rail safety and rail privatisation in Britain', inaugural lecture, Imperial College London, 2004.

Evans, Geoffrey, Heath, Anthony and Payne, Clive, 'Class: Labour as a catch-all party?' in G. Evans and P. Norris (eds.), *Critical Elections*, London: Sage Publications, 1999.

Fielding, Steven, *The Labour Party: Continuity and Change in the Making of 'New' Labour*, Basingstoke: Palgrave Macmillan, 2003.

Finegold, David, Keep, Ewart, Miliband, David, Raffe, David, Spours, Ken, and Young, Michael, *A British 'Baccalauréat'*, Education and Training Paper no. 1, London: Institute for Public Policy Research, 1990.

Fisher, J., 'Money matters: the financing of the Conservative Party', *Political Quarterly*, 75 (2004).

Foley, Michael, *The Rise of the British Presidency*, Manchester, Manchester University Press, 1993, 2000.

Foster, Christopher D., *British Government in Crisis*, Oxford: Hart Publishing, 2005.

Franklin, Bob, 'The hand of history: New Labour, news management and governance', in S. Ludlam and M. J. Smith (eds.), *New Labour in Government*, Basingstoke: Macmillan, 2001, pp. 130–44.

'A Damascene conversion? New Labour and media relations', in S. Ludlam and M. J. Smith (eds.), *Governing as New Labour: Policy and Politics under Blair*, Basingstoke: Palgrave Macmillan, 2004, pp. 88–105.

Fraser of Carmyllie, Lord, *Holyrood Inquiry: Final Report*, Edinburgh: HMSO, 2004.

Gaber, Ivor, 'Going from bad to worse: Why Phillis (and the Government) have got it wrong', paper presented at the conference 'Can Vote, Won't Vote: Are the Media to Blame for Political Disengagement?', Goldsmiths College London, 6 November 2003.

Gamble, Andrew, *Between Europe and America: the Future of British Politics*, Basingstoke: Palgrave Macmillan, 2003.

Garner, Richard, 'Warm words and £95,000 for sacked exams watchdog', *Independent*, 6 February 2003.

Gelman, Andrew and King, Gary, 'Why are American presidential election polls so variable when votes are so predictable?' *British Journal of Political Science* (1993) 23: 409–51.

Glaister, Stephen, *British Rail Privatisation – Competition Destroyed by Politics*, Occasional Paper 23, Bath: Centre for Regulated Industries, 2005.

Glaister, Stephen and Travers, Tony, *Governing the Underground: Funding, Management and Democracy for London's Tube*, Bath: Centre for Regulated Industries, 1997.

Glaister, Stephen, Scanlon, Rosemary and Travers, Tony, *A Fourth Way for the Underground?* London: Greater London Group, London School of Economics, June 1998.

Getting Partnerships Going: Public Private Partnerships in Transport, London: Institute for Public Policy Research, April 2000.

Glees, Anthony, 'Evidence-based policy or policy-based evidence? Hutton and the government's use of secret intelligence', *Parliamentary Affairs*, 58:1 (2005): 138–55.

Glennerster, Howard with Korman, Nancy and Marslen-Wilson, Francis, *Planning for Priority Groups*, Oxford: Martin Robertson, 1983.

Goodman, Alissa and Webb, Steve, *For Richer, For Poorer: The Changing Distribution of Income in the United Kingdom 1961–1991*, London: Institute for Fiscal Studies, 1994.

Goodman, Alissa, Myck, Michael and Shephard, Andrew, *Sharing in the Nation's Prosperity? Pensioner Poverty in Britain*, Commentary 93, London: Institute for Fiscal Studies, 2003.

Graham, Hilary (ed.), *Understanding Health Inequalities*, Buckingham: Open University Press, 2000.

Greer, Scott L., *Territorial Politics and Health Policy: UK Health Policy in Comparative Perspective*, Manchester: Manchester University Press, 2004.

Gregg, Paul and Wadsworth, Jonathan, 'Workless households and the recovery', in R. Dickens, P. Gregg and J. Wadsworth (eds.), *The Labour Market Under New Labour*, Basingstoke: Palgrave Macmillan, 2003, pp. 32–9.

Gregg, Paul, Waldfogel, Jane and Washbrook, Elisabeth, 'That's the way the money goes: expenditure patterns as real incomes rise for the poorest families with children', in John Hills and Kitty Stewart (eds.), *A More Equal Society?* Bristol: The Policy Press, 2005.

Grice, Andrew, '"Mr Targets" on a mission to reform Whitehall', *Independent*, 6 January 2003.

Guha, Krishna, 'Expulsion row keeps Morris trapped in spotlight', *Financial Times*, weekend 12–13 October 2002.

Hagerty, Bill 'Cap'n spin *does* lose his rag', *British Journalism Review* 11:2 (2000): 7–20.

Hallin, Daniel, *The Uncensored War*, Oxford: Oxford University Press, 1986.

Halper, Stefan and Clarke, Jonathan, *America Alone: The Neo-Conservatives and the Global Order*, Cambridge: Cambridge University Press, 2004.

Hargreaves, David, *Review of Curriculum 2000 – QCA's Report on Phase One*, London: Qualifications and Curriculum Authority, July 2001.

Review of Curriculum 2000 – QCA's Report on Phase Two, London: Qualifications and Curriculum Authority, December 2001.

Harmer, Harry, *The Longman Companion to the Labour Party 1900–1998*, London: Addison Wesley Longman, 1999.

Harris, Robert, *Gotcha! The Media, the Government and the Falklands Crisis*, London: Faber & Faber, 1983.

Hassan, G., Gibb, E. and Howland, L. (eds.), *Scotland 2020: Hopeful Stories for a Northern Nation*, London: Demos, 2005.

Henig, Simon and Baston, Lewis, *Politico's Guide to the General Election 2005*, London: Methuen, 2005.

Hennessy, Peter, *The Prime Minister. The Office and its Holders*, London: Allen Lane, 2000.

'An end to the poverty of aspirations? Parliament since 1979', unpublished paper, November, 2004.

Hill, Christopher, *Cabinet Decisions in Foreign Policy: the British Experience October 1938–June 1941*, Cambridge: Cambridge University Press, 1991.

'Foreign policy', in Anthony Seldon (ed.), *The Blair Effect*, London: Little, Brown, 2001.

'Renationalizing or Regrouping? EU Foreign Policy since 11 September 2001', *Journal of Common Market Studies* 42:1 (2004): 143–63.

Hills, John, *Inequality and the State*, Oxford: Oxford University Press, 2004.

Hills, John and Stewart, Kitty (eds.), *A More Equal Society? New Labour, Poverty, Inequality and Exclusion*, Bristol: The Policy Press, 2005.

HM Treasury, 'Modern Public Services for Britain, Investing in Reform' (Comprehensive Spending Review), Cm 4011, London: The Stationery Office, 1998.

UK Membership of the Single Currency: An assessment of the five economic tests, Cm 5776, London: HM Treasury, June 2003.

2004 Spending Review: Public Service Agreements 2005–2008, Cm 6238, London: HM Treasury 2004.

Funding the Scottish Parliament, National Assembly for Wales and Northern Ireland Assembly, 4th edn, London: HM Treasury, 2004.

Securing Good Health for the Whole Population, London: HM Treasury, 2004.

HM Treasury and Department of Health, *Tackling Health Inequalities: Summary of the 2002 Cross Cutting Review*, London: HM Treasury and Department of Health, 2002.

Holden, Russell, *The Making of New Labour's European Policy*, Basingstoke: Palgrave Macmillan, 2002.

House of Commons Committee of Public Accounts, 'London Underground Public Private Partnerships', HC466, London: The Stationery Office, 2005.

House of Commons Committee on Transport, Local Government and the Regions, 'London Underground', HC387, London: The Stationery Office, 2002.

House of Commons Education and Skills Committee, *Minutes of Evidence for Wednesday 24 October 2001, Rt Hon Estelle Morris MP, Secretary of State for Education and Skill*, London: The Stationery Office, 2001.

Individual Learning Accounts, London: The Stationery Office, May 2002.

Oral Evidence on Wednesday 14 January 2004, Rt Hon Charles Clarke, London: The Stationery Office, October 2004.

Secondary Education, London: The Stationery Office, March 2005.

House of Commons Transport Committee, *The Performance of the London Underground*, HC94, London: The Stationery Office, 2005.

House of Commons Transport Select Committee, *The Future of the Railway*, HC145, London: The Stationery Office, 2004.

Humphreys, James, 'The Iraq dossier and the meaning of spin', *Parliamentary Affairs* 58/1 (2005): 156–70.

Hutton, Lord, *Report of the Inquiry into the Circumstances Surrounding the Death of David Kelly, C.M.G.* (Hutton Report) HC247, London: The Stationery Office, 28 January 2004.

Hyman, Peter, *1 out of 10, From Downing Street Vision to Classroom Reality*, London: Vintage, 2005.

Jackson, Ben and Segal, Paul, *Why Inequality Matters*, Catalyst Working Paper, London: Catalyst, 2004.

Janis, Irving, *Groupthink: Psychological Studies of Foreign Policy Decisions and Fiascoes*, Boston, MA: Houghton Mifflin, 1982.

Johnston, Ron, Pattie, Charles, Dorling, Danny and Rossiter, David, *From Votes to Seats*, Manchester: Manchester University Press, 2001.

Kampfner, John, *Blair's Wars*, London: Free Press, 2003.

Kaye, Robert P., ' "OfGov": A commissioner for government conduct?', *Parliamentary Affairs*, 58:1 (2005): 171–88.

Keegan, William, *The Prudence of Mr Gordon Brown*, London: Wiley, 2003.

Kelso, Alexandra, '"Where were the massed ranks of parliamentary reformers?"– "attitudinal" and "contextual" approaches to parliamentary reform', *Journal of Legislative Studies* 9 (2003): 57–76.

King, Anthony (ed.), *Leaders' Personalities and the Outcome of Democratic Elections*, Oxford: Oxford University Press, 2002.

King's Fund, *Audit of the Labour Government's Health Record*, London: The King's Fund, 2005.

Kuhn, Raymond 'The first Blair government and political journalism', in R. Kuhn and E. Neveu (eds.), *Political Journalism: New Challenges, New Practices*, London: Routledge, 2002, pp. 47–68.

Labour Party, *Partnership in Power*, London: Labour Party, 1997.

21st Century Party, London: Labour Party, 1999.

Le Grand, Julian, *Motivation, Agency, and Public Policy*, Oxford: Oxford University Press, 2003.

Le Grand, Julian and Vizard, Polly, 'The National Health Service: crisis, change, or continuity?' in H. Glennerster and J. Hills (eds.), *The State of Welfare: The Economics of Social Spending*, Oxford: Oxford University Press, 1998.

Lea, Ruth, 'Whatever happened to the Golden Legacy?', London: Centre for Policy Studies, March 2005.

Lees-Marshment, J., 'Mis-marketing the Conservatives: the limitations of style over substance', *Political Quarterly* 75 (2004).

Lewis, Jane and Surender, Rebecca, *Welfare State Change: Towards a Third Way?* Oxford: Oxford University Press, 2004.

Lewis, Justin and Brookes, Rod, 'Reporting the war on British television', in D. Miller (ed.), *Tell Me Lies: Propaganda and Media Distortion in the Attack on Iraq*, London: Pluto Press, 2004, pp. 132–43.

Lewis-Beck, Michael, *Economics and Elections: The Major Western Democracies*, Ann Arbor: University of Michigan Press, 1988.

Liddle, Roger, *The New Case for Europe: The Crisis in British Pro-Europeanism – and How to Overcome It*, London: Fabian Society, 2005.

Lindsay, Craig, 'Labour productivity: labour market trends', London: Office for National Statistics, November 2004.

Lloyd, John, *What the Media are Doing to Our Politics*, London: Constable, 2004.

London Underground, 'London Underground and the PPP – The First Year', 2004.

Ludlam, Steve, and Smith, Martin, *Governing as New Labour: Policy and Politics under Blair*, Basingstoke: Palgrave Macmillan, 2004.

MacDonald, R. and Hallwood, P., 'The economic case for fiscal federalism in Scotland', Glasgow: Fraser of Allander Institute, 2004.

Machin, Stephen, McNally, Sandra and Meghir, Costas, 'Improving pupil performance in English secondary schools: Excellence in Cities', *Journal of the European Economic Association*, 2:2 (2004): 396–405.

Mair, Peter, 'Partyless democracy', *New Left Review* 2 (2000).

McKay, Stephen and Collard, Sharon, *Developing Deprivation Questions for the Family Resources Survey*, Personal Finance Research Centre, Bristol: University of Bristol, 2003.

McKnight, Abigail, Glennerster, Howard and Lupton, Ruth, 'Education, education, education . . .: an assessment of Labour's success in tackling educational inequalities', in John Hills and Kitty Stewart (eds.), *A More Equal Society?* Bristol: The Policy Press, 2005.

McLean, I., 'The national question', in A. Seldon (ed.), *The Blair Effect: The Blair Government 1997–2001*, London: Little Brown, 2001, pp. 429–47.

The Fiscal Crisis of the United Kingdom, Basingstoke: Palgrave Macmillan, 2005.

McLean, I. and McMillan, A., *State of the Union*, Oxford: Oxford University Press, 2005.

McLean, Iain, Spirling, Arthur and Russell, Meg, 'None of the above: the UK House of Commons votes on reforming the House of Lords, February 2003', *Political Quarterly* 74 (2003): 298–310.

Micklewright, John and Stewart, Kitty, *The Welfare of Europe's Children: Are EU Member States Converging?* Bristol: The Policy Press, 2000.

Mulgan, Geoffrey, 'Lessons of power', *Prospect*, May 2005.

'My time in the engine room', *Prospect*, May 2005.

Murray, Alasdair and Wanlin, Aurore, *The Lisbon Scorecard V. Can Europe Compete?* London: Centre for Economic Reform, 2005.

National Audit Office, *The New Deal for Young People*, London: The Stationery Office, February 2002.

Individual Learning Accounts, London: The Stationery Office, October 2002.

Tackling Cancer in England: Saving more lives, London: National Audit Office, 2004.

National Institute of Economic and Social Research, *National Institute Economic Review*, London: Sage Publications, April 2005.

National Statistics, 'A report on the 2002–2003 Expenditure and Food Survey', London: The Stationery Office, 2004.

NESS (National Evaluation of Sure Start), *The Impact of Sure Start Local Programmes on Child Development and Family Functioning: A Report on Preliminary findings*, London: Institute for the Study of Children, Families and Social Issues, Birkbeck College, 2004.

Neustadt, Richard, *Alliance Politics*, New York: Columbia University Press, 1970.

Norman, Peter, *The Accidental Constitution: The Making of Europe's Constitutional Treaty*, Brussels: EuroComment, 2005.

Norris, Pippa, 'Gender: a gender-generation gap?' in Geoffrey Evans and Pippa Norris (eds.), *Critical Elections*, London: Sage Publications, 1999.

Norris, Pippa (ed.), *Britain Votes 2001*, Oxford: Oxford University Press, 2001.

Norris, Pippa and Lovenduski, Joni, 'Why parties fail to learn: electoral defeat, selective perception and British party politics', *Party Politics* 10:1 (2004): 85–104.

Norton, Philip, 'Parliament', in A. Seldon (ed.), *The Blair Effect: The Blair Government 1997–2001*, London: Little, Brown, 2001.

Norton, Philip, 'Cohesion without discipline: party voting in the House of Lords', *Journal of Legislative Studies* 9 (2003): 57–72.

O'Leary, Brendan, 'The Belfast Agreement and the Labour Government', in Anthony Seldon, (ed.), *The Blair Effect: The Blair Government 1997–2001*, London: Little Brown, 2001, pp. 449–87.

Oborne, Peter, 'Blair downgraded the Labour whips – and now he is paying the price', *Spectator*, 17 January 2004.

'The mean machine', *Spectator*, 20 November 2004.

The Rise of Political Lying, London: Free Press, 2005.

Oborne, Peter and Walters, Simon, *Alastair Campbell*, London: Aurum, 2004.

Ofsted, *Specialist Schools: A Second Evaluation*, HMI 2362, London: Ofsted, February 2004.

Parliamentary Joint Committee, 'Report on the Draft Mental Health Bill', House of Commons and Lords, 23 March 2005.

Pearce, Nick and Paxton, Will (eds.), *Social Justice: Building a Fairer Britain*, (London: IPPR, 2005).

Peston, Robert, *Brown's Britain*, London: Short Books, 2005.

Phillis, Bob, *An Independent Review of Government Communications*, London: The Stationery Office, 2004.

Phythian, Mark, 'Hutton and Scott: a tale of two inquiries', *Parliamentary Affairs* 58:1 (2005): 124–37.

Pollard, Stephen, *David Blunkett*, London: Hodder & Stoughton, 2004.

Pollock, Allyson M., Price, David, Talbot-Smith, Alison and Mohan, John, 'NHS and the Health and Social Care Bill: end of Bevan's vision?', *British Medical Journal* 327 (2003): 982–5.

Portillo, Michael, 'The Conservatives undone by their Victor Meldrew Manifesto', *Sunday Times*, 24 April 2005.

Power, Anne and Willmot, Helen, 'Bringing up families in poor neighbourhoods under New Labour', in John Hills and Kitty Stewart (eds.), *A More Equal Society?* Bristol: The Policy Press, 2005.

RAC Foundation, 'Motoring towards 2050', London: RAC Foundation, 2002.

Review of Intelligence on Weapons of Mass Destruction, Report of a Committee of Privy Counsellors, chaired by Lord Butler of Brockwell (Butler Report), London: The Stationery Office, 14 July 2004.

Richard of Ammanford, Rt. Hon. Lord (chairman), *Commission on the Powers and Electoral Arrangements of the National Assembly for Wales*, Cardiff: National Assembly, 2004.

Riddell, Peter, *Parliament Under Blair*, London: Palgrave, 1998.

    Parliament Under Blair, London: Politico's, 2000.

    Hug Them Close: Blair, Clinton, Bush and the 'Special Relationship', London: Politico's/Methuen Publishing, 2003.

Robinson, Peter, Hawksworth, John, Broadbent, Jane, Laughlin, Richard and Haslam, Colin, *The Private Finance Initiative: Saviour, Villain or Irrelevance?*, Working Paper of the Commission on Public Private Partnerships, London: Institute for Public Policy Research, 1999–2001.

Rose, Richard, *The Prime Minister in a Shrinking World*, Cambridge: Polity, 2001.

Royal Commission on Long Term Care, *With Respect to Old Age*, London: The Stationery Office, 1999.

Runciman, W. G. (ed.), *Hutton and Butler: Lifting the Lid on the Workings of Power*, Oxford: Oxford University Press, for the British Academy, 2004.

Sainsbury Centre for Mental Health, *Money for Mental Health*, London: Sainsbury Centre, 2003.

Sambrook, Richard, 'Tragedy in the fog of war', *British Journalism Review* 15:3 (2004): 7–13.

Sassi, Franco, 'Tackling health inequalities', in John Hills and Kitty Stewart (eds.), *A More Equal Society?* Bristol: The Policy Press, 2005.

SBC Warburg, 'Railtrack Share Offer, Prospectus', London, 1996.

Scott, Derek, *Off Whitehall: A View from Downing Street by Tony Blair's Adviser*, London: I.B.Tauris, 2004.

Sefton, Tom and Sutherland, Holly, 'Inequality and poverty under New Labour', in John Hills and Kitty Stewart (eds.), *A More Equal Society?* Bristol: The Policy Press, 2005.

Seldon, Anthony, *Major: A Political Life,* London: Orion, 1997.

    Blair, London: The Free Press, 2004 (2nd edn, 2005).

Seldon, A. (ed.), *The Blair Effect: The Blair Government 1997–2001*, London: Little, Brown, 2001.

Seldon, Anthony and Snowdon, Peter, *The Conservative Party: An Illustrated History*, Stroud: Sutton Publishing, 2004.

Select Committee on Intelligence, *Report on the U.S. Intelligence Community's Prewar Intelligence Assessments on Iraq*, Washington, DC: US Senate, 7 July 2004.

Shaw, Eric, *The Labour Party since 1979*, London: Routledge, 1994.

Smee, Clive, 'Speaking truth to power', Nuffield Trust Lecture delivered at the Royal Society of Arts, 1 February, 2005.

Smith, David, 'Brown to break record', *Sunday Times*, 6 June 2004.

Smith, Trevor, '"Something old, something new, something borrowed, something blue." Themes of Tony Blair and his government', *Parliamentary Affairs* 56 (2003): 580–96.

Smithers, Alan, 'Education policy', in Anthony Seldon (ed.), *The Blair Effect*, London: Little, Brown, 2001, pp. 405–26.

England's Education: What Can be Learned by Comparing Countries? London: Sutton Trust, May 2004.

Snowdon, Peter and Collings, Daniel, 'Déjà vu? Conservative problems in historical perspective', *Political Quarterly* 75 (2004).

Social Exclusion Unit (SEU), *New Commitment to Neighbourhood Renewal: National Strategy Action Plan*, London: Cabinet Office, 2001.

Excluded Older People, London: ODPM, 2005.

Stephens, Philip, *Tony Blair, The Price of Leadership*, London: Politico's/Methuen Publishing, 2004.

Stevens, Robert, *University to Uni*, London: Politico's, 2004.

Stevens, Simon, 'Reform strategies for the English NHS', *Health Affairs* 23:3 (2004): 37–44.

Stothard, Peter, *30 Days: A Month at the Heart of Blair's War*, London: HarperCollins, 2003.

Strategic Rail Authority, *Everyone's Railway: The Wider Case for Rail*, London: SRA, 2003.

Sunderland, John, 'Annual Dinner speech', London: CBI, 17 May 2005.

Sutherland, Holly, *Poverty in Britain: The Impact of Government Policy since 1997. An Update to 2004–5 using Microsimulation*, Cambridge: Microsimulation Unit, University of Cambridge, 2004.

Taylor, Robert, 'Britain's world of work: myths and reality', Future of Work Programme, London: Economic and Social Research Council, 2003.

Thomson, Alice, 'We lost but the Conservatives are back in the game', *Spectator*, 19 May 2005.

Tomlinson, Mike, *Inquiry into A Level Standards*, Interim Report. London: Department for Education and Skills, September 2002.

Inquiry into A Level Standards, Final Report, London: Department for Education and Skills, December 2002.

14–19 Curriculum and Qualifications Reform, Working Group on 14–19 Reform, Progress Report, London: Department for Education and Skills, July 2003.

14–19 Curriculum and Qualifications Reform, Working Group on 14–19 Reform, Interim Report, London: Department for Education and Skills, February 2004.

14–19 Curriculum and Qualifications Reform, Working Group on 14–19 Reform, Final Report, London: Department for Education and Skills, October 2004.

Tomlinson, Sally, *Education in a Post-Welfare Society*, Buckingham: Open University Press, 2001.

Toynbee, Polly and Walker, David, *Better or Worse? Has Labour Delivered?* London: Bloomsbury, 2005.

Trench, A. (ed.), *The State of the Nations 2001: The Second Year of Devolution in the United Kingdom*, Exeter: Imprint Academic, 2001.

Has Devolution Made a Difference? The State of the Nations 2004, Exeter: Imprint Academic, 2004.

Tumber, Howard and Palmer, Jerry, *Media at War: The Iraq Crisis*, London: Sage, 2004.

Vaitilingam, Romesh. *The UK's Productivity Gap: What Research Tells Us and What We Need to Find Out*, Swindon: Economic and Social Research Council (ESRC), September 2004.

Wanless, Derek, *Securing Good Health for the Whole Population*, London: HM Treasury, 2004.

Wilkinson, Richard, G., *Unhealthy Societies: The Afflictions of Inequality*, London: Routledge, 1996.

Wlezein, Christopher and Norris, Pippa (eds.), *Britain Votes 2005*, Oxford: Oxford University Press, 2005.

Woodward, Will, 'Bargepole jibe angers teachers', *Guardian*, 25 June 2002.

INDEX